The World of Business

Fourth Edition

The World of Business
A Canadian Profile

Authors

Terry G. Murphy

Jack Wilson

David Notman

NELSON

™

THOMSON LEARNING

Australia • Canada • Mexico • Singapore • Spain • United Kingdom • United States

NELSON

THOMSON LEARNING ™

The World of Business: A Canadian Profile
Fourth Edition
by Terry G. Murphy, Jack Wilson, and David Notman

NELSON THOMSON LEARNING

Director of Publishing
David Steele

Senior Managing Editor
Nicola Balfour

Proofreader
Lisa Dimson

Production Coordinator
Sharon Latta Paterson

Cover Design
Peter Papayanakis

Printer
Transcontinental Printing Inc.

FIRST FOLIO RESOURCE GROUP, INC.

Program Manager
Fran Cohen

Developmental Editors
Geraldine Kikuta
Brenda McLoughlin
Dayne Ogilvie
Evelyn Steinberg

Production Editor
Debbie Smith

Art Direction/Interior Design
Tom Dart

Permissions
Erinn Banting

Photo Research
Robyn Craig

Composition
Alana Lai
Greg Duhaney

Copy Editor
Amanda Stewart

Research
Matthew Gourlay
Amanda Stewart

Review Process
Natalie McKinnon

National Library of Canada Cataloguing in Publication Data

Murphy, Terry G., 1940–
   The World of Business: A Canadian Profile

4th ed.
Previous eds. by Terry G. Murphy, et. al
ISBN 0-17-620140-8

1. Business. 2. Canada—Commerce. I. Wilson, Jack II. Notman, David. III. Title.
HF5351.W67 2001   658
C2001-930418-8

The brand names and photos that appear in this book do not represent endorsements, but rather are business-related examples relevant to the content of the text.

Acknowledgments

We are extremely grateful to many educators and specialists from the business and financial sectors who provided current data, reviewed portions of the manuscript, and offered suggestions to help make this fourth edition of *The World of Business* the best ever! The suggestions and comments made by these business and education representatives have helped make this book as correct, as accurate, and as user-friendly as possible. These contributors are listed on a separate page, and we thank them most sincerely.

Special thanks to Fran Cohen and her hard-working and committed staff. Thanks also to David Steele for perceiving that there was a need for a fourth edition to support curriculum and provide students and teachers with an exciting new resource. Also, sincere thanks to Mike Czukar for his vision in making teachers across Canada aware of our new fourth edition. Thanks also to the members of the K.C.V.I. Business Department (Greg Hunt, Vance Grekul, and Huw Davies) for their patience and assistance.

To my wife, Katherine (Kit); Jamie and Laura; Karen, Russell, and our first granddaughter, Macy Elizabeth, and to my mother, Louise—*TGM*

In memory of my sister, Linda, and my mother, Rosalind Margaret. To my father who introduced me to the world of business—*JW*

To my mom and dad. Thanks for giving me my love of business and my love of writing—*DN*

To Gerry Amirault, a business educator, a mentor, an inventor, and an inspiration to each of us—*TGM, JW, DN*

Reviewers

Kathi Bogue, Thames Valley District School Board, ON

Annice Blair, Durham District School Board, ON

Darlene Brindley, Simcoe County District School Board, ON

Diana Caringi, Ottawa-Carleton Catholic District School Board, ON

Ron Dawe, Lewisporte/Gander School District, NF

Joanne De Laurentiis, Mondex Canada, ON

Kathleen Elliott, Kawartha Pine Ridge District School Board, ON

Gordon H. Graham, Business Consultant, ON

Vance Grekul, Limestone District School Board, ON

Roy McMillan, formerly of Halton District School Board, ON

Ron McNamara, Windsor-Essex Catholic District School Board, ON

Lorianne Mendola, Hamilton-Wentworth Catholic District School Board, ON

Diane Mitchell, Avon Maitland District School Board, ON

Jamie Murphy, The Hospital for Sick Children Foundation, ON

Rob Notman, Murray-Axmith, ON

Mark O'Connor, Ottawa-Carleton Catholic District School Board, ON

Ann Pepin, Simcoe County District School Board, ON

John Pownall, York Region District School Board, ON

Linda J. Routledge, Canadian Bankers Association, ON

Wayne Roswell, Toronto District School Board, ON

Michael Schultz, Peel District School Board, ON

Marion Spino, Hamilton-Wentworth District School Board, ON

Margaret Stewart, Limestone District School Board, ON

Michael D. White, Northern Peninsula/Labrador South School District, ON

Jim Willson, Toronto District School Board, ON

Preface

To the student,

You are beginning your study of the world of business and you will face many choices and challenges as we move into the 21st century. With a global economy, the Internet, rapid technological advances, and an ever-changing workplace, it is important that you understand how the business world operates. Small businesses provide three of every four jobs in Canada, and future employees must be creative thinkers, problem solvers, and life-long learners. You must understand how the vital role of business in Canada and in the global economy will contribute to the ability of Canadian businesses to remain competitive and operate efficiently. You must also acquire a sound background in personal finance and ways in which to spend, save, and invest your money wisely. *The World of Business*, fourth edition, has been written to help you reach these goals.

Features of the Fourth Edition

Chapter Opening Profiles highlight a Canadian or a Canadian company whose business activities reflect the main ideas of each chapter.

Before You Begin questions and activities open each chapter. They are designed to build on your prior knowledge or begin a discussion about what you will be reading.

Stretch Your Thinking questions appear boxed in the margins throughout the text. They will help you develop your critical and creative thinking and inquiry skills.

Reflect on Your Learning questions and activities appear at the end of each chapter. Often, they link back to the "Before You Begin" to help you see what knowledge and attitude changes you have acquired through the study of the chapter.

E-activities appear throughout each chapter and link to the Nelson Thomson Learning Web site. These activities will help you use the Internet effectively to research business topics. The notes at the Nelson Web site connect the Internet research activity with chapter topics, concepts, and skills, and contain references to relevant sections of the chapter and its features.

Contemporary Issues in Canadian Business are presented in a Point/Counterpoint format, presenting both sides of a particular business-related issue. This feature includes a real life example and questions and activities that explore the issue in greater depth. There are 10 issues scattered throughout the text.

Career Focus features appear in the first chapter of each unit. They will provide you with basic information on career searches, how to apply for a job, and how to handle a job interview.

We hope that you will find *The World of Business* interesting, challenging, and stimulating as you begin your involvement in the world of business studies, both in school and throughout your lives.

Terry G. Murphy
Jack Wilson
David Notman

March, 2001

A Note from the Publisher: The brand names and photos that appear in this book do not represent endorsements, but rather are business-related examples relevant to the content of the text.

Table of Contents

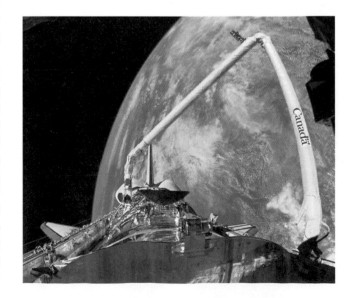

THE ROLE OF BUSINESS

Chapter 1 Understanding Business
Chapter 2 Business and the Consumer
Chapter 3 Starting a Business
Chapter 4 Business and the Community

"Successful businesspeople monitor social trends, adopt new technologies, compare themselves to the competition, and listen and watch with an open mind."

Human Resources Development Canada, "Could You Succeed in Small Business?," 1999

CHAPTER

1

UNDERSTANDING BUSINESS

STUDENT EXPECTATIONS

After completing this chapter, you will be able to

- define a business in both a formal and an informal manner
- distinguish between goods and services, essential goods and essential services, and luxury goods and luxury services
- identify and define the three kinds of economic resources
- explain how citizens are both producers and consumers of goods and services
- describe the concepts of demand and supply and the conditions that create each
- explain how needs, wants, and demand create opportunities for business
- explain how profit and competition affect businesses
- define interdependence and explain how businesses and consumers are interdependent
- apply the decision-making model in a business environment

Profile

Manoucher Etminan: entrepreneur and designer of breads.

THE BREADMAN

Manoucher Etminan has the hands of a baker. But he'll be the first to tell you that he isn't one. Instead, he will tell you in his rich Iranian accent that he is a designer of breads. And since Etminan has built a multimillion-dollar business baking hand-made specialty breads, nobody is likely to dispute this claim.

As a child in Iran, Etminan loved poetry and painting, but as he grew up, he felt these were impossible ways to support himself. He was working as a successful computer hardware importer when Iran's revolution (1979–1988) forced him and many others to leave the country. Etminan came to Canada and took a job waiting tables, but he longed for the opportunity to run his own business once again.

He started off by making old-fashioned-looking jars of a Persian pickle called *torshi*, and worked out a deal with Holt Renfrew to supply the store with nearly 1000 jars a month. His big moment, however, came in 1983 when he saw an opportunity to sell specialty breads. He says, "At that time, people went to the store to choose their vegetables, their cans, even their dog food, but not their bread. There was one shelf and all the breads looked the same." Many who knew him were skeptical, he says, but one friend lent him $6000, which enabled him to get his business off the ground.

When an early alliance with a baker didn't work out, the businessperson and artist became a baker himself. He baked his first breads by recalling the way his mother did it in Iran. "From there on, I started realizing that, 'Hey, I'm not a baker, I'm a designer.' When I design bread, I think of shape, style, for afternoon, for morning, for pizza, for sandwich, whatever."

Etminan went against the "grain" when establishing his business; it's a method he now recommends. He began with nothing but an idea and his own love of bread. But by skillfully tapping into

CONTINUED →

the growing market for gourmet foods, he has created great demand for a product where many thought it impossible to do so. "It's fine and good to start with an idea that everyone thinks will be a winner," he says, "but when the time comes that people start saying, 'No, it cannot work,' you will really have to fight and believe in yourself. It's a beautiful thing when you get there, because everyone was telling you you were wrong."

Etminan wants to be remembered as someone who rescued bread from the hands of large companies selling preservative-filled loaves at cheap prices. His specialty breads, which sell for as much as $7 a loaf, are more expensive than typical bread. Yet his sellers confirm that he has had plenty of imitators. And the soft, doughy breads have acquired legions of fans.

"They're delicious," says Paul Biggs, head chef at Le Sélect Bistro, a French restaurant in Toronto. "We get in trouble if we try to take one of them off the menu. Our customers ask why."

Manoucher's specialty breads are marketed to upscale food markets and gourmet restaurants.

All of Etminan's breads are handmade and packaged for export by 30 or 40 employees at his bakery in Toronto, Ontario. His daughter Henny has worked with the company since 1994. "He's never done a thing according to what others have told him. He's just gone with his gut. He's got a really good instinct for what he does," she says of her father.

The walls of the outer office display handwritten letters from satisfied customers, attesting to Etminan's success. As for the breads, "they bring smiles to people's faces," he observes. "When an old woman comes to me and says, 'Mr. Manoucher, so happy to meet you, you have done wonderful work,' that's the whole world to me."

About This Profile

1. What makes Etminan's products different from most of the other breads on the market?
2. Why did Etminan think that people would be interested in buying his specialty breads?
3. Why do you think many people thought that his business would fail? Why has he succeeded?

What Is Business?

Think about different businesses that you're familiar with. What do they have in common? Use your ideas to define "business."

In 2000, the Canadian Cancer Society's daffodil campaign raised over $6.2 million for cancer research.

Is a lemonade stand set up by two 10-year-olds an example of a business? Yes, it is. Roots Canada is a multinational corporation that employs thousands of people. Is Roots an example of a business? Absolutely. Businesses come in many different forms and sizes. But no matter how small or how big, they operate with the express purpose of making a profit for their owners. A formal definition of a **business** is as follows: an organization that produces or sells goods or services to satisfy the needs, wants, and demands of consumers for the purpose of making a profit.

A business can also be described informally by

- the type of ownership. For example, businesses that have two or more owners, or partners, are called partnerships. (See Chapter 3 for more information on types of ownership.)
- the goods it produces or services it offers. The Ford Motor Company produces cars, while All Languages provides translators and interpreters for over 100 languages.
- the different functions that it performs in its community. For example, the Canadian Cancer Society offers support and raises funds to help people who have cancer.
- the types of jobs it provides. A meat packing company, for example, provides jobs to farmers, inspectors, packaging manufacturers, and truck drivers.

Think about what business has done for you today. For example, the food you eat for lunch is a product of the combined efforts of farmers, food processors, retail outlets, and perhaps cafeteria workers. Your school was also constructed through the cooperation of hundreds of businesses. Some provided raw materials such as lumber, nails, and shingles; others provided skilled labourers to construct and equip the building.

Computer repair, plumbing, painting, and hair cutting are just a few of the services provided by businesses in Canada. The stores that sell goods to your family and the transportation companies that deliver the goods to the store are other types of business ventures. There are as many different types of businesses as there are ways to describe them.

People who take a risk and start businesses to solve a problem or to take advantage of an opportunity are called **entrepreneurs**. Often, entrepreneurs go into business to satisfy a need that is not being met in the marketplace. They recognize that an unsatisfied need is an opportunity for a business venture. Businesses cannot exist without the people who start them, manage them, and work in them. But without people to buy their goods or services, businesses would have no need to produce anything.

GOODS AND SERVICES

Businesses provide goods and services to supply people with the things that they need and want in their everyday lives. A **need** is an item that is necessary for survival such as food, clothing, or shelter. A **want** is an item that is not necessary for survival, but it adds pleasure and comfort to life. We will take a closer look at needs and wants in Chapter 2. Most **goods** have a dollars-and-cents, or monetary, value. The monetary value of a particular good may change over time. An old pair of sneakers, for example, might not be worth as much as a new pair, but the sneakers still might be of some use and value. Goods are produced and you can touch them. Something that you can see and touch, like a good, is referred to as a **tangible** item.

Most **services** also have monetary value because people are willing to pay for them. However, services are considered **intangible** because they do not result in a product that you can touch. When you visit your dentist or play a round of golf, for example, you are paying for intangible services, not tangible goods. Some services are unpaid, such as those provided by volunteers doing community service work. Such services are very valuable to not-for-profit organizations and particularly to those people in need who are helped. A **not-for-profit organization** is a business that does not seek to make a profit. It is usually a charitable organization that helps numerous people, such as a community food bank or the United Way.

Take a walk through a "big-box" home-improvement store, like Home Depot. You will see several thousand different goods—painting supplies, kitchen cabinets, lawncare products, lighting fixtures, and barbecues. Almost anything that you can think of for the home is available for sale at Home Depot. These goods are available because of the combined efforts of many businesses. For example, the kitchen cabinets consist of nails, brackets, lumber, varnish, and handles. These individual goods are assembled so that the kitchen cabinets can be sold as one unit.

Home Depot also provides many services. Employees offer advice on the goods available for sale, answer questions such as which paint is best for outdoor furniture, or make exchanges or returns. Like many home improvement stores, Home Depot provides a delivery service for its customers. Employees also conduct "How to" seminars to teach their customers special skills, such as putting up drywall.

E-ACTIVITY

Visit
www.business.
nelson.com
and follow the links
to find out more
about
not-for-profit
organizations in
Canada.

A Home Depot employee conducts a "How to Wallpaper" seminar.

Some stores have another business on-site to provide other products or services. Many Home Depot stores, for example, also have a Harvey's hamburger franchise. This additional service makes it convenient for customers to eat and shop. While having lunch, customers may think of other goods that they want to buy before they leave. Having two or more businesses under one roof is commonly referred to as **co-branding**. Co-branding allows businesses to share space, reducing the costs of operation and increasing the opportunity for profit.

Essential and Luxury Goods and Services

Essential goods and **essential services** are things that we need for survival. Essential goods include food, clothing, and shelter. Utilities such as heating, lighting, and water are examples of essential services. **Luxury goods** and **luxury services** are enjoyable but not necessary for survival. Home entertainment centres and swimming pools are two examples of luxury goods. Taking a limousine ride or visiting a spa are examples of luxury services.

Is getting a hair cut an essential service or a luxury service?

Flip through your Yellow Pages telephone directory. You will see advertisements for many different businesses that provide hundreds of products for your consumption: DVD players, computers, large and small appliances, clothing, sporting and exercise equipment, jewellery, watches, automotive supplies, and many more. Some of these goods are essential and others are luxuries. You will also find advertisements for services such as computer programming, dry-cleaning, decorating, moving, tax preparation, and flower arranging. Which of these services do you consider to be luxuries?

Economic Resources

Goods and services do not just suddenly appear in the marketplace. Goods must be created from basic components. Providing services requires skill and effort. **Economic resources**, also commonly referred to as **factors of production**, are the means through which goods and services are made available to consumers. There are three kinds of economic resources: natural resources, human resources, and capital resources.

Natural resources are those raw materials that come from the earth, water, and air. Soil, iron ore, gold, oil, trees, wildlife, agricultural products, fish, and oxygen are all examples of natural resources used in the production of goods and services.

Human resources (sometimes referred to as "labour") are the people who work to create the goods and services. Some examples are farmers, factory workers, construction workers, Web site designers, investment bankers, teachers, nurses, and pilots. The human component is so important that many businesses have established a human resources department to manage their employees. (See Chapter 7 for more information on human resources.)

Capital resources are the third factor of production. They include buildings, equipment, tools, trucks, and factories. Capital resources usually last for a long period of time and often require a substantial investment on the part of a business. In addition to purchasing buildings and equipment, businesses also require money, another capital resource, to buy the raw materials and services they use to produce their own product or service.

In most cases, it takes a combination of all three economic resources to create the goods and services that businesses provide. But what if there isn't enough of one of these economic resources? Oil is a natural resource whose supply seems to fluctuate. As a result, the price of oil goes up and down. Businesses rely on this natural resource—if it is not going to be available in the same quantities as before, alternatives need to be found. Concern about depleting oil reserves has led to the development of other forms of energy, such as nuclear power, which can provide the power for running businesses. Because of pollution, we do not have an unlimited supply of clean air, water, and land. Since our resources are limited, we are limited in what we can build and produce.

Producers and Consumers

Most businesses provide either goods or services designed to satisfy consumer needs and wants. For example, a computer manufacturer is a **producer** of a product, while a computer-repair shop is a provider of a service. The people who buy computers, along with those who have their computers serviced at computer-repair shops, are known as **consumers**. Companies that can attract more consumers to their place of business will have more opportunities to generate sales and make a profit.

A person can be both a producer and a consumer of the same product. When a computer-store owner combines component parts to make computer systems, he or she is a producer. However, when the same owner uses a personal computer for accounting, inventory, pricing, and sales, he or she is a consumer.

STRETCH YOUR THINKING

What related products and services could a computer store sell to attract consumers?

ACTIVITIES FOR ...

INFORMATION	CONNECTION	EXTENSION
1. a) What is the formal definition of a business?	**b)** Give an actual business example for each of the four informal ways of describing a business.	**c)** Ask two business owners how they would define a business.
2. a) Complete this statement: "Without _____ , businesses would have no need to produce anything."	**b)** Select a local business. Find out who started it, who the managers are, what their titles and duties are, and what the duties of three workers are.	**c)** Find out how many businesses operate in your community. What percentage of those businesses are considered small businesses? What is the definition of a small business?
3. a) Define "co-branding."	**b)** List a business in your community that has co-branded.	**c)** In your opinion, will more businesses co-brand in the future? Give reasons to support your answer.
4. a) Identify three essential goods and three essential services.	**b)** Can the same service be essential to one person but a luxury to another? Explain, using an example.	**c)** Would you prefer to run a business that provides essential goods and services or one that offers luxury goods and services? Explain your choice.
5. a) What is another name for "factors of production"?	**b)** What natural resources are in or near your community? Are any of them at risk? Explain.	**c)** How can money function as a capital resource for both producers and consumers?

Demand, Supply, and Price

The amount of a good or service that we demand, the amount of a good or service that suppliers supply, and the price of a good or service all affect one another. Let's examine the relationship between demand, supply, and price.

DEMAND

Demand is the quantity of a good or service that consumers are willing and able to buy at a particular price. Since each of us has different needs and wants, we each have different demands. When we buy a particular good or use a particular service, we are expressing a demand for it. Usually, consumers will increase the quantity demanded of a good or service as prices decrease. As prices increase, the reverse is true. This relationship is called the **Law of Demand**.

Four Conditions That Create Demand

Several conditions create a demand. First, the consumer must be aware of or interested in the good or service. Businesses usually address this condition by advertising their good or service. Other conditions involve having an ample supply of the good or service available for the consumer and establishing prices that are reasonable and competitive. Finally, accessibility is critical. The good or service must be conveniently located for the consumer to purchase. In fact, many businesses attribute their success to "location, location, location."

Factors That Affect Demand

Many factors affect demand. The demand for a good or service can be affected by a change in consumers' income. Generally speaking, as incomes increase, people buy more of a product than before. For example, a raise in pay may result in some people buying an extra TV, taking an extra holiday, or buying more clothes. However, for some goods, the opposite may be true. An increase in income may result in the purchase of fewer groceries and an increase in the purchase of restaurant meals.

A second factor that affects demand is a change in consumers' tastes. The fashion industry is a good example of how quickly the demand for certain products or styles increases while the demand for others decreases. Popular music, too, depends on consumers' tastes. A song that is popular today may be gone from the charts tomorrow.

A third factor that affects demand is a change in expectations of future conditions. For example, if consumers expect that either prices or income will increase in the future, they will often purchase more now. For most goods and services, this will result in an increase in demand. However, if they expect the opposite to occur, demand will decrease.

Lastly, a change in population will affect demand. An increase in population will create an increase in the need for housing, cars, roads, waterworks and sewers, schools, hospitals, clothes, and nearly every good and service imaginable. Also, as certain segments of the population increase, demand for goods associated with those segments will increase. Presently in Canada, there is an increase in the population of people over the age of 55. As a result, the demand for health care, sports activities such as golfing and curling, and housing in the form of adult lifestyle and retirement homes is increasing. (See Chapter 6 for more information about the connection between characteristics of different populations and demand.)

SUPPLY

If the goods and services we demand can be provided at prices we are willing to pay, businesses will supply them. **Supply** is the quantity of a good or service that businesses are willing and able to provide within a range of prices that people would be willing to pay. Businesspeople recognize consumers' needs and wants and try to provide the goods and services to satisfy them—at a profit, of course. Some businesses are more efficient than others. Take, for example, a particular group of businesses that produce similar goods in the same market. Those businesses that are more efficient will produce more goods for the same price as businesses that are less efficient. Generally speaking, as prices increase, producers will be able to use the increased revenue to put more goods and services on the market. With higher prices, they can afford to pay overtime, expand their factories, hire another shift, and buy more productive equipment. This relationship of increasing the quantity supplied as prices increase is called the **Law of Supply**.

Conditions That Affect Supply

The supply of a good or service is affected by the cost of producing it and, to some extent, by the price people are willing to pay for it. Occasionally, a business will try to create demand for a new product or service simply by supplying it for sale in the marketplace. Although this strategy involves risk, it also produces an opportunity for enormous profits if a demand is created.

There are many factors that affect supply. The first is a change in the number of producers. If a particular product seems to provide attractive profits, new businesses will soon start to produce that product. The result is that more of these products will enter the market. As a result, if demand remains the same, prices will be lower because of the increased competition.

A second factor affecting supply is the price of related goods. For example, if the price of wheat decreases, farmers may shift production from wheat to corn or soybeans. As the price of steel increases, car and

STRETCH YOUR THINKING

What changes in technology used in space exploration have affected the supply of products in your home or school?

appliance manufacturers may switch to using more plastic. As the price of gas increases, consumers may switch to smaller, more fuel-efficient automobiles or, if possible, use more public transit.

A change in technology is a third factor affecting supply. As computer chip technology has improved, computers have become much more powerful, much lower in cost, and affordable to many more consumers. This improvement has drastically changed the supply of PCs worldwide.

The fourth factor affecting supply is a change in expectations. This affects producers as well as consumers. Producers must always plan ahead to forecast sales, production, financing, and so on. Many producers try to predict economic conditions and consumer demand for two to five years in advance. As conditions change, they must adjust their plans accordingly. Imagine the planning and forecasting that must take place before a new car rolls off the assembly line, or a new tenant moves into a new office tower or apartment complex. Each decision that is made in the planning process can have an effect on other, related businesses. (See Chapter 7 for more information on planning.)

The last factor that affects supply is a change in costs of production. If a local baker can find a lower-cost source of sugar and flour, he or she can produce more products for the same cost of production. Suppose a student is setting up a lawn service and has $2000 to purchase lawn mowers. If each lawn mower costs $500, the student may buy four mowers, hire four workers, and arrange contracts to put the four employees to work. However, if a new source of suitable mowers is found at $400 each, five mowers can be purchased and five workers hired.

A store owner orders more stock from his supplier in anticipation of a sale.

PRICE

Price is determined by many factors, including both demand and supply. And as you have seen, both demand and supply change as a result of the actions of consumers and producers. If consumer demand for a good or service is high while the supply of that same good or service is low, prices will tend to be higher. Conversely, if consumer demand for a good or service is low while the supply of that good or service is high, prices will tend to be lower. Prices tend to fluctuate, sometimes rapidly, because demand and supply are constantly changing. For example, during the fall season, businesses have a large supply of fall and winter goods for sale. Prices of these goods usually remain higher during this time period. Then, as winter comes to an end, businesses will put these goods on sale to clear them out and make room for spring and summer stock. (See Chapter 5 for more information on the relationship between demand, supply, and price.)

Price is also influenced by the cost of producing a good or service. For example, if the cost of producing DVD players were low enough that they could be sold for $50 each, many of us would want to own one. Low prices tend to increase consumer demand. On the other hand, if ballpoint pens cost $50 each, most of us would be forced to use pencils. High prices tend to decrease the quantity of goods and services that consumers will buy. In other words, high prices usually decrease demand.

ACTIVITIES FOR ...

INFORMATION	CONNECTION	EXTENSION
1. a) Identify the four conditions that create demand.	**b)** Think of the things that you and your friends buy or would like to buy. What products are in high demand among your age group? Why are they in demand?	**c)** Give an example of a business that created demand for a product simply by supplying it for sale in the marketplace. What was the product? How did the market-place respond?
2. a) What factors affect the supply of a product or service? What factors affect the price?	**b)** Give an example of a product whose price tends to fluctuate. How does this fluctuation affect people's purchases?	**c)** At one time, hand-held calculators were expensive to purchase. Explain how changes in supply and demand have affected the price of these calculators.

Career Focus 1: Who Am I?

THE CANADIAN WORKPLACE: AN INTRODUCTION

The Canadian workplace has changed considerably during the past 10 years, and it will continue to do so throughout the 21st century. The jobs held by today's workers are constantly changing, too. Many jobs are being eliminated, while other jobs will cause the work, and the workers, to change. Often, these changes require employees to develop new skills or to be retrained.

There are many reasons for these changes. Companies merge, new technology influences how workers perform their jobs, and new Canadians from all over the world enrich the workplace with their experience and expertise. All these changes contribute to the ability of Canadian businesses to remain competitive and operate efficiently.

CAREER PLANNING

An **occupation** is a specific job. It is something you do in order to provide a good or service. People are hired to fill jobs and are paid for the work that they do. A **career** is the path toward a goal in life that is fulfilled through an occupation or series of occupations. **Career planning** is the process of studying careers and career options; assessing your talents, abilities, and preferences; and then deciding on a future career based on this personal assessment.

Occupations are often classified into two very broad groups: white-collar and blue-collar. **White-collar workers** handle and process information. They may spend a great deal of time interacting with other people. White-collar workers perform professional, managerial, and clerical work. **Blue-collar workers** are involved in operating machinery and equipment. They are employed in factories, in machine shops, and on construction sites. However, the increased use of computers and information

technology is changing the role of the blue-collar worker. Today, many jobs require additional levels of education and training.

SELF-AWARENESS

In a few years, you will need to choose a career—and you must be prepared. How can you tell what you want to be and do?

You must examine your likes and dislikes, skills and abilities, talents, personality, and values. Using these factors as guidelines, you will need to research the types of jobs that are available in your chosen field and the educational requirements for these jobs. Finally, you will need to learn the best way to go about getting a job. The Career Focus sections, found in the first chapter of each unit in this book, are designed to assist you in this process.

KNOW YOURSELF

Before planning a career, you must be able to answer this question: "Who am I?" The first step in planning is to conduct a self-assessment of your skills and goals, and then choose a career that suits and interests you.

What activities do you enjoy most? What do you least like to do? Do you enjoy working and playing with others as part of a team, or would you rather do things alone? Do you enjoy leadership roles? What are your hobbies and interests?

Many experts believe that everyone has **multiple intelligences**. There are eight types of intelligence; everyone has some intelligence in all eight areas, but each person has three or four areas that are dominant or stand out. Realizing what your dominant intelligences are can help you better understand your strengths and make sound decisions about your future.

Another helpful resource is "Employability Skills 2000+," which is

E-ACTIVITY

Visit
**www.careers.
nelson.com**
and follow the links
to other Web sites
about careers.

published by the Conference Board of Canada. "Employability Skills 2000+" organizes the critical skills, attitudes, and behaviours needed for the world of work into three categories: academic, teamwork, and personal management skills. Canadian employers use this skills profile as a guideline when they are considering which workers to hire. You can use it to figure out which skills you need in order to get (and keep) a job. Developing your employability skills will also enable you to progress in the world of work—whether you work on your own or as part of a team.

There are many advantages to making initial career decisions while you are still in school. One advantage is that you have a lot of good information available to help you select the right courses and start planning your career. But because the decisions you make today will likely change over time, you should keep your options open and make course selections that will prepare you for a variety of possible careers.

Something to Think About

1. Read "Employability Skills 2000+," published by the Conference Board of Canada, and answer the following questions:
   a) What are your academic, teamwork, and personal management skills? Identify at least one skill from each category.
   b) What characteristics reflect a positive attitude?

2. Look at Figure 1.1. Think of what you know about yourself. Then answer the following questions:
   a) What are my interests?
   b) What are my most dominant intelligences?
   c) What are my least dominant intelligences?
   d) How have my intelligences helped me develop my skills?
   e) How is this information useful in my career planning?

Figure 1.1

Multiple Intelligences

Verbal/linguistic intelligence
- using language to present your ideas, to express your feelings, or to persuade others

Logical/mathematical intelligence
- reasoning, logical thinking; handling mathematical problems

Visual/spatial intelligence
- creating and interpreting visual images; thinking in three dimensions

Bodily/kinesthetic intelligence
- feeling and expressing things physically; doing hands-on work

Musical/rhythmic intelligence
- creating and feeling a rhythm to express a mood; detecting and analyzing musical themes

Intrapersonal intelligence (within the self)
- understanding your own thoughts and feelings in a very clear way

Interpersonal intelligence (between people)
- understanding the feelings, needs, and purposes of others

Naturalist intelligence
- understanding nature, seeking patterns in the way nature works; classifying things

Profit and Competition

The goal of business is to make a profit by supplying goods and services to meet consumer demands. A business must earn some profit to be successful. **Profit** is the income that is left after all costs and expenses are paid. **Expenses** are those expenditures that are involved in running a business, such as wages, as well as those assets that get "used up" in the process, such as a car. **Costs** are the amount of money required for each stage of production, such as the cost of raw materials. For example, if a store sells goods for $500 and costs and expenses total $350, the profit on the sale of those goods is $150. As costs and expenses increase, the owner's profit gets smaller. Businesses, therefore, try to keep costs and expenses as low as possible by being efficient and well organized. One of the largest expenses for a business is its payroll, or the wages it pays its employees. If a business decreases its staff to save on expenses, profits may increase. However, if there are not enough employees to serve customers, sales could decrease and profits could actually decline. (See Chapter 5 for more information on increasing profit and controlling costs and expenses.)

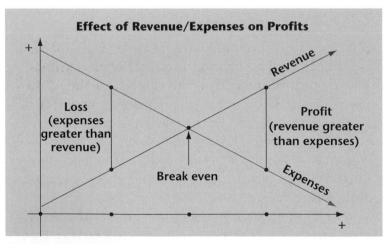

Figure 1.2 Profit can increase or decrease, depending on how much a business spends on costs and expenses.

Making a profit enables a business to put more money back into the operation for expansion and growth. Some businesses might choose to use profits to provide better goods or improved services. Profit also gives the owner money to spend on personal needs and wants. If a business does not make a profit but the owner is still able to pay all debts, the business is **solvent**. Solvency means having the ability to pay your debts and meet financial obligations. Business losses or failure to make a profit will eventually force an owner to close the operation. In 1999, insolvency led to the closure of Eaton's department stores all across Canada, though seven stores have since reopened under the ownership of Sears. Ideally, a business meets all of its debt obligations and also makes a profit.

Have you ever wondered why the price of a new car begins at about $15 000 and goes up from there? Demand and supply certainly have an influence on price, but so does **competition**. If only one company offered cars for sale, that company could set the price and consumers would have to pay it if they wanted a car. In reality, however, many companies sell cars and compete for car-buying consumers. This competition helps keep car prices at a reasonable level. In Canada, free enterprise and competition among businesses is encouraged and promoted. **Free enterprise** is an economic system in which economic resources are privately owned and decisions about what to produce are made freely by individual owners. (See Chapter 4 for more information about free enterpise.)

Consumers can benefit from competition among businesses in several ways. Lower prices are one obvious benefit. Businesses constantly monitor their competitors so that they can match or better the price of their competitors' goods or services. Gas stations change their prices on a regular basis to make sure that they remain competitive. Higher-quality goods and services are another benefit. Businesses are always looking for a competitive edge. If a business can "build a better mousetrap," both the business and the consumer will benefit. Lastly, competition among businesses can lead to the development and introduction of new products.

KEY TO BUSINESS SURVIVAL

A business cannot survive unless it produces goods or services that people need or want. In Canada, consumers can choose from thousands of different products and services. Your choices, combined with those of all other Canadians, determine what goods and services will be produced and in what quantities. These choices also determine which businesses will be successful. If people decide that they no longer want or need snowmobiles, companies will sell fewer and lower production of them. With lower consumer demand, some businesses that manufacture snowmobiles could not survive.

Over the years, many products become **obsolete**, which means they are no longer in use. Either people no longer want or need these products, or new and improved products replace them. Treadle sewing machines, steam-powered locomotives, wringer washing machines, manual typewriters, Beta VCRs, and 8-track cassettes are a few goods that have become obsolete. Services can also become obsolete. In the early 1900s, all street lamps were gaslights. Each night, a lamplighter would light each lamp by hand. Coal and ice were delivered to homes so that people could heat their houses and keep their food cold. These services are no longer provided because they are no longer needed or wanted.

Businesses are always looking for ways to produce new and better products and to provide better services to consumers. Successful businesses change as the wants and needs of consumers change. These same businesses pay attention to basic business survival tactics such as risk taking, innovation, and adaptability. You will learn more about these survival tactics in later chapters.

INTERDEPENDENCE

Our society is **interdependent**, which means we rely on the goods and services provided by thousands of different businesses to satisfy our needs and wants. Businesses are also highly interdependent. A clothing manufacturer, for example, buys the goods and services of many other businesses to produce a final product. To make a pair of jeans, the manufacturer relies on other businesses to provide the denim, thread, zippers, buttons, rivets, and sewing and cutting machines that it requires. The shopping list for a large manufacturing company would include raw materials, machinery, replacement parts, office supplies, and cleaning and repair services. Small businesses also rely on others. The neighbourhood variety store relies on the suppliers of many different products to stock its shelves. The local bakery buys flour, sugar, eggs, and other ingredients from several businesses and advertises in newspapers run by still other businesses. For such a system to run smoothly, cooperation is a necessity.

The consuming habits of Canadians tell businesses what goods and services consumers want, when they want them, where they want them, and how much they are willing to pay for them. Businesses use this information to provide goods and services in sufficient quantities to satisfy consumer demands. However, businesses can only respond to the demands of consumers and consumer groups if it is possible and profitable for them to do so. Businesses need you and you need businesses.

Decision-Making Model

Making timely business decisions is more than a matter of good fortune, although even the most successful businessperson welcomes a bit of luck from time to time. One important business decision is determining how much inventory a business must carry to satisfy the needs and wants of consumers. **Inventory**, sometimes called stock, is the quantity of goods and materials kept on hand. If a business keeps too much inventory, a lot of financial resources are tied up. As a result, that money is no longer available to generate income for the business. If the inventory consists of chocolate bars and potato chips, stocking up on inventory would probably not be a major investment. However, if the business is a car dealership, there could easily be millions of dollars invested in inventory. A car dealership could have four versions of the same model car in four different colour combinations available

for sale. If the dealership had to pay for these cars in advance and if they did not sell quickly, a lot of the dealership's money would not be available for other purposes. A decision-making model could help the owner with this problem.

You can use the five-step **decision-making model** that follows as you proceed through *The World of Business*. It is not necessary to use this model when you make simple decisions like what to wear to school, especially if your school policy outlines a specific dress code. However, if you are considering a purchase that involves a lot of money, such as a new computer, you may find the model helpful as an organizer. The decision-making model may also assist you in making personal decisions, such as which career to pursue or which postsecondary institution to attend.

Figure 1.3 How does the decision-making model help you make better choices?

THE DECISION-MAKING PROCESS

GOOD DECISION

1. Define the decision.
2. Identify alternatives.
3. Evaluate alternatives.
4. Make a decision and take action.
5. Evaluate the decision.

PROBLEM

1. **Define the decision to be made.** How many vehicles should a car dealership keep on the lot to satisfy consumer demand?

2. **Identify the alternatives.** One alternative would be to have several models of each type of vehicle available. A second alternative would be to have only one model of each type of vehicle available.

3. **Evaluate the advantages and disadvantages of each alternative.** One advantage of having many vehicles available is that it gives consumers a number of choices. Consumers can choose from a variety of models and colours. Possible disadvantages include the cost of purchasing many vehicles and finding space to display and store them.

   An advantage of having only one model on hand is that the smaller inventory will not tie up a lot of financial resources. The dealer may be able to afford to spend more on advertising. On the other hand, if competitors have larger inventories, consumers may decide to shop at dealerships that offer more choice.

4. **Make a decision and take action.** If all possible alternatives are identified and if the advantages and disadvantages of each alternative are very carefully considered, an informed decision can be made. It is time to take action and live with the decision. What decision might the car dealer make?

5. **Evaluate the decision.** After some time has passed, it is wise to review the decision. If a mistake was made, reconsider the alternatives and take appropriate action. As you review your decision, new alternatives may surface.

ACTIVITIES FOR ...

INFORMATION	CONNECTION	EXTENSION
1. a) Define "profit."	**b)** One way that consumers benefit from competition among businesses is by having access to new or improved products in the marketplace. Identify two of these new or improved products.	**c)** How might increased competition affect profit?
2. a) Define "obsolescence."	**b)** Think of a business in your community that used to provide a product or service that is now obsolete. Describe how changes in demand or supply for that product affected the business.	**c)** Interview an entrepreneur to determine which of the following survival tactics he or she has used in business, and why: risk taking, innovation, and adaptability.
3. a) Give an example that shows how businesses are interdependent, and another example that shows how businesses and consumers are interdependent.	**b)** Select a business familiar to you. Draw a diagram to illustrate how it relies on at least six other businesses.	**c)** What kinds of problems would a business encounter if the employees of one of the businesses it relies on went on strike? What measures could the business take to make sure that it continues to meet consumer demand?
4. a) Which step is the most critical in the decision-making process?	**b)** Identify a decision that is about to be made by a local business. If you were the owner of this business, what decision would you make? Use the decision-making model to outline your choices and help you arrive at the best alternative.	**c)** How would you go about evaluating a decision that has already been made and carried out?

Review

Knowledge and Understanding

1. Match each of the following terms to the correct definition:

   consumers   producers
   demand   profit
   essential goods   service
   luxury goods   supply

   a) Items you require to survive.

   b) The quantity of a good or service that consumers are willing and able to buy at a particular price.

   c) The quantity of a good or service that businesses are willing and able to provide within a range of prices that people would be willing to pay.

   d) The people who buy goods and services.

   e) Goods that are nice to have but are not necessary for survival.

   f) The amount of money left over after all costs and expenses have been taken away from a business's income.

   g) Something provided by a waiter, a store clerk, or a cab driver.

   h) Individuals or businesses that make goods to meet the needs and wants of consumers.

2. Look through the chapter for other new terms and their definitions. Write each term on a card and its definition on another. Use the cards to play a game of "Concentration."

3. Copy the chart below into your notebook. Complete the chart by identifying three competing businesses for each category. For example, under the category of fast-food restaurants, you might list McDonald's, Burger King, and Harvey's as the competing businesses.

	Competing Businesses		
Category	**1**	**2**	**3**
Fast-food restaurants			
Pharmacies			
Department stores			
Hotels			
Airlines			
Service stations			
"Big box" stores			
Computers			
Tire dealers			
Banks			

4. In-line skates are a finished product made up of many goods. List the goods that are used to make in-line skates.

5. Explain how someone can be both a producer and a consumer of the same good or service.

6. "Businesses need you and you need businesses." Explain the statement, citing examples from your own experiences and the experiences of your family.

Thinking and Inquiry

1. The decision-making model presented in this chapter has five steps. Demonstrate how you would use these five steps in each of the following situations:
   a) selecting courses to complete your diploma
   b) deciding whether to take a part-time job while attending school

2. "Businesses sometimes take advantage of consumers." Give an example that supports this statement. Prepare a brief argument supporting or criticizing the action taken by the business in your example.

3. "Consumers sometimes take advantage of businesses." Give an example that supports this statement. Prepare a brief argument supporting or criticizing the action taken by the consumer in your example.

4. The demand for a product or service can change overnight. Why might demand change so quickly? How would the price and supply of this product be affected?

Communication

1. Choose three categories of businesses from Question 3 in Knowledge and Understanding. Interview students, teachers, family members, and friends to find out where they shop for each category. Why do they prefer buying goods and services from these businesses? To prompt their thinking, ask about quality, price, selection, convenience, service, and other factors. Then, meet with a partner to discuss the results of your interviews. What factors seem to be most important in people's decisions of where to shop? With your partner, write a report of your findings. Share your report with the class.

2. Several community agencies provide services to students in your school. Investigate one of these agencies and the services it provides. Design a poster telling about the agency. Display it by the guidance office, in the cafeteria, or in the library.

Application

1. Many goods and services that are common today will not be available 10 years from now. List 10 goods or services that you think will be obsolete in 10 years. Give reasons for your choices. What goods or services might replace these obsolete ones?

2. Work in a group of not more than four students to discuss and answer the following "What if" questions:
   a) What if all businesses closed their operations for a two-week period?
   b) What if all consumers had unlimited amounts of money to spend?
   Create a third "What if" question that relates to the contents of this chapter. Exchange this third question with another group.

REFLECT ON YOUR LEARNING

1. Think back to the definition of "business" you wrote for the Before You Begin question on page 5. How has your definition changed after reading this chapter?

2. In your own words, state three important ideas that you learned in this chapter. How do they relate to the profile of Manoucher Etminan?

CHAPTER
2
BUSINESS AND THE CONSUMER

STUDENT EXPECTATIONS

After completing this chapter, you will be able to

- demonstrate how businesses respond to needs and wants
- analyze how needs, wants, values, and goals affect consumer spending
- understand how choice affects you as a consumer
- identify the key factors that influence what consumers buy
- identify three key factors that determine how consumers buy
- describe the concepts behind e-commerce
- explain how a business can get established online

Steve Debus, owner of Mōdrobes.

MŌDROBES: CLOTHING THE MODERN WORLD

Young designer/entrepreneur Steve Debus's funky urban sportswear clothing line, Mōdrobes, is booming. He went from sales of $70 000 in his first season to $3 million in 1999, and he is intent on making Mōdrobes the next Levi's. But he's definitely not going the denim route. Explains Steve: "Denim is not a fit for the modern world! People sit at computers now rather than working in factories and need something more comfortable, a little more lightweight. That's where I thought we would fit perfectly."

Mōdrobes has taken off because of Steve's back-to-basics marketing style. Staying current with young customers means marketing where they meet. So on Canada Day 1999, Steve set up shop at Edgefest in Barrie, Ontario, one stop on a nine-city, cross-country series of rock concerts. In Barrie, with a two-storey booth, Steve and staff sold their clothes to a captive audience of 30 000 who flock to gatherings like this.

From there, the Mōdrobes travelling road show made stops at Edgefests all the way to Vancouver. These concert sell-a-thons were a lot of fun—and profitable. But that's not all: They also created huge demand. Steve launched retail outlets in Toronto to deal with the soaring local sales. He also started selling wholesale to stores across Canada. Plus, he was doing all the designing himself.

Faced with almost unrelenting growth, what was a stretched-thin entrepreneur to do? By late July, Steve's solution to his growth crisis seemed to be … ignore it. The call of the road was too strong. This time he headed to Woodstock '99 in Rome, New York. For the first time ever, Mōdrobes sold in the U.S. Despite deplorable conditions and many technical difficulties, American kids bought Mōdrobes in droves.

CONTINUED →

The Woodstock experience just added to Steve's master marketing plan. After all, did anyone see a Gap outlet there? Steve's analysis: "No one else will do it. No one will take that risk. You start to become part of that atmosphere. It's not a reckless brand. It's a legend of your own. It's more than clothing. It's a lifestyle."

The next step in Steve's marketing plan was to customize for his customers, so that not every retailer sold the same styles. For example, Steve designed a new Mōdrobes pant, with drawstrings and an extra pocket, for his biggest customer, Athlete's World stores. For the price of a small modification, Steve is able to keep the Mōdrobes line in the "coolest clothing" category.

After such a frenzied summer, was it time to slow down? Not likely. Next on the dance card for Mōdrobes: a two-month-long tour of university campuses. Steve Debus is just a guy who can't say "No" to growth. "Our biggest challenge for the future is being able to maintain this level of energy doing all these events as well as being able to maintain the operation of business, having the supply flow out to the stores. That's the key to whether or not we'll succeed. I'd rather not be a traditional company. I'd rather do all those things or nothing." And Mōdrobes is succeeding. It now has four retail outlets in Toronto, sells wholesale to 450 other stores across Canada, and distribution in the U.S. is growing. What could be next?

About This Profile

1. "People sit at computers now rather than working in factories and need something more comfortable." Do you agree that consumers need the kind of clothing that Mōdrobes sells? Explain why or why not.

2. How does Mōdrobes's advertising strategy differ from that of other clothing companies such as Gap? Why do you think this strategy has been effective in attracting teenage consumers?

Today's Consumer

BEFORE YOU BEGIN

How do you think your needs, wants, values, and goals are reflected in the goods and services you buy? Make a note of your ideas so that you can return to them at the end of the chapter.

In Chapter 1, we looked at how businesses try to satisfy consumer wants and needs by providing goods and services. In Canada, billions of dollars worth of goods and services are bought, sold, and exchanged each day. But for businesses, satisfying consumers is not always easy. Often, consumers are not sure what they need and want.

We are all consumers, but no two consumers are identical. We each have our own needs, wants, values, and goals. Francine comes from a family that struggles to make ends meet. Her parents cannot help with university expenses, so she studies hard to earn scholarship-level marks. She does occasional work at an animal shelter and intends to study veterinary medicine. Helmut contributes most of his money from his part-time job to his family because his father's business went bankrupt. Helmut's marks are suffering, but his family is desperate. Farhana comes from a prosperous family. She spends all her spare time training in track and field, and spends a great deal of money on equipment and travel expenses to sports meets. She is driven to achieve a career in sports.

NEEDS AND WANTS

Needs are necessities; they are the goods and services you must have to survive. Wants, no matter how urgent they may seem, are not necessary for survival. The difference between needs and wants sometimes gets blurred. Needs and wants differ from person to person. Today, many Canadian families feel that their basic needs go beyond food, clothing, and shelter to include television, radio, a car (or two), and a computer. Goods and services that were once considered wants become needs.

Without employment, most people could not pay for their basic needs, let alone satisfy their wants. For many, employment is so important for survival that it must be added to the list of basic needs.

In Canada, most people feel that getting an education is a basic need.

Satisfying Needs and Wants

If you were to conduct a survey, you might find that most people say all they want from life is to be healthy, happy, and successful. However, if you ask a more specific question, for example, "What things do you need to be healthy, happy, and successful?," you may find that the list of wants is much longer. In-line skates, fashionable clothing and hairstyles, vacations, CD and DVD players, movies, computer games, cell phones—for some people, these items seem to be essential to life. These are just a few of the thousands of goods and services competing for the attention and pocketbooks of consumers.

How you satisfy your needs and wants depends on your lifestyle and financial resources. Deciding whether or not to satisfy a want usually involves answering these types of questions:
• Do I really need it?
• Where would I buy it?
• Is there much variety to choose from?
• How much can I afford to spend?
• Should I wait for it to go on sale?
• Is it possible that someone may buy it for me?

VALUES AND GOALS

Values are based on what you believe is important in life. Personal experiences influence our values, as does the behaviour of family members, friends, classmates, and other people in the community. Personal values often change after a significant emotional event, such as the loss of a friend or relative. All of a sudden, something that seemed so important is not as critical. Traumatic events like this affect people at different times in their lives, which is another reason why values differ from person to person.

Goals are closely related to values. A goal is something that you work to achieve. For example, if you value good health and fitness, your goal might be to maintain or improve your physical condition. To achieve this goal, you might take a brisk walk every day, join a sports team, or enroll in a fitness club. Goals can be **short term** (achieved in the near future) or **long term** (achieved years later). Saving money to purchase your favourite group's latest CD is a short-term goal. Saving money to pay for your college or university tuition is a long-term goal. It is wise to have both types of goals. Focusing on a few goals and celebrating the achievement of those goals can be very satisfying.

CHOICES

Like most consumers, you are probably financially unable to buy all the goods and services you need and want. Therefore, it is necessary to make choices. For example, you may need winter boots and also want new running shoes. Which item should you buy—the boots or the shoes? Could you buy both? The cost of the goods, the available styles and sizes, and any special deals will help you make your choice. Of course, the amount of money that you choose to spend (or are able to spend) will chiefly determine what you buy.

Each day, you make choices, some of which may involve spending money. Many everyday choices are easy to make, for example, what you will wear to school, eat for lunch, or watch on television. For such choices, there are unlikely to be any major consequences no matter what you decide. Other choices are important and require careful consideration. For example, choosing a career requires a great deal of research and decision making; an inappropriate choice could have long-term effects. (The five-step decision-making model on pages 18–20 is helpful whenever you need to make a serious decision.)

The high cost of products and services—particularly in housing—has forced many families to be careful about what they buy. Unwise choices can be costly. Decision-making skills are more important than ever. For some families, making the right decisions can be the difference between paying the rent or not. For most Canadian families, however, making good choices simply means being able to sustain their lifestyle.

These consumers listen to CDs in the store to help them choose what to buy.

Family Lifestyles

Changing family lifestyles, including family size and family responsibilities, have a major impact not only on how much people spend but on what they buy. For example, because of the rising cost of products and services, many families require two incomes to satisfy their wants and needs. As a result, most families are rushed for time. Businesses have responded with goods and services that save time, are convenient, and improve efficiency. Food products that can be prepared by popping them into the microwave are an example of a type of good that has become very popular.

ACTIVITIES FOR ...

INFORMATION	CONNECTION	EXTENSION
1. a) Distinguish between a need and a want, and a value and a goal.	**b)** Identify one need and one want that you had three years ago. Name one need and one want that you have now. Describe how your values have changed.	**c)** Interview your principal, school administrator, or a senior staff member to find out what the school's goals are for the current school year. How will the school go about achieving these goals? Then, ask about the school's long-term goals and how these will be achieved.
2. a) Describe four choices that you made in the past week.	**b)** Describe three choices that you have made that required very little thought and three choices that required a great deal of thought.	**c)** Describe how your needs, wants, values, and goals influence the choices you make when buying goods and services.
3. a) How do changing family lifestyles affect how much people spend and what they buy?	**b)** Identify five goods and five services that save time, improve efficiency, or provide convenience for consumers today.	**c)** "If you make the right decisions, you may not have to change your lifestyle expectations a great deal." Ask a teacher, a parent or guardian, and a businessperson to each give you an example of a decision they made that proves this statement.

Why We Buy

Consumer decision making is the process of choosing among all the alternatives available in the marketplace. Sometimes, however, trade-offs are necessary—the expensive vacation is cancelled in order to save money for college or university, or the new car purchase is delayed to pay for repairs to a leaky roof.

We all buy products for different reasons, but there are six key factors that influence consumer buying decisions: income and price, status, current trends, customs and habits, safety, and promotion.

INCOME AND PRICE

The amount of money consumers have to spend has a big influence on what they buy. A low-income family has to spend a larger portion of its income on basic necessities (food, clothing, and shelter) than a high-income family. People who are responsible for children or aging parents often make different consumer and financial decisions than do people without these obligations. Families with more available income can invest, travel, and spend more on entertainment and recreation.

Price is still the most important consideration for consumers. It greatly influences the types and quantities of products and services that consumers buy. Some consumers believe that the higher the price, the better the product, but this is not always true.

Today, consumers expect good value for the money they spend. Most will not pay more than what they believe an item is worth. Price alone, however, is not the only consideration. Quality, service, warranty, convenience, and variety in selection are also important factors.

STATUS

You may know people who brag about how much they paid for a product. They must have the biggest and the best, the latest and the greatest of everything. They feel that owning these items improves their status, making others admire or at least notice them. This desire to flaunt purchases to impress others is called **conspicuous consumption**.

Some people buy goods simply because neighbours or friends have done so. Or, they may want to be the first in the neighbourhood to have something new or unusual. Others buy large homes, luxury cars, or swimming pools because they think owning these things is proof of success or status. Unfortunately, some consumers purchase these expensive items even when they can't afford them and seldom use them.

Did You Know?

A person who earns an average salary of $27 800 spends approximately 56% of his or her income on food, shelter, water, electricity, fuel, household operation, and health care. A person who earns an average salary of $64 700 spends approximately 38% of his or her income on these same expenses.

CURRENT TRENDS

Although jeans and T-shirts remain fashion basics, it is the different, or "in," look that lures both teenage and adult consumers into retail stores. For many people, clothing helps create an image. For teens, clothing is often seen as an indicator of status, popularity, or being part of an exclusive group. As a result, clothing is a key area of youth spending. You might even be strongly influenced by your friends to buy something you don't really want. This type of influence is called **peer pressure**. Teenage peer pressure comes into play most often at school and in social settings. Buying to belong is a common motive in the buying patterns of young people and a popular strategy in product advertising targeted at teens.

Staying in style can be costly. The latest fashions quickly become obsolete and are replaced by something new. You can easily spend hundreds of dollars putting together a single outfit that will soon be thrown out or forgotten because it is out of fashion. Keeping up with the latest trends often leads to unwise purchases.

BUSINESS —FACT—

The teen market responds to fashion trends more than any other segment of society.

Teenage Consumers

Canadian businesses see teens as a major market. As a group, this generation of teenagers has more money to spend than any previous generation of teenagers. Not only do teens directly contribute to the Canadian economy, they also influence parents' or guardians' spending patterns. Whether it's clothing, groceries, sports equipment, television sets, vehicles, electronic equipment, personal computers, or vacations— what teens want often decides what the family gets.

Businesses target teens for another reason. Teens are usually in the process of establishing their own identities, independent of the family. Although they regularly buy items such as soft drinks, clothing, CDs, and personal grooming products, teens have no strongly established buying patterns. That's why marketers often design advertising and sales promotions aimed at teens. If companies can establish buying habits and loyalties to certain products and services now, they may have customers for life.

CUSTOMS AND HABITS

Family, religion, community, and customs often affect consumer choices. For example, weddings, birthdays, and baby showers are customary gift-giving times. In fact, special occasions and certain holidays result in dramatically increased consumer spending. Without proper planning, holiday spending can also lead to disastrous consumer debt.

Habit also plays a part in what you buy. You may buy a particular magazine each week or month, rent a videocassette every Friday, go out to a movie every week, or eat at the same fast-food outlet every day. These behaviours are habits—they are formed over time and done repetitively, often with very little thought.

SAFETY

Product safety has become a major public and consumer issue, and often reflects the purchases that consumers make. Parents are extremely concerned about their children's safety when they purchase items such

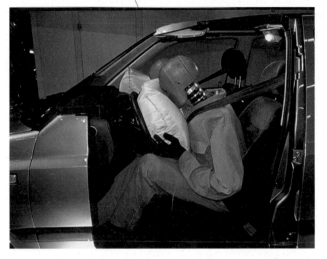

Crash test dummies are used to test a car's safety.

as cribs, car seats, highchairs, and baby carriages. Safety has also become a major concern for car buyers and manufacturers. As a result, air bags, antilocking brakes, and other safety devices are now common features of most vehicles.

Canada is recognized worldwide for its excellent product standards. Canadians have come to expect a high level of safety, effectiveness, and quality in the goods they buy. Many of these items must meet safety standards established by government and industry. The Canadian Standards Association (CSA) is a not-for-profit, voluntary-membership association. It is involved in developing standards for safety and in certifying products. CSA standards are supported by producers and consumers, and are widely used by industry and commerce. They are often incorporated into government regulations, particularly in areas of health, safety, building construction, and the environment. You will read more about health and safety regulations in Chapter 5.

Is It Always Safe?

Even products developed for safety may be unsafe under certain circumstances. For example, many air bags deploy at such a great force that they can injure children in the front seat or drivers who cannot maintain a distance of 25 cm between the steering wheel, where the air bag is located, and their breastbone. Transport Canada offers suggestions for ways to minimize the risk posed by air bags, and has a program to deactivate air bags for those who cannot minimize the risk.

PROMOTION

E-ACTIVITY

Can advertising be harmful? Visit www.business. nelson.com and follow the links to learn about organizations that uncover the truth behind ads.

Business advertising and promotion are designed to influence consumer spending and create a desire for products and services. Strong competition in the global marketplace has led to more sophisticated promotional techniques. For one thing, advertisers now use the Internet to attract customers to businesses and products in very different ways. Through advertising, consumers learn about the many products and services available to them.

Sometimes, advertising methods are deceptive. Consumers are led to believe, for example, that a certain product or service is far superior to another, when in fact little or no difference exists. False or misleading advertising comes in many different forms. One form, known as **lifestyle advertising**, shows attractive, healthy, successful, and appealing people using the product or service that is being promoted. The ads suggest that if you use the product or service, you will be just like these ideal people and, instantly, your lifestyle will improve. Advertisements for soft drinks, snack foods, jeans, and athletic shoes often use this technique. To be a smart consumer, a person has to pay careful attention to the intention of advertisements and not be taken in by the unrealistic expectations they promote.

ACTIVITIES FOR ...

INFORMATION	CONNECTION	EXTENSION
1. a) Name six factors that affect buying decisions.	**b)** Choose a product. When buying that product, which of the six buying factors most affects your final decision?	**c)** Have you ever made a buying decision based on one factor, then regretted your decision? Tell about the experience.
2. a) What is the function of the Canadian Standards Association?	**b)** Does the CSA support consumers, businesses, or both? Explain your answer.	**c)** Using the Internet, research the CSA and similar organizations in other countries. How are their missions the same? How are they different? Create a visual or print presentation about the CSA or a similar organization using the organization's logo and its mission statement to describe its work.

Taking Care of Business

Business decisions would be very simple and predictable if all consumers only made purchases to satisfy the three basic survival needs: food, clothing, and shelter. Obviously, however, some businesses satisfy much more than just basic needs; they focus on consumer wants. If every consumer "needed" a particular good or service, then the potential market for that good or service would be enormous. As a result, those businesses offering it could be very profitable. On the other hand, businesses that focus on a specific consumer want, perhaps luxury cars, would find the demand much more limited. Deciding which products or services to offer requires careful thought and, in some cases, a great deal of risk taking.

Not only do businesses have to decide which products and services to offer, they must also decide how much to charge. This is one of a business's most important tasks. As discussed in Chapter 1, pricing is determined by supply and demand. If a good or service is not priced very competitively, consumers will shop elsewhere.

BUSINESS RESPONSES TO CONSUMER BEHAVIOUR

Businesses try to determine how much customers will buy to satisfy their needs and wants. By studying customers' behaviour patterns, a business can create an environment that will promote sales and, as a result, increase profit opportunities. Three factors determine how customers buy: the amount of time a customer spends in a store, the amount of contact time between customers and sales personnel, and the amount of time a customer must wait to pay.

Time Spent in a Store

The amount of time a shopper spends in a store is perhaps the most important factor in determining whether or not a customer will buy. Consumer research surveys show that the longer a business can keep a customer in the store, the greater its chances of making a sale.

BUSINESS
—FACT—

Businesses try to increase the amount of time customers spend in their stores by providing a welcoming environment, including wide aisles, suitable music, free samples, and babysitting services.

Table 2.1 Time Spent in a Store		
	Buyer	**Non-buyer**
Electronics store	9 min 29s	5 min 6s
Toy store	17 min	10 min

Contact Time

How much time do customers spend with a store employee while they are in the store? If this contact time, or **interception rate**, is increased, the opportunity for making a sale also increases. A business that has fewer employees to "intercept" potential customers is likely to have lower sales rates than a store that is fully staffed with friendly and approachable salespeople. Employees can help customers find the goods or services they are looking for. They can also recommend complementary products to increase the customer's total purchases and answer any questions they might have.

Waiting Time

Even customers who reach the checkout counter satisfied with the goods and services they have chosen may quickly become impatient and irritable if they have to wait a long time to pay. In today's world, most people are extremely busy and pressed for time—they are less likely to shop at a particular store if they see that there is a long lineup or if they have experienced slow service at that store in the past. Long lines discourage customers and could result in a loss of business.

BUSINESS IN A CHANGING MARKETPLACE

Today, the Internet has created a new kind of marketplace and a new form of business. It is known as **e-commerce**, which stands for "electronic commerce." In today's electronic marketplace, consumers and sellers can conduct business without ever meeting face to face. To go shopping, all you need is Internet access. Most traditional businesses may be open 12 hours a day for six days a week. E-businesses are generally "24/7"—they are open 24 hours a day, seven days a week.

Setting Up an E-Business

To conduct e-commerce, a business needs an actual physical space in which to operate. Electronically, the first thing the business needs is a **Web site** to conduct e-commerce transactions. It also needs a **domain name**—a catchy and simple Internet address—if it wants to present the business professionally to potential customers. This Internet address lets potential customers connect with the business **online**. Once a business Web site is created, **Web pages** are necessary to advertise the goods or services that are for sale. Some small businesses do this design work themselves, but larger businesses usually hire professional Internet-service businesses to do this work. E-businesses also need a method of processing payments. If it is more convenient for them, online businesses may hire other businesses to assist them with their payment process.

**Visit
www.business.
nelson.com**
and follow the links
to learn how
businesses register
domain names.

Once all this is accomplished, e-businesses can measure their success in different ways. Sales and profits are a critical indicator, but e-businesses can also gauge the popularity of their Web site by keeping track of the Web site hits. **Web site hits** measure the number of people who visit the Web site. They are a reflection of whether the business's online presence has become well known and popular.

More and more people are ordering groceries from online grocery stores, such as grocerygateway.com. They can choose from a variety of products, as shown on this screen.

Deciding Whether to Buy Online

Many goods and services are selling well on the Internet, and the volume of sales is increasing rapidly. Some products that sell particularly well online include CDs, health products, books, software, and hardware. Clothes, jewellery, toys, and gift items are also gaining popularity online. Frequently used online services include banking and investing, distance education, airline bookings, and travel planning. Of course, the Internet has also created a market for many new types of services, such as Web page design and Internet security services.

Table 2.2 Approximate E-commerce Revenue for 2000 and Projected E-commerce Revenue for 2004		
Region	2000	2004
North America	$795.0 billion	$5.5 trillion
Asia Pacific	$84.0 billion	$2.5 trillion
Western Europe	$136.0 billion	$2.4 trillion
Latin America	$6.3 billion	$128.0 billion
Rest of world	$4.7 billion	$104.7 billion

As more businesses go online, consumers will be faced with a staggering number of goods and services. In the "real world," consumers can touch the goods they are considering buying. They can meet the people offering services. E-commerce, however, takes place in cyberspace, where nothing is tangible. As a result, consumers are cautious about placing their trust in e-businesses. Research indicates that many consumers make buying decisions online but then buy offline. (See Chapter 10 for more information about online shopping, and Chapter 13 for information about banking online.)

The Top Five Reasons That People Hesitate to Purchase Goods Online

According to a recent survey, consumers are reluctant to buy products online because they
- worry about unreliable or dishonest retailers (81%)
- do not want to deal with the hassle of returning goods (72%)
- worry about their credit card number being misused (69%)
- think they are going to get a lot of junk mail (63%)
- want to see and touch what they buy (62%)

ACTIVITIES FOR ...

INFORMATION	CONNECTION	EXTENSION
1. a) Identify the three factors that determine how consumers buy.	**b)** Think about your recent shopping experiences. Give examples of how these three factors have affected your buying behaviour.	**c)** Given the importance of these three factors, why might a business choose not to address them?
2. a) Define "e-commerce."	**b)** Identify ten domain names with which you are familiar. What good or service does each Web site provide?	**c)** What factors do you think might contribute to a customer visiting or revisiting a Web site? What factors might discourage a customer from visiting or revisiting a Web site?
3. a) List the top five reasons why people do not buy online.	**b)** "Consumers seem to do research online to help them make buying decisions, but they do their actual buying offline." Explain how this statement does or does not apply to you and your family. Has your family's attitude toward online shopping changed over time? Explain why or why not.	**c)** Interview students and staff at your school to find out about their online purchases. Make a list of products they have purchased online and a list of products they have just researched online. Why are they willing to buy certain products online but not others? Compare their reasons to the top five reasons for not buying online cited on this page.

Review

Knowledge and Understanding

1. Match each of the following terms to the correct definition:

   conspicuous consumption   interception rate
   domain name   lifestyle advertising
   e-commerce   Web site

   a) A place on the Internet which a business can call its own and use to sell products and services to consumers.
   b) A form of advertising that shows attractive, healthy, successful, and appealing people using the product or service that is being promoted.
   c) The average amount of time that each customer will spend with a salesperson in a store.
   d) An address on the Internet that allows people to identify a business.
   e) Buying things to impress other people.
   f) The electronic marketplace used for conducting business over the Internet.

2. Define "short-term goals" and "long-term goals." What are some of your short-term and long-term goals?

3. What steps must a business take to establish itself online?

Thinking and Inquiry

1. Prepare a one-page report describing how your needs and wants would change if you moved to a warm, sunny island such as Bermuda.

2. Give three examples to demonstrate how businesses respond to consumers' needs and wants.

3. "Young people influence the spending patterns and buying decisions of others, namely parents and guardians." Research this statement by interviewing your parents or guardians. Summarize your findings by creating a list of goods and services purchased because of this "teenage pressure."

4. "If companies can establish teenage buying habits and loyalties to certain products and services now, they may have customers for life." Explain this statement and give an example of how it applies to you. What would it take to break your buying habit and, in turn, destroy your loyalty to that brand of product or service?

Communication

1. You and your classmates have made many choices and decisions over the past few days. In a small group, make a list of these. Use the headings "Choices Presented" and "Decisions Made." Discuss how the decisions were made. Did the person carefully weigh the advantages and disadvantages of each alternative (as outlined in the decision-making model)? Or, did the person make a snap decision? Was the result of the decision positive or negative?

2. Identify three current trends or fads that have caught teenagers' interest recently. How long has each trend been around? Is this trend a passing fad or will it become part of everyday culture? Then, create a radio or television advertisement that encourages teens to adopt the trend. Present your ad to the class.

3. Lifestyle advertising can create unrealistic expectations. Find one example of this type of advertising in each of the following media: magazines, newspapers, radio, television, and the Internet. Meet with a partner to share your findings. Explain how each advertisement is unrealistic and possibly even misleading.

Application

1. Do some research about current fashions. You might look online, browse through fashion magazines, watch fashion programs on TV, or talk to people who work in clothing stores. Record your answers to the following questions:
   • What are the current fashions?
   • What fashion advice are the experts offering?
   • Who are these experts?
   • Are you going to buy these fashions? Why or why not?
   Present your findings in a written report.

2. After getting permission from a business owner, conduct an on-site survey with another class member to determine consumer behaviour patterns. Use a stopwatch and personal interviews to gather data about the time spent in a store, contact time, and waiting time. Summarize your findings in an oral presentation.

3. Conduct an Internet search using "e-commerce" as your keyword. How many Web site hits did this search produce? Select one of these Web sites and write a one-page summary of the consumer information available on this site.

4. Buying a car the "old-fashioned" way typically involves the following steps:
   • driving to a car dealership
   • strolling around the lot to check out the merchandise
   • kicking the tires to check for durability
   • taking a test drive
   • negotiating the price
   • getting financing
   • trading in your old car (if you have one)
   • signing papers
   Today, researching, comparison shopping, and purchasing can all be done online. Describe the steps involved in buying a car online. How is shopping for cars on the Internet both similar to and different from the eight-step procedure outlined above? Which procedure do you prefer? Ask your classmates, parents, and teachers which method they prefer. Make an oral presentation to your class comparing the old and new ways of car buying.

REFLECT ON YOUR LEARNING

1. Look at your answers to the Before You Begin question on page 27. Now that you've read the chapter, have any of your ideas changed? Explain why or why not.

2. Analyze Mōdrobes's product based on the six factors affecting consumers' buying decisions. Would you buy this product? Explain why or why not.

CHAPTER 3

STARTING A BUSINESS

STUDENT EXPECTATIONS

After completing this chapter, you will be able to

- explain the most common reasons for going into business
- define debt financing and equity financing
- distinguish between types and forms of business ownership
- explain why people may choose to establish one type of business rather than another
- identify different ways of starting a new business
- compare the features of sole proprietorships, partnerships, corporations, and cooperatives
- distinguish between the different types of corporations

Profile

(left to right) Michael Sponagle, Morgan Hicks, Mary Middleton, and Carrie Donovan of the Post Road Tea Room.

YES PROGRAM BREWS OPPORTUNITY

Entrepreneurship is the specialty of the day, everyday, at the Post Road Tea Room. Located in Mount Uniacke, Nova Scotia, the tea room is the brainchild of four friends who own and operate it themselves. The idea originated from a Maritime studies class project at Windsor Regional High School. Today, Morgan Hicks, Mary Middleton, Michael Sponagle, and Carrie Donovan (who are now in university) are partners in a thriving tea room business.

It all started with the Uniacke Estate Museum Park, which is operated by the Nova Scotia Museum. Visitors could not buy food on the park grounds. That inconvenience started the four friends thinking. Originally, they considered a vendor cart. But once they discussed it further, the idea changed to a tea room. "We got together and were talking about it and thought it would be kind of a cool idea," says Morgan.

After presenting the idea to their classmates, the four teens made a proposal to Nova Scotia Museum members. "I'm sure the museum was pretty skeptical when we first approached them," says Morgan. "I mean, I was 14 at the time and the others were 15." But the museum people were impressed with the calibre of their presentation. "They said it had the quality of a presentation by fourth-year university students," says Mary. The museum accepted their proposal.

CONTINUED →

The next step was to find funding. Their search led them to the Youth Entrepreneurial Skills (YES) program, which provides loans to students wishing to set up and operate their own business. The Post Road Tea Room qualified for a loan of $2000—enough to cover startup costs such as tables, chairs, and teas. The operators were given space in the kitchen area of Uniacke House.

In addition to selling tea, the Post Road Tea Room also sells retail merchandise from the Nova Scotia Museum on commission. "Instead of paying rent, we sell their stuff," says Morgan. "We missed out on June last year, but we still managed to make a gross profit of $13 000. We made about $4000 in net profit because we had to pay off the loan and other expenses."

One of the major benefits of starting your own business is that it makes the job search much easier. Says Mary: "It was good to start early. Now we have something and we don't have to go out and look for a job every summer."

While making tea and sandwiches may take up most of her day, Morgan believes that her experience running the tea room has given her greater confidence in dealing with money. "I learned a lot of stuff about finances. Stuff that I didn't understand before, but now I feel like I could talk to a banker and know what I'm talking about."

And she said that as long as the museum will have them, the Post Road Tea Room will continue to operate. "We can only run it for as long as we're students; that was part of the deal. So we're going to have to pass it on, later on." The tea room continues to enjoy success each summer, with an average of 150 people passing through its doors every day to satisfy their cravings for Wild Berry Zinger, I Love Lemon, or Earl Grey tea.

"Now I feel like I could talk to a banker and know what I'm talking about."

About This Profile
1. Why did Morgan Hicks, Mary Middleton, Michael Sponagle, and Carrie Donovan decide to go into business?
2. What costs were involved in starting the business? What other costs would be required to operate the tea room?
3. What questions might the loans officer have asked about the Post Road Tea Room before deciding to offer the students a loan?
4. How have these students benefited from operating their own business?

Going into Business

With a partner, speculate about the types of decisions businesspeople must make before opening a business. Record your ideas and revisit them at the end of the chapter.

Many young people have already experienced some of the advantages and disadvantages of being in business. Starting and running a business takes motivation, commitment, and talent. Before deciding to go into business, you have to do a lot of research and planning. What types of businesses are most likely to succeed? Should you start an e-business or is it better to stick with the traditional "bricks and mortar" approach? This chapter will address many of the questions that can help you decide if going into business is the right decision for you. However, because the business environment is so complex, everything that you'll need to know before starting a business can't be explained here. As you do your research and planning, you can locate many other sources that provide useful information. Chapters 15 to 17, which focus on entrepreneurship, will also help you.

WHY START YOUR OWN BUSINESS?

Have you ever worked for someone else and thought that you could do a better job if you were in charge? While many people spend their entire lives working for someone else and enjoy it, others hope to advance in the organization until they become the boss. That way, they can be the ones responsible for making final business decisions. A faster way to become the boss is to start your own business.

Many people go into business to achieve financial independence. In the beginning, having your own business is usually difficult financially—you need to spend quite a bit of money to get a new business off the ground. This money usually comes from your personal savings as well as from others who have loaned you money to help with startup costs. But once the business begins to generate a profit, you are the primary beneficiary. If your business is successful, you will likely earn more money than you would working for someone else's company.

Starting your own business gives you the opportunity to use your skills and knowledge and to be creative. Some businesses are launched by an innovative idea for a product or service. For example, when magnetic tape appeared in the marketplace as a device to store information, no one imagined that CDs and DVDs would come along later to replace it. Perhaps you have an innovative product in mind to replace the DVD?

As you consider starting a business, there are a number of questions you might ask to help you make a decision:

- What are my skills best suited for?
- Where can I find information about businesses of this kind?
- What are the startup costs? How much money will I need? What will I need it for?
- Where can I find financing?
- What level of risk can I expect?
- What steps are involved in running this business? How complex is it? What would I need to know? What would I need to be able to do?
- What resources would I need?
- Should my business be home-based?

What Are My Skills Best Suited For?

Your experiences in school, in your private life, and possibly on the job have provided you with ideas, skills, and knowledge. Starting your own business gives you the opportunity to pursue these ideas and employ these capabilities. For example, if you enjoy doing small renovation projects, you might want to start a summer business building patio decks, fixing or erecting fences, or doing painting or staining jobs. If you would like the opportunity to be creative and achieve financial independence, then you should consider what business would be "just right" for you.

Where Can I Find Information About Businesses of This Kind?

Imagine that you're thinking about going into business. Where can you find information that will help you make a good decision? It's important that your information be accurate and current. Libraries, existing businesses, trade associations, government resources, and the Internet are possible sources of free information.

Industry Canada, a department of the federal government, provides a comprehensive Internet site called Strategis for Canadian businesses and consumers. Strategis gives Canadians direct access to valuable business and consumer information sources, timesaving interactive tools, and a large number of online and e-commerce services. A businessperson can use Strategis to find new markets, business partners, and technologies, or to learn about risk factors that may apply to the business venture. Strategis offers information on business opportunities and market analysis, promoting and improving your business, and contacts and events. This information is organized according to business categories or sectors. Strategis also gives advice on doing business both in and outside Canada.

Another source of information for businesspeople is Statistics Canada, which collects statistical information. For example, if you are interested in starting a business related to environmental affairs, you can see whether this area is a growing field. To do so, you might find out how much the environmental affairs sector contributes to Canada's total gross domestic product (GDP). The **gross domestic product** is the total dollar value of all goods and services produced in a country during one year. It measures how a country's economy is performing. (See Chapter 15 for more information about researching different kinds of businesses.)

What Are the Startup Costs?

Where will you get the money to start a business? In Chapter 1, money was identified as one of the economic capital resources needed to run a business. You will need money to pay the rent or mortgage, to pay for other expenses such as salaries and advertising, and to buy goods needed for sale. You will also need money for day-to-day operations and to pay debts.

Startup money is available through two kinds of sources—debt financing and equity financing. You can borrow money to run your business (**debt financing**). You can also use money from your savings or from investors (**equity financing**). Each method of financing has both advantages and disadvantages. If you borrow a large sum from a bank, for example, you may find it difficult to repay on time. With equity financing, on the other hand, you must invest your own savings in the business or be willing to obtain funds by setting up the business as a partnership or corporation. (More information on partnerships, corporations, and other forms of business ownership is found later in this chapter.) Using equity financing often means giving up part of the ownership of the business.

Where Can I Find Financing?

Debt financing isn't automatically available. **Financial institutions**, such as banks, trust companies, and credit unions, lend money to businesses. Before they do, however, they assess several factors. They check the applicant's past credit history and review the company's business plan. They also try to judge whether the owner has the skills necessary to achieve the company's objectives. This information will help the lending institution predict how successful the business will be and whether the applicant will be able to repay the loan. (See Chapter 17 for more information on financing a business.)

STRETCH YOUR THINKING

If you were a loans officer, what questions would you ask a person applying for a loan before making a decision about the application?

What Level of Risk Can I Expect?

Starting and operating a business can be a risky undertaking, even if you've done preliminary research and planning. Let's say you wanted to start a lawn-care and snow-clearing business. Here are some situations that you might encounter:

- A homeowner might be dissatisfied with the quality of your lawn-care service and refuse to pay you.
- Your new partner might make a commitment to a customer that is unacceptable to you.
- You might hire an employee who fails to do the job properly. Terminating this employee might lead to legal action for wrongful dismissal.
- A supplier might be late delivering the snow blower that you ordered, preventing you from fulfilling your commitments.
- You might use a product that kills your customer's lawn and results in a lawsuit for damages.

These types of risks could put you in financial difficulty. For example, the loss of customers or their failure to pay might mean that you are unable to repay a loan or pay for the snow blower and other supplies. Eventually, you may lose the capital that you invested and be forced out of business.

What other risks might this teen encounter as he operates his snow-clearing business?

What Steps Are Involved in Running This Business?

Some types of businesses are more complex than others. Usually, a complex business requires people with a variety of skills to start and run it successfully—especially when operating the business involves many different steps. In a manufacturing company, for example, someone has to determine what raw materials are necessary to make the finished product. Someone needs to ensure that those raw materials are available when needed; otherwise, production comes to a halt.

Someone has to determine how many employees are required for the various stages of production. Having too many employees is costly; having too few slows production. And on it goes. In a complex operation, "someone" may in fact be several people.

What Resources Would I Need?

Cash, inventory, supplies, furniture and fixtures, computer hardware and software, equipment, tools, vehicles, and buildings are some resources that you may require to set up and run a business. As the owner, you must determine what resources you require and how much financing you will need to acquire them. This process is called **forecasting**.

Every three months or so, you will also need to figure out how much projected revenue you will likely have. (**Revenue** is the amount of money you will gain from the sale of the product.) You will compare this amount with your total expenses and costs. It's very important to accurately monitor the business over the three-month period to detect any problems that should be considered in the next forecast.

Should My Business Be Home-based?

Home-based businesses—sometimes called "soho" (short for "small office, home office")—are not a new idea. However, technological advances over the past two decades have changed how these businesses operate. Computers, scanners, video equipment, camcorders, and access to the Internet have transformed the home office into a "virtual" office.

Working out of the home may mean fewer meetings to attend, no office politics, and less time spent on the telephone or running from office to office. Running your business from home also means you can wear casual clothes—who's to know that you're sitting at your desk in jeans and a T-shirt!—and save on clothing and dry-cleaning costs. Not everyone, however, would enjoy working from home. Some people need personal contact; others need the discipline of a traditional work environment.

Today, many types of online businesses are home-based. For example, many cartoonists who work from home have their own Web sites. At these sites, customers can view samples of the cartoonist's work and purchase copies. Customers may also be able to submit online requests for customized illustrations and cartoons.

STRETCH YOUR THINKING

Would a home-based business suit your personality? Why or why not?

| --- | --- | --- |
1. a) Why do people go into business?	**b)** Interview local business owners to find out why they went into business. Are the reasons they give similar to the ones mentioned in the text, or do they identify other reasons? Has owning their own business lived up to their expectations? Why or why not?	**c)** Working with a "business partner," list the skills and knowledge that you each possess that would contribute to a successful business operation. Then, identify any skills or knowledge that you still need. How could you acquire these skills and knowledge?
2. a) What are business risks?	**b)** Return to the list of potential risks involved in the lawn-care and snow-clearing business (page 48). Work with a partner to discuss how you would respond to each situation.	**c)** Interview a businessperson about business risks. Find out how he or she has handled problems similar to the ones identified on page 48. Summarize your findings and report back to the class.
3. a) Define "debt financing" and "equity financing."	**b)** Make a list of all the financial institutions in your community where you could borrow money if you were to start a business.	**c)** Work in groups of three. Two people role-play partners applying for a business loan. The third person role-plays the loans officer of a financial institution. Obtain and complete a loan application form from a financial institution to help with your role-play.

Types of Businesses

Once you decide to go into business, you have to decide what type of business you want to own. Do you want to produce something? sell something? offer a service? A **manufacturing business**, like General Motors of Canada, produces a product from materials and provides this product to retailers who then sell it to consumers. A **retail business** buys goods and resells them to consumers to satisfy consumer needs and wants. Club Monaco is one example. A **service business** tries to satisfy the needs and wants of consumers by providing a service. Magicuts, a hair salon, is an example of a service business. A retail business is also a service business.

A General Motors employee, working in the final assembly department, checks the trim on a truck.

You must also decide if you want to start a new business, buy an existing business, or buy into a franchise. You should research each alternative and assess your chances of succeeding with each option. Will you be able to raise enough money to establish a new business? If you're considering taking over a business, is the business located in a good area? If you decide to buy a franchise, do you understand the details of the agreement you will be signing with the franchiser?

FRANCHISES

In a franchise operation, one business, the **franchiser**, licenses the rights to its name, operating procedure, designs, and business expertise to another business, the **franchisee**. In this way, a franchisee buys a licence to operate a ready-made business and is often provided with a fully operational facility. The franchiser and the franchisee are independent businesses affiliated for this agreement only.

Franchise businesses are very popular in the business community. They offer brand recognition that consumers find more and more appealing. Hotels, motels, fast-food restaurants, and automobile dealerships are a few examples of franchise operations.

Before a franchise is awarded, the franchisee must meet many requirements. The most basic of these is the franchise fee, which is paid to the franchiser. These fees can range from thousands to millions of dollars. The more successful the franchise, the higher the franchise fee. Imagine having to pay $350 000 for a well-known coffee franchise before you even sold your first cup of coffee!

BUSINESS —FACT—

Canada has more franchise units per capita than any other country. The franchise sector employs at least 1 million people and chalks up sales of $100 billion a year. There are 1300 franchisers in Canada and nearly 64 000 franchise outlets.

In addition to the initial franchise fee, the franchisee pays a monthly fee for being part of the franchise family. This franchise fee might be 5% of total monthly sales. The franchisee also has to pay the franchiser for national and local advertising (roughly 1% of monthly sales). Moreover, all supplies have to be purchased centrally through the franchiser. This type of quantity buying should work to the benefit of the franchisee by reducing the cost of supplies and providing uniform quality.

Some franchisers require the franchisee to go through a training period to learn how to do business according to their standards. In this way, the quality of brand recognition is guaranteed. For example, a visit to Tim Hortons anywhere in Canada means fresh coffee and friendly service. Despite high franchise fees and monthly costs, it is not uncommon for franchise operations to be very successful. (See Chapter 16 for more information on franchises.)

Hungry customers wait in line at a Harvey's/Swiss Chalet franchise.

Types of Business Ownership

Another way to classify businesses is by type of ownership. There are four main types of ownership: sole proprietorships, partnerships, corporations, and cooperatives. Each type of ownership has its own advantages and disadvantages.

SOLE PROPRIETORSHIPS

A **sole proprietorship** is a business owned by one person, normally referred to as a "proprietor." The proprietor has many different responsibilities within the business. For example, the owner of a bicycle store usually buys the merchandise, sells to customers, does the accounting, arranges displays, and cleans the store. The owner owns all the equipment in the store, and might own the building. Money to open and run the business usually comes from the owner's savings or from a loan. If the business does well, the owner enjoys all the profits. If the business does poorly, the owner is responsible for all the losses. The owner may even lose his or her home and other personal belongings. This is called **unlimited liability**.

BUSINESS
—FACT—

A business could begin as a sole proprietorship, then reorganize as a partnership, and eventually evolve into a corporation. It might go through several organizational changes over a period of time.

PARTNERSHIPS

A **partnership** is a business operated by two or more individuals who want to share the costs and responsibilities of running a business. For

example, lawyers who specialize in different areas of law, such as civil, divorce, real estate, corporate, family, and wills and power of attorney, will form partnerships so that they can serve a wider client base. The terms of their partnership are recorded in a **partnership agreement**.

There are different kinds of partnerships. A **general partnership** is the most common form. In a general partnership, all partners have unlimited liability for the firm's debts. Unlimited liability means that each partner could be held responsible for the other partner's debts. In a **limited partnership**, on the other hand, partners have **limited liability**. They are only responsible for paying back the amount that they invested in the partnership. Even if the business fails, their personal savings and other assets cannot be used to pay the partnership's debts.

These new partners shake hands after signing a partnership agreement. The agreement includes details about how much each person invested in the partnership and the degree to which each partner will share in the profits or losses.

CORPORATIONS

A **corporation** is a type of business whose ownership is divided into many small parts, called **shares** or **stock**. Individuals who buy shares become owners of the company and are called **shareholders** or **stockholders**. The more shares a shareholder owns, the greater the control he or she has. Because there are so many owners, a **board of directors** is put into place to run the corporation.

Shareholders have limited liability. If the business fails, they lose only the amount that they've invested in shares. If the business earns a profit, some of it may be used to expand the company. The rest is paid out to shareholders in the form of a **dividend**. The amount of the dividend paid for each share is calculated by dividing the total profit paid out by the total number of shares owned by shareholders.

Types of Corporations

There are different types of corporations. In a **private corporation**, only a few people control all the shares and, therefore, the business. Stocks in the company are not listed for sale on a **stock exchange**, a trading market where stocks are bought and sold. On the other hand, a **public corporation** raises money by making shares available to thousands of people through selling stocks on the stock exchange. These individuals become the owners of the business.

People with only a few shares of a stock have little influence on a company's policies. Major shareholders, on the other hand, can have a considerable impact because each share gives them one vote. A **Crown corporation** is a business operated by the provincial or federal government. Some examples of Crown corporations are the Business Development Bank of Canada, Via Rail, Atomic Energy of Canada Limited, Canada Post, and the Canadian Broadcasting Corporation. Towns and cities can also be incorporated. They are organized as businesses, or **municipal corporations**, to provide services to the local citizens.

COOPERATIVES

A **cooperative** is a business owned by the people, or members, who buy the products or use the services that the business offers. The motive for operating a cooperative is service, not profit.

Like a corporation, a cooperative is run by a board of directors, and the members of the cooperative own shares. Unlike a corporation, however, each member has only one vote, regardless of the number of shares owned. Another major difference is that the profits of a cooperative are distributed according to how much each member spends at the cooperative. For example, a member who buys $5000 worth of goods or services will receive a dividend five times as large as someone who buys $1000 worth of goods or services.

The cooperative model has been adapted to almost every form of business in Canada. Consumer cooperatives, retail cooperatives, and

Members of Mountain Equipment Co-op, which sells outdoor equipment such as backpacks, camping gear, and outdoor clothing, wait in line to pay for their purchases.

E-ACTIVITY

What other Canadian examples of cooperatives can you find? How could you become a member? Visit www.business. nelson.com and follow the links to find out.

worker cooperatives are three such adaptations. A local credit union where members pool their savings so that they can provide themselves with financial services at a reasonable cost is an example of a consumer cooperative. Retail cooperatives, like IGA (Independent Grocers' Association) and IDA (Independent Druggist Association), act as buying organizations for members. A worker cooperative is created to provide work for its members. The Sleepless Goat (a coffee shop in Kingston, Ontario) is an example of a worker cooperative. In Canada, most cooperatives in the healthcare, childcare, and housing sectors are not-for-profit cooperatives.

ADVANTAGES AND DISADVANTAGES OF DIFFERENT TYPES OF BUSINESS OWNERSHIP

Table 3.1 summarizes the advantages and disadvantages of different types of business ownership. Which type of business ownership would you prefer, and why?

Table 3.1 Types of Business Ownership

	Sole Proprietorship	Partnership	Corporation	Cooperative
Features	• one owner	• two or more owners • written partnership agreement	• many shareholders • one vote per share • board of directors	• owned by members • each member has only one vote regardless of number of shares • board of directors
Advantages	• be your own boss • easy to start and end • profits to owner	• more capital and financing • shared responsibilities	• limited liability • transfer of ownership is simple	• less expensive goods/services • easily set up
Disadvantages	• unlimited liability • financing may be difficult • owner may not be familiar with all aspects of business	• unlimited liability in general partnerships • partner disagreements	• timely and costly startup • people who own only a few shares don't have a lot of influence on how the company is run	• decision-making process could be difficult

Top 10 Checklist for Startups

1. Are you ready to start a business? Know what you want and understand what's involved. Be willing to devote long hours to your endeavour.

2. Have you done your homework? Conduct research to ensure there's a need for your product or service. Be sure market conditions can support your business. Talk with friends, family, and advisers to obtain business information. Government agencies, trade associations, and other organizations offer services and programs to help get businesses started.

3. How will you utilize your skills and compensate for your weaknesses? Evaluate your personal qualities and skills. Use your talents and recognize the areas you need help with.

4. What form of ownership will your business take—sole proprietorship, partnership, corporation, or cooperative?

5. How will you promote and market your business? How are you going to distinguish your business from the competition?

6. What is your pricing strategy? What does the price say about your product (and its quality versus that of the competition)? Think about what you'll charge people for your product or service. Estimate your break-even point, revenues, and expenses.

7. Have you prepared a detailed business plan? (See Chapter 17.)

8. What funding sources will fuel your enterprise? Secure sufficient financial resources for startup and operations.

9. Where will you locate? Pick a business location that makes sense for you and your customers.

10. How will your business operate on a daily basis? How will you deliver your product or service and manage your business? Figure out what you'll need for the day-to-day smooth functioning of your business.

Business Responsibilities

All types of businesses and forms of business ownership come with responsibilities for the owner. Before opening, you, as the owner, should do the following:

- Decide where the business will operate. You may need to lease space.
- Determine whether the business needs employees and, if so, how many. You will need to become familiar with your obligations as an employer, such as paying employment insurance.
- Find out where supplies and startup materials can be obtained and under what terms.
- Find out if the business is subject to any specific legal restrictions.
- If you are taking over a preexisting business, you must find out if the business has any remaining debts and whether the new owner is responsible for repaying them.

Once the business is up and running, you have another set of responsibilities—including a great deal of paperwork. Order forms for goods, sales receipts, and tax forms need to be completed. As the owner, you also oversee accounting procedures, inventory control, and the maintenance of employee records and files. Or you may prefer to hire an accountant. While computers have facilitated much of this paperwork, the tracking and recording of information must be accurate and up to date so that the business can make timely decisions.

ACTIVITIES FOR ...

INFORMATION	**C**ONNECTION	**E**XTENSION
1. a) What is the difference between types of businesses and types of business ownership?	**b)** Identify two examples of manufacturing, retail, and other service businesses in your community. What type of ownership does each business have?	**c)** In a group, discuss why a business might reorganize and change its type of ownership.
2. a) Define the terms "franchisee" and "franchiser."	**b)** Keep a "franchise diary" for two weeks. Record the names of the franchises you visit, the items you purchase, and the amount you spend. Total your purchases and compare your franchise-spending habits with those of your classmates.	**c)** Using the Internet, advertisements for startup franchises in the financial section of the newspaper, or a personal contact, find out the startup fee for each of the following franchises: Burger King, Apple Auto Glass, and Home Depot. If you have difficulty finding one of these, substitute another franchise.
3. a) What are the advantages and disadvantages of partnerships?	**b)** Identify a business partnership in your community. Ask the partners what they think the greatest advantage and greatest disadvantage of a partnership is. Prepare a one-page report of your findings.	**c)** With a classmate, prepare a list of points you would want to include in a partnership agreement for your lawn-care or snow-removal business. Try to anticipate and address any problems or disputes that might arise during the partnership.
4. a) Identify and describe four types of corporations.	**b)** List the businesses whose products and services you bought in the past week. How many of these businesses are corporations? Classify these corporations as public, private, Crown, or municipal.	**c)** Choose one of the Crown corporations mentioned on page 54. Prepare a radio advertisement that tells what services the corporation provides.

Review

Knowledge and Understanding

1. Match each of the following terms to the correct definition:

   cooperative   partnership
   corporation   public corporation
   Crown corporation   sole proprietorship
   debt financing

   a) A business owned by shareholders.
   b) Financial institutions provide this type of financing for business owners to help them run the business, purchase inventory, and expand the business.
   c) A business with one owner.
   d) A business with two or more owners.
   e) A form of business that is owned by members who purchase products from or use the services of the business.
   f) A business that sells shares of its stock on the stock exchange.
   g) A government-owned business.

2. If you owned a small business, which type of corporation—public or private—would be most appealing to you? Why?

3. How is owning one share in a cooperative different from owning one share in a public corporation, for example, in terms of voting or receiving dividends?

Thinking and Inquiry

1. How does government benefit from providing free services and help to the business community?

2. As a franchisee, what business responsibilities and risks might you encounter? What might be your risks and responsibilities as a franchiser?

3. What do you think is the biggest disadvantage of a partnership? Why?

4. If you had the choice to finance your business using debt or equity financing, which one would you select? Explain your choice.

Communication

1. Invite to your class a representative from a sole proprietorship, a partnership, a corporation, and a cooperative. Ask each representative to talk about his or her type of business ownership and to provide an overview of its advantages and disadvantages. Introduce each representative to your class, giving some information about the types of products or services that the business offers. Class members should be prepared to ask the businesspeople questions.

2. Refer to the "Top 10 Checklist for Startups" on page 56. In small groups, select a business in your community and interview the owner(s). Ask if the owner used a similar checklist when starting the business. Does the owner think that the checklist is useful? Identify any questions not on the list that a new businessperson should consider.

Application

1. Working with a partner, select two businesses in your community that have the same type of ownership. Gather information about each business's startup costs, the availability of financing, the complexity of production, and the business's resource requirements. Which of these businesses would you prefer to own? Record your findings in a chart and briefly summarize the reasons for your choice.

2. This chapter outlines a number of important questions that you must ask yourself before going into business:
   • Why do you want to own your own business?
   • What type of business do you want to own?
   • Do you want to start a new business, buy an existing business, or buy into a franchise?
   • What type of business ownership would you prefer?
   Choose one of these questions and apply the decision-making model (on pages 18 to 20) to arrive at a decision.

REFLECT ON YOUR LEARNING

1. Review your answers to the Before You Begin question on page 45. How would you answer this question now that you've read this chapter?

2. What skills have you acquired in school (or elsewhere) that would help you start or run your own business?

CHAPTER 4

BUSINESS AND THE COMMUNITY

STUDENT EXPECTATIONS

After completing this chapter, you will be able to

- describe the type of economic system that Canada has
- distinguish between private and public ownership
- explain how a public–private partnership works in a business environment
- describe how privatization can affect both public and private sector businesses
- describe how businesses generate wealth, jobs, and income
- identify and explain the phases of a business cycle
- understand how businesses affect quality of life on the job site and in the community

Emmie Leung stands in front of a wall of paper about to be recycled.

GARBAGE GURU

When Emmie Leung talks trash, people listen. A pioneer in the field of recycling, Leung has built her company, International Paper Industries (IPI), from a one-woman operation to a multimillion-dollar business with four processing facilities in the Vancouver area.

After completing a business degree at the University of Manitoba in 1976, Leung left Winnipeg to start her venture on the West Coast. Her friends reacted with skepticism. In 1976, few people in North America had given any thought to recycling. "Everybody's attitude was consume, consume, consume," recalls Leung. In contrast, the young graduate had grown up in Asia where reusing and recycling were part of everyday life. She could have settled in California where a growing environmental movement was already taking root, but Leung had already decided that Canada was home. "I liked the culture of this country," she explains. "For this lonely soul, there was nothing better than a friendly atmosphere."

In the beginning, work was hard and progress was slow. But Leung broke new ground—she convinced municipalities to participate in her unusual plan of collecting and recycling newspapers and, later, plastic, glass, and tin. "I started with a penny," is how

CONTINUED →

she describes her experience. "Then there were two pennies, then four. At first, the pennies weren't accumulating very fast."

In 1982, Leung moved into her first plant just as recycling began to take off. The public, government, and industry were becoming more interested in recycling. This concern translated into a growing market for a greater variety of recyclable products. Thanks to Leung, the infrastructure for collection and processing was already well established in Vancouver.

IPI's success is partly the result of Leung's approach, exemplified by the company motto "Market first, collection second." From the start, Leung ensured that her raw materials were not only available and transportable, but marketable and saleable as well. "What is the point of collecting fancy garbage?" she asks. "Everything we touch we are able to divert to the right use. We are able to find markets for even the most challenging items."

Nowadays, those items are the innumerable types of plastic that are slowly beginning to be recyclable. According to Leung, only 30% of plastics are currently processed into new products. IPI has also begun to address the problem of garden waste. Branches, clippings, and leaves are collected separately, processed in the industrial composting system, and sold as fertilizer.

Lately, Leung's biggest challenge has been competition from other companies vying for a place in the relatively volatile market for "natural resources, the second time around." At the same time, IPI continues to expand. Under the name Halton Recycling, it runs operations in several Ontario cities. Someday, Leung hopes to have operations in Winnipeg as well, a city for which she still has a soft spot.

From the start, Leung ensured that her raw materials were not only available and transportable, but marketable and saleable as well.

About This Profile
1. How did the public, government, and industry help Leung's business take off?
2. What products are made from recycled newspapers, plastic, glass, and tin?
3. What types of jobs might Emmie Leung's company create? What other benefits might a recycling business bring to a community?

Economic Systems

In what ways is government involved in the business community? Make a note of your ideas so that you can return to them at the end of the chapter.

Several different types of economic systems operate in the world today. An **economic system** is the way government and businesses work together to provide goods and services to consumers. Because the economic resources that are used to produce goods and services are limited, the amount of goods and services that can be produced is also limited. For example, a car company can produce only a certain number of vehicles because it has only a certain number of workers, factories, pieces of equipment, and steel. Human wants, however, are relatively unlimited. Consequently, government agencies and businesses need to answer three major economic questions:

1. What goods and services should be produced?
2. How should these goods and services be produced?
3. For whom should the goods and services be produced?

Let's see how three model economies—pure command, pure market, and modern mixed—address these three basic economic questions.

PURE COMMAND ECONOMY

In a **pure command economy**, such as a communist system, the government owns the natural resources, farms, factories, machinery, offices, and most businesses. It controls all economic decision making and provides the answers to all three economic questions. The government decides what goods and services will be produced, how they will be produced, and for whom they will be produced. The government also establishes wages and benefits.

PURE MARKET ECONOMY

In a **pure market economy** (also called a free market, free enterprise, or capitalist system), the actions of buyers and sellers of goods and services direct the economic system. In other words, the marketplace decides the answers to the three economic questions. Consumers determine what will be produced by the dollars they spend. Competition among producers dictates how goods and services will be produced. Consumers affect this process by seeking competitive prices. Consumers in competitive markets also answer the "For whom?" question—they reward producers by buying their goods and services and increasing business incomes.

What's Free About Free Enterprise?

In a free enterprise system, a business is "free" to establish a place of operation and is encouraged to make a profit. Consumers are "free" to buy goods and services when and where they choose. Profit and competition are two features of free enterprise. (See Chapter 1.) Other features include freedom to own private property and freedom of choice. Freedom to own **private property** means that individuals and businesses can own, use, or dispose of things of value. **Freedom of choice** means that individuals can make their own choices as long as they don't break any laws. They can start or invest in any business they wish, and produce any product or service they choose, in any way they choose, as long as they act legally.

MODERN MIXED ECONOMY

In reality, no economic system operates in a pure form. In fact, economies are mixed. They contain elements of both models in varying proportions. Such economies are known as **modern mixed economies**. Figure 4.1 shows the position of several countries in terms of their mix of market and command systems. Canada's economy, for example, is primarily a market system, but includes aspects of the command system. In Sweden, the government plays a larger role in the economy.

Figure 4.1

Range of Economic Systems

Market Economy — United States, Canada, Sweden ... North Korea — Command Economy

ACTIVITIES FOR ...

INFORMATION	CONNECTION	EXTENSION
1. a) What are the three major economic questions?	**b)** Why does a company with limited resources need to answer the three major economic questions? Explain, using an example other than a car manufacturer.	**c)** In a three-column chart, summarize how command and market economies answer each of the three economic questions.
2. a) What are the characteristics of a free enterprise system?	**b)** If Canadians were not allowed to own private property and did not have freedom of choice, what impact would this have on business?	**c)** Even though businesses have many freedoms under our economic system, there are many activities that they are not free to do. For example, businesses are not allowed to provide an unsafe environment for workers. List five other activities that businesses are not allowed to do.
3. a) Define "modern mixed economy."	**b)** Give an example that shows how the Canadian economic system is a modern mixed economy.	**c)** Why might it be desirable for a country to have elements of both a command and a market economy?

The Private and Public Sectors

Canada's modern mixed economy has a private and a public sector. In the **private sector**, businesses are individually owned and operated. Their purpose is primarily to make a profit. In the **public sector**, different levels of government provide services to Canadians. Schools, public utilities, and hospitals are three examples of services provided by public sector businesses. The purpose of these businesses does not usually include making a profit.

Public ownership may be undertaken for a variety of reasons. For example, to protect cultural industries from too much American influence, the federal government created the Canadian Broadcasting Corporation (CBC) in 1936 and the National Film Board (NFB) in 1939.

Petro-Canada was established as a Crown corporation in 1975 to give the federal government a strong presence in the oil industry and to help develop new Canadian energy resources. (The federal government sold 80% of Petro-Canada to the private sector in 1995.) Another Crown corporation, Human Resources Development Canada (HRDC), was set up to provide training programs for individuals and startup funding for businesses.

Part of the CBC's mandate is to tell stories that reflect the diversity of Canada, and to build bridges among Canadians who live in different regions and speak different languages.

OTHER BUSINESS COMBINATIONS

In addition to private and public ownership, there is an unofficial third sector: public–private partnerships. When the private sector and public sector go into business together, a public–private partnership is formed. This partnership attempts to combine the best features of private ownership and public control. As well, businesses that were once owned by the public sector are sometimes privatized—they are sold to or taken over by the private sector.

Public–Private Partnerships

Public–private partnerships, sometimes called P3s, are businesses from the public and private sectors that have pooled resources and gone into business together. Public–private partnerships form because a proposed business venture or project is simply too big for one sector to assume. The construction of the Olympic villages in Montreal and Calgary, for example, involved partnerships between the public and private sectors. In Atlantic Canada, a partnership composed of Canadian and international business groups as well as the federal government constructed Confederation Bridge. This structure, which links the provinces of New Brunswick and Prince Edward Island, is the world's longest bridge over ice-covered waters.

Another advantage of P3s is that risks and responsibilities are shared between the private and public sectors, giving the business venture a better chance at success. P3s permit private and public businesses to take advantage of each other's expertise and resources. Furthermore, a private business may want to partner with a public business to benefit from the power and influence that the public business has in the marketplace.

The 12.9 km Confederation Bridge opened on May 31, 1997. It has bridge patrol and surveillance 24 hours a day, as well as a monitoring station that provides information on weather conditions such as wind speed, wind direction, air temperature, road temperature, and humidity.

Privatization

Privatization occurs when a publicly owned business or industry is sold to the private sector. A government may decide to privatize a service because it feels that the private sector could do a better job, or because the government is losing money providing that service. The newly privatized business then operates like any other business in the private sector.

Privatization can be accomplished in one of two ways: The government can stop providing a service directly and rely on the private sector to deliver the service, or the government can sell its assets to private buyers. **Assets** are things of value that a business owns.

Any federal, provincial, or municipal government service can be privatized. For example, in the fall of 1998, the Ontario government passed Bill 35 to deregulate Ontario Hydro. Power generation and hydro sales and service became competitive industries. Consumers in Ontario can now purchase their electricity from whomever they choose.

Alberta is experimenting with the privatization of education by introducing charter schools. A **charter school** is a school that is run by a private business while receiving funds from the provincial government. The school is accountable for money spent. If the school does not meet standards and guidelines set by the government, its charter can be taken away and it will cease to exist as a business.

ACTIVITIES FOR ...

INFORMATION	CONNECTION	EXTENSION
1. a) Define "private sector" and "public sector."	**b)** List examples of services provided in your community by the public sector and by the private sector.	**c)** Choose a public sector business and find out why it was established. How successful has it been in achieving its objectives? Present your results in an oral report—perhaps from the point of view of someone analyzing the business.
2. a) What is a P3?	**b)** Think of a private sector business in your community. Give an example of how it might benefit by partnering with a business in the public sector.	**c)** Find out about a project in your community that was the result of a partnership between public and private business. When was the project undertaken, and why? Design a poster that gives five interesting facts about the project.
3. a) Why might a public business privatize?	**b)** What do you think would happen if a public swimming pool were privatized? Consider both the quality of the service and the cost to you, the consumer.	**c)** Research a business in your community that has been privatized. What effect has the privatization had on the community, for example, on price, quality, variety, number of employees, and taxes paid?

Contemporary Issues in Canadian Business

THE ISSUE: PUBLIC SECTOR PRIVATIZATION

What is privatization?

Privatization occurs when businesses that are owned by the government are sold to the private sector. Police services, the post office, local health units, social service agencies, public utilities, and local water services are all examples of government-owned, or public sector, businesses. In most cases, these businesses can continue to operate even if they do not make a profit. Their operating costs are paid by money the government receives through taxation. If these businesses were in the private sector and did not make a profit, they would quickly shut down. But if they *were* in the private sector, would they operate more efficiently and be more profitable?

In many cases, the debate about privatization centres on this question: Whom can the public trust to provide the best service at the best possible price? Let's examine the two sides of this issue.

Point

Many people who support privatization argue that private sector businesses provide better services at lower prices than public sector companies. One reason for this is that many public sector businesses are monopolies. A **monopoly** is a business that is the only supplier of a particular good or service to consumers. Since no one else provides the good or service, the monopoly doesn't have to work as hard to improve the quality of its product, and it can charge whatever price it wants (as long as consumers will pay it). However, if a public service is sold to the private sector, or if a partnership is established with the private sector, competition may be introduced in the marketplace. This competition can mean lower prices and improved quality for consumers.

Private sector businesses are often more efficient than public sector businesses. In 1996, Transport Canada privatized its air navigation service (ANS). NavCanada, a private sector company involved in air traffic control and flight information, bought ANS from the federal government for $1.5 billion. NavCanada implemented many changes that made the system more efficient, including eliminating 1100 jobs, mostly in administrative areas, and consolidating six regional offices into two to avoid duplication of services. Because of these and other changes, it now costs less to fly in Canada than it would if the ANS were still operating Canada's air traffic control system.

Whom can the public trust to provide the best service at the best possible price? Since prices and services both improve when there's pressure from competition, the answer seems to be that consumers will be served better by a private company than by one in the public sector.

Counterpoint

Most private buyers who acquire public sector businesses have fewer financial resources than the government. This means that the private buyers often have to look for ways to save money. Saving money may mean providing poorer-quality service, increasing the cost of the service, or reducing the number of staff.

Perhaps the biggest drawback of privatization is the increased cost to the consumer. With increased costs, people who have more money may get better service than people who are poor, and some people may no longer be able to afford the service at all. What would happen if, for example, public libraries were privatized? In most places, local residents do not have to pay anything to belong to a public library (although the library does charge a small fee for overdue materials). However, if the library were privatized, it would need to make a profit to survive, and membership fees would likely be implemented. Residents might also have to pay a fee each time they took materials out of the library. And, of course, overdue charges would still apply. Under private ownership, residents would be charged a fee for most of the services that public libraries now offer for free.

And, what happens if a privatized business fails? The federal government sold Air Canada to the private sector in 1988. Since then, Air Canada has taken over Canadian Airlines and increased its market share. (See Chapter 6 for more information about market share.) But Air Canada has also had many problems. Customers have complained about poor service, long waits, and scheduling conflicts. Prices of fuel have increased and Air Canada's profitability has suffered.

When a public sector company has financial troubles, it can turn to the government for additional funding that will help it continue to do its job. When a private sector company runs out of money, it has to raise prices, cut services, or go out of business altogether. For this reason, many people believe that public sector organizations that offer vital services, such as health care, should not be privatized.

A Real Life Example

A two-tier health care system provides two levels of health services. At one level is the public health care system, which provides free medical services to all Canadians. The second level of health services is provided by private businesses, which charge a fee.

Alberta's Health Care Protection Act (Bill 11) became law on May 10, 2000. The new law gives regional health authorities the option to contract out minor surgical procedures under certain conditions. It extends public funding to private clinics that offer overnight surgery. It also allows private facilities to charge patients for services that go beyond what the government considers necessary.

Will the Alberta law improve health care delivery? According to a study conducted by the Fraser Institute, private hospitals are more efficient

than government-run facilities. The study also found that increased competition among hospitals actually enhances health care delivery because more attention is paid to such things as cleanliness and bedside manner. But will the poor have the same access to health care as the rich? Many people oppose the Health Care Protection Act because they believe that it will lead to the privatization of more and more services. Eventually, people may have to pay a user fee for many of the health services that are now guaranteed under the Canada Health Act.

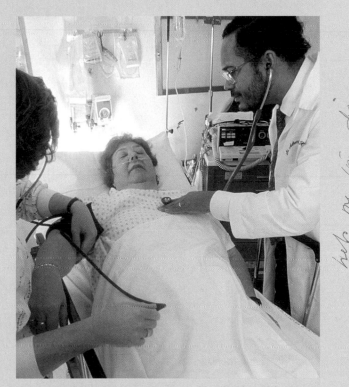

Do you think patients receive better medical care in a private hospital?

Questions and Activities About This Issue

1. Other than ANS and Air Canada, what government businesses have been privatized? Has privatization worked for these new private sector businesses?

2. Do other provinces have legislation similar to Alberta's Health Care Protection Act? What is the federal government's position on privatized health care?

Impact of Businesses on the Community

The first part of this chapter looked at the Canadian economic system, briefly studied its features, and distinguished between the public and private sectors. This is the "big" picture. The "smaller" picture illustrates what impact businesses from both sectors have on the community.

GENERATION OF WEALTH

When a person decides to open a business, many "wheels" are set in motion. If, for example, the new business plans to occupy existing building space, renovations may be necessary to make the space suitable for the new operation. The work space has to be designed; rooms may have to be constructed or altered; walls may need painting; and everything must be cleaned thoroughly.

Usually, the renovation involves many people with various skills. An architecture firm designs the work space; a renovation firm does the construction work; painters paint the walls; a cleaning company makes sure everything is washed and dusted, ready for opening day. These tasks represent only the "behind the scenes" work. Other jobs might include stocking shelves with inventory, adding furniture and fixtures to the work area, setting up computer hardware and software, installing phone and cable lines, and making sure that office supplies are available.

The owners of a new business meet with an architect to look at the blueprints and calculate renovation costs.

The architects, construction workers, painters, and cleaners all receive money for their work. Their payment can be considered "level one" money. They then apply, or spend, this money in many ways. The architect uses the funds to pay rent; the construction worker buys groceries; the painter repays debts to a bank; the cleaning person spends the money on a winter vacation. This money can be referred to as "level two" money. Each time this money changes hands, a business or consumer is affected in some way. The "money trail" could be followed to even further "levels" as the original funds continue to change hands. (See Figure 4.2.)

Figure 4.2 Generation of Wealth

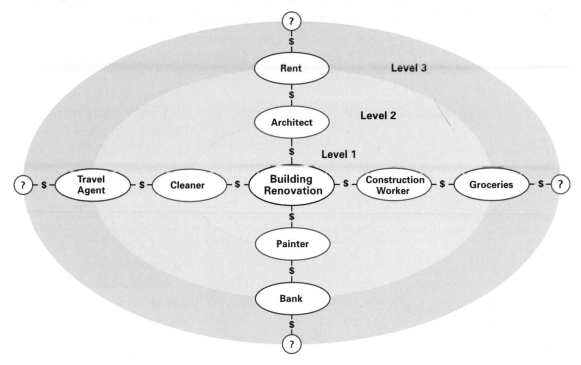

GENERATION OF JOBS

Have you looked at the classified ads in a newspaper or searched the Internet for employment opportunities lately? When businesses establish themselves or expand in a community, they create jobs. The job market is influenced by several factors: consumer demand, changes in business cycles, technological improvements, and competition. Sometimes, these factors produce negative results such as job loss; at other times, the factors have positive effects on employment opportunities.

Consumer Demand

When consumers indicate that there is a demand for a good or service, businesses try to meet that demand. In response to increased consumer interest in electronics, for example, businesses have responded with many new products, such as PlayStation2, the i2000 digital phone, and an interactive robot named RoboNagi. Each new product requires human resources to produce, market, and sell it to consumers. In other words, the new products create job opportunities.

If consumer demand shifts, jobs may be eliminated. For example, in the 1980s, animal-rights protests decreased consumer demand for fur and hurt fur exports. This decreased demand led to the loss of many jobs. Similarly, if a product becomes obsolete because of a disappearing demand, jobs may be eliminated in the workforce.

STRETCH YOUR THINKING

The fur industry is experiencing a revival. It now employs over 80 000 Canadians, 90% of whom are trappers. In groups, discuss both sides of this issue: animal rights versus jobs.

Business Cycles

The Canadian economy has its ups and downs: The economy fluctuates in cycles. A **business cycle** has four phases: trough, recovery, peak, and recession. Business cycles usually last from eight to ten years, but the length of time between each phase varies considerably.

Figure 4.3

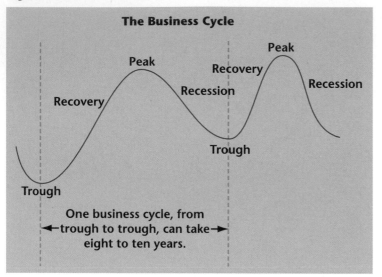

The Business Cycle

One business cycle, from ←trough to trough, can take→ eight to ten years.

During the **trough** phase of a business cycle, economic activity is at its lowest level. Many people are unemployed. Those who are employed are uneasy about the economy and reluctant to part with their money. Given low sales in the marketplace, businesses have difficulty making a profit, banks are reluctant to lend money, and bankruptcies increase.

Eventually, the business cycle enters a **recovery** phase. Demand for goods and services increases as people begin to replace existing goods. With the increase in demand, existing stock is depleted and businesses have to increase production. This increases job opportunities. With growing confidence in the economy, people spend more money.

With growing employment and increased wages, the business cycle enters the **peak** phase. The economy experiences prosperity and reaches the highest point in the business cycle. People begin investing in speculative ventures and buying real estate and stocks, and prices of goods and services increase.

Unfortunately, this phase does not last forever. Optimistic producers overestimate market demands and overproduce. This leads to worker layoffs and a decline in consumer spending. Eventually, the economy begins to slow. The business cycle has entered the fourth stage, a **recession**. As the recession worsens, the business cycle once again enters the trough phase.

If the economic situation becomes severe, a recession can lead to a **depression**. During a depression, unemployment is high, prices decline, businesses fail, and economic activity is greatly reduced. The Great Depression, which began in 1929, was worldwide. It lasted 10 years. Fortunately, Canada has not experienced a depression of this magnitude since then.

BUSINESS —FACT—

Because business cycles are unpredictable and the length of each phase is uncertain, it is difficult for businesses and consumers to plan for the future.

Technological Improvements

Businesses have taken advantage of changes in technology to increase the efficiency of their operations. Computers have altered the way business is done. Changes in technology have resulted in job loss, but many new jobs have also been created. For example, automated bank machines (ABMs) have made banking more convenient for consumers, but they have reduced the number of tellers needed in financial institutions. However, employees are needed to build, service, and maintain the ABMs. In this way, banking machines have created many new types of jobs.

Competition

In a free enterprise economy, businesses need to be competitive to survive. One of the most effective ways to compete is to charge less than other competitors. In order to charge less for the same product or service, businesses must become more efficient, use fewer resources, and make better deals with suppliers. Sometimes, becoming more efficient means trimming jobs.

GENERATION OF INCOME

Income, or revenue, is the money that a business has received or expects to receive. Most businesses try to find as many different sources of income as possible. These include
- selling goods or services
- earning interest on money held in a bank account. For example, if customers pay a business immediately but the business takes 90 days to pay its bills and places the money in a bank account, the money will earn interest.
- investing extra funds in short-term interest-earning investments (Chapter 8 deals with generating business income and Chapter 11 deals with saving and investing in greater detail.)

Not only do businesses earn income, they generate income for the government through the taxes that they pay—including property taxes and taxes on profits—and through the taxes that their customers pay—sales taxes. The government can then use this income to provide more services to the community.

STANDARD OF LIVING

The wealth, jobs, and income that businesses generate for themselves and for the communities they serve have an impact on people's

standard of living. **Standard of living** is the way a person lives as measured by the kinds and quality of goods and services that person can afford.

The standard of living for a high school graduate just entering the business world is probably quite different from that of a successful businessperson. The amount of money each of these individuals has to spend on needs and wants accounts for much of this difference. However, a higher standard of living does not necessarily mean a better standard of living; that assessment depends on a person's viewpoint. While some people may feel that owning a house and car represents a higher standard of living than renting an apartment and taking public transportation, not everyone would agree. The apartment dweller, for example, may prefer to spend weekends on the golf course or boating instead of being burdened with yard work. And the transit rider may have strong environmental views.

Some people feel that taking the streetcar represents a better standard of living because public transportation reduces pollution and traffic congestion, and costs less than owning a car.

QUALITY OF LIFE

The quality of a business environment has a direct impact on the life of the workers in that environment. High-quality work environments provide employees with a range of opportunities. Factors that contribute to a positive work environment include adequate incomes with regular raises, benefits packages, health and social services, educational and recreational programs, advancement opportunities, and profit sharing options. (See Chapter 7 for more information on employee benefits.)

Businesses also have an impact on the quality of life in a community. In most cases, businesses have a positive effect, creating wealth, jobs, and income. Businesses also make it convenient for local consumers to obtain goods and services at a fair price. At the same time, businesses can have a negative impact on a community. Consider the effect that the construction of a new airport would have on a nearby residential area. While building the airport would certainly provide wealth, jobs, and income, there would also be a cost. Airplanes taking off and landing would increase noise and air pollution, and diminish the quality of life of the residents living nearby.

STRETCH YOUR THINKING

Besides people moving, what other shifts have you noticed in your community? How have they affected businesses?

THE CHANGING COMMUNITY

When businesses move, the wealth, income, and jobs in a community are affected. Over the past couple of decades, businesses in communities all across Canada have shifted their locations as the urban scene has changed. When people began moving out of downtown areas into the suburbs, many businesses also abandoned the downtown core to move their operations into suburban mall locations. The malls provide enclosed environments and free parking for consumers. The downtown areas found it difficult to attract new businesses to replace those that had left. As a result, downtown cores entered a difficult period.

In recent times, urban renewal programs have improved many downtown cores. This process, known as **gentrification**, includes replacing run-down housing with luxurious high-rise condominiums. Many single people and childless couples with high incomes choose to live in these new buildings, which are close to work and entertainment. The increase in the number of residents with high incomes has had a positive impact on the business community in these downtown areas. As shifts like these take place, job opportunities shift accordingly.

A Closer Look

All businesses, no matter how big or small, whether in the private or public sector, have an impact on the community. Let's examine some of the main businesses in the city of London, in western Ontario. If these businesses are successful, the community benefits through employment opportunities, money spent and invested in the community, revenue generated through the collection of taxes, and quality of life. However, if these businesses fail, wealth, jobs, and income are lost, and quality of life suffers. The closure of a large business that employs hundreds of people can devastate a community.

CITY SERVICES

The city of London operates many businesses that provide services to the community. These include fire and police departments, garbage pickup and recycling, public transit, road construction, and the collection of commercial and residential taxes. Each service benefits the people of London. For example, the fire and police departments protect London's citizens and their property. Garbage pickup and recycling help keep the city clean and preserve the environment. Road construction and public transit ensure that people and goods move through the city safely and efficiently. With the commerical and residential taxes that the city collects, it is able to continue providing services to the people who live there.

Sometimes, instead of using its own employees to provide a service, the city of London hires outside contractors. For example, it might be more efficient for the city to hire a private paving company to do road repairs. The practice of subcontracting work to other companies is known as **outsourcing.**

HEALTH AND EDUCATION

Education and health care are important businesses in London. There are public and separate school systems, private schools, and institutions of higher learning such as Fanshawe College and the University of Western Ontario. Health-related businesses include pharmacies, the London Health Sciences Centre, the London Regional Cancer Centre, and the Middlesex-London Health Unit.

Not only do these businesses provide the people of London with quality education and health care, but they attract further investment to the community. This generates even more jobs, wealth, and income. For example, more than $70 million is spent every year in London on research activities at public and private health institutions, such as the London Health Sciences Centre, the John P. Robarts Research Institute, the Lawson Health Research Institute, and the London Regional Cancer Centre.

Approximately 23 000 full-time students are enrolled at the University of Western Ontario. What types of jobs are created to meet these students' needs?

CULTURE AND RECREATION

Many public and private businesses in London focus on culture and recreation. Londoners can visit art galleries, museums, movie theatres, libraries, and historic sites. They can play baseball or soccer, swim, skate, bike, or bowl. These activities enrich their cultural life and contribute to their physical well-being.

TOURISM

Many businesses in London sell goods and services not only to the people who live there, but to tourists. These businesses include museums, galleries, and historic sites; restaurants and hotels; car rental firms and taxi companies; and book shops and clothing stores. Tourists generate additional wealth, income, and jobs for the residents of London.

To help businesses in the tourism industry, London has an organization called Tourism London. It is run and supported by tourist businesses in the private and public sector. Tourism London works to promote London as a tourist destination and, therefore, bring additional business to its members. It also offers its members many benefits, including

• continuing education about the tourist industry
• advice on marketing and advertising
• identifying new opportunities for tourist businesses
• help in forming partnerships with other tourist businesses

E-ACTIVITY

Visit
www.business.
nelson.com
and follow the links
to learn about the
work of the
Canadian Chamber
of Commerce.

London's Chamber of Commerce

Like most cities, London has a chamber of commerce where citizens and visitors can go to find out about services and activities in the community. The chamber of commerce also offers important services to businesses, including professional and business development and opportunities to network with other businesses. Other agencies in the community, such as the London Economic Development Corporation, have been established to attract new businesses and industries to the city. By encouraging and supporting businesses, these organizations also contribute to the community.

ACTIVITIES FOR ...

INFORMATION	**C**ONNECTION	**E**XTENSION
1. a) In what different ways do businesses have an impact on the community?	**b)** Using the information in the text as a guide, describe what impact the opening of a new restaurant would have on your community.	**c)** Create an illustration similar to Figure 4.2 that shows how your spending affects the community.
2. a) What factors influence the job market?	**b)** How many jobs have been gained or lost in your community over the past year? Identify reasons for this job gain or loss.	**c)** Give an example, other than in the banking industry, where a technological improvement has led to both a job loss and a job gain.
3. a) Identify and explain the phases of a business cycle.	**b)** What impact would each phase of the business cycle have on your community?	**c)** Which of the four phases of the business cycle best describes where the Canadian economy is today? In which stage of the cycle do you think Canada will be in two years? Explain your reasoning.
4. a) Define "standard of living."	**b)** "A business can have both a negative and positive effect on a community." Explain this statement, using an example other than an airport.	**c)** Gentrification is a controversial issue. Residents who have lived in an area for many years may have to move because they can't afford to live in the new luxury homes. Research this issue and present arguments to support both sides. You may wish to use a point/ counterpoint approach. Then, debate your findings.
5. a) List some services that the private and public sectors provide in London, Ontario.	**b)** How do these services affect life in the community, from the point of view of both business and quality of life?	**c)** Contact the chamber of commerce in your community. Use the categories "city services," "culture and recreation," "health and education," and "tourism," to find out what services are available for local residents.

Review

Knowledge and Understanding

1. Match each of the following terms to the correct definition:

   business cycle   private sector
   economic system   privatization
   modern mixed economy   standard of living

   a) A system that enables government and business to work together to provide goods and services to consumers.
   b) A sector represented by individually owned and operated businesses.
   c) The way you live as measured by the kinds and quality of goods and services you can afford.
   d) It consists of four phases—trough, recovery, peak, and recession.
   e) A process whereby government-owned businesses are sold to the private sector.
   f) An economy that combines the features of more than one economic system.

2. Name the three types of economic systems and identify their characteristics.

3. Using the telephone book as a resource, name two public service agencies or departments for each of the three levels of government.

Thinking and Inquiry

1. If workers produce fewer goods and services than expected, what effect will this lower production have on the nation's standard of living?

2. If you were in charge of tourism in your city, what four things would you do to attract tourists? Use specific examples where possible.

3. Imagine that many auto and steel plants close throughout Canada. Thousands of workers lose their jobs in a relatively short period of time. If the country has been enjoying prosperous times, into what phase of the business cycle might it now be headed, and why? Describe other conditions that might occur.

4. Why is outsourcing becoming more popular in the business world? What problems might outsourcing cause?

5. "If you use your earnings to raise your standard of living by spending, saving, and investing, you are, in turn, supporting the business community." Explain this statement, giving examples.

Communication

1. Central City's chamber of commerce and economic development council have persuaded a computer manufacturing and processing plant to open in the city's industrial park. The company expects to employ 300 people. Write a letter to the editor of the local paper listing at least five ways that you think the city would benefit from the new business.

2. Communist countries like China and Cuba do not encourage free enterprise. With a small group, discuss the disadvantages for businesses and consumers in these countries. What advantages can you think of?

Application

1. Interview the partners of a public–private partnership in your community or in the surrounding area. Find the answers to the following questions:
   a) How long has this partnership been in operation?
   b) How has it benefited each party?
   c) What problems have arisen and how were they resolved?
   d) Would the partners recommend a public–private partnership to other businesses?

2. How do businesses affect the quality of life in your community? To find out, visit three businesses. Talk to employees and to people who buy goods or services from each business. Create a plus/minus chart to show your findings. Based on your findings, which one of the businesses would you recommend for an award for improving the quality of life in your community? Present an award that you designed to that business.

REFLECT ON YOUR LEARNING

1. Return to the Before You Begin question on page 63. Have your ideas about this topic changed after reading this chapter? Explain.

2. Explain what makes Emmie Leung's company, International Paper Industries, a free enterprise.

UNIT 2

DOING BUSINESS IN CANADA

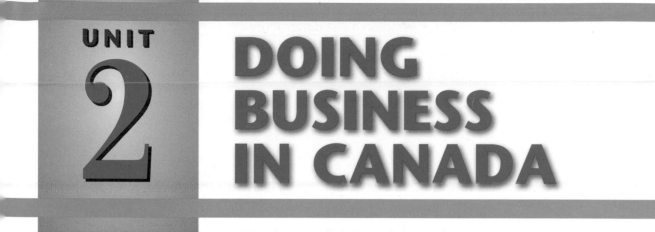

Chapter 5 What Makes a Successful Business?
Chapter 6 Competitive Environments
Chapter 7 Human Resources and Management
Chapter 8 The Role and Functions of Accounting
Chapter 9 The Role and Functions of Marketing

"A business exists to create a customer."
Peter Drucker, author and economics consultant to the Canadian government

WHAT MAKES A SUCCESSFUL BUSINESS?

STUDENT EXPECTATIONS

After completing this chapter, you will be able to

- define business success
- demonstrate an understanding of the profit equation
- show how a business can increase profits
- identify the personal factors influencing the success of Canadian businesses
- discuss what effects economic factors have on a business's success
- analyze the forces of supply and demand and explain how they determine market prices
- describe reasons for government policies and actions relating to regulations of markets and business activities
- give reasons for a business's failure

Profile

Saskatchewan-born Marcia Kilgore gives a facial at Bliss Spa in New York City.

THE "BLISS" OF BEING A SUCCESSFUL BUSINESSPERSON

Marcia Kilgore is the founder of the fashionably funky Bliss Spa. In four short years, Kilgore's business has grown from a single location in SoHo (a trendy district of New York City) into a profitable international line of beauty and skin-care products that are sold online and through a catalogue that goes out to over a million consumers. Her client list reads like a who's who of show business. Among the celebrities who line up for her facials or get rubbed, peeled, and wrapped at her spa are Oprah Winfrey, Julia Roberts, Uma Thurman, Jennifer Lopez, and Madonna.

Kilgore spends a typical day tending to the endless details of her company. She still gives facials (now only two mornings a week), trains the staff, develops new products, and writes all the humorous advertisements for her mail-order catalogue, called *BlissOut* (for example, Bliss Serious Seaweed Cellulite Soap: "Forget the rope, this is soap with hope"). She also personally answers complaint letters. "People come into Bliss now and they don't just expect a great massage, they expect it to change their lives," says Kilgore. "It's hard because people have heard so much about Bliss, they always expect it to be perfect. And when it was really small, I really could make everything perfect. I had 20 hours a day when I could be awake, when I would work on everything, constantly."

Kilgore was born in the small town of Outlook, Saskatchewan, 75 km south of Saskatoon. She and her two sisters were raised to be fearless and to feel that they were as smart as anyone else. In 1987, the 18-year-old Kilgore moved to New York to join her sister Jodi, who was working as a model. The hectic pace of New York City suited Kilgore. She started hanging out with Jodi's friends in the star-studded fashion world, contacts that would come in handy later on. In 1990, after taking an esthetician's course, Kilgore started doing facials on the floor of her tiny apartment. Soon, word spread about her "magic hands" and her ability to cure pimply skin. Kilgore couldn't keep up with the demand. She started expanding, renting more rooms to run the business, and hiring more staff to help her out.

CONTINUED →

> **Marcia Kilgore's client list reads like a who's who of show business. Among the celebrities who line up for her facials at her spa are Oprah Winfrey, Julia Roberts, Uma Thurman, Jennifer Lopez, and Madonna.**

She also figured out where the real money is made in the beauty business: mail-order sales of those skin-smoothing, blemish-busting creams and lotions. As word of mouth spread, Kilgore started to gain a reputation in the fashion industry. In the spring of 1996, a small article about Kilgore and her fun facials appeared in *Vogue* magazine. It was no accident. Kilgore realized early on that exposure in a fashion magazine was exactly the type of publicity she was looking for. She worked hard to make sure that the magazines knew who she was and what she was selling, turning many of the magazines' editors into regular Bliss clients. After the *Vogue* piece, her phones started ringing. At one point, she was so busy that 500 clients had to be put on a waiting list.

As an entrepreneur, Kilgore has taken an old concept and given it a new twist. Spas, after all, have been around for a long time. But to Kilgore they were often stuffy and intimidating. In July 1996, when she opened Bliss Spa, she turned that attitude on its head. She did away with the snootiness, and instead designed a spa with a relaxed and playful atmosphere. "A lot of spas are hushed and clinical," says Eleni Gage, beauty editor of *InStyle* magazine. "You feel like you're going to the doctor for a checkup. Marcia has made Bliss upscale but not fancy." At Bliss, spa-goers can enjoy wacky furniture and a pedicure room painted like a Caribbean beach scene. The sign on one door in the massage area asks that the door be closed gently since "the thump, thump, thump is not very spa." In the lounge, there are brownies and white wine. To stressed-out women, she offers fun-sounding treatments like the "Tunnel of Rub" and the "Carrot and Sesame Body Buff."

Since opening, the SoHo spa has doubled in size. Bliss now employs approximately 300 people in two locations in New York City. Hundreds of customers cycle through the spas' robe rooms and saunas each day, paying for treatments such as the two-hour Deep Sea Detox, where clients are wrapped in hot French seaweed. Plans are under way to open more spas in California and London.

About This Profile

1. How would you describe Marcia Kilgore's personality? Do you think that these characteristics make her a better businessperson? Why or why not?
2. Why do you think Bliss Spa has been so successful?

What Is Business Success?

BEFORE YOU BEGIN

Discuss the following with a partner: Should profit be the only motive for running a business?

Roots, Tim Hortons, and Sobeys are all successful Canadian businesses. What does it mean to be successful? For one thing, these businesses are still in operation. A sure sign of an unsuccessful business is the "Going out of Business" sign in the window. But success means more than just staying afloat.

Business success is measured in four ways. The most important gauge is profit since a business will fail without it, but to be considered successful a business should also demonstrate social responsibility by making a contribution to its community and society. Since the people who work for the business have their own way of evaluating the success of the company, successful businesses need to develop employee satisfaction. Finally, a successful business must provide its owner or operator with some degree of personal satisfaction.

PROFIT

Most often, describing a business as successful means that it is profitable. A successful business makes money; an unsuccessful business does not. An unprofitable business will not continue operating for long.

A business makes a profit by selling its goods and services for more than the costs and expenses required to produce them. For example, if you made some tomato sauce from tomatoes you grew in your garden and then sold it in jars to your classmates, you would have to sell the sauce for more than it cost you to make it in order to make a profit. This process is not as simple as it sounds.

The tomato plant cost $10 and yielded 30 tomatoes, 25 of which were usable. Therefore, each usable tomato cost 40¢. But you also had to drive to the nursery to purchase the tomato plant. The gas cost $2. The wear and tear on the car cost 50¢. These costs and expenses add an extra 10¢ per tomato, increasing the cost of each tomato to 50¢. Each jar of sauce holds 8 tomatoes, which means that the tomatoes in the sauce cost $4.

Other costs and expenses include the jars, the wax for sealing them, and the electricity for the stove to heat the sauce and sterilize the jars. Also take into account the salt, sugar, and spices for the sauce. Consider, too, the household expenses, such as lighting and heating the kitchen for as long as it takes you to make the sauce. To these costs and expenses, add the portion of household insurance and mortgage interest, or the portion of apartment rent, that was used for your time in the kitchen. You must also account for the use of pots, pans, bowls, and knives, the transportation costs to buy the jars and spices, and the

BUSINESS —FACT—

Microsoft, the world's largest software maker, made a net profit of $9.4 billion (U.S.) in 2000.

water that you used for sterilization and cleaning up. And then there's your time—the time it took you to

• buy the plants, jars, wax, and ingredients for the sauce
• tend the tomato plant and harvest the tomatoes
• make the sauce and put it in jars
• label the jars and sell them

Suppose by this time, the sauce has cost you $9 a jar to make.

If you sell the jars for $10 each, you will make $1 per jar. Your crop was 25 tomatoes and it takes 8 tomatoes to make 1 jar of sauce. Therefore, you could make 3 jars of sauce and earn $3 profit. Is your business successful? What if you broke a jar? What if the cold summer lowered your yield? What if the cost of sugar went up? What if no one wanted to spend $10 for a jar of tomato sauce?

Of course, you could sell your tomato sauce for $5 a jar. Five dollars is a reasonable price for tomato sauce. And you would sell a lot of sauce. You would be successful as far as sales were concerned. But you would not be profitable, and your business would eventually fail.

Profit is often expressed as a **return on sales**. If you sell 1000 jars of sauce at $10 a jar, your sales would be $10 000. If your total profit is $1000, then you would have a 10% return on sales [($1000 ÷ $10 000) × 100]. For every dollar you receive through sales, you get to keep 10¢. Many successful businesses work on very low returns on sales percentages. The major supermarket chains, for example, are still very successful with a 2% return because of the high volume of sales they make each day.

To make a profit on tomato sauce, you have to sell the sauce for more than it cost you to manufacture it.

The Profit Equation

Successful businesses account for their expenses very carefully. Keeping accurate financial records is one of the functions of the accounting department, which will be studied in more detail in Chapter 8.

Profit can be calculated using the **profit equation**.

Profit = Selling Price – Cost of Goods Sold – Expenses

There are several ways to increase profit. You can increase your revenue by increasing the selling price. You would make more profit as long as your sales remain the same. But, as you read in Chapter 1, a price increase often decreases demand. You can keep the selling price the same and sell more, but to increase sales you would probably have to spend money on advertising and promotion. The money spent to promote your product would increase expenses, not profit. The most effective and efficient way for most businesses to increase profit is to decrease expenses.

Controlling Expenses

Henry Ford did not invent the automobile—but he did make the manufacturing of the automobile so efficient that the costs of the product went down and the demand for it went up. His assembly line concept became the way most factories operated. Soon, the modern industrial age was born. Ford took advantage of the principle of **economies of scale**, which means the more products you can make using the same factory, the cheaper each product becomes.

Figure 5.1 Since variable costs increase as the quantity produced increases (and as fixed costs stay the same), total costs of production also increase.

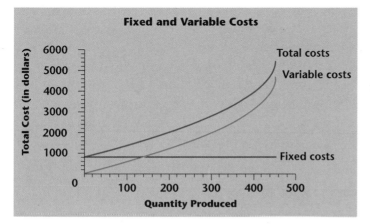

Let's look at your tomato sauce again, this time using the principle of economies of scale. Instead of one tomato plant, imagine that you had planted 100 and made 300 jars of sauce. The costs of the jars, ingredients, and wax are all dependent on the number of jars of sauce made. One hundred tomato plants will probably cost almost 100 times what one tomato plant costs (although there are often discounts for volume buying). Because the costs of these materials and ingredients change with the quantity of sauce made, they are called **variable costs**. But there are some expenses that do not change with quantity. These are called **fixed costs**. Some household expenses, such as insurance and mortgage, would be the same for one jar of sauce as they would be for 100 jars. As you make more jars of tomato sauce, your variable costs will increase but your fixed costs will stay the same. Therefore, the more jars of tomato sauce you make, the less they cost per jar to produce, and the more profit your business makes. Successful businesses control their expenses through economies of scale.

Another method of controlling expenses and making more profit is through budgeting and cost cutting. Businesses try to control expenses by setting budgets based on expected sales with a desired profit in mind. A **budget** is a plan for wise spending and saving based on income (sales) and expenses. If the sales of the business do not match expectations, then expenses must be scaled back to ensure that the profit equation is in balance. The business may spend less on advertising, payroll, or other controllable expenses. However, cuts in one area may lead to problems in other areas. For example, if you used a cheaper quality of glass jar, you may get more breakage, decreasing overall profit. (See Chapters 8 and 10 for more information on budgeting.)

STRETCH YOUR THINKING

Would a budget help you? Keep track of your expenses for a week or a month. How would you use this information to make better use of your spending money?

SOCIAL RESPONSIBILITY

A profitable business can have a major impact on its community. Many businesses donate goods, services, or money to both local and national charities. They sponsor public service advertisements to raise awareness about issues of concern to the public. They often provide work experience or cooperative education for students at both the secondary and postsecondary levels.

Of course, there are several reasons for this community involvement. Often, the business's owner or board of directors feels strongly about an issue and decides to help. At other times, the business may hope that gaining good publicity or a positive community reputation will attract more customers. Some businesses can claim charitable donations as a tax deduction, which enables the business to save money. In many cases, it is a combination of these factors that prompt businesses to be good **corporate citizens**.

You might decide to donate several jars of your tomato sauce to a local food bank, or sponsor a Meals on Wheels program for the senior citizens in your community. Another way of measuring a business's success, then, is to look at how much of a contribution it makes to the community.

EMPLOYEE SATISFACTION

National magazines in both Canada and the United States often publish lists of the best companies to work for. Imagine for a moment that you are the owner of one of these companies. When employees stay with your business because they like the working environment or the conditions of employment, your business is successful in two ways: First, it is very expensive to train employees. If a well-trained employee stays with your business, it is less expensive and more productive for you. Second, having a reputation as a good employer gives your business a positive image.

To improve the working environment, some companies offer on-site fitness facilities.

As you will see in Chapter 7, there are many ways to achieve employee satisfaction. Good salaries, medical benefits, employee discounts, and generous vacation packages are examples of compensation that your business can offer. Employee satisfaction also depends on the working environment. Is it a safe, healthy, and enjoyable place to work? Do the employees get along? Do they take pride in their work or in the company? Both the compensation and the working environment need to be good if employee retention is going to be high. And if employee retention is high, your business can certainly be called successful.

PERSONAL SATISFACTION

Possibly the ultimate measure of a business's success is whether or not the owner is satisfied with the business. For many people, owning a business gives them an opportunity to work in areas they enjoy. If you love books, owning a bookstore, buying rare books and selling them to dealers, or operating an Internet book review site might be some of the things you would like to do. You need to make a profit only so that you can continue running the business. Often, the most successful businesses did not start out to make huge profits or become major corporations. Many successful businesses were started by people who simply loved what they did. If making tomato sauce became an everyday chore that you hated to do, you would soon lose interest in the business. But if you enjoyed making sauce and you knew that you made the best tomato sauce in the country, then, regardless of the amount of profit you made, your business would be successful.

ACTIVITIES FOR ...

INFORMATION	CONNECTION	EXTENSION
1. a) What is the profit equation?	**b)** Think of a local business that you are familiar with. How could it increase profits?	**c)** How might a business create problems for itself by cutting back too much on expenses?
2. a) Using return on sales as a scale, which company made more profit: Company A which made $10 000 on $100 000 in sales? Company B which made $30 000 on $400 000 in sales?	**b)** Select an industry with a number of major companies in it (the automobile industry, for example). Compare the annual reports of three major competitors to see which company is the most profitable.	**c)** Using annual reports, outline the five-year profit trend for three major competitors. Use return on sales to measure the profits of each company. Are there profit trends developing in any of the companies? in the industry?
3. a) Besides calculating profit, how else can you measure the success of a business?	**b)** Interview a local business-person to find out what personal satisfaction he or she finds in owning a business.	**c)** If you had a business, what personal satisfaction might you get from it?

Contemporary Issues in Canadian Business

THE ISSUE: CORPORATE SOCIAL RESPONSIBILITY

What is corporate social responsibility?

Companies exhibit corporate social responsibility (CSR) through their values, their ethics, and the contributions they make to their communities. **Values** are the company's beliefs about what is important. **Ethics** are the principles of morality or rules of conduct under which the business operates. Because CSR was started by businesses (the government did not force companies to become more socially responsible), it is considered to be a grassroots movement. In Canada, a CSR approach to doing business is becoming more common.

Being a CSR company means, first of all, believing that profit is only one of the reasons for being in business. CSR companies practise ethical behaviour and make every effort to support their beliefs by adhering to the following CSR principles:

- providing a safe and healthy work environment
- adopting fair labour policies
- protecting the environment
- being truthful in advertising
- practising fair pricing
- donating to charity

Providing a safe and healthy work environment, for example, could mean investing in an employee wellness program. Such a program might offer employees flexible hours, professional development opportunities, or on-site daycare or fitness facilities.

CSR companies also believe that it is important for businesses to be socially responsible to their customers and communities. One way companies can contribute to their communities is by sponsoring a local club, team, or activity. Shell Canada is one company that has set an example on a larger scale. It has established the Shell Environmental Fund to raise money for projects such as cleaning up a local stream or setting up a community recycling program. Shell contributes up to $5000 per project. To date, the environmental fund has granted more than $7.5 million. Some business analysts predict that CSR will be the most important business issue of the 21st century.

If CSR is so important, should the government introduce laws to force every company to act in socially responsible ways? People have different views on this question.

Point

Many companies have adopted and acted upon CSR principles because they believe in them. For these companies, CSR has become an important part of their philosophy or mission statement. As well, consumers are demanding that companies become much more socially responsible. According to a recent Conference Board of Canada study, 60% of Canadians say they have chosen to do business with a company because it was more socially responsible than its competitors.

There's no need to force companies to adopt CSR policies, because treating customers and employees fairly and helping the community is just good business sense. Satisfied customers will return and bring others with them. Good employees will be attracted to responsible companies, and will be less likely to leave. Community projects provide an opportunity for the company to improve its public image and to save money on taxes and advertising.

As a result, well-managed companies will move toward CSR on their own, while companies that don't adopt CSR policies will soon be left behind. Laws are not needed to enforce participation in activities that offer such clear benefits to the companies involved.

Counterpoint

When a company sponsors a community project, donates a percentage of its profits to a local charity, or practises fair pricing for its customers, it is making sacrifices in terms of profits. Because managers and shareholders may be reluctant to make these sacrifices on their own, government legislation may be necessary to encourage socially responsible decision making. In fact, in Canada, laws are already in place to ensure that companies offer their employees safe working environments and fair treatment. There are also laws to ensure truth in advertising.

Along with government legislation, government funding could help encourage CSR projects. Some projects are simply too costly for smaller companies. For example, providing an on-site daycare facility may promote a healthy and safe work environment, but the facility would be expensive to build and maintain. The high cost of running an employee daycare probably explains why a recent Conference Board study found that only 15% of 220 Canadian public and private sector employers surveyed provided daycare facilities for their staff.

According to the Buffet Taylor National Wellness Survey report, for every dollar spent on an effective workplace wellness program, employers can realize a return of more than $6. Yet, despite the apparent benefits, many companies are unwilling to spend the money. Government legislation and financial support, in the form of grants, loans, or tax rebates, would encourage more companies to take steps that would provide long-term benefits for employees, shareholders, and the community.

A Real Life Example

G.A.P (Great Adventure People) Adventures Inc. is a travel company owned by Bruce Poon Tip. He founded the business in 1990 with the goal of providing overseas tours that respect and protect local communities and their environments. People who travel through G.A.P also get to experience their host country in a unique way—travellers stay in private homes or guesthouses rather than hotels. This type of accommodation minimizes the amount of ecological interference that tourism can cause. It also enables travellers to gain a greater understanding of the country's people and culture.

Recently, Poon Tip voluntarily gave up a very profitable part of his business. He cancelled a popular tour to Myanmar (formerly Burma) because he felt that the political conditions in that country violated his company's philosophy. He had no power to change these conditions and, therefore, he chose to leave.

The socially responsible choice is not always the easiest choice—but making tough decisions and sticking to your principles are what CSR is all about.

Bruce Poon Tip

Questions and Activities About This Issue

1. Research a company in your community that has a socially responsible program. How long has this company's program been in place? What impact has it had on your community?

2. A public company wants to devote more of its resources to social responsibility. With a partner, role-play opposing views. One of you is the CEO of the company. The other represents the shareholders who want to see a large return on their investment. Plan your argument before you begin.

Factors Affecting Business Success

Business success is never a matter of luck or accident. Success depends on several things: personal factors, economic conditions, and the influence of the government. Although personal factors are the only ones that can be controlled directly by the owner or manager, it is crucial for business leaders to understand, anticipate, and adapt to both economic conditions and the influence of government.

PERSONAL FACTORS

People who create businesses (entrepreneurs) are often quite different from those who can run or manage businesses successfully. A person can have a great idea and expend a lot of energy in starting a new business, but that same person may lack certain personal characteristics that are important in running a successful business. Starting a business and running a business each require separate sets of characteristics. (We will deal with the characteristics of successful entrepreneurs in Chapter 15.)

Successful businesspeople must grow their businesses, not simply plant them. To grow, a successful business requires people with the following personal traits: desire for control, vision, passion, perseverance, and teamwork.

Desire for Control

Successful businesspeople like to be in charge. They like to make the important decisions in life. Many people are content to let others direct them, tell them what to do, and pay them well for doing it. There is a high degree of security in living life this way. People who start businesses do not enjoy working for others and will give up the security of being employed for the independence of running their own businesses.

A successful businessperson must also like directing others. To keep the business running smoothly, a hundred different things must be done in a day. The successful businessperson must delegate tasks that need to be done. Delegating means telling others what they should do. If you cannot delegate, you will end up doing most of the work, and you will not have time to make the important decisions that will determine the future success of the business.

STRETCH YOUR THINKING

How are the factors affecting business success like or unlike those required for success in school?

A Company with Vision

When the owners of Roots, Michael Budman and Don Green, decided to outfit the entire Canadian Winter Olympic team in 1998, they knew they were not just giving away merchandise. Hundreds of millions of people around the world saw the now-famous red Roots cap, and millions of fans wanted one. The cap was one of the most successful products in the world that year. The Roots team had the vision not just to buy ads on the Olympic programs or give money to Canadian Olympic teams, but also to place its products in a sporting event of the highest calibre. Not only did sales soar, but Roots's reputation grew as well. It repeated its clothing giveaway during the 2000 Summer Olympics in Sydney, Australia, with equal success.

The 1998 Canadian Winter Olympics team, led by freestyle skier Jean-Luc Brassard, is outfitted by Roots.

Vision

A person with vision (in the business sense of the word) sees opportunities that others do not see. He or she recognizes the potential demand for a service or product that is not currently available and acts to fill that gap.

Passion

Success in business requires a commitment of time that often takes people away from family, friends, recreational activities, and the normal routines of their daily lives. Successful businesspeople must have a passion for what they do in order to work as hard as they do for so little material reward (at least in the beginning). It is their love of the product or the process (or both) that keeps successful businesspeople going.

Perseverance

Perseverance is not just staying with a task for a long time; it is staying with a task long past the time that most people would have quit. Successful businesspeople are often faced with reasons to give up. These hardships include long hours, family pressures, personal stress, and market uncertainty. It is much easier to work for someone else's company, where there is a guaranteed salary and the working hours are defined. But a businessperson who sticks with it and overcomes the obstacles can be very successful.

Teamwork

No one can be successful in business without the ability to work with other people. Businesspeople need to work with suppliers, customers, and their own employees. Owning or managing a business requires the development of teams as well. The successful owner or manager will be able to attract people with different skills, abilities, and personality types. Most important, the manager will be able to get employees to all work together to achieve the goals of the business. In order to develop effective teams, a successful leader must be a coach, a negotiator, a motivator, a teacher, and a counsellor. Shyness, rudeness, arrogance, lack of empathy, rigidity, and lack of a sense of humour are all personal characteristics that make teamwork difficult, and therefore, they can be obstacles to business success.

To be successful, businesspeople must motivate their employees to work together as a team.

THE SUCCESSFUL BUSINESSPERSON

As we have seen, it is no accident that certain people are successful in business and others are not. There is a "business personality," a set of personal attributes that indicates a high likelihood of business success. Perhaps you have what it takes to be successful in business. Do you
- like to take control?
- see opportunities when others do not?
- become enthusiastic about an activity or a product?
- stick to a task when even your friends back away and the obstacles seem insurmountable?
- enjoy being with different types of people?

Many of these personal traits can be developed, however; so even if you are missing some of these characteristics at the moment, if you are interested in business, you can work to improve your personal business skills.

ACTIVITIES FOR ...

INFORMATION	**C**ONNECTION	**E**XTENSION
1. a) What are the five personal factors that can lead to business success?	**b)** Use the five factors for business success to rate your business personality.	**c)** Outline a plan for developing your business personality.
2. a) Which personal factor do you think is the most important one for business success? Explain.	**b)** Interview a local business-person to get his or her reaction to the list of personal factors that affect business success. Which factor does he or she think is the most important one?	**c)** Read a recent magazine or newspaper article about a successful businessperson. Based on your reading, can you add any personal factors to the five already studied?
3. a) Give an example of a businessperson who illustrates each of the five personal factors for success.	**b)** Work with a group. In your community, find an example of a business to illustrate each of the five personal factors for success. (You will need to find five businesses.) Give reasons for your choices.	**c)** Can the five factors for success be used to predict success in school? at work? with personal relationships? Explain.

Economic Conditions

Economic factors that affect business include supply and demand, labour market conditions, and inflation. These factors cannot be controlled by individuals, but they can be anticipated. Successful businesses know how to adapt to economic changes.

SUPPLY AND DEMAND

As you read in Chapter 1, one of the economic factors that affects the marketplace is the relationship between supply and demand. As the supply of a particular good or service increases, the price usually decreases if the demand remains the same. This price decrease is the result of increased competition, which promotes more and better research, cheaper manufacturing or distribution methods, and price reductions based on economies of scale. The lower prices, as well as increased availability in the market, increase the demand for the product. As the price drops and competition heats up, businesses that are barely competitive (**marginal businesses**) start to leave the marketplace because they cannot make enough profit. Some businesses may need to change their direction or product line. Others lose so much money that they actually fold.

Price decreases occur over time, and it is very difficult to predict how long it will take before some businesses can no longer maintain their necessary profit levels. Manufacturers and distributors, for example, can be profitable for some time, but they must always be aware that the profit picture could change at any time. A good businessperson will watch developments in the supply/demand relationship very carefully.

Figure 5.2 Supply has a dramatic impact on the price of goods if demand remains the same.

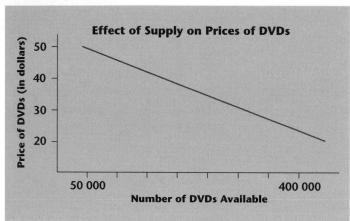

Until fairly recently, no one supplied movies in the DVD format. There were no DVD players on the market and therefore there was no demand for movies in the DVD format. As more DVD players were purchased, the demand for movies formatted to fit them increased. Because supply was low and the demand was relatively high, the price of DVDs was high. This situation made DVDs very profitable and encouraged other companies who owned movie libraries to release their products on DVD. As the supply increased, competition in the manufacturing and distribution of the DVDs increased, and the price gradually began to fall. Eventually, the profit potential in the manufacturing of DVDs will be attractive only to those major and efficient manufacturers who have already invested in the factories, machinery, and technology. Companies who entered the market late or who wish to enter the market now will have a very difficult time making a profit.

By controlling the supply of a particular product and waiting for the demand to increase, a business can charge a price that is much higher than the actual costs. **Price fixing** occurs when, without government permission, businesses in a particular industry get together in order to set a price for their product rather than letting the forces of competition determine the price. Sometimes, this is done by setting supply quotas. A **supply quota** is the amount of a good that producers are allowed to supply. (More information on quotas is provided later in this chapter and in Chapter 18.) Canada has laws that prevent price fixing, as you will see on page 104. However, some of these industries are not in Canada, and they can form groups legally. Groups that form to control the supply and, therefore, the price of a product or service within a particular industry are called **trusts** or **cartels**. One of the most famous cartels is the **Organization of Petroleum Exporting Countries (OPEC).**

What Is OPEC?

OPEC is an intergovernmental organization dedicated to the stability and prosperity of the petroleum market. OPEC membership is open to any country that is a substantial net exporter of oil and that shares the ideals of the organization. OPEC has 11 member countries: Algeria, Indonesia, Iran, Iraq, Kuwait, Libya, Nigeria, Qatar, Saudi Arabia, the United Arab Emirates, and Venezuela. The OPEC member countries currently supply more than 40% of the world's oil. They also possess about 78% of the world's total proven crude oil reserves.

An oil refinery.

E-ACTIVITY

Visit www.business. nelson.com and follow the links to learn about the unemployment rate in Canada and other countries. Compare the rates. In which country would you be interested in opening a business?

LABOUR MARKET CONDITIONS

The availability of skilled labour is an economic factor that businesses cannot control. It is dependent on the educational system in a particular region, the number of people of working age in that region, and the number of businesses competing for their skills. The supply and demand factor is at work here as well, in that businesses compete for the labour supply by offering higher wages, better working conditions, or excellent benefits packages.

The **unemployment rate** measures the number of able-to-work people who don't have jobs as a percentage of the labour force. The **labour force** includes all those working and looking for work. If the unemployment rate is high (over 5%), then the availability of labour is also high. As the supply of labour increases, employers can offer lower wages and still have numerous applicants for open positions. There are many regional and seasonal variations in the unemployment rate. Canada's Atlantic provinces suffer rates of high unemployment as their fishing and mining industries decline. The retail industry experiences higher demand for labour during the Christmas season. It is important to note that there could be a difference in the availability of unskilled labour and the availability of skilled labour. Simply looking at the unemployment rates will not inform a business about the type of labour available in the community.

Successful businesspeople usually examine the unemployment rate in a particular community before establishing a business there. A business will often qualify for government **subsidies** if it locates in an area of high unemployment. The government offers these subsidies to help lower the unemployment rates in economically depressed areas. A business wishing to take advantage of these subsidies, in the form of tax breaks, low-interest loans, or actual government grants, must be willing to invest money in training programs because much of the available labour will not have the skills necessary for the new business. The government also provides interest-free loans to students to help them start a summer business. As well, it provides subsidies to businesses to encourage them to hire students during the summer months.

INFLATION

Inflation occurs when the price of many products goes up while the **purchasing power** of money—the amount and quality of goods and services that money can buy—decreases. This decrease in the purchasing power of money happens for many reasons. Low interest rates make credit attractive, which increases consumer spending. Increased spending increases demand, which in turn increases prices and causes inflation. Tax cuts that encourage production or consumer spending can also stimulate a rapid increase in consumer demand that will fuel inflation. Low unemployment rates mean more jobs; more jobs mean more people are earning salaries that are being spent on consumer goods; more spending leads to increased demand, increased prices, and, ultimately, inflation.

The problem with an inflationary period is that the money that a consumer has to spend is not worth the same amount in the marketplace from one year to the next. Some countries have experienced periods of runaway inflation so severe that the purchasing power of money was reduced within days or even hours. If the price of a pair of running shoes, school supplies, pizza, and a movie increases by 10%, your salary or your savings will not buy as much. For you, the high prices are annoying until your wages go up or the interest on your savings is increased, but for many people on fixed incomes (retired people, people on social assistance) inflation is a more serious problem.

Inflation has very serious consequences for businesses

When too many stores sell competing products, some businesses can no longer make a profit and they are forced to close.

E-ACTIVITY

Visit www.business.nelson.com and follow the links to learn the current inflation rate in Canada and in other countries. Compare the rates.

because they have to spend more for the products and services they need. Businesses must then pass these price increases on to the consumer to ensure that they maintain the necessary profit levels to stay in business. Often, as inflation increases, consumers reduce spending. When their wages and salaries do not keep pace with rising prices, consumers can no longer afford all the goods and services that they were willing and able to buy in the past. At this point, some businesses start to lose sales and become unprofitable. Losses are especially great for restaurants, car dealers, home construction businesses, and luxury-goods manufacturers and retailers because these businesses offer goods or services that are expensive or not essential. A successful business will be able to manage expenses and keep cost cutting to a minimum during inflationary periods. It will concentrate on providing service to its existing clients, trying to keep prices reasonable, and trying to attract new customers.

The cure for inflation is often as bad as the problem. Borrowing and spending need to be controlled. The government will step in and raise interest rates to make it less attractive to borrow money, or it will raise taxes. If the government can slow spending, then inflation can be controlled. The problem is that sometimes these measures severely reduce consumer spending. When consumer spending slows, the economy goes into a recession. As you read in Chapter 4, during a recession, consumer demand decreases, businesses cannot make a profit, and many businesses fail, resulting in increased unemployment. With a reduction in available wages, spending decreases even further, more people are put out of work, and the recession gets worse. Controlling the economy is a delicate balancing act.

ACTIVITIES FOR ...

INFORMATION	**C**ONNECTION	**E**XTENSION
1. a) What is "unemployment rate"?	**b)** What is the current unemployment rate in your area?	**c)** "Companies locate in countries that can provide available, cheap labour." Evaluate this statement from the perspective of all the people involved (for example, the owner of the company, a consumer, and a worker at the company).
2. a) Define "inflation."	**b)** If the inflation rate in Canada were to increase to over 300%, what effect would it have on you and your family?	**c)** As a businessperson, how would you react to a period of inflation? a period of recession?

CAREER FOCUS 2: IDENTIFYING JOB SOURCES

SOURCES OF JOB INFORMATION

You will probably have seven or more jobs during your working life. Your first job will help you find out a great deal about yourself, your career goals, and work in general. You may get a part-time job during the school year to gain work experience and earn personal spending money, or you may need a full-time summer job to start saving for college or university.

Today's job market is in a constant state of change, as you saw in the first Career Focus on pages 14–15. Despite the confusion, however, career information is plentiful and simple to use if you know where to find it. The following information will help you get started.

Open and Hidden Job Markets

According to Human Resources Development Canada (HRDC), only 15% of available jobs are advertised. This is the **open job market**—employers advertise a job opening, receive applications or résumés from interested job seekers, and then interview applicants to fill the jobs. However, nearly 85% of available jobs are never advertised anywhere. These unadvertised jobs are called the **hidden job market**. Employers may use recommendations from current employees to find new employees, and job seekers can learn about openings through word of mouth. Employers may also reconsider résumés that have been submitted to them by job seekers in the past. Through these methods and others, positions are very often filled without an opening ever being advertised.

GUIDANCE/STUDENT SERVICES DEPARTMENTS

Your counsellors and teachers can help you in a job search. Work experience and cooperative education ("co-op") placements, for example, allow you to combine your studies with work in a "real world" setting. Through these experiences, you will become familiar with employer expectations, workplace procedures, possible career opportunities, and concrete applications of your in-school studies. Your teachers may also receive notices of job vacancies from employers.

NEWSPAPER ADVERTISEMENTS

Most local newspapers have a "Help Wanted" or "Careers" section that lists a variety of jobs. Reading this section of your newspaper will give you a good idea of the jobs that are in demand in your community and will help you discover what qualities employers are looking for in potential employees. Most employers now require applicants to use e-mail or fax machines to submit their applications, so be prepared to use these methods to contact employers.

NETWORKING

The process of meeting and getting to know people in a business that you are interested in is called **networking**. Friends and relatives can be excellent sources of job information, and they can direct you to contacts who may be of further help to you. Employers often prefer to hire someone who is recommended by one of their own employees rather than take a chance on a total stranger, so it helps to get to know people in businesses that interest you. Usually, networking provides a forum to seek advice, not a specific job. Be willing to give help as well as receive it. And be sure to follow up on leads. There is an old saying: "It isn't what you know; it's who you know." If you have a large network of contacts, you'll likely have more opportunities.

THE INTERNET

The Internet is the fastest-growing source of information about job opportunities and career planning. Many Web sites are dedicated to providing career information to potential job seekers. Career Gateway, an Ontario Ministry of Education Web site, is one source for you to investigate. Many online databases provide access to current information on occupations and sources of education and funding. One example is workopolis.com, jointly sponsored by *The Globe and Mail* and *The Toronto Star*. It is Canada's largest job site, listing over 35 000 jobs. There are also job-search programs available online that ask questions about your skills, interests, and level of education. Then, the computer matches your profile with appropriate jobs and gives you information about each opening.

HUMAN RESOURCES CENTRES

Human Resources Development Canada (HRDC) is the federal government department responsible for the Canadian work force. Located in communities across Canada, HRDC's human resources centres provide information and services pertaining to all aspects of the employment market. By visiting an HRDC human resources centre, you will gain valuable support and access to a broad range of employment resources. Also, HRDC maintains several Web sites that contain job postings from across Canada, as well as extensive advice and assistance for job seekers.

OTHER SOURCES

Visiting companies in a given area to inquire about job openings is called "walking the beat"—you can submit your résumé to a potential employer in person and complete an application on site. Also, career days and job fairs offer other opportunities to obtain information about various companies and the types of jobs they offer. If a particular company interests you, see if it would be possible for you to "job shadow" or volunteer there. These types of opportunities can give you a better idea of exactly which options you would like to pursue in the future.

Be realistic when looking for a job; you might not be able to find the "perfect" first job. However, any job will help you find out more about yourself and about some aspects of being an employee.

Job seekers search for information online and in brochures at a local HRDC office.

Something to Think About

1. Prepare a list of your interests and aptitudes. Then brainstorm jobs that might be appropriate for you. Make point-form notes about the resources and training you require to pursue your career possibilities. Which source of job information will provide you with the best lead in attempting to achieve your career goals?

2. Explain how you could use your own version of networking to find a job.

3. Your best friend says to you, "I can't get a job because I don't have any experience, and I can't get experience because I don't have a job." What advice would you give your friend so that he or she won't get discouraged about finding a job?

Government Influence

STRETCH YOUR THINKING

Analyze a grocery bill for your family. What taxes are added? What percentage of the total does each tax represent?

E-ACTIVITY

Visit **www.business. nelson.com** and follow the links to find out which products have only one tax added to them.

As you have just seen, the government influences business a great deal. In a truly free market economy, government influence would be minimal. But Canada does not have a strictly "free" market in a number of ways and for a number of reasons. The various levels of government in Canada impose taxes on consumers and on businesses, control the distribution of many goods and services, and enforce numerous regulations that businesses must obey.

TAXES

In order to pay for all the government services that we have come to expect, such as education, health care, police and fire protection, highways, and the court system, the government needs money. The main source of revenue for all levels of government is taxes. There are the obvious taxes like sales taxes—the **goods and services tax (GST)** and the **provincial sales tax (PST)**—and income taxes, but there are also taxes that are less obvious. Gasoline, liquor, and cigarettes are examples of products that have extra taxes added. Luxury goods have a special tax. **Imports**—goods and services from other countries that are brought into Canada for sale—often have a **customs duty** added, which is a form of taxation. (See Chapter 18 for more information on imports and custom duties.) Businesses dealing in these sorts of products need to be aware that the prices they charge for the items must include these hidden taxes. This factor may make the businesses less competitive and less profitable. As taxes go up, the available income for consumer spending goes down, while government spending usually goes up.

CONTROL OF DISTRIBUTION

The government plays a dual role in how products are distributed. In some cases, the government wants to control the supply of a product, especially products that are consumer necessities, like milk. To prevent price increases and to encourage stability of supply, the government creates marketing boards. For most other products, like soft drinks, running shoes, and automobiles, the government wishes to encourage a free market and opposes control of supply. Therefore, the government has passed antitrust legislation. The government also controls the money supply through the Bank of Canada. And, through licensing and permits, the provincial and municipal governments control what businesses are allowed to open, who is allowed to open them, and where they are allowed to open.

Marketing Boards

Marketing boards operate in every province or territory in Canada, regulating the supply of certain agricultural products through a system of quotas. Marketing boards control the distribution, manufacturing, and processing of the product. They grade and standardize for quality, regulate or buy a farm's entire quota, and, in some cases, sell the total output of all the farms to manufacturers, processors, and distributors at a standard price. They also promote the product to increase demand. Marketing boards may perform some or all of these tasks.

In Ontario, for example, there are five agricultural products that are controlled totally by marketing boards: chicken, eggs, turkey, tobacco, and milk. The most famous is the milk marketing board, called the Dairy Farmers of Ontario. This group is responsible for the "Drink Milk. Love Life" marketing campaign. These advertisements encourage consumers to drink more milk, thereby increasing the overall demand. The marketing board also promotes milk consumption in cooking: Each year, it publishes a calendar featuring recipes that call for milk. Note that these advertisements do not promote a particular brand of milk or a specific dairy. They simply encourage the increased use of the product, improving demand for the entire industry.

In order to be a dairy farmer or operate a dairy in Canada, you must belong to a milk marketing board. No dairy can produce milk for sale in Canada unless the farm has been approved by the marketing board. Dairy farmers are given strict quotas that tell them how much milk they can produce. If they exceed these quotas, the product cannot be sold and must be destroyed or stored. Anyone wishing to enter the market or increase production must buy his or her quota from dairy farmers wishing to sell some of theirs. If no farmer wants to part with his or her quota, no new producers will be added. These control measures ensure stability of supply and price.

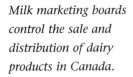

Milk marketing boards control the sale and distribution of dairy products in Canada.

Drink Milk. Love Life.

Antitrust Legislation

For products other than agricultural, the government takes exactly the opposite position: No attempt should be made to control the supply of any product or service by any business or group of businesses, nor should there be any attempt made by groups of businesses to control prices. Some companies, such as Future Shop or Microsoft, are large enough that they can influence the market on their own. Other companies may want to operate as a unified group in order to control the supply and influence prices. In Canada, any effort to control the supply, price, or distribution of products and services in the marketplace, without government approval, is not permitted under the federal Competition Act. The **Competition Act** encourages free and open competition, one of the fundamental principles of a free market system. (See Chapter 6.)

Other Federal Acts That Regulate Canadian Business

The Consumer Packaging and Labelling Act
The Fair Wages and Hours of Labour Act
The Transportation of Dangerous Goods Act
The Hazardous Products Act
The Canadian Environmental Protection Act
The Export and Import Permits Act

Money Supply

The **Bank of Canada**, established by the federal government in 1934, is Canada's central bank. The Bank of Canada is located in Ottawa and has regional offices in most provinces.

The Bank of Canada regulates the money supply in this country, setting the cost of borrowing for the major banks. The individual banks then use this set rate to determine the interest rate for their customers. The Bank of Canada also regulates how much money is in circulation at any given time. "Money" includes cash (coins and bills) and deposits in financial institutions. The Bank tries to ensure that the money supply grows fast enough to permit business production and employment to grow, but not so fast that it causes inflation. The Bank prints more money when it wants to devalue the dollar and recalls more dollars when it wants to decrease the money supply and increase the value of the dollar. Changes in the growth rate of the money supply have a major impact on interest rates, on the level of saving and spending in Canada, and on the exchange value of the Canadian dollar. (See Chapters 10 and 12 for more information about the Bank of Canada and Chapter 18 for more information about exchange rates.)

Licensing and Permits

The government also regulates who does business in Canada by means of licensing and permits. Businesses working with food, drugs, liquor, lodging, transportation, entertainment, broadcasting, tobacco, and firearms (as well as many other types of businesses) need special permission to operate. The owner must apply for this permission and pay for it as well. A person wishing to operate a television station, for example, must apply for a licence to the Canadian Radio-television and Telecommunications Commission (CRTC) before he or she can start a station. Anyone doing business in Canada must have a GST number and a **provincial sales tax number** (except in provinces without sales tax). Municipal governments control where a business can locate by passing **zoning regulations**. Each area of the city is divided into zones where people are supposed to manufacture goods (industrial zones), sell goods and services to consumers (commercial zones), or live (residential zones). You can only establish a business in an area of a town or city zoned for business use.

OTHER REGULATIONS

Canada has many different regulations that protect the consumer. Because of consumer demand, the old philosophy of *caveat emptor* or "Let the buyer beware" has been replaced by the belief that consumers should be protected from unsafe products, poor-quality products, and unethical business practices.

Health and Safety Regulations

In Canada, the Food and Drug Act requires extensive testing of all new food and drug products placed on the market. Regulations also exist for electrical products, children's clothing, furniture, toys, chemicals, cleaners and other toxic substances, automobiles, and many more. Manufacturers or importers need to be familiar with the safety standards and be sure that the products they are making or selling conform to government specifications. Failure to meet these standards could endanger both the consumer and the business. Large fines and even criminal charges could result. In one case, a manufacturer of children's pyjamas used a very flammable liquid to treat the cotton used in the manufacturing of the product. As a result, many children playing near fireplaces or other open flames were severely burned when their pyjamas burst into flames. Not only was the manufacturer sued for millions of dollars, but the stores that sold the product were sued as well.

Quality Control

The right of a business to compete with other businesses by providing lower-quality merchandise at a lower price is a fundamental part of trade. The government does, however, set standards in various industries, notably agricultural products (including meat, fruit, vegetables,

E-ACTIVITY

Have you seen "ISO 9001" and "ISO 9002" banners on some buildings? Visit www.business. nelson.com and follow the links to learn what ISO means and why companies are proud to display these banners.

eggs, and dairy products) and clothing, to ensure minimum standards and consumer confidence. Clothing manufacturers, for example, must conform to Canadian standard-size charts and to various labelling requirements that provide symbols for the garment's care, even if the product is not made in Canada. If, on the other hand, you bought a VCR that did not work properly and was not under warranty, you must try to get your money back from the store or the manufacturer without government assistance. In most cases, consumers looking for bargains need to remember the *caveat emptor* rule and be very cautious. Some examples of laws that set standards for Canadian goods or goods sold in Canada are the Canada Agricultural Products Standards Act, the Fish Inspection Act, and the Textile Labelling Act.

In most cases, consumers looking for bargains need to remember the caveat emptor rule and be very cautious.

Ethical Business Practices

Businesses will often try to get the most profit for the goods and services they sell. They also try to maximize sales, attracting the consumer with special promotions and advertising. Some businesses mislead consumers and try to trick them into buying something. Under the Competition Act, fraud and deceptive business practices such as the following are prohibited in Canada:

- false or misleading advertising
- advertising a bargain price for merchandise that is unavailable for sale in a reasonable quantity ("bait and switch" selling)
- placing two different prices on a product and selling it to the consumer at the higher price (double ticketing)

In Ontario, the **Business Practices Act** protects consumers from fraud and from salespeople who mislead consumers about the quality of the merchandise or the terms of the sale. The **Consumer Protection Act** regulates door-to-door selling by providing a two-day cooling-off period (meaning that the consumer can cancel any contract signed with a door-to-door salesperson, as long as it is done in writing within two business days from the time the contract was first signed). The act also prohibits the practice of referral selling (meaning that no door-to-door salesperson can offer a discount on merchandise in exchange for the names of friends who may be prospective clients). All provinces have enacted similar legislation. However, the length of the cooling-off period varies from province to province.

INFORMATION	CONNECTION	EXTENSION
1. a) List several ways in which governments control business?	**b)** Interview a local business-person. Ask him or her to list and comment on five government regulations that affect his or her business.	**c)** Is there too much government control of business or not enough? Discuss.
2. a) Which government regulation is most necessary? Explain.	**b)** Select one of the acts listed in this section of the chapter. Research the act and report on how it affects local business.	**c)** How do Canadian government regulations on business compare to those of any other country? Select one country for comparison and prepare a brief report.

Why Do Businesses Fail?

Why should we look at business failure? At some point in your life, you will own, work for, invest in, or depend upon one or more of these businesses. Also, we can learn from analyzing businesses that fail because the reasons for their failure are often well documented. Reasons for failure are usually more obvious than reasons for success. They include lack of skill or knowledge, expanding too quickly, lack of capital, and an inability to stay competitive.

LACK OF SKILL OR KNOWLEDGE

Business courses in high school, community college, or university provide some of the skills necessary to run a business. Experience in business provides the rest. It is unrealistic to assume that without these skills you can operate a successful business. It would be like asking a person who has never learned to be an electrician to wire your house.

Business failure often results from a lack of one of the two major business skills: marketing or accounting. The marketing experts are often good at promotional ideas, creative advertising, and colourful, eye-catching displays. Marketers can read the market, predict demand, and select products that will be popular. They spot trends and fads, know styles and fashions, and can appreciate a good product design or package graphic. Most marketers are adept at sales techniques. They know how to reach customers and how to talk to them. Often, they are experts in their product field. (See Chapter 9 for more information about marketing.)

BUSINESS —FACT—

At least half of new companies in Canada go out of business before their third anniversary, and only one-fifth of them survive a decade. Roughly one out of every four new firms won't make it past its first birthday.

Accountants hold the purse strings of a business. They set budgets and **buying quotas** (limits on the amount of money a business should spend on inventory) that ensure the business has the right amount of inventory on hand and on order. They help negotiate terms, pay invoices on time, take advantage of purchase discounts, and factor transportation costs into the overall expenses. Accountants keep financial records, which can be used to predict the sales targets for the next day, month, or year. The major goal of the accountant is to make sure the business is profitable. (See Chapter 8 for more information about accounting.)

Often, a businessperson will be skilled in either marketing or accounting, but not both. The marketer will often overspend to get sales, while the accountant is often overly cautious and won't spend enough. A businessperson who does not have both skills will find it very difficult to remain in business. If you do not have one of these skills yourself, then it is necessary to hire or form a partnership with someone who does. Take, for example, the "retro" restaurant with a '70s theme, modelled after the movie *Saturday Night Fever*. The owner had a vision of a restaurant with real disco balls, servers outfitted in '70s glitter and shine, lots of chrome and glass, and disco music playing all the time. When it was finished, it was beautiful, but the costs were so high that it couldn't make a profit and failed after a year and a half. The marketing was right, but no one did the accounting. If the owner had hired a good accountant, limits would have been placed on spending, and the business would have had a much better chance for success.

EXPANDING TOO QUICKLY

Many successful businesses decide to expand, develop new products or distribution channels, franchise, or acquire other businesses. If these decisions are based on thorough research and are financially responsible, they will often make the business more profitable by opening up new markets, taking advantage of economies of scale, or diversifying. Some businesses become successful so fast that they try to grow too quickly without analyzing their expansion plans. When rapid expansion occurs, a business will often forget the reasons for its initial success.

Take, for example, the homemade ice-cream business that made small batches of its product from fresh ingredients. The store had a window into the production room where the customer could watch the ice cream being made. The store even made its own waffle cones. The store was very successful and the owners thought that they could expand the concept to a number of different locations, even to different cities. However, they could no longer supply all the ice cream for their new locations, so they had it mass-produced. The new stores

Orbitz, a soft drink introduced by Clearly Canadian, is an example of an unsuccessful product launched by a successful business.

were not as popular because the original concept of homemade ice cream was no longer there. The cost of construction and opening expenses were not recovered, and the business quickly went bankrupt.

Forgetting your origins can cause even established businesses financial difficulty. Coca-Cola changed its formula in 1984 and was forced by consumer pressure to bring the old Coke back as Coca-Cola Classic. The ill-fated new Coke, or Coke II as it was eventually called, was never successful and was finally taken off the market. McDonald's thought it could be a pizza parlour as well as a "burger joint." This attempt at diversifying was a very expensive mistake. Consumers could not associate the famous hamburger restaurant with pizza, and McDonald's dropped the product from its menu after spending millions of dollars on the research and equipment to bring the product to market. Both companies seemed to temporarily forget the products that made them great.

Some businesses are so large that change happens very slowly. Many companies require a new product to go through lots of market research and testing before they make it available for sale. Such was the case with Clairol's Short 'n' Sassy shampoo. By the time the company brought the product to market, the short hairstyles that prompted its introduction were no longer as popular and the product failed.

LACK OF CAPITAL

Businesses that fail often say that they "just ran out of money." Running out of money is often the result of failure to budget properly for the first year's operating expenses. Experienced businesspeople suggest that no one go into business without one full year of operating expenses in reserve. Initial capital comes from personal savings, bank loans, investors, partners, friends, and family. It is needed to buy inventory, pay for construction, remodelling, and furnishing, and cover all the other expenses involved in opening. If the business is profitable, revenue from sales will eventually cover the operating costs … *eventually*.

A small gift store opened in March with $50 000 in initial capital. Buying and installing fixtures and stocking the store cost $40 000, and the owners felt good that they had $10 000 left over. The revenue from sales in the spring and summer months was 10% less than predicted. The store was new, and customers were just beginning to discover it. The operating expenses, including rent and salaries, came to $20 000 per month. The store only cleared $18 000 per month to cover expenses. The owners were hoping to make it until Christmas, which would account for 50% of their yearly sales, but because the business was costing them $2000 per month to stay open, they only had enough capital to get them into the summer. No one would lend them more money, so they had to sell off their remaining inventory and close down. Had this business made it until Christmas, it may have been wildly successful; but the owners were underfinanced, which means they did not have enough money to carry them through their startup.

INABILITY TO STAY COMPETITIVE

Small businesses often account for their failure by blaming larger businesses. The real problem, however, is the inability of the smaller business to stay competitive. Businesses can compete using their product mix, product quality, service, price, location, reputation, or expertise. If a big store has better prices, then the little store offers better service. If the big store has a wide product mix, the little store hires product experts to sell to customers. Creative businesses will often find a way to stay competitive, while marginal businesses will go under. Often, the only reason for a small business's success in a particular area or community is the fact that there is no competition for its market.

A small bookstore recently went out of business and blamed one of the big-box stores for its demise. **Big-box stores** are the new retail giants. They sell a wide variety of products at very low prices and offer many services not found in smaller stores. Indigo is an example of a big-box store in the book category. The small bookstore had a wonderful selection of mystery books and a loyal following, but it began losing customers when the big-box store opened. As the customers trickled away, the owner decided to close down. The store could have been transformed into a mystery lover's bookstore, offering a much wider selection of classic mysteries, a bit of atmosphere, an expert staff, better advertising, and an Internet mystery book club, complete with book reviews and the latest titles that could be ordered online. The owner was not willing, or was not able, to compete in this manner, and chose to close.

There is an old saying: "Those who do not learn from past mistakes are bound to repeat them."

Learning from Failure

As businesses succeed from day to day, the owners rarely have time or reason to ask themselves, "What is going right?" But as a business fails, the question that is always asked is "What went wrong?" Obviously, the time to ask this question is before the problem gets so big that there is no way to correct it. Even successful businesses should take frequent opportunities to evaluate their position.

There is an old saying: "Those who do not learn from past mistakes are bound to repeat them." This is especially true in business. Many companies go to great lengths to hide their mistakes for several reasons. Consumers tend to desert a failing product or business. Rumours that a business is about to go under will often force the event, as consumer confidence disappears and sales stop. Even if a business is strong and has many products, it may still want to hide the mistakes, putting on a perfect front for the public. In attempting to hide the problems, businesses often ignore them, deny that they are happening, or attribute the cause of the problem to forces outside their control. A company cannot learn from its failures if it doesn't admit to having them.

The 3M company encourages and supports its employees' "failures." The company recognizes that valuable learning comes from experimentation, and that the definition of experimentation must include the word "failure." The Post-it Note was a product that came out of an adhesive that failed to stick very well. An innovative product designer did not hide the fact that this glue didn't work as well as the scientists had hoped it would. Instead, he saw the potential in having a product that would stick well enough to stay on paper, but not stick so much that it would damage the paper when it was removed. Post-it Notes were born.

ACTIVITIES FOR ...

INFORMATION

1. a) List four reasons for business failures.

2. a) Select three companies or products mentioned in this section of the chapter that were unsuccessful. Give a reason for the failure of each business you selected.

CONNECTION

b) Provide an example that illustrates each of the reasons for business failures.

b) Select a failed product or company from the following list:
• Consumers Distributing
• Crystal Pepsi
• Hires Root Beer
Research the reasons for the failure, and prepare a case study outlining what happened.

EXTENSION

c) Describe a failure that you have had. What were the reasons for it? What did you learn from It?

c) From your reading and research, select a product or business that you think may fail within the next five years. Give reasons for your prediction.

Review

Knowledge and Understanding

1. Match each of the following terms to the correct definition:

   economies of scale   profit equation
   fixed costs   unemployment rate
   inflation   variable costs
   marketing boards

   a) Revenue – Cost of Goods Sold – Expenses.
   b) An economic principle that states that the more products that are made by the same factory, the lower the cost to produce each product becomes.
   c) Expenses that do not change with the quantity made.
   d) Government organizations that regulate the supply of agricultural products.
   e) The measurement of the number of able-to-work people who do not have jobs, expressed as a percentage of the labour force.
   f) The economic term used when prices of many products go up while the purchasing power of money goes down.
   g) Expenses that change with the quantity made.

2. Explain how businesses benefit from economies of scale.

3. Why are marketing boards used in Canada?

4. What effect does the unemployment rate have on availability of labour? on wages and benefits?

Thinking and Inquiry

1. How do supply and demand affect market prices? How do they affect the willingness of businesses to produce products?

2. Why do governments develop policies and actions that regulate markets and business activities?

3. Develop a business analysis chart that could be used to evaluate a business's potential for success or failure.

4. Using the school library, the Internet, the local library, or local business resources, collect a variety of business success stories. Do these businesses share any common characteristics that have helped them achieve their success? Explain.

5. Prepare a questionnaire that could be used to interview a successful local businessperson about his or her success.

Communication

1. Prepare a report on a successful business. Use headings such as Purpose, History, Financing, Equipment, and Employees. The report should contain appropriate illustrations, interviews, business analysis charts, and copies of e-mails and letters sent and received during your research.

2. Assume the role of a dairy farmer. Prepare a monologue in which you describe the advantages and disadvantages of belonging to a milk marketing board.

3. Using the Internet and other sources, research Canada's inflation rate over the past 15 years. Graph your findings and prepare a report to present what you found.

Application

1. Select a product from the list below. What is its current price? What are the prices of two similar products? What was the price of this product last year at this time? Explain why the price has or has not changed.
   a) one litre of Shell Bronze gasoline
   b) one dozen extra large eggs
   c) one ounce of gold
   d) one roundtrip fare on Air Canada economy class, from Halifax to Vancouver
   e) a Burger King Whopper

2. Do you think you would be successful in business? Why or why not?

REFLECT ON YOUR LEARNING

1. Rank the factors affecting business success in order of importance, in your opinion. Discuss your reasoning with a partner.

2. Do you think Canada is a good place in which to do business? Support your answer with evidence from this chapter.

STUDENT EXPECTATIONS

After completing this chapter, you will be able to

- explain the benefits of competition
- describe how products compete with one another
- describe how service businesses compete with one another
- compare competing companies based on their levels of consumer service and the quality of their goods and services
- describe competitive and consumer markets
- explain the concept of market share
- explain how a business can be affected by the number and quality of competitors in a market
- identify the factors that contribute to a competitive image

Profile

(left to right) Gary Stuart, Gurval Caer, Lee Feldman, and Francis Chan.

WHAT A BLAST!

It still blows Gary Stuart away. Whenever he returns to the Vancouver headquarters of Blast Radius, the Web site development and e-business consulting company he cofounded in 1996, he is astounded by its growth. "Every time I come over here," Stuart says, "I see another five faces I've never seen before."

It's a long way from the cramped one-bedroom apartment where the seven guys who started it all set up shop. Only four of the founders remain: Stuart, Gurval Caer, Lee Feldman, and Francis Chan. The rest dropped out while Blast Radius struggled in obscurity before hitting the big time in early 1999. Now, the firm ranks as one of North America's up-and-coming full-service Web boutiques, having snagged such big-name clients as Nike, Casio, Universal Studios, and Atlantic Records. The company no longer has to dig for the work; the work comes to it—so much so, that fewer than 20% of applicants are taken on as clients.

It was in January 1996, while sitting around a coffee table in the one-bedroom apartment, that the founders of Blast decided to aim high: to design Web sites for global companies in the entertainment, consumer electronics, and sports industries and become the experts on the 12- to 34-year-old demographic.

But how do you take on the world from a living room in Vancouver when you've got no money and the head offices of many of your chosen clients are in New York? Stuart solved the latter issue by moving to New York to set up a satellite office. Meanwhile, the six other founders pooled their limited finances—less than $10 000 in total—and moved into a nearby house with dedicated office space. To make extra money, Caer taught Java programming part time and Chan poured coffee on Saturday nights at a café. "It forced us to be ruthless with ourselves and to understand how to improve when we didn't win business," says Caer. "Lack of capital became a key success factor."

In March 1999, Blast Radius caught its big break. That's when the Dover, New Jersey–based Casio Inc. put up for review the brand extension site of its premier watch brand, G-Shock. Blast Radius wasn't even among the agencies asked to compete, until one of the

CONTINUED →

original contenders dropped out. The team took its best shot, going up against top-tier firms like the site's incumbent, Razorfish. "When the partners of Blast Radius came in, they showed us that they had researched the brand and how it compared to others," explains Mike McCormick, Casio's Internet services manager. "They said, 'This is who we think your target market is, this is what we know about them, and this is what we think a Web site could look like.' The other agencies did not do that."

When Blast Radius won the contract, the company entered the global stage. Deals with the likes of Lego and Nike soon followed. In every case, the end product is the result of an exhaustive strategic planning process. Blast Radius forces clients to question every aspect of their Web site's plan so that it is focused on the experience of the target user. "Clients don't have to buy in to our vision, but Blast Radius is going to help them look at their business differently, perhaps redefine the type of interaction that they're having with their customers," says Feldman.

The founders are equally vigilant with their own business. Big fees are nice, but securing the right clients and building a reputation is what really counts. "We're deploying a clients-for-life approach," says Michael Dingle, executive vice-president of client development. "We've got to be sure they want us to be around."

Targeting the 12- to 34-year-old demographic also fits Blast Radius's own corporate culture. Most creative young designers want the chance to work on sites for the global brands they wear themselves, like Nike and Casio. On the flip side, such companies want to appeal to precisely that demographic—so they turn to the cool designers at Blast Radius. "They get this place," says Keith Peters, Nike.com's director of content development. "They're really good about bringing ideas to us. It means they kind of represent us—they understand the brand."

> *Blast Radius ranks as one of North America's up-and-coming full-service Web boutiques, having snagged such big-name clients as Nike, Casio, Universal Studios, and Atlantic Records.*

About This Profile

1. Who are Blast Radius's clients? What service does Blast Radius offer them?
2. What do you think of Blast Radius's strategy of "securing the right clients and building a reputation"? What drawbacks might there be in such a strategy?
3. Why do you think that so many big companies, like Nike and Casio, try to reach the 12- to 34-year-old age group? What other types of companies (other than the ones mentioned above) would be "right" for Blast Radius? Explain why.

The Need For Competition

BEFORE YOU BEGIN

Why do you think that there are so many similar products in the marketplace? How does this competition affect buyers? producers?

The last time you looked for a pair of running shoes, were you overwhelmed by the choices you had? Nike, Fila, Reebok, New Balance, and Asics are just a few of the brand names that are on the market. Once you decided on a brand, did you choose cross-trainers, basketball shoes, aerobic shoes, hiking shoes, or another of the scores of other types available? As you were making your selection, did you stop and wonder at the wide assortment? Do we really need all that choice? These choices provide competition among retailers. In a free market economy, competition is necessary for a variety of reasons; so necessary, in fact, that the Canadian government has passed regulations to guarantee a competitive marketplace.

GOVERNMENT REGULATION

As you read in Chapter 5, the government introduced the Competition Act to govern business conduct in Canada. This act promotes competition in the marketplace by stopping anticompetitive practices. Most businesses, both small and large, are governed by this act. The act contains both criminal and civil provisions. Criminal offences are considered more serious than civil law matters, and result in more serious consequences for offenders.

Criminal Offences

The Competition Act considers unfair pricing practices to be criminal offences. One of these practices is conspiracy to fix prices, or price fixing. As you read in Chapter 5, in **price fixing**, competitors agree on the prices that they will charge their customers, in an effort to reduce competition.

Bid rigging is another unfair pricing practice. Bids and **tenders** are a way of choosing a company to provide goods or services while at the same time preventing corruption and favouritism. When government departments and private sector companies need to select a company to provide goods and services, they put out a call or request for bids or tenders. Companies interested in bidding for the business submit sealed bids that are supposedly secret. The winning bid is usually the lowest.

Sometimes, one or more bidders may try to narrow the competition by agreeing not to submit a bid. Or two or more bidders may agree to submit bids that they have prearranged among themselves. Both these scenarios are considered bid rigging. Suppose, for example, that the school board decides to replace all the windows in your school. Three window manufacturers get together and decide that this time Company A will get the job, next time Company B, and so on. Then, Company A submits a very high bid, but Companies B and C submit even higher bids. Companies B and C purposely overbid so that the job will go to Company A, the lowest bidder. However, Company A still recieves a higher-than-usual price.

Civil Law Matters

When a dominant firm engages in anticompetitive activities that substantially lessen competition in a market, it is known as an **abuse of dominant position**. For example, a large cheese manufacturer floods a particular market with cheeses priced much lower than those of a small local cheese factory. The large manufacturer can absorb the loss of revenue by keeping its cheese prices high in other markets. The small local company, however, cannot compete with the lower prices. It might even be forced to close, eliminating the large manufacturer's local competition. The large manufacturer will then resume charging higher prices.

Another unlawful matter under the Competition Act is **exclusive dealing**. Exclusive dealing occurs when a manufacturer requires a dealer to carry its products, essentially shutting competitors out of the market. Suppose the manufacturer of a popular toy only agrees to sell the toy to a dealer who carries 80% of its other products. By taking up the dealer's valuable shelf space, the manufacturer effectively eliminates others from distributing competing products in that store.

Refusal to deal is also unlawful. Suppose a kite distributor sells its products to a large store but refuses to also sell to a smaller store located nearby. The distributor may fear that if it sells to the smaller store, the larger store will stop carrying its kites. To protect its sales, the distributor refuses to deal with the small store, forcing it out of business. The distributor's actions are against the law because its refusal to sell means that the small store cannot obtain adequate supplies of a product it needs to stay in business.

A **merger** occurs when two or more companies join together, either because one has purchased a controlling interest in the other(s) or because the companies have combined their interests. If a merger might restrict competition, it must be approved in advance by the Competition Bureau. The merger between Air Canada and Canadian Airlines is an example. In Canada, mergers that involve non-Canadian companies must also have prior approval. (See Chapter 20 for more information on mergers.)

BUSINESS —FACT—

In 2000, Air Canada was accused of slashing fares below their cost in order to drive a smaller airline out of business. The Competition Bureau issued a cease-and-desist order against Air Canada, ordering the company to stop anticompetitive pricing.

BENEFITS OF COMPETITION

Competition contributes to our economy by encouraging the creation of new businesses. One business starts with an idea, for example, a machine that records and plays television programs. Someone else thinks of a way to improve the product—by adding a remote control—and a new business opens to produce the new model. Still another business begins to manufacture a model with a playback system that provides sharper slow-motion images.

These businesses also lead to other businesses. Companies start manufacturing videocassettes. Other companies start making video cameras. Video rental stores open. Each of these businesses encourages competition. Competition in the video rental business, for example, has lead to larger video stores that provide better and larger selections, better service, and "extras" like magazines and snacks. Each new business provides jobs and salaries, and is dependent on even more businesses.

One of the most effective ways to compete is by charging less than other competitors for the same product or service. To charge less, businesses must become more efficient and increase their **productivity**, which means that the company uses the same resources to produce more or better products or services or produces the same number of goods or services with fewer resources.

To improve its productivity or its product, a business may have to develop something new. Many businesses have a research and development (R&D) department that supports scientists and technicians who work on new ideas. This research often leads to new and improved products. These improvements are then used by other researchers to make even more improvements. The rapid development of cancer-treating drugs, new varieties of plants, better metals, and so on are a direct result of business research. (See Chapter 7 for more information on R&D departments.)

The wide selection offered to consumers in the marketplace is a direct result of competition and research. Consumers have a choice of product styles, product types, price, and quality. Without competition, there would be little or no choice for the consumer. Root beer, for example, was developed to provide consumers with a new soft drink flavour. Moreover, each brand of root beer—Mug, Dad's, Barq's, and Cott—is a little different from the others.

What new businesses may have started because of this product?

Many of us have been dissatisfied with poor service from a store or other business. When we are unhappy with the service, we often shop at another business nearby. It costs a lot of money to attract customers, but it costs even more to lose them. Over the past few years, many businesses have increased their level of service in an effort to remain competitive.

Competition, then, provides many benefits both to individual consumers and to our society as a whole. Competition leads to better products at better prices, new technology that improves our standard of living, and improved service and selection. Competition is an integral part of our economy. No wonder it is protected by our government.

The Importance of Good Service

Good service has a huge impact on a company's revenue. Imagine that you are a business traveller who uses the services of the same hotel chain 50 times a year. How much will you spend on these hotel stays after 10 years, if each visit costs $200? What if, on your recommendation, your company sends its large sales force of 100 people to stay in that hotel chain each time they travel? If the employees log 5000 hotel stays per year, how much money will your company spend on this hotel each year? over 10 years? Now imagine that the hotel chain's service deteriorates. The coffee is missing from the hotel room, the morning paper fails to arrive at the door, or the checkout procedure takes too long. Your company might take its business elsewhere. Think of all the revenue that the hotel chain would lose!

This hotel features a lavish restaurant where attentive service is emphasized.

ACTIVITIES FOR ...

INFORMATION	CONNECTION	EXTENSION
1. a) What criminal offences and civil law matters does the Competition Act cover?	**b)** Select an industry and identify the dominant business in it. What makes this business dominant?	**c)** Choose one of the criminal offences or civil law matters in the Competition Act. If a local business uses this unfair or illegal business practice, what penalties might it face. What impact would the crime have on the community?
2. a) What is a tender?	**b)** Find several examples of "Call for Tenders" advertisements in your local newspaper. What kinds of businesses and organizations put out calls for tenders?	**c)** Using one of the "Call for Tenders" advertisements that you collected in Question 2b), outline specific things that a business would have to consider if it were to bid for the job.
3. a) List four benefits of competition.	**b)** Illustrate how competition has benefited you and your community recently.	**c)** What are some disadvantages of competition?

Competition Among Products

The most obvious type of competition is competition among similar products. All products compete for the consumer's money in some way. If you have $25 and decide to spend it taking a friend to a movie, each theatre and each movie competes for your money. Once you spend $25 on the movie, that $25 is gone—you can't spend it on anything else. So it's not just movies and theatres that compete for your $25; CDs, pizzas, clothes, and any other products that you might buy also compete for your money. This type of competition is called **indirect competition** because the products or services are not directly related to each other. Every business is in competition with every other business for your **discretionary income**. Discretionary income is the income you have that is not committed to paying for basic necessities, such as food, clothing, and shelter. **Disposable income**, on the other hand, is used to pay for basic necessities. It is the amount of income left after taxes have been paid.

Products that are very similar are in **direct competition**. The consumer chooses among them because of minor differences. There really is not a large difference between two brands of sunscreen—they both have the same sun protection factor, both are waterproof, and both are non-greasy. These products compete mainly on image, a topic that will be covered later in this chapter. Other products compete directly in more obvious ways, through quality, price, design, features, and benefits.

QUALITY

"Build a better mousetrap and the world will beat a path to your door." This old expression means that if you improve the quality of your product, you will attract more customers. Vacuum cleaners that pick up more dirt, skateboards with better wheels, and jeans with higher-grade denim are all examples of products that are of better quality than other similar products. Many established brand names take pride in their quality … and consumers depend on it.

PRICE

The most obvious way to compete directly with a similar product is by charging less than your competition charges. If the quality is the same but the price is different, consumers will very often buy the less expensive product. Imagine that you were shopping for blue jeans and found two pairs of the same quality. Both pairs fit and looked good, but one pair cost $10 less than the other. Which one would you buy?

DESIGN

Most often we think of style and design in relation to clothing. Jeans, for example, come in many different styles—slim fit or wide leg, button fly or zipper, straight leg or flare. Every detail is part of the design, from the colour of thread used in the stitching to the colour of the denim itself. Each fashion designer hopes that the consumer will like his or her designs the best.

Clothing is not the only thing that is designed. Every product has a design component. We often buy one product instead of another because we like the way it looks. For example, all cars will transport us from one place to another, but many of us would prefer to get there in a Porsche.

Package design is one way to compete for the customer's attention. The shape of the bottle, the way a can opens, the picture on the box, the built-in handle on the jar: These are all examples of design choices that can give a product a **competitive edge**, or an obvious advantage over the competition.

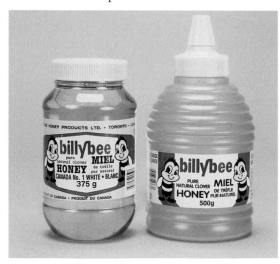

Billy Bee honey is sold in both a glass jar and a distinctive hive-shaped bottle.

FEATURES

By improving or changing features of products, such as the material used in construction, the scent, the size, or the flavour, businesses can make their products more competitive. You might buy a foam pillow instead of a feather one because you are allergic to feathers. You might use one fragrance instead of another because you like the way it smells. You might purchase Cocoa Krispies instead of Raisin Bran because you like the taste of chocolate better than raisins. You might buy the large box of detergent instead of the small one so that you will not have to shop for detergent as often. Without competition, we might all eat the same cereal, wear the same fragrance, and sleep on the same pillows (even if they made us sneeze).

BENEFITS

People buy most products for a particular purpose—towels for drying, blankets for warmth, microwaves to cook food quickly. But some towels are more absorbent than others, some blankets are warmer, and some microwaves cook food faster. Each product has different benefits that help it remain competitive. A product that can do more or perform better than another product will have a competitive edge.

ACTIVITIES FOR ...

INFORMATION	CONNECTION	EXTENSION
1. a) Explain the differences between direct and indirect competition.	**b)** Divide a piece of paper into two columns. In the first column, list 10 things that you would buy if you won $100. In the second column, provide at least two brand names for each item you listed. Which column would you title "Direct Competition"? Which column would you title "Indirect Competition"?	**c)** Think of a retail store that you know. How does it deal with both direct and indirect competition?
2. a) List five ways that products compete with one another.	**b)** Select two competitive products. Explain how they are competitive.	**c)** Other than the five ways products compete that you listed in Question 2a), for what other reasons would you purchase one product over another similar product?

Contemporary Issues in Canadian Business

THE ISSUE: ACHIEVING A BALANCE IN THE MARKETPLACE

What does it mean to achieve a balance in the marketplace?

Achieving a balance in the marketplace means accommodating the needs of consumers, businesses, and society as a whole—with the minimum amount of government regulation. Consumers want quality goods and services, lots of selection, and fair prices. They also want goods or services to be available when and where they want them. Businesses attempt to meet these demands so that they can remain competitive and make a profit. Sometimes, however, in order to make a profit, businesses may be tempted to neglect regulations, such as safety standards, labour codes, emission limits, and waste disposal policies.

Government and consumer groups act as watchdogs to ensure that consumers and businesses operate within limits. The government enacts laws to protect consumers and the environment. Organizations like Pollution Probe and Environment Canada provide support, guidance, and direction for consumers and businesses. Many times, a decision about what and how to produce something revolves around one basic question: "How much will it cost?" Recycling, for example, costs money. Someone has to pay for it. Should this cost get passed along to consumers or should businesses and the government also share in the cost?

Some people believe that businesses can effectively regulate themselves; others believe that consumer groups and the government need to "help" businesses establish their priorities. Let's use the example of environmental concerns to examine the two sides of this argument.

Point

First, does Canada really have a pollution problem? Some might argue that since Canada is so big and since many parts of the country remain virtually untouched, Canada does not have a serious pollution problem. Second, businesses are not the only polluters; private citizens also pollute. Third, not having to comply with laws and standards would permit businesses to produce goods and services at cheaper prices and to remain more competitive. Fourth, many businesses are already actively addressing environmental concerns by recycling and, in some cases, composting waste. By doing so, they are also creating jobs. According to the Institute for Local Self-Reliance, one job is created for every 15 000 tonnes of solid waste deposited in a landfill each year. If a similar amount is composted, seven jobs are created. If recycled, that material would generate nine jobs in collection and processing alone.

Counterpoint

If businesses didn't have to comply with government legislation, would they even be concerned with environmental issues? Environmental concerns were virtually ignored by businesses until the 1970s. It was not until 1971, when the federal government established the Department of the Environment and adopted a regulatory approach to managing environmental concerns, that businesses began to take action to help the environment. Even then, many businesses resisted regulations, considering them unnecessary and expensive. Furthermore, if businesses were truly serious about protecting the environment, they would design more goods that could be safely reused or recycled. Businesses would also give environmental concerns a higher profile in their short- and long-term plans, reporting progress on these goals in their annual reports, along with their financial data.

A Real Life Example

Litter is a big problem in many communities across Canada, even in communities that have a "blue box" recycling program. But who is responsible for this litter? Should businesses be blamed for packaging goods in inappropriate containers? Should consumers take responsibility for not disposing of these containers in an acceptable manner? Or does the government need to step in and pass laws that regulate both business and the consumer?

In the 1970s and early 1980s, Prince Edward Island had a serious litter problem. Discarded soft drink and beer containers were cluttering the province's roadsides, polluting the environment, and diminishing the natural beauty of the island. As a result, the government passed a law in 1984, the Environmental Protection Act, which banned all carbonated beverages that were not sold in refillable bottles.

How did businesses react? One local soft drink manufacturer, Seaman's Beverages, embraced the new legislation and has thrived because of the law. Seaman's had always used refillable glass bottles. Coca-Cola and Pepsi, on the other hand, preferred to sell their products in aluminum cans and plastic containers. They did not want to build new bottling plants in Prince Edward Island just to address the limits of this new law. As a result, Seaman's is now the only soft drink bottler in Prince Edward Island (the company bottles Pepsi products as well as the Seaman's brand). Any Coke products consumed in Prince Edward Island are bottled in Quebec and shipped to the island. Thanks to the Environmental Protection Act, Seaman's has been able to survive as an independent business against the multinational giants. Seaman's Beverages is also the proud recipient of the Prince Edward Island Environmental Award and the first soft drink company in North America to recieve the Eco Logo Award. Most importantly, each year, PEI's bottling policy is able to divert more than 40 million beverage containers from landfills. These bottles are refilled and reused over and over again.

One of Seaman's most popular products is its Olde Fashioned Orange drink. It is packaged in a bottle that has been refilled many times.

Questions and Activities About This Issue

1. Do you support the point or the counter-point position? Explain why.
2. Have other provinces passed acts to protect the environment? If so, how do they compare with Prince Edward Island's law? What effect have they had?

Service Competition

Every business provides some type of service. Some companies offer extra services to attract customers. This kind of extra service is called **value-added service**. A service is intangible. When you see a movie, for example, you may laugh, cry, or be frightened. You take home an experience from the theatre rather than something that is solid or concrete (unless you bought popcorn, which is a product not a service).

THE SERVICE SECTOR

Businesses that provide mainly services are said to be in the **service sector**. Statistics Canada divides the service sector into 11 classes.

Table 6.1 The Service Sector

Type of Business	Examples
Trade (includes both retail and wholesale)	Clothing stores, wholesalers
Transportation and warehousing	Delivery companies, warehouses
Finance, insurance, real estate, and leasing	Banks, insurance agents, real estate brokers
Professional, scientific, and technical services	Advertising agencies, accounting services, architectural services
Management, administrative, and other support	Employment agencies, cleaning services, security
Educational services	Teachers
Health care and social assistance	Doctors, dentists, government assistance
Information, culture, and recreation	Movies, concerts, travel
Accommodation and food services	Hotels, restaurants, coffee shops
Public administration	Government
Other services	Automobile and machinery maintenance and repair, personal care services, laundry services, photo finishing services

COMPETITION IN THE SERVICE SECTOR

Competition in the service sector is different from competition for similar products. Convenience, degree, selection, reputation, and price are important aspects of competition in the service sector.

Convenience

Think of all the ways you could travel to another Canadian city. You could fly, take a train, drive, or take a bus. Each method varies in terms of convenience. An airplane will get you to your destination quickly, but airports are often far outside the city you are visiting. Trains and buses, on the other hand, usually pick up and drop off passengers downtown, but they are much slower than airplanes. Driving yourself is tiring and means you have to find parking when you arrive at your destination. A person selecting one of these transportation methods might use convenience to decide which method to choose.

Usually, people do not want to spend a lot of time looking for a service, so the location of a business is very important. As you read in Chapter 1, if a business is close to the consumer or if it can be reached with ease, it is likely to be more popular than a similar business that is hard to locate. Some examples of businesses that try to attract customers through convenience are car rental companies that offer pickup and delivery, companies that promise pizza delivery in less than 40 minutes, hotels that offer express check in and checkout, 24-hour fitness centres, and doctors who make house calls.

Degree of Service

Spending $350 per night for a hotel room might seem excessive if all you were paying for was the use of a room for the night. Hotels that can charge this much and still be fully booked must offer a very high degree of service. Luxury hotels provide dry cleaning, shirt pressing, and shoe polishing. You can have your hair styled, nails manicured, and body massaged. These hotels have well-equipped fitness centres, excellent restaurants, and entertainment lounges. Room service will deliver meals from a full menu, 24 hours a day. A courtesy desk will arrange tickets to concerts, tours, and theatrical productions for you. Hotel employees will pick up your shopping, walk your dog, and bring your car to the front door. They will provide the newspaper of your choice from most major cities and offer the use of a computer, fax machine, photocopier, and personal secretary.

Many businesses compete with others of the same type by offering more services. Other businesses compete by offering fewer services. Customers know that service costs money. If only a few services are provided, customers will not have to pay as much.

BUSINESS —FACT—

A business listed first in the Yellow Pages makes itself more convenient to find. In fact, many companies choose names such as A-1, Ace, or AAA so that they will appear at the top of the listings!

Selection

Businesses compete by offering more selection. The selection can be wide, meaning that a large number of different brands or types of merchandise are carried, or it can be deep, meaning that the store carries an assortment of one specific product. For example, a music store with a **wide selection** might carry jazz, classical, country, hip-hop, folk, techno, rock, and soundtrack compact discs. The store could also carry all the CD titles of a popular artist and have several copies of each available. This store would have a **deep selection** as well. Most stores are usually wide or deep but rarely both.

Reputation

Since no one can see or touch what a service business sells, it is important that the business have a good reputation. Customers who receive good service *might* tell others about their experience. Customers who receive bad service almost *always* tell others about it. Evaluations of different services also appear in magazines, newspapers, and television reviews. Movies, books, CDs, travel destinations, restaurants, and many other businesses are evaluated by experts in each field. A good review may bring new business. A bad review can ruin a business.

Price

Price is the only deciding factor where product competition and service competition are the same. If two services are similar, the business with the lowest price has the competitive edge. For example, if two dry cleaners clean clothes equally well, customers will give their business to the less expensive dry cleaner.

THE PRODUCT/SERVICE MIX

Retail stores provide services that add value to the products they sell. These include delivery, installation, extended warranties, alterations, advice, carryouts, gift-wrapping, and free parking. Many stores provide coffee or relaxation areas. Some have a cafeteria or restaurant. Every service that a store offers gives consumers another reason to select that store instead of another.

On the other hand, many service businesses also sell products. Movie theatres sell popcorn, video stores sell candy, veterinarians sell pet food, universities sell sweatshirts, and salons sell hair care products. The right product/service mix can increase sales to existing customers. It can also attract new customers by helping the store be competitive.

ACTIVITIES FOR ...

INFORMATION	**C**ONNECTION	**E**XTENSION
1. a) Name the 11 classes of business in the service sector.	**b)** Give an example of each of the 11 classes of service-sector businesses in your community.	**c)** Choose one business in the service sector. Make a list of all the services it provides. Exchange lists with a partner. Add more ideas to your partner's list.
2. a) List the five ways that service businesses compete.	**b)** Select two businesses that provide the same service in your community. In a chart, rate them on a scale of your own making. Use the five ways service businesses compete as criteria. Which business is better?	**c)** Role play a critic reviewing a movie, television program, restaurant, book, or CD. After your role play, ask your audience what impact your review had on their spending decisions. Discuss the power of reviews.
3. a) Describe five services that retail stores offer consumers.	**b)** What services are provided by two of your favourite retail stores?	**c)** Is one of your favourite retail stores missing a service that you think might make shopping there more fun, convenient, or positive? Write a letter to the store manager or to the public relations department of the store's head office, outlining the benefits the store would receive by offering the service.

The Competition for Markets

Every new product introduced into the market has the potential to replace a product that is already there. This is because there is a limit to the total number of consumers, to the number of consumers who use a particular type of product, and to the number of consumers who use a specific brand of that product. Businesses look at similar products that other businesses make to determine the nature of the competitive market. They also study the potential users of the product to determine how to compete in the consumer market. The same principles apply to services, as well.

THE COMPETITIVE MARKET

The **competitive market** consists of specific types of products as well as the businesses that manufacture these products. The amount of money consumers spend annually on these specific products defines the size of that market in dollars. For example, the athletic footwear market in Canada and the United States includes all the manufacturers and importers of athletic shoes. The total market is worth approximately $15 billion. Each manufacturer has to consider how it can compete with every other manufacturer to get a portion of that $15 billion.

THE QUEST FOR MARKET SHARE

STRETCH YOUR THINKING

Why do you think that Nike has such a commanding lead in the athletic footwear market?

A business's **market share** is the percentage that one business's product takes of the total dollars spent by consumers on similar products. Table 6.2 shows that Nike's market share for athletic footwear was 37.92% in the period from January 1 to October 15, 2000. If the total amount spent on athletic footwear was $15 billion, then Nike's share was approximately $6 billion. Nike had the largest share of any of its competitors. Adidas was its closest competitor, with a 14.98% share.

Table 6.2 Athletic Footwear Market Share

Manufacturer	2000	Manufacturer	1999
Nike	37.92%	Nike	42.03%
Adidas	14.98%	Adidas	17.52%
Reebok	10.95%	Reebok	11.14%
New Balance	9.96%	New Balance	5.84%
K-Swiss	2.84%	K-Swiss	3.95%
Timberland	2.58%	Timberland	2.60%
Asics	2.19%	Asics	1.44%
Skechers	2.08%	Saucony	1.31%
Saucony	1.65%	Lugz	1.10%
And 1	1.41%	Converse	1.07%
Other	13.44%	Skechers	1.05%
Total	100.00%	Avia	1.04%
		And 1	0.91%
		Other	9.00%
		Total	100.00%

The athletic footwear market is made up of many smaller pieces, or market segments. A **market segment** is a part of the overall market that has similar characteristics. For example, the overall athletic footwear market is composed of the basketball shoe segment, the cleated shoe segment, the aerobic shoe segment, the court and fitness shoe segment, and so on. Nike, for example, has more than a 70% share of the basketball shoe segment. (See Chapter 17 for more information about market segments.)

A company can increase market share in two ways. The first is by increasing the size of the overall market. When Simon Whitfield won a gold medal for Canada in the triathalon event at the 2000 Summer Olympics, the sport increased in popularity in Canada. This new popularity meant that many new runners, swimmers, and cyclists entered the market for athletic shoes, swimsuits, and cycling shoes. The size of each market expanded because all these new athletes needed proper clothing. The increased sales gave competing companies of each product a chance to attract more customers, thereby increasing their market share.

Table 6.2 illustrates the second way to increase market share: by taking sales away from competitors. Over a two-year period, Nike lost 4.11% of its market share. This market share did not simply disappear. New Balance, Asics, Skechers, Saucony, and And 1 took parts of it. Market shares are like pieces of a pie. If five people are sharing the pie and one person gets half, all the others get much smaller pieces. In the athletic shoe pie, Nike got a smaller piece when New Balance, Asics, Skechers, Saucony, and And 1 took bigger pieces.

THE CONSUMER MARKET

Companies also compete by studying the **consumer market**, or the types of consumers who buy their products. These consumers can be identified in at least two ways: by demographics and by lifestyle.

Demographics

Demographics is the study of obvious characteristics that categorize human beings. Businesses use demographics to target specific consumers. Examples of demographic variables are age, gender, family life cycle, income level, and ethnicity and culture.

Age

Teens want computer games; seniors buy tickets to the symphony. Children want toys; adults are interested in cars. Age defines our tastes, as well as our needs and wants. Some age groups are consumers, but not often customers. For example, an adult, most often a parent,

STRETCH YOUR THINKING

Besides its use in studying consumer spending patterns, why might the study of demographics be important?

usually directs his or her child's purchases. Businesses consider this adult a **gatekeeper**, or a person who makes buying decisions for others. Cereal makers compete by selling their products to the gatekeepers, advertising that their cereal is low in sugar or has added vitamins for good health. However, cereal makers also know that children have some influence over the decisions that their gatekeepers make, so these companies also target young people in their advertisements.

The most important consumer group to most businesses is the **baby-boom group**. Baby boomers are people who were born after World War II, roughly between 1947 and 1961. Shortly after the war, hundreds of thousands of couples who had postponed their weddings got married and started a family, which generated a dramatic but temporary growth in the population. The children born in this period grew older together and stimulated the consumer market along the way. As teens, the baby boomers influenced the music industry with the birth of rock 'n' roll. As adults with young families, they made the minivan popular. Indeed, many of the major trends in the last 50 years were started by the baby boomers.

People born in the 1960s and 1970s made jogging strollers popular when they became parents.

Gender

Many products, like jeans and athletic shoes, are worn by both genders. However, businesses that sell jeans and shoes still distinguish between their men's and women's product lines. The businesses market their men's athletic shoes to the male market and their women's athletic shoes to the female market.

In the area of shopping, gender roles have changed a great deal. At one time, women did the family grocery shopping and men purchased the family car. Today, the act of shopping is becoming a task for males and females alike, and purchase decisions are more likely to be shared. Many successful businesses have recognized this change. Many products that were formerly targeted at females (detergents, disposable diapers, food products) or males (cars, power tools, sporting equipment) are now being advertised and sold successfully to both genders.

Family Life Cycle

Newly married couples need furniture. Parents with a new baby need a crib, carriage, and car seat. A couple with three teenagers wants to save for their children's college or university education. Retired seniors want to travel. Your stage in the family life cycle often determines your wants and needs. Businesses are aware of this demographic. They compete for consumer dollars in different ways for various groups. For example, a cruise could be a honeymoon for a newly married couple, a break for a couple with a baby, a family holiday for a couple with teenagers, or a retirement escape for a senior. The advertising, destination, onboard activities, and meals will all depend on the type of customers the cruise is trying to attract.

Income Level

Consumers are often grouped by how much money they have or earn. This grouping affects what products or services a business tries to sell them. Products such as Kellogg's Corn Flakes are targeted at consumers in every income bracket, but a Mercedes automobile could only be purchased by wealthy customers. Businesses have many ways of determining the income of specific groups of consumers. One way is to look at the postal codes of affluent, or upper-income, neighbourhoods. If a consumer has an address in this postal code, it is likely that he or she has a high income. Similarly, a business can look at written programs for ballets, book readings, and other special events in the community to find out who sponsors these events. Or, if a business wants to target a particular high-income group, it might place an advertisement in a certain type of publication.

Businesses that make or sell luxury goods and services are interested in the wealthy customer, but most manufacturers and retailers make and sell products to consumers with average incomes. These businesses are mainly interested in competing for the discretionary income that almost all consumers possess. They sell their products and services to everyone.

Many Canadian cities have neighbourhoods with stores and businesses that target a particular ethnic group.

Ethnicity and Culture

Canada has a diverse population with a wonderful mix of customs and traditions. Many cities have ethnic communities with stores and businesses that target the various wants and needs of a particular ethnic group. These businesses compete for a cultural market by importing goods from the consumer's country of origin or producing goods reflective of that country. The food service sector has a multitude of restaurants that reflect different cultural tastes in food. Newspapers and magazines in Canada are available in over 100 different languages. Of course, many of the products and services that first attracted the business of a specific ethnic group now compete for the business of all Canadians. Italian restaurants, for example, certainly have many non-Italian customers.

Lifestyle

Lifestyle is less obvious than demographics but equally important to businesses competing for specific groups of consumers. **Lifestyle** is the way people live, which includes their values, beliefs, and motivations. The study of lifestyles is called **psychographics**. Lifestyles are categorized as either introverted or extroverted.

Introverted

Introverted consumers are interested in their own self-concept. These potential customers challenge themselves, develop a unique identity, are interested in personal statements in fashion, and have personal causes. Businesses competing for the introvert's attention will stress personal growth and experience as a feature of the products they sell or the services they provide. An introverted consumer may take a ride in a hot air balloon to see the sunset from another angle or buy a new coat because it is warm enough to go winter camping.

Extroverted

Extroverted consumers are very interested in the opinions of others. This prospective market is interested in what is trendy or fashionable, works hard to achieve, and uses products to reward that achievement. To attract this market, a business will emphasize the popularity of a product. An extroverted consumer may take a hot air balloon ride to have something to talk about or buy a new coat because it is the latest fashion.

Did You Know?

"Introverted" and "extroverted" are also terms used to describe personality types. Introverts tend to keep to themselves, while extroverts are outgoing. How do these definitions relate to the definitions used in the field of psychographics?

Consumer Tracking

Where do businesses get their information about the consumer market? Much of it comes from you. Merchants collect and store information from your transactions in their data warehouses. Warranty cards and surveys that you complete give companies more personal information. And when you log on to a Web site, "cookies" and other tracking software may be implanted on your hard drive. These devices will follow you as you surf online, recording even more details about you and your lifestyle. Businesses use these and other gathering methods to target customers for existing and new products.

INFORMATION	**C**ONNECTION	**E**XTENSION
1. a) Briefly describe the competitive market and the consumer market.	**b)** Choose a product. Name some businesses that compete in the same market. What demographic does each business's product cater to?	**c)** You are designing a new type of cell phone. What similar cell phones exist in the competitive market? How will you give your product the competitive edge? What demographic will your product appeal to?
2. a) Explain the term "market share."	**b)** Research market share data for any product other than athletic shoes.	**c)** Select a product (other than athletic shoes) and describe how you would increase the market size.
3. a) List the five demographic groups.	**b)** Using an advertisement from a magazine, identify the demographic groups targeted by the product being advertised.	**c)** Work in groups of three. Choose a product that has traditionally been marketed to a male audience. One person makes up an ad that appeals to males, the second makes up an ad that appeals to females, and the third makes up an ad that appeals to both genders. Repeat with a product that has traditionally been marketed to females. Discuss the similarities and differences among each set of ads. Do gender-specific ads contribute to sexism?

Competitive Images

One of the most powerful competitive tools that any business has is its **image**—the way the consumer sees the business or thinks about the products that the business makes or sells. When the difference between products is minor, the consumer's image of the product is very important.

CREATING AN IMAGE

Some businesses spend hundreds of thousands of dollars to create an image. Others spend very little. In either case, three things can be part of the image: a brand name, a logo or trademark, and a slogan.

STRETCH YOUR THINKING

Which is more important to you when deciding which cola to drink—taste or image? Why?

Brand Name

A **brand name** is a word or group of words that a business uses to distinguish its products from competitors' products. The brand name is the most important part of a product or company's image because it is how the company is identified. If you buy a bottle of Jones Soda Root Beer for the first time and really enjoy it, the company will want you to remember the name for a number of reasons. They may want you to purchase this soft drink again. If you can't recall the name, you could easily buy a competitor's product instead. If you're talking to friends about beverage preferences and mention Jones Soda to them, you're giving the company free publicity. Or you may like the one flavour from Jones Soda enough that you want to try other flavours from that company. Brand names should be distinctive and stand out from the competition. They should also be easy to remember.

What images do these products suggest to you?

The brand name should also say something about the product. Ivory soap suggests whiteness and purity; Zest soap suggests energy and wakefulness. Some names signify quality, such as Alpo Prime dog food or Taster's Choice coffee. Other names offer a clue as to the ingredients, like Jell-O or Rice-a-Roni. Brand names such as Sprite and Joy are fun and whimsical. Some product names are associated with real or imaginary people, for example, Laura Secord or Miss Vicki. In any case, a brand name should have a positive association with the product and communicate a positive image.

However, some brand names don't seem to say much about the product itself. For example, the names Dial and Lever 2000 do not suggest any quality related to soap. Peter Pan peanut butter is given a name that has no association or identification with the product at all. With names like these, consumers often need some other device to help them remember what the product is.

Logo or Trademark

Many products combine their name with a special symbol that is associated with the product. This symbol is called a **logo** or **trademark**. The logo or trademark helps the product compete for consumer awareness. Peter Pan peanut butter, for example, has a cartoon of Peter Pan on the label. Its logo indicates that the product is aimed at young people.

Logos take three different forms. The first is a monogram, which is a stylized writing of the company's initials or a combination of initials and numbers. IBM (International Business Machines), KFC (Kentucky Fried Chicken), or 3M (Minnesota Mining and Manufacturing Company) are all examples of monogrammatic trademarks. Some companies

McDonald's golden arches logo is recognized around the world.

use monograms to update an image that has become outdated or undesirable. KFC wanted to de-emphasize the word "fried" in its original name; IBM wanted consumers to associate its name with computers rather than adding machines; and 3M had moved far from its roots as a sandpaper manufacturer.

Other companies use visual symbols as logos. These are usually line drawings of people, animals, or things. Tony the Tiger, Toucan Sam, and Snap!, Crackle!, and Pop! are all pictures that represent Kellogg cereals and help children remember them. The swan is a symbol that Scott Paper uses for its White Swan paper products, including paper towels and napkins, to indicate the products' softness. Sprite uses a combined lemon and lime (a limon?) to illustrate its flavour. A strong visual symbol in combination with a well-chosen brand name can communicate a great deal about a product before a customer even tries it.

Many companies select an abstract symbol as a logo. Abstract symbols are shapes that carry a visual message but are not representative of actual things. Some symbols seek to communicate a company's initials but are obscure enough to be considered abstract. Often these types of logos are difficult to remember. Many are not distinctive enough to stand out from all the other symbols. However, the Nike "swoosh" is an abstract symbol and is one of the world's most famous logos.

Slogan

The reason that the Nike "swoosh" and the Lever 2000 and Dial names are remembered by consumers is largely a result of the third method of brand identification, the slogan. A **slogan** is a short, catchy phrase that is always attached to the company's name and logo. For Nike, we remember "Just Do It"; for Lever 2000 we remember "For all your 2000 body parts"; and for Dial we remember "Aren't you glad you use Dial? Don't you wish everybody did?" Each slogan is a small advertisement for the product, communicating that Nike believes in the importance of exercise (and therefore running shoes), that Lever 2000 washes your whole body, and that Dial is a deodorant soap.

USING THE IMAGE

Once an image is created using either a brand name, logo, or slogan (or a combination of these), a business must decide how best to use this image. Obviously, brand identification on packages, company letterhead, and Web sites is important, but the image can also be used effectively with promotional activities and brand extension.

Brand Identification

Once a company develops a name, slogan, or logo for a product, everything associated with that product should carry the identification. If the name is written in a distinctive style, such as Coca-Cola or Pepsi, the name should always be written that way. If there are specific colours associated with the brand, these colours should appear on everything associated with the product. Some brands develop a distinctive design for the package. That, too, becomes part of the brand's identification. No consumer should ever have to guess whether this is the product they want. Competition is so fierce that no company wants its product to get lost on a store shelf, especially after spending a great deal of money on promoting the brand.

Promotional Activities

Every advertisement should emphasize the product's image. The brand name should be mentioned often. The slogan should be repeated or incorporated into a **jingle**, a short, catchy tune that uses the slogan and is easily remembered by the consumer. The logo should be featured prominently. Even the package should be shown if there is one.

All public relations material, such as catalogues, brochures, price lists, sales literature, letters, and annual reports, should carry the name, slogan, and trademark of the company. The material should be printed using the identifying colours. Business cards should be designed using all the corporate image devices.

Sales promotion materials should feature all the parts that make up the competitive image. Signs, banners, coupons, and all giveaways, such as T-shirts, pens, calendars, watches, and golf balls, should carry the company's logo, name, and slogan. Consumers should know the product and remember it when they wish to make a purchase.

Brand Extension

When the image created for one product is transferred to other products made by the same company, it is called **brand extension**. Ivory soap calls its dishwashing detergent Ivory liquid. Consumers who like the soap transfer the image of purity and cleanliness to the detergent. The company uses the same logo and brand identification to help convey the same impressions that the original product established. President's Choice soft drinks led to President's Choice cookies, ice cream, and hundreds of other products. Each product displays the President's Choice name and logo.

Competition is so fierce that no company wants its product to get lost on a store shelf, especially after spending a great deal of money on promoting the brand.

THE ROLE OF MARKETING

It is not enough to simply create a positive image for the product. The image must be communicated to the customer in a way that is both understood and remembered. One role of marketing is to transmit the desired image to the selected target markets through creative advertising. If a company is trying to increase its market share by making the consumer think that its product is better than the competitors', that company needs to emphasize how its product is different from the others (even if the only difference is one of image). Products that target specific demographic groups need to make sure that their image is appropriate for that group.

Nike always communicates an image that says it is better than its competition, but Nike uses different images to target different consumers. The marketing campaign designed for teenaged basketball players is much different from the campaign targeted at middle-aged runners. Soccer shoes are advertised in a different way than aerobics shoes. But all these images are associated with the Nike name, the Nike "swoosh," and the slogan "Just Do It." (Chapter 9 will discuss the role of marketing in much greater detail.)

ACTIVITIES FOR ...

INFORMATION	CONNECTION	EXTENSION
1. a) What are the three parts of a competitive image?	**b)** Select five different products. Describe each product's image and tell how it is created.	**c)** How does advertising support the image of any one of the products you selected in Question 1b?
2. a) What are the three types of logos?	**b)** Provide five examples of each type of logo.	**c)** Create a game that allows other students to match logos with the companies that the logos represent.
3. a) Define brand extension.	**b)** Give five examples of brand extension.	**c)** Research a case where brand extension did not work. Explain the case, and tell why you think brand extension did not work.

Review

Knowledge and Understanding

1. Match each of the following terms to the correct definition:

   brand extension   image
   competitive edge   lifestyle
   competitive market   market share
   consumer market   price fixing
   demographics   service sector

   a) The way the consumer sees the business or thinks about the products that the business makes or sells.
   b) An obvious advantage over the competition.
   c) Businesses that provide mainly services.
   d) When the image created for one product is transferred to other products made by the same company.
   e) The way people live, which includes their values and beliefs, and what motivates them.
   f) The study of obvious characteristics that categorize human beings.
   g) The percentage that one company's product takes of the total dollars spent by consumers on similar products.
   h) Specific types of products as well as the companies that manufacture these products.
   i) When competitors agree on the prices that they will charge their customers to reduce competition.
   j) The types of customers who buy a company's products.

2. Explain how a company creates a competitive image for a product.

3. How is market segment related to market share?

4. How can a business be affected by the number and quality of competitors in the market?

Thinking and Inquiry

1. Explain how a business can be affected by the number and quality of competitors in a market. Use a specific example to support your explanation.

2. Select a product that is sold in your local supermarket. Analyze the competitiveness of this product by answering the following questions:
   a) What makes the product you chose competitive?

b) What competitive image does the product project? How is this image established?

c) What demographic groups does this product appeal to?

d) What products are most directly competitive with your product?

e) What is the name of your product's main competitor?

3. Using the research tools available in your school or local library, report on how a product's competitive image has changed over time. Be sure to select a product that has been around for more than 25 years. Why have these changes occurred over the years? How did they help the product stay competitive?

Communication

1. What factors are most important to you when purchasing similar products? similar services? Discuss your answer with a classmate.

2. Create a competitive image for a new breakfast cereal, using an original brand name, logo, and slogan. Present your competitive image to a small group. Invite the group to offer constructive feedback about the competitiveness of the image.

Application

1. Choose a product whose market share has increased over the past year, for example, New Balance athletic shoes. (See Table 6.2.) Investigate and offer an explanation for the increase in the market share.

2. Choose a particular brand of a product, for example, a specific brand of soft drink or jeans. Assume you are the marketing/advertising director for this brand. Draw or describe an advertisement you would create to increase this brand's market share. What demographic segments would you want to notice your ad? How would you try to make sure these groups notice it?

REFLECT ON YOUR LEARNING

1. Do you think that it is right for government to legislate competition? Explain.

2. Think about a product or service that a company has convinced you to buy. How did that company's product or service gain the competitive edge over similar products or services?

CHAPTER 7

HUMAN RESOURCES AND MANAGEMENT

STUDENT EXPECTATIONS

After completing this chapter, you will be able to

- identify factors that influence employees' attitudes and the quality of their work
- list different types of compensation
- explain the function and importance of a human resources department
- list the rights of employees and employers
- explain the composition and function of an organization
- read and understand an organization chart
- describe the role of management
- describe different management approaches and how they influence productivity

Profile

Walter Arbib and Surjit Babra, partners in SkyLink Aviation Inc.

DON'T SHOOT, WE'RE THE GOOD GUYS

SkyLink Aviation Inc. is one of only a few aviation companies in the world that specializes in flying humanitarian relief supplies anywhere, anytime, and under any conditions. While few Canadians know the company by name, many have heard of its missions. In October 1999, SkyLink transported Canadian peacekeepers destined for East Timor to Australia. Earlier that year, SkyLink pilots dodged bullets as they flew the first food drop into Kosovo days before the North Atlantic Treaty Organization (NATO) ceased its bombing runs in June. SkyLink was also the first Western airline allowed to land in North Korea in April 2000, when the U.S. government hired it to deliver potato seeds to the famine-ravaged country.

SkyLink's founder, Walter Arbib, is a former Israeli travel agent who decided to move to Canada in 1988. In Toronto, he partnered with Surjit Babra, who was running an air travel wholesale business in Toronto. Babra was born in India and lived in the U.K. before moving to Canada in 1979.

One year after Arbib came to Canada, the partners won their first United Nations (UN) contract: providing transportation for troop rotations to Namibia to keep the peace and oversee the country's first free election. SkyLink leased planes to fly peace-keepers into the civil-war-ravaged African nation, and soon the company's responsibilities grew. It began flying troops within the country, and used its ticket-brokering capabilities to organize vacations for soldiers on leave. The mission was one of the most successful in UN peacekeeping history. The warring factions were separated, and observers ensured the subsequent election was run fairly.

SkyLink's pilots and work-around-the-clock field managers are the backbone of the company's success. Arbib has recruited a mixed bag of combat-tested Russian aviators and Canadian bush pilots accustomed to working under extreme conditions. Pilots earn a base salary of between $60 000 and $70 000, plus hefty expenses.

But the greatest risks come not from the assignments they've been contracted for but rather from the dangerous emergency missions that arise while they're in the field—missions that SkyLink is

CONTINUED →

not always paid for. "Don't get me wrong, we are not here to be a philanthropic organization. We are here to make money," says Arbib. "But when you are in the situation and someone asks for help, what do you do? Stand by and do nothing? Of course not."

Although they don't draw gunfire or put their lives on the line, the company's office employees in Toronto are essential in getting any SkyLink flight off the ground. When a government or humanitarian organization calls for bids, SkyLink staff members often have less than three hours to determine if they can fulfill the mission requirements. Once a contract is awarded, SkyLink has only hours to get its plane in the air or, if none of its aircraft is available, to lease one. While it could take several days to secure the paperwork needed for a flight through normal channels, SkyLink employees will call aviation officials at home in the middle of the night to secure fly-over and landing permits. Even a simple thing like insurance is not so simple when you're flying into war zones and disaster areas. Now the company has its own in-house broker who can insure flights 24 hours a day.

But according to John Abood, contract officer for the U.S. Agency for International Development, a desire to do whatever it takes to ensure that relief supplies make it into the hands of those who desperately need them is essential. "I have been in fields where farmers have lost their crops, people have lost their homes, or everything has been knocked down by a hurricane," he says. "I take very personally the needs of those people and I look for contractors who feel the same way. SkyLink handled some airdrops for us into Kosovo during the end of hostilities there and their plane was shot at. Did that deter them from continuing their contract? No, it did not."

Arbib has mixed emotions about SkyLink's growth. When business is good, it means somewhere in the world there are people suffering from either a natural disaster or their inability to resolve conflict without war and violence. But it also means that, with SkyLink involved, suffering is alleviated a little more quickly. "I could have gone into a normal business and sent tourists on holiday," Arbib says. "Nothing compares with the satisfaction I get when I turn on the television and see disasters and wars and know that we are there helping."

With SkyLink involved, suffering is alleviated a little more quickly.

About This Profile
1. Compare SkyLink with a typical airline.
2. If you owned a business like SkyLink, what skills and qualities would you want your employees to possess? Explain your answer.

People and Productivity

BEFORE YOU BEGIN

What factors contribute to a positive work environment? Make a note of your ideas so that you can review them at the end of the chapter.

One of the most important resources a business has is the people it employs. In Chapter 6, you learned about productivity. To increase productivity, a business must use the same amount of resources to produce more or better goods and services. Increasing productivity is an enormous challenge. Successful business owners and managers know that to achieve their goals, they have to manage the people who work for them effectively. Businesses must also be able to find skilled labour, train their employees, and develop a work environment that leads to positive employee attitudes and job satisfaction.

THE LABOUR MARKET

The **labour market** is where employers (buyers of skills) meet employees (sellers of skills). Employers look at the labour market to determine what occupations and skills are available, what education and training is provided in the community, and what the economic conditions are in the area. Employees look at the labour market to find potential employers, determine the types of skills in demand, and find out what the employment rate is in the community. Both the employer and employee want to know what wage rates are offered to employees and what kinds of jobs will be popular in the future. Predictions about jobs are called **occupational forecasts**.

The following scenario demonstrates the labour market in action: The Bread Basket plans to open a bakery in a small New Brunswick city. It needs labour that falls into several categories. It needs dishwashers and kitchen help. These jobs are considered **unskilled labour** because little training is required. It needs cashiers. A cashier position falls into the category of **semiskilled labour** because it requires some instruction. The bakery also needs cake decorators. Cake decorating is an example of **skilled labour** because employees require training from an educational institution or through previous employment. It must also hire **professional labour**, highly trained people with specific occupations, such as accountants and electricians. The most important professional that The Bread Basket needs, however, is a baker. The person hired must have work experience and be skilled at baking bread and desserts. Because the city's community college offers a program for bakers, there are likely trained bakers in the area. But bakeries are popular here, which may mean that the good bakers are already working.

STRETCH YOUR THINKING

Would you open a business in a small community where several businesses already offer the same good or service? Tell what advantages and disadvantages there might be.

When Emily Green graduates from the community college program, she notices a want ad for a baker in the local paper. She applies for the job; the interview goes well; and The Bread Basket offers Emily the position, with a starting salary of $450 a week. Emily knows two other graduates—one works locally for $400 a week; the other works in a larger city and earns $600 a week. Emily, who was recognized by her college for her superior baking skills and who knows that good bakers are in short supply, asks for $500 a week. She also asks the bakery to develop a career plan that will provide for her promotion and growth. The bakery agrees and hires Emily.

THE IMPORTANCE OF PRODUCTIVITY

What deal is made between the employer and employee? In the case of The Bread Basket, the employer offers to pay Emily to perform specific tasks—to bake bread, bagels, and pies. It agrees to pay her $500 a week to do these tasks. Although the deal does not state that Emily must produce a certain quantity and quality of goods, the bakery wants her to be a productive worker. If Emily makes 1000 items during a five-day week, the average labour cost for each item is 50¢ ($500 ÷ 1000). If she makes more items at the same salary, the average cost per item goes down and the bakery makes more profit. The Bread Basket, then, wants Emily to increase productivity.

But Emily feels she is already working very hard. The ovens are extremely hot, and she wants one more 15-minute break each day. This extra break could mean the number of items she bakes will decrease, and the cost of each item will increase. The bakery would make less profit. Clearly, the bakery and the baker need to come to an agreement about the number of items that can be expected, or find a way to use time more efficiently, in order to produce the same amount of items in less time.

THE IMPORTANCE OF SKILLED LABOUR

It is important for businesses to hire people who can do the job or be trained to do the job. The more skill an employee already has, the less a business has to invest in training. Skilled employees can mean savings for a business because they usually provide a better product or service. For example, if its bread is better than the competition's bread, The Bread Basket can charge more for its product. The bakery's reputation improves and the number of customers increases. A business must balance the quality of product or service that it would like to provide with the amount of money needed to hire the skilled labour necessary to attain that quality.

Emily proudly displays some of the many types of bagels she bakes.

THE IMPORTANCE OF A POSITIVE ATTITUDE

Happy employees often make more or better products than unhappy ones. When Emily is grumpy and tired from the heat, her productivity declines. As she struggles to finish the day and get home to her air-conditioned apartment, she works at a slower pace and the quality of her baked goods suffers. Emily's mood also upsets other workers and affects the whole bakery. Giving her an extra break, air-conditioning the kitchen, and letting her go home early on hot days are a few of the things the employer could do to keep Emily happy—and more productive.

ACTIVITIES FOR ...

INFORMATION	CONNECTION	EXTENSION
1. a) What is the labour market?	**b)** Why might employers and employees be interested in occupational forecasts?	**c)** What job interests you? Use occupational forecasts on the Internet, in the library, or from your school's guidance department to determine if the demand for this type of job will decrease, remain the same, or increase between now and the time you enter the labour market.
2. a) Why is productivity important?	**b)** Do you think that extra breaks for employees could increase productivity? Explain your answer.	**c)** What other factors might increase an employee's productivity? What factors might decrease it?
3. a) How does hiring employees who are already skilled contribute to business savings?	**b)** Make a list of 10 jobs. Exchange your list with a partner. For each job on your partner's list, tell whether it is considered unskilled labour, semiskilled labour, skilled labour, or professional labour.	**c)** Choose a job that you think you would like to do. What skills do you need to do this job? How will you obtain them? Be specific.
4. a) Why is encouraging a positive attitude among employees important?	**b)** Interview three employees you know about their job and their work environment. How satisfied are they at work? What effect does their attitude have on their productivity?	**c)** How does your attitude toward school or individual classes affect your productivity? Explain. How could you improve your productivity?

Creating a Positive Attitude in the Workplace

Employees who have positive attitudes often achieve job satisfaction and stay with employers for longer. Businesses can help employees achieve job satisfaction by providing good compensation, maintaining a safe and healthy workplace, offering employee benefits, and providing opportunities to grow and advance in the company.

COMPENSATION

The most important consideration for employees is usually the amount of money they are paid, or compensation. As you read in Chapter 5, because the labour market is competitive, **compensation** is affected by supply and demand. For example, if many companies need staff with hi-tech training but few people in the job market have this training, technology skills will be highly priced. The greater the demand for a particular skill, the higher the compensation. Compensation can take many forms.

Hourly Wages

One of the most common payment methods, especially for part-time employees, is the hourly wage. Rates range from the minimum wage paid to unskilled or semiskilled labour to hundreds of dollars an hour for skilled or professional labour. **Minimum wage** is the lowest hourly wage an employer can pay an employee. Hourly wage employees often receive an increased rate of pay if they work **overtime**, which means working more than regular work hours or on holidays.

Salary

A **salary** is a fixed amount of money that employees receive on a regular schedule, such as weekly or monthly. Often, it is expressed as a yearly amount. A business advertising for an accountant, for example, may offer "$57 000 a year." Salaried jobs often do not specify how many hours employees will have to work, but employees are expected to complete their tasks. If finishing these tasks requires them to work more hours, no overtime is paid.

Salary plus Commission

In some sales jobs, especially retail, employers pay the employee a percentage of his or her sales. This **commission** is usually quite small, and is in addition to salary or hourly wages. Commission is an **incentive**

that encourages employees to work harder. For example, an employee earning a 1% commission, earns an extra $30 if he or she sells $3000 in goods. A higher commission usually means the salesperson is paid a lower salary or hourly wage.

Straight Commission

Straight commission is a form of compensation that is based solely on the employee's sales. Most often, people who sell to wholesale businesses or large industries, as well as people who sell high-priced items such as cars and houses, are paid straight commission. Employees can make a great deal of money from straight commission if they are talented salespeople, but if sales fall off or if they have to take days off because of illness, they may earn little or no income.

Incentive Bonus

Many businesses offer employees a **bonus**, or reward, for good performance. Sometimes, this type of reward is called "variable pay." Companies set performance goals (also called **sales quotas** or targets) for each employee. If the employee meets the goal, he or she receives extra cash, a trip, a car, or something else of value.

Performance-Based Pay

Performance-based pay is calculated on the amount of a particular product that an employee can make. Also known as **piecework**, this form of compensation is widely used in the clothing industry. Piecework rewards skill and speed: The more products employees can make for the business, the more money they can earn for themselves. However, performance-based pay can also lead to severe abuses. In parts of the world that suffer from poverty, some employers offer very little compensation for piecework. In some cases, factories employ children, who will work for almost nothing. Some piecework factories become known as **sweatshops**. Not only are wages low, but employees are forced to work in unsafe and unhealthy conditions.

On the other hand, many reputable businesses use piecework. It allows employees to work at home with their own equipment, for example, a sewing machine, oven, or computer, and to set their own pace. It also allows people with family responsibilities to earn money at home.

Fee for Service

Construction, catering, and cleaning businesses often receive a fee-for-service form of compensation. They estimate how much it will cost in terms of time and materials to do a job, and then build in an additional fee to ensure that they earn a profit. With this estimate, the person who hires them, their employer, knows how much to expect to pay for the whole job. To prevent misunderstandings, the employer and employee sign a written contract. This contract usually offers some kind of guarantee and states the costs, time of completion, materials required, and so on.

Royalty or Licensing Fee

If you write a book, record a song, or have an idea that you can sell, you may receive a **licensing fee** or **royalty**. Both terms refer to a payment for the use of ideas and creativity. For example, imagine that you created a successful cartoon character and that a T-shirt business wants to put your character on its product. You could rent your character to the company, and it could pay you a portion of the sale price from each T-shirt sold. Although the percentage is often small (between 1% and 5%), you don't risk losing any money if the T-shirts don't sell. The company that leases your idea (**the licensee**) assumes that risk. In other cases, you may be paid a fixed licensing fee. You receive the same amount of money regardless of how many T-shirts the company sells. That would be to your advantage if the company does not sell a lot of T-shirts, but you might lose out if sales of the T-shirts are high. In other cases, you might be paid a fixed licensing fee as well as a percentage of sales. (See Chapter 16 for more information on licensing agreements and royalties.)

Stock Options

Businesses often offer shares as a form of compensation to attract desirable employees. The business gives employees an opportunity to buy company shares at a lower-than-market price. These shares are called **stock options**. Employees benefit from stock options because they can purchase the company's stock at a preset price for a given period of time, even if the stock's market price increases during that time. Companies benefit from issuing stock options because employees who own part of the company often work harder and stay longer than those who do not have an ownership stake.

HEALTH AND SAFETY

Federal and provincial laws require businesses to provide and maintain a healthy and safe work environment. Besides their legal responsibility to do so, it makes sense for businesses to provide this kind of environment. A sick or injured employee has to take time off work and is unproductive during that period. An employee injured on the job may also take the employer to court. Businesses that focus on health and safety also create positive employee attitudes.

STRETCH YOUR THINKING

If a company wanted to license one of your ideas or creations, would you prefer a fee based on percentage of sales or a fixed licensing fee? Explain your answer.

Health

Businesses suffer a double loss when an employee becomes ill. First of all, they lose the worker's skill and productivity. Second, many businesses provide **sick pay**: They continue to pay full wages to the employee while he or she is absent due to illness. Because businesses benefit from healthy employees, many companies offer **wellness programs**. These programs promote the physical and emotional well-being of employees and help reduce absenteeism. The more provisions an employer makes for employees' well-being, the more likely the employees will remain healthy and productive.

Table 7.1 Health and Wellness Programs

Health Area	Wellness Programs
Fitness programs	lunch-hour exercise programs; fitness-club memberships; fitness breaks instead of coffee breaks
Antismoking programs	awareness campaigns; support for quitting; "quitting" or "terminating" bonuses
Addiction treatment	paid time off for treatment; space and time for counselling programs; emotional support to addicted workers and their families
Job stress	planned social activities and special events; relaxed dress code; flexible hours; working from home (telework); job sharing (two or more employees share the same job and split the salary)
Counselling	financial, marriage, and bereavement (loss of a loved one) counselling
Growth	job-related or extension courses; leave for further education; paid registration at conferences; professional development opportunities
Other benefits	paid vacations; sick leave; bereavement and personal days (moving, errands, child or elder care, etc.); employee discounts; company car; health, dental, and optical plans; group life insurance, long-term disability, and accidental death benefits; daycare; profit sharing; expense accounts; free parking

Husky Injection Molding Systems

Husky Injection Molding Systems Ltd., in Bolton, Ontario, is a leader in running wellness programs which aim to boost productivity. For example, the cafeteria provides low-cost health food and charges a premium for junk food. This encourages workers to eat better, which keeps them fitter and allows them to work better. Husky also provides other benefits, including an on-site fitness centre.

Safety

Employers in Canada are legally required to maintain a safe workplace. Part Two of the Canada Labour Code (CLC) and various provincial acts govern occupational health and safety. This legislation is intended to prevent accidents, injury, and disease related to employment activities. According to the legislation, employees have the right to

• be informed about known or foreseeable hazards in the workplace

• help identify and resolve job-related problems in safety and health

• refuse dangerous work if they have reasonable cause to believe that a situation constitutes a danger

Some foreseeable hazards involve the use of equipment. The employer must ensure that all equipment is safe and that employees who use it have the proper training. The potential dangers of some types of equipment—table saws, for example—are obvious. But even office equipment can be harmful. Using a computer improperly can lead to a very painful injury called **carpal tunnel syndrome**. In its most severe form, this condition can cause crippling pain that shoots from the hands, up the arm, and as far as the shoulder.

Employers should also make certain that all dangerous chemicals and toxic waste are properly stored, and that employees know how to safely handle these substances. First aid equipment must be available, and employees should be trained in first aid procedures. The workplace should be free of hazards, such as unsafe electrical connections, slippery floors, and sharp edges. Employees should also be instructed in proper lifting techniques to avoid back injury. (Always bend at the knees and lift with the legs, rather than the back.) The workplace should be kept clean, with nothing left in the aisles or on the floor that might cause others to trip.

If an employee is injured on the job, a workers' compensation board pays the employee while he or she is recovering, provides additional medical coverage, and may arrange and pay for rehabilitation. The employer contributes premiums for this form of occupational insurance. If workers are injured on the job, it becomes very expensive for the business to hire and train replacement employees. The reputation of the business also suffers, making it hard for the company to attract good employees. If a particular business has a high number of injuries, the government may also investigate and lay charges if violations of safety rules are found.

ACTIVITIES FOR ...

INFORMATION	CONNECTION	EXTENSION
1. a) List the nine methods of compensation.	**b)** For each method of compensation, find a business that uses that method of payment.	**c)** What method of payment would you prefer to receive? Why?
2. a) List 10 employee benefits that a business might provide.	**b)** What benefits would most interest you? Why?	**c)** Choose a business in your community. Find out what employee benefits it offers.
3. a) How can a business help maintain its employees' good health?	**b)** Describe how a local business helps maintain its employees' good health.	**c)** "Ergonomics" is the science of designing equipment that minimizes a worker's fatigue and discomfort while maximizing productivity. Find out about some products that have been ergonomically designed. How do they make it easier for workers to do their jobs?
4. a) What are some common workplace hazards?	**b)** Draw a diagram to show the effect that hazards in a workplace would have on a business and its employees.	**c)** Using information from the Internet, library, local business contacts, or the workers' compensation board, develop a safety checklist for your school or another workplace with which you are familiar.

Contemporary Issues in Canadian Business

THE ISSUE: GENDER DISCRIMINATION IN THE WORKPLACE

What is gender discrimination?

The expression "**glass ceiling**" describes the invisible barriers that women face as they approach senior leadership positions in companies, as well as the barriers faced by visible minorities or people with disabilities. In the case of women, the barriers are due to gender discrimination, and they make it difficult for women to become corporate managers and presidents. The barriers are invisible because the company does not openly discriminate. In other words, a business is not likely to have an official policy of not appointing women to these positions, but it may nevertheless treat its male and female employees differently in less obvious ways. Invisible barriers may arise in selection and recruitment practices, job assignments, performance evaluations, decisions about salaries, and the working environment of the company. For example, if a company does not give its female employees the opportunity to serve on high-profile task forces and committees, women may not be able to get the experience they need to advance to higher-level positions within the company.

Some people believe that these barriers still exist in the workplace; others feel that although barriers did exist in the past, discrimination is no longer an issue for women in business today. Let's examine the two sides of this issue.

Point

Those who argue that gender discrimination in the workplace is intact point out that there are still very few women in high-level management positions in Canada's biggest corporations. If gender discrimination doesn't exist, why are there no women serving on the boards of directors in two-thirds of the top 500 Canadian companies? In fact, only 13 of these companies have women at the top.

Moreover, businesses that claim to be "equal opportunity employers" are not always committed to this principle. Many businesses do make an effort to actively recruit women staff members, but their promotion practices may not parallel their hiring practices. As long as men are still promoted more often than women, women will be at a disadvantage in the workplace.

Negative stereotypes are yet another barrier that women must overcome. Although these stereotypes are diminishing over time, some continue to exist in today's business world. Many people still believe that women are less committed to their jobs, are unwilling to work long hours, are unwilling to relocate, lack quantitative skills, and value their family lives more than their jobs.

Counterpoint

In 1998, women accounted for just over 45% of the Canadian workforce, and 43% of managers and administrators in Canadian businesses and professions were women. Just two decades earlier, women accounted for only 29% of Canada's managers and administrators. These statistics seem to suggest that women are making tremendous progress in the workplace and are no longer hindered by gender discrimination.

Women have also made significant achievements as entrepreneurs. A *Profit* magazine survey found that Canada's top 100 women entrepreneurs generated business revenues of $1.7 billion in 2000. At the same time, their businesses employed over 19 000 workers. These success stories indicate that Canadian women are finding opportunities to pursue jobs at the highest level of business.

E-ACTIVITY

Visit www.business.nelson.com to learn more about women entrepreneurs and the glass ceiling in the Canadian workplace.

Most people who argue that gender discrimination is irrelevant in today's workplace don't deny that it once existed. But they feel that important changes have been made to remove gender discrimination from the workplace. Women have successfully lobbied for changes that have improved their status in the business world, and they are now able to compete on an equal basis for management and high-level positions.

How have women learned to survive in a once male-dominated business environment?

Mentoring and networking are two methods women have used to break through the glass ceiling. Mentoring occurs when one person acts as an advisor to another, fostering the skills needed for success in a business environment. A mentor can answer questions, provide advice and directions, and assist with career advancement. Women also support one another by establishing networks both inside and outside the business environment. Networks take one-on-one mentoring to another level. Because networks are composed of several people, women who belong to a network are able to draw on the talents, advice, and assistance of many different people.

Maureen Kempston Darkes, president and general manger of General Motors of Canada.

A Real Life Example

In July 1994, Maureen Kempston Darkes became the first woman president of a major automotive manufacturing business. She was appointed president and general manager of General Motors of Canada and vice president of General Motors Corporation.

Hard work and perseverance have enabled Kempston Darkes to rise to the top. She also emphasizes the importance of teamwork—pointing out that those who cooperate with fellow employees, help out coworkers when needed, and try to find ways to contribute to their companies will find it much easier to climb the corporate ladder.

As president of GM Canada, one of Kempston Darkes's main objectives is to create a more diverse and equitable workplace. She advocates an "open door" management style that encourages employees to share their ideas and actively participate in the

company. And she also believes that managers need to be aware of and guard against discrimination based on gender, ethnicity, age, or any other factor that would not affect an employee's ability to do his or her job.

Questions and Activities About This Issue

1. Barriers to women exist not only in the business world, but also in society and government. Give an example of one non-business barrier that affects women.
2. Identify five different ways for a company to discourage discrimination among its employees.

The Role of the Human Resources Manager

Many large companies have a human resources manager who is responsible for coordinating all the activities involving the company's employees. These activities include determining when a new employee is required and what skills this employee should have. The human resources department searches for applicants, conducts interviews, and selects the best candidate. Training new employees, organizing ongoing training for all employees, creating programs that will help retain good employees, and handling worker transitions are other areas for which the human resources manager may be responsible.

DETERMINING THE NEED FOR A NEW EMPLOYEE

Human resources managers predict their company's personnel needs. They determine how many employees will be needed when a company first opens, and how many additional people will have to be hired if the company expands. They can forecast their company's **employee turnover**, the rate at which employees leave the firm voluntarily either for another job or to retire. They can also predict how their company's personnel needs will be affected by new technologies, changes in hiring practices, and shifts in economic conditions.

When a vacancy occurs, the human resources department tries to hire a qualified person from within the company to fill the position. This usually involves checking employee records. The records should show length of service, skill level, training received, and performance evaluations. If there are no suitable candidates within the company, the human resources department hires a person from outside. A business that is expanding or just starting out will also have to hire people from outside.

To better understand this process, imagine a local computer company with a staff of 20 people. The business grows rapidly, and it soon needs someone to head its new industrial sales division. One of its programmers knows the needs of the industrial market inside out, and the company promotes her to head this division. But the new sales division also needs salespeople. No other employees can be moved from their current jobs without creating problems, so the company decides to hire from outside.

STRETCH YOUR THINKING

What types of businesses do you think have the highest employee turnover? What factors do you think are responsible for this high turnover?

Looking for the Right Employee

The method a human resources manager uses to find an employee depends on the qualifications required for the job. A company may
- advertise in newspapers, journals, and magazines
- recruit on university and college campuses
- post the job at Human Resources Development Canada (HRDC)
- post the job on an online recruiting site such as Workopolis
- post the job on the company Web site
- use high school or university co-op programs
- hire an employee search firm (often called a **headhunter**)
- use an employee referral program
- search the files of recent job applicants

A computer company looking for a sales representative, for example, may place an advertisement in the classified ads section of local and national newspapers—most people looking for jobs check the newspapers for job opportunities. An ad in a computer-trade magazine will also reach the targeted labour market. A job posting on the business's Web site or an online recruiting site will attract people who regularly use the Internet. An employee referral program may be an effective way to find qualified workers. Many human resources managers feel current employees have the best connections to people working in similar jobs at other companies. It might make sense for the computer company to hire the services of an employee search firm that specializes in the computer industry. Campus recruiting is not the best option—although many university and college graduates possess the required computer skills, most lack sales experience. High school co-op students also lack the needed experience. HRDC tends not to be a good source of highly qualified people in the computer industry. Because this is a new position within the company, applicants who recently applied for other positions probably aren't qualified for this one, so their applications won't be reconsidered.

The Application Process and the Interview

The human resources department receives submissions from hopeful applicants. These often include a completed application form, a cover letter that asks for an interview, and a résumé listing the applicant's education, experience, interests, and abilities.

Ultimately, the business decides to hire or not hire an applicant based on an interview conducted by the human resources manager or another member of the human resources department. Usually, the manager of the department where the new employee will work also

Did You Know?

According to recent surveys, career search activities are the second largest use of the Internet.

Did You Know?

You can learn more about applying for a job and going to job interviews by reading the Career Focus features in Chapters 10 and 15 and by attending your classes in career studies.

attends the interview. The interview team meets the applicant and asks questions to determine the applicant's personality, work habits, values, interests, and other qualities. After all the interviews have been conducted, the interview team rates each applicant. The team often conducts several rounds of interviews to narrow its choice. An applicant may be asked to come in for a second or even a third interview. The final step before hiring an employee is to conduct a reference check. The interviewer calls the applicant's references to verify the information in the application or to ask further questions.

JOB TRAINING

The human resources department coordinates orientation and training for all new employees. During **orientation**, new employees meet other employees and tour the workplace. The department introduces the business's policies on compensation, work hours, benefits, rules of behaviour, dress codes, health and safety procedures, and so on. New employees receive training on equipment that they will use. Many companies also provide ongoing training, particularly in new technology, software, and equipment. Some arrange motivational presentations and provide training in stress management, increasing productivity, and management skills. These businesses believe in keeping employees happy, well qualified, and up to date in their skills.

KEEPING GOOD EMPLOYEES

Employers invest a great deal of time and expense to search for, hire, and train new employees. It makes sense, then, for employers to try to retain productive and valued employees. High employee turnover can result in costly problems. Not only does the search for new employees have to begin again, but employees are less productive during training because they are just learning how to do their jobs. As you learned, lower productivity means significantly lower profit for the business.

In a competitive labour market, businesses try to attract experienced employees, often from competitors. Some companies now go well beyond the usual compensation methods and offer special benefits, known as **perks**. Casual dress codes are more common. Some companies now provide daycare services; others let employees set up playpens in their office. Because fitness programs have positive effects on employee attitudes, more businesses offer on-site gym facilities. Companies arrange for massage therapists to make office calls. Special food is ordered for the staff kitchen. Reading rooms that look and feel like living rooms are arranged. And if you need a rest, some businesses even have nap rooms.

Departures, Dismissals, and Retirement

All employees eventually leave the business they work for. The human resources department tries to make their transition easier, regardless of its cause. An employer who helps an employee make a transition protects the reputation of the firm and maintains a good relationship with the employee.

Departuress

Some employees leave their jobs voluntarily. Their departure could be based on personal or family needs, job dissatisfaction, or a better opportunity elsewhere. The employer can help in the transition by providing a letter of recommendation for the employee or by agreeing to act as a positive reference. The human resources department can arrange exit counselling. During the **exit interview**, an employee can discuss his or her future goals and make sure that leaving is the best way to achieve these goals. The employer should ensure that there is no ill will. The company may also ask departing employees for their opinions about how the work environment could be improved. Since the employees are leaving, they may be prepared to provide honest, valuable feedback.

Dismissals

Sometimes, employees leave a job involuntarily: A business decides that an employee is not fulfilling duties as required, and dismisses him or her. Prior to this point, however, employers record in an employee's personnel file any problems or concerns that might lead to dismissal, for example, lateness, absenteeism, or poor work habits. Many firms conduct corrective interviews. During a **corrective interview**, the employer discusses problems with the employee and, together, both parties make a plan for improvement. All conversations with the employee during the corrective interview should be summarized and signed as accurate by both the employer and the employee. After a set period of time, the employee must show improvement or face dismissal.

Companies also dismiss employees to cut back expenses. This type of dismissal is called **employee layoff**. Companies with unionized employees lay off workers in order of **seniority**. This means that employees with fewer years of service are let go first. In non-unionized companies, the business usually lays off the employees who are least essential to its day-to-day operations.

Many companies provide a **severance package** to a dismissed employee. This package often contains a final payment, which usually depends on the amount of time the employee has worked for the business. For example, an employee might receive one week's salary for

STRETCH YOUR THINKING

Why is it important for a business to document steps taken to improve an employee's performance?

every year of service. The company may also provide **outplacement counselling** to ease the employee's transition by helping him or her search for a new job.

Retirement

Retirement normally occurs when an employee voluntarily withdraws from the labour market. Often, retirees have reached a certain age, such as 55, when they qualify for a pension. A **pension** gives the employee income once he or she no longer works for the company. Throughout the employee's time at the company, both the employer and the employee contribute to the pension. In some cases, people retire from one job and receive a pension, only to use their pension to start their own business. Because the Canadian population is living longer and remaining healthy, retirement may soon become just another career move for many people.

ACTIVITIES FOR ...

INFORMATION	**C**ONNECTION	**E**XTENSION
1. a) Outline the role of the human resources manager.	**b)** What qualities and training do you think a human resources manager should have?	**c)** Interview a human resources manager in person, on the phone, or by e-mail to find out what he or she considers to be the greatest rewards and challenges of the job.
2. a) What methods can a business use to find new employees?	**b)** Use advertisements from local newspapers, the Internet, HRDC, and other resources to prepare a list of available jobs in a field that interests you.	**c)** Develop a list of 10 qualities that a human resources manager might look for in a potential employee. Ask a human resources manager what qualities he or she looks for. Compare your lists. Develop a poster to illustrate the key characteristics of a good employee.
3. a) What types of training do most businesses provide?	**b)** Using your own experience, a classmate's experience, or the experience of a family member, describe the training provided for a specific job.	**c)** Nortel, a large Canadian communications firm, awards its workers with special points that they can convert into money or use to buy goods, gift certificates, tickets to sports events, and trips. Do some research to find out what other kinds of perks Canadian businesses offer their employees.
4. a) List three reasons why employees might leave a company.	**b)** Find out about a company layoff in your community. What was the cause of the layoff? What kind of severance package were the employees offered?	**c)** Role play an exit interview between an employee and a human resources manager. Consider the topics that should be covered as well as the tone of the interview.

Rights in the Workplace

As mentioned on page 152, employees have rights. Many of these rights are based on the Universal Declaration of Human Rights, adopted by the General Assembly of the United Nations on December 10, 1948. The following articles, or sections of the declaration, are sometimes known as the Universal Employee Bill of Rights.

Universal Declaration of Human Rights

Article 4. No one shall be held in slavery or servitude; slavery and the slave trade shall be prohibited in all their forms.

Article 23. (1) Everyone has the right to work, to free choice of employment, to just and favourable conditions of work, and to protection against unemployment.

(2) Everyone, without any discrimination, has the right to equal pay for equal work.

(3) Everyone who works has the right to just and favourable remuneration, ensuring ... an existence worthy of human dignity....

(4) Everyone has the right to form and to join trade unions....

Article 24. Everyone has the right to rest and leisure, including reasonable limitation of working hours and periodic holidays with pay.

Article 25. (1) Everyone has the right to a standard of living adequate for the health and well-being of himself and of his family, including food, clothing, housing, medical care, and necessary social services....

Article 26. Everyone has the right to job training. Job training shall be free, at least in the elementary and fundamental stages....

Flags of its member countries fly outside the United Nations building in New York City.

THE RIGHTS OF THE EMPLOYEE

The provincial and federal governments have drafted legislation that sets out employment standards for workers in the private and public sectors. The legislation sets out provisions for the following:
- the minimum age for employment
- hours of work
- minimum wages
- overtime, holiday, and vacation pay
- paid public holidays
- parental leave
- individual and group terminations of employment
- the recovery of unpaid wages

In addition to employment standards, each province has human rights legislation. Human rights codes make it illegal to harass or discriminate against an employee or potential employee on the grounds of gender, race, religion, sexual preference, physical disability, age, and so on. These characteristics are called **protected grounds**. Denying someone an interview, a job, or a promotion because of religion, gender, or physical disability is job **discrimination**. **Harassment** occurs when specific people or groups are made to feel threatened or uncomfortable because of who they are. Harassment can include making rude jokes, offensive comments, and inappropriate sexual suggestions. Employees who experience discrimination or harassment can complain to the appropriate human rights body.

STRETCH YOUR THINKING

Are the articles proclaiming employee rights in the Universal Declaration of Human Rights actually practised in the real world? Explain.

THE RIGHTS OF THE EMPLOYER

Employers have the right to hire, dismiss, and promote employees, and to establish conditions of employment that best serve their business goals. In doing so, they must not discriminate on the grounds protected by human rights legislation. Specifically, employers have the right to
- decide what their employment needs are
- require that employees have job-related qualifications and/or experience
- hire, promote, and assign the most qualified person for a position
- establish standards for evaluating job performance
- require that employees adhere to clearly defined job descriptions and performance criteria
- discipline, demote, or dismiss incompetent, negligent, or insubordinate employees
- set employment terms and conditions
- establish salary and wage scales either independently or through negotiations

1. a) Describe the rights of the employee.

b) Why do you think that it is necessary to have legislation that protects the rights of employees?

c) Using the Internet or the local library, look at your province's legislation on employment standards. What are the paid holidays? How long is parental leave? How many hours make up a regular work week?

2. a) Describe the rights of the employer.

b) Choose three employer rights. Tell why it is important for the employer to have each right.

c) Who has more rights: the employee or the employer? Explain.

Organization and Management

What is an organization? An **organization** is a method of combining people, finances, and physical resources. A business organization is designed to acquire, store, transform, and distribute goods and services to achieve a business's objectives. Every business has some sort of organizational structure that outlines what tasks need to be done and who will perform them. Even a sole proprietorship must organize its resources to meet its goals.

ORGANIZATIONAL STRUCTURES

Most businesses are structured into departments. With this type of organization, called **departmentalization**, similar activities are grouped together to achieve related goals. Most departments are formed on one of five bases:

- **Function**: A soft-drink business might be organized into bottling, sales, and shipping departments. A dry-cleaning business might have cleaning, wrapping, and customer-service departments.
- **Geography**: A clothing manufacturer might have eastern, central, and western divisions. Different sales representatives would be assigned to each region.
- **Product**: Retail stores often create departments according to product. For example, in a clothing store, there could be departments for pants, sweaters, and accessories. A music store might have departments for hip-hop, alternative, soundtrack, classical, rap, and rock music. As well, many large businesses create departments for certain

brands. For example, a cereal company might have a separate department for each brand of cereal. This type of departmentalization is often called **brand management**.

- **Customers:** Some companies focus their departments on different categories of customers. A food-distribution company might have a department that sells to airlines and railways (its transportation department) and a department that sells to high school cafeterias, prisons, and university food services (its institutional department).
- **Time:** Many businesses, such as convenience stores and cleaning companies, have a night shift and a day shift. These shifts can form the basis for departments.

Organization Charts

In order to see how a company is organized, most firms develop an organization chart. An **organization chart** graphically shows how the company is structured, including

- lines of authority (who reports to whom)
- how the business is departmentalized
- the relationship of one department to another
- various positions in the business

Sometimes, the chart also shows what tasks need to be performed so that the business can achieve its goals.

Figure 7.1

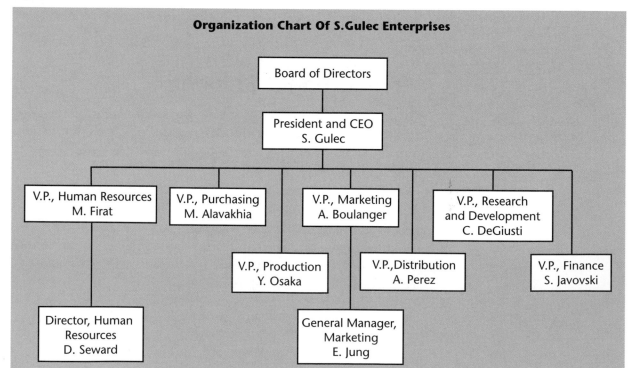

Notice that in Figure 7.1, each box represents one person or one department that is managed by one person. Only one line connects that person to one other person in the organization. This represents a basic principle of management: No employee should have more than one boss. Most businesses base their organization on this formal structure.

Work Teams

Many businesses are adopting a work-team organizational approach. A **work team** is made up of qualified people from different departments in the organization who are grouped together for a specific task. All members of the team are still responsible to their departments, but for a specific time they are also responsible to the work team. Once the work team achieves its goal, the team disbands and members return to their departments. While a work team is operational, an employee will usually have two managers: a department manager and a work team manager.

Informal Business Structures

The **informal structure** of a business is based on who really speaks to whom. There is rarely any kind of chart for this organizational structure. For example, many businesspeople discuss company decisions in car pools. One car pool may bring together the head of the marketing department, the accounting clerk, a sales representative, and a production worker. During the two hours they spend in the car each day, they make a number of decisions, completely outside formal channels. The informal structure may also come into play during dinner parties, lunches, coffee breaks, and rounds of golf.

After eating breakfast together, these coworkers discuss a new business project.

HOW MANAGEMENT FUNCTIONS

Management tries to achieve a company's goals by deciding how best to use the business's human, financial, and material resources. Management performs five major functions for any business: planning, organizing, directing, controlling, and staffing.

Planning

Planning is the process of setting realistic goals for a business—both short-term and long-term—and deciding how best to achieve them. Goals are occasionally social and always economic. (See Chapter 5 for

STRETCH YOUR THINKING

Besides corporate social responsibility, what other social goals might a business set for itself?

information on corporate social responsibility.) The long-term economic goal of any business is to maximize profits. Short-term goals are often expressed as a sales or income target. For example, a business may plan to increase sales by 10% in the next quarter or to increase profit by 5% in the next year.

Managers must understand these goals and develop strategies to achieve them. If a beverage company plans to increase sales by 10%, all of its managers have to work to meet this goal. The marketing manager creates a promotional plan. The sales manager arranges new contracts with companies who will distribute the beverages. And the production manager arranges the necessary resources to produce an increased amount of the product.

Organizing

Each department within a company has its own manager, who is responsible for organizing the department. That manager determines tasks and duties for the department and establishes relationships with other departments to help achieve the company's goals. The manager also writes job descriptions for each member of the department so that each employee is aware of his or her role.

A business's executives organize department managers. These executives are called **divisional managers** or vice presidents. As upper-level managers, they set company policy, determine corporate objectives, and decide on the best way for a company's directors (its chief executive officer, president, and board of directors) to communicate with the various department heads.

Directing

Managers direct when they focus employees on achieving objectives and motivate their staff to accomplish these objectives. Directing is also called leading. There are two main types of leaders. **Autocratic leaders** do not allow employees to participate in decision making, while **democratic leaders** provide opportunities for employees to contribute to the decision-making process. Most leaders fall somewhere between purely democratic and purely autocratic leadership.

Motivating

This chapter has already discussed different kinds of compensation and benefits that businesses can offer employees. Compensation can be a strong motivating factor. Some employees work harder to receive a pay increase. Others work hard so that they will be moved to a well-decorated office. Some people are more interested in a longer vacation.

In other words, motivation means different things to different people. A skillful manager discovers how to best motivate each employee, and uses these motivating factors to increase employee productivity.

Communicating

Directing others means letting them know what needs to be done. A good leader communicates directions, urgency, corporate values, plans, and goals clearly and effectively. Failure to do so may mean that tasks are not done at all or that they are poorly done. A task completed improperly wastes labour. Employees will have to redo the task, and the company's reputation may be damaged.

Encouraging Participation

Many progressive businesses allow employees to direct the training, promotion, and dismissal of other employees in their department. This type of employee participation is called **decision ownership** because the people affected by the decision (**stakeholders**) get to make the decision. In a beverage company that practises decision ownership, telephone receptionists, for example, may contribute to decision making about promoting sales representatives because they talk to customers every day and know which sales representatives the customers are satisfied with. Not only can employee participation result in better decisions, it can improve staff motivation. Many employees enjoy the sense of purpose that comes from being involved in making decisions.

Controlling

Controlling is the method managers use to increase, maintain, or decrease the resources that they are allocated. The number of employees in a department, the amount of money the department receives, and the extent of its physical supplies are all based on the budget it is given. If the department fails to reach its goals, its budget may be cut and resources reduced. If the department exceeds its goals, more resources are required and usually supplied. If the department simply reaches its target, little changes. The budgeting process, in other words, is a very important means of control.

Staffing

The staffing function of management was covered in depth earlier in this chapter. Large companies can have an entire department devoted to staffing and other areas of human resources (the human resources department). In small businesses, the owners usually perform the human resources functions by themselves. In fact, many small business owners perform all the management functions without assistance.

STRETCH YOUR THINKING

What disadvantages might there be to decision ownership? Share your ideas with a partner.

MANAGING RESOURCES

As has been discussed in detail in this chapter, a manager's ability to hire, train, direct, and motivate good employees is one of the most important skills he or she can possess. But businesses have other resources, besides human resources, that must also be managed.

Purchasing

The purchasing manager negotiates deals for the supply and delivery of **raw materials** (which the manufacturer transforms into another product), equipment, supplies, and goods for resale. If a beverage company's purchasing manager negotiates a small reduction in the price of sugar, for example, 5¢ per kilogram, it may not seem like a big savings. But if the company uses 2 000 000 kg of sugar a year, the reduction is considerable. The company will save $100 000 a year! A good purchasing manager also arranges for inventory to arrive when it is needed. **Just in time** delivery reduces shipping costs and warehouse needs.

Production

The production manager ensures that a business makes the things it is supposed to make. The production manager balances many activities, from arranging for raw materials to be processed into a finished product to packaging and storing that product. The production manager often has to arrange and coordinate plant maintenance, shift scheduling, machinery repair, and technological improvements.

Marketing and Distribution

Marketing and distribution managers try to ensure that whatever the production department produces gets sold. The marketing manager develops sales strategies, which include advertising, promotional activities, and publicity. The distribution manager (who is often the marketing manager as well) focuses on sales, often attempting to improve product distribution through direct sales efforts (sales representatives) or indirect ones (vending machines, catalogues, and Internet sales). Marketing and distribution will be covered in greater detail in Chapter 9.

Research and Development

As you read in Chapter 6, research and development (R&D) departments create new products or services, or come up with new and better ways to produce the same product or service. An R&D department's work is sometimes based on feedback from the marketplace. A company will conduct studies to find out what consumers like or dislike about their product, or what new products they would like to see. Then, R&D managers analyze and interpret the market data and give direction to their department. They also prepare reports that help the purchasing, production, and marketing managers make decisions for their departments.

Finance

The **comptroller**, or manager of the financial department, is often an accountant. His or her major responsibilities are keeping records of the company's financial transactions and controlling the company's money, which includes setting the budget of each department along with the department manager.

ACTIVITIES FOR ...

INFORMATION	**C**ONNECTION	**E**XTENSION
1. a) List five ways that organizations departmentalize.	**b)** Find an example of each type of departmentalization in a local business.	**c)** Describe ways in which your family is an organization.
2. a) What are the five components of a typical organization chart?	**b)** Develop an organization chart for a small local business or for your school.	**c)** Using the Internet or company brochures, find the organization chart of a major company. In a short report, explain how the chart represents the business's organization.
3. a) What are the five functions of management?	**b)** Interview the manager of a local business. Ask him or her for specific examples of each management function that he or she performs in a typical day.	**c)** How do you manage yourself? What planning, organizing, directing, controlling, and staffing will you need to do in the next year? in the next five years?
4. a) List three styles of leadership.	**b)** Ask a manager of a local business to describe his or her leadership style.	**c)** Imagine doing a task that you • hate, for example, cleaning the kitty litter box • feel so-so about, for example, doing the dishes • love, for example, polishing your trophies In what different ways could your manager (mother, father, teacher, older sister, etc.) motivate you to perform those tasks? Which motivators would be most effective? Explain.

Review

Knowledge and Understanding

1. Match each of the following terms to the correct definition:

   commission   labour markets
   compensation   management
   harassment   piecework
   incentive   salary

   a) Where buyers of skills (employers) meet sellers of skills (employees).
   b) The amount of money employees are paid.
   c) A fixed amount of money paid to an employee on a regular schedule.
   d) A form of compensation based on the amount of an employee's sales.
   e) Something added to compensation to encourage employees to work harder.
   f) A form of compensation based on the amount of product an employee makes.
   g) When specific people or groups are made to feel uncomfortable because of who they are.
   h) Those responsible for achieving an organization's goals by directing the allocation and use of the organization's human, financial, and material resources.

2. Describe the relationship between employers and employees in the labour market.

3. What legislation exists at the provincial and federal levels of government to protect the rights of employees in Canada? Outline the rights that are provided for employees in the various laws.

4. When searching for a job, many people look only at the classified ads section of a newspaper. Why might this not be the best way to find out about job opportunities?

5. Describe the hiring process.

6. How does departmentalization affect a business's organization?

Thinking and Inquiry

1. What is the definition of a part-time employee in your province? Why do many businesses like to hire part-time employees?

2. Talk to an older family member or friend about an excellent manager that he or she has had. What qualities made that person an excellent manager?

3. Do you agree that a firm's most important asset is its human resources? Explain your response.

4. What occupations do you think will draw top salaries in 2025? Why?

Communication

1. Does performance-based pay encourage sweatshops? Research and debate this issue.

2. Design a poster promoting workplace safety. Display it in your school.

3. Invite at least two human resources managers to your class. Ask them to discuss training for new employees, programs that promote employee development and growth, and employee benefits at their workplace. Prepare specific questions to ask in advance, and make notes during the presentations. Then, working in small groups, use your notes to develop a list of programs and benefits that you could reasonably expect from employers in your area.

4. Prepare an illustrated report that profiles a local manufacturing business. Be sure to show each of the business's departments as well as each department's responsibilities.

Application

1. Select various job advertisements from a local or national newspaper. Group the ads according to whether they require unskilled, semiskilled, skilled, or professional labour. What types of compensation packages are mentioned for each type of job? For two of the ads, write a profile of the ideal employee. Other than these ads, how else and where else should each company look for the ideal employee?

2. Imagine that you are negotiating the compensation of an all-star professional athlete. What might you ask for as part of the compensation package?

3. Using a national newspaper or the Internet, find an advertisement for two careers in human resources, one in Canada and one outside Canada. Using a step diagram, flow chart, or time line, map a possible career path that would lead you to each job. Be specific about where and how you would obtain the requirements for the job. Share your career paths with the class in a discussion forum.

4. After getting permission, job shadow the manager of a local company for a day. Record your observations and prepare a report on the manager's style. Be sure to share your comments with the manager.

5. Interview a person who is retired. How did his or her life change because of retirement? What are the major benefits? What are the major drawbacks?

6. Find out about your province's human rights legislation. What are the prohibited areas of discrimination? Look in local newspapers or on the Web site of your province's human rights organization to find out about a case of discrimination. Prepare a report outlining the case and stating the result. Do you think that the case was settled fairly? Explain.

REFLECT ON YOUR LEARNING

1. Review your answers to the Before You Begin question on page 145. Now, describe what you would consider an ideal place to work. Support your answer with ideas from this chapter.

2. Consider SkyLink, the company profiled on pages 143–144. What could the company do to keep its employees? How might it create a positive attitude in the workplace? Why is this attitude important to SkyLink's productivity? What health and safety issues should SkyLink consider?

STUDENT EXPECTATIONS

After completing this chapter, you will be able to

- demonstrate an understanding of the functions of accounting
- state the purpose of an annual report
- explain the differences among service, retail, and manufacturing accounting systems
- identify the key elements of a balance sheet
- use a balance sheet to analyze the success of a business
- identify the key elements of an income statement
- use an income statement to analyze the success of a business
- explain the composition and purpose of a statement of cash flow
- describe how effective accounting and financial statements contribute to business success

The owners of Polar Magnetics pose with their giant muscle magnet on the side of a car.

ELVIS LIVES

Javier Espinal is strolling through the large storage area of his Toronto factory, casually inspecting Polar Magnetics Inc.'s inventory of "trinkets and trash." The carefully stacked merchandise ranges from key chains, wall plaques, coasters, place mats, and reusable stickers to the company's biggest seller: fridge magnets.

Shelves groan under the weight of thousands of magnets displaying the likenesses of a veritable "Who's Who" of pop culture. There's the trendy (Britney Spears and the Backstreet Boys), the classic (Marilyn Monroe and the Three Stooges), the forever cool (Elvis Presley and Woody Woodpecker), plus a host of others from fruit to fish. Judging by the amount of inventory awaiting shipment, the company is in superb shape to supply its growing number of retail accounts. But then Espinal, the company's cofounder and vice president of product development and licensing, comes upon a rack piled haphazardly with a bunch of magnets—all of them coated in dust. "Oh, that's garbage, man, pure garbage. By the time we finally got the licence to do them, they were dead," Espinal says. "They" are the Spice Girls, the pop group that was the hottest thing in the known universe, just around the time when Polar got the licence for them in 1998. Then, Ginger Spice left the group and the Spice Girls' popularity fizzled. Espinal couldn't even give the stuff away. Such turns in trendiness are part of the cycle of pop culture. Luckily for Espinal and his partners—Mike Boland, president, and Lucian Pateopol, vice president of production—Polar Magnetics has notched far more hits than misses.

The company began in the early 1990s. One day, on a whim, Espinal made a fridge magnet of former Toronto Maple Leaf winger Wendel Clark by cutting out his photograph and laminating it on a small piece of wood. He then carved the wooden slab to match the photo's dimensions, stuck on a magnetic backing and, presto, the "Funky Chunky" fridge magnet was born.

Espinal created more magnets and gave them away as gifts to family members and close friends. They were an immediate hit, and many recipients urged him to think about actually selling them.

Espinal met Boland at the end of 1992, and they soon formed

a partnership. (The third partner, Pateopol, joined in 1995.) The company's big break came in 1995 when Boland struck a deal with the Graceland gift shop in Memphis, Tennessee. The shop bought 1500 magnets, all of them adorned with Elvis images. The gift shop priced the magnets at about U.S. $10 apiece, and in less than three weeks the magnets sold out. Graceland put in another order—this time for 2500.

Elvis opened the door. Licensing deals with the estates of James Dean, Marilyn Monroe, the Beatles, and the Three Stooges soon followed. In September 1995, the company moved into a larger factory. Sales soared from $25 000 in 1994 to $1.2 million in 1996.

Licensing is a risky game. The trick is to know early on which properties to back. (The more popular the property, the more expensive the licence.) A good or bad decision often means the difference between a profitable or money-losing year. That became apparent by October 1997. Boland received a phone call from a licensing company representing an edgy new animated TV series. The show was the then-unknown *South Park*. Based on industry buzz, Boland decided to sign a deal that allowed Polar to become one of the original *South Park* licensees.

It was a wise decision. *South Park* was a monster hit for the company. Between November 1, 1997 and March 31, 1998, Polar sold more than $3 million worth of *South Park* merchandise. But perhaps they learned too much from those bratty *South Park* boys. "It made us so much money so fast that we became fat, dumb, and happy," Boland says. "It gave us a false sense of security," and led the Polar principals to make some regrettable business decisions. Like the Spice Girls.

In the long run, Polar plans to achieve a 50–50 split between licensed and non-licensed merchandise—which should help the company through the ups and downs of pop culture trends. Then again, there's always the chance that everything old will become new again.

About This Profile

1. Why is it important for Polar Magnetics to keep up with the latest trends? How do changes in trends affect Polar's inventory?
2. Why does Polar want to produce more non-licensed products? Explain how this change might affect the company's expenses and profit.

The Accounting Function

BEFORE YOU BEGIN

Look back to the profile of Polar Magnetics. On a piece of paper, make two columns: "Expenses" and "Assets." In the "Expenses" column, list all the expenses Polar might have. In the "Assets" column, list all the things of value that the company might own.

Accounting is the process of recording, analyzing, and interpreting the economic activities of a business. In accounting, any business activity involving money is recorded as a **transaction**. A transaction occurs when something that has value is exchanged for something else that has value. A business pays an employee $80 in exchange for eight hours of work; a customer buys (or exchanges) a computer printer for $250; a clothing manufacturer sells 100 sweaters to a retail outlet in exchange for $5000. The monetary part of these exchanges can be paid in cash, by cheque, or on credit. Accounting principles are based on the fact that at least two things happen during any transaction. When the business pays $80 for labour, for example, it decreases its cash and increases its expenses. What two things happen during the sale of the computer printer? of the sweaters?

A business can conduct hundreds—even thousands—of transactions daily. For example, a supermarket might serve several thousand customers on a busy Saturday. In addition to customer transactions, businesses conduct many other types of monetary exchanges on a regular basis. These include paying staff; paying bills, such as heat and electricity; and buying and storing inventory. Because each transaction affects a business's finances, companies keep records of these transactions. This type of record keeping is done for several reasons: accountability, budgeting, taxation, and preparation of financial statements and annual reports.

ACCOUNTABILITY

While doing business, a great deal of money passes through the control of many different people. To make sure that this money doesn't get lost or stolen, businesses have security systems. Usually, each transaction is recorded. This record ensures accountability. **Accountability** means that employees who handle or have access to cash are responsible for it and must explain any losses or discrepancies.

All businesses guarantee accountability through bookkeeping. **Bookkeeping** is a method of recording all transactions for a business in a specific format. Cash register receipts are one way that retail businesses record transactions. In addition, bookkeepers use **invoices** (bills for goods and services either bought by or sold to the business), bank statements, and cheque records to account for all business transactions.

BUDGETING

Accurate transaction records give a business information that it can use for budgeting. As you read in Chapter 7, when a business budgets, it allocates money to various areas of the business. To budget accurately, the business has to be able to estimate both sales and expenses. For example, a retail store needs to predict the total sales for the Christmas season. It can then give the purchasing department a budget to buy inventory, the human resources department a budget to hire seasonal staff, and the advertising department a budget to promote the store.

When the season is over, budgeted forecasts can be checked against actual sales. If sales figures were underestimated, the buyer would not have bought enough, and the store would have run out of inventory. If sales were overestimated, the store would have remaining inventory. This leftover inventory costs the store money. The company already paid for it, and now it will take up storage space even though it won't generate any revenue. The business may try to reduce inventory by putting leftover items on sale—but even if the items do sell, they generate less in sales revenue than they would have if sold at the regular price. If actual sales fell far below the budgeted predictions, labour and advertising expenses would also have been too high. In this case, the company probably suffered a loss and didn't make a profit.

The best way a company can predict sales figures is to analyze all the records of transactions for the same period in previous years. The retail store, for example, consults records for the past few Christmas seasons. If the outlook for the coming year is good, the store could increase the budget accordingly. The buyer might also check how much inventory remained at the end of last year's season.

TAXATION

All businesses operating in Canada have to pay taxes on their profits or earnings. The government requires every business to keep a set of books that include accurate accounting records of every business transaction as well as a yearly income statement, which shows the company's profit (or loss). This income statement must be included with the necessary tax forms, and taxes must be paid to the Canada Customs and Revenue Agency (formerly Revenue Canada) and to the province(s) in which the business operates.

Individual shareholders of any corporation also pay taxes on profits earned through dividends paid by the corporation. Investors pay tax on any substantial gain they make by selling corporation stocks. This income is called a **capital gain**, and it occurs whenever you sell a stock for a price that is higher than what you paid for it.

STRETCH YOUR THINKING

The Christmas buying season represents 60% to 70% of toy sales in North America. How might toy manufacturers and retail stores that sell toys plan their budgets to prepare for the Christmas season?

BUSINESS —FACT—

More and more, a company's "books" are kept on computer rather than on paper.

FINANCIAL STATEMENTS

Financial statements are reports that summarize the financial performance of a business. Normally, a business prepares three financial statements (four, if the business is a corporation) at least once a year. These statements are the balance sheet, income statement (or statement of earnings), and cash-flow statement. Each will be discussed in more detail later in this chapter. A corporation also prepares a statement of shareholders' equity.

Financial statements indicate the business's economic health to interested parties. These parties, or stakeholders, include management, owners, investors, shareholders, and the government. In a corporation, the owners and the shareholders are one and the same. Each group has reason to be interested in the state of the business. Management wants to see if good decisions have been made. Owners want to check profit. Investors want to check the return on their investment. Shareholders want to judge the future strength of the business. Government wants to collect taxes.

ANNUAL REPORTS

Financial statements are presented to shareholders and potential investors in the form of an **annual report**. Most often this is a glossy publication that opens with a letter to shareholders from the chief executive officer (CEO) and the chairperson of the board of directors. (Often, a company's CEO and chairperson of the board are the same person.) The annual report summarizes the year's activities and tells how the company achieved its goals (or why it did not). New product launches, expansions, new international markets, sales of corporate divisions, and acquisitions of other companies are described and sometimes lavishly illustrated.

Many annual reports are not only attractive, they are also interesting and innovative. For example, Ben & Jerry's (an international business that makes ice cream) recently published its annual report as a colouring book, complete with crayons. Company shareholders automatically receive the annual report, but most businesses will supply a free copy to anyone who is interested. As far as the business is concerned, we are all potential investors. Providing free copies of the annual report is one way a business can advertise and promote the company, and possibly attract new investors. (You will learn more about advertising and promotion in Chapter 9.)

ACTIVITIES FOR ...

INFORMATION	**CONNECTION**	**EXTENSION**
1. a) What is accounting? Why is it important to a business?	**b)** Choose a local business. With a partner, brainstorm at least 10 different types of transactions that the business might make.	**c)** For each of the 10 transactions you listed in Question 1b, state what two things happened. (For example, cash went down and labour expenses went up.)
2. a) Why do businesses need to keep financial records?	**b)** Interview the owner or manager of a local business to find out how he or she budgets for his or her business.	**c)** With a partner, examine a tax form that businesses need to complete for the Canada Customs and Revenue Agency. Talk about terms you understand. List terms that you do not understand. At the end of the chapter, look back at your list to see which terms remain unclear.
3. a) What are financial statements? Who might be interested in them, and why?	**b)** Obtain a copy of an annual report from a company that interests you. Browse through the report to see what financial statements it includes.	**c)** If you were going to invest money in a business, how much would you rely on its annual report to make your decision? What other sources might you consider?

Accounting for Various Types of Businesses

The kinds of activities that a business is involved in help determine the accounting method that the business uses. Businesses fall into certain categories because they conduct specific types of transactions. The record-keeping system that each business uses has to accommodate these different kinds of transactions. Let's look at the three major types of businesses: service (excluding retail), retail, and manufacturing.

SERVICE BUSINESSES

Service businesses require the simplest type of accounting. What these businesses sell is intangible. For example, you may pay $11 for a movie ticket, but you're not paying for the ticket itself. You're paying for permission to enter the theatre. The ticket is only proof that you paid.

Imagine that you have a snow-removal business. Recording your transactions would be simple: gas purchases for the snow blower,

This business not only provides a service by renting out videos; it also sells goods such as chocolate bars, magazines, previously viewed movies, and computer games. As a result, it uses service-business and retail accounting methods.

BUSINESS
—FACT—

A typical payment term for retail businesses is "2/10, net/30." The manufacturer or wholesaler offers the retailer 30 days to pay for the inventory (net/30), but will give the store a 2% discount if the store pays within 10 days (2/10). A retailer who purchases $5000 worth of inventory can save $100 if he or she pays within 10 days.

equipment costs and repairs, and customer payments for the snow-clearing service. If you clear a driveway for $25, you record that your cash has increased by $25, and so has your sales revenue. Buying $10 in gas means that your gas expenses go up and your cash goes down.

A pure service business has no product inventory to record. Your snow-removal business sells only the services you provide. The absence of inventory is the main difference between a pure service business and any other type of business. Few businesses today, however, are pure service businesses. Consider that movie again: the theatre also sells chocolate bars and snack foods.

RETAIL AND PRODUCT-SALES BUSINESSES

Because retail businesses sell products to consumers, they use some accounts in their accounting systems that service businesses do not use. Retail businesses buy inventories of goods and keep track of them once they arrive. As in other service businesses, retail businesses also record revenue, costs, and expenses.

Retail stores often buy inventory on **credit**, which means that they pay for the goods they receive at a future date. The manufacturers, wholesalers, and importers from whom they buy their inventory state terms for payment. Often, suppliers offer a discount to stores that pay their bills early. The store must record the terms and dates accurately to take advantage of the discounts. Missing the due dates can increase business costs dramatically.

Inventory control is also important. Businesses check that the quantity of goods actually shipped matches the quantity of goods recorded on the shipper's invoice. As inventory sells, businesses deduct it from the quantity they have on hand to provide an accurate, up-to-date total. At least once a year, companies physically count the inventory to check that records are accurate.

Every retailer starts the fiscal year with inventory on hand. A **fiscal year**, or business year, is any 12-month operating period.

Often, but not always, the fiscal year corresponds to the calendar year. For example, a fiscal year might begin on April 1 and end on March 31 of the following year. Imagine that you own a shoe store. At the start of your fiscal year, you have $50 000 worth of inventory. In other words, your inventory cost $50 000. Throughout the year, your store updates styles, replaces sold stock, and prepares for seasonal changes by purchasing $75 000 worth of additional inventory. During the year, then, the store has a total of $125 000 worth of inventory to sell.

One year later, a physical, or actual, count of the inventory shows that your shoe store has $40 000 in unsold inventory to start the next fiscal year. If this amount is subtracted from the cost of goods available for the year ($125 000), the store must have sold goods that cost $85 000. In retail accounting, this amount is expressed as the **cost of goods sold**.

Beginning Inventory	$50 000
Inventory Purchased	+ 75 000
Cost of All Goods Available for Sale	$125 000
Ending Inventory	– 40 000
Cost of Goods Sold	$85 000

If the store has $150 000 in sales revenue, this revenue is generated entirely by the goods sold. Because $85 000 worth of goods was sold to bring in $150 000 in sales, the store makes a gross profit of $65 000. **Gross profit** is all the money left over after deducting the cost of goods sold from the revenue, but before deducting the business expenses that helped generate the revenue.

Sales Revenue	$150 000
Cost of Goods Sold	– 85 000
Gross Profit	$65 000

The store must now use a portion of the gross profit to pay expenses such as rent, salaries and wages, supplies, and advertising. Once these expenses are deducted from the gross profit, the amount of money left over is called the **net profit**, or **net income**. If the expenses are $25 000, then the net profit would be $40 000.

Gross Profit	$65 000
Expenses	– 25 000
Net Profit	$40 000

Net profit is the amount of money the storeowner can declare as income for income tax purposes. As you learned in Chapter 3, if the company is a corporation, net profit is divided among shareholders in the form of dividends.

Retail is not the only type of business that uses this accounting method. Wholesalers and importers use it as well. These businesses do not manufacture goods; instead, they buy inventory from manufacturers and resell it to other companies or stores. Wholesalers and importers calculate the cost of goods sold just as retail stores do. (See Chapter 9 for more information on wholesalers and importers.)

MANUFACTURING BUSINESSES

Because manufacturing businesses make products, their accounting needs are far more complex than those of retail and other types of service businesses. Manufacturers not only use the normal accounting categories of these types of businesses; they need systems that account for their inventory of raw materials, inventory of goods in process, direct labour, and inventory of finished goods. These factors must all be considered when calculating profit.

Raw Materials

As you read in Chapter 7, raw materials are the goods a manufacturer purchases and transforms into another product. Sometimes, these "raw" materials are unprocessed, for example, wheat, sugar cane, or fish. At other times, the materials are semifinished or processed goods, such as flour, sugar, or fish meal.

To accurately track expenses, the accounting department calculates the cost of raw materials used in production, much as a retail store calculates the cost of goods sold. For example, a bakery might use 500 mL of flour, 250 mL of milk, and 50 mL of sugar to produce one loaf of bread. The cost of each loaf will be affected by the cost of each raw material. (The tomato sauce example in Chapter 5 outlined the costs of raw materials in detail.)

BUSINESS
—FACT—

Some manufactured products can be used as raw materials, for example, tires, bottles, or nails.

Goods in Process

At the end of each day, most manufacturing businesses have materials that are only partly processed. A bakery, for example, may have bread dough. The dough has used up the raw materials and, eventually, it will become bread, but as dough it cannot be accounted for as either a raw material or a finished product. Manufacturing accounting, therefore, keeps track of **goods in process**. This category records the costs of all the partially finished goods at inventory time, which is normally the end of the fiscal year.

Direct Labour

In manufacturing, labour is not only an expense of doing business; it is also an ingredient in the finished product. If a baker bakes 200 loaves in an hour and is paid $20 an hour, each loaf includes 10¢ worth of the baker's labour (200 ÷ 20 = 10). The baker's work is called **direct labour** because it is directly involved in the manufacturing process. In a manufacturing business, the cost of direct labour is added to the cost of the finished product.

Direct labour is different from labour in departments that are not directly involved in the manufacturing process, for example, in human resources or marketing. Labour in these departments is known as **indirect labour**. It is not included as a cost of the product. As in retail and other service businesses, the costs of indirect labour are deducted from the gross profit.

Finished Goods

One of the main functions of accounting in a manufacturing business is to calculate the cost of a finished product. This cost is then used to calculate a selling price that generates a profit. To calculate the cost of a finished product, the accountant first calculates the cost of raw materials and then adds the cost of the direct labour used to make the finished goods. Finally, the accountant adds in the **factory overhead**, or the expenses involved in operating all the production facilities, for example, utilities, rent, and insurance. The total of the costs of raw materials, direct labour, and factory overhead equals the cost of the finished goods.

Cost of Raw Materials + Cost of Direct Labour + Factory Overhead = Cost of Finished Goods

The formula is quite simple. But imagine how complex the accounting system of a large manufacturing company would be. McCain's, for example, must calculate the cost of each product it makes. Each product will have a different cost. McCain's frozen orange juice, for example, will not cost the same as its frozen lemonade.

1. a) Why do retailers need a different kind of accounting system than other kinds of service businesses?

b) Why is inventory control important to retailers?

c) What business in your community would use both retail and service-business accounting methods? Why would it need both?

2. a) What accounting categories do manufacturers use that retail and other service businesses do not use?

b) Why must a manufacturer consider each of the categories you mentioned in Question 2a?

c) Calculate the actual cost of a sandwich that you would have for lunch. Share your findings with a classmate to check each other's work for possible omissions. How can you reduce the costs of the sandwich? Explain.

The Balance Sheet

A **balance sheet** is a financial statement that shows the financial position of a business on a single, specific date. It is a snapshot of the business at a given moment in time—what you see today is different from yesterday and will be different again tomorrow. The balance sheet does not indicate whether a business has made a profit, only whether it is financially strong. The balance sheet does this by presenting the assets, liabilities, and owner's equity at a specific moment in time.

ASSETS

As you read in Chapter 4, assets are things of value that are owned. An owner can sell assets, use them, give them away, or leave them to heirs. Some assets, such as cars, are often purchased on credit. Buying something on credit does not make it any less of an asset because it is still the owner's property. He or she can drive it anywhere or paint it any colour. If the owner sells the car, however, he or she must pay the lender any money owed on the car. (See Chapter 14 for more information on credit.)

Businesses also have assets: inventory, cash, vehicles, buildings, machinery, office equipment, and so on. Money owed to a business is also considered an asset because the business can expect to receive payment of these debts. Debts owed by customers, suppliers, etc. are called **accounts receivable**, or simply **receivables**. Businesses use

Did You Know?

Business assets can include logos as well as patents and trademarks, which indicate ownership of ideas, formulas, or designs that the business developed.

Office furniture, telephones, computers, and even binders are all part of this business's assets.

their assets to conduct their affairs. For example, they manufacture goods with the machinery, sell their inventory at a profit, or use their cash to invest in the company.

Businesses categorize their assets into two types: current assets and long-term (or capital) assets. **Current assets** are the things a business owns that disappear quickly, usually in less than one year. A store's inventory, for example, is sold within a few months, or a soft drink manufacturer's supply of sugar gets used within a few weeks. Receivables become a cash asset when payments are received. Businesses spend cash (the most current asset of all) on a daily basis.

Long-term assets or **capital assets**, such as furniture, vehicles, equipment, property, and fixtures, are all assets that businesses keep for a long time. Often, these long-term assets are crucial. If a manufacturing business does not have the machinery to make its product, for example, it will not be able to do business.

Cash is perhaps the most valuable asset for a business because it has **liquidity**. A liquid asset can be easily exchanged for any other asset or turned into cash. On the other hand, machinery used in manufacturing is not liquid: It can never be sold, unless it is being upgraded or replaced, and cannot easily be exchanged for cash.

BUSINESS
—FACT—
Businesses list assets on their balance sheet in order of liquidity.

LIABILITIES

Liabilities are the debts of a business. Businesses acquire debt in two main ways. One way is by purchasing inventory and supplies on credit. This kind of debt is called **accounts payable**, or simply **payables**. Businesses can also acquire debt by borrowing money from investors, banks, or other financial institutions. This kind of debt is called **loans payable**, or **notes payable**.

Businesses pay off some debts, such as invoices for merchandise inventory, very quickly. These kinds of debts are recorded as **current liabilities**. In some cases, however, businesses borrow with a longer repayment period. For example, a new **mortgage loan** (a debt taken on to purchase real estate) will not be repaid for decades. These types of debts are called **long-term liabilities**.

EQUITY

The third element of the balance sheet is **owner's equity**. This is the owner's investment in the business, or the financial portion of the business that actually belongs to the owner. As an example of owner's equity, consider a family that purchases a house for $150 000. The family makes a $40 000 down payment and takes out a mortgage loan for the remaining $110 000. The owner's initial equity in the house is $40 000.

As the owner makes mortgage payments, the amount owing on the house becomes less and less. Equity in the house grows. Once the mortgage is paid off, the house is pure equity; in other words, the family owns it completely. Similarly, a business may start out with high liabilities. As the business grows, however, it can pay off its liabilities and increase its equity. Owner's equity is expressed on the balance sheet in many different ways. Equity in corporations is known as **shareholders' equity** because the shareholders are the only owners.

The Accounting Equation

You may have noticed that assets, liabilities, and owner's equity are related to each other. But how, exactly? Think back to the example of the house. As an asset, the house had a mortgage liability that prevented the full value of the house from being equity. When it was purchased, the $150 000 asset had a $110 000 mortgage. The equity in the house was $40 000—the amount of the family's down payment. This relationship can be expressed as an equation:

$$\text{Assets} = \text{Liabilities} + \text{Owner's Equity}$$

This equation can also be expressed as follows:

$$\text{Owner's Equity} = \text{Assets} - \text{Liabilities}$$
$$\text{Liabilities} = \text{Assets} - \text{Owner's Equity}$$

Measuring Business Success with Balance Sheets

Management uses balance sheets to see any changes that have taken place within a business and to identify any problems or challenges that the business faces. Figure 8.1 shows a comparative balance sheet for Baxter–Hunt Medical Supplies, for February 29, 2000 and February 28, 2001.

Figure 8.1

Baxter–Hunt Medical Supplies
Comparative Balance Sheet

	February 28, 2001		February 29, 2000	
ASSETS				
Current Assets				
Cash	$ 47 000		$ 27 000	
Accounts Receivable	65 000		39 000	
Merchandise Inventory	125 000		210 000	
Supplies	26 000		18 000	
Total Current Assets		$263 000		$294 000
Capital Assets				
Furniture	$ 34 000		$ 34 000	
Equipment	154 000		127 000	
Delivery Trucks	150 000		180 000	
Total Capital Assets		338 000		341 000
TOTAL ASSETS		$601 000		$635 000
LIABILITIES AND OWNERS' EQUITY				
Current Liabilities				
Accounts Payable	$100 000		$125 000	
Long-term Liabilities				
Bank Loan	70 000		100 000	
TOTAL LIABILITIES		$170 000		$225 000
Owners' Equity				
Emily Baxter	$215 500		$205 000	
Jessie Hunt	215 500		205 000	
TOTAL OWNERS' EQUITY		431 000		410 000
TOTAL LIABILITIES AND OWNERS' EQUITY		$601 000		$635 000

According to Figure 8.1, Baxter–Hunt has had a big increase in cash, from $27 000 in 2000 to $47 000 in 2001. Baxter–Hunt's managers may decide that it needs to make better choices for what it does with cash beyond what is needed for day-to-day operations. For example, the business might pay off some of its liabilities, thereby reducing the interest it pays on its loans. Or it could acquire another asset, perhaps investing some of the money in bonds that pay a good interest rate. This type of investment would generate more income for the business: $25 000 invested at 8% would yield $2000 in one year.

The balance sheets would also show outside investors and banks that the owners' equity increased in the past year. Because liabilities also decreased by $55 000, Baxter–Hunt is in a good position to borrow money. Bankers or other creditors would also look at the business's liquidity to determine its ability to pay current liabilities without having to borrow or sell assets. Bankers, other creditors, and management use different calculations to analyze a business's liquidity. The two most basic calculations are those that determine working capital and the current ratio.

STRETCH YOUR THINKING

Figure 8.1 shows that the owners' equity increased from $410 000 on February 29, 2000 to $431 000 on February 28, 2001. Why might outside investors and bankers be interested in this information?

WORKING CAPITAL

Businesses should be able to pay all their debts when they are due. If a business cannot meet its payroll obligations on time, employees may quit. If rent is paid late, the landlord might obtain a legal notice to evict the business. A business that doesn't pay suppliers on time will have to pay extra money in interest penalties; the supplier may even stop shipping goods to the company. **Working capital** indicates a business's ability to pay its short-term debts. The formula is as follows:

Working Capital = Current Assets – Current Liabilities

In Figure 8.1, you can see that Baxter–Hunt's working capital for 2001 is $163 000 ($263 000 – $100 000 = $163 000). A bank would consider this amount of working capital a strong indication that the business can repay a short-term loan.

CURRENT RATIO

The **current ratio** shows how many dollars of liquid assets (cash or near cash) a business has for every dollar of short-term debt. It is calculated by dividing the total current assets by the total current liabilities.

Current Ratio = Total Current Assets ÷ Total Current Liabilities

The current ratio allows creditors and investors to tell very quickly whether a business can meet its short-term financial obligations. No investor wants to put money into a business that could be forced to close by creditors. Using Figure 8.1, you can calculate the current ratio for Baxter–Hunt in 2001: $263 000 ÷ $100 000 = 2.63. In other words, Baxter–Hunt has $2.63 of current assets for every $1 of current debt. This ratio indicates the debt could be paid off quickly if necessary. A current ratio that is too high may indicate poor management. For example, if a company's current ratio is 4 : 1, the company might have too much inventory or too many outstanding receivables that may be hard to collect.

ACTIVITIES FOR ...

INFORMATION	**C**ONNECTION	**E**XTENSION
1. a) What is a balance sheet? What aspects of a company's financial position are shown on a balance sheet?	**b)** Describe the differences between assets and equity.	**c)** List assets and liabilities that a business might have. Exchange your list with a partner. Tell whether each asset and liability is considered current or long term.
2. a) Identify the three parts of the accounting equation. What does each part refer to? How are these parts related?	**b)** Using an annual report, find a business's total current assets, total long-term assets, total assets, current liabilities, long-term liabilities, total liabilities, and owners' or shareholders' equity. Arrange the totals to illustrate the accounting equation.	**c)** What changes have taken place in the company you selected in Question 2b since the previous year? What might this indicate to management?
3. a) What two calculations measure a business's liquidity?	**b)** Calculate the working capital and current ratio for the company you selected in Question 2b.	**c)** Assume you are a potential investor for the company you selected in Question 2b. Using the working capital and current ratio, analyze the ability of your selected company to meet its short-term debt obligations.

The Income Statement

An **income statement** is a financial statement that shows a business's profitability over a stated period of time. Management can prepare income statements to track profit daily, monthly, or quarterly (every three months). Businesses are required by law to prepare an income statement at the end of every fiscal year. Every income statement shows revenue and expenses. As you learned earlier in this chapter, retail and other sales businesses must also show the cost of goods sold, and manufacturing businesses must show all the costs involved in making the finished product as well as the cost of goods sold.

Figure 8.2 shows a comparative income statement for Baxter–Hunt Medical Supplies. You will notice that, like for other sales businesses, this comparative income statement gives information on revenue, cost of goods sold, gross profit, operating expenses, and net profit.

Figure 8.2

Baxter–Hunt Medical Supplies
Comparative Income Statement

	For the Year Ending February 28, 2001		For the Year Ending February 29, 2000	
REVENUE				
Sales		$395 000		$338 000
Sales Returns		5 000		4 000
TOTAL REVENUE		$390 000		$334 000
COST OF GOODS SOLD				
Inventory March 1, 2000	$210 000		$300 000	
Purchases	65 000		70 000	
Goods Available for Sale	275 000		370 000	
Inventory February 28, 2001	125 000		210 000	
TOTAL COST OF GOODS SOLD		150 000		160 000
GROSS PROFIT		240 000		174 000
OPERATING EXPENSES				
Salaries	$108 000		$ 81 000	
Delivery Expenses	22 000		20 000	
Rent	38 000		38 000	
Telephone	3 800		3 400	
Utilities	3 200		3 200	
Insurance	4 800		4 800	
Advertising	19 000		15 000	
Interest and Bank Charges	1 200		2 400	
Supplies	6 000		4 200	
TOTAL EXPENSES		206 000		172 000
NET PROFIT		$ 34 000		$ 2 000

REVENUE

A business earns revenue, or income, from the sale of goods or services. It can earn this revenue from various sources. A beauty salon may get sales revenue from haircuts, perms, and hair colouring. It could sell shampoo, conditioner, and other beauty products. Baxter–Hunt sells oxygen, scalpels, and other supplies to hospitals, drug stores, and seniors' homes. It could also rent crutches and wheelchairs to customers who need these items on a temporary basis. Other revenue could be generated from interest on Baxter–Hunt's investments.

COST OF GOODS SOLD

An income statement includes information for a specific period of time on the cost of goods sold. The cost of goods sold is calculated using information collected from the balance sheet, from invoices that detail the year's purchases, and from the physical inventory count at the end of the fiscal year.

The merchandise inventory recorded on last year's balance sheet is the beginning inventory figure in the cost-of-goods-sold section. A business determines this figure by physically counting the inventory at the end of the fiscal year. For example, the merchandise inventory of Baxter–Hunt for the year ending February 29, 2000 is $210 000. (See Figure 8.1.) Therefore, $210 000 is the beginning inventory figure in the cost-of-goods-sold section of the income statement for the year ending February 28, 2001. (See Figure 8.2.) **Purchases** show the total amount of the goods bought by the business in a year. Purchases are calculated by examining invoices for the year, as recorded in the books of the business.

GROSS PROFIT

Gross profit was discussed earlier, but it is important to review it here. Once the cost of goods sold has been deducted from total revenue, a business is left with its gross profit. If no other expenses were involved in generating revenue, the owner can keep whatever money is left over after income taxes are paid.

OPERATING EXPENSES

Businesses almost always have expenses related to selling the goods and services they make or provide. These costs are called operating expenses or overhead. **Operating expenses** are the costs of operating the business during the period the sales took place. It is important that all the costs—and only the costs incurred for the specific period—are included in the statement. Accurate profit reporting can only be achieved if all the costs of doing business in a particular time period are matched with the revenue generated during this same period. This is called the **matching principle**.

NET PROFIT

As you read earlier in this chapter, net profit is gross profit minus operating expenses, or the amount of revenue left over after all expenses are deducted. Net profit increases equity. If the company's cash position allows, the company can pay down debt, make distributions to owners, buy assets that will help it expand operations, or make other investments.

Measuring Business Success with Income Statements

STRETCH YOUR THINKING

If an income statement shows a major increase in sales, what decisions might a business make as a result? What if the business shows a major decrease in sales?

If a balance sheet is a "snapshot" of a given moment in the life of a business, an income statement is a "movie" that tells about the company over a period of time. Owners or managers look at income statements to measure profitability and to see how expenses, paid from potential profit, are being managed. The comparative income statements for Baxter–Hunt (Figure 8.2) show that in both 2000 and 2001, Baxter–Hunt made a profit, but the profit in 2001 was much higher. What could account for this increase in profit? Baxter–Hunt's advertising expense increased in 2001, but advertising may have stimulated the increase in sales. The salary expense also went up by $27 000. If this expense was paid to a manager who helped the business achieve higher profits, it was money well spent.

Sales at Baxter–Hunt increased by $57 000 from 2000 to 2001. This increase in sales is significant, but it is positive only if it is followed by an increase in profit. Management looks at income statements to measure profitability. If the business has not lost money or broken even, then it has made a profit. Profit needs to be measured carefully. Two important ways to measure profit are to calculate the rate of return on net sales and the gross profit percentage.

RATE OF RETURN ON NET SALES

Rate of return on net sales indicates, as a percentage, the portion of business sales that are kept as profit. It is calculated by dividing net profit by total revenue.

> Rate of Return on Net Sales = (Net Profit ÷ Total Revenue) × 100%

Let's assume that a business makes $20 000 in profit. Whether this amount of profit is considered good or bad depends on how much revenue was taken in to produce that profit. If $20 000 is made on $100 000 in total revenue, the rate of return is 20% [($20 000 ÷ $100 000) × 100% = 20%]. If it took $200 000 in revenue to make $20 000, then the rate of return is 10% [($20 000 ÷ $200 000) × 100% = 10%]. A higher rate of return on sales means a more profitable company. In 2000, Baxter–Hunt had a very poor rate of return [($2000 ÷ $334 000) × 100% = 0.6%]. In 2001, the rate of return improved substantially [($34 000 ÷ $390 000) × 100% = 8.7%].

GROSS PROFIT PERCENTAGE

By expressing gross profit as a percentage of total revenue, management can see how much of its potential profit pays for product and how much pays for expenses.

> Gross Profit Percentage = (Gross Profit ÷ Total Revenue) × 100%

If a business has a high gross profit percentage, it means the business is earning a high margin on its sales. **Margin** is the difference between the cost of the product and the selling price of the product. The business should concentrate on managing expenses. If it does so successfully, the net profit will rise. But, if the gross profit percentage is low, then the business needs to try to reduce the costs of the products it buys, or charge more for the products it sells.

In 2000, Baxter–Hunt made $174 000 in gross profit, and its total revenue was $334 000. (See Figure 8.2.) Therefore, its gross profit was 52% [($174 000 ÷ $334 000) × 100%]. In 2001, its gross profit was 62% ($240 000 ÷ $390 000) × 100%]. This means that in 2000, 48% of Baxter–Hunt's revenue paid for goods sold (100% – 52% = 48%), and 52% was left to cover expenses. In 2001, Baxter–Hunt only used 38% of its revenue to pay for the goods that it sold (100% – 62% = 38%), leaving 62% of the revenue to pay for expenses. Management and investors would be very pleased to see that Baxter–Hunt can keep over 60% of its revenue to pay its expenses and share as net profit.

ACTIVITIES FOR ...

INFORMATION	CONNECTION	EXTENSION
1. a) What is an income statement? What are the key elements of an income statement?	**b)** How are each of the following calculated: total revenue, cost of goods sold, gross profit, total expenses, and net profit?	**c)** If Baxter–Hunt only rented equipment to people who needed it and was, therefore, a pure service business, how would its income statement be different? Be specific.
2. a) List three ways that a business can increase profit.	**b)** Give at least five specific ways that Baxter–Hunt could increase its profits.	**c)** What do you think Baxter–Hunt should do with its profit?
3. a) What two measurements are used to indicate a firm's profitability? How are these measurements calculated?	**b)** Using an annual report from any company you choose, calculate the rate of return on net sales for that company. Compare your results with those of at least three other classmates. In your group, rank the companies in terms of which made the most money. Then rank the companies according to which one had the highest rate of return on sales. Do the lists match?	**c)** Consider the companies you examined in Question 3b. In which company would you like to invest? Why?

Cash Flow

Cash flow is the movement of cash in and out of a business. The **statement of cash flow** reports on a business's cash flow over a stated period of time. For example, a business might prepare a projected statement of cash flow to estimate the amount of cash it will likely receive in a given period of time and the amount of regular and extra expenses it will have to pay in that time. Sources of cash include sales, interest received from investments, accounts receivable that will be collected, the sale of capital equipment, new loans, and investments. Regular expenses such as rent, payroll, accounts payable, interest payable, and insurance can be listed fairly accurately. Extra payments such as the purchase of capital assets and payment of loan principal are harder to predict but must be carefully considered.

By examining the cash-in and cash-out sections of a statement of cash flow, a business must predict whether it will have enough cash to meet obligations. If it will not, the business must take steps to correct the problem. These steps could include extra investment (for example, an infusion of capital from the owner, a short-term loan from a bank, or finding a partner or investor), reducing inventory purchases (to keep accounts payable down), and increasing activity to collect accounts receivable. At the end of the stated period, the budgeted cash flow is updated to include the actual numbers. In this way, predictions can be validated or changed as needed. Annual reports include a more complicated type of statement of cash flow that summarizes a business's cash-in and cash-out transactions and its cash position at the beginning and end of the fiscal year.

Big-Box Stores and Cash Flow

Big-box stores, such as Business Depot, often operate in a way that enables them to generate a positive cash flow. How do they do this?

Most big-box stores ask customers to pay in cash or use a credit or debit card. Using these methods of payment means that the stores do not have to wait for their money (accounts receivable). Instead, the stores get their money (sales revenue) up front. On the opposite side of the cash flow, big-box stores often take as long as possible to pay their own bills (accounts payable). In the interim, they may invest their "customers' cash" to make "money on money." In many cases, these stores actually make as much or more on their money-on-money investments as they do from selling the goods in the stores. A business with a positive cash flow has more money on hand than it needs to meet all of its short-term commitments. A positive cash flow is an objective that almost every business strives to achieve.

A FINAL MEASURE OF SUCCESS

An owner's equity in a business is an investment. By spending the time and effort to run the business, risking capital, and worrying daily about its success or failure, the owner hopes to see a return on his or her investment. What kind of return can an owner reasonably expect? To consider a business successful, the return should be equal to or greater than the return if the owner had simply put the money in a savings account or invested the money in a bond or mutual fund.

Businesses use the **rate of return on average owner's equity** to determine their success. This figure is calculated by dividing a business's net profit by the average owner's equity.

Rate of Return on Average Owner's Equity = (Net Profit ÷ Average Owner's Equity) × 100%

First, calculate the average owner's equity for two years. To do this, add the owner's equity from two consecutive years and divide by two. For example, using Figure 8.1, the average owner's equity for Baxter–Hunt was $420 500.

Average Owner's Equity = (Total Owners' Equity for 2000 + Total Owners' Equity for 2001) ÷ 2
= ($410 000 + $431 000) ÷ 2
= $841 000 ÷ 2
= $420 500

The second step is to divide the business's net profit by the average owner's equity, and then multiply the result by 100 to convert this figure to a percentage. Using Figure 8.2, Baxter–Hunt's rate of return on average owner's equity for the year ending February 28, 2001 was 8.1%.

Rate of Return on Average Owner's Equity = (Net Profit ÷ Average Owner's Equity) × 100%
= ($34 000 ÷ $420 500) × 100%
= 0.081 × 100%
= 8.1%

Can Baxter–Hunt Medical Supplies earn more? Depending on current interest rates, the state of the economy, and the risk level of the company's investments, the answer is "perhaps." By leaving the equity in the business, the owners of Baxter–Hunt have some control over what it earns. The business is growing and earning more profit each year. The opportunities for equity growth within the business seem greater than the opportunities for the same equity growing in investments outside the business. By this measure, then, Baxter–Hunt Medical Supplies is a successful business.

ACTIVITIES FOR ...

INFORMATION	**C**ONNECTION	**E**XTENSION
1. a) Define "cash flow."	**b)** Why is it important to consider cash flow?	**c)** Predict and record your actual cash flow for one month.
2. a) Why would a business owner want to know the rate of return on average owner's equity?	**b)** What steps could a business take if it did not have enough cash to meet its financial obligations?	**c)** If you could earn the same rate of return by operating a business as by leaving the money in a savings account, what would you do? Consider the pros and cons of each decision.

Review

Knowledge and Understanding

1. Match each of the following terms to the correct definition:

   balance sheet   liquidity
   fiscal year   net profit
   gross profit   operating expenses
   income statement   owner's equity
   liabilities   revenue

   a) The cost of doing business for a particular period.
   b) All the money left over after deducting the cost of goods sold from the revenue, but before deducting the business expenses that helped generate the revenue.
   c) All the money a business receives from the sale of goods or services.
   d) A financial statement that shows the profitability of a business over a stated period of time.
   e) A business year.
   f) How quickly assets can be turned into, or generate, cash.
   g) The owner's investment in the business.
   h) The money left over once operating expenses have been deducted from gross profit.
   i) A business's debts.
   j) A statement that shows the financial position of a business on a single, specific date.

2. Your business started the month of November with $140 000 in inventory, had total revenue of $82 000 for the month, ended November with inventory of $145 000, and made purchases throughout the month equalling $37 000.
   a) What was your gross profit for November?
   b) If your business had operating expenses of $41 800, what was the rate of return on net sales?
   c) Your business had current assets of $320 000 and current liabilities of $80 000. Calculate the working capital and the current ratio.

Thinking and Inquiry

1. Increasing sales can increase profit in a business. Suggest how a business might increase sales. When would increasing sales not increase profits?

2. Describe how owner's equity is related to liability.

3. What is the dollar difference between the Total Liabilities and Owners' Equity sections on the 2000 and 2001 balance sheets of Baxter–Hunt Medical Supplies (Figure 8.1)? How does this figure relate to Baxter–Hunt's income statement for 2001 (Figure 8.2)? Explain your findings.

4. In what ways is a balance sheet related to an income statement?

Communication

1. Use pictures from magazines, old annual reports, publications from businesses in your community, or pictures that you've drawn to illustrate the differences between a manufacturing business, a retail business, and other service businesses that affect each type of business's accounting methods.

2. Prepare a summary and critique of an annual report. Focus on the annual report as a document, not on the business itself. You might consider the following questions:
   • How informative was the CEO's letter to the shareholders?
   • How lavish was the use of colour?
   • How interesting was the report?
   • What other aspects of the report would catch the eye of a potential investor?
   Discuss your impressions with a small group.

3. Select a business. Collect several years' worth of the business's annual reports. Assume the role of a corporate director and prepare a report summarizing the company's successes and failures during the period. Present your report as if you were at a directors' meeting. Predict whether the company is heading toward success or failure.

Application

1. Examine Table 8.1. Why is the "Actual Sales" box not completed for 2001?

Table 8.1 Sample Inventory Budget for a Retail Store

Year	Actual Sales	Budgeted Sales	Inventory Budget
1999	$152 000	$145 000	$75 000
2000	$158 000	$160 000	$80 000
2001		$165 000	$82 500

E-ACTIVITY

Visit
www.business.
nelson.com
and follow the links
to learn more about
the accounting
profession.

2. Using an accounting text in your school, the Internet, the local library, or any other resource, find one more financial measurement that a business can use to determine its economic health. Apply this measurement to Baxter–Hunt Medical Supplies. Prepare a short report on your findings. Share the report with a small group.

3. Find out what an accountant does and what education an accountant requires by interviewing a local accountant, job shadowing an accountant for a day, or by working in an accounting office as a cooperative placement.

REFLECT ON YOUR LEARNING

1. Go back to the Before You Begin question on page 176. What things would you now add to your lists of expenses and assets?

2. Find out what types of financial records your family keeps. What information is on these records? How do these records help your family manage its money?

THE ROLE AND FUNCTIONS OF MARKETING

STUDENT EXPECTATIONS

After completing this chapter, you will be able to

- explain the role and importance of marketing
- describe traditional and non-traditional product life cycles
- analyze the role of brand management throughout a product life cycle
- demonstrate an understanding of business strategies used to manage brands
- compare various methods of marketing research
- explain the process of product development
- give examples of distribution methods
- describe the role of advertising in business
- give examples of activities used to promote sales

Profile

Andy Levy (left) and Jonathan Levy, cofounders of Mastermind Educational Technologies.

CERTAIN TOYS ARE US

Scene 1: Toys "R" Us—the Barbie section, midday. Myles Munshaw and his five-year-old daughter saunter through the canyons of brand name products. There are summer specials up front, Sega down that aisle, dolls over here. Munshaw's daughter gets to choose a toy today for having braved a needle at the doctor's office. Munshaw is not particularly interested in customer service. The little girl will find what she wants, which is to say she'll find the brand name goods. "She likes everything she sees on TV," he muses.

Scene 2: Mastermind—an hour later. Tanya Dorbyk has two boys, wears a crisp grey business suit, and looks to be in a terrific hurry. But not to worry: Mastermind has five sales clerks on high alert, answers at the ready. The store looks like a thoughtfully stocked playroom. That suits Dorbyk, who hates the toys promoted on Saturday morning cartoons. She wants something different, with an educational twist and a shelf life of more than a week. "I don't want my kids to be into all that stuff [on TV]," she says. "I'd prefer to get something they don't have." And come to think of it, she'd prefer it gift-wrapped, which the smiling, apron-wearing staff at Mastermind will do for free.

Welcome to the two solitudes of the toy industry. One—dominated by Toys "R" Us and Wal-Mart—is sustained by brand name toys, whose sales are driven by television advertising, Disney's merchandising blitzes, and the latest trends in the schoolyard. The other—populated by independent stores and a few mid-sized chains—is the "specialty retail" sector, which focuses on pricier, higher-quality, trend-proof toys.

Mastermind Educational Technologies Inc., a Toronto-area chain that won the Canadian toy industry's prize for top retailer in 1999, operates on the specialty side. It's a pioneer, in fact, although specialty lately has become all the rage in the toy industry. With nine locations and an e-tailing operation (mastermindtoys.com), Mastermind is the ambitious parent's toy store of choice. Its stock includes science and craft kits, children's books, and gorgeous, but very expensive, wooden train sets.

CONTINUED →

So choosing toys for a chain such as Mastermind must be one of the most fun things an adult can do, right? Jonathan Levy, who cofounded the chain with elder brother Andy and serves as the head buyer, says, "The toy industry is a serious, competitive business. But we try not to let the fun come out of it." He and Andy travel extensively to international trade shows to find the newest and best stuff. Judging by the reputation he's developed among suppliers, he's still tapped in to the original point of toys. "They joke that if it flies, bounces, or can be thrown, I'll stop at the booth," he says, flashing a grin.

Although mass merchandisers now account for at least 65% of the country's $1 billion in toy sales, Mastermind has managed to remain competitive. "They know their market," says Graham Kennedy, publisher of Toronto-based *Toys and Games Magazine*. The Levys offer neighbourly service, and merchandise their wares in a kid-friendly style that contrasts sharply with the industrial shelving of the big-box stores. They provide display models and bathrooms. The former encourages return business, the latter long visits.

During one Christmas season, Mastermind was the only Canadian retailer to stock a new high-concept contraption called Music Blocks. This toy allows toddlers to scramble prerecorded classical tunes by manipulating coloured cubes. The company sold 700 units, at a hundred bucks a pop, presumably to those parents who've come to believe the faddish theory that Mozart makes better babies.

While they've passed on many trendy toys, like the Pog discs from several years back, Mastermind does sell Pokémon merchandise. "You can't pull in your horns and say, 'I'm not going to carry Lego because Wal-Mart carries Lego,' " says Jonathan. But they make choices and avoid picking fights with the mass merchandisers.

"The toy industry is a serious, competitive business. But we try not to let the fun come out of it."

About This Profile

1. What types of products does Mastermind sell? Who are its main competitors?
2. How does Mastermind remain competitive in the Canadian toy industry?
3. What group of consumers is the target market for Mastermind?
4. If you were a buyer for Mastermind, what sorts of products would you look for? How could a toy manufacturer convince you that its product was right for Mastermind?

The Role and Importance of Marketing

BEFORE YOU BEGIN

List the different ways that businesses try to influence your buying decisions through advertising and marketing.

Marketing is the term used to describe all the activities involved in getting goods and services from the businesses that produce them to the consumers who wish to purchase them. Marketing includes research, development, sales, distribution, advertising, and promotion. It does not include the actual production of goods and services.

Without marketing, not much would get sold. Consumers wouldn't know what goods and services were available. They wouldn't know about new trends or fashions, or how products have been improved. Manufacturers wouldn't know what to make. Importers, wholesalers, and retailers wouldn't know what to carry. Marketing is important to all businesses—it often means the difference between success and failure. Marketing ensures that businesses actually sell the goods and services they offer.

BRAND MANAGEMENT: THE PRODUCT LIFE CYCLE

Every product has a brand. In Chapter 6, you learned how brands help businesses and their products establish an identity in the competitive marketplace. In Chapter 10, you will learn how stores and businesses create different kinds of brand names for different markets. The primary function of any business's marketing department is to manage that business's brand or brands. Marketers create plans for distributing, promoting, pricing, and developing the business's brand(s). They also help put these plans into action.

To effectively market a brand, marketers must know where the brand is in terms of the **product life cycle**. The traditional product life cycle consists of five parts: product introduction, growth, maturity, decline, and decision point. A graph of the product life cycle, which can also be called the **style curve**, illustrates product sales over time. Almost all products are popular for a period of time and then their popularity declines. Some products, from automobiles to fashions, are designed to be in style for only one season.

Figure 9.1

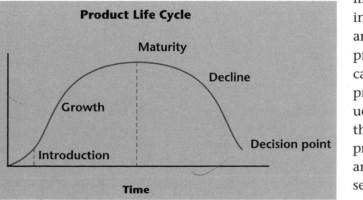

Product Introduction

The product enters the marketplace through a product introduction, often called a **launch**. Sometimes, businesses introduce a product nationally or even internationally. At other times, they introduce their products by city, region, or province. At the introduction stage of the product life cycle, consumers don't even know that the product exists. The business needs to inform them about the product's features, availability, package design, and brand identification. Usually, curious or adventurous consumers (or consumers who like to be the first to own new products) buy the product first.

Marketers often call these first consumers **early adopters**. Other consumers look to early adapters, or trendsetters, for style information. Trendsetters can be celebrities, sports heroes, politicians, or even students in your school. Professional athletes often help businesses introduce new products. When a television star wears a new hairstyle, for example, fans of that star often copy him or her. Other early adopters copy the clothing and dress styles worn by famous people at celebrity events such as award shows.

During the introduction stage, marketers focus on selling to early adopters. Early adopters tend to read style magazines such as *Flare*, *Cosmopolitan*, or *GQ*. They attend parties, galas, openings, award ceremonies, and charity events. Their photos appear in newspapers and magazines, and they're regularly followed by celebrity news and entertainment programs.

Dress designers, jewellery manufacturers, hair stylists, cosmetics companies, and many other businesses often provide their products to early adopters for free—and not just to the rich and famous. In the U.S., for example, Nike supplies free basketball shoes to star players on high school teams. If these basketball players wear the shoes, other early adopters may see the product and want to try it, too.

Many products, however, are introduced without elaborate planning. A new yogurt, for example, doesn't need the same publicity as a new designer's fashion line. In the case of a new yogurt, advertising campaigns and sales promotions (including free trials) promote the product in its introductory stage. (Advertising campaigns and sales promotions will be discussed later in this chapter.)

Growth

Once early adopters find and use a new product, others soon try it and sales increase rapidly. The original kick scooter, called "The Razor," is an example of a product that moved through the introductory stage very rapidly. JD Corporation introduced the scooter in Taiwan and Japan in 1996, then in North America in 1998. The product attracted

STRETCH YOUR THINKING

How do styles become popular in your school? For what new product would you be considered an early adopter?

the interest of early adopters, and its popularity skyrocketed in only a couple of years.

During the growth stage, marketers manage their products very carefully. As a product's popularity increases, competitors enter the market. These competitors modify the original product either by adding features and improving quality or by making a similar product more cheaply and offering it at a lower price. Within two years of the Razor's introduction, other brands of kick scooters flooded the market, including Vapor, Just-Go, Flying, and Royce Union. The marketers at JD Corporation had to keep a close eye on the competition.

A fight for market share usually leaves casualties. If a business doesn't make a profit on a particular product, it either moves into other product lines or it fails. The businesses that survive advertise and distribute their products as widely as possible. Consumers see the product everywhere—those who want to buy the product know what to buy and where to buy it.

BUSINESS
—FACT—

Many brands fail simply because there are not enough buyers in the market.

Maturity

At the maturity stage, growth is flat—it does not increase or decrease. New consumers replace those who leave to purchase a competing product. Companies manage mature products through continued advertising. This advertising keeps the brand in the public eye and reminds consumers of the advantages this product has over the competition. Kellogg's Corn Flakes, Coca-Cola, and Ganong chocolates are all products at the maturity stage.

By the time a product reaches maturity, the manufacturer has long since paid for all the major costs of production and product development. Because a mature product has established, effective distribution methods, the costs of sales and distribution are low. As a result, products at the maturity stage usually make large profits. Businesses can use income generated by their mature products, often called **cash cows**, to develop and fund new products.

Decline

At some point, most products fail to attract new customers to replace the customers who leave to buy other brands. As sales decrease, the product enters the decline stage. Seasonal changes or new competition may cause a temporary decline. But if the decline continues, businesses research their markets to determine whether consumers are actually rejecting the brand. A small change in price or a new advertising campaign can reverse a temporary decline. If, on the other hand, consumers just decide to no longer buy the brand, then the business has a serious problem.

At the final stage of the product life cycle, the decision point, marketers make very important brand-management decisions. Often, they reformulate, repackage, and reintroduce a "new and improved" product. For example, an old brand of liquid detergent could reenter the market with a convenient new pour spout.

Most often, however, decision-point management involves new promotion and repricing. An advertising agency, for example, might develop a campaign to target a new segment of the market. If the campaign succeeds, the brand becomes more popular. A lower price may also boost the brand's popularity. If these marketing strategies work, the brand regains its original sales figures. If the decline continues in spite of efforts to stop it, the manufacturer discontinues the product and removes it from the market.

NON-TRADITIONAL PRODUCT LIFE CYCLES

Many products do not go through the stages of the traditional product life cycle. There are at least three non-traditional product life cycles: fad, niche, and seasonal. These life cycles are shown in Figure 9.2.

Fads

A **fad** is a product that is extremely popular for a very short period of time. You may remember the Tamagotchi craze in the late 1990s. Tamagotchis were digital pets on a key chain that you could "hug" and "feed" by pushing buttons. If you didn't care for the Tamagotchi properly, it "died." The fad lasted about six months, and then it died. Even so, many imitation products entered the market during this short period.

Companies can make or lose a great deal of money on fads. If a business can sell most of its stock and get out of the market for this product just as the fad reaches its peak, the business will make an excellent profit. Many fad marketers—especially imitators who create a cheaper version of the fad, called a **knockoff**—enter the market at the wrong time, or stay too long. When a fad dies, it dies very quickly, and many businesses get caught with a large product inventory that no one wants to buy.

STRETCH YOUR THINKING

Think of a product whose popularity has declined. Who is the target market for this product? Who else might an advertising agency target to increase sales?

Before the Tamagotchi craze died, this girl had received five Tamagotchis as gifts.

Figure 9.2

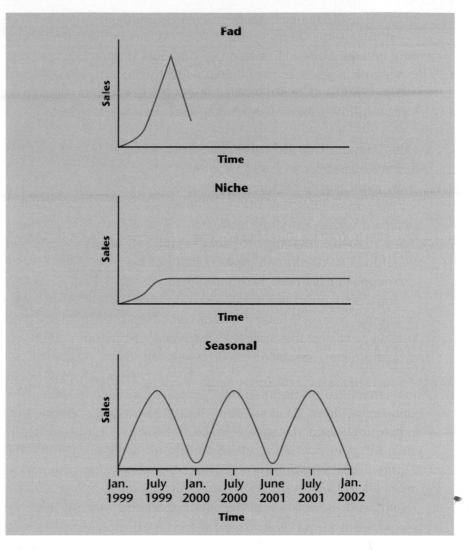

Niches

Some products have a very short growth stage that leads to a solid, but not financially spectacular, maturity stage. These products have a **niche**—a section of the market in which they dominate and into which very few competitors enter. Niche marketers usually invent their products and hold exclusive patents or formulas. By the time other businesses can invent a competing product, the original manufacturer has already distributed its brand to most of the businesses or stores that wish to purchase it. Competitors, then, have no one to sell their product to. Often, niche marketers manufacture specialty parts. Recently, niche marketers have shown rapid growth in the high-tech industry, manufacturing specialized computer parts for large computer firms.

Barriers to Entry

Many factors prevent competitors from being profitable in a given market. These factors, called **barriers to entry**, include the small market size, the cost of research and development, advertising expenses, factory and equipment costs, design costs, lack of distribution channels, and the cost of raw materials. High barriers to entry usually mean that competitors don't enter a market, leaving a niche marketer alone.

Seasonal

Try to sell a Christmas tree the day after Christmas, or a snow blower on the hottest day in August. Ice-cream parlours have lineups from July to the end of August, but are often closed in January and February. These examples demonstrate that many products are popular only during a specific time or season. The product becomes popular again only when the season returns. The new season, however, brings with it new styles. Even Christmas ornaments change in style from year to year. Retailers, wholesalers, importers, and manufacturers of seasonal products need to make the most of their selling season. These businesses must keep adequate stock. However, if they have too much inventory left over at the end of the season, many of the products will be out of style when the season starts again the next year. This balancing of product quantity with sales is called **inventory management**.

ACTIVITIES FOR ...

INFORMATION	**C**ONNECTION	**E**XTENSION
1. a) Define "marketing."	**b)** Choose a product that you purchased recently. Create a poster that illustrates all the marketing activities involved in getting that product from the manufacturer to you.	**c)** Describe the relationship between the marketing department of a business and the other departments.
2. a) List and briefly describe the five stages of the traditional product life cycle.	**b)** Choose five products. Tell what stage of the traditional product life cycle each product is in. Explain your reasoning.	**c)** Research a product that is no longer manufactured or sold, for example, a toy. Why do you think the business decided to discontinue the product?
3. a) Describe three non-traditional product life cycles.	**b)** For each of the non-traditional product life cycles, name five products that go through that cycle.	**c)** Assume that you invented a new product. Briefly describe any barriers to entry into the market that you can anticipate.

Brand Management Strategies

To market their products effectively, marketers develop brand management strategies. A **strategy** is a plan for achieving goals. Most marketing strategies try to increase brand awareness, sales, and market share. There are two major marketing strategies: the push strategy and the pull strategy.

The Push Strategy

Usually, a manufacturer's customers are not people who shop in a store. The manufacturer's customers are importers, wholesalers, and retailers who buy large quantities of goods and resell them through channels of distribution. **Channels of distribution** are the paths of ownership that goods follow as they pass from the producer to the consumer. These channels will be discussed later in this chapter.

The main goal of the **push strategy** is to sell products to the retailer. The retailer then sells the product to the consumer. Marketers who use the push strategy want their products to occupy good retail floor or shelf space. Consider Jones Soda, a relatively new soft drink that is manufactured in British Columbia. If the Jones Soda Co. wants you to buy its products, it must make them available for you to purchase. In Halifax, retailers may be less likely to place Jones Soda on their shelves. They already carry Coke, Pepsi, Canada Dry, and other soft drinks made locally. Why would they devote space, which could be used to sell well-known products, to an unknown and unproven brand?

The marketers of Jones Soda could offer the Halifax retailer a special deal—the company might sell to the retailer at a lower price, which could increase the store's gross profit. Jones Soda might offer a special cooler to display the soft drinks so that the store doesn't have to rearrange shelf space in order to make room for the new product. Or the company might offer incentives, such as trips or prizes, to the store that sells the most Jones Soda products. Sometimes, the manufacturer pays the retailer a special fee to help offset the costs of advertising and rearranging the shelves to stock a product. This fee is called a **shelf allowance**, and it is quite controversial.

Recently, Jones Soda used an innovative push strategy to distribute its product—the company placed special coolers in trendy clothing stores to attract the attention of young people shopping. The purpose of this strategy was to get these young shoppers to try the drink. At the very least, the coolers made the main target market (young people)

STRETCH YOUR THINKING

Why do you think shelf allowances are so controversial? Look back to information about the Competition Act in Chapter 6 to help you with your response.

aware of Jones Soda and linked the product with trendy fashions. And because the clothing stores had no floor space committed to selling other brands of pop, Jones Soda didn't have to compete with other soft-drink companies.

THE PULL STRATEGY

The **pull strategy** attempts to increase consumer demand directly, rather than appealing to retailers. If a manufacturer can convince consumers that they want or need a product, consumers will insist that local retailers carry the product. This demand pulls consumers into stores, looking for the product. The retailer sees the demand and orders in great quantity. Most often, businesses create this kind of brand awareness through advertising and promotional activities.

Push, Pull, or Both?

Consumers often buy products that they see and like, regardless of the brand (as long as they are willing to pay the price). For example, most people do not pay attention to the brand of coffee mugs, dishtowels, or pencils that they buy. It makes sense, then, for marketers to focus on selling these products to retailers rather than advertising to consumers. These marketers use only the push strategy.

The pull strategy, on the other hand, cannot be used alone. It is always used with a push strategy. When the manufacturer spends a great deal of money on advertising and promotion (pull strategy) to create consumer demand and awareness (push strategy), it is usually easier for the manufacturer to sell its product to the retailer.

ACTIVITIES FOR ...

INFORMATION	**C**ONNECTION	**E**XTENSION
1. a) What is the main goal of the push strategy?	**b)** What advantages and disadvantages are there to a retailer in devoting shelf or floor space to an unknown and unproven brand?	**c)** Interview the owner of a local retail store. Collect samples of ads, flyers, or other materials that demonstrate the types of push strategies that manufacturers use to sell their products to the store.
2. a) How is the pull strategy different from the push strategy?	**b)** Why can a pull strategy not be used on its own?	**c)** Choose a product. Tell what strategy or strategies you would use to manage that product.

Marketing Research

Marketing research is the collection and analysis of information that is relevant to the marketing strategy. There are several different types of marketing research, including consumer, market, motivation, pricing, competitive, product, and advertising research. Marketers do not use every type of research in every situation. Instead, they select which type to use based on what information they require, how they want to collect the information, and what they are going to do with the information after it has been analyzed.

CONSUMER RESEARCH

Consumer research discovers what type of product consumers want, and predicts overall sales potential for that product. Researchers use primary-data collection methods, such as phone surveys and personal interviews, to get actual consumer opinions. **Primary data** is current information that researchers collect and analyze for a specific purpose. **Secondary data** is information that others have collected. Researchers reinterpret this information for their own or their clients' purposes.

What comments might this focus group make about different types of audiocassettes?

One of the most popular forms of consumer research is the focus group. A **focus group** is a company-arranged meeting of potential consumers. Marketers observe the focus group during an organized discussion. The meeting usually lasts a few hours, and there is often an incentive for consumers to participate. For example, the company might offer participants a meal, product samples, or money. Before Nike introduced a line of soccer shoes in North America, it had to determine that there was a large enough market for the product. Nike organized several focus groups of soccer players. Interviewers asked people of various ages and skill levels questions in a group discussion. With the participants' permission, Nike marketers observed and taped the discussion. (See Chapter 17 for more information about consumer research.)

MARKET RESEARCH

Market research identifies specific groups of consumers who would use a particular product or service. Then, marketers create profiles of these groups using demographic and psychographic studies.

MOTIVATION RESEARCH

Motivation research analyzes the psychology of consumer behaviour. This type of research helps marketers determine what kind of advertising and promotion they should use to sell their products to their chosen target markets. Motivation research examines both the emotional (the way we feel) and the rational (the way we think) motives that influence our buying decisions. It tries to find out why we buy.

PRICING RESEARCH

Pricing research establishes the prices that businesses charge for their products. Pricing research helps the marketer determine if the company can sell the product for a competitive price and still make a profit. Pricing research also looks at how different prices affect demand and, consequently, sales. The relationship between price and sales isn't simple. Often, it makes sense to introduce a product at a low price to help establish it in the market. At first, the profits may be low, but as the product's sales increase, so do profits.

COMPETITIVE RESEARCH

Competitive research studies all similar products on the market. By studying the competition, businesses can avoid repeating the mistakes of other businesses. Marketers also look for opportunities in areas where competition is weak or absent.

PRODUCT RESEARCH

Product research examines each detail of a product or service, and analyzes what impact these details might have on the market. Product research examines things like colour, packaging, flavour, size, texture, scent, design, and sound. Today, for example, many food products that were once sold in cans come in packages that are easier to open. This type of packaging was designed to accommodate elderly consumers who have difficulty using can openers.

ADVERTISING RESEARCH

Advertising research provides information on the most effective ways to get a message about a product to potential consumers. This research normally involves finding ways to reach the consumer and then measuring the effectiveness of these methods.

Links Between Types of Marketing Research

The different types of marketing research link together. Consumer research identifies products that people want—consumers say they want soup in a bottle. Market research identifies the consumer target market—senior citizens. Motivation research determines why senior citizens want to buy soup in a bottle—The container is visually appealing; it pours single servings; the screw top keeps the soup fresh; and the package is easy to use. Pricing research decides on a competitive and profit-generating price—$2.49 a bottle. Competitive research determines that no other company currently markets soup in a bottle. Product research establishes that soup should be packaged in a clear plastic bottle so that consumers can see what's inside. Advertising research reports on the various magazines and television programs that are popular with seniors so that the company knows where and when it should run advertisements.

Product Development

Marketing research helps a business decide what type of product to make. The product-development team then creates the product by designing it, packaging it, and branding it.

PRODUCT DESIGN

Every product on the market today was designed by product designers. Product designers choose materials, shape these materials, and fit them together. Ultimately, they decide on the final look of the product. Designers use two principles to create products: form and function.

BUSINESS —FACT—

Product designers also create product features that you cannot see, such as the flavour of a soft drink or the scent of a perfume.

Form

Form is what the product looks like. It's the shape of the product, its colour and the patterns or pictures on it, and the material used to make it. For example, a Jeep is made up of right angles, while a Volkswagen Beetle is all curves. An umbrella can be red with green leaves or plain black. A jar can be made of glass or plastic. A product's form is what makes it different from other similar products.

Function

Function is what the product is designed to do. A bowl's function may be to hold soup, cereal, or cake mix. In other words, all bowls do not perform the same function. In almost every case, form follows function—a product is designed to look the way it does because of what it is supposed to do. A bowl for cereal is smaller than a mixing bowl. A bowl for a dog's water has a wide base so that it won't slip on the floor. A child's cereal bowl has pictures of bunnies on the bottom. In each case, however, the bowl has watertight sides and base because its primary function is to hold a liquid. A bowl is shaped like a bowl because it needs to function as a bowl. Think of the mess if your soup bowl was designed with a large hole in the bottom!

PACKAGING

When designing a package, product developers consider the package's functions. Packages protect the product from light, dirt, germs, air, water, tampering, and damage. A good package also makes it easy for the consumer to use the product, for example, cartons with spouts, bottles with handgrips, or resealable cereal bags. Consumers may also identify a particular product by the shape or colour of the package design. The traditional Coca-Cola bottle is one of the most identifiable packages in the world.

Package labels also help consumers identify the product, and can make the product stand out from the competition. An attractive label can help sell a product. For example, Arizona Iced Tea shrink-wraps colourful plastic labels around the entire bottle. This labelling method, which results in a bottle that attracts consumers' attention, has helped sales. Labels also provide information about a product's size, weight, ingredients, and nutritional content.

Arizona Iced Tea's packaging is designed to catch consumers' attention.

Through the Jones Soda Web site, consumers can order personalized cases of soft drinks and even design their own labels.

BRANDING

As part of overall product development, marketing people need to create a brand identity that fits the target consumer market. Compare two soft drinks: Arizona Iced Tea and Jones Soda. Each product has a totally different brand personality. Jones Soda has a simple name, black-and-white labels to which consumers can add their own photos, long-necked bottles, and a fortune-cookie-type prediction under each cap. The Jones Soda brand appeals to consumers looking for a personalized, "cool" product. Arizona Iced Tea, on the other hand, appeals to a different market. Its colourful labels, extra large bottle, and name suggest health and quality. (Arizona is a U.S. state that is known as a desireable place to go for personal health and well-being.)

ACTIVITIES FOR ...

INFORMATION

1. a) List and briefly describe the seven types of marketing research.

2. a) What is the difference between primary and secondary data?

3. a) Explain what "form follows function" means.

CONNECTION

b) Think of a product that is sold today. What do you think marketers discovered when they conducted their research? Consider the product's features, its price, who the target market is, and how the product is advertised and promoted.

b) Tell whether information gathered from each source is primary or secondary data: Web sites, surveys, interviews, magazines, questionnaires, and encyclopedias. What other sources offer primary data? secondary data?

b) Find pictures of five different forms of products that perform the same function (shoes, for example).

EXTENSION

c) Using the Internet, Yellow Pages, library, or other resources, locate a marketing research firm. Profile what the firm does for clients, who its clients are, and what research methods it uses.

c) With a small group, develop and administer a survey that collects primary data about your class's opinions on an issue. Interpret the data and present it in a graphic format.

c) Select a product. Evaluate the effectiveness of its design, packaging, and brand.

Sales and Distribution

Sales and distribution are often considered to be the same as marketing, and most marketing departments *do* focus on these two activities. Sales transfer the ownership of a product from one person or business to another person or business. Distribution gets the product to the consumer.

CHANNELS OF DISTRIBUTION

On page 209, channels of distribution were defined as the paths of ownership that goods follow as they pass from the producer to the consumer. They are the methods that a business uses to sell and distribute its products. A product does not change as it moves through channels of distribution (also known as a **distribution chain**). If a product does change in any way, it has reached the end of that particular channel. For example, a farmer sells wheat to a business that stores grain. Because it does *not* change the product, the storage company is part of the wheat's distribution chain. The storage company then sells the wheat to a flour mill, and the mill processes the wheat into flour. Because the mill *does* change the wheat into another product, the channel of distribution for the wheat ends, and a new channel of distribution for the flour begins.

A marketer can use three types of channels of distribution: direct, indirect, and specialty channels.

BUSINESS
—FACT—

Before becoming the end product used by consumers, raw materials often travel through several channels of distribution, and are transformed into new products at various stages.

Direct Channels

Selling directly to the consumer is the simplest form of distribution. It has a number of advantages. Other channels of distribution use **intermediaries**, or businesses that take possession of the goods before consumers do. Intermediaries add costs to a product so that they make a profit. Eliminating intermediaries cuts out these costs.

Direct channels of distribution connect buyers to the businesses providing the goods or services. This connection is known as a **maker-user relationship**. Through this relationship, consumers can inform businesses about their needs. Consumers may also feel more confident because they know the actual source of the products they are buying. Farmers' markets, roadside produce stands, factory outlets, factory-owned stores (such as Jacob clothing stores), bakeries, homemade ice-cream parlours, and many other businesses use direct channels of distribution.

Shoppers buy fresh fruit at a farmers' market.

Indirect Channels

Indirect channels of distribution have one or more intermediaries. These intermediaries might be importers, wholesalers, or retailers.

Importers

Many foreign businesses want to sell their products in Canada. An **importer** searches for these businesses, negotiates distribution deals with foreign manufacturers, buys the manufactured merchandise, stores it in Canada, if necessary, and then sells it. This arrangement makes it easier for foreign businesses to ship their goods to Canadian customers. Sometimes, importers only arrange delivery of foreign products to Canadian businesses. In this way, they assume no risk in buying the goods.

Normally, importers hire a sales force to sell the products across Canada. When an importer actually buys the foreign merchandise and distributes it nationally, the foreign business usually gives the importer exclusive rights to the product. Having exclusive rights means that no other business can buy or sell these products in Canada. An exclusive distribution deal is usually for a year or more. (Importing will be studied more closely in Chapter 18.)

Wholesalers

Wholesalers buy goods from producers or importers and resell the goods to retailers. Retailers use wholesalers, rather than buying directly from suppliers, for a number of reasons. Manufacturers often require retailers to purchase a minimum quantity of goods. Smaller stores may not have the space or money to buy in such large quantities. Wholesalers can afford to buy in volume, and will sell to retailers in much smaller quantities. As well, wholesalers are usually located close to retailers, which means wholesalers can provide storage space and reduce transportation costs. Retailers who use wholesalers, however, often pay more for a product than those who buy directly from the manufacturer.

Retailers

In the distribution chain, retailers link directly to consumers. Retailers buy merchandise that consumers want, have it in stock when consumers want it, and display the merchandise so consumers can examine it in an easy-to-reach location. (Different types of retailers are discussed in greater detail in Chapter 10.)

STRETCH YOUR THINKING

Why would an importer want to have exclusive rights to a product? Why would a manufacturer want to give exclusive rights to an importer?

Specialty Channels

A **specialty channel of distribution** is any indirect channel of distribution that does not involve a retail store. There are many different specialty channels, including vending machines, telemarketing, catalogue sales, e-commerce, and door-to-door sales.

Vending Machines

Vending machines sell everything from soft drinks to blue jeans. Some vending machines sell French fries; others sell ice cream. Some dispense videos; others squirt perfume. Marketers can place their products in vending machines where consumers work, study, shop, rest, eat, or travel. As well, if the manufacturer owns the machine, it dispenses only the manufacturer's product—there is no competition unless a rival producer's machine is nearby.

Telemarketing

With telemarketing, marketers use the telephone to sell products or services. Telecommunications companies that offer low long-distance rates, for example, may phone potential consumers to ask them to switch telephone companies. Many charities also solicit donations over the phone. Carpet-cleaning companies, promoters selling restaurant coupons, and many other businesses use the telephone to sell their products and services to consumers.

Businesses often hire a telemarketing company to create a sales pitch. A **sales pitch** is a scripted sales presentation that anticipates all possible consumer responses. Telemarketing companies hire people with good speaking voices to call consumers and make the pitch. Sometimes, the company selects phone numbers at random. At other times, it selects phone numbers from a list of potential customers whose numbers have been collected from coupons, contest entry forms, or surveys that consumers completed. The main problem with telemarketing is that it often annoys consumers, which may lead to negative reactions to the product or service being marketed in this way.

Catalogue Sales

Catalogues often feature merchandise from various retailers or catalogue distributors. Catalogues from retailers, like Sears, provide information about merchandise that consumers can purchase by mail, phone, or visiting the store. Catalogue distributors sell only by mail, and they only buy products that are related to their theme or target market. The Canadian Wildlife Federation, for example, sells products with a nature theme. It offers these products to consumers only through its catalogues. Catalogues are expensive to produce because they are usually printed in colour, and photos of products are taken by professional photographers. But catalogue businesses can be very successful, as American companies like L.L. Bean and J. Crew demonstrate.

Did You Know?

People are often unaware that by filling out a survey or by entering a contest, their names and phone numbers may be added to telemarketing call lists.

E-commerce

As you learned in Chapter 2, many businesses now sell their products online. E-commerce, or "e-tailing" as it is sometimes called, is the newest specialty channel of distribution. Online shopping offers consumers convenience and competitive prices while eliminating expensive intermediaries. If, as is predicted, more manufacturers start to sell goods directly to consumers via the Internet, distribution costs will become much lower and the price of products should decrease for consumers. However, as you also read in Chapter 2, e-commerce has met with some consumer resistance.

Today, retailers, wholesalers, and importers are considering the impact that e-commerce has on their businesses. Many retailers now maintain Web sites so that consumers can shop in person or online. The Gap, Indigo, and HMV are just a few of the hundreds of retailers making efforts to stay on top of the e-commerce revolution.

Door-to-door Sales

In the past, many companies distributed their products through door-to-door sales. Today, this method of distribution is much less common although some businesses, such as Amway and Avon, still sell door to door. As well, a number of charitable organizations solicit donations door to door. For the most part, this distribution method is no longer effective because most people now work outside their home—they aren't at home to answer the door when a salesperson visits. And if door-to-door sales representatives visit potential customers in the evening or at dinnertime, consumers can become very annoyed.

ACTIVITIES FOR ...

INFORMATION	CONNECTION	EXTENSION
1. a) What is the difference between direct and indirect channels of distribution?	**b)** What businesses in your community distribute goods or services through direct channels? Why do they distribute their goods in this way?	**c)** Work with a partner. Interview two or three wholesalers in your area. What type of goods do they carry? To whom do they distribute? Why do their customers use their services rather than another distribution method?
2. a) List and briefly describe five specialty distribution channels.	**b)** Make a list or bring in samples of catalogues that you have at home. What are some advantages of catalogue shopping? What are some disadvantages?	**c)** In a small group, discuss an Internet shopping experience that you or someone you know had. Tell about the product, the price compared to the price in a retail store, the efficiency of delivery, the name of the company, and so on.

Advertising and Promotion

Advertising is the paid-for promotion of a business's goods and services over a variety of mass media to a target market of consumers.

Today, ads are placed in all kinds of places—even on public buses.

Businesses pay a great deal of money to advertise, and they carefully control what their ads say. In other words, an advertisement gives only the advertiser's point of view. **Publicity** is media information about a business that the business doesn't pay for. Publicity can be either positive or negative. As a result, it is more believable than advertising. Many companies try to control their publicity by hiring public relations firms. Public relations firms try to influence the media to use only positive stories about their clients. In fact, public relations firms often write and distribute positive stories about the businesses they represent, hoping that the media will use them.

We see, hear, and read hundreds of advertisements every day. Ads are played during movie previews at the cinema and during our favourite television programs each night. We hear advertising messages on the radio when we wake up. We read ads on buses and in subway stations; in magazines, newspapers, and flyers; and on the Internet.

PURPOSES OF ADVERTISING

As you learned earlier in this chapter, most businesses believe that advertising is needed at every stage of a product's life cycle. In the introductory stage, advertising creates brand awareness. Advertisements tell consumers the name of the product, what the product does, why the consumer should buy it, and where the consumer can purchase it.

To get the product into the growth stage, advertising encourages consumers to try the product. This is known as **brand trial**. Often, advertisements offer low introductory prices or special deals. They may also urge consumers to "buy now!" As the product moves up the growth curve, competition becomes a concern. At this stage, advertisements promote brand preference. This type of advertisement claims that a product is superior in certain areas, using words such as "better," "best," "greatest," and "most." When a product reaches maturity, advertising keeps the product's name in consumers' minds, reminding them that the product is still on the shelves.

When the product starts to decline, a business will often try to stop the fall by increasing the advertising for the product. If the new promotion campaign fails to halt the drop, the business can reformulate the product, find a new use for it, repackage it, or simply promote it more aggressively. Advertising would support any of these decisions by repositioning the brand—changing the way consumers thought about the product to encourage them to try it again. Advertisements at this stage use phrases such as "new and improved," "new larger size," and "new lemon fresh scent."

TYPES OF ADVERTISING

Most often, advertising is classified by the type of media that is used to carry the message: direct-to-home, out-of-home, radio and television (broadcast media), newspapers, and magazines.

Direct-to-home

Any advertising message that comes to your home, such as a flyer or catalogue, is a **direct-to-home advertisement**. Advertisements on the Internet, which are quite new, are also considered direct-to-home advertisements. Businesses are still testing the effectiveness of Internet advertisements, which are usually interactive graphic banners across Web pages. Consumers do not ask or pay for direct-to-home advertisements, and residents often ignore them or throw them out.

What aspects of this Levi's ad, in Toronto, catch consumers' attention?

Out-of-home

Out-of-home advertising is any advertising message that the consumer is supposed to receive while not at home. These messages are sometimes carried on billboards, which can reach 100% of a city's mobile population if the advertiser rents the right number of billboards. Out-of-home ads are also shown in buses, subways, and transit shelters. Some advertisers have their ads painted on the outside of buses, making each ad a billboard in transit. These ads attract consumers' attention during the commute to and from work, school, shopping, or entertainment. Clever advertisements also provide an interesting diversion for bored or weary travellers.

Radio

Because the radio is often playing in the background, many people call it the "go anywhere" medium. Clock radios wake us up; car radios entertain us on the way to school or work; desk radios keep us amused while we work; radios at the cottage or beach help us relax. Effective radio advertisements skillfully use words and sound effects to draw us in. Although we may never have seen a flying crocodile, we can certainly imagine one when it's described. In fact, you're probably imagining one right now. (What kind of sound effect would you use?)

Television

Because television combines words, sounds, and images, it is an extremely effective advertising medium. It is also very expensive. Nonetheless, television has the size of audience that many businesses want. Millions of people watch popular television shows and sporting events. Some programs appeal to a particular group of consumers. Others reach a large, general audience. If a television advertisement is creative and well made, a large percentage of the target audience will remember the product's name, and many will purchase the product. If an advertisement is especially creative, it may become popular in itself.

Newspapers

Businesses advertise in both local and national newspapers. Small companies usually advertise in just local papers, while large companies might advertise in both local and national papers. It can be expensive to place a large ad in a newspaper, but inexpensive to place a small ad in the classified section.

Magazines

Magazines offer advertisers many advantages over newspapers. Magazines print colour advertisements, which attract consumers to the product. Many advertisers use specialty magazines to target specific groups of consumers. They advertise products that appeal to skiers, for example, in *Ski Magazine*. *Flare* has advertisements for fashions for young women. Advertisements for stores that sell bridal gowns appear in *Brides* magazine. Other magazines target specific demographics. There are magazines for men, women, business executives, new parents, young people, and senior citizens. General interest magazines, such as *People* or *Maclean's*, have enormous readerships and appeal to a large cross section of people.

> ### Did You Know?
>
> **A 30-second commercial spot during the televised broadcast of the 2001 Super Bowl football game cost an average of U.S. $2.3 million.**

Table 9.1 Advantages and Disadvantages of Advertising Media

Media	Advantages	Disadvantages
Direct-to-home	Highly segmented markets Easy to measure effectiveness Stimulate action Hidden from competition	Often considered junk mail Expensive
Out-of-home	Low cost Can repeat message High visibility	Increasingly regulated Messages are short Seldom have viewer's complete attention
Radio	Highly mobile Relatively low cost Highly segmented markets	Messages limited to audio Often do not have listener's full attention
Television	Reach large audiences Low cost per viewer Sight, sound, and motion combined Highly segmented markets	High total cost
Newspapers	Large circulation Can carry response vehicles (coupons)	Lower print quality Short life Limited market segmentation Compete with many other advertisements
Magazines	Long life span Excellent print quality Can carry response vehicles High pass-along rate Highly segmented markets	High cost

SALES PROMOTIONS

A **sales promotion** is any attempt to sell a product. Many advertisements are sales promotions, especially those that promote brand trials. Other advertisements, however, only create brand awareness in the minds and memories of consumers. A sales promotion encourages consumers to buy a product by using coupons, contests, premiums, samples, and special events.

Coupons

Coupons offer consumers money off the price of a product. When a consumer presents a coupon at a checkout counter, the cashier treats it as cash. On average, Canadian consumers are exposed to more than 1200 coupons a year. Most coupons end up in the trash. Advertisers measure the effectiveness of a coupon promotion by the **redemption rate**, or the percentage of coupons that consumers actually use. An average redemption rate is 5%. In general, the larger the value of the coupon, the higher the redemption rate.

Contests

Contests are an exciting way to increase brand recognition and brand sales. By law, businesses must organize contests so that anyone can enter—the business cannot require consumers to buy a product in order to enter a contest. As a result, you often see "no purchase required" included in contest rules. Businesses, however, can make it easier for consumers who buy the product or service to enter contests. Purchasers of the product may receive an entry form at the cash register, for example, or receive a game card to scratch or collect.

There are laws that forbid the use of gambling in contests. Contests must either require people to demonstrate a skill, for example, drawing a logo, thinking up a name, responding to a quiz, or answering a skill-testing question—usually a simple math problem. Consider the Tim Hortons "Roll Up the Rim to Win" contest. People could enter their name in the contest by writing to the Tim Hortons head office, but most consumers bought coffee in specially marked cups and "rolled up the rim" of the coffee cups themselves to see if they had won a prize. Contestants did not have to exhibit a skill to enter, but winners did have to answer a skill-testing question.

Premiums

Premiums are giveaways—something a consumer gets free with the purchase of a product. Premiums can be unrelated to the product, for example, a free CD with the purchase of a certain amount of coffee or a free T-shirt with the purchase of a case of pop. To establish brand recognition, these free products usually carry the company's logo.

Many businesses encourage brand loyalty by giving free products to regular customers. Coffee and sandwich shops, florists, video-rental businesses, and CD retailers issue **customer loyalty cards**. These cards are stamped each time the customer buys the business's product. When the card is completed, the consumer is entitled to a free product. Because the consumer must buy the product to get the premium, this method of promotion ensures sales.

E-ACTIVITY

Visit www.business. nelson.com and follow the links to find out about about different contests. What prizes are offered? What do you have to do to win? What are the chances of winning?

Samples

Samples encourage brand trial. Usually, samples are small, "trial" sizes of the product being promoted. Often, the company distributes these samples door to door. Sometimes, marketers hire product-sampling businesses to set up booths in supermarkets, big box stores, and shopping centres. They give out samples of the product to shoppers passing by. They also provide information about the product, its price, and where it can be found in the store. Sampling is a very effective method of sales promotion, and it usually results in increased sales. Costs are very high, however.

Special Events

Marketers organize special events to attract customers and increase product sales. Authors visit bookstores to autograph their newly published books. Sports heroes, television stars, actors, and music celebrities take part in special events that promote their athletic shoe, new perfume, new movie, or new CD. Sometimes, special events also include other types of sales promotions, such as contests, premiums, and samples. The main purpose of a special event is to excite consumers, encourage their participation, and, ultimately, get them to buy the product. Consumers are more likely to buy if they are having fun.

ACTIVITIES FOR ...

INFORMATION	CONNECTION	EXTENSION
1. a) How are advertising and publicity alike? How are they different?	**b)** Find an advertisement that marketers are using at each stage of the product life cycle.	**c)** Think about all the places that you see, hear, and read ads. Do you think that all this advertising is necessary? Explain your answer.
2. a) In what different media do advertisements appear?	**b)** "Lead time" is the amount of time between when you plan to put an ad in a given medium and when the ad actually appears. Which media have a short lead time? a long lead time? Is a short lead time an advantage or a disadvantage? Explain.	**c)** What types of advertising do you pay most attention to? Why? Compare your responses with those of a small group of classmates.
3. a) Name five methods of sales promotion.	**b)** List the pros and cons of each type of sales promotion.	**c)** Describe one type of sales promotion that you have used or participated in. Was it an effective method of sales promotion? Why?

Review

Knowledge and Understanding

1. Match each of the following terms to the correct definition:

   advertising   publicity
   channels of distribution   pull strategy
   marketing   push strategy
   product life cycle   sales promotion

   a) This term describes all the activities involved in getting goods and services from the businesses that produce them to the consumers who wish to purchase them.

   b) A marketing strategy whose main goal is to increase consumer demand directly.

   c) Positive or negative information about a business that the media prints or broadcasts by choice.

   d) Any attempt to sell a product.

   e) It consists of five stages: product introduction, growth, maturity, decline, and decision point.

   f) The paths of ownership that goods follow as they pass from the producer or manufacturer to the consumer.

   g) A marketing strategy whose main goal is to sell products to the retailer.

   h) The paid-for promotion of a business's goods and services over a variety of mass media to a target market of consumers.

2. Why is marketing important?

3. How do the purposes of advertising relate to the product life cycle?

4. Name a specialty channel of distribution that wasn't mentioned in this chapter.

Thinking and Inquiry

1. Give an example of a product that is managed using both push and pull strategies. Why do you think marketers chose to manage the product in this way?

2. Businesses study the competition so they can avoid repeating the mistakes of other businesses. What specific factors might they be studying?

3. Choose three products. Tell a partner as much as you can about each product's form.

4. Profile a business that uses e-commerce exclusively, for example, grocerygateway.com or e-Bay. When did this business start? How successful has it been? How successful do you think it will be in the future?

5. Make a collage of advertisements found in local newspapers. Make another collage of advertisements found in national newspapers. What types of businesses advertise in local newspapers? in national newspapers?

6. In your opinion, which media do you think would be most effective to advertise a new breakfast cereal? Explain your reasoning.

Communication

1. Create a flow chart or diagram to explain how coffee, sugar, flour, or any other raw material finds its way from its origins into your home.

2. As a class project, design and administer a marketing survey to find out the most popular fast-food restaurant in your area. Interpret the results of the survey and then prepare a report to share your findings. Design a "First Annual Most Popular Fast-Food Restaurant Award" and present it to the restaurant.

3. Visit a magazine store, the periodicals section of your local library, or use the Internet to find 10 magazines that appeal to very different readerships. Create a three-column table. In the first column, list the title of each magazine. In the second column, note the target audience of the magazine. In the third column, write down the name of a product that was advertised in the magazine that appeals to the target audience. Mix up the order of your information. Ask a classmate to try to match the magazines, audiences, and products.

4. Find one example of a responsible advertisement and one example of an advertisement that you find offensive, sexist, demeaning, or inappropriate in some way. Explain the reason for both of your choices in a short presentation to a small group.

5. With a partner, brainstorm a list of careers related to marketing. Then, each of you can choose one career to research.
   • What level of education is required?
   • What skills do you need?
   • What specific tasks are involved in the job?
   Meet with your partner to discuss whether this career interests you, and why.

Application

1. For one week, keep track of all the vending machines that you see. What different products do they sell? Are there any products that you would not want to buy from a vending machine? Explain your answer.

2. Select one product that you purchased in the past month. Analyze your reasons for buying it. How did advertising, packaging, display, distribution, and brand-management strategies affect your decision?

3. With a small group, choose a target market. Design packaging for a new breakfast cereal that is aimed at that market. Consider the following:
   • How you can make the design more attractive?
   • How can you make the design more functional?
   • How does the design meet the needs of your target market?

REFLECT ON YOUR LEARNING

1. What impact does advertising and promotion have on your buying decisions? Give examples to support your answer.

2. Choose a product that you think isn't as popular as it could be. List five things that you would do to market the product more effectively. Use ideas from this chapter to help with your answer.

UNIT 3

PERSONAL FINANCE

"The secret of getting ahead is getting started."

Anonymous

CHAPTER 10

MONEY: EARNING, SPENDING, AND MANAGING IT

STUDENT EXPECTATIONS

After completing this chapter, you will be able to
- list the four major functions of money
- explain why the dollar's purchasing power changes
- summarize ways in which you can earn income
- identify major factors that influence a job's income level
- identify and apply the criteria needed to make effective purchasing decisions
- identify the types of expenses that individuals and households typically incur
- demonstrate personal budgeting and financial planning skills
- set goals and create a personal budget and financial plan

Profile

Annette Vershuren, president of Home Depot Canada.

THE WAR FOR YOUR HOME-IMPROVEMENT DOLLARS

They are both 44, energetic, youthful looking, and immensely proud of where they came from. Annette Verschuren is a former Cape Breton farm girl raised by Dutch immigrant parents. John Kitchen is the son of a Toronto building-supplies merchant who likes to say he grew up with "sawdust in his veins." Despite very different backgrounds, their career paths have brought them face to face as rivals in one of the hottest retail battles in the country—the fight to dominate the $25-billion-a-year home-improvement market. Verschuren is president of Toronto-based Home Depot Canada, while Kitchen is Ontario vice-president of Surrey, B.C.-based Revy Home Centres Inc. Kitchen turned up the heat recently with newspaper ads declaring his company "proudly Canadian" and American-owned Home Depot as "hardly Canadian." Verschuren's response: "This thing will be won by providing great service, not negative advertising."

Southern Ontario is the principal battlefield in this war between suburban big-box stores—some the size of football fields—which typically carry over 50 000 different products, everything from nails and lumber to Jacuzzis and chandeliers. Retail analysts say the victors will be the companies with the deepest pockets, especially since two Quebec-based home-improvement giants—European-owned Reno-Depot Inc. and dealer-controlled Rona Inc.—have also moved into the Ontario market, with Reno-Depot operating under the Building Box brand. And what happens in Ontario will determine what happens in hardware retailing across the country, the analysts say. They predict that only two of the four big-box companies will survive, and both will become national chains dominating Canada's suburbs.

The most aggressive combatants are operating at fever pitch. A home-improvement centre usually has up to 600 parking spaces and sits on about four hectares of land. In two Greater Toronto locations, Home Depot and Revy have opened giant stores right across the street from each other, and observers warn that such competition is leading to overbuilding. By the start of 2001, Home Depot had

CONTINUED →

67 stores open, each employing an average of 200 people, in all provinces except New Brunswick, P.E.I, and Newfoundland. Verschuren plans to expand to those provinces by 2004.

One reason that warehouse-style stores are growing so quickly, insiders say, is because they attract far more female customers than traditional hardware and building supply outlets. In addition to basic products such as lumber, plumbing, and electrical goods, they carry many items for finishing a home, such as paint, kitchen cabinets, and light fixtures. And all are trying to make their stores more appealing to women. Rona, for example, incorporates four to six decor boutiques to break up the big-box format of long rows of merchandise stacked on shelves from the floor to the ceiling. Revy uses female actors in radio ads and reserves parking spots near the front doors for expectant mothers as well as those with young children. "Women are usually the decision makers in home improvements," says Kitchen. "Give them a store where they feel comfortable and they drive that shopping."

The big-box stores have put many smaller, independent competitors out of business, experts say, but they have not driven all of them out. Far from it, in fact. Home Hardware Stores Ltd. is now the largest chain in this sector of the retail industry, with nearly 1100 outlets and 1999 sales of $2.9 billion, compared with Home Depot's $2.3 billion. Home Hardware has flourished, chief executive officer Paul Straus says, because its dealers own their stores and maintain close contact with customers. "No one knows the market better than people working in the community every day," he argues.

Home Hardware plans to stick with small- and medium-sized stores, says Straus, and most retail analysts would agree with that strategy. The field of giants, they say, is already too crowded, and casualties are inevitable. "We're going to have an all-out war," says retail consultant Richard Talbot. "But it's going to end with two national brands." For now at least, consumers can expect very competitive pricing in the grand cathedrals of home improvement.

One reason that warehouse-style stores are growing so quickly is because they attract far more female customers than traditional hardware and building supply outlets.

About This Profile
1. How are stores like Revy and Home Depot different from stores like Home Hardware?
2. Why might big-box retailers be especially popular in the suburbs?
3. What types of consumers are likely to shop at smaller, Home Hardware-type retailers? Who is more likely to shop at big-box stores?

What Is Money?

Do you control money or does money (or the lack of it) control you? Discuss this question with a partner and make notes about both sides of the question.

Did You Know?

On average, the Royal Canadian Mint manufactures 600 million pennies each year.

"Money makes the world go 'round." At least, that's what the song from the play and movie *Cabaret* says. Without money, businesses could not operate, and consumers could not buy the goods and services they need and desire. But what exactly is money and how does it function in a modern economy?

FORMS OF LEGAL TENDER

Under federal law, **legal tender** must be accepted as payment for goods and services. The two main forms of legal tender are coins and paper money, specifically, 1¢, 5¢, 10¢, 25¢, $1, and $2 coins, and Bank of Canada notes (or "bills") at face value. Cheques and credit cards, although widely used and accepted as payment, are not legal tender. No law states that they must be accepted as payment, but they are seldom refused.

Coins are **minted**, or manufactured, at the Royal Canadian Mint headquarters in Ottawa or at the Mint's Winnipeg branch. The Government of Canada decides when and if to issue new coins. For example, in 1989, the government replaced the $1 paper note with a $1 coin. In 1996, it replaced the $2 paper note with a $2 coin. Coins are much more durable and, therefore, more cost effective.

The Bank of Canada issues paper money, also known as **bank notes**. The Bank issued its first notes in separate French and English versions in 1935. In 1937, it released a redesigned, bilingual series. The Bank of Canada does not run its own facilities to print bank notes. Instead, it uses two privately owned, high-security printing companies.

New Canadian Bank Notes

In January 2001, the Bank of Canada began issuing a new series of Canadian bank notes; the last series had been introduced in 1986. The $10 bill was introduced in January 2001, with other denominations being introduced up to 2004. The new bills are the same colour as the old ones, and they still feature Queen Elizabeth II and Canada's prime ministers on the front, but the portraits are updated. New designs on the back of the notes reflect Canada's culture, history, and achievements. (The backs of the 1986 bills featured Canadian birds.)

Special Features of Money

Canada's new bank notes have state-of-the-art security features to discourage high-tech counterfeiting. (**Counterfeiting** is the

The $10 bill released in January 2001 is called "Remembrance and Peace-keeping." Sir John A. Macdonald appears on the front, and war veterans, children, and peacekeepers appear on the back.

production of fake money.) These features include the following:

- **Raised ink, called intaglio.** On a new $10 note, the large number 10, the words BANQUE DU CANADA • BANK OF CANADA, the portrait, and the coat of arms are all raised.
- **Iridescent maple leaves.** When you tilt the bank note, the three maple leaves seem to turn gold.
- **A hidden number.** If you hold the new $10 note at eye level and tilt it to a 45° angle, the number 10 becomes visible.
- **Fluorescence.** If you hold the new $10 note under fluorescent light, the coat of arms and the words TEN • DIX and BANQUE DU CANADA • BANK OF CANADA glow blue over the portrait. White security fibres, which are invisible in normal light, become red. Blue fibres that are visible in normal light don't glow.

These features make Canadian bank notes even more secure than before.

The new notes also have features that make it much easier for blind and vision-impaired people to distinguish between the different denominations. Each denomination has a unique texture and feel so that people can recognize it by touch alone. Canada is one of the first countries in the world to incorporate these tactile features in its paper bills.

STRETCH YOUR THINKING

Not all cultures have—or had—economies based on money. The Aboriginal cultures of Canada's Northwest Coast, for example, had a gift-based economy. How do you think this economy worked? Could it work today?

THE FUNCTIONS OF MONEY

For many people, money is simply a medium of exchange used to buy goods and services. But money also represents a standard of value, a store of value, and a standard of future payment.

Medium of Exchange

When people exchange money for goods and services, money functions as a **medium of exchange**. Money makes it possible to obtain goods and services without having to **barter**, or trade, for them. Imagine that you want to buy a computer game but you have no money; all you have to trade or exchange is your time and services. If the owner of the computer software store needs some work done in the store, such as stocking shelves or cleaning, you can earn your game. If not, you will have to find an employee who does need your services. With money, you have a greater choice of where to buy your computer game because any software store will accept it. Money also allows you to buy a greater range of products.

Standard of Value

Most societies use money as a **standard of value** to determine how much goods and services are worth. If you find a computer software store that will let you work to earn a computer game, you and the owner will have to decide how many hours of work will be exchanged for the game. It might be difficult to agree on a value for such different things. Money, on the other hand, makes it easy to compare the value of one thing with the value of another. The value of all goods and services is measured by their price.

4 hours of labour   @ $7-an-hour wages   =   one $28 computer game

Store of Value

In an economy that uses bartering, fresh fruit, vegetables, and dairy products may be exchanged for goods and services. They would be considered currency. In this economy, it would be impossible to save your currency. Because fresh food does not stay fresh very long, these perishable goods would have to be traded quickly. Money, however, can be stored or saved for use in the future. Therefore, it is a **store of value**. Money allows you to purchase a computer game whenever you want. If you learn that the software store is going to have a sale in two weeks, you can save your money until then. By waiting, you can store, or save, the value of your money for two weeks, and then buy the game at a reduced price.

Standard of Future Payment

Money also functions as a **standard of future payment**. Imagine that you want to buy a new mountain bike that costs $500. You have $100, which you use as a down payment. The store agrees to let you pay off the balance of $400 over the next 10 months, but charges you $50 in interest. Your total debt, then, is $450, and your monthly payment is $45 a month for 10 months. Your money has thus served as a basis or standard of future payments.

MONEY'S CHANGING PURCHASING POWER

Money is convenient because it is light and easy to carry and store. Money's true value, however, is its purchasing power. The paper used to print our currency is virtually worthless, as are the "precious" metals used to make coins. Our "silver" coins (nickels, dimes, and quarters) no longer contain silver. Just a few cents' worth of metal is used to make a toonie. In other words, our currency has almost no value in itself. It is worth something only because we accept that it has a specific value—two nickels equal 10¢, four quarters equal $1, ten $10 bills equal $100, and so on.

Money's true value is its purchasing power.

Although money serves as a standard of value, its purchasing power changes as prices for goods and services change, as you read in Chapter 5. In general, prices tend to rise (inflation), so the dollar buys less from one year to the next. Today, $10 buys much less than $10 did 30 years ago. You have probably noticed that the prices of clothing, magazines, and movie tickets have increased over the past few years. The purchasing power of a dollar even changes from season to season. For example, every winter, Canadians pay higher prices for fresh fruit and vegetables than they do during the warmer months.

The Pros and Cons of Inflation

With inflation, consumers have to pay higher prices for the goods and services they buy. In turn, as employees, they want to earn more money to maintain their standard of living. But, if salaries and wages increase faster than prices, businesses tend to hire fewer workers and unemployment increases. As a result, consumers spend less and businesses have less income and profits.

However, a mild rate of inflation (1% or 2% a year) can stimulate the economy. Wages often increase at a slower rate than the prices of goods and services. Therefore, businesses can sell their goods and services at prices that are high compared to the labour costs that they pay. Under these circumstances, producers make higher profits, which often means expanded production and higher rates of employment. More jobs means more consumer spending, and the overall demand for goods and services increases.

ACTIVITIES FOR ...

INFORMATION	**C**ONNECTION	**E**XTENSION
1. a) What is legal tender?	**b)** What security features do bank notes have, other than those listed on page 234?	**c)** Some people suggest that the $5 bill should be replaced with a coin. Survey people in your neighbourhood about this possibility. Prepare a report to share with a small group. Your report should present your survey results and outline the proposal's advantages and disadvantages.
2. a) List the four functions of money.	**b)** Beaver pelts and playing cards were once used as forms of currency in Canada. Why do you think these forms of currency were used? Why do you think they disappeared from use?	**c)** How does the purchasing power of money today compare with the purchasing power of money in the past? Find examples of goods and services you could buy with $100 in 1950, 1960, 1970, 1980, 1990, 2000, and today.

Earning Money

Where does money come from? Where does it go? What do people do with their money? Because most goods and services cost money, people need money to live. For some people, most of the money they earn is used to pay for necessities such as food, rent, and clothing. People who have higher incomes can afford to spend more money on non-essential items like vacations and DVD players. Regardless of your income level, it is a good idea to have a financial plan so that you can get the most out of the money you earn. (Money management will be discussed later in the chapter.)

SOURCES OF INCOME

People receive income from many different sources. For some young people, an allowance may be a source of income. Income also includes money that you receive for work that you do, money that you earn on savings and investments, and money that you receive from government social assistance programs.

STRETCH YOUR THINKING

With a partner, role-play a 15-year-old asking a parent or guardian for an allowance or allowance increase. Consider these questions: Should teens receive allowances? How much should an allowance be? Is it fair for someone to receive an allowance if his or her friends do not?

Allowances

Some of you may receive an allowance from your parents or guardians. An allowance allows you to buy things and do things, but it also teaches you about money management, responsibility, values, setting goals, and planning. Getting an allowance early in the week, for example, forces you to plan ahead for the weekend. Receiving a regular, but limited, source of income can also help you learn to

- consider the cost of goods and services
- make spending choices
- appreciate the goods and services you buy

There is no "right" time to start an allowance because children develop concepts about money at different ages. Some people say that an allowance should start when a child begins school. Others suggest that a child should receive an allowance even earlier. Most experts agree that, if a family can afford it, children should receive an allowance by the age of seven or eight. They suggest allowances should increase at a regular time, perhaps on birthdays or at the start of the school year. They should also be given at a set time—weekly or even monthly.

The amount of an allowance and how long it should continue are issues that divide many people. Some people say that the amount should match the amount the child's friends receive; others suggest $1 for each year of age. But does a 4-year-old really need $4 a week? Is $16 enough for a 16-year-old? Another factor to consider is what the allowance will be used for. Will it pay for school supplies and lunches, or clothes and entertainment? Should parents and guardians base their child's allowance on the amount of work that the child does around the house? Is it a kind of wage? Parents and guardians consider these factors when determining how much allowance to give their child.

Employment Income

During your lifetime, most of your income will come from working for an employer or for yourself as an entrepreneur. In Chapter 7, you learned about different forms of employment income, including salary, wages, commission, piecework, and profit sharing. You also learned about different employee benefits, including medical insurance, paid holidays, and paid sick days.

Regardless of your form of income, many factors affect the amount of money you earn. The pay you receive depends on the type of work you do and your level of education and skill. In today's workplace, most jobs require at least a high school diploma.

Many other factors influence what you earn, including
- work experience
- length of time on the job
- reliability and work habits
- how up-to-date your skills are
- demand for your skills
- labour market conditions
- employment rate
- salaries negotiated by unions
- job competition
- your employer's level of success

Reading a Paycheque

Today, many employers deposit wages and salaries directly into an employee's bank account. (See Chapter 13 for more information on direct deposits.) Other employers pay employees by cheque. Either way, the employer issues an earnings statement, which explains earnings and deductions. It is important to know how to read a pay stub, and to understand the difference between **gross pay** (the total amount of money earned) and **net pay** (the amount received after deductions).

How to Read a Pay Stub

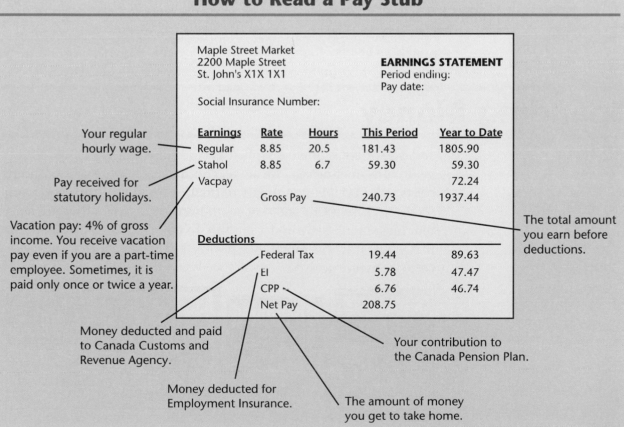

Maple Street Market
2200 Maple Street
St. John's X1X 1X1

EARNINGS STATEMENT
Period ending:
Pay date:

Social Insurance Number:

Earnings	Rate	Hours	This Period	Year to Date
Regular	8.85	20.5	181.43	1805.90
Stahol	8.85	6.7	59.30	59.30
Vacpay				72.24
Gross Pay			240.73	1937.44

Deductions		
Federal Tax	19.44	89.63
EI	5.78	47.47
CPP	6.76	46.74
Net Pay	208.75	

Your regular hourly wage.

Pay received for statutory holidays.

Vacation pay: 4% of gross income. You receive vacation pay even if you are a part-time employee. Sometimes, it is paid only once or twice a year.

The total amount you earn before deductions.

Money deducted and paid to Canada Customs and Revenue Agency.

Your contribution to the Canada Pension Plan.

Money deducted for Employment Insurance.

The amount of money you get to take home.

Savings and Investment Income

Savings plans and investments are other sources of income. You earn interest on money in a savings account. The longer the money stays in the account, the more interest it earns. In addition, if you purchase stocks in a company, you share in the profits the company makes. (Saving and investing will be examined in greater detail in Chapter 11.)

ACTIVITIES FOR ...

INFORMATION	**C**ONNECTION	**E**XTENSION
1. a) Name three sources of income.	**b)** "The pay that an employee receives is often not the pay that he or she has earned." Explain this statement, using the pay stub on page 239 as a reference.	**c)** Choose three factors that affect employment income. Interview the owner of a business to find out how these factors affect an employee's pay.
2. a) List three reasons for giving allowances to children.	**b)** Imagine that you are the parent or guardian of a young child. Would you give your child an allowance? If you would give your child an allowance, at what age would he or she first receive it? How much would the allowance be? Explain your answers.	**c)** With a partner, discuss the following questions: What benefits might a teen get from having a part-time job that he or she wouldn't get from receiving an allowance? Does an allowance offer any benefits over a part-time job? Should a teen who has a part-time job still receive an allowance?

Spending Money

Today's society is often described as (and sometimes criticized for) being consumer-driven. We are all consumers, and the new economy offers us a never-ending supply of exciting and innovative goods and services. These goods and services, however wonderful they are, mean that most families are under pressure to be more careful about what they buy—and how much they pay for it. Unwise choices can have costly consequences.

What does this cartoon tell you about society's attitude toward consumer spending?

COMPARISON SHOPPING

Before buying anything, smart consumers compare. You can find almost every available product at more than one store. So, it is important to shop around before you buy and compare the price, quality, and special features of a product offered in one store with those of the same (or a similar) product in several other stores. By **comparison shopping**, you'll get better value for your money when you make a purchase.

Price and Quality

Comparison shopping does not always mean paying the lowest price. It means selecting the least expensive product or service that best suits your needs and wants. At times, quality may be more important than price. If you want the product to last for many years, you may spend less money in the long run if you pay more for a high-quality product now. High-quality sports equipment, electronic components, and automobiles generally last much longer than lower-quality goods.

Features

Sometimes, the features of goods and services are the most important consideration. Imagine that you need a new bike to get to school. You live in a hilly area, so you need a bike with at least 21 gears. A bike with fewer gears costs less, but you'll likely arrive at school tired and sweaty from working so hard to make it over the hills. In this case, you should shop at several stores to compare features, quality, and price—you want to find the best deal on a bike with at least 21 gears. You may be able to find a good-quality bike with the features you want in your price range, or you may have to make a tradeoff— perhaps buying a bike with more features, but paying more than you expected.

Comparison shopping does not always mean paying the lowest price. It means selecting the least expensive product or service that best suits your needs and wants.

Services

It's important to check what services different retail stores offer. If you're making a large purchase, for example, will the store deliver it to your home? If delivery service is available, is it free or is there a charge? What type of guarantee, or warranty, does the product have? A **guarantee** is the manufacturer's or dealer's promise, usually in writing, that a product is of a certain quality. It may apply to the entire product or to parts only. It usually promises that the product or defective parts will be replaced free of charge for a certain period of time—the first 90 days or the first year after the purchase date, for example. You may also want to research the store's reputation for follow-up services, such as repair or replacement of defective products.

Another consideration is whether the store sells goods on a cash-only basis. If the store accepts payment on credit, are all major credit cards accepted? Can you get a discount if you pay in cash? If prices are almost identical in all stores, you may want to choose the store nearest you or the store that has the best services or reputation. If the product costs less at a store far from your home, you may still decide to buy the product at a local store. The cost of transportation for follow-up services, such as tune-ups for a car, could easily cancel any money saved on the purchase price.

Young Kings of a Toy Empire

There was no reason to think the day would go badly. Spin Master Toys had done remarkably well that holiday season, selling 400 000 units of the Air Hogs Sky Shark—a motorized Styrofoam airplane powered by compressed air. It was Boxing Day 1998, and Ben Varadi had come into the office to do a bit of work.

(left to right) Anton Rabie, Ronnen Harary, and Ben Varadi display an assortment of Spin Master toys.

Instead, he was swamped by calls all day. Most of the customers who called were angry that the planes' fragile wings had snapped in crashes the first time their kids had played with them. In the following weeks, Spin Master voluntarily shipped more than 100 000 replacement wings to irate customers. It also made changes to the design. It was a tough initiation for Varadi and his two partners, Anton Rabie and Ronnen Harary, as their first major success seemed to be turning to disaster. But they went on to sell more than three million Air Hogs and cemented themselves as a force to contend with in the global market for toys. Furthermore, notes Harary, Spin Master today employs six customer service agents to attend to "any product issues that happen to arise."

Planning and Comparing

Besides visiting stores, you can usually compare the prices and features of a particular product and find out about delivery terms and follow-up services by looking at catalogues and newspaper advertisements, phoning stores that sell the product, or doing research on the Internet. Sometimes, it is helpful to ask the opinion of people who have already used the product or service. In addition, product reports in consumer magazines, such as *Consumer Reports* and *MoneySense*, can provide vital information. *The Globe and Mail* and other large daily newspapers often run consumer-information features as well. You can access these sources at your local library or on the Internet.

WHERE TO BUY

The Canadian marketplace offers a vast number of goods and services and a wide variety of places where consumers can purchase them. Where you choose to buy depends on your needs and wants, and on the retailers in your community.

Shoppers in Victoria, British Columbia, wait for one of the seven new Eatons stores, relaunched by Sears, to open. When Sears reopened the stores in 2000 after Eaton's went out of business, they changed the spelling from "Eaton's" to "Eatons." This new spelling reflected a more modern image.

Department Stores

Department stores, also known as full-service stores, offer a wide variety of goods and services to their customers, with an emphasis on customer service. The Bay, Sears, and Eatons are a few examples of department stores. Although prices may be higher than at discount stores, department stores offer more customer conveniences. These conveniences may include home delivery of large items, telephone-ordering services for customers with accounts, gift-wrapping, fast replacement or repair of defective or damaged items, and regular advertising in the local media that keeps consumers informed about sales and other money-saving events.

Discount Stores

Discount stores are noted for low prices on well-known brands of products. These stores buy in large quantities, and their success is based on a high volume of sales. Usually, discount stores offer fewer customer conveniences and services than department stores. If service is less important to you than low prices, you may prefer shopping at discount stores.

Factory Outlets

Factory outlets are popular all over North America because they often offer consumers bargains. Goods sold here come directly from the manufacturer. Some goods have minor flaws that prevent them from being sold for full value in department stores. Many other goods are of top quality. At factory outlets, careful consumers can find good bargains on products by well-known manufacturers.

Specialty Stores

Specialty stores carry only a specific group or line of products. Computer, clothing, shoe, music, and pet stores are examples of specialty stores. They are generally small in size, and prices from store to store vary widely for the same type of product. Some specialty stores are known for quality and high prices, while others feature goods at discount prices.

Supermarkets

For most consumers, **supermarkets** are their first choice for buying food and some household products. Supermarkets carry a wide variety of items. Many different manufacturers make these products, which include national, private, and generic brands. (See page 250 for more information on different types of brands.)

This specialty retailer sells bikes and related products, and also provides repair services.

Convenience Stores

Convenience stores are usually small neighbourhood stores that stock popular foods, essential household products, magazines, newspapers, and other handy items. Examples include Mac's, Hasty Market, and 7-Eleven stores. Convenience stores are much smaller than supermarkets and carry far less stock. They are usually open for longer hours than supermarkets (often 24 hours a day) and stay open on holidays. Prices are usually higher than at supermarkets because convenience stores do not buy in large quantities. Consumers also pay for the convenience of a store's location and its extended hours.

Warehouse Clubs

Warehouse clubs are stores that sell bulk quantities of products at prices that are much lower than those of most supermarkets or other types of stores. Shoppers pay a membership fee to join a warehouse club, which sells everything from meat and produce to electronic equipment. These outlets are usually very large, plain, and functional—there are no frills. Customer service is minimal to help keep prices low. Costco is an example of a warehouse club.

Big-Box Stores

As you read in Chapter 5, **big-box stores** are a relatively new category of stores. Some, such as Costco (which is also a warehouse club, as mentioned above), resemble department stores and supermarkets. Others, such as Home Depot and Indigo, resemble large specialty stores. They sell a wide variety of products at very low prices. Consumers shop here for price and selection. Another common name for this type of store is "category killer" because when a big-box store picks a category of product to carry in depth, for example, hardware at Home Depot or books at Indigo, other smaller stores have difficulty competing.

Online Shopping

As you read in Chapters 2 and 9, e-commerce is the latest shopping option for consumers. Today, thousands of businesses and millions of individuals are taking advantage of buying and selling on the Internet.

With e-commerce, consumers can go from store to store in search of a good or service without ever leaving home. Comparison shopping and product research have never been easier. As well, shopping online gives consumers access to items that they may not be able to find in local stores. And if they can't find the item they're looking for, there are countless e-auction houses where they can search for the item or place a wanted notice. E-commerce is changing the way people buy and sell everything from books to cars.

The Most Popular Web Sites

In 2000, the most popular Web sites among Canadian shoppers were, in the following order

1. Chapters.ca
2. Sears.ca
3. Amazon.com
4. FutureShop.ca
5. eBay.com
6. ColumbiaHouseCanada.com
7. Staples.ca
8. Indigo.ca
9. BarnesandNoble.com
10. RadioShack.ca

Contemporary Issues in Canadian Business

THE ISSUE: ONLINE SECURITY

How safe are we when we're shopping online?

The Internet is rapidly gaining ground as a serious competitor for traditional retail stores and shopping malls. However, in stores, customers deal face to face with people who can assist them before, during, and after the sale. Also, a store may offer a range of payment options, including cash, debit cards, cheques, and credit cards. Online, people often deal with unknown retailers and usually make payments by entering their credit card numbers.

The lure of online shopping is the opportunity to purchase whatever you need, 24 hours a day, seven days a week. With a click of the mouse, you can order anything—from out-of-print books to a vacation in Switzerland. On the other hand, the Internet also offers a wide range of opportunities to people who are less than honest. In 1999 and 2000, for example, many customers lost their money when they unknowingly participated in fraudulent "online auctions."

Often, online customers must enter personal and financial information into the computer in order to make a purchase. Are adequate safeguards in place to help protect their interests? Let's examine two contrasting points of view on this issue.

Point

When online shopping was introduced, consumers were a bit nervous. Many used the Internet to research products that interested them, and then did their shopping offline. Soon, the businesses that people patronized offline began setting up Web sites of their own. This made people more comfortable with the idea of online shopping because they could make purchases from companies they already knew and trusted. Today, most major retailers have Web sites, as do many small local businesses.

Another reason to feel secure is that privacy legislation and security methods are constantly being introduced and updated. In Canada, the Personal Information Protection and Electronic Documents Act sets regulations for the collection and trading of information about consumers and private individuals. When this act came into effect in 2001, it applied only to federally regulated industries, such as broadcasting and banking. However, through related provincial legislation, it will be extended to all provincially regulated industries as well.

The security of credit card information is a special concern for online shoppers. A process called **encryption** helps many online businesses protect people's card numbers. Each number is translated into an unreadable format called **ciphertext**, which can only be decoded using a specific key.

What if goods are ordered but not received? The province of Ontario is currently considering passing a law to establish a 30-day delivery rule. This law would give Internet shoppers the right to cancel a contract if goods or services are not provided within 30 days of the date specified in the contract.

Over time, online shopping is gradually becoming safer for consumers. As long as customers exercise reasonable caution—giving credit card numbers and personal information only to established businesses or businesses that offer appropriate protection—then there is no need for concern about the safety of online transactions.

Counterpoint

The Personal Information Protection and Electronic Documents Act states that companies must get a person's consent before collecting, disclosing, or selling personal information. It also gives individuals the right to view, revise, and revoke information that has been collected about them. However, the legislation does *not* deal with non-commercial transactions or personal health information, nor does it protect information that Canadians send to Web sites outside Canada. As a result, Canadians who shop online are still vulnerable to having their personal, health, or credit information distributed or sold to other Internet marketers.

In addition to privacy issues, there are other concerns that make online shopping more difficult to safeguard, and that could put consumers at risk:

• The customer and retailer could be thousands of kilometres apart, so delivery problems might occur.

• If the customer and retailer are in different time zones or speak different languages, direct communication will be difficult.

• There are often unexpected costs involved in exchanging currencies, shipping orders, or paying customs duties that greatly inflate the cost of an order.

• The Web site could be a fictitious one, and the order would never arrive.

Given these problems, it makes sense for Canadians to continue to rely on traditional retailers for most of their shopping needs.

A Real Life Example

One of the many things that consumers buy online is stocks. To help them make decisions, they often join chat rooms to "hear" people's opinions about the stocks they're considering buying. However, some individuals and businesses share information in the chat room that is purposely misleading. This information affects the way consumers view the stock and, consequently, their purchases.

A Vancouver-based business, MindfulEye.com now provides an Internet chat surveillance service that helps companies discover whether anyone is giving out misleading or inaccurate information about their stocks. They've developed software that "listens" to online commentary about client companies, determines the true meaning of words in context, and then reports on what it hears. In a world where information flies around the globe in a matter of moments, it's important for investors to have accurate information they can rely on as they make important decisions.

Questions and Activities About This Issue

1. Online auctions are one of the most common forms of Internet fraud. Identify some other types of Internet fraud that might occur.

2. MindfulEye's software helps deal with security issues, but is it fair to "listen in" on people's online conversations and report the results to companies that were mentioned? Write a point/counterpoint response to this question.

Career Focus 3: Applying for a Job

RESEARCHING JOB OPPORTUNITIES

Imagine that you're researching jobs on an Internet job site. You search the jobs available in your area and then narrow the search to the types of jobs that interest you. Now you're ready to apply for several job openings.

PREPARING YOUR RÉSUMÉ

For most jobs, you'll be asked to submit a résumé that tells the employer who you are, what you know, and what experiences you've had that will help you do the job. Many Web sites offer advice on résumé writing that can help you stay informed about current practices and expectations.

Your résumé is your primary personal-marketing document. It should convince a potential employer that you are capable and knowledgeable, and that your abilities will be an asset to his or her organization. Before you write your résumé, research the employer to find out as much as possible about the business. This information will help you tailor your résumé to suit the employer's needs, and will enable you to show why you are the best person for the job. Your résumé should include

- your name, address, telephone number, and e-mail address (if you have one)
- your education history, including any relevant courses you've taken and any awards you've received
- special skills, such as computer expertise, that will help you do the job
- a chronological list of work experiences, including full-time and part-time jobs, as well as volunteer work
- a list of your skills and abilities placed in order of importance (if you haven't had much work experience)

RÉSUMÉ TIPS

According to a recent survey, 50% of Canadian executives usually spend 5 minutes or less screening the résumés of job applicants. Only 17% routinely spend more than 10 minutes. Clearly, then, it's very important to keep your résumé short and to the point—all on one page if possible. Make sure your résumé is simple and clear, without long descriptions. Try to focus the reader's attention on how your skills will be useful in the job you're applying for.

Expect to do several edits or rewrites, and to adjust your résumé slightly each time you apply for a new job. Adjusting your résumé will help you make sure that the skills you highlight are the right ones for each job.

Sometimes, employers will ask for a list of references, such as former employers, teachers, or adult friends, who can provide the employer with more information about your education, work habits, and character. When you list references, be sure to ask each person on the list if he or she is willing to be contacted by your potential employers. Try to choose people who can be counted on to give a positive recommendation.

Finally, be sure to have someone else review your résumé before it's printed in final form.

PREPARING YOUR COVER LETTER

A job application or résumé should always be accompanied by a brief cover letter that explains why you have applied for the job. Your letter and résumé should be neatly word-processed and should not contain any spelling or grammatical errors. The letter introduces you, identifies the job you're applying for, and highlights the skills, experiences, and accomplishments that make you the best person for the job. It also provides a chance for you to show that you've done some research about the company.

Your letter is probably the first thing the employer will see, even before your résumé; it should leave the employer with a desire to meet you in person. Make your letter sound friendly and personal—not like a form letter—and close by expressing the hope that the employer will contact you for an interview.

Macy Elizabeth Spencer
123 Maple Street
Hometown, Ontario
X1Y 2Z3
(234) 555-6789
mespencer@email.ca

Job Objective: Part-time accounting clerk

Main Qualifications:
> Computer and Internet skills
> Computerized accounting background
> Honest and trustworthy
> Willing to learn and to help
> Excellent school attendance record

Education:
> Central High School
> Graduated June 30, 2001
> Ontario Scholar

Business Courses Completed:
> Introduction to Information Technology in Business (Grade 9)
> Introduction to Business (Grade 10)
> Introduction to Financial Accounting (Grade 11)
> Introduction to Entrepreneurial Studies (Grade 11)
> Organizational Studies (Grade 12)

Work Experience:
> 2000–2001   Record clerk, ABC Books and Cards
> part-time cooperative education placement (1 year)
> 1999–2000   Sales clerk, Roundstone Clothing
> 15 hours weekly (1 year)

Other Activities:
> Assistant coach, junior girls' basketball (2 years)
> Volunteer, Rideaucrest Seniors' Home (1 year)

Accomplishments and Awards:
> 2000–2001   Top graduating student
> 2000–2001   President, Students' Association
> 1999–2000   Treasurer, Students' Association

References: References will be supplied on request

STRETCH YOUR THINKING

When national brands, private brands, and no-name brands are all available, suggest reasons why a consumer might choose one over the others. Are national brands necessarily of higher quality, as many consumers think?

WHAT TO BUY

How do you decide what to buy? Manufacturers offer consumers a wide variety of choices and brands. Choosing among these alternatives can be difficult, especially since the choices can sometimes be deceptive.

Brand Names

As you learned in Chapter 6, manufacturers give their products or product lines brand names. A business creates its brand name to help build consumer loyalty to its product. Many brand names are advertised nationally and are sold in most communities. These **national brands** (or **name brands**) appear on virtually any product you can think of, including clothing, shoes, food, and electronics. Some examples of well-known brands are Canada Dry, Roots, and Sony.

Some stores sell products with their own brand names. These **private brands** (or **store brands**) are manufactured by other companies, but are sold as the store's brand name. Examples include President's Choice (Loblaws), Select (Safeway), and Craftsman (Sears) products. Generally, store brands offer quality products at prices that are lower than name brands. By buying store brands, you can save money and still get a high-quality product.

Finally, some supermarkets carry **no-name brands** (or **generic brands**). These goods are sold in plain packaging that doesn't identify the manufacturer. Because the packaging is very basic, these products cost less to produce than name brand and private brand products. Savings are passed on to consumers in the form of lower prices.

WHEN TO BUY

Do you need to buy your item immediately? Can you wait for a sale? When goods are on sale, their price should be lower than the regular selling price. Although it is illegal, a few retailers sell goods at regular prices but advertise them as sale items. If you have any doubts as to whether a price is a sale price, do some comparison shopping to see what other stores are charging for the same product. Most stores use two basic types of sales to attract consumers: clearance sales and promotional sales.

Clearance Sales

As you read in Chapter 1, at the end of a season, stores usually reduce prices on seasonal stock they have left over. Stores hold **clearance sales** (or end-of-season sales) to make room for new merchandise. For example, clothing stores usually have sales in January and in June or July. Many people buy next year's Christmas cards and wrapping paper at Boxing Day sales, when prices are often reduced to 50% of the regular price. Car dealerships usually lower prices in August and September, just before new models arrive in October. However, you may not find exactly what you want at a clearance sale. Because the store is clearing out its leftovers, selection is limited. You have to decide which is more important to you: a lower price or getting exactly what you want.

Promotional Sales

Stores hold **promotional sales** for a number of reasons. A retailer may want to publicize the opening of a new store or new location. The retailer hopes you will become a regular customer at that store. A retailer also uses sales to draw you into a long-established store, hoping that you will also buy products that are not on sale. Manufacturers might put their goods on sale when they want to introduce a new product. If you like the new product, the manufacturer hopes you will buy it again—at the regular price.

Secondhand Shopping

Secondhand shopping lets you save money while supporting the three Rs of waste management—reduce, reuse, and recycle. You might

Buying at stores such as Goodwill means the money you spend helps support charitable groups that work to improve life for the less fortunate in our communities.

consider making your purchases at "nearly new" stores in your community, through the classifieds in your local newspaper, or at garage sales. Perhaps your school has recycling sales or garage sales to raise funds for various purposes. You might not have to go too far to find exactly what you want.

The obvious advantage of secondhand purchases is that they cost much less than new items. You can find secondhand bargains that will provide you with years of service and pleasure. On the other hand, the disadvantage of secondhand purchases is that they come with no guarantees or return policies. Also, you might not find the item in exactly the colour or style that you want.

AVOIDING IMPULSE BUYING

The time you spend planning purchases usually pays off in savings. Taking your time means slowing down, visiting more stores (real or online), and giving yourself a chance to look for the best values. A smart shopper refuses to be hurried into buying anything. With careful planning, you can avoid buying things that you really don't want or need.

Some consumers can't seem to stop buying impulsively; these people put little or no thought into their purchases. Most people indulge in **impulse buying** at some time. For example, have you ever been in a music store and bought a CD because you heard it being played in the store and liked it at the time? Most of us have also impulsively bought chocolate bars, gum, or magazines from displays at supermarket and drugstore checkout counters. In fact, these stores deliberately place these types of items at the checkout counter, hoping that you will buy them on impulse.

Impulse buying can be a mistake for many reasons. If you're on a tight budget, you might not have enough money left for essential items after you've given in to an impulse. Most impulse purchases cost you more than purchases made after you've taken the time to comparison shop. People who buy on impulse also end up with many items that they don't really need or want. The biggest disadvantage of impulse buying is that you waste money.

ACTIVITIES FOR ...

INFORMATION	CONNECTION	EXTENSION
1. a) What are some advantages of comparison shopping? What are some disadvantages? What factors should you consider when comparison shopping?	**b)** For which product might price be the most important factor for you when shopping? When is quality the most important factor? features? services?	**c)** Think of an expensive item that you might like to buy now or in the future. Visit three stores or go online to comparison shop. Make a chart of your findings. Decide where you would make your purchase, and why. Use the decision-making model on pages 18–20 and "Questions for the Smart Shopper" on page 241 to help you make your choice.
2. a) List nine different types of stores where consumers can buy goods and services. What are the features of each type of store?	**b)** How many of the types of stores studied in this chapter are in or near your community? Which are the most common? In which type of store do you prefer to shop? Why?	**c)** Choose one type of store. Use your Yellow Pages or the Internet to locate different retailers of this type in or near your community. How are these retailers similar? How are they different?
3. a) Describe the differences between a promotional sale and a clearance sale.	**b)** Choose three of the nine types of stores discussed in this chapter. Visit one store of each type. Classify its products as name brands, private brands, and/or generic brands. Based on these observations, what conclusions can you make about the wants and needs of each store's customers?	**c)** Prepare a report outlining the pros and cons of impulse buying.

Managing Money

STRETCH YOUR THINKING

Would you consider building a house without blueprints? Would you plan a driving trip to Florida or California without using maps and planning a route? How is the way you earn, spend, save, and invest your money like these two examples?

Some people are described as being "good with money." They were not born that way. To be able to earn and use their money effectively, they developed a money management plan. **Money management** refers to the daily financial activities connected to using your limited income to satisfy all your needs and wants. It means getting the most for your money through careful planning, saving, and spending. Money management is a very important part of your education. You may already have begun to form ideas about money management by observing how adults close to you earn and spend money.

Whether you earn $2000 a year or $200 000, it is very important to know how much money you have to spend and where you spend it. It is equally important to know what you want to achieve. Setting up a budget is the first and most important step in developing your money-management plan.

BUDGETING

As you learned in Chapter 5, a **budget** is a plan for wise spending and saving based on income and expenses. With a budget, you can organize and control your financial resources, set and realize goals, and decide in advance how your money will work for you. A budget can be as simple or as complicated as you want to make it. You can make a daily, weekly, or monthly plan. If you receive a paycheque every other week, you might develop a two-week budget to make sure that your money will last until your next payday.

Deciding what to do with your allowance is one example of budgeting. Think of your allowance as a whole that can be broken into parts. (See Figure 10.1.) It makes sense to consider a "savings" component. For example, why not save 10% each time you get your allowance? If donating is important to you, set aside another set percentage (a "donating" component) for a charitable or religious contribution. The remaining portion of your allowance could be divided into two parts. Your "mad money" is the portion that you can spend on whatever you want. Your "planned spending" is for items that you know you will need, for example, school supplies and lunches.

Figure 10.1 *Budgeting Your Allowance*

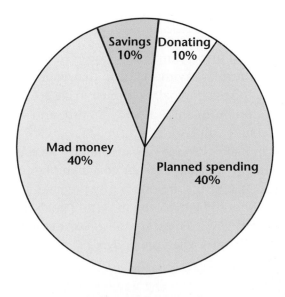

Because many people feel that budgeting involves going without, "pinching pennies," or not having any fun, they avoid the subject completely. What they don't understand is that creating and following a budget can actually help them find the money for the things they really want. Think of budgeting as financial planning for your dreams and wants. Budgeting gets money to work for you, rather than the other way around. Thinking in this way may provide you with the motivation you need to get started.

The time to begin managing your money is now, regardless of how much or how little you have. During your lifetime, you will probably earn well over $1 million. If you graduate from college or university, or develop skills through postsecondary training, you will probably earn even more.

One million dollars may seem like a fortune, but it really isn't. You'll have to pay for essential needs such as food, clothing, and shelter. You'll also want to save for future expenses and emergencies. You'll likely need to buy or lease a car, or pay for public transportation to get to work. You'll use some of your money to buy wants or non-essential goods and services.

Planning means setting goals and establishing the financial targets that enable you to reach those goals. To be able to plan, you first need to know your total income and expenses. Then, figure out how much you need to put aside regularly to keep your targets in sight. Budgeting is all about planning. Fortunately, with practice, most people can learn how to create and stick to a budget.

Setting Goals

In Chapter 2, you saw that we all set both short-term and long-term goals, and that one person's goals may be quite different from another person's goals. Setting up your financial plan requires you to establish goals and to identify whether those goals are short-term goals or long-term goals. Budgeting is more than just setting goals, however. In addition, you need to develop a regular savings plan so that your budget is realistic. To achieve a long-term goal, you must make a strong commitment to save a minimum amount *every* month, and you must decide what that amount will be.

Goals should be realistic and achievable. They should also be specific and have a clear time frame.

Goals should be realistic and achievable. They should also be specific and have a clear time frame. For example, your goal could be to save $50 a month for the next 24 months. If your family prepares a budget together, each member should be involved in setting goals and in identifying the most important goals. These are the goals that you will work toward first. Table 10.2 shows a sample budget for one family.

Table 10.1 The Pappas Household's Income and Expenditures for One Month

Budgeted Household Income / **Budgeted Distribution of Savings and Expenditure**

Month	Date	Theo's net income	Teresa's net income	Total	Savings	Food	Clothing	House-hold	Transpor-tation	Health/Personal	Rec. & Ed.	Gifts	Misc.	Total
		$2280	$2550	$4830	$900	$600	$275	$1255	$675	$200	$400	$150	$375	$4830

Actual Household Income / **Actual Distribution of Savings and Expenditure**

Month	Date	Theo's net income	Teresa's net income	Total	Savings	Food	Clothing	House-hold	Transpor-tation	Health/Personal	Rec. & Ed.	Gifts	Misc.	Total
Jan.	1				$900									$900
	7					$110	$70	$50	$55	$50	$125			$460
	14	$1140		$1140		$130	$45	$50	$50	$100	$45			$420
	15		$1275	$1275								$40	$25	$65
	16							$1030				$50		$1080
	17								$425					$475
	21					$100	$80	$50	$40		$80		$50	$350
	28					$150	$80	$120	$50	$55	$45		$75	$575
	29											$75		$75
	31	$1140	$1275	$2415										
TOTALS		$2280	$2550	$4830	$900	$490	$275	$1300	$620	$205	$295	$165	$150	$4400

Balance = Total Household Income − Total Payments
= $4830 − $4400
= $430

Preparing a Budget

Some budgets are very simple records of how much money you have, how much you plan to save, and how much you plan to spend. You can also prepare a budget using computer software programs that allow you to alter input data in order to predict your future financial results. A useful budget should not take much time to prepare, but it should still be specific enough to let you know what is happening with your money.

Calculating Income

The first step in preparing a budget is to determine the amount of money that you receive every month. If you don't know this amount, it is very difficult to plan and budget accurately. Your incoming funds are fairly predictable: your allowance, if you receive one; your pay-cheque, if you earn one; and interest on savings and investments, if you have any.

Calculating Expenses

Ater calculating your monthly income, calculate your regular monthly expenses. It's important to keep a complete record of how much you spend and what you spend it on. If you can't be exact, estimate. Get a receipt for everything you buy, from snack food at school to movie tickets on the weekend. If you can't get a receipt, make a note of what you spend so that you have a record of every purchase.

Many people who budget divide expenses into two categories: fixed expenses and variable expenses. Fixed expenses occur regularly and usually can't be adjusted. For most families, these expenses include items such as rent or mortgage payments and car payments. Variable expenses, such as food, clothing, utilities, personal care, and entertainment, are living expenses that differ from month to month. Your family also has to consider other expenses: income tax, home repairs, car repairs and servicing, medical and dental expenses, vacation planning, gifts, and so on. Family members may set aside some money each month to cover these expenses, or they may just budget for such expenses during the month they occur.

Reviewing Your Budget

At the end of the month, review your spending plan so that you can compare your actual spending with the budgeted amounts. You may be surprised at just how much it costs you to buy the things you want, or you may find that you're doing too much impulse buying. You need to know where your money goes. If you're spending more than you earn, you need to adjust your expenses or increase your income. If you have money left over, you could add to your savings.

Use your expenses for the past few months as a basis for creating your budget. As you develop your budget, continue to record expenses for several months. By regularly reviewing your expenses, you'll see areas where you can reduce spending without altering your lifestyle too much. You may also be able to increase your savings. Understanding and, if necessary, changing your spending habits are the keys to successful budgeting.

If you've trimmed and cut expenses but still can't meet your savings goals, reevaluate the goals. You may want to change the time frame or adjust the goal itself. You may have to take a shorter vacation this winter, or postpone it until next year. You may have to buy a less expensive car or use public transportation instead. Try to think ahead to the day when you can finally take that vacation or get that new car. With smart budgeting, these goals are within your reach.

Figure 10.2 *What additional expenses would you need to consider if you were planning to move out on your own?*

Sample Budget for One Month

INCOME

Take-home pay (babysitting, part-time job, etc.)	$_____
Other income (allowance, gift)	$_____
Total Income	$_____

EXPENSES

Clothes	$_____
Books, magazines, video rentals, etc.	$_____
Eating out (school lunches, dinner, coffee, etc.)	$_____
Entertainment (sports, movies, etc.)	$_____
Hobbies	$_____
Transportation (public transportation, taxis, car, etc.)	$_____
Other expenses (computer games, Internet access, etc.)	$_____
Total Expenses	$_____

SAVINGS

Total Income – Total Expenses	$_____

ACTIVITIES FOR ...

INFORMATION	**CONNECTION**	**EXTENSION**
1. a) Describe the steps involved in creating a budget.	**b)** Visit at least two financial institutions to get information on budgeting and money management. Which materials did you find most useful, and why? Share this information with your family.	**c)** With a partner, role-play a situation in which you try to persuade someone to start a budget.
2. a) Give some examples of fixed and variable expenses.	**b)** Using Table 10.1, identify the Pappas family's fixed and variable expenses. In which categories did expenditures exceed the budgeted amount? In which categories were they less than the budgeted amount?	**c)** Based on the information in Table 10.1, create a budget for the Pappas family for February. What would you change? What would you keep the same? Why?

Review

Knowledge and Understanding

1. Match each of the following terms to the correct definition:

   budget   legal tender
   comparison shopping   money management
   gross pay   net pay
   impulse buying

   a) The amount of money you receive from your employer after deductions are made.
   b) Buying an item on the spur of the moment with little thought.
   c) Comparing the price, quality, and special features of one product with those of another product.
   d) The daily financial activities connected to using your limited income to satisfy all your needs and wants.
   e) The total amount of money earned.
   f) A plan for wise spending and saving based on income and expenses.
   g) Coins and bank notes that must be accepted as payment for goods and services.

2. Explain why the dollar's purchasing power changes.

3. How would you adapt Figure 10.1 to suit your needs?

4. What factors might you consider when deciding where to shop?

5. What advantages are there to buying goods on sale? What disadvantages are there?

6. What actions can you take if you find that your monthly expenses are consistently greater than your monthly income?

Thinking and Inquiry

1. Do you think that a businessperson who sells good products or services wants well-informed customers? Explain your answer.

2. "If you only spend money on things you really need, you will always have money for the things you really want." Do you agree with this statement? Why or why not?

Communication

1. Interview an older relative or neighbour, or visit someone in a retirement home. How has inflation affected this generation? You might ask questions such as the following:
   - When you were a teenager, what was the cost of a newspaper, a soft drink, an ice cream, a chocolate bar, and a movie ticket?
   - Did you receive an allowance? If so, how much? Did you earn money from part-time work? If so, how much did you earn?
   - How has inflation affected your quality of life?
   - Did you plan in advance for protection against inflation?

   If possible, videotape or audiotape your interview. Use basic editing to make a presentation for your classmates. You could also present your findings as an essay, a newspaper article, or an oral presentation.

2. Find articles on budgeting and financial planning on the Internet, in newspapers or magazines, and in local business resources. Place your articles in a scrapbook, and highlight the key parts of each one. Below each article, write one or two summary sentences.

Application

1. People who develop online-shopping Web sites believe that in the next 20 years, the Internet economy will revolutionize the way we work, live, play, and shop. Brainstorm with friends and family how the Internet will change our lives.

2. Using budgeting software and a computer spreadsheet program, input data to create your own personal budget for one month. Record your expenses throughout the month. Then, compare your budgeted estimates with your actual expenses. Revise your budget and continue inputting data for another month. How do you think your budget would change if your take-home pay increased by $50 a month? by $100 a month? Share your findings with your classmates.

REFLECT ON YOUR LEARNING

1. Reread the notes you wrote in response to the Before You Begin question on page 233. Has your opinion changed about whether you control money or whether money controls you? What ways do you use to "control" money? Which of these methods do you find most helpful? Why?

2. What characteristics or skills do you possess that would help you plan and follow a budget? Consider your personality, talents, and any skills you have acquired through school, work, volunteering, and so on. What could you do in your everyday life that would help you improve your planning and budgeting skills?

CHAPTER 11

SAVING AND INVESTING

STUDENT EXPECTATIONS

After completing this chapter, you will be able to

- outline the main reasons for saving money
- explain why it's important to have a savings plan
- compare the benefits of saving and investing
- identify various types of investments
- explain how investing in stocks is different from investing in bonds
- explain why people invest in mutual funds
- explain why people invest in real estate and collectibles
- demonstrate an understanding of the factors that affect the value of money over time
- identify the financial institutions in your community and the services they offer for saving and investing

Profile

Julie Charbonneau's job at McDonald's has allowed her to start investing for her future.

HOW ABOUT A SAVINGS PLAN WITH THAT BIG MAC?

Many teens have part-time jobs—hauling heavy bags to shoppers' cars at the grocery store or clearing tables at the local greasy spoon. What do they do with their earnings? Buy clothes? Stock up on CDs from their favourite band? Buy a used car?

Julie Charbonneau of Orleans, Ontario (about 15 km east of Ottawa) probably had similar thoughts about how to spend her money when she began her part-time job. But with a little help from her mother, she took a big step. An unusually big step. She began to plan for retirement. Two years ago, Julie started investing a small slice of earnings from her job at the local McDonald's restaurant in a mutual fund. The goal: to lay the foundation for a decent level of retirement income. She's 18 now, and that investment of $80 a month—$40 of her own, $40 from her mother—has grown to about $2000.

The $40 contribution is but a small piece—8%—of the $500 she earns each month at McDonald's. So it doesn't interfere with her other spending habits or savings goals. Julie has put the vast bulk of the retirement funds in the Fidelity Canadian Asset Allocation fund. She also has a few hundred dollars in Canada Savings Bonds. At first, Julie's mother held the funds in trust for her, but now that she's 18, Julie has control of the money. Now, a $2000 portfolio is not going to get the blood racing on Bay Street, in the centre of Toronto's financial district. Nevertheless, you have to start somewhere. "It's just a long-term investment so I will have money when I retire," says Julie, who works about 20 hours a week. A recent promotion has her helping train other restaurant staff members.

Julie plans to pursue postsecondary education and a career as a dental hygienist. Once she begins to bring home bigger dollars, she intends to boost her retirement contribution. Many of her friends, she says, just don't get her savings plan. "I often tell my friends about it and they're like, 'Yeah, I'll think about it in 10 years.' I say, 'That's a waste of time. Do it now. It adds up.' " Clearly, Julie understands the impact of investments compounding over time. Even if she makes no further investments, today's $2000 could grow to

CONTINUED →

Chapter 11 • Saving and Investing **261**

more than $74 000 by the time she retires at age 65, assuming an 8% rate of return, compounded annually.

Julie's mother, Christine Charbonneau, encourages her daughter to invest for retirement. She planted the retirement investing seed, but she did not push. It was up to Julie to call the family's investment advisor, arrange a meeting, select the investment, and get the program set up. "If I can teach my daughter one thing in life, it's how to manage her finances, especially when she gets into the older years," Ms. Charbonneau says. Had she started to invest when she was Julie's age, she'd be able to retire at 45.

Getting into the habit of saving early is crucial, says Jerry Fryer, an advisor at an Ottawa-area financial planning firm. He assists Julie and also does work for her parents. "She's focused on putting a portion of her paycheque aside and accumulating savings. If she can keep that discipline throughout her life, she's going to be in good shape," Mr. Fryer says. As he points out, "A lot of the new companies out there don't have pension plans, and basically you're on your own to save for retirement."

Mr. Fryer has several clients under 18. For this group, he prefers to find "relatively conservative investments, like a balanced fund, that are going to provide some consistency in returns." While there's no financial reward to him today, Mr. Fryer hopes that when Julie opens a registered retirement savings plan sometime in the future, she'll turn to him for advice. Moreover, Mr. Fryer adds, deferred sales charges could hurt returns for a young person who needs to pull money out much earlier than expected because goals change. "I don't want them to feel constrained if they want to take money out in few years."

Not to worry. That thought probably hasn't even entered Julie's mind.

Clearly, Julie understands the impact of investments compounding over time.

About This Profile
1. Why is it important to start saving for retirement early?
2. Julie Charbonneau sees her $2000 portfolio as a long-term investment. What short-term savings goals might Julie have?
3. Jerry Fryer says that young people may need "to pull money out much earlier than expected because goals change." What if Julie decides that she wants to become a dentist instead of a dental hygienist? How would this change in goals affect her financial planning?

The Need for a Savings Plan

BEFORE YOU BEGIN

Do you save money? Is saving money when you're in school important? Why do you think so? Why is it sometimes difficult to save money, even when you have a savings plan?

Some day you may want to buy an MP3 player, go backpacking in Europe, or attend college or university. These things are expensive and you'll need to save part of your income to be able to pay for them. When you put money aside in a systematic or regular way to reach a financial goal, you have a **savings plan**. How much you save, what you save, and where you save are important decisions. Developing a savings plan should be a basic part of your financial future.

Saving is putting money aside for future use. It is the opposite of consuming. How much of your earnings you save is your decision. No matter how young you are, saving part of your earnings or unexpected windfalls (such as gifts of money) is a good habit to develop. Many employers help you save by deducting a specified amount of money from your paycheque and depositing it directly in your bank account. If you start saving on a regular basis now, you'll find it easier to save when you're older and earning more money.

WHY PEOPLE SAVE

People save for many reasons: emergency needs, short- and long-term goals, security, and future needs.

Emergency Needs

For a snowboarding weekend, you need to think about the cost of meals, transportation, lift tickets, accommodation, entertainment, and miscellaneous items.

What would happen if unexpected events affected the main income earner in your family? There could be sudden expenses and a loss of family income. Insurance offers protection against risks such as an accident, serious illness, or losing a job, but it doesn't always fully cover the loss. Savings can help a family meet expenses during an emergency. The importance of saving to prepare for emergencies or unexpected hardships is what lies behind the familiar expression "saving for a rainy day."

Short- and Long-term Goals

Many people save money to pay for short- and long-term goals. As you read in Chapter 2, short-term goals are usually intended for the purchase of inexpensive items within a short period of time. A long-term goal requires you to save for a year or longer to pay for more expensive items. If you have a specific goal in mind, it's much easier to save. Anytime you think of spending the money that you have in your savings, just remember your savings goal.

Security and Future Needs

Knowing that you have money saved for unexpected emergencies, special opportunities, and future needs can give you a sense of security and satisfaction. An important savings goal for many people is to have extra income for their retirement years. People who are free from worries about money are happier people.

How Much to Save

At one time, financial experts suggested that families should have savings equal to three or four months' income. Another guideline was saving 10% of annual income. Unfortunately, such guidelines are difficult for many people to follow, especially in periods of inflation and high unemployment.

Only you can determine how much you can save. If you do not have a particular savings goal, try to save as much as you can each week or each month. The important thing is to save on a regular basis and to develop a plan that works for you. Everyone should have a personal savings plan. Having a little money saved is better than having none saved at all!

Selecting a Savings Plan

A teen, saving for a mountain bike, deposits money into her savings account.

Deciding what to do with the money you save requires effort and thought. You could keep your savings in a jar or hidden under your mattress so that when you need it, the money will be readily available. However, you'll always have the same amount of money as you had before. In fact, inflation will reduce the purchasing power of your money, as you saw in Chapter 10.

A variety of savings plans are offered by chartered banks, trust companies, credit unions, or *caisses populaires*. (You'll learn more about these financial institutions in Chapter 12.) All savings plans operate similarly. They are intended for people who do not plan to withdraw money very often while they are saving toward a goal. A **withdrawal** is the act of taking money from your account.

Besides saving, you probably want your money to increase in value. One way to make your money grow is by investing. **Investing** is committing money in order to gain a financial return. When you invest your money, you use your savings to earn more money or extra income. Your money can be invested in stocks, bonds, and other long-term investments. All these options are discussed in this chapter.

BENEFITS OF SAVINGS PLANS

The savings plans of financial institutions offer many benefits. They earn interest on your money, while keeping your money safe and insured against loss.

Earnings and Yield

When you deposit money in a financial institution, you are actually lending the institution your money. The financial institution will pay you interest on your **deposit** in order to be able to lend it to other customers who want to borrow it. **Interest** is money you receive over time for letting others borrow your money. It is also the price that you pay over time for borrowing money.

When interest is expressed as a percentage of the original investment, it is called **rate of return** or **yield**. It is usually based on a one-year time period. Say you deposit $1000. If the $1000 earns interest at the rate of 5% a year, you would earn $50 interest [($1000 × 5) ÷ 100 = $50]. Your total investment is now worth $1050. The $1000 is the original investment. The $50 is the amount of interest. The 5% is the rate of return, or yield.

Earnings on savings plans vary depending on how often interest is calculated and paid. Usually, the more often interest is paid, the greater the interest that is earned. Therefore, the return on the money is larger. Earnings on savings plans also depend on how interest is calculated. **Simple interest** is calculated only on the **principal**, or the amount you deposited. (See Chapter 14 for the formula for calculating simple interest.) **Compound interest** is caluclated on the amount saved plus any interest already earned. As interest is added to the principal, your savings increase. More interest is earned on each payment period because you are earning interest on interest, as well as interest on principal.

STRETCH YOUR THINKING

If you invest $1000 and it earns a rate of return of 10%, what amount of interest would you earn? What amount of interest would you earn if the rate of return were 4%?

Calculating Compound Interest

If you deposit $1000 in a savings plan for 5 years at 5% interest compounded annually, interest is calculated as follows:

Beginning of Year	During the Year	End of Year
Year 1	$1000.00 + (5% of $1000.00 = $50.00) = $1050.00	
Year 2	$1050.00 + (5% of $1050.00 = $52.50) = $1102.50	
Year 3	$1102.50 + (5% of $1102.50 = $55.13) = $1157.63	
Year 4	$1157.63 + (5% of $1157.63 = $57.88) = $1215.51	
Year 5	$1215.51 + (5% of $1215.51 = $60.78) = $1276.29	

Even small amounts of money deposited each month grow when interest is compounded. If you deposited $1 a day in a savings plan at 5% interest compounded daily, you would have just over $4700 at the end of 10 years. Compounding makes your savings grow faster than simple interest. Interest can be compounded daily, monthly, quarterly, semiannually (twice a year), or annually. The more often the compounding occurs, the more your savings grow.

A good savings plan should earn a reasonable rate of interest. The yield varies according to the risk involved. Higher yields go hand in hand with greater risks. You should compare interest rates to see where you get the best yield, with a level of risk that you are comfortable with.

Safety

Most savings-plan deposits in banks, trust companies, and loan companies are protected by the Canada Deposit Insurance Corporation (CDIC), an agency of the federal government established in 1967. You do not have to pay for deposit insurance; the financial institutions that hold your accounts pay for it. Each depositor's money is automatically insured to a maximum of $60 000, including principal and interest.

This $60 000 maximum is the total amount insured on deposits in *all* your accounts at *all* branches of the same financial institution. If you have $50 000 in one account and $40 000 in another account with the same institution, $30 000 of your money will not be covered by the insurance.

$$\$50\ 000 + \$40\ 000 = \$90\ 000$$
$$\$90\ 000 - \$60\ 000 = \$30\ 000$$

So, if you have more than $60 000 and you want all of it to be protected, you should make deposits in several different institutions.

Accounts at credit unions are also insured by deposit insurance or deposit guarantee corporations. The extent of protection varies from province to province. For example, the Nova Scotia Credit Union Deposit Insurance Corporation (NSCUDIC) insures deposits up to $250 000, while the Deposit Insurance Corporation of Ontario (DICO) insures deposits to a $100 000 maximum. British Columbia deposits are also insured up to $100 000.

Liquidity

An important feature of some savings plans is that, in an emergency, you can withdraw money quickly and without notice. A savings account, for example, has liquidity. Land, a home, a valuable painting: These assets are not considered liquid since it would be difficult to sell them quickly. Should you need money in an emergency, you might even have to sell these items at less than their fair value. For this reason, it is important for investors to try to keep some liquid investments.

ACTIVITIES FOR ...

INFORMATION	CONNECTION	EXTENSION
1. a) Why do most people save money? List three reasons.	**b)** What advice would you give to people who are unable to save money regularly?	**c)** Outline a personal savings plan. Explain how and why you developed it in this particular way.
2. a) What are three benefits to having a savings plan?	**b)** Explain to a partner why a savings plan earns more with compound interest than with simple interest.	**c)** Why might people want investments, such as land or valuable paintings, that are not liquid?

Common Savings Plans

Savings plans are a basic and popular part of most financial planning. They are easy to open and they pay a fixed rate of interest, while protecting your money against loss. Although the various savings plans may differ from one institution to another, the most common types are savings accounts, term deposits, guaranteed investment certificates (GICs), registered retirement savings plans (RRSPs), and registered education savings plans (RESPs).

SAVINGS ACCOUNTS

A savings account is a safe vehicle for savings of any amount. Savings accounts are intended for people who want to save money while earning some interest. Many financial institutions require a monthly minimum balance in some types of savings accounts before paying any interest. The rate of interest paid and the way the interest is calculated vary among institutions and types of accounts. Interest rates rise and fall with the economic conditions in the country.

Interest may be calculated
- daily and paid at the end of each month
- on the average account balance during a specific period
- on the minimum monthly balance, and deposited in your account semiannually on April 30 and October 31

No matter how it's calculated, the interest paid on savings accounts is the lowest rate of interest paid on all types of investments.

The Rule of 72

A simple way to estimate how your money will grow is by using the **Rule of 72**. To find out how many years you will need to double your money if you let your investment compound, divide 72 by the interest rate on your investment. For example, if your investment earns interest at a rate of 8%, your money will double every 9 years (72 ÷ 8 = 9).

TERM DEPOSITS AND GUARANTEED INVESTMENT CERTIFICATES

Term deposits and **guaranteed investment certificates (GICs)** are both savings plans in which you deposit a fixed sum of money for a specific length of time, or term, at a fixed rate of interest. Terms range from 30 days to five years. Usually, the shorter the term, the greater the deposit required and the lower the interest rate.

Some financial institutions sell both term deposits and GICs. Term deposits offer a lower rate of interest than GICs because they can be redeemed, or cashed in, early. Most GICs are locked in, which means they cannot be cashed in early. There are exceptions, however. Certain GICs can be redeemed on the anniversary date of their purchase.

Other financial institutions do not offer term deposits. Instead, they sell GICs that can be redeemed early and GICs that are locked in. GICs that can be redeemed early offer a lower interest rate than GICs that are locked in. When considering term deposits and/or GICs, it's important to shop around and compare options and interest rates at various institutions.

STRETCH YOUR THINKING

What are the basic differences between savings account deposits and term deposits or GICs?

Registered Retirement Savings Plans

The federal government introduced the **registered retirement savings plan (RRSP)** in 1957 to encourage people to save for retirement. RRSPs help you save money by allowing you to invest a portion of your yearly income without paying taxes on it. Your contributions to the plan are allowed to grow, along with interest earned, on a tax-free basis until you withdraw the funds. When you withdraw the money, you must pay income tax on it. Although you are allowed to withdraw funds before your retirement years, it would not be in your best financial interest to do so. Since your income after retirement is usually lower, your tax rate will likely be lower. The government limits how much money you can contribute to your RRSP each year, depending on whether you and your employer also contribute to a pension plan. Self-employed people and those without a company pension plan can make larger RRSP contributions than employees with company pension plans.

The best time to contribute to your RRSP is early in the tax year so that you can benefit from the interest that will accumulate over the course of the year. Many people make monthly contributions directly from each paycheque. Begin early and invest regularly. Because of compound interest, small amounts invested frequently can actually grow faster than larger sums of money invested less often. The income you earn on your investment can also be reinvested, earning you additional income.

This couple used money from their RRSP to purchase their first home. With the "Home Buyers' Plan," you are allowed to withdraw up to $20 000 from your RRSP to purchase your first home. You will not be taxed as long as you return the money to your RRSP within 15 years.

The Benefits of Early Savings

You might think you're too young to be concerned about retirement. Well, check it out and you'll be surprised.

When Sarah was 19, she started her RRSP. Her annual contributions were $2000 for eight consecutive years, earning her a growth of 10% per year, compounded. After the eighth year, Sarah decided to attend university and she stopped making contributions.

That year, Sarah's friend Anthony started his RRSP, at the age of 27. Anthony also contributed $2000 annually, earning the same compounded rate of interest each year. Anthony continued contributing until he was 65 years old. Sarah had made only eight contributions, totalling $16 000, while Anthony had made 39 contributions, totalling $78 000. Which person do you think ended up with more money?

The answer is Sarah. Her contributions started compounding interest eight years earlier than Anthony's. As a result, at the age of 65, Sarah's RRSP was worth $1 035 161, while Anthony's was worth $883 185.

Figure 11.1

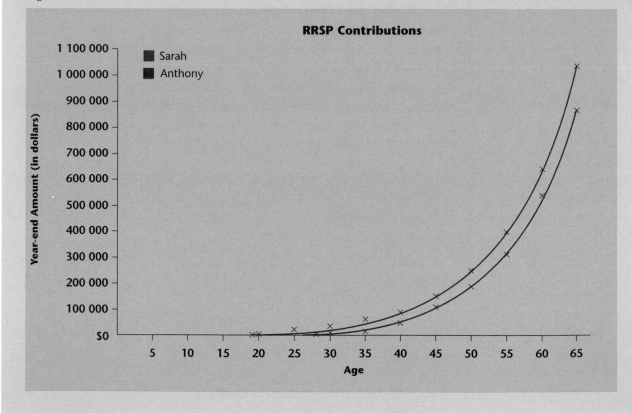

REGISTERED EDUCATION SAVINGS PLANS

The **registered education savings plan (RESP)** is another tax-sheltered plan designed to help finance postsecondary education. Parents, grandparents, aunts, uncles, or anyone else who wants to help a child save for educational costs can contribute to an RESP. The child is called the beneficiary because he or she is the one who will benefit from the savings plan. The beneficiary must be a resident of Canada.

Unlike an RRSP contributor, the person making contributions to an RESP does not get any tax benefit. However, the income earned from investing in these contributions grows tax-free until the beneficiary is ready to attend a college, university, or other approved postsecondary institution on a full-time basis. Then, he or she withdraws the money. Because students usually have limited incomes, they pay little or no tax when the funds are withdrawn. The government limits the amount that a person can contribute to an RESP each year, and sets a maximum limit for the total RESP contribution. To help with the increasing costs of education, the government contributes a set amount for every dollar saved in an RESP.

With rising tuition fees and increasing costs for housing, books, meals, travel, and other expenses, many students may find that postsecondary education is not financially possible. Yet, more and more jobs now require a postsecondary education—and this trend will likely continue. It's important to start preparing for your future education now. One way to do so might be through an RESP. Even though you're already in high school, it's not too late for a relative to establish an RESP for you, if he or she is financially able and willing to do so. Remember how compounded interest adds up!

With the costs of post-secondary education rising, more and more people are turning to RESPs to help finance students' education.

More About RESPs

If you're the beneficiary of an RESP but you don't go on to a postsecondary institution, you have the following choices:

- Appoint a different beneficiary.
- Withdraw the contributions made to the plan; however, taxes and a 20% surcharge may apply.
- Transfer the RESP proceeds into your RRSP, provided certain conditions are met.
- Donate all or part of the RESP funds to an educational institution.

Costs of Postsecondary Education

Tables 11.1 and 11.2 show the estimated costs of postsecondary education and the amount of monthly savings needed for students living at home and away from home. The calculations assume a 5% annual increase in education costs (which takes into account inflation) and four years of education. They also assume an 8% rate of return on any investment savings. There are no additional investments once the child starts college or university. The savings are withdrawn once a year for four years. At the end of four years, with inflation and annual investment income taken into consideration, there are no savings left.

Table 11.1 Student Living at Home

The estimated cost of postsecondary education is based on $4000 per year. This includes tuition and books. (All figures are rounded.)

Years until child attends a postsecondary institution	Estimated cost of four-year college or university program	Monthly savings needed
2	$17 000	$650
4	$19 000	$330
6	$21 000	$225
8	$23 000	$170
10	$25 000	$140
12	$28 000	$115
14	$30 000	$100
16	$34 000	$90
18	$37 000	$80

Table 11.2 Student Living Away From Home

The estimated cost of postsecondary education is based on $10 000 per year. This includes tuition, books, and room and board. (All figures are rounded).

Years until child attends a postsecondary institution	Estimated cost of four-year college or university program	Monthly savings needed
2	$42 000	$1600
4	$46 000	$820
6	$51 000	$560
8	$56 000	$425
10	$62 000	$345
12	$68 000	$290
14	$75 000	$250
16	$83 000	$220
18	$92 000	$200

INFORMATION	**C**ONNECTION	**E**XTENSION
1. a) Why are savings accounts a basic part of most people's financial planning?	**b)** You are looking for a financial institution in which to open a savings account. What questions should you ask?	**c)** What characteristics of savings accounts make them especially good for students?
2. a) In what different ways might interest rates on savings accounts be calculated?	**b)** Visit a local financial institution and find out the interest rates paid on different savings accounts. Present your findings in a one-page report.	**c)** Financial institutions usually pay a higher interest rate on special savings accounts than they do on regular accounts. Why can they do this?
3. a) How does a term deposit or cashable GIC differ from a non-cashable GIC?	**b)** At your local financial institution, find out about the interest rates on term deposits and/or GICs. Present your findings in a chart.	**c)** Why do term deposits and cashable GICs have lower interest rates than non-cashable GICs?
4. a) What are the main advantages of an RRSP and an RESP?	**b)** What types of registered plans does your local financial institution offer?	**c)** RRSPs are advertised extensively in January and February. Explain why.

Common Forms of Investments

Even though your money earns interest and is protected against loss in a financial institution, it may still lose purchasing power over time. The same item that costs $100 today might cost $110 in the future because of inflation. If you want a greater and faster yield on your investment, you should consider other possibilities. These include purchasing government or corporate bonds, buying stock in corporations or mutual funds, acquiring real estate, or investing in collectibles. Each investment has a different level of risk and expected return. Some investments tend to be "safer" than others. With safe investments, you have a better chance of keeping your original investment, but the yield may be low. Investments with a high yield are often considered more risky.

Investing has two major advantages over saving: Investments often produce a higher rate of return than savings plans, and investments can grow at or exceed the inflation rate. The major disadvantages of investing are that there is some degree of risk and the yield is not guaranteed. You can also lose all your money if an investment fails.

Investors, therefore, usually look for investments that provide security and a reasonable and steady rate of growth. If you have only a small amount of savings, you shouldn't take big risks. Only consider risky investments if you're prepared for the possibility of losing part of your savings. Investors looking for safety in their investments should know that their return will not be as high, but they don't run the risk of losing some, or all, of their investment.

CANADA SAVINGS BONDS

E-ACTIVITY

Visit
www.business.
nelson.com
and follow the links
to find out about
CSB interest rates
for current and past
years.

You can buy CSBs from October to April at most financial institutions and through most investment dealers.

A **Canada Savings Bond (CSB)** represents a loan made by you to the Government of Canada. The Government of Canada will repay you the value of the bond plus interest earned on or before the maturity date. The **maturity date**, printed on the face of the bond, is when the bond becomes due and is paid. Provincial and municipal bonds are also available, but CSBs are most commonly purchased.

There are several definite advantages of purchasing CSBs. First, they're guaranteed by the Government of Canada. Also, they're very liquid; they can be cashed at any time. If you cash your bonds within the first three months of purchase, you'll receive only the face value of the bond. The **face value** is the amount that appears on the front of the bond that the government promises to pay you at maturity. After the first three months, you'll receive the full face value plus all interest earned since you purchased the bond.

Another advantage is that CSBs can be purchased through payroll deduction. This makes it simple and convenient for Canadians to save for their goals from each paycheque. Finally, CSBs can be purchased for as little as $100.

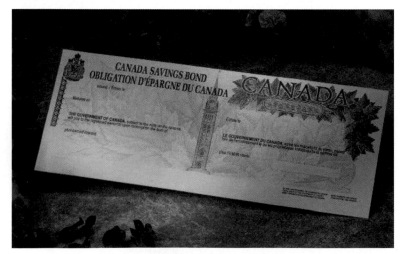

Since 1998, investors have been able to purchase a second type of Canada Savings Bonds—the Canada Premium Bond. This bond has the same security and guarantees as the CSB, but it offers a higher interest rate because it can only be cashed on the anniversary of the issue date or during the 30 days after that date.

CORPORATE BONDS

Business corporations often need money to increase production, expand their operations, or introduce new products. They raise some of the money by selling **securities**: corporate bonds and shares of stock.

Just as people who buy Canada Savings Bonds lend money to the federal government, people who buy corporate bonds lend money to the corporation. A **bond** is a definite promise to repay borrowed money on a certain future date, along with interest. It is guaranteed by specific assets of the company issuing the bond.

Bondholders receive a fixed interest payment each year, based on the reputation and credit rating of the corporation and on the general interest rates in Canada when the bonds are issued. Bond yields must be high enough to provide serious investors with a reasonable return on their investment.

If bondholders want their money back before the bonds mature, they can sell them to other investors, through investment dealers, at the current value, or **market value**. This amount may be more or less than the bond's face value, depending on what other investors will pay. In this way, corporate bonds are a little less liquid than savings accounts and CSBs. Although some bonds change in price, such changes are generally slight. People who purchase corporate bonds rather than short-term, high-yield investments generally do so for the regular interest income.

INVESTING IN STOCKS

As you've just learned, when you invest in bonds you lend money to a government or a large corporation. Investing in stocks is different. When you invest in a stock, you become a part owner, or shareholder, of that company. Shareholders share both the risks and rewards of the company. Companies sell shares to raise money to become established or to continue to expand and grow. As you read in Chapter 3, if a business is profitable, part of the profits may be divided and paid to the shareholders in the form of dividends, based on the number of shares they hold.

Unlike bonds, stock shares do not have a maturity date. They can be held as long as the shareholder desires. Stock prices can go up or down from day to day, even from hour to hour. They are determined by supply and demand. If there are more orders to buy a given stock than offers to sell it, prices will rise. When the demand for and prices of stocks are high, we say it is a **bull market**. If the offers to sell exceed the orders to buy, prices will fall. In these circumstances, we say it is a **bear market**. The stock price reflects the investors' overall opinion of the company's prospects. This opinion is influenced by earnings and growth prospects, news of new products or planned services, and the general state of the economy.

Companies issue two different types of stock—common shares and preferred shares. Each type offers distinct advantages to the shareholder.

Common Stock

Most available stock is common stock. **Common stock** gives its owner a voice in the operation of the business. Common shareholders have the right to attend the company's annual meeting and to vote on company matters. Shareholders hoping to influence company policy are likely to purchase as much common stock as they can afford since each share equals one vote.

If the company makes a profit, common shareholders will share in that profit only after bondholders and preferred shareholders have been paid. If any profit remains, common shareholders will see the value of their shares rise or they will be paid dividends. If the company suffers a poor year or markets decline, share values will fall and dividends are unlikely.

Preferred Stock

Preferred stock has certain advantages over common stock. The main advantage is that preferred shareholders are paid first if the company makes a profit. The dividends paid to preferred holders are set at a fixed rate, which is usually a higher yield than dividends paid on common shares. Another advantage is that if the corporation goes out of business and the inventory, equipment, and other assets are sold, preferred shareholders will get back their investment before common shareholders, but after bondholders. This is why they are called "preferred" shareholders. Finally, there is less risk in owning preferred stock since prices tend to be more stable and dividends are fixed. But there is less chance of big gains in years of high profit. Also, preferred shareholders usually have no voting rights within the corporation.

Both common and preferred shares are liquid because they can be bought or sold on the open market at any time. Companies with long records of regular dividend payments, stable growth patterns, and active trading of their shares are called **blue chip companies**. Large, well-established companies with long records, such as Bell Canada International, Imperial Oil, TransCanada Pipelines, and Weston, are examples. They are much less risky than **growth companies**, which reinvest their profits into their operations rather than pay shareholder dividends. If the company goes out of business, shareholders are liable,

STRETCH YOUR THINKING

Corporations of all sizes issue common shares to raise money. Generally, the smaller the corporation, the higher the risk. Why do you think this is generally the case?

or responsible, only for the amount they invested. As you learned in Chapter 3, this is known as the principle of limited liability.

The Stock Exchange

Most stocks are bought and sold through stockbrokers and investment dealers. These licensed financial experts will advise you on which stocks to buy and sell, and when. They charge a fee, or commission, which pays for the broker's salary and for services their firm provides. Commission rates vary, with the current average being about 2.5% of the order's value.

Shareholders tell their broker the prices at which they are willing to sell their shares. Interested buyers tell their brokers what they would be willing to pay for these shares. The buyers and sellers adjust their bidding and asking prices until they reach a satisfactory price.

Investors buy and sell stocks, usually with the help of stockbrokers, through the stock exchange. The Toronto Stock Exchange (TSE), founded in 1861, handles over 80% of all share trading in Canada. About $2 billion shares are traded daily. The Canadian Venture Exchange (CDNX) was formed when the Vancouver and Alberta Stock Exchanges merged in 1999. CDNX was launched with some 2300 listed companies active in the resource (mining and oil and gas), industrial, technology, manufacturing, and financial services sectors. CDNX's headquarters are in Calgary, while its trading and operations office is in Vancouver. Other exchanges in Canada are in Montreal and Winnipeg.

Visitors learn about the Toronto Stock Exchange at this interactive display.

Stocks are often listed on more than one exchange. In the United States, the best known exchanges are the New York Stock Exchange and the Nasdaq (National Association of Securities Dealers Automated Quotations) in New York City. Opened in 1971, Nasdaq is the market for high-tech stocks and emerging technologies. Plans are underway for a Nasdaq Europe and a Nasdaq Japan, which will ultimately link up with Nasdaq in the United States and Canada.

Stock exchanges are not-for-profit organizations owned and operated by their member companies or brokerage firms. For example, the TSE is governed by a 15-member board and owned by over 100 member brokerage firms. To qualify for membership, a company must buy a seat and pay an annual membership fee as well as a fee for each transaction its traders make. Only member brokers can use the facilities of a stock exchange. When selecting a brokerage company, it's a good idea to select one that is a member of one of the Canadian exchanges or the Investment Dealers Association of Canada.

Stock Quotations

A stock quotation consists of two prices. The **bid price** is the highest price anyone is currently willing to pay for a particular stock. The **ask price** is the lowest selling price that another investor is willing to accept for that stock. The current prices of the more common and popular stocks are listed in most daily newspapers. These stock quotations usually list the highest and lowest price paid for the stock during the current year; the highest and lowest price paid for the stock the previous day; the last, or closing, price of the stock that day; the change in price from the previous day's closing price; and the number of shares traded during the most recent trading session.

How to Read Newspaper Stock Quotations

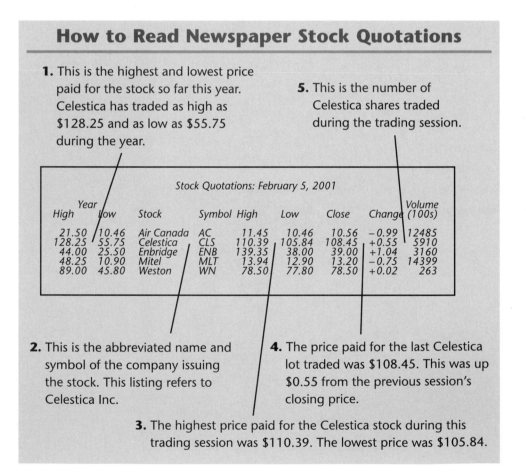

1. This is the highest and lowest price paid for the stock so far this year. Celestica has traded as high as $128.25 and as low as $55.75 during the year.

5. This is the number of Celestica shares traded during the trading session.

Stock Quotations: February 5, 2001

Year High	Low	Stock	Symbol	High	Low	Close	Change	Volume (100s)
21.50	10.46	Air Canada	AC	11.45	10.46	10.56	−0.99	12485
128.25	55.75	Celestica	CLS	110.39	105.84	108.45	+0.55	5910
44.00	25.50	Enbridge	ENB	139.35	38.00	39.00	+1.04	3160
48.25	10.90	Mitel	MLT	13.94	12.90	13.20	−0.75	14399
89.00	45.80	Weston	WN	78.50	77.80	78.50	+0.02	263

2. This is the abbreviated name and symbol of the company issuing the stock. This listing refers to Celestica Inc.

4. The price paid for the last Celestica lot traded was $108.45. This was up $0.55 from the previous session's closing price.

3. The highest price paid for the Celestica stock during this trading session was $110.39. The lowest price was $105.84.

MUTUAL FUNDS

If you want to invest in stocks but don't have the time or patience to follow the stock market carefully on a daily basis, you can buy units in a mutual fund. A **mutual fund** is a pool of money from many investors that is set up and managed by an investment company to buy and sell securities of other corporations.

Mutual fund companies sell many different types of funds. It's important to understand the differences between them in order to make the choice that's best for you.

When you invest in a mutual fund, professional investment managers make day-to-day decisions for you. They research the marketplace and economic conditions around the world before selecting securities to buy and sell. For this service, you pay management fees and additional fees for buying and selling securities. Some funds are no-load funds. This means that no fees of any kind are charged to buy and sell funds or to move investments among different funds. When selecting a fund, make sure that you know what types of fees you'll be paying and how they'll be paid.

Mutual fund managers select investments from many different companies at the same time, which spreads the risk over a large number of securities. If one stock in the fund does poorly, others might do well enough to balance the loss. However, there is no guarantee against loss, and the investment is not protected by the CDIC even if your purchase was made through a financial institution whose savings deposits are insured by CDIC.

Hundreds of mutual funds are available today. These include growth funds, balanced funds, global funds, money market funds, and real estate funds. Most funds now use sophisticated computer programs to move investments among various groups, to adjust to varying economic conditions, and to provide the best rate of return for investors. Even though a professional manager is making decisions for you, you should follow how your fund is doing to ensure that you're getting a good return on your investment. You can see how your mutual fund is performing by looking at the financial pages of your daily newspaper, the financial reports issued on a regular basis by your fund, and the Internet.

Online Investing

With the rapid growth of the Internet, online investing has become more and more popular. Many claim it is less expensive and more convenient than using a financial planner or stockbroker. New Internet companies and long-standing investment firms and financial institutions offer a wide variety of services on the Internet.

You can now receive stock quotations for companies and buy and sell stock directly from your computer. Many investment firms provide tips for the novice and allow you to maintain an investment portfolio right on their Web site. Through e-mail, message boards, and newsgroups, investors can exchange data and knowledge of companies. By investing online, you are your own financial planner.

However, online investing has some definite disadvantages. Acting as your own financial planner, you do not benefit from the advice of a financial expert. Without proper research, you may buy or sell stocks too quickly, since trading is as quick as clicking your computer mouse. Also, your lack of experience in making sound investment decisions could result in serious financial losses. Moreover, when you read data online, you do not always know who is actually writing this information; it could be a skilled fraud artist. Investors need to be careful about investment scams and get-rich-quick swindles.

If you're interested in buying certain stocks, do some research first. Check out the company's annual reports, financial statements, company news, and background on how the stock has performed recently. You can get valuable information from credible sources, including many on the Internet, and then decide whether to invest online or through a traditional stockbroker.

E-ACTIVITY

**Visit
www.business.
nelson.com
and follow the links
to sites that offer
online investing.**

Socially Responsible Investments

A recent concern for some investors is a company's policy on social responsibility. Some investors will only buy securities of companies whose business policies contribute to a community's well-being. These policies might support environmental protection, advancement of women and minorities, employment of older workers and those with disabilities, a healthy and safe workplace, employee wellness, and so on. These investors are satisfied with a fair return knowing that their investment is also helping improve the quality of life for employees and society.

REAL ESTATE

Although savings plans and securities are popular investments, many investors want to see, use, and enjoy their investments. For this reason, they choose to invest in real estate and collectibles.

Real estate is land and anything attached to it. It may involve the purchase of a house, cottage, condominium, or piece of property. For most people, buying a home will be their single most expensive purchase. Nothing requires more careful planning and selection. When you buy a home, you need to consider the cost of maintaining it as well as the amount of the monthly mortgage payment, taxes, and insurance. Another investment opportunity is buying income property, such as an apartment or a commercial building, and renting it to tenants.

COLLECTIBLES

If you collect baseball or hockey cards, you may have an investment. Any item of personal interest to a collector that can increase in value over time is a **collectible**. A collectible will increase in value only if it is popular and hard to find, or if it is produced in a limited edition so that the demand for it far exceeds the supply. Maybe you or someone you know collects comic books, antiques, dolls, stamps, coins, glass bottles, or a variety of other items. Think of almost any item and there is probably someone somewhere who collects it.

The main advantage of collecting is the personal pleasure you get from the process of buying, storing, arranging, and displaying what you collect. Many collectors form clubs or organizations where they meet to buy, trade, sell, and display their prized collections. For many investors, collectibles combine an interesting and enjoyable hobby with a potential investment.

Remember, though, that collectibles do not provide dividends or interest. You will not realize a return until you sell the item, and to sell, you need to find someone who wants to buy your collectible at a price satisfactory to you. Thus, many experts suggest that you only collect items you really enjoy. Investing in

Carlos Delgado plays first base for the Toronto Blue Jays. After becoming one of the top hitters in the American League, his baseball card increased in value.

collectibles requires as much serious effort and study as any other investments discussed in this chapter.

No matter what you purchase, investing money has both rewards and risks. You should not invest money that you need for your basic living expenses in case you lose your investment. Before you invest, check the following features or benefits: safety, rate of return, liquidity, and potential growth of the investment. Wise consumers comparison shop for an investment just as they do for goods and services.

ACTIVITIES FOR ...

INFORMATION	CONNECTION	EXTENSION
1. a) What are four advantages of Canada Savings Bonds as an investment? Which advantage do you think is the most important? Why?	**b)** Find the maturity dates and interest rates on the last two issues of Canada Savings Bonds. Which issue was the better investment? Why?	**c)** Find the maturity dates and interest rates for your province's savings bonds. How do they compare with Canada Savings Bonds as an investment over the same period of time?
2. a) How is investing in stocks different from investing in bonds?	**2. b)** How does common stock differ from preferred stock, with regard to security, voting, and dividends? Record you ideas in a chart. Which type of stock would you rather purchase? Explain your reasoning.	**c)** Ask parents, guardians, or other adults about investing. Have they invested in stocks or bonds? Why or why not? If they have investments, what kind are they? Why did they choose these types of investments?
3. a) What is considered real estate?	**b)** List five specific real estate opportunities in your community today.	**c)** Using your local newspaper and interviews with realtors and neighbours, research how property values have changed in your community in the last year and in the last five years. Prepare a report on your findings to share with the class.
4. a) What are collectibles? List five examples.	**b)** Do you own any collectible items? If you do, why did you choose to collect these particular items?	**c)** Choose a collectible that interests you. Find out its original cost and its value today. By what percent has the value of your collectible increased or decreased since you purchased it?

Review

Knowledge and Understanding

1. Match each of the following terms with the correct definition:

   collectible   preferred stock
   common stock   saving
   interest   securities
   investing

   a) Putting money aside for future use.
   b) Stock that has priority in the payment of dividends.
   c) Any item of personal interest that can increase in value over time.
   d) Stock that carries voting privileges.
   e) A general term for stocks and bonds.
   f) The price paid for the use of money over a period of time.
   g) Committing money in order to gain a financial return.

2. Role-play a savings or investment scenario with a partner. For example, one person could be a client and the other person could be a financial advisor, offering investment advice. Use at least four terms from the list above in your role-play.

3. Copy the following chart onto a blank sheet of paper. Complete the chart using the terms "poor," "fair," "good," "very good," and "excellent."

Investment	How Safe?	How Liquid?	Rate of Return?
Savings accounts			
Term deposits/Cashable GICs			
Noncashable GICs			
Registered retirement savings plans			
Registered education savings plans			
Canada Savings Bonds			
Corporate bonds			
Common stocks			
Preferred stocks			
Mutual funds			
Real estate			
Collectibles			

Thinking and Inquiry

1. Why does a savings account grow even when you don't deposit any more money into it?

2. Stocks are not as safe an investment as savings plans. Why, then, do many people still buy stocks?

3. Su Mei Cheng wants to invest in stocks that will be highly liquid, very safe, and earn a high yield. Is she likely to find such an investment? Why or why not? What advice would you give Miyoshi to consider when buying stocks and bonds?

4. What effect do each of the following have on the value of money over time: simple interest, compound interest, rate of inflation, saving, and investing?

Communication

1. "Since all savings accounts are basically the same, it really doesn't matter in which financial institution you open your acount." Debate this statement with a partner. One partner should argue that the statement is true, the other that the statement is false. Use the information in this chapter to support your arguments.

2. With a group, brainstorm the advantages and disadvantages of various types of saving and investment plans for different types of goals. Be prepared to share this information with the class and defend your decisions.

3. Working with a partner, try to find 10 articles or stories that describe why people save and invest. (Your local newspaper, current magazines, the school library, and the Internet are some possible resources.) Highlight or summarize the key points in the articles. Bring the articles to class and share them with your classmates. Prepare either an oral report or a bulletin board display based on the theme "Why People Save and Invest."

Application

1. Decide on a goal for which you might save money. Is it a short-term goal or a long-term goal? What might be the best savings plan to meet this goal?

2. John Anderson has just inherited $15 000. He is 24 years old, has graduated from a college business program, and works as an assistant manager in a retail store. John shares a two-bedroom apartment with a friend, and regularly saves 5% of his monthly paycheque. He wants to invest his inheritance in safe, secure

investments because he doesn't want to lose money. But he also wants a good yield on his investment. The only major expense that John plans is a one-week holiday in the Caribbean. From what you learned in this chapter, what advice would you give John about how to invest his $15 000?

3. Using the local newspaper or an Internet site that provides listings of stocks traded on a major stock exchange, select five stocks that interest you. Find answers to the following questions:

   a) What was the high and low price for each stock today?
   b) How many shares of stock were traded today?
   c) What was the high and low price for each stock so far this year?

   For two of your choices, follow the prices for one month. At the end of the month, plot the price changes on a line graph. Can you explain why the price changed as it did during the month? Prepare a report summarizing your findings, indicating which of your stocks you would recommend for an investment, and why. If possible, include newspaper articles or Internet articles that provide additional background on your stocks.

REFLECT ON YOUR LEARNING

1. Think about the different types of investments discussed in this chapter. Which ones were you familiar with before reading this chapter? What new information did you learn?

2. In 1910, Stephen Leacock wrote a humorous story, "My Financial Career," that has become a classic about the overwhelming feeling of intimidation when conducting business with a bank. Visit www.business. nelson.com and follow the links to this story. Read the story, then talk about it with a partner. In what ways do you identify with the feelings of the author? How is banking today similar to and different from the way it was in 1910?

STUDENT EXPECTATIONS

After completing this chapter, you will be able to

- explain the importance of the Bank Act
- define branch banking
- describe the relationship between the Bank of Canada and Canada's chartered banks
- compare the functions of chartered banks with those of trust companies, *caisses populaires*, and credit unions
- identify the main financial institutions in Canada
- explain the importance of financial institutions to our personal lives and to the business community
- outline the procedures for opening an account in a financial institution

Profile

PERSONAL TOUCH BANKING LIBRE-SE ROYA

Sharlyn Ayotte banks at one of the audio bank machines she helped develop.

SOUND OF MONEY IS SWEET MUSIC AT LAST

The automated banking machine at the Royal Bank branch at 99 Bank Street, in Ottawa, looks quite ordinary, performing all the mundane tasks that such machines do. It dispenses cash, ejects receipts, and accepts bill payments. However, this machine is actually the culmination of one Ottawa woman's hard work. What distinguishes it from other such machines is that it is an audio machine, intended for the blind or visually impaired. The users will certainly know it is extraordinary because, for many of them, it will be the first time they have used a banking machine unaided for a simple task that those with sight daily take for granted.

Sharlyn Ayotte is the president of T-Base Research and Development Inc., the Ottawa company she formed seven years ago to attack such problems that confront the blind. Ms. Ayotte, 45, lost her sight nearly 20 years ago in the space of just 10 months to a degenerative disease. She now has only five percent peripheral sight. The audio bank machine, developed in collaboration with the Royal and NCR Canada, is one of her company's greatest achievements.

T-Base has worked with the Royal since 1994 on the development of information packages the bank supplies its customers in Braille and large-print formats, and as audio cassettes and computer diskettes. So, it was T-Base that the bank approached to work on its touch-banking service for the blind.

The machine is the first of its kind in Canada, perhaps even the world. T-Base devised the audio aspect of the ABM, a raised metallic square, in the centre of which is a jack for the client's headset. The Royal is supplying the headset earphones, similar to those used by portable CD players, as part of its audio banking kit.

Inserting the headset jack activates the ABM so that, instead of using the screen directions for transactions, the client can use the

CONTINUED →

same metal keypad everyone uses to punch in a PIN. "It's the same as a telephone answering system," Ms. Ayotte says. "Press 1 for this, press 2 for that, and so on."

Ms. Ayotte worked in computer programming and computer sales before forming T-Base. The experience served T-Base well for the Royal's audio machine. T-Base designed the audio script, the methodology to access the audio files, and the system's bilingual wav (pronounced wave) file sound bites, and then got the whole thing up and running in 10 months. "It's a great company," says Chuck Wilson, senior manager of the Royal's Direct Banking Network in Toronto. "This was quite a complex undertaking, and it has worked out fantastically well."

It was the loss of her sight and one year of constantly badgering the federal government that prompted Ms. Ayotte to form T-Base to produce multiple-format information for the visually impaired. In 1992, the government passed legislation that gave people the right to obtain information in whichever format they needed. That meant the government would provide, for example, different information formats for health, safety, security, economy, employment, and transportation services.

Ms. Ayotte's requests for information in a 10-month span that year cost the government $90 000. "It was all information that was readily available to the public, but I needed to have it, too, as a blind person, to run a business," she says. "I was driven to despair by what I had to go through. I'm an in-your-face kind of girl. Something had to be done, so I did it." And that was the birth of T-Base. Today, the company employs eight full-time staff and has 30 consultants.

"I think the audio machine is going to be hugely successful," Ms. Ayotte says. "I just love it. It works like a dream." The Royal, too, believes it is going to be popular and that there will be demand not only from those who are visually impaired, but also from those who might prefer to use the banking machine aurally instead of visually, for example, people who have a reading disability. The Royal has installed other audio bank machines in Canada, and T-Base has created talking ABMs for the U.S.

> *"I'm an in-your-face kind of girl. Something had to be done, so I did it."*

About This Profile

1. How does the audio bank machine differ from other ABMs?
2. What factors motivated Ms. Ayotte and the Royal Bank to develop an audio bank machine? Why was this a sound business decision for the Royal Bank?

The Need for Financial Institutions

BEFORE YOU BEGIN

Tell a partner what you know about opening a savings account. How much money do you need? How do you withdraw money or make deposits to your account?

When someone says, "I need to go to the bank to get some money," that person may not mean a bank as you know it. They might be referring to another one of Canada's financial institutions or to an automated banking machine. The main deposit-taking institutions in Canada are chartered banks, trust companies, *caisses populaires,* and credit unions. All these financial institutions are essential to our economy. They accept deposits, encourage saving, and keep our money safe. They provide loans to individual consumers and to businesses, and each day, they handle millions of cheques relating to business transactions. They also offer a wide variety of other services to their customers.

Each institution differs in the services it provides, the methods it uses, and its hours of operation. However, all invest and lend their customers' savings, and charge fees for many of their services. To use these institutions effectively and to get the best value for your money, you need to understand how they work and what services they offer. Details about the various services will be examined more fully in Chapter 13.

EARLY BANKING IN CANADA

Canada's Aboriginal people and early European settlers had no need for financial institutions because they didn't use money. Instead, they traded or bartered for goods and services. Over time, however, Canada became more involved in trade and commerce, creating a need for coins, paper currency, and, eventually, a system of credit. These developments meant that it was important for the money supply to be managed in an orderly way.

In 1817, a group of merchants established the first bank in Canada—the Montreal Bank. Its purpose was to accept deposits and make loans. Eventually, it became the Bank of Montreal. By Confederation in 1867, 35 banks were operating in Canada. Since 1867, many new banks have been established and others have merged, or joined together. For example, in 1955, the Bank of Toronto and the Dominion Bank merged to form the Toronto Dominion Bank. In 1891, the Canadian Bankers Association (CBA) formed to serve chartered banks and the banking industry in Canada.

Aboriginal peoples and early European settlers trade at Fort Pitt, NWT.

THE BANK ACT

The Canadian Constitution of 1867 gave the federal government control over money and banking. As a result, the government created a common, unified banking system—all banks in Canada had to operate under similar rules. In 1871, the federal parliament passed Canada's first bank act. The Bank Act outlines the rules and regulations that banks have to follow. All banks in Canada receive a charter from the federal government, which means that the government gives the bank the authority to operate. For this reason, Canadian banks are known as **chartered banks**. Only a chartered institution that operates under the Bank Act can call itself a "bank."

The Bank Act outlines the procedures for opening new banks and forming mergers, and gives other details about what banks can and cannot do. The act also states that banks must make regular reports to the federal minister of finance. In addition, the Office of the Superintendent of Financial Institutions (OSFI) monitors the banks' operations to keep track of how they are doing financially. At least once a year, the OSFI examines the records kept at each bank's head office. It also inspects bank branches on a regular basis.

Every few years, the federal government reviews and revises the Bank Act. The review and revision process ensures that the act continues to meet the needs of society and the business community. For example, the 1980 revisions allowed foreign banks to operate in Canada for the first time. The 1997 revision made financial services more convenient for and accessible to consumers. In February 2001, the federal government introduced a new revision (Bill C-8). This bill was designed to provide consumers with improved services and protection. For example, under Bill C-8, financial institutions will have to be more accountable to their customers, and a Canadian Financial Services ombudsman will be appointed to handle complaints from individuals and small businesses. As well, Bill C-8 contained provisions that would enable Canadian financial services providers to compete in a rapidly changing marketplace.

CANADIAN BANKING TODAY

Banks are businesses, just as retail stores and manufacturing companies are businesses. Banks sell services and earn profits on these services. They earn most of their revenue by charging interest on money they loan to consumers, businesses, and government. They also invest a portion of the money that individuals and businesses deposit with them. The banks earn interest on these investments, which contributes to their profits.

E-ACTIVITY

Visit
www.business.
nelson.com
and follow the links
to find resources
that the Canadian
Bankers Association
offers to help young
people learn about
banking.

The 1980 revisions to the Bank Act established two classes of banks—Schedule I and Schedule II banks—to encourage more competition. Canadian shareholders own the Schedule I banks. Shareholders can trade their shares openly on the major Canadian stock exchanges. In many ways, Schedule I banks are like any other corporation: They are owned by a large number of shareholders who invested their money in the bank in order to receive a share of its profits.

Schedule I Banks

Canada has eight Schedule I banks. The country's major banks—known as the "Big Six"—hold 92% of all bank assets and are the core of Canada's banking system. These banks are identified with an asterisk (*) below.

- Bank of Montreal*
- The Bank of Nova Scotia*
- CIBC (Canadian Imperial Bank of Commerce)*
- Canadian Western Bank
- Laurentian Bank of Canada
- National Bank of Canada*
- Royal Bank of Canada*
- Toronto Bank Financial Group (formally Toronto Dominion Bank)*

Schedule II banks are mostly foreign-owned banks that are controlled by a small number of shareholders. Generally, Schedule II banks don't offer shares to the public. Schedule II banks have the same powers as Schedule I banks. However, the government sets limits on the number of branches that each Schedule II bank can have and on the total amount of assets that these banks are allowed to hold. Examples of Schedule II banks include the Amex Bank of Canada, the HSBC Bank of Canada (formerly Hongkong Bank of Canada), the First Nations Bank of Canada, and ING Bank of Canada.

BRANCH BANKING

Each Schedule I bank has a head office in one of Canada's main cities. Each head office determines overall bank policy and is connected to thousands of bank branches across Canada. Canadian banks have also established branches in more than 40 foreign countries. This system of banking is called **branch banking**.

Banks in the United States

In the United States, banks operate under a local, or "unit banking," system. The majority of banks are separate institutions that are owned and operated locally. Most American cities and towns have several different banks that do business primarily in that city or town. As a result, there are more than 8000 different banks in the United States. Although American banks offer basically the same services as Canadian chartered banks, most are not part of a unified, national system.

Branch Banking Today

Branch banking has played a vital role in the development of Canada. It offers residents of both small communities and large cities the same services at the same cost. Branches provide financial links between small communities and major financial centres. Also, customers can go to any branch of their bank anywhere in Canada and, with proper identification, make transactions as easily as at their home branch.

Another advantage of the branch banking system is that a bank can diversify, or spread out, its loans among various segments of the economy to reduce the degree of risk. As a result, poor economic conditions in one area may affect the local branch, but this will be balanced by the better conditions in other areas. Each branch, no matter how small, is also fully supported by the expertise and services of the bank's head office.

Branch banking is undergoing a change. Banks are finding that branch banking may not be as viable as it once was. To stay competitive, they are closing branches, and are encouraging customers to use automated banking machines (ABMs), or to conduct financial transactions by phone or online. (More information on ABMs appears later in this chapter. Information on telephone banking and online banking appears in Chapter 13.)

THE BANK OF CANADA

In Chapter 10, you learned that the Bank of Canada issues Canada's paper money. The Bank of Canada is not a chartered bank—customers cannot open accounts in or borrow money from this bank. (The chartered banks can borrow money from the Bank of Canada, but they seldom do.) Although it offers no direct services to the general public, the Bank of Canada helps keep the Canadian economy as stable as possible.

As you read in Chapter 5, the most important function of the Bank of Canada is to regulate the money supply. Sometimes, the Bank of Canada raises or lowers the bank rate to control the money supply. The **bank rate**, also called the **prime lending rate**, is the minimum rate of interest that the Bank of Canada charges for loans it makes to chartered banks. Because chartered banks borrow very little and very rarely from the Bank of Canada, raising or lowering the bank rate is actually a symbolic move—it suggests to chartered banks that they raise or lower their interest rates to borrowers. If interest rates rise, fewer businesses and consumers will take out loans. On the other hand, if interest rates drop, borrowing money becomes more attractive to businesses and consumers. The Bank of Canada announces its new bank rate several times a year. The release of this figure is major economic news.

ACTIVITIES FOR ...

INFORMATION	CONNECTION	EXTENSION
1. a) What is the purpose of the Bank Act?	**b)** Explain how the Bank Act affects consumers and society as a whole.	**c)** Why do you think that American-owned banks in Canada are subject to fewer regulations than other foreign-owned banks? Is this fair? Explain your reasoning.
2. a) What is the difference between Schedule I and Schedule II banks?	**b)** Which Schedule I and Schedule II banks are in or near your community?	**c)** Use the Internet or conduct a personal visit to compare a Schedule I and Schedule II bank. How are they the same? How are they different?
3. a) What is branch banking? List three advantages of branch banking.	**b)** Survey your community to find out how many different bank branches exist. Do you think they are all necessary? Why or why not?	**c)** Do some research to find out how branch banking is changing. Prepare a report to show your findings.

Contemporary Issues in Canadian Business

THE ISSUE: BANK MERGERS AND ACQUISITIONS

What role do mergers and acquisitions play in Canadian banking?

Canada has six major national banks that have developed through more than 40 mergers and acquisitions over the past 130 years. As you read in Chapter 6, a **merger** takes place when two or more businesses join together, either because one takes over the other or because they combine their assets. When one business takes ownership of another, usually by buying a controlling share in the company, it is called an **acquisition** or **takeover.**

In 1998, two bank mergers were proposed: The TD Bank sought to merge with the Canadian Imperial Bank of Commerce, and the Royal Bank of Canada planned to join forces with the Bank of Montreal. However, under the Bank Act, the federal minister of finance was required to approve the mergers before they could go forward. The minister withheld his approval because the government did not believe that the mergers were in the best interest of the Canadian public. Why were the mergers not approved?

The four Canadian banks involved in the proposed mergers, along with Scotiabank and National Bank, are known as the "Big Six." Together, these banks account for well over 90% of the banking business that takes place in Canada. If the minister had approved the mergers, the "Big Six" would have become the "Big Four," significantly limiting the choices available to Canadian banking customers.

Events in 1998 polarized opinions about the role of the government in regulating bank mergers and acquisitions. Some people believe that banks should be free to make their own decisions about how to grow and expand so

they can compete in the global market. Others believe that regulations are needed to protect customers and bank employees from potential negative results. What are some arguments on both sides of this issue?

Point

In today's global economy, banking is an international business. There are currently 38 foreign banks operating in Canada, while Canadian banks generate nearly 50% of their annual earnings outside Canada. Mergers allow Canadian banks to compete with large foreign banks—especially those from the United States.

As financial institutions around the world have grown, Canadian banks have lost ground in comparison. In the early 1980s, there were three Canadian banks listed among the world's 50 largest; by 1999, Canada's largest bank, CIBC, had dropped to 55th place. If CIBC and the TD Bank had merged in 1998 as planned, the resulting institution would have become the ninth largest bank in North America and the 21st largest in the world, with assets of over $460 billion.

Larger banks have a number of advantages over smaller competitors. They have more money to spend and to lend, more locations, more staff, and access to larger markets for their services. They also have more money that they can use to acquire new technology—an important asset at a time when Internet banking is expanding rapidly. Keeping Canadian banks strong ultimately means keeping more jobs in Canada and making a greater contribution to the Canadian economy. To stay strong, the banks need the freedom to grow through mergers and acquisitions.

Counterpoint

A survey conducted in November 1998 indicated that people believed the proposed bank mergers would benefit bank shareholders more than customers. The Council of Canadians, an independent citizens' interest group, agreed. The Council's view was that "bigger banks will make a bad situation worse. Jobs will be lost; services will be cut; and Canadians will be held hostage by an even more monopolized industry."

Fewer banks could mean fewer choices for customers, higher fees, and less personal service. The impact would be especially great on small businesses and rural communities. With larger banks, owners of small businesses might find it more difficult to get the loans they need. With branches closing in smaller communities, people might have less access to bank services, and it might be difficult for bank staff who have been laid off to get new jobs.

A Real Life Example

On January 10, 2000, the Toronto Dominion Bank made a takeover bid to acquire Canada Trust Financial Services Inc. The minister of finance approved the bid, and TD Canada Trust was born on February 1, 2000.

Since the merger, former TD customers have experienced some service improvements, including the fact that branches across the country are now open longer hours. And, Canada Trust customers have indicated that they are more satisfied since the merger. The bank itself has gained market share in areas such as personal deposits, credit cards, personal loans, and mortgages. Bank president Ed Clark says that these results are just the opposite of what merger specialists predicted. The specialists said that two things would happen—customer satisfaction would decrease and market share would decline. Interestingly, neither result has occurred.

Because TD and Canada Trust had complementary strengths, the merger appears to have been a winning situation for everyone—but changes are on the way. First, TD Canada Trust plans to streamline account options, offering all customers only one line of accounts (the former Canada Trust menu selections). Then, over the next 30 months, the bank will shrink its branch network by 275 branches, eliminating 4900 full-time positions, or about 10% of its work force. Clark expects that most of these positions can be eliminated as people retire or take extended leaves of absence, and that layoffs will be kept to a minimum. According to Clark, customer satisfaction is still the bank's top priority, followed closely by employee morale and increased earnings for shareholders.

Ed Clark (right), president of Canada Trust, and Charles Baillie (left), chairman of TD Bank Financial Group, seal the TD–Canada Trust merger with a handshake at a press conference in Toronto.

Questions and Activities About This Issue

1. Find out what further impact the TD Bank–Canada Trust merger has had on customers and on the bank itself.
2. The Bank Act is continually being revised to address changing conditions in Canadian banking. If you were in charge of the current revisions, would you change the provision that bank mergers must have the approval of the minister of finance? Why or why not?
3. Research the evolution of a large Canadian bank. What strategies have helped this bank grow?

Other Financial Institutions

The chartered bank is the most common type of financial institution in Canada, but it is not the only one. Trust companies, credit unions, and *caisses populaires* also play an important role in Canada's economy. With the passage of Bill C-8, insurance companies and money market and mutual fund dealers will also be able to offer many of the same deposit-taking services that banks now provide.

TRUST COMPANIES

Trust companies were first established in Canada in the late 1800s to manage and invest the funds entrusted to them by consumers. Today, they also provide many banking services, such as loans and savings and chequing accounts. Because their services are similar to those offered by banks, trust companies are sometimes called "near banks."

In addition to basic banking services, trust companies provide other financial services. They assist customers with the purchase and sale of real estate, administer the estates of deceased people, and maintain trust accounts for charitable organizations and minors.

Either the federal or the provincial government grants a trust company the right to operate. However, the Bank Act does not regulate trust companies; instead, each province and the federal government specify the types of investments that these institutions can make with their customers' money. As with chartered banks, the Canada Deposit Insurance Corporation (CDIC) protects depositors' accounts in a trust company.

CAISSES POPULAIRES AND CREDIT UNIONS

In 1900, Alphonse Desjardins established the first Canadian *caisse populaire* in Lévis, Quebec. This institution promoted the benefits of cooperation and thrift. It opened with a single deposit of 10¢. A few years later, the credit union movement, promoting cooperation and credit facilities for the average person, began in Atlantic Canada. The movement gained momentum and spread across the country. Credit unions soon appeared in Ontario and in the West.

Caisses populaires and **credit unions** are organized and owned by groups of people who agree to pool and share their resources. Members share a common bond of association, such as a profession, place of employment, geographic area, cultural or ethnic background, or religion. Both *caisses populaires* and credit unions belong to the World Council of Credit Unions.

Table 12.1 Credit Unions and Caisses Populaires in Canada

Province	Number of Credit Unions	Total Locations	Total Members
British Columbia	74	334	1 445 000
Alberta	78	192	504 564
Saskatchewan	143	333	555 000
Manitoba	66	164	410 000
Ontario	278	633	1 370 116
New Brunswick	25	33	86 800
Nova Scotia	52	85	160 134
Prince Edward Island	10	13	54 246
Newfoundland	11	35	36 424

Province	Number of Caisses Populaires	Total Locations	Total Members
Manitoba	9	30	34 699
Quebec	1110	1600	5 000 000
New Brunswick	56	88	200 800

Caisses populaires and credit unions receive deposits, lend money, offer chequing services, and provide investment products, such as RRSPs and GICs, in most of their branches. They offer competitive interest rates on deposits and loans. If you want to borrow money from a *caisse populaire* or credit union, you must have some savings deposited in that institution. A small committee of members determines how much you will be able to borrow.

Caisses populaires and credit unions have some unique features. They provide services only to members and their families. To become a member, a person must purchase at least one share in the institution. When members make collective decisions, each member has one vote. All members are equal owners regardless of how many shares they hold. Since members are shareholders, credit unions can respond in unique ways to the special needs of their members. For example, during periods of economic difficulty, some credit unions in parts of Canada have developed innovative loan repayment options to accommodate individual members' needs.

Provincial legislation gives *caisses populaires* and credit unions the right to operate, and establishes maximum rates of interest on deposits and loans. Since both *caisses populaires* and credit unions are not-for-profit organizations, they return any profits they make to their members in the form of dividends or rebates at the end of the year. Provincial governments protect the depositors' accounts through legislation.

BUSINESS
—FACT—

In 2000, there were more than 775 credit unions operating in Canada, with more than 4.4 million members.

1. a) Why are trust companies called "near banks"?	**b)** Why might someone prefer to use the services of a trust company rather than a bank?	**c)** Research a trust company by searching the Internet, visiting a local trust company, or inviting a representative of a trust company to speak to your class. Prepare a detailed report on the trust company, explaining how it is similar to and different from a bank.
2. a) What is a *caisse populaire*? a credit union?	**b)** Give examples of *caisses populaires* and/or credit unions that are organized around each type of bond mentioned on page 296.	**c)** How do credit unions differ from banks and trust companies? How are they similar? Record your findings in a two-column table. Tell why you think credit unions are growing in popularity.
3. a) How do you become a member of a *caisse populaire* or credit union?	**b)** Some staff members at credit unions are volunteers. Find out about the different jobs they perform.	**c)** Do some research to find out why *caisses populaires* and credit unions have historically been more popular in some parts of the country than others.

About Accounts

All of Canada's deposit-taking institutions accept and hold deposits. The institution holds this money in an account until the depositor needs it. As you learned in Chapter 11, people open savings accounts because they want to save money and earn interest on it. Interest rates vary from account to account, depending on the minimum balance required and whether or not cheques can be written on the account.

The steps involved in opening an account are basically the same in all financial institutions. Usually, you need only a minimal amount of money. A savings account can be in your own name, giving you full control. A **joint account** can be opened in the name of two or more people, such as a married couple or a parent and child. Withdrawals from joint accounts may require one or more signatures, depending on the wishes of the people who open the account.

OPENING AND ACCESSING AN ACCOUNT

When you open an account, the financial institution asks you for certain personal information, including your full name and home address, date of birth, telephone number, and occupation. You also need to show two current pieces of identification containing your signature and, if possible, your photograph. Acceptable identification includes a driver's licence, credit card, employer identity card, passport, or student card. You must fill out a **signature card** to provide a sample of the signature you will use when you deposit and withdraw money, write cheques, and engage in other financial transactions. If you wish to change your signature at any time, you have to give the financial institution a copy of your new signature. Finally, you usually receive a card which you can use to conduct transactions in a financial institution or at an automated banking machine. You can also use the card as a debit card. (See Chapter 13 for more information on debit cards.)

Your signature card is kept at the branch of the institution where you opened your account. When you conduct a transaction at that branch, tellers may verify your signature by checking your signature card. Usually, however, they check the signature on the back of your ABM card.

Social Insurance Numbers

The Government of Canada requires financial institutions to ask for your social insurance number (SIN) when you open an account that pays interest. The institution must issue an income tax slip for any account that earns more than $100 in interest per year, and the depositor must declare this income on his or her tax return. The institution could be fined if it does not ask for your SIN, and you can be fined if you refuse to provide it. However, if you are under 18 years of age, you only have to provide your SIN if you earn or receive investment income that totals more than $2500 a year.

Passbooks

The financial institution may give you a **passbook** to keep a record of account transactions. Your account has a unique number, which appears in your passbook. Your passbook shows all deposits, withdrawals, transfers of money, service charges, and any interest earned on your account. You can have your passbook updated any time you take it to the financial institution or at certain automated banking machines. Institutions also provide monthly account statements instead of passbooks. (See Chapter 13 for more information about account statements.)

Making a Deposit

You can deposit money into your account at a financial institution or at an automated banking machine. At a financial institution, you deposit money by having the teller input information—including your account number and the amount of the deposit—electronically or by filling out a deposit slip. (The financial institution keeps the deposit slip for its records.) Then, you give the teller the item(s) being deposited. The teller will give you a receipt for the transaction, which you should keep for your records, and/or update the information in your passbook.

An ABM card cannot be used without a PIN.

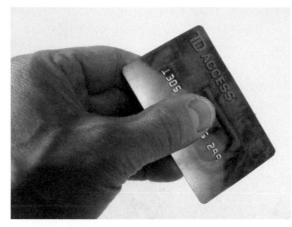

At an automated banking machine, you input the deposit information electronically. **Automated banking machines (ABMs)** are computer terminals that allow customers to deposit or withdraw funds, pay bills, transfer funds from one account to another, and check their account balances. ABM users need an ABM card, which has a magnetic strip on the back, and a **personal identification number (PIN)**. The PIN is a confidential electronic signature, similar to your signature on your signature card. To use an ABM, insert your card and then enter your PIN. Via an electronic network, the ABM checks the validity of the card and the PIN. After this is done, simply follow the on-screen instructions to carry out your deposit. The ABM prints out a transaction record of your updated account balance. The transaction is generally processed the same day (if you make the deposit before 3:00 p.m.) or the next day (if you make the deposit later than this time). There may be holds on cheques deposited at ABMs or branches, depending on the terms of your account agreement. (See Chapter 13 for information on cheques.)

Making a Withdrawal

When you want to make a withdrawal, you can go to a financial institution, where a teller will input your request electronically, or you can fill out a withdrawal slip. The teller will give you the money and, as with a deposit, give you a receipt for your transaction and/or update your passbook. If your account has chequing privileges, you can also withdraw money by writing a cheque on that account.

You can also make a withdrawal at an ABM. Just insert your card, enter your PIN, and follow the on-screen instructions. The machine will give you the money, update your account balance, and print a transaction record.

BUSINESS
—FACT—

ABMs dispense more than $2.5 billion in cash daily through an estimated 850 000 terminals around the world.

Security Tips for Using ABMs

- Your ABM card is a key that opens your account(s) and is for your use only. Keep it in a safe place and never lend it to anyone.
- Be creative when selecting a PIN. Always avoid the obvious: your name, phone number, date of birth, and so on.
- Keep your PIN a secret. Never disclose it to anyone, including bank staff, police, clerks, or merchants, and never write it down—memorize it!
- You cannot use your ABM without the correct PIN. In fact, after a number of incorrect PIN entries, the ABM will keep your card until you claim it later at your financial institution.
- Only conduct ABM transactions when and where you feel secure. If you are uncomfortable for any reason, do it later or at another location.
- To ensure privacy when conducting an ABM transaction, use your hand or body to prevent others from watching you enter your PIN.
- After completing an ABM transaction, remember to take your card and transaction record.
- When making a withdrawal from an ABM, count the cash that you receive and put it away immediately.
- If your card is lost, stolen, or retained by an ABM, notify your financial institution immediately. Most institutions offer a toll-free telephone number or 24-hour service for lost or stolen cards.
- Robbery is rare at ABMs. If it does happen, remember that your safety comes first. Report the incident to the police and to your financial institution.

ACTIVITIES FOR ...

INFORMATION	CONNECTION	EXTENSION
1. a) What is a joint account?	**b)** Would you prefer to have an account in your own name or a joint account? Explain your reasoning.	**c)** Interview three adults you know. Do they have a joint account? If so, with whom? Why did they open a joint account? Prepare a list of reasons and compare your findings with your classmates.
2. a) What is the purpose of a signature card?	**b)** How is a signature card similar to a PIN?	**c)** Visit a financial institution in your community to find out what specific information you need to provide when opening an account. Why does the institution need this information?
3. a) List three ways to withdraw money from your account.	**b)** If you wanted to withdraw money from an account, would you go to a financial institution or use an ABM? Explain why.	**c)** Do most customers today go to their financial institution to withdraw money, or do they use an ABM? Use the Internet or interview a bank employee to find out. How have withdrawal methods changed over the past 10 years?

Review

Knowledge and Understanding

1. Match each of the following terms to the correct definition:

   bank rate   passbook
   branch banking   signature card
   credit union   trust company
   joint account

   a) An account used by two or more people.
   b) A financial institution owned and controlled by its members.
   c) A financial institution's record of how you write your name.
   d) A financial institution that manages estates, acts as a trustee in business transactions, and provides many of the financial services provided by banks.
   e) A banking system with a head office and interconnected outlets.
   f) The minimum interest charged by the Bank of Canada for loans to banks.
   g) A customer's record of the transactions in an account.

2. What is the Bank of Canada? How does it differ from a chartered bank? What is the relationship between the Bank of Canada and chartered banks?

3. Describe to a partner how to open a bank account. Have your partner tell you whether you missed any steps.

Thinking and Inquiry

1. Why are financial institutions important to you and your community?

2. Why did Canada develop a branch banking system rather than a unit banking system?

3. When the Bank of Canada rate falls, who benefits the most? Why? Who benefits the least? Why?

4. What information is printed on an ABM transaction record? Why is each piece of information important?

5. Using the Internet and other resources, find out what has happened with Bill C-8 and what effect it has had on financial institutions.

Communication

1. Why do most Canadians open some type of account in a financial institution? Work in groups of three or four and brainstorm as many different reasons as possible. Then, place the reasons in order from the most important to the least important. Select one person from your group to write your ordered list of reasons on the board or on a flip chart. Compare and discuss the various group lists, noting similarities and differences. As a class, develop a final "Top Five Reasons for Opening an Account" list.

2. Find out more about Canada's first *caisse populaire*. Present your findings in role as one of the first members of this *caisse populaire*.

Application

1. Imagine that you inherit $1000 on the condition that you deposit it in a savings account. Use the Internet or contact representatives from local financial institutions to determine where you should open your account. Use information that you learned in Chapter 11 to help you answer the following questions:
   • How is interest calculated? How often is it added to your account?
   • Do you have the option of using a passbook or getting a monthly statement? Which would you prefer?
   • Are there advantages to opening the account at a chartered bank, trust company, *caisse populaire*, or credit union? If so, what are they?
   Once you answer these questions, prepare a table or chart with the heading "Comparison of Savings Plans at Financial Institutions." Be prepared to present your findings to the class, outlining where you would open your account, and why.

2. Safoora and Reema are sisters who are roommates at university. They are thinking about opening a savings account, but they aren't certain if they should open a joint account or two separate, individual accounts. What advice would you give them? Why?

REFLECT ON YOUR LEARNING

1. How has the information in this chapter helped you understand the similarities and differences among financial institutions? What did you know before? What do you know now?

2. Since the different types of financial institutions discussed in this chapter offer many of the same services, are they all necessary? Will each type of institution continue to exist in the future? Explain your answer.

CHAPTER 13

FINANCIAL SERVICES AND FUTURE DIRECTIONS

STUDENT EXPECTATIONS

After completing this chapter, you will be able to

- describe the main types of transaction accounts
- demonstrate how to reconcile a transaction account
- list the six essential elements of a cheque
- list the main steps in writing and endorsing cheques
- explain how a cheque is cleared
- describe and evaluate the major services offered by financial institutions
- give examples of the increased use of technology by financial institutions
- explain how electronic funds transfers are used to make payments

Profile

Sarah and her brother research GICs using the CBA's online resources.

THERE'S SOMETHING ABOUT MONEY

Like many young people, 15-year-old Sarah Park's experience with the world of banking and financial services was limited. Although her parents had opened an account for her at a local bank when she was quite young and had given her a weekly allowance, Sarah rarely thought about her financial future. "My allowance was small and I usually spent it pretty quickly on things like snacks or CDs, so I never had too much money in my account. But last summer I got a job at a restaurant and managed to save quite a bit. By the end of August, I had almost $800."

Soon after Sarah returned to school in the fall, she participated in a Canadian Bankers Association (CBA) seminar as part of her business class. The CBA is the professional association of Canada's banking industry. In 1998, the organization decided that it needed to make banking more accessible to young people, and to make teens aware that financial planning and management should be an important part of their life. The seminar, called "There's Something about Money, " is presented by local volunteers from the banking industry in communities across Canada. It introduces students to basic financial planning by focusing on three situations that many students will encounter someday: paying for postsecondary education, starting a new business, and beginning a career.

After the seminar, Sarah started thinking differently about her money. "Before the CBA presentation, I really just considered the bank as a place to keep my money. I didn't realize that banks offer so many different types of accounts and services. I started to wonder if I should be putting more thought into what I do with my money."

Sarah then decided to check out the CBA's Web site. It offers banking information that is designed to teach young people about topics such as setting financial goals, investing, and obtaining loans. The information is presented in ways that students will find

CONTINUED →

interesting and fun; many of the online features and activities are interactive. For example, Sarah clicked on the "Shopping for a Bank Account" feature and filled out a checklist that helped her decide what kind of account she needed. After completing the checklist, the program created a personal "profile," which identified the key features Sarah should look for when choosing a bank account. The site also has links to the Web sites of most of Canada's major financial institutions, making it easy for students to start "shopping" right away.

Sarah says she would definitely recommend the CBA's youth materials to other students. She also advises asking others for assistance—teachers, relatives, and representatives from local financial institutions. "My older brother has been a big help," says Sarah. "He's in university now and has been saving money from his part-time and summer jobs for a long time. He's also taken out loans to help him pay for school, so he's had to deal with banks a lot."

On her brother's advice, Sarah used some of the money she made during the summer to purchase a GIC. She figures that if she can set aside money in a GIC, which accumulates a guaranteed rate of interest, she will have more choices when she graduates in a few years. "I'm not sure if I want to go to college or university as soon as I finish high school. I might take a year off to do some travelling before I go back to school. Either way, I'll be able to put the money toward something that's important to me."

About This Profile

1. How is the Canadian Bankers Association trying to get young people interested in banking and financial planning?
2. Why is it important for young people to learn all they can about banking and financial services?
3. Besides basic bank accounts, what other services do you think financial institutions offer? How might these services be useful to teens?
4. Do you think that a GIC was a good investment for Sarah? Explain.

Transaction Accounts

Intense competition has led to many changes in the financial-services industry. One sign of these changes is the increased variety of services that financial institutions now offer customers. These services include a greater variety of transaction (formerly chequing) accounts.

REASONS FOR TRANSACTION ACCOUNTS

As you read in Chapters 11 and 12, people open savings accounts primarily to earn interest on the money that they save. They open **transaction accounts**, on the other hand, so that they have a place where they can keep money they will use to pay for everyday needs. With a transaction account, they can pay for goods and services with cash, cheques, or debit cards. They can also pay bills using an ABM, telephone banking, and online banking. (You will learn more about debit cards, telephone banking, and online banking later in this chapter.)

When you open a transaction account, the institution gives you a **transaction register**, which is similar to a blank passbook. Each time you deposit or write a cheque; deposit or withdraw cash; use your debit card; or pay a bill through the ABM, telephone banking, or online banking, you should record the details in the transaction register. Keeping this record ensures that you always know how much money is in your account.

Using your transaction register, you can keep track of your balance after each transaction.

Bank of Montreal Banque de Montréal				AMOUNT OF CHEQUE / RETRAITS	AMOUNT OF DEPOSIT / DÉPÔTS	BALANCE / SOLDE	
DATE	NO.	PARTICULARS / DÉTAILS				$ 513.47	
Jan 12 2001	153	To / Bénéf.	The Jeans Store	69.95			
		For / Objet	Jeans			BAL./SOLDE 443.52	
31		To / Bénéf.	Part-time pay		125.00		
		For / Objet				BAL./SOLDE 568.52	
Feb 3		To / Bénéf.	ABM Withdrawal	40.00			
		For / Objet				BAL./SOLDE 528.52	
10	Debit	To / Bénéf.	The Bike Shop	34.50			
		For / Objet	Helmet			BAL./SOLDE 494.02	
17		To / Bénéf.	ABM Deposit		50.00		
		For / Objet				BAL./SOLDE 544.02	
18		To / Bénéf.	Service Charge	3.60			
		For / Objet				BAL./SOLDE 540.42	
		To / Bénéf.					
		For / Objet				BAL./SOLDE	

TYPES OF TRANSACTION ACCOUNTS

As with savings accounts, transaction accounts may be held by one person only or jointly by two or more people. Although the names of transaction accounts differ from one financial institution to another, the two most common types are the straight transaction account and the transaction-savings, or combination, account. For businesses, there is another kind of transaction account: the current account.

Straight Transaction Accounts

The straight transaction account is a simple way to pay personal and household bills. Because this type of account is not meant for savings, most financial institutions pay no interest on account balances.

Transaction-Savings (Combination) Accounts

As with a passbook, withdrawals on an account statement appear in the debit column; deposits appear in the credit column.

If you want an account that enables you to save money but still pay expenses, consider opening a **combination account**. This kind of account is part transaction and part savings; you can write cheques, make debit transactions, and also collect a small amount of interest. Interest is calculated on the minimum account balance during a specific time period, and is usually paid monthly. For example, if your monthly account balance ranges from $50 to $2500 during the month, interest will be paid only on the $50—that is your minimum balance during this month.

With both straight transaction and combination accounts, the financial institution levies a **service charge**, or processing fee, on each cheque unless you have a service plan that includes processing cheques, debits, and other withdrawals. (See page 320 for more information on combination service packages.) The institution may allow some free withdrawals if you keep a minimum balance in your account. The number of free withdrawals and the required minimum balance differ among institutions.

Depending on the financial institution, customers receive either a passbook or a detailed monthly account statement. An **account statement** is a computer printout that lists the amount of every transaction by the date it was processed. The statement totals the transactions and provides the balance in your account on the statement date.

Scotiabank™

Your Branch
123 Any Street
Your Town, Province   12345
A1B 2C3   (123) 456-7890

Aileen C Love
192 Main Street
Your Town, Province
A1B 2C3   ACCOUNT NUMBER
12345 5678901

STATEMENT OF	FROM	TO	PAGE
DIS GETTING THERE	2001/01/01	2001/01/31	1

DESCRIPTION	WITHDRAWALS/DEBITS	DEPOSITS/CREDITS	DATE M D	BALANCE
BALANCE FORWARD			0101	11196
POINT OF SALE PURCHASE DAIRY QUEEN KANATA ON	320		0109	10876
POINT OF SALE PURCHASE PHARMAPLUS DRUG MART #220KANATA ON	455		0111	10921
ABM DEPOSIT BRIDLEWOOD #1 KANATA ON		5000	0116	10921
ABM DEPOSIT RIDEAU & WILLIAM 2 OTTAWA ON		10000		
POINT OF SALE PURCHASE THRIFTYS #J138 OTTAWA ON	6899		0120	14022
POINT OF SALE PURCHASE AMC THEATRES #37030# KANATA ON	1600			
POINT OF SALE PURCHASE PAYLESS SHOES #5986 KANATA ON	399		0122	12023
POINT OF SALE PURCHASE SHOPPERS DRUG MART #09 KANATA ON	240			
POINT OF SALE PURCHASE LOBLAWS #203 KANATA ON	975		0123	10808
POINT OF SALE PURCHASE LOBLAWS #203 KANATA ON	847		0126	9961
INTEREST			0050131	9966

SCOTIABANK'S ICAN FINANCIAL PLAN. WE'LL WORK WITH YOU TO SET YOUR PRIORITIES AND BUILD A PLAN TO GET AHEAD FINANCIALLY. LET'S TALK TODAY. VISIT YOUR NEAREST BRANCH.

NO. OF DEBITS	TOTAL AMOUNT - DEBITS	NO. OF CREDITS	TOTAL AMOUNT - CREDITS	NO. OF ENCLOSURES	MORE ITEMS ON PAGE
8	117.35	3	105.05	0	

GST REGISTRATION NO. R105195598

Cancelled Cheques

A **cancelled cheque** is a cheque that has been cashed and paid by the financial institution. Your financial institution stamps each cancelled cheque with the date the money was taken from your account. The institution either returns these cheques with your monthly statement, provides photocopies of the cancelled cheques along with the statement, or stores the cheques for future reference. Cancelled cheques are considered legal proof of payment; you can use them to prove that you paid a bill.

Current Accounts

Current accounts are for businesses. To open a current account, a business must be registered with the provincial and/or federal government, and the account must be in the business's name. The financial institution that holds the account pays no interest on account balances and charges a service fee for each deposit, withdrawal, and cheque. At the end of the month, cheques are returned to the business, with the statement. Most financial institutions provide a deposit book that contains duplicate deposit slips for clients. The institution keeps one copy of the deposit slip and stamps the other as a receipt for the business.

RECONCILING THE STATEMENT

The balance on your monthly statement may not agree with the balance recorded in your transaction register on the statement date. Checking your records and bringing the two balances into agreement is called **reconciliation**. It is important to prepare a reconciliation each month so that you know your current account balance. You need to be sure that you have enough money to cover any financial transactions that you've made or that you're going to make soon.

If you write a cheque and there are "not sufficient funds" in your account to cover it, it becomes an **NSF cheque**. Because NSF cheques must be processed manually, they are costly for financial institutions. Most institutions levy a service charge on them. Charges range from $20 to $25. If you pay a business with an NSF cheque, that business might charge you a fee as well.

Steps in a Reconciliation

Follow these steps to reconcile your account:

1. In your transaction register, check off all the financial transactions that appear on your account statement.

2. List any cheques and withdrawals that are in your register but that are not on your statement. These amounts represent withdrawals that have occurred since the statement was prepared and cheques that have not yet cleared through your account. Cheques not yet cashed and deducted from your account statement balance are

Did You Know?

An NSF cheque is sometimes called a "rubber cheque" because it "bounces back to you."

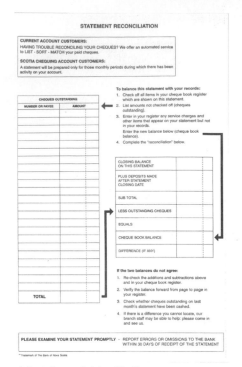

STATEMENT RECONCILIATION

CURRENT ACCOUNT CUSTOMERS:
HAVING TROUBLE RECONCILING YOUR CHEQUES? We offer an automated service to LIST - SORT - MATCH your paid cheques.

SCOTIA CHEQUING ACCOUNT CUSTOMERS:
A statement will be prepared only for those monthly periods during which there has been activity on your account.

CHEQUES OUTSTANDING	
NUMBER OR PAYEE	AMOUNT
TOTAL	

To balance this statement with your records:
1. Check off all items in your cheque book register which are shown on this statement.
2. List amounts not checked off (cheques outstanding).
3. Enter in your register any service charges and other items that appear on your statement but not in your records. Enter the new balance below (cheque book balance).
4. Complete the "reconciliation" below.

CLOSING BALANCE ON THIS STATEMENT	
PLUS DEPOSITS MADE AFTER STATEMENT CLOSING DATE	
SUB TOTAL	
LESS OUTSTANDING CHEQUES	
EQUALS	
CHEQUE BOOK BALANCE	
DIFFERENCE (IF ANY)	

If the two balances do not agree:
1. Re-check the additions and subtractions above and in your cheque book register.
2. Verify the balance forward from page to page in your register.
3. Check whether cheques outstanding on last month's statement have been cashed.
4. If there is a difference you cannot locate, our branch staff may be able to help: please come in and see us.

PLEASE EXAMINE YOUR STATEMENT PROMPTLY · REPORT ERRORS OR OMISSIONS TO THE BANK WITHIN 30 DAYS OF RECEIPT OF THE STATEMENT

* Trademark of The Bank of Nova Scotia

Most financial institutions print a reconciliation form on the back of your monthly account statement.

outstanding cheques. Calculate the total of these cheques and withdrawals.

3. List any deposits that are in your transaction register but that do not appear on the account statement. These amounts are usually deposits made since the statement was prepared. Add this total to the closing balance of your account statement.

4. Subtract the total in Step 2 from the total in Step 3.

5. Enter into your transaction register any transactions on the statement that are not already in your transaction register, for example, interest, services charges, debit card purchases, and ABM transactions. Then, calculate the register's new balance. The balance at the end of Step 4 should match the balance at the end of Step 5. If the balances do not agree, carefully recheck your work. If you haven't made any errors and the balances still don't agree, contact your financial institution.

ACTIVITIES FOR ...

INFORMATION

1. a) List the main types of transaction accounts.

2. a) Why do financial institutions issue passbooks or monthly statements for accounts?

CONNECTION

b) Why is a cancelled cheque a valuable financial record?

b) Explain why the balance in your transaction register and on your account statement may not agree. What can you do to figure out your current account balance?

EXTENSION

c) Use the Internet or visit a local financial institution to find out what types of transaction accounts are available, and what service charges are involved in each one. Present your findings in a table. Indicate which transaction account is most appropriate for you, and why.

c) Ask your teachers, parents or guardians, or other adults you know about their experiences reconciling account statements. Has there ever been a discrepancy that they couldn't account for? How was it resolved?

Writing Cheques

The winning curling team at a competition in Fredericton holds up a large cheque showing the amount of its prize money.

A cheque does not have to be written from a cheque-book, nor even on paper. You can write a cheque on almost anything and it will still be valid, as long as it contains a few basic elements, described below. Financial institutions have accepted cheques written on some very unusual materials—a roofing shingle, the hide of a cow, an envelope, and even a large piece of white spruce. They might charge an extra fee to process an unusual cheque, however, since they cannot handle these types of cheques electronically.

CHEQUE ESSENTIALS

All cheques must have the same basic information: the date; the names of the payee, drawee, and drawer; the amount of the cheque in numbers and words; and the account number from which the money is to be drawn.

Figure 13.1

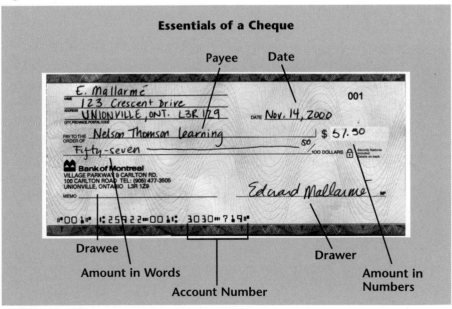

Date

All cheques must show the date, month, and year. Most financial institutions do not accept cheques more than six months after the date shown on them. These cheques are known as **staledated cheques.**

Postdating a cheque means putting a date on the cheque that is later than the actual date when the cheque is written. If someone presents a postdated cheque before the date written on it, the institution will refuse to cash it. For example, a cheque dated September 15, 2002 is not valid for cashing until this date.

Payee

The **payee** is the name of the person or business to whom the cheque is written. Write the payee's name at the extreme left side of the "Pay to the order of" line, followed by a line to fill in any blank space. Filling in this space prevents somebody from changing the name or adding another name. Be sure to spell the payee's name correctly so that the person or business will not have difficulty cashing the cheque.

Drawee

The **drawee** is your financial institution. Its logo, name, and address are usually preprinted on the front of the cheque. In this way, the payee's financial institution knows which institution will honour the cheque.

Drawer

The **drawer**, or the person from whose account the money will be taken, must sign the cheque on the line in the bottom right corner. The signature should be identical to the one on the drawer's signature card.

Amount

The amount of the cheque must appear in both numbers and words. Write the numbers close to the dollar sign to prevent someone from adding more numbers in front of the true amount. Write the amount in words as far left as possible, followed by a line to fill in the blank space. Write the number of cents above the /100. To indicate no cents, place small marks (xx) or zeros (00) above the /100.

The amounts in numbers and words must agree. Most financial institutions will not cash a cheque if the amounts are not the same or show a big difference. If they do cash the cheque, they usually cash it for the amount written in words.

Account Number

If you are writing a cheque that is not preprinted, insert your account number where indicated. Your account number indicates from which account the money is to be drawn.

STRETCH YOUR THINKING

If the amount of a cheque written in words differs from the amount written in numbers, why do you think the financial institution will cash the amount written in words?

Tips for Writing Cheques

When writing a cheque, keep the following in mind:

- To ensure that you don't forget to update your transaction register, record the cheque in your register before you even write it.
- Write the cheque in ink—pencil is too easy to change. Many businesses and organizations use computer-printed cheques.
- If you make a major error, destroy the cheque and write another. If you make only one small error, draw a line through the mistake and write the correction above or beside it. Initial the change to show that you made it.
- Never sign a blank or incomplete cheque. A **blank cheque** has no details filled in. If someone finds a blank cheque that you've signed, he or she could insert his or her name and an amount. If you've signed the cheque, the financial institution will cash it.
- Avoid making cheques payable to "Cash" unless you're at your financial institution. If such a cheque is lost or stolen, anyone can cash it.

STOPPING PAYMENT

If a cheque you have written is lost or stolen, or if you do not want it cashed for some reason, you have the right to stop payment on that cheque. Immediately notify your financial institution that you want a **stop payment** order issued on the cheque. Give them the details on the cheque. Although this action does not officially stop the cheque from being processed, it does delay payment until you can fill out the proper form. This form requires your account number, the date the cheque was written, the cheque number, the payee's name, the exact amount, and your signature. The financial institution usually charges a fee to stop payment on a cheque.

If payment is stopped because a cheque has been lost, write another cheque to replace it. The replacement should have a new date and cheque number to distinguish it from the original.

ENDORSING A CHEQUE

Before a cheque can be cashed, deposited, or transferred to another person, the payee must endorse it. An **endorsement** is the payee's signature on the back of the cheque. Often, the signature is written in a preprinted area in the upper right corner.

A signature proves that the payee has received payment for the cheque or given it to a third party. To endorse a cheque, sign your name in ink. The name you sign should be exactly the same as the one written on the front of the cheque. If the name on the cheque is different from the one on your signature card, you will need to sign twice: once to match the name on the front of the cheque and a second time to match your official signature.

A **blank endorsement** contains only the payee's signature. Anyone can legally cash a cheque with a blank endorsement, so sign this type of cheque only when you are ready to cash or deposit it.

A **restrictive endorsement** limits or restricts what can be done with the cheque. The most common restrictive endorsement is "For deposit only to the account of," written above the signature of the payee. Since a cheque with this endorsement can only be deposited into the payee's account, if the cheque is lost and someone else finds it, that person cannot cash it. When you deposit an endorsed cheque, you should also write your account number under your endorsement. Businesses often use rubber stamps to endorse cheques deposited to their accounts.

THE CHEQUE-CLEARING SYSTEM

In the 1980 revision of the Bank Act, the federal government established the Canadian Payments Association (CPA) to develop and oversee the settling of accounts among Canadian financial institutions. All banks are required to join the CPA. Also, any other institution that accepts deposits may join the CPA.

Clearing is the processing of cheques and the settling of account balances among financial institutions. Every day, representatives of financial institutions exchange cheques and computer records through their regional data centres. No money, however, actually changes hands. After being sorted, cheques are shipped to the individual financial institutions. The individual institutions process the cheques further and take the money from the drawers' accounts. Branches receive most cheques, regardless of how far they have to travel, no later than two days after they are deposited. (See Figure 13.2 for more information on the cheque-clearing process.) Cashing a cheque involves about 20 different processes. The labour required for these processes represents a significant part of the operating costs of any financial institution.

Cheques move through the clearing process quickly and accurately. Magnetic ink character coding, electronic and digital equipment, and computer terminals linked to increasingly fast central computers have improved the speed and efficiency of this process.

E-ACTIVITY

Visit
www.business.
nelson.com
and follow the links
to learn more about
the Canadian
Payments
Association.

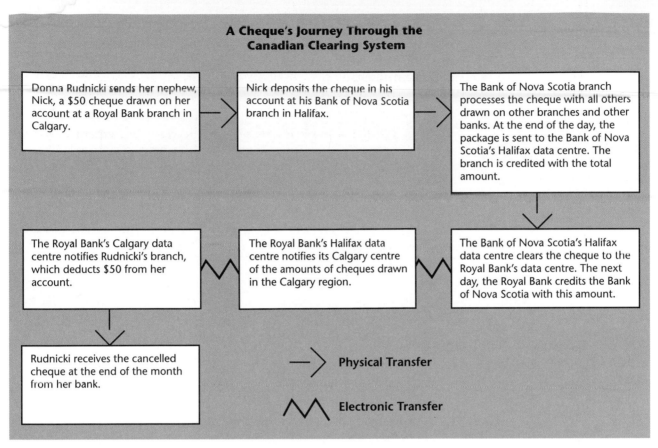

A Cheque's Journey Through the Canadian Clearing System

Donna Rudnicki sends her nephew, Nick, a $50 cheque drawn on her account at a Royal Bank branch in Calgary.

Nick deposits the cheque in his account at his Bank of Nova Scotia branch in Halifax.

The Bank of Nova Scotia branch processes the cheque with all others drawn on other branches and other banks. At the end of the day, the package is sent to the Bank of Nova Scotia's Halifax data centre. The branch is credited with the total amount.

The Royal Bank's Calgary data centre notifies Rudnicki's branch, which deducts $50 from her account.

The Royal Bank's Halifax data centre notifies its Calgary centre of the amounts of cheques drawn in the Calgary region.

The Bank of Nova Scotia's Halifax data centre clears the cheque to the Royal Bank's data centre. The next day, the Royal Bank credits the Bank of Nova Scotia with this amount.

Rudnicki receives the cancelled cheque at the end of the month from her bank.

→ **Physical Transfer**

⋏⋏ **Electronic Transfer**

Figure 13.2

Magnetic Ink Character Recognition

Across the bottom of any preprinted cheque is a string of coded numbers, or an encoding line. This line is printed in special ink and is needed for **magnetic ink character recognition (MICR)**. When an institution processes a cheque through an electronic sorting machine, the encoding line is magnetized. The code contains the cheque number, the institution and branch numbers, and the account number. Two more codes are added during clearing: the amount and type of transaction.

HOLDS ON CHEQUES

Your financial institution may put a **hold** on a cheque that you deposit. With a hold, there is a delay before you can take the money in cash. The hold gives the institution time to clear the cheque and to make sure that you or the financial institution on which the cheque is written does not present a risk. If your institution knows you well and you have a good record with them, you are less of a risk. Holds are a way for financial institutions to ensure that the person or business who wrote the cheque is willing and able to cover its value.

If you earn interest on money in your account, it is paid even if funds are being held. Holds simply protect you and your financial institution against losses from NSF cheques or cheques written for illegal purposes.

ACTIVITIES FOR ...

INFORMATION	**CONNECTION**	**EXTENSION**
1. a) List the six essential elements of a valid cheque.	**b)** Why might someone write a postdated cheque?	**c)** Why do you think financial institutions generally won't accept cheques that are more than six months old? Do you agree with this policy? Explain your position.
2. a) Why must cheques be endorsed before cashing or depositing them?	**b)** What should you do if you think a cheque that you wrote has been lost or stolen?	**c)** Find out more about magnetic ink character recognition (MICR). Present your findings in an illustrated diagram.
3. a) Describe how a cheque is cleared.	**b)** In 1995, paper-based payments (mainly cheques) accounted for 80% of all transactions processed by the Canadian Payments Association. By 2000, they accounted for less than 50%. What do you think accounts for this difference?	**c)** Conduct research on the Internet or visit a financial institution to find out about its policy on holds for cheques. How long does it normally take for cheques to pass through the cheque-clearing system? What criteria does the financial institution use to assess risk in clients? Prepare a report to share with your classmates.

Other Financial Services

In addition to different kinds of transaction accounts, financial institutions offer many different services. Some of the more popular services are loans, lines of credit, credit cards, direct deposits, money orders and drafts, night depositories, overdraft protection, preauthorized bill payments, safety deposit boxes, traveller's cheques, and combination service packages. The types and costs of services vary from institution to institution.

LOANS

Financial institutions lend money to consumers, businesses, and to all three levels of government. Loans range from small personal loans to the multimillion—or multibillion—dollar financing of corporate megaprojects such as the construction of business towers. Loans, in fact, are the most important financial service that financial institutions provide. The interest from loans is a major source of income for financial institutions, and competition among institutions to lend money is very keen.

Institutions lend money only if it seems likely that the loan will be repaid on time. Term loans, student loans, credit cards, lines of credit, and mortgages are the most common forms of loans. A **term loan** involves borrowing money and paying it back at a specified time. The interest rate on the loan can be a fixed rate, which is set for the specific length of the loan, or it can rise and fall with general interest rates. (See Chapter 14 for more information about loans.)

LINES OF CREDIT

When it comes to money management, a smart way to make the most of your purchasing power is to establish a line of credit with your financial institution. A **line of credit** is a form of instant access to credit that has been arranged between you and your financial institution. It is a one-time approved loan that allows you to borrow up to a prearranged amount. It is like having cash on hand when you really need it. With a line of credit, you pay interest only on the exact amount you borrow and only for the number of days that you use the money. The interest rates are much lower than basic credit card rates. (See Chapter 14 for more information about credit.)

CREDIT CARDS

Millions of Canadians regularly use credit, or charge, cards to buy goods and services. These cards offer a convenient and handy alternative to paying cash or writing personal cheques. Many of Canada's financial institutions offer one of two major credit cards: Visa or MasterCard. More than 30 types of these cards are available, with various features, fees, and interest rates. Visa and MasterCard are known as all-purpose cards because they can be used worldwide to make purchases and to obtain cash from ABMs. (See Chapter 14 for more information on different types of credit cards and their use.)

DIRECT DEPOSITS

The **direct deposit** service transfers funds from an outside source directly into a specific account that you designate. For example, if you are expecting money from the government, such as an income tax refund or a monthly pension cheque, you can arrange payment by direct deposit. As you read in Chapter 10, many employers also pay employees through direct deposit. Direct deposits give you instant access to your money and eliminate any holds on cheques.

MONEY ORDERS AND DRAFTS

A **money order** is a form of payment similar to a cheque. The issuing institution guarantees to pay the amount shown on the order to the payee. The guarantee also protects the payee (and the sender) in case the money order is lost or stolen. You can purchase a money order up to a certain amount—usually $1000—from a financial institution or from Canada Post. Money orders are also available in foreign currencies. (You may have to pay a small service charge for the money order.)

A **draft** is similar to a money order except that it is issued only by financial institutions, usually for larger amounts. Some financial institutions no longer differentiate between money orders and drafts—they issue only drafts, regardless of the amount. Unlike cheques, money orders and drafts are not held. As a result, they guarantee the payee instant access to his or her money.

Money orders and drafts are completed in triplicate. The issuer fills in the amount, while the sender fills in the name of the payee, the date, and the sender's name and address. The payee receives the main copy of the money order or draft, the issuing institution keeps one copy for its records, and the sender keeps the third copy as a receipt.

NIGHT DEPOSITORIES

Most branches of financial institutions have a night depository facility, or chute. The **night depository** chute allows customers to make deposits or drop off important financial documents at any time—24 hours a day, seven days a week. This means that businesses do not have to hold large amounts of cash overnight on company premises. As a result, the risk of theft and insurance costs are reduced. Customers place their deposits in locked pouches or bags and then drop them into the chute, which is

One of the advantages of night depositories is that customers don't have to wait while their deposit is being processed.

secure. During business hours, a branch employee accesses these deposits with a special key and processes them. The customer does not need to be present while the deposit is processed.

OVERDRAFT PROTECTION

Even the most careful depositor occasionally runs up an overdraft. Having an **overdraft** means that you write a cheque for more money than you have in your account. For example, if you write a cheque for $300 and your account balance is $250, your account overdraft is $50. In some cases, the financial institution refuses to pay the cheque and returns it marked NSF. With overdraft protection, the institution will lend the depositor the $50 so that the payee can cash the cheque. Institutions usually charge the depositor for this service.

PREAUTHORIZED BILL PAYMENTS

If you have regular monthly bills, such as loans, a mortgage, cable TV, or insurance, you can arrange to make payments automatically through your financial institution. If you give a company written permission to make a **preauthorized debit**, the business can make regular and automatic withdrawals from your account. This type of payment is convenient because you don't need to write cheques as frequently, submit postdated cheques, or pay bills through the ABM, telephone banking, or online banking. Preauthorized payments can also help you prepare your monthly budget.

For regular bills that vary in amount from month to month, the business must provide you with notice of the amount to be debited from your account at least 10 days before payment is due. You should always keep track of what you owe, however, and record the payment in your transaction register to make sure that you have enough money in your account.

STRETCH YOUR THINKING

How can preauthorized payments help you prepare your monthly budget?

SAFETY DEPOSIT BOXES

Most financial institutions offer safety deposit boxes. Individuals and businesses can use these fireproof, metal boxes to store important documents and valuables, such as birth certificates, stocks and bonds, insurance policies, wills, collector coins, jewellery, and home-ownership papers—though deposit insurance does not cover the contents of safety deposit boxes. Financial institutions are not allowed to know what is in a box. Only the person renting the box, or a person legally named by the renter, can open it. Two keys are required: the renter's key and the institution's key. Rental rates vary according to the size of the box.

TRAVELLER'S CHEQUES

When travelling, your money can easily be lost or stolen. And if you travel outside Canada, few people or businesses will accept your personal cheques. **Traveller's cheques**, however, are accepted almost anywhere in the world because they are difficult to forge or alter. Three of the most common brands of traveller's cheques are American Express, Visa, and Thomas Cook.

Traveller's cheques resemble ordinary cheques and are available in various amounts, although $20, $50, and $100 cheques are the most common. Sometimes, financial institutions impose a service charge of 1% when you purchase traveller's cheques. However, they often waive this fee for customers with certain types of accounts.

Traveller's cheques, such as this American Express traveller's cheque, are available in euros and other foreign currencies.

When you buy a traveller's cheque, you must sign it in the presence of the seller. Later, when you want to use the cheque, you must fill in the date and the name of the payee, and sign it again for the person cashing it. This person can then compare the two signatures to be sure they were written by the same person.

The institution issuing the traveller's cheques gives you a separate record on which to list the numbers of your cheques. Then, when you use each cheque, record the name of the payee and the date. Keep this record current and separate from your cheques. Report any lost or stolen cheques to the nearest financial institution that sells traveller's cheques. Most institutions will quickly replace your cheques if you can identify which ones were lost or stolen.

COMBINATION SERVICE PACKAGES

Most financial institutions offer their customers package plans that provide a range of services for a flat monthly fee. The most basic plans allow a certain number of cheques and withdrawals each month. The most comprehensive packages usually include unlimited free chequing privileges, personalized cheques, overdraft protection, a MasterCard or Visa card, a credit that covers part of the rental cost for a safety deposit box, free electronic transactions, and a preferred rate on personal loans.

Combination service plans are ideal for people who use most of the services included in the package. To decide if a combination service plan is for you, determine the separate costs of the services that you use most often. Then, compare the total of these costs with the monthly cost of the service package.

BUSINESS
—FACT—

Financial institutions often waive fees for volunteer, not-for-profit, and school groups.

Most financial institutions offer a youth plan, which gives young people a certain number of free in-branch and electronic transactions. Full-time postsecondary students may apply for a special reduced-fee plan, while seniors over 59 or 60 may find a free package plan that offers other benefits as well.

E-ACTIVITY

Visit
**www.business.
nelson.com**
and follow the links
to compare monthly
service fees at
various financial
institutions.

SHOPPING FOR A FINANCIAL INSTITUTION

When you are ready to open an account, visit different financial institutions in your area to compare what each one has to offer. Every financial institution has its own products and services, all of them differently named, priced, and packaged. As a consumer, be as careful in selecting your financial institution as you would be in making any major purchase. Consider reputation, convenience, fees, types of services available, and your level of comfort. Also keep in mind that many people use more than one financial institution to help them manage their affairs. All financial institutions provide brochures describing their accounts, charges, and other commonly used services.

ACTIVITIES FOR ...

INFORMATION	**CONNECTION**	**EXTENSION**
1. a) List some services provided by Canada's financial institutions.	**b)** Of the financial services discussed in this section, which do you think are the most important to teens? Why?	**c)** Find out about new services offered by financial institutions. Why are these services important to clients? to financial institutions?
2. a) How are money orders and drafts similar to and different from cheques?	**b)** Why is it better for a traveller to use traveller's cheques instead of cash or personal cheques?	**c)** Ask your parents or guardians if preauthorized payments are available for the regular monthly bills they pay. Do they pay these bills through preauthorized payments? Why or why not?
3. a) What is a combination service package?	**b)** Work in groups of three or four. Each group member researches combination service packages at a different financial institution. What services are included? What quantity of services is offered? How much does each plan cost? Record your findings in a group chart. Then, use your answer to Question 1b to help you choose the package that would be most appropriate for young people.	**c)** Ask your parents or guardians what financial services they use. Find out if they would benefit from a combination service package. Present your findings to them.

Technology and Financial Institutions

Canada's financial institutions have to deal with a continually growing volume of daily transactions. They must also create and offer competitive new services to meet the demands of individual consumers and corporate clients. As a result of these pressures, financial institutions have turned more and more toward computer technology and away from manual, face-to-face transactions.

In a single year, Canadian businesses handle more than one billion cheques. The huge cost associated with processing these cheques has led businesses and financial institutions to devise methods that reduce the number of cheques needed. One way to decrease these costs is to encourage customers to make electronic transactions, including bill payments, withdrawals, and deposits.

Automated machines provide services more quickly, conveniently, and accurately than the old manual methods. Automation has made services such as ABMs, instant computer updates of passbooks or monthly statements, and the transfer of funds at the push of a button commonplace. The **electronic funds transfer system (EFTS)** is a computerized system of electronic deposits and withdrawals. It provides customers with faster and less costly service, while reducing the need for cash and cheques.

BUSINESS —FACT—

In 2000, more than 85% of all banking transactions in Canada were done electronically.

SHARED ABM NETWORKS

Financial institutions introduced ABMs in Canada in 1970. Today, you can find them in supermarkets, airports, train and bus stations, malls, gas stations, and convenience stores. Many banks, trust companies, credit unions, and *caisses populaires* are part of a shared ABM network. In addition to providing customers with ready access to their accounts, shared networks save individual institutions the cost of installing their own ABMs at additional locations. Usually, customers must pay a service charge to their own financial institution for each transaction carried out at another institution's ABM. The three main shared ABM networks in Canada are Interac, Cirrus, and Plus. The largest is Interac, a Canadian network which has been in operation since 1986. Many Interac members are linked with Cirrus and Plus, international ABM networks that provide cardholders with access to their accounts while travelling abroad.

DEBIT CARDS/DIRECT PAYMENT

In 1993, **Interac Direct Payment (IDP)** became available across Canada. With direct payment, consumers can use their ABM cards as **debit cards** to pay retailers on the spot for goods and services, rather than paying cash, writing cheques, or using credit cards. Direct payment is similar to using an ABM. ABM transactions directly transfer money between your accounts, or transfer funds to you in the form of cash. With direct payment, money is transferred directly from your account to the retailer's account. The security tips that apply to using ABMs also apply to using debit cards. (See Chapter 12.)

Today, with the increasing use of wireless technology, IDP consumers often use debit cards to pay for purchases or services outside retail stores. For example, in some cities, you can use IDP to pay for taxi rides or pizza delivered to your home. The customer passes, or "swipes," his or her card through a card reader. On a hand-held electronic device, the customer checks the amount of the sale. If the price is correct, the customer presses one key to confirm the amount and another key to indicate the account from which funds are to be taken. The customer then enters his or her PIN (the same as the one used for the ABM). If there is enough money in the account to cover the purchase, the money is immediately debited from the customer's account and credited to the retailer's account. For each direct payment transaction, customers may have to pay a service charge to the institution that issued the card.

People who do not like to buy on credit may prefer to use a debit card as a way to make a "cash" purchase without having to carry large amounts of cash or cheques. More than 300 000 merchants in Canada offer direct payment. Its use has grown in every major retail category, from grocery stores to restaurants. The most frequent debit-card users are 18- to 24-year-olds. Fifty-five percent of this group say that it is their number one way to pay for purchases.

TELEPHONE AND ONLINE BANKING

Technological innovation in banking has led to greater customer convenience. Telephone banking, for example, now lets customers bank at any time and anywhere a telephone is available. To use telephone banking, you need an account, a bank card, and a telephone. Visit your local financial institution or call its toll-free number to get started. Once your account is set up, all you have to do is dial the telephone-banking phone number and follow the voice instructions to use a variety of services. Each institution offers different services. Service charges also vary, depending on how much you use the services and the balance of your account.

Most financial institutions also offer online banking for clients who prefer computer banking. Again, services are usually available 24 hours a day, seven days a week, from anywhere that customers have Internet access. All services available through telephone banking are also available online. Internet banking, however, has added options such as the ability to buy RRSPs, download files, and print out financial data. Financial institutions may or may not charge a monthly service fee for online banking, depending on your account balance and how often you use the service.

Once you are connected to the financial institution online, you enter your PIN and then follow step-by-step instructions to complete transactions. Generally, banking online is more convenient than traditional banking, and service charges are lower. Online banking is also beneficial for financial institutions because online accounts involve less paperwork and require fewer staff to service them. Institutions use a variety of names to describe their online banking services, including home banking, e-banking, Web banking, and Internet banking.

Table 13.1 Pros and Cons of Online Banking

Pros	Cons
A wide range of services is available.	Access to a computer and Internet access are necessary.
Most services are available 24 hours a day, seven days a week.	Power failures and technical problems can disrupt service.
Transactions are quickly executed and confirmed.	Time is required to become familiar with programs and procedures.
Detailed financial information is available.	Privacy and security may not be guaranteed.
Tools are provided for tracking money and financial planning.	Personal contact between customers and staff at financial institutions is reduced.

ELECTRONIC BILL PRESENTMENT

Many financial institutions offer electronic bill presentment. With **electronic bill presentment**, customers can have everything from phone bills to cable bills sent, or "presented," over the Internet to their computer. Paper copies of these bills continue to be mailed if requested, but many customers choose computer-only delivery.

In 1998, six of Canada's top financial institutions created e-route inc., an integrated electronic system that links financial institutions, billers, and customers. The e-route inc. system delivers bills to customers via their financial institution's Web site. Once customers log on, they can call up their bills, review them, and decide when and how to pay. The system also delivers a variety of non-bill statements and notices, including investment account statements and mutual fund sales confirmations. As electronic bill presentment develops, clients will be able to link directly with billers to get more information. These direct links will also be an advantage to billers, who will be able to contact customers virtually anywhere via the Internet. Similarly, Canada Post's EPOST service allows Canadians and businesses to receive and send mail, receive and pay bills, access information and government forms, and much more—all online.

Wireless Online Banking

In 1999, three of Canada's largest chartered banks launched wireless banking for their clients. The remaining major banks followed in 2000. Wireless banking provides flexibility for customers on the move. With cellular phones, laptop computers, and personal digital assistants (PDAs), such as the Palm Pilot, banking is literally just a touch away. You can review your credit card transactions while riding on the bus, transfer funds between accounts while shopping at the mall, or check your stock portfolio while standing in line at the supermarket.

Wireless bill presentment allows customers to receive and pay bills on cellular phones, pagers, and other devices. Soon, voice recognition will allow customers to talk to their financial institution's computer to access accounts, pay bills, and so on. Some experts have even suggested that within the next decade, customers will be able to bank through their microwave or refrigerator.

Smart Cards

Smart cards have been used as cash substitutes for phone cards and transit cards.

A **smart card** looks like an ABM card or a credit card, but has a powerful microchip. It can store different applications, including e-cash, or electronic cash. E-cash is an alternative to regular cash, cheques, debit cards, and credit cards. Every time a cardholder makes a purchase, the amount of the transaction is deducted directly from the balance on the smart card. Unlike debit cards, no PIN is required to access a remote financial institution. The smart card system transfers money directly from the buyer to the seller.

Various companies, including Mondex, Microsoft, and Visa, have developed e-cash applications. E-cash offers many advantages over cash and cheque transactions, including convenience, faster and easier transactions, and lower handling costs for retailers and financial institutions. E-cash applications from different companies offer different features. For example, the Mondex e-cash system

- keeps a record of the last 10 transactions and an up-to-date balance
- enables cardholders to lock the cash value on their smart card with a special code so that their e-cash cannot be stolen
- can store five currencies at one time
- allows cardholders to reload cash on their card via a phone, an ABM, or the Internet

Some companies, including Mondex, have developed operating systems that enable a single smart card to combine applications that meet the specific needs of the cardholder. For example, a single smart card could provide e-cash, be used as a credit card, and store information about customer loyalty programs.

THE FUTURE OF FINANCIAL SERVICES

Although more and more financial transactions are being done electronically, there will always be times when you will have to visit a branch of your financial institution, and there will always be some people who prefer the direct contact with employees of the financial institution.

Canada will probably never be a cashless (or cheque-less) society. Many Canadians will continue to write cheques for costly transactions, such as paying rent. And they will continue to use cash—probably coins—to buy low-priced goods or services, such as snack foods, newspapers, bus fares, and so on. Cash is still the only universally accepted form of payment and the simplest way to exchange value. As well, many Canadians are still reluctant to accept the electronic transfer of funds, or do not use credit or debit cards because of personal beliefs and values. For these reasons, financial institutions must continue to offer customers the choice of using cash and cheques.

No matter what a person's personal preferences are, coins and bank notes are no longer the only form of money available. Cheques, debit and credit cards, telephone banking, online banking, and smart cards were all developed to give people increased access to their money and new ways to use it. One thing is certain: electronic and digital technology will continue to transform financial institutions and the way Canadians use and think about money.

Electronic and digital technology will continue to transform financial institutions and the way Canadians use and think about money.

ACTIVITIES FOR ...

INFORMATION	**C**ONNECTION	**E**XTENSION
1. a) Explain how electronic funds transfers are used to make payments.	**b)** Compare electronic funds transfers with regular banking. What are the main advantages and disadvantages?	**c)** Conduct research on the Internet or interview an employee of a financial institution to learn more about electronic funds transfers. Using the information you find, predict how electronic funds transfers will develop over the next 10 years.
2. a) What is the main difference between using a credit card and a debit card?	**b)** It costs less for a financial institution to process a debit card transaction than it does to process a cheque. Why do you think this is the case?	**c)** With a small group, survey five consumers and five retailers to determine why they do, or do not, use debit cards. Prepare a report that compares and contrasts the retailers' responses with the consumers' responses.
3. a) What is online banking?	**b)** As electronic bill presentment develops, billers will be able to supply customers with graphically rich electronic bills that also serve as interactive marketing tools. Why will these kinds of bills be important to billers?	**c)** In Chapter 2, you learned that many Canadians are reluctant to make purchases over the Internet. Do you think they are any more or less reluctant to do their banking online? Explain your answer.

Review

Knowledge and Understanding

1. Match each of the following terms to the correct definition:

   cancelled cheque   payee
   drawee   postdating
   drawer   reconciliation
   outstanding cheque   service charge
   overdraft   stop payment

   a) The person from whose account a cheque is taken.
   b) The process of checking your financial institution's statement against your account records to ensure that they agree.
   c) A cheque that has been cashed and paid by the financial institution.

d) The financial institution on which a cheque is drawn.

e) A processing fee charged by a financial institution for a particular service.

f) A cheque that has not yet been cashed and deducted from your statement balance.

g) The person or business to whom a cheque is payable.

h) An order instructing a financial institution not to pay a certain cheque.

i) This results when someone writes a cheque for more money than is in his or her account.

j) Putting a date on a cheque that is later than the actual date.

2. Explain to a partner how to write and endorse a cheque.

3. Imagine that you pay your telephone bill by cheque. Six weeks later, you get an overdue notice from the telephone company. What should you do?

Thinking and Inquiry

1. List the types of banking services that each of the following would most likely use:
- your school's student council
- an entrepreneur planning to open a new small business
- a band in which you play lead guitar
- your grandparents

Give reasons for your answers.

2. Why should you still have to pay a service charge when you use an ABM, a debit card, telephone banking, or online banking?

Communication

1. While high-tech banking provides consumers with convenience and speed, it also collects massive amounts of information on consumers. Should such information be private, or should it be made available to financial institutions and businesses? Hold a debate to discuss this issue.

2. Visit a financial institution or use its Web site to learn about online and wireless banking at that institution. What online services does it provide? What service charges are involved? What services does the institution expect to offer in the future? Compare your results with the results of at least three classmates who investigated other institutions. Prepare a bulletin board display of your findings.

Application

1. According to your transaction register, the balance in your straight transaction account is $865.84 on October 31. You have just received your monthly account statement and cancelled cheques, and your statement indicates that your balance as of October 31 is $989.24. In comparing these records, you observe the following differences:
    - According to the statement, Cheque 103 for $89.80, Cheque 104 for $187.50, and Cheque 107 for $48.60 have not yet been cashed.
    - A $200 deposit you made on October 30 does not appear on the statement.
    - A deduction of $2.50 for a service charge appears in the statement. This deduction isn't recorded in your register.

    Using this information, determine your current account balance.

2. Interview a staff member from a local financial institution about his or her position. Prepare appropriate questions in advance. Your questions should address the following points:
    - job description and responsibilities
    - educational requirements
    - personal qualities required to do the job effectively
    - possibilities for advancement
    - salary range for the position
    - reasons for considering this career

    Prepare a report on the career you investigated. Your report should combine different presentation formats, for example, a written summary, a chart, and a clip from a video or audio recording.

REFLECT ON YOUR LEARNING

1. In this chapter, you learned about different ways to pay bills. Make a list of the different ways. Which form of payment do you prefer? Explain.

2. Choose a partner for this activity. Imagine that a financial institution has hired you and your partner to help it plan new services for one of the following groups: your age group, your school, or your community. What services would you suggest for this group? Keep in mind what you learned in this chapter about the kinds of services available and future directions in banking.

CONSUMER CREDIT

STUDENT EXPECTATIONS

After completing this chapter, you will be able to

- explain what credit is
- describe ways in which consumers, businesses, and governments use credit
- explain the advantages and disadvantages of credit
- outline the main types and sources of credit
- identify and give examples of three common types of credit cards
- calculate the total cost of credit on a variety of loans
- describe the process of establishing a personal credit rating and applying for and obtaining credit

Profile

Cutting back on monthly expenses and making a budget helped Günseli reduce her debt.

AVOIDING THE DEBT TRAP

For many people, graduating from college or university marks their official entry into the "real world." The transition can be difficult at the best of times, but for those who have accumulated a large debt from student loans, it can be overwhelming.

Today, the cost of postsecondary education is higher than it has ever been. More and more students are forced to look beyond their own or their parents' savings in order to finance their education. The result is that more students are taking out loans, and these loans are for larger amounts. In fact, in Canada, the average student now graduates with a debt of $25 000. Günseli Akol is all too familiar with this situation. In 1999, she graduated from university, with a Bachelor of Arts degree, having borrowed almost $20 000 along the way.

"As I was going through school, I didn't really worry about the amount of money I was borrowing," says Günseli. "All my loans were government-sponsored, so I didn't have to make any payments as long as I was in school full-time. I don't think I fully understood how in debt I was until I received my notice of repayment in the mail. All of a sudden, I realized that I owed $20 000 and had no idea how I was going to pay it back."

Students who receive federal or provincial student loans are not required to start making payments until six months after they finish full-time studies. But, sometimes, it takes longer than six months to find a suitable job. Günseli had worked part-time as a cashier at a grocery store to earn some extra money while she was in school, but she planned to quit as soon as she found a job in her field. "I thought it might take a couple of months, but six months after I graduated, I was still working at the store and had no promising job leads—only now I was supposed to start making my loan payments. I didn't know how I was going to find the money—I was only earning enough to pay for food, rent, and other necessities. I totally panicked."

Fortunately, people who find themselves in Günseli's position do have options. She applied for interest relief, which is offered by

CONTINUED →

both the federal government and by many provincial governments. Under this program, students who do not have enough income to make their loan payments can postpone them for a specified period of time. During this time, the government pays the interest (or a percentage of the interest) on the loans. Günseli was approved for six months of interest relief, which gave her the time she needed to find a job in her field—after over a year of searching.

With the income from her new job, Günseli was able to start making regular payments on her loan. "I had really been struggling with my finances for the last year or so," says Günseli. "For the first few months after I got my new job, I just enjoyed not having to worry about money all the time. But after the novelty wore off, I started to seriously consider what I could do to reduce my debt load."

"First, I decided to keep my job as a cashier, in addition to my new full-time job. I worked two or three shifts a week at the store, usually on the weekends. This gave me some extra money and allowed me to increase the amount of my loan payments. Then, I made a budget and tried to cut back expenses wherever I could; I moved to a smaller apartment and really tried to watch what I spent." In this way, Günseli was able to make larger payments on her loan, and she was still able to save some money each month.

In a year, Günseli had managed to save about $6000. "I had planned to use this money to go on a vacation, but I decided it could wait for another year. Instead, I used the money to pay off part of my loan. I figured that the money I'd save on interest costs would more than make up for the vacation."

In fact, Günseli has been able to cut her total debt in half in a relatively short period of time. "It hasn't been easy because I've had to work a lot of extra hours and have put off buying things or doing things that I really would like," she says. "But in the end, I think it's worth it. I've reduced the total amount of money I'll have to pay back by thousands of dollars, and I also spend less time worrying about my debt load now that it's so much smaller."

"I've reduced the total amount of money I'll have to pay back by thousands of dollars, and I also spend less time worrying about my debt load now that it's so much smaller."

About This Profile

1. What actions did Günseli take to reduce her debt?
2. Imagine that, instead of applying for interest relief, Günseli had just decided not to make payments on her loan because she couldn't afford to. How might this decision have affected her financial future?

The Wonderful World of Credit

In a small group, brainstorm reasons for using credit. What are the main advantages and disadvantages of using credit? Make a note of your responses so you can return to them at the end of this chapter.

"Buy now, pay later" is a phrase that is frequently used in retail advertising. "Will that be cash or credit?" are often the first words that cashiers say to a customer. Almost without thinking, many customers respond, "Put it on my plastic." Other customers, however, have a little voice telling them to always pay in cash. In Shakespeare's play *Hamlet*, the character Polonius advises Laertes, "Neither a borrower nor a lender be/For loan oft uses both itself and friend." Polonius makes credit sound like a very bad idea. But is it? What exactly is credit? Who uses it and why? What are the advantages and disadvantages of using credit?

WHAT IS CREDIT?

At some point in their lives, most people need credit. **Credit** is the privilege of using someone else's money for a period of time. It is widely accepted as a substitute for ready cash. Using credit means that a transaction takes place between a creditor and a debtor. A **creditor** is any person or business that grants a loan or sells on credit. A **debtor** is any person or business that buys on credit or receives a loan.

Credit can be good or bad. It can be a very helpful tool in a money management plan, but it can also result in financial disaster. Used wisely, credit lets people maintain a comfortable standard of living without spending all their current income or draining their savings. But for those who borrow beyond their ability to repay the debt, credit can bring financial difficulties.

WHO USES CREDIT?

Nearly everyone uses credit. Consumers use credit extensively, as do businesses and governments. Consumers use credit to buy expensive items, such as a home, car, home entertainment centre, or major appliance. They use credit to buy less expensive items too, such as DVDs, theatre tickets, and restaurant meals, because it is often more convenient than cash. Consumers also commonly use credit to pay for vacations and, sometimes, to make investments or pay off other debts.

Businesses may use long-term credit to purchase land, buildings, and equipment, while entrepreneurs use loans to start new business ventures. Businesses may also borrow money for short-term reasons. For example, a business may need to use credit while it waits for goods in stock to be sold or for credit customers to pay for their purchases. Businesses also use credit to buy goods for sale or to purchase raw materials and supplies.

Table 14.1 Total Business and Consumer Credit in Canada (in Millions of Dollars)

Year	Business Credit	Consumer Credit (Excluding Mortgages)
1996	575 825	128 383
1997	626 443	141 322
1998	693 907	156 365
1999	732 989	167 625
2000	784 204	N/A

All three levels of government—federal, provincial, and local—borrow money to provide goods and services to citizens. For example, governments borrow money to build schools, hospitals, highways, airports, and buses, and to pay the salaries of government employees.

ADVANTAGES OF CREDIT

Everyone who uses credit benefits from it in some way. For consumers such as you and your family, some of the benefits include the following:

1. **Instant enjoyment**. Credit allows consumers to buy, enjoy, and use goods and services immediately and pay for them in the future. For example, a family could buy a sport utility vehicle (SUV) on credit and begin using it right away. On the other hand, it might take the family many years to save enough money to buy the SUV with cash—the very years, perhaps, when the SUV would be most useful.

2. **Convenience**. Credit can replace the need for cash or cheques, which is very convenient when shopping or travelling. Many consumers then pay the balance in full at the end of the month.

3. **Emergencies**. In an emergency, credit can be very handy. For example, if your car breaks down during a trip, you might not be able to afford to have it repaired unless you can use credit. Or if you are suddenly out of work, you may be able to use credit to pay for purchases until you are working again.

4. **Savings**. Credit allows consumers to take advantage of sales, giving them the opportunity to buy goods of a higher quality than they might usually be able to afford. With expensive items such as automobiles and appliances, the savings can be quite high. However, consumers should make sure that the amount they save by buying

BUSINESS
—FACT—

Businesses often offer customers credit. This option benefits both businesses and customers. Customers can buy more than they would if they were paying cash, which increases sales and profits for businesses.

on sale is greater than the interest charges they will pay for buying on credit.

5. **Credit rating**. Buying on credit is one way to establish a credit rating. A **credit rating** is an indication of the level of risk that consumers, businesses, or governments will pose if credit is granted to them. You can earn a good credit rating by making your payments in full and on time. A good credit rating allows consumers to make major purchases on credit. (Credit ratings will be discussed in more detail later in this chapter.)

6. **Purchase record**. When you use credit, you receive a monthly statement that lists all your purchases. This statement is a useful record that can help you budget your money and trace your spending.

DISADVANTAGES OF CREDIT

Although credit has many advantages, it also has major disadvantages. These include the following:

1. **Credit costs**. There are costs involved in buying on credit that are not involved when paying cash. Businesses that offer credit must keep a detailed accounting system that records credit sales and credit payments. If customers do not pay on time, there are additional costs and losses for the business. These costs are passed on to all customers in the form of higher prices. Because credit increases the cost of doing business, stores that sell on a cash-only basis can offer goods at lower prices than those that offer credit. An additional cost of using credit is the interest charges that are added to the purchase price after a period of time. (The interest costs of credit will be further discussed later in this chapter.)

2. **Impulse buying**. With easily available credit, many consumers may not bother to comparison shop or check advertisements carefully. Rather than looking for the best deal, they buy impulsively.

3. **Overbuying**. Credit allows consumers to make more purchases or more expensive purchases than they need or, at times, can afford. Buying an expensive large-screen TV, for example, is easier when consumers can just say, "Charge it." If they had to pay cash, they might buy a smaller, less expensive TV.

4. **Financial difficulties**. Consumers can get carried away with credit and lose track of their monthly spending. Too many impulse purchases—for example, paying $4500 for a TV rather than $750—can mean a consumer gets buried in bills and cannot make his or her payments. A budget and money management plan can help people make sure that they don't spend more than they can afford.

To Use or Not to Use?

Before buying anything on credit, ask yourself these key questions:
- Do I really need this item, or is it an impulse purchase?
- Is this item a good buy or should I comparison shop?
- How much could I save if I paid cash?
- If I pay cash, how long will it take me to save enough money?
- How much interest will I pay if I use credit?
- Can I afford the monthly credit payments?
- How will the use of credit affect my budget?
- Is this purchase a wise use of credit?

   Your answers to these questions will help you determine if you should use credit, and how much credit you can realistically afford. Just pausing long enough to ask yourself the questions means you will probably use credit more wisely.

ACTIVITIES FOR ...

INFORMATION	CONNECTION	EXTENSION
1. a) What is credit and who uses it?	**b)** What do the statistics in Table 14.1 say about the role of credit in Canadian life?	**c)** What do you think Polonius meant when he said "loan oft uses both itself and friend"? Do you agree or disagree?
2. a) List five advantages of buying on credit.	**b)** What advantages to buying on credit do you think are most important? Arrange your list of advantages from the most to least important. Compare your list with a partner. Discuss any differences.	**c)** Why might it be a good idea for people who always pay cash to purchase a few things on credit?
3. a) List four disadvantages of buying on credit.	**b)** Do you think the advantages of credit outweigh the disadvantages? Explain your answer.	**c)** With a partner, debate the advantages and disadvantages of credit from the viewpoint of a small business owner. How might credit benefit the business? How might credit hurt it?

Types and Sources of Credit

During your lifetime, you will probably borrow money and make many purchases on credit. People with a regular, steady income have a variety of credit options. The type of credit they use depends on their needs, wants, and goals, and on the types of purchases they make. Buying a snowboard, for example, presents different credit needs than buying a car. Buying a house or a condominium requires another type of credit financing. The five most common types of credit are charge accounts, credit cards, installment sales credit, consumer loans, and mortgage loans. Each type of credit has its own advantages and disadvantages. You should look at each form of credit carefully to decide which type best suits your needs and budget.

CHARGE ACCOUNTS

A **charge account** is a contract between a consumer and a retailer for sales in the retailer's stores. A charge account at the Bay, Canadian Tire, Eatons, Sears, or Zellers, for example, is a contract that allows the consumer to buy goods at these stores on credit. Based on the consumer's credit rating, the retailer sets an upper limit for credit purchases. Retailers and businesses issue charge cards to encourage consumers to shop at their stores rather than at a competitor's store.

Because customers can use these retail charge cards only at the issuing store, they are known as single-purpose cards. Some stores encourage consumers to get and use the cards by offering special sales that are available only to retail charge card holders. Major oil companies, such as Esso, Shell, and Texaco, also issue their own credit cards, and offer users special deals and bonuses.

Charge accounts come in different types. A 30-day charge account requires full payment within 30 days. A **revolving credit account** allows consumers to charge purchases at any time, but they must pay a minimum monthly payment until the account is paid in full. Interest is charged on the remaining balance at the end of each month.

Layaway Plans

Some retailers offer layaway plans. With a **layaway plan**, the store sets the product aside while the customer makes equal payments for a set number of weeks or months until the price has been paid in full. The retailer often charges interest for this service. Consumers should be certain that they want the product because many retailers will not

BUSINESS —FACT—

Revolving credit is popular because it is flexible and convenient, but it can also tempt consumers to overspend.

refund payments if consumers change their minds about the purchase during the layaway period.

CREDIT CARDS

Credit cards are so popular that the average Canadian today carries at least three different cards. In fact, there are more than 600 issuers of credit cards in Canada. There are three basic types of cards: charge cards issued by retailers (discussed on the previous page), bank-issued credit cards, and cards issued by travel and entertainment companies. All three are popular, but bank-issued credit cards account for the largest percentage of consumer spending.

Why might this person have more than one Visa and MasterCard?

Except for retail charge cards, credit cards are universal, or multipurpose; they can be used to purchase goods and services at retailers, hotels, airlines, dental offices, and many other places. Many people like to use these cards when they are travelling so that they do not have to carry as much cash with them. Millions of businesses around the world accept several cards. By doing so, these businesses attract more customers and increase their sales.

Using a credit card is like taking out a short-term loan—it is important to be aware of terms and conditions as well as options. Some cards are free, while other cards involve annual or transaction fees to cover expenses. Cards range from basic no-frills cards with low interest rates, to "gold" and "platinum" premium cards that offer benefits such as travel and car rental insurance. Many premium cards also offer programs that allow customers to collect points for air or rail travel and other rewards.

Bank-Issued Credit Cards

Bank-issued credit cards, such as Visa and MasterCard, are probably the most popular credit cards. Financial institutions issue cards to customers whose credit ratings meet certain standards. Based on the customer's credit rating, the financial institution sets a credit limit for each individual. If the balance owing on the card is paid in full every month, no interest is charged. Otherwise, customers must make a minimum monthly payment on the outstanding balance. With both Visa and MasterCard, interest is calculated immediately on cash advances, but interest is only charged on purchases 21 days after the statement date.

STRETCH YOUR THINKING

Interview a local merchant to find out what transaction fees are charged on different bank-issued credit cards.

The credit extended in a bank-issued card comes from depositors' savings. Since the financial institution must pay depositors interest on their savings, credit cards must make a profit for the issuers. This profit comes from the difference between the interest the financial institutions pay depositors and the interest they receive from borrowers. In addition, merchants pay the issuing institution a transaction fee (a percentage of the purchase price) each time a customer uses the card to pay for a good or service.

As stated earlier, consumers like bank-issued credit cards because they are widely accepted. As well, customers receive one monthly bill that lists their purchases. Retailers like bank-issued credit cards because it is the banks, not the retailers, that have to determine and assume the risk of granting credit to the customer. Retailers also like the fact that they receive their money promptly.

Ten Steps to Stay Fraud Free

With more than 38 million credit cards in use, credit card fraud has become a serious concern in Canada. Credit card fraud comes in several forms, including stolen cards, counterfeit cards, and false credit card applications. To avoid becoming a victim of fraud, police and business organizations recommend that consumers follow these steps:

1. If your credit card is programmed to access an ABM, memorize your PIN and never write it down.

2. Never leave credit cards unattended in the workplace—it is the number one place for thefts.

3. Never leave credit cards in your car—the second most likely place for card thefts.

4. Always be sure that your credit card is returned to you after you make a purchase.

5. When travelling, keep your cards with you or place them in a safe location.

6. Report lost or stolen credit cards immediately.

7. Sign the back of your new credit card as soon as you get it and destroy all old cards.

8. Make a list of all your cards and their numbers.

9. Always check that the charges on your monthly statements were made by you.

10. Only give your credit card number over the phone if you are dealing with a reputable company or if you initiated the call yourself.

Travel and Entertainment Cards

American Express, Diners Club International, and Discover are used widely for hotels, airline tickets, car rentals, meals, concert and theatre tickets, and other consumer purchases. Because consumers use these cards to pay for such services and products, they are called travel and entertainment cards. Businesses often use these prestigious cards for expense accounts. Subscribers to these cards usually pay a yearly membership fee that is higher than the fee charged for bank-issued cards. Some travel and entertainment cards require that payment be made in full each month.

INSTALLMENT SALES CREDIT

Installment sales credit is a credit plan that requires a purchaser to make a down payment and fixed regular payments, with finance charges added to the purchase price. Consumers making expensive purchases, such as furniture, appliances, or a vehicle, often find this kind of credit plan ideal. First, a repayment plan is drawn up in the form of a conditional sales contract between the buyer and the seller. This contract normally includes the terms of the purchase and payment details, including finance charges. Usually, the buyer makes a down payment of at least 10% of the purchase price.

Installment credit is more complicated to use than a charge account or credit card, which simply requires the buyer to hand over a card to the salesperson. With installment sales credit, the buyer must fill out a credit application, be approved as a credit risk, and then sign a detailed sales contract each time he or she makes a purchase. The buyer *does* get possession of the goods as soon as the contract is signed, but ownership of the goods stays with the seller until all payments are made.

CONSUMER LOANS

Consumer, or personal, loans can be used to finance purchases of almost anything other than a home. Home buying is usually financed through a mortgage loan, which will be discussed on the next page. A consumer loan is an alternative to charge accounts, credit cards, and installment sales credit for purchases such as a computer system, family holiday, car, or home renovations. Types of loans include term loans, demand loans, and student loans. Each type of loan provides a number of repayment options. Consumer loans can be obtained from most of Canada's financial institutions.

Term Loans

As you read in Chapter 13, a **term loan** is a form of installment credit in which the borrower agrees to make fixed monthly payments over a set period of time, or **term**. Usually, the term is from one to five years. The biggest advantage of a term loan is that payments can be arranged to fit the borrower's budget. The total amount to be repaid includes the amount borrowed plus finance charges. Because terms and repayment details differ among financial institutions, it is important to consider the kinds of interest rates that the institutions offer. With a fixed-rate loan, the interest rate is set in advance for the full term of the loan. In a variable-rate loan, the interest rate changes because it is linked to the prime lending rate. (See Chapter 12 for more information about the Bank of Canada's prime lending rate.)

Leasing is another way to acquire the use of an asset. A **lease** is an agreement to rent something, such as a car or computer system, for a period of time at an agreed price. Leases are similar to term loans because they require a customers to make regular payments over a fixed period of time. Unlike a loan, however, leasing is actually a long-term rental—the borrower doesn't own the asset at the end of the lease. Usually, the customer does have the option to buy the asset at its "residual value," or the worth of the asset at the end of the lease. This value is normally set when the contract to lease is signed.

Demand Loans

A **demand loan** is a special kind of short-term loan with flexible terms of repayment. Demand loans are usually granted to borrowers who have a strong relationship with their financial institution and who have security or collateral to guarantee the loan. **Collateral** is something of value that the lender can take and sell if the loan is not repaid on time. Examples of collateral include savings, property, jewellery, or other valuable assets. With demand loans, borrowers can choose whether or not to make regular payments or to pay the full amount at any time. The lender can also "demand" full payment from the borrower at any time.

Student Loans

Student loans are guaranteed by both the federal and provincial governments and are available through most financial institutions. Canada Student Loans are usually interest-free until six months after graduation, when repayment is expected to begin. Canada Student Loan applications are available at most guidance/student services offices in high schools, as well as at most colleges and universities. Almost any full- or part-time student can apply for a student loan, as long as his or her courses and institutions are approved. For students

E-ACTIVITY

Visit
www.business.
nelson.com
and follow the links to learn more about the Canada Student Loans Program.

who are still dependants, their family's financial background determines whether or not a loan is granted.

MORTGAGE LOANS

Buying a home is the largest purchase that most people will ever make, and it usually requires a special kind of loan. A **mortgage loan** is a long-term credit plan for buying property. The period to repay mortgage loans is usually 20–25 years. The **mortgage** itself is a legal document in which the purchaser pledges the property as collateral for the loan. Different mortgage options are available that offer flexibility and choice in terms, interest rates, and length of time. However, the terms of the loan and the interest rate are renegotiated several times during the length of the mortgage because of changing interest rates.

ACTIVITIES FOR ...

INFORMATION	**C**ONNECTION	**E**XTENSION
1. a) List the five most common types of credit.	**b)** Use the Internet to find examples of retail stores that offer charge accounts or cards. How do these stores benefit from offering this method of payment?	**c)** Imagine that you need to make a large purchase, such as a new computer. What form of credit would you prefer to use to finance this purchase? Why?
2. a) What is a multipurpose credit card?	**b)** Many businesses prefer to provide and accept credit cards rather than accept personal cheques. Why do you think this is the case?	**c)** Visit a financial institution in person or online to find out what credit cards it offers. List the main types of cards available, the fees involved, and the rates of interest. Prepare a report on your findings In your report, tell which card you would use, and why.
3. a) What is installment sales credit?	**b)** How does installment sales credit differ from a charge account or credit card?	**c)** Why might people prefer installment sales credit over using a credit card?
4. a) List three types of consumer loans.	**b)** Would you prefer to have a fixed-rate loan or a variable-interest loan? Explain why.	**c)** Find out what types of mortgage loans a local financial institution offers. What are the advantages and disadvantages of each type?

The Cost of Credit

Credit is very popular with consumers, but it does involve a cost. Several factors affect the amount of interest that consumers pay for credit. The **principal**, or the amount of money borrowed, is the chief factor in determining the interest cost. Other factors include
- the term for repaying the loan
- current interest rates
- inflation and general economic conditions
- security or collateral
- risk and credit rating

When you borrow, shop around for the best deal, just as you would for a consumer purchase. Remember, financial institutions make their profits on loans, and they compete for customers. You might even ask for a lower interest rate than the first one offered. If you are a first time borrower, however, you will not likely get the lowest rate available.

PRINCIPAL AND TERM

Obviously, the more money you borrow and the more credit you use, the more you pay in interest charges. Interest is applied to the amount of money that is owed. The term of the loan also determines the interest rate. Short-term loans, usually up to one year, generally have a lower interest rate than long-term loans. Short-term loans have lower rates because the shorter period allows lending institutions to predict interest rates, economic conditions in Canada, and inflation rates with some accuracy. Long-term loans are riskier for lenders because they cannot accurately predict long-term economic trends. As a result, lenders charge higher interest rates for long-term loans.

As you can see from Table 14.2, borrowing costs less if you repay a loan over a shorter term. In this example, by making larger payments over a term of three rather than five years, a borrower can save more than $1000 in interest charges. Borrowing also costs less if you make extra payments.

STRETCH YOUR THINKING

An old saying states that if you owe the bank $15 000 but cannot pay it back, you have a problem. If you owe the bank $15 million and cannot pay it back, the bank has a problem. In your own words, explain what this statement means.

Table 14.2 Cost of Borrowing $10 000 for a Car

Amount of Loan	Term of Loan	Interest Rate	Monthly Payment	Total Paid	Total Interest Paid
$10 000	5 years	9.00%	$207.63	$12 457.80	$2457.80
$10 000	3 years	9.00%	$318.08	$11 450.88	$1450.88

How to Calculate Simple Interest

If you are considering arranging a loan, it helps to know and use a few formulas. A formula for quickly calculating simple interest is as follows:

I (interest) = P (principal) × R (interest rate) × T (time)

For example, if you borrow $3000 at 7% interest for one year, your simple interest payment would be as follows:

I = $3000 × .07 × 1
  = $210

In other words, if you borrow $3000 over one year at 7% interest, you would repay a total of $3210 ($3000 + $210). If you borrowed the $3000 for three years, your simple interest calculation would be $210 × 3 = $630. You should always know the total cost of your loan, which is P + I.

Financial institutions, however, do not calculate the interest on a loan using this simple formula. They must take into account any amounts repaid during the term of the loan, and charge interest only on the amount outstanding. Financial institutions must provide borrowers with a payment schedule that includes the total number of payments and the monthly payments for principal and interest.

SECURITY OR COLLATERAL

Depending on the principal involved and the borrower's credit rating, collateral may be required as security for a loan. When a borrower offers a home, a car, or stocks and bonds as collateral, the risk of the loan is reduced because the lender can sell this security if the borrower fails to repay the loan. Offering collateral usually allows a consumer to borrow a larger amount at a lower interest rate than he or she could without this form of security.

RISK AND CREDIT RATING

The borrower's credit history and credit rating also affect the cost of a loan. A borrower who has a record of borrowing money and repaying it promptly will probably get a competitive interest rate from the lender. An applicant who has no record of borrowing, or a record that indicates he or she is unreliable, may be denied a loan or charged a higher interest rate. The process of applying for credit and the importance of a credit rating will be discussed in the next section of this chapter.

INFORMATION	CONNECTION	EXTENSION
1. a) List five factors that affect the interest rate of a loan.	**b)** "Long-term loans are riskier for lenders because they cannot accurately predict long-term economic trends." What economic trends might this statement refer to? What impact would they have on interest rates?	**c)** Use the Internet or interview a representative from a financial institution to determine how interest rates for personal loans have changed over the past 10 years. Prepare a report on your findings, including a graph that plots interest rates over this time.
2. a) What is collateral?	**b)** List several examples of things that could be used as collateral. Which item do you think a loans officer would consider most valuable? Why?	**c)** Conduct research at the library or on the Internet to find out what governments offer lenders as collateral for the money that they borrow.
3. a) What is the formula for calculating simple interest?	**b)** Explain how length of term and interest rate affect the total amount of money a borrower has to repay.	**c)** Students who do not qualify for a government loan can still apply for a loan at a financial institution. Invite a loans officer from a local financial institution to discuss how these loans are similar to and different from government loans.

Applying for Credit

Before going to a financial institution to apply for credit, borrowers should be organized. They should know the principal amount of the loan they need and the term. They should also be clear on the kind of repayment schedule they can afford. It is important that borrowers have an accurate picture of income and expenses to show a loans officer. Borrowers who present detailed and organized information will have a much better chance of success in applying for credit. Lenders want to be assured of two things: that borrowers can repay the debt and that they are willing to do so.

THE CREDIT APPLICATION

A **credit application** is an information form that a borrower must complete before being granted a loan, charge account, or credit card. The completed credit application helps the lender make a decision about granting credit or approving a loan. Borrowers must be accurate and honest in providing information. They must also sign the application. Their signature gives the lender permission to check the accuracy of the information and to conduct a complete credit check.

CREDIT WORTHINESS

Before lenders decide whether or not to grant credit or a loan, they evaluate a potential borrower's **credit worthiness**, or the borrower's ability to assume and pay back credit. In their evaluations, lenders consider the **three Cs of credit**: character, capacity, and capital.

Character

Character refers to a borrower's willingness to repay a loan when it's due, as well as his or her reliability and trustworthiness. Answers to questions such as the following help a lender determine a borrower's character:
- Do you pay your bills on time?
- Have you used credit before?
- How long have you lived at your current address?
- Where do you work, and how long have you held your present job?

The lender looks at the borrower's answers for signs of responsibility and stability. The lender's assessment of character must answer a basic question: "Will the borrower repay the debt?"

STRETCH YOUR THINKING

Why might a lender be concerned if you've changed jobs or moved often?

Capacity

Capacity refers to a borrower's ability to make payments on time and to pay a debt when it is due. Answers to questions such as the following help a lender determine a borrower's capacity:
- Do you have a permanent job?
- How much do you earn?
- Do you have any dependants?
- What are your current living expenses?
- How much money do you presently owe?

If a borrower's income is unsteady or low, he or she may not be able to handle more—or any—credit. Even with a high income, a borrower may not be able to handle more credit because of other debts. The lender asks this basic question in assessing a borrower's capacity: "Can the borrower repay the debt?"

What information does the credit application request?

MasterCard®* Application

Bank of Montreal

Please choose one of the following MasterCard options by initialing your choice.
If no initial appears, this application will be for the Standard card.

If you are already an AIR MILES™ Collector, please provide your Collector Number.

8

Bank of Montreal
Branch Transit
King & Yonge
6 King St. W.
1-2411 Toronto, Ont. M5H 1C3

Standard card [initial]   Gold card [initial]
If you would like to add Low Rate Option, please initial [initial]
You can add one of the following Reward Options by initializing your choice
AIR MILES Reward Program [initial]   FirstHome Program [initial]
If you are adding the AIR MILES Reward Program, choose the reward level by initializing below
Earn 1 reward mile/$40 in purchases [initial]   Earn 1 reward mile/$20 in purchases [initial]
If you would like to add the Out-Of-Canada Medical Insurance Option to the Gold card, please initial [initial]
Please initial if you are a student [initial]

For internal use only:
Source Code:

To qualify for the Gold MasterCard card, your family income should be $40,000 or more. Personal information you provide is protected under the Bank's "Your Privacy" Code.
Please see reverse for which we ask for your information. Please print clearly and complete in full.

TELL US ABOUT YOURSELF

| Mr. Miss Dr. | First Name | | Initials Last Name |
| Mrs. Ms. | | | |

Social Insurance Number (optional)   Date of Birth M M / D D / Y Y   No. of dependents excluding spouse   Area Code Home Telephone   Area Code Business Telephone

Permanent Address   Apt. number   City   Province   Postal Code

Time at this address years months   own rent school dormitory board live with parents   Your portion of monthly rent/mtge/board while: at permanent home address $ at school address $

School Address (if different from present address)   Apt. number   City   Province   Postal Code

Previous Address (if at present address less than 2 years)   Apt. number   City   Province   Postal Code   # years

Correspondence English French   Send statement to Permanent Address School Address Business Address

TELL US ABOUT YOUR EMPLOYER

Name of present employer   Time with this employer years months   Gross monthly salary $ Other monthly income $ Source of other income

Present employer's address   City   Province   Postal Code

Present Occupation   Self-employed Part-Time Full-Time Seasonal

Previous employer (if with present employer less than 2 years)   Previous Occupation   # years

TELL US ABOUT YOUR FINANCES

Name of bank/financial institution   Account Number   Chequing account Savings account Investment account

Address   City   Province

Name of Creditor – Loan/Credit Card   Monthly payment $ Name of Creditor – Loan/Credit Card   Monthly payment $

Name of Creditor – Loan/Credit Card   Monthly payment $ Name of Creditor – Loan/Credit Card   Monthly payment $

FOR SPOUSE/CO-APPLICANTS (COMPLETE THIS SECTION ONLY IF AN ADDITIONAL CARD IS REQUESTED FOR THE SPOUSE/CO-APPLICANT)

Spouse/Co-applicant's first name   Initials   Last Name

Name of Spouse/Co-applicant's employer   # years   Occupation

Employer's address   City   Province   Postal code

Gross Monthly Salary $ Other Income $ Date of Birth M M / D D / Y Y

TELL US ABOUT YOUR COLLEGE/UNIVERSITY (COMPLETE THIS SECTION ONLY IF YOU ARE A STUDENT)

Name of University or College   Course of Study   Enrollment status Part-Time Full-Time

What year are you in now?   How many years have you completed?   Duration of current program? (in years)   When do you expect to graduate? M M / Y Y   Did you previously graduate from another college/university? yes no   If yes, graduation date M M / Y Y

Please list your gross monthly income from all sources.   Employment $ Scholarship/Grant $ Family Assistance $ Savings $ Other $ Source of other income

Employment income listed above is Past Present Future   If past, please provide date M M / Y Y

By signing this application I accept notice in writing and consent to you obtaining or exchanging any information about me at any time from the credit bureau, my employer or other person in connection with any relationship between us or those which you or I wish to establish.
I/We have read the terms and conditions on the reverse and agree to be bound by them.

Signature of Applicant   Date M M / D D / Y Y   Signature of Spouse/Co-applicant if additional card required   Date M M / D D / Y Y

Completed application may be: handed in at any Bank of Montreal branch; faxed to 1 888 454-3578; or folded, sealed and mailed.   BM/GC

Capital

Capital is the value of a borrower's assets. Capital can be used to repay a loan if income is unavailable. Answers to questions such as the following help a lender determine a borrower's capital:

• How much money do you have in a savings account?
• What assets do you have and what is their value?
• What investments do you have that could be used as collateral?
• Do you own or rent your residence?

The value of a borrower's capital gives a lender concrete evidence of whether or not the borrower will be able to meet his or her credit obligations. In assessing a borrower's capital, a lender asks this basic question: "What does the borrower have of value that could be sold if he or she does not repay the debt?"

CHECKING THE CREDIT APPLICATION

In most cases, lenders check the information on a credit application. They contact employers to verify length of employment and earnings. They contact financial institutions and retailers to confirm information about existing accounts and loans. Lenders also contact other creditors for information on any unpaid accounts or loans that the borrower might have. This credit check indicates how the borrower has met past financial obligations. In other words, the credit check basically determines the borrower's credit worthiness.

CREDIT BUREAUS

Lenders may also check a borrower's credit worthiness using a credit bureau. A **credit bureau** is a business that gathers credit information on all borrowers in a particular region for the purpose of selling that information to credit grantors, or lenders. Retail stores and financial institutions are the main customers of credit bureaus.

Canada has two major credit bureaus: Equifax Canada, founded in 1919, and Trans Union of Canada, which has been in business since 1989. Because most national and international creditors are registered with both bureaus, credit reports from both firms probably hold similar information. Both Equifax and Trans Union maintain a coast-to-coast network of offices, and charge annual fees to users as well as a fee for each credit report requested.

Credit bureaus do not rate or evaluate borrowers. They simply gather information on borrowers, then keep the information in credit bureau files for seven years. After this time, the information is removed.

STRETCH YOUR THINKING

Credit bureau files must not contain any personal information on the borrower's medical background, race, creed, colour, ancestry, religion, or political connections. What might happen if credit bureaus issued reports with this information?

Credit bureaus obtain their information from three major sources:

1. **Consumer information**. Consumers supply this information when they complete credit or loan applications that require personal information, such as place of work, address, and date of birth.

2. **Major credit grantors**. Financial institutions and other credit-granting businesses regularly transmit payment histories to credit bureaus. This information shows whether a borrower's payments are current or overdue, and whether action has ever been taken to collect unpaid loans.

3. **Public records**. Bankruptcies and court judgments are matters of public record. Borrowers who have filed for bankruptcy or who have had a court rule against them may receive lower credit worthiness ratings.

Some people distrust credit reporting because they see it as an invasion of their privacy. If consumers always pay cash, however, they will have no credit record. Generally, the credit reporting system benefits both businesses and consumers. Businesses know they can use credit reports to make sounder decisions about whether or not to grant credit. Consumers benefit because lenders are able to make quicker credit decisions, which makes buying on credit fast, easy, and safe for qualified applicants.

A good credit rating is an extremely valuable asset. It should be carefully protected.

CREDIT RATING

As you read earlier in the chapter, a credit rating is an indication of the level of risk that consumers, businesses, or governments will pose if credit is granted to them. In other words, a credit rating is a measure of your credit worthiness. Credit ratings exist because businesses that extend credit share the information they gather with other businesses, especially the regional credit bureau. Some lenders, in fact, refer to the credit bureau's report as the credit rating.

A good credit rating is an extremely valuable asset. It should be carefully protected. If credit is used unwisely, it will result in a poor credit rating. A good credit rating results when a consumer
- carries no outstanding balance on credit cards
- pays all bills on time
- keeps debt to a reasonable level, based on income and assets
- has taken out a loan, and met all payment obligations on time
    A lower credit rating results when a consumer
- often pays bills late
- has too many credit cards
- owes large sums of money as well as a mortgage

- applies for many loans or credit cards in a short time period
- has declared personal bankruptcy

Getting a Credit History

Getting a loan or credit can be very difficult for students. Usually, students have no credit history and, therefore, no credit file or credit rating. The absence of a credit history makes it difficult for a lender to determine credit worthiness. You can, however, start to build a credit history even while you are a student in high school. As you have learned, lenders consider trustworthiness and reliability to be important character traits. Good marks and regular school attendance help establish these qualities. Teachers can also indicate to lenders how a student is doing in school. Lenders often view positive behaviour as an indication that a student is likely to succeed in future education and in the job market. Holding a job, and staying with a job for a steady period of time, can also help students establish a good credit record.

A simple way to create a credit record is to buy something on credit and pay the bill within 30 days. In this way, you can begin a good credit record and pay nothing in interest charges. If you expect to borrow in the future, consider taking out a small loan before you need larger credit financing—for a car or computer system, for example. Repaying the smaller loan on schedule will help you establish a good credit rating.

Checking Your Credit File

As a consumer, you are entitled to a copy of all the information that a credit bureau holds about you. In fact, many consumers check their file on a regular basis. Those who are unsure of their credit rating, have been denied credit, or plan to apply for a large amount of credit might want to check their file. A bad credit rating not only affects credit; it can be a deciding factor in job and apartment applications as well.

To get a copy of your credit file, contact Equifax or Trans Union in person, by mail, or by fax, and provide the following information:
- your full name and address
- your previous addresses (if you've been at your current address for less than five years)
- your date of birth
- your social insurance number
- a phone number
- photocopies of both sides of two pieces of identification (driver's licence, birth certificate, passport), including one with your signature

BUSINESS —FACT—

The Personal Information Protection and Electronic Documents Act came into effect on January 1, 2001. Among other things, this federal legislation ensures that all consumers in Canada have access to the contents of their credit file.

E-ACTIVITY

Visit
www.business.
nelson.com
and follow the links
to learn more about
how to get a copy
of a credit report.

Normally, you will receive a copy of your credit report by mail within three weeks. Because credit information is confidential, it will not be given over the phone.

As a consumer, you have the right to dispute any information in your credit file. Normally, you must complete a form to request corrections which you send back to the credit bureau. You may be required to provide more information or proof before any corrections are made. If you find an error in your credit file but no longer have any proof, what happens next depends on where you live. Each province has its own consumer protection laws concerning credit bureaus. If an error is corrected, however, the credit bureau must notify all credit grantors who have inquired about your credit worthiness within a specified number of months.

GETTING OUT OF DEBT

One of the disadvantages of credit is that it can lead to financial difficulties. If credit consumers cannot pay their bills on time, the worst thing they can do is panic and try to avoid creditors. Doing so will only make the crisis worse. Instead, they can take simple steps to help make the situation manageable. They can

- contact creditors immediately and explain their difficulties
- be honest and realistic, and work with creditors to make a plan for paying the debts
- pay a portion of what is owed in overdue payments, if possible

A financial crisis is also a wake-up call to review spending habits, financial goals, and lifestyle. It is important to remember that a budget is the key to personal financial planning, but it will work only if it is realistic and changes are made when necessary. A consumer with several debts should consider a **consolidation loan**, which combines all debts into one consumer loan. A loan and repayment schedule can usually be developed with the financial institution that will reduce monthly payments to a manageable level, over a longer term. The interest rate charged on a consolidation loan will probably be lower than the interest rate charged on credit card and charge account balances.

It is best to consider a consolidation loan when it is combined with credit counselling. **Credit counselling services** are not-for-profit organizations that provide unbiased assistance to individuals and families experiencing money and credit problems. Credit counsellors help clients look at their personal financial situation, discuss their options, and develop a course of action. Counsellors can offer advice on budget planning, and can contact creditors to arrange debt-management plans and reduced payments.

BUSINESS
—FACT—

Credit Counselling Canada was formed in 2000 to bring together provincial not-for-profit credit counselling agencies and provincial debt-payment programs. This association was formed to provide all Canadians with access to a national standard of credit counselling services.

INFORMATION	CONNECTION	EXTENSION
1. a) What two things do lenders want to know before making a decision about granting credit?	**b)** Look at the credit application on page 347. What information would be on your credit application form?	**c)** Visit at least three retail stores (in person or online) that grant credit. Get a copy of each store's credit application. Prepare a report that notes which elements are common to all the forms and which are unique.
2. a) List the three Cs of credit.	**b)** Why is each of the three Cs of credit important? Which do you think is the most important? Why?	**c)** Look at the required information on the credit applications you collected in Question 1c. Group the information to determine which questions provide answers to the applicant's character, capacity, and capital.
3. a) What is a credit rating? Why is it so important?	**b)** As a high school student, what could you do to begin to establish a credit rating?	**c)** Imagine that you are deeply in debt and decide to use a credit counselling service. With a partner, role-play and, if possible, videotape the dialogue that might occur between the counsellor and the debtor. What are the main concerns of the counseller? of the debtor?

Review

Knowledge and Understanding

1. Match each of the following terms to the correct definition:

capacity   creditor
capital   credit rating
character   credit worthiness
collateral   debtor
credit   mortgage

a) An evaluation of a person's ability to assume and repay a debt.
b) Anyone who buys on credit or receives a loan.

c) A legal document in which the purchaser of a property pledges the property as collateral for a loan.

d) A person or business that grants a loan or sells on credit.

e) A borrower's ability to carry a debt and pay the debt when it is due.

f) An indication of the level of risk that a consumer, business, or government poses to a creditor.

g) Assets that are offered as security for a loan.

h) A borrower's reliability and willingness to repay a debt when it is due.

i) The value of a borrower's assets that could be used to repay a debt.

j) The privilege of using someone else's money for a period of time.

2. Describe ways in which consumers, businesses, and governments use credit.

3. What are some key questions that consumers should ask themselves when deciding whether to use credit?

4. Identify and give examples of common types of credit cards.

5. Why should a person protect a good credit rating?

6. What is the purpose of a credit bureau? Who uses it?

Thinking and Inquiry

1. Canada's credit system is based partly on trust. Who does the trusting: the creditor or the debtor? Explain.

2. Working in pairs, discuss the meaning of the following statement: "A good credit rating is like having money in the bank."

3. Do you agree or disagree with the following statements? Explain why.
   - "If goods were sold only for cash, prices would be lower and everyone would be better off."
   - "If I can't pay cash for something, it means I can't afford it, so I won't buy it."
   - "I buy on credit whenever I can because credit increases sales and is good for businesses."
   - "You should use credit sometimes; it helps you establish a credit rating, which may be useful in case of emergency."

4. Why do you think that interest rates on credit cards are higher than on many other kinds of loans?

Communication

1. Do you think that teenagers should be given credit cards? Debate this issue with a partner.

2. Using a library, the Internet, newspapers, magazines, or local business resources, collect information on credit, consumer debt, credit bureaus, and credit ratings. Place your articles in a scrapbook, highlighting the key passages. Write one or two sentences explaining each article and its message.

3. Does it concern you that so much personal data is available in an individual's credit file? Why or why not? In small groups, discuss the issue of protecting the privacy of consumer information. Make notes and compare your ideas with other groups.

Application

1. Imagine that you are planning to buy a new computer system for $5000, and that you plan to use credit to finance your purchase. Explore different credit plans and rates of interest offered by at least three different creditors. In a chart, show the total amount of your purchase (principal + interest) using each plan. Prepare a report of your findings, indicating which credit source you would use and why. Share your findings with others in the class.

2. Using the Internet or a national newspaper, look for advertisements for employment opportunities in the credit field. Using a step diagram, flow chart, or timeline, map a possible career path that would lead you to each job. Be specific about where and how you would obtain the requirements for the job. If possible, interview people involved in the credit field for further information. Share your career paths with the class in a career discussion forum.

REFLECT ON YOUR LEARNING

1. Reread the notes you wrote in response to the Before You Begin question on page 333. How have your ideas changed now that you've read this chapter?

2. Imagine that you want to borrow $3000. This is your first loan application. What things have you done that could help a lender judge your trustworthiness and reliability according to the three Cs of credit?

BECOMING AN ENTREPRENEUR

"Entrepreneurship is the most difficult thing you will ever do. Remember one thing: If you're loyal to your vision, you will probably make it work."

Frank O'Dea, founder of The Second Cup Coffee Company

CHAPTER 15

WHAT IS AN ENTREPRENEUR?

STUDENT EXPECTATIONS

After completing this chapter, you will be able to

- explain the term "entrepreneur"
- compare an entrepreneur with an enterprising person
- identify characteristics and skills associated with successful entrepreneurs
- explain how entrepreneurial characteristics and skills can be applied to all types of endeavours
- describe the lives and achievements of several Canadian entrepreneurs
- identify goods and services produced by entrepreneurs in your community
- analyze your own entrepreneurial strengths and interests
- investigate opportunities for entrepreneurship within your school or community using a variety of techniques and methods

Profile

Sue Randall (front) leads skiers through Gros Morne National Park.

DREAMS COME TRUE

There's nothing like spending endless hours exploring the backcountry of Newfoundland and Labrador. For Sue Randall, it's a way of life. Sue co-owns and operates Gros Morne Adventure Guides. The company provides everything from sea kayaking and hiking adventures to backcountry skiing and snowshoeing.

Born in Gander, Sue completed a physical education degree at Memorial University in St. John's. She taught phys. ed at Pasadena Academy and at the Deer Lake community recreation centre. She later went on to instruct a two-year adventure tourism course at the College of the North Atlantic. So why the leap into business? "Lifestyle," she says. "Being an entrepreneur was appealing—running my own business, setting my own hours, and ultimately being my own boss." In 1990, Sue, along with partner Bob Hicks, started the trek into the world of business. "There's a lot of opportunity here in the province, but it takes a lot of time and effort." Sue had to keep a full-time job while she was getting the business off the ground.

Sue and Bob certainly had an ideal location for their service. With the ocean a few minutes walk from Sue's house in Norris Point, and Gros Morne National Park just a short drive away, they had all the natural resources that they could handle … and more. All they had to do was make themselves known. Sue and Bob did a lot of promotion, advertising what they had to offer. They prepared pamphlets, advertised on the Internet, and, of course, relied on word of mouth. All the effort paid off. In 1998, they won the Hospitality Newfoundland and Labrador Tourism Award.

Sue says a lot of their success is due to the prime location of the business. Gros Morne National Park is a UNESCO World Heritage site. Its scenery encompasses the dramatic transition from the sea-coast to the towering rock walls of deep, landlocked fjords, to the arctic alpine of the Long Range Mountains. Its outstanding geological features rank it among the most significant natural areas in the world, and northern species like arctic hare, woodland caribou, rock ptarmigan, alpine campion, and diapensia exist here. The mix of

CONTINUED →

ocean, mountains, and arctic alpine offers the adventure traveller such diversity in scenery and landscape that it is hard to match anywhere else in North America.

A good location alone, however, does not ensure success. Says Sue: "We take great pride in creating an excellent quality service." Gros Morne Adventure Guides provides trained guides, instruction, meals, and accommodation. "Newfoundland and Labrador have everything that I like," says Sue, glancing through her window. "It's pristine, it has a rich culture, and it's a great place to live." But she adds: "It takes a lot of hard work to start a business here. You have to do your homework; you must persevere and take advantage of technology. Just believe in your dream and do it."

"Being an entrepreneur was appealing— running my own business, setting my own hours, and ultimately being my own boss."

Bob Hicks (front) and a fellow kayaker pass an iceberg in Notre Dame Bay, in Newfoundland.

About This Profile

1. How did Sue's background in physical education prepare her for her entrepreneurial venture?
2. Why do you think Sue wanted a business partner?
3. Why does Sue advise entrepreneurs to do their homework, persevere, and take advantage of technology?
4. What factors have made Gros Morne Adventure Guides a success?

The Entrepreneur

Some people seem to be naturals at starting businesses, projects, and organizations. Create a list of characteristics you think these people possess, and list some of the skills you think they need to succeed.

Unit 2 of this textbook opens with a quotation from Peter Drucker: "A business exists to create a customer." This statement is surprising; it forces you to rethink the relationship between businesses and customers. It also helps you understand how businesses are created. This chapter will look at what motivates and inspires the people who start new businesses and organizations.

WHAT IS AN ENTREPRENEUR?

As you read in Chapter 1, an **entrepreneur** is a person who starts a venture to solve a problem or take advantage of an opportunity. A **venture** is a business enterprise involving some risk, in expectation of gain. Entrepreneurs always set goals for their ventures. These goals are specific and defined. For example, Taisha started a business to sell personal digit assistants (PDAs), such as Palm Pilots. She recognized an opportunity and started a venture to take advantage of a trend in the hope of making a profit.

WHAT IS AN ENTERPRISING PERSON?

Enterprising people bring entrepreneurial characteristics to the workplace or to other organizations. They do not, however, start a venture themselves—or assume most of the risk. Enterprising people contribute to someone else's venture by seeing problems that need to be solved or opportunities that the business can exploit. They organize themselves, work teams, or committees to help solve these problems or take advantage of the opportunities. The enterprising person often takes charge without being asked, particularly if the business encourages an enterprising spirit among its employees. In Chapter 5, you learned that the 3M company turned one of its product failures (an adhesive) into a product success (Post-it Notes). The 3M company encourages enterprising employees. In fact, 3M scientists are allowed to spend part of their time on projects of their own choice.

Enterprising people are very important to businesses. They often save the businesses time and money, or create new ideas that help businesses achieve profit goals. Enterprising people can also be found in clubs, classrooms, and committees. For example, Fred organized an information presentation to combat drinking and driving. He used the presentation as a way to help solve a problem in his community. He organized resources and set specific goals. Fred was enterprising.

ENTREPRENEURIAL CHARACTERISTICS

Not everyone is entrepreneurial. Many people are comfortable working for others, and they look for stability and security. Other people are driven to make changes. It is these people who become entrepreneurs. All entrepreneurs possess similar characteristics. They are risk takers, and they are perceptive, curious, and imaginative. They are persistent goal setters who are hard working. They are self-confident, flexible, and like to be independent.

Risk Taker

If you had $50 000, you could do several things with it. You could buy a new car with the money. You could give it to charity. You could invest in Canada Savings Bonds or other safe investments, or you could invest in areas that are less safe. As you read in Chapter 11, risky investments often promise better financial rewards than safer investments. With risky investments, however, you could lose all your money.

Entrepreneurs often take on a high degree of risk. Because there are no "sure things" in business, every business faces risk. A failed business can mean bankruptcy for its owners, leaving them with few or no business and personal assets. Not everyone can cope with this stress.

Successful entrepreneurs minimize and manage risk. Business owners research opportunities to be sure they have covered all the potential problems. Some risks are simply unacceptable. For example, it would not be acceptable to bet all your business capital on a horse race or at a casino. In these examples, financial success depends only on luck. On the other hand, if you have a plan to produce and distribute a product that you know people will buy, starting a factory to manufacture this product is an acceptable risk. If you've done the research and acquired the knowledge and skills to make the factory efficient, there's a good chance that you'll be able to earn a profit on the money you've invested.

Perceptive

Entrepreneurs do not avoid problems. Instead, when faced with problems, they welcome them as opportunities or challenges. When Canadian soft-drink manufacturer Cott Corporation started out, it had a problem. How could it hope to compete with Coke and Pepsi, the two giants in the soft-drink industry? Gerald Pencer, Cott's entrepreneurial CEO, was very perceptive. Research indicated that soft drinks were one of the biggest selling items in supermarkets. Pencer decided to develop Cott as a **private label** bottler. Cott contracted with supermarkets and other retail stores to manufacture a variety of soft drinks that could be packaged under the retailer's brand, such as President's Choice at Loblaws or Master Choice at A&P. (See Chapter 10 for more information on private brands.) Cott's product challenged Coke and Pepsi by developing a whole new method of distribution— one that allowed retailers to make more profits by offering consumers a much cheaper soft drink. Today, Cott is the fourth largest beverage manufacturer in the world.

Curious

Entrepreneurs like to know how things work. Before American Ray Kroc, founder of the McDonald's fast-food franchise, got into the restaurant business in the 1950s, he worked as a salesperson. One of the products he offered was a multimixer, a blender that could make five milkshakes at a time. Two of Kroc's customers, the McDonald brothers, ordered many of these machines. Kroc wondered why. Instead of simply sending out the order, Kroc decided he needed to see what kind of restaurant used so many mixers. When he saw the restaurant in operation, Kroc immediately perceived that the McDonald brothers had a formula for producing good, inexpensive food. They had created a kind of food assembly line that could deliver meals to customers in a matter of minutes. Kroc suggested that he could open additional restaurants for the McDonald brothers and translate their

Did You Know?

Gerry Pencer's entrepreneurial spirit never deserted him, even after he was diagnosed with a fatal brain tumor in 1997. Before he died, Pencer created The Gerry & Nancy Pencer Brain Trust to raise funds for cancer support and research. In 1998, the Pencer Brain Tumor Centre, a leading treatment centre and research facility, opened at Toronto's Princess Margaret Hospital.

"fast food" concept into a business venture. In 1961, he bought out the McDonald brothers. Ray Kroc's curiosity made him a very successful businessperson—his McDonald's restaurant chain spread throughout the United States and, eventually, the world. He was a leader in the development of the modern franchise system.

Imaginative

Entrepreneurs are creative. They imagine solutions to problems and create new products or generate new ideas. Entrepreneurs have a vision.

Cirque du Soleil

In 1984, childhood friends Guy Laliberté and Daniel Gauthier joined forces to create Cirque du Soleil. Before Cirque du Soleil's arrival, North American circuses stuck to a basic formula: lots of animal tricks, a few acrobatic stunts, and horn-honking clowns who climbed out of miniature cars, sprayed each other with water, and performed various other slapstick comedy routines. Laliberté and Gauthier took the traditional circus and turned it on its head. Part opera, part dance, part circus, Cirque du Soleil mixes dark humour and eerie imagery with live music, pyrotechnics, and complex choreography. For decades, traditional circus fare was targeted at families with young children. Cirque du Soleil, with its more sophisticated brand of entertainment, taps into a much wider audience. Today, Cirque du Soleil is celebrated throughout the world for its innovative ideas, designs, and performers. It has also expanded into new ventures, such as retail outlets and entertainment complexes.

Persistent

Rarely is a new venture successful right away. Often, dealing with bureaucracy, making mistakes in the market, confronting criticism, and having money, family, or stress problems are part of the entrepreneurial experience. Many people would say "Enough!" and give up. True entrepreneurs stick with their ideas until they're sure that they've tried everything to make the venture work.

The success of Maureen Mitchells, founder of Winnipeg-based CanTalk Canada, proves that persistence pays off. As a former journalist and international marketing consultant, Mitchells realized that communication is key in today's global marketplace. Her idea was to offer fast, over-the-phone language interpretation and translation services to companies in the tourism, financial services, and hospitality industries. However, in 1995, these industries showed little interest in her project. Mitchells was not deterred. Instead of giving up, she simply altered her plan. She focused on developing a niche market, providing foreign-language operator services to companies in the telecommunications sector. Today, CanTalk Canada offers services in 93 languages to 160 countries, and employs 150 people who manage over 300 000 calls a month. And while CanTalk's biggest clients are still the telecommunications companies, Mitchells is gaining more and more clients in finance and tourism.

Goal-setting

For many entrepreneurs, one success may not be enough. In fact, entrepreneurs are often motivated primarily by the excitement of starting a new venture. They set a goal, then develop a venture to achieve that goal. Once the goal is achieved, a new goal needs to take its place. Most often, setting a new goal means starting a new venture.

The cofounders of Roots, for example, are always looking for new opportunities. In the early days, Michael Budman and Don Green made Earth Shoes. Then, they developed a line of clothing and opened a chain of retail stores to sell the clothing and leather goods. Other Roots ventures include a Roots resort, furniture store, Paris-based magazine, airline, and designer vitamins. In this way, the ongoing restlessness of the Roots cofounders has helped make them two of Canada's most famous entrepreneurs.

Hard-working

Entrepreneurs see the task in front of them, but do not let hard work deter them. During the Christmas season, for example, a retailer may work 16 hours straight for days in a row. If a new plant is opening or a special order needs to be filled, a factory owner may not get home for days. To succeed, entrepreneurs need a great deal of energy.

The owner of a hardware store calls his suppliers to check the date of the next shipment.

"When life deals you lemons, make lemonade." Explain why this saying is perfect for entrepreneurs.

Self-confident

Entrepreneurs believe in themselves. In order to take risks and work so hard, entrepreneurs must be certain that their ideas are worth the effort. Doubts may exist, but the self-confidence of entrepreneurs takes care of these doubts. Denise Meehan, founder of Lick's Homeburgers and Ice Cream, has this kind of confidence. Meehan learned a great deal about running a business from her parents, who operated a tourist retreat in Sturgeon Falls, Ontario. Meehan became involved in the business at an early age, and customers often complimented her on her approach to service. These early experiences gave Meehan the confidence to open her own business—a restaurant that offers high-quality hamburgers and homemade ice cream. She strongly believed that her commitment to high standards of food, service, and atmosphere would mean success. In 1980, Meehan got a $5000 loan and opened the first Lick's restaurant. Her idea took off, and there are now more than 20 Lick's restaurants across Ontario.

Flexible

There are no sure things in business. The only thing an entrepreneur can count on is that things will change, sometimes for the better, sometimes for the worse. A true entrepreneur looks at change as an opportunity. He or she must be flexible in order to adapt to changing trends, markets, technologies, rules, and economic environments.

The Flexibility to Change

Ali Jaffri and two partners realized that pager companies weren't catering to younger clients. So in 1995, they founded The Pager Clinic to fill the gap.

Competition in the wireless industry is fierce. In one mall, Jaffri has 13 direct competitors. He believes flexibility and awareness are key to survival. "You have to be aware of the industry you are in at all times. We are always anticipating what is coming next," says Jaffri. "The best advice I can give is not to be stubborn. You have to realize that your business is going to change."

Ali offers one other reminder to entrepreneurs on how to cope with a changing marketplace: "The key is not your product, it is your management team and how aware you are of what is going on in your industry," he insists. "You need to recognize what is selling, what isn't, and what the new developments are. Just be on your toes at all times."

STRETCH YOUR THINKING

Could Guy Laliberté and Daniel Gauthier have started Cott Corporation? Could Ali Jaffri have started Roots? Could Denise Meehan have started The Pager Clinic? Why or why not?

Independent

The most common entrepreneurial characteristic is the desire for independence. Entrepreneurs do not like to be told what to do. They need to control their own lives and make their own decisions. People with an entrepreneurial personality find it hard to work in a controlled environment. As a result, they would not likely enjoy working on an assembly line or in the military.

Entrepreneurs' need for independence helps them achieve their goals. No one possesses exactly the same characteristics. It is the particular mix of characteristics in each entrepreneur that defines each new project. Moreover, each entrepreneur may only succeed in his or her personal ventures. Entrepreneurs, then, must find their own opportunities, make their own plans, and create their own solutions. Each venture is a reflection of the independent entrepreneur who started it.

Because creative, entrepreneurial people are so independent, businesses can find it very difficult to attract them. To encourage **intrapreneurship** (entrepreneurial spirit within a business or an organization), many businesses allow employees a great deal of independence. Some businesses also use team or work-group management styles, as you read in Chapter 7.

ACTIVITIES FOR ...

INFORMATION	CONNECTION	EXTENSION
1. a) What is an entrepreneur?	**b)** Describe in detail how you could turn an entertainment or sports event, a party, or a vacation into a venture.	**c)** In what ways could you be entrepreneurial in your school? in your classroom? Create a proposal, and convince either your entire school or your class to support your venture.
2. a) What is an enterprising person?	**b)** Explain why enterprising employees save businesses time and money.	**c)** With a partner, make a list of things that a business could do to encourage an enterprising spirit in its employees.
3. a) List, with brief descriptions, 10 characteristics of entrepreneurs.	**b)** Describe the entrepreneurial characteristic that you think is the most important. How might this characteristic lead to success in business?	**c)** Find a magazine or newspaper article, Web site, or television program that profiles an entrepreneur. Find as many entrepreneurial characteristics in the profile as you can. Explain how the person being profiled illustrates each characteristic.

Contemporary Issues in Canadian Business

THE ISSUE: ETHICS IN THE WORLD OF BUSINESS

What role should ethics play in business?
Ethics is a matter of knowing the difference between right and wrong and then choosing to do the right thing. Businesses face ethical questions every day concerning the products or services they sell, and how they deal with people inside and outside the company. Many companies choose to operate according to a **code of ethics**—a document that explains specifically how employees should respond in different situations.

A code of ethics is especially useful when problems arise. For example, in the mid-1970s, someone contaminated several bottles of Tylenol with poison. Johnson & Johnson, the manufacturer of Tylenol, followed its code of ethics and pulled every package of the product off the shelves, even though it was very expensive for the company to do so. Johnson & Johnson also changed its packaging so it would be much more difficult for someone to contaminate the product in the future. The recall and repackaging effort cost the corporation about $100 million, but it also showed customers that the company cared about their safety.

Does every business need a code of ethics? Let's examine both sides of this issue.

Point

Imagine that you're the manager of an electronics store. You have an opportunity to buy a number of inexpensive television sets from a company that's going out of business, but if the sets don't work properly, customers won't be able to return them or buy parts to fix them. The company salesperson suggests that you can sell the sets at a sale price, with a "no returns" policy, and that most customers probably won't ask about a warranty if you don't bring up the subject first. You see a chance to make a significant profit, and you're tempted.

When you consult your code of ethics, you see that several parts of the code apply to the current situation:

• All products offered for sale must be of an acceptable quality.
• Customers may return any product within 30 days of sale and are entitled to a full refund or exchange.
• Sales offers must disclose the exact nature of what is being offered.

Based on what you've learned from the company salesperson, you decide not to buy the discount television sets. Because of your code of ethics, your store will continue to maintain its reputation as a source of high-quality products.

A code of ethics helps different people approach problems in the same way. Many companies have gone beyond simply writing a code, and have established educational programs to help employees learn to behave more ethically. Program topics range from making personal calls during business hours to handling employee layoffs.

When a number of companies follow similar codes of ethics, their actions may lead to changes in the law. For example, in the past, ethical considerations have led to laws that have eliminated child labour, outlawed price fixing, and upheld employee rights.

Ethical behavior is based on values such as trustworthiness, respect, responsibility, caring, justice, and good citizenship. It is not enough for companies simply to say that they support these values. They also need a code of ethics to show employees and customers how such values are reflected in the company's day-to-day operations.

Counterpoint

The problem with a code of ethics is that it isn't always easy to draw the line between right and wrong. Is it wrong for a businessperson to give a client a gift because that client has been a valued customer over the past year? Is it wrong for a politician to make a phone call to a bank manager to help a friend obtain a business loan?

Rather than referring to a written guideline, all ethical people really need to do is ask themselves, "If we take this action, will anyone suffer as a result?" For example, if the retailer described earlier had bought and sold the discount-price television sets, customers (and the business's reputation) would have suffered. The ethical answer could easily have been determined without reference to a written code.

In Canada, detailed codes for business behaviour are clearly laid down by law, but it's still possible to behave unethically while staying within the law. Like the law, no code of ethics can provide guidance for every possible situation.

Although codes of ethics may sometimes help people make decisions, they are not conclusive guides to distinguishing between right and wrong, and they are not necessary for every company. Instead, people should rely on their own judgment about how the situation will affect themselves and others.

A Real Life Example

The Canadian Information Processing Society has a written code of ethics. The following statements are agreed to by all members of the society as a condition of membership.

Code of Ethics

I acknowledge that my position as an information processing professional carries with it certain obligations, and I will take diligent personal responsibility for their discharge.

P) **To the public:** I will endeavour to protect the public interest and strive to promote understanding of information processing and its application, but will not represent myself as an authority on topics in which I lack competence.

M) **To myself and my profession:** I will guard my competence and effectiveness as a valuable possession, and work at maintaining them despite changing circumstances and requirements. Furthermore, I will maintain high personal standards of moral responsibility, character, and integrity when acting in my professional capacity.

C) **To my colleagues:** I will treat my colleagues with integrity and respect, and hold their right to success to be as important as my own. I will contribute to the professional knowledge of information processing to the best of my ability.

E) **To my employer and management:** I will give faithful service to further my employer's legitimate best interests through management's direction.

C) **To my clients:** I will give frank and careful counsel on matters within my competence, and guard my clients' confidential information and private matters absolutely. In my capacity as a provider of products or services, I will provide good value for my compensation, and will endeavour to protect the user of my product or service against consequential loss or harm.

S) **To my students:** I will provide a scholarly education to my students in a sympathetic and helpful manner.

Questions and Activities About This Issue

1. Review your school's guidelines for student behaviour. How are these guidelines similar to the code of ethics a business might have? How are they different?

2. Search through magazines and newspapers to find a current ethical issue that affects the business world. Discuss the issue with a partner. Then write a point/counterpoint analysis of the situation.

Career Focus 4: The Job Interview

Purpose of an Interview

In the third Career Focus on pages 248–249, you learned how to apply for a job. If you're lucky, you may be invited to an interview with your potential employer. This interview is your opportunity to show the employer why you're the best person for the job. In a way, an interview is like a sales call, except that instead of selling a product, you're selling yourself and your skills. It's up to you to convince the interviewer that you have what his or her business wants and needs.

To do well at the interview, you'll have to convince the interviewer that
- you're qualified for the job
- you have the motivation and ambition to get the job done well
- you'll fit in with the other employees you'll be working with

Remember that an interview is a two-way exchange of information. It's an opportunity for the interviewer to learn more about you, but it's also a chance for you to learn more about the job and about the company you'll be working for.

Preparing for the Interview

Prepare for the interview in the same careful way you prepared your résumé and cover letter. Start by finding out as much as you can about the company. Read the annual report or visit the company's Web site. If the employer is a retailer or restaurant, visit the workplace. What are the employees doing? What is the work environment like?

Use networking to find out as much as you can about the company, its reputation, and how it treats its employees. This type of preparation is important because it shows the employer that you're interested in the job and that you have initiative. It may also help you decide whether or not you really want the job.

Interviews make most people nervous, but it's easier to be confident when you're well prepared. Reread your résumé and cover letter, and focus on what you have to offer. The interviewer may ask questions about your skills, values, interests, accomplishments, education, work experience, and personal goals, such as the following:
- What courses do you like best in school? Why?
- What extracurricular activities have you participated in? Why did you choose those activities?
- How would you describe yourself? How would others describe you?
- What do you know about our company? Why do you want to work for us?
- What is your greatest strength? weakness?
- How could you improve yourself?
- What experience do you have working with a team?
- With so many applicants, why should we hire you?

The interviewer is also likely to ask if you have any questions. Your questions will help to convince the interviewer that you are sincerely interested in the job, so it's a good idea to prepare a few in advance. Possible questions include the following:
- What would my responsibilities be?
- What would you expect of me in the first six months?
- What are the company's plans for the future?
- What are the possibilities for advancement? How long would it take?
- What will my salary be? (Don't bring this up too early in the interview.)
- What training do you provide?
- When will you decide who gets this job?

Interview Tips

There are several tips that can help you make the most of your interview.
- Dress appropriately for the job. Don't be too formal or too casual.
- Go alone. Don't take friends or family with you.
- Make sure you know when the interview will take place and how to find the location.
- Plan to arrive a few minutes early. Be sure to leave extra time in case you run into any problems with traffic or other delays on the way.

- When you arrive, take time to focus and calm down.
- When you meet the interviewer, give a firm handshake. Make eye contact and smile during the introduction.
- Be pleasant and enthusiastic, but avoid talking too much. Don't say more than you're asked to say.
- Listen carefully to each question and give a brief but complete answer.
- Try to be aware of your body language, facial expressions, and tone of voice.
- Remember to thank the interviewer at the end of the interview and to reaffirm your interest in the job.

AFTER THE INTERVIEW

Send a thank-you note promptly to the interviewer, expressing your enthusiasm for the job and your appreciation for the interview.

Whether or not you get the job, it's good to think about what went well—or not so well—during the interview. If you get the job, this process will help you gain a better sense of what your employer expects of you. If you don't get the job, what you've learned may help you with other interviews.

If you get the job, you'll likely hear back from the employer in a few days. If no one calls you, call the interviewer back after about a week and ask what happened. If you didn't get the job, ask for advice about how you could do better next time.

There are many reasons why an employer might choose one candidate over another, but most people who make a sincere effort eventually find the right job. However, many employers say that there are a few applicants they would *not* hire under any circumstances. These may include people who
- have a sloppy personal appearance
- fail to demonstrate a keen interest in the job
- seem unable to outline clear thoughts and answers
- have poor manners
- avoid eye contact
- fail to ask any questions about the job or the company
- appear to be too focused on money

It may be disappointing not to get the job, but many very successful people have had the same experience. The important thing is to learn from

what happened and to make changes that will make the interview process go better next time.

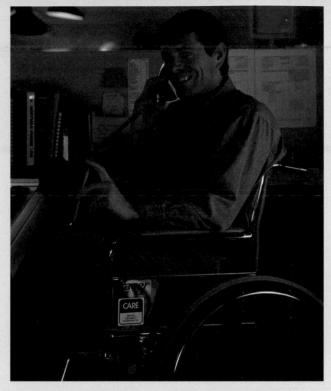

This man found out the day after his interview that he got the job.

Something to Think About

1. List some specific things you can do to ensure that you have a positive interview.

2. In the third Career Focus, you were asked to prepare a sample application for a job you found on an Internet job site. With two partners, role-play and, if possible, videotape a mock interview for this job. One partner acts as an interviewer, another as an observer, and the third person takes the role of the job applicant. The observer should evaluate the effectiveness of the interview and be prepared to offer suggestions to both the interviewer and the applicant.

   Be sure to give copies of your résumé and cover letter to the other members of your group. After the interview is complete, change roles and repeat until everyone in the group has been interviewed.

Entrepreneurial Skills

Having a **skill** means that you have the ability to do something specific. Carpenters have woodworking skills, chefs have cooking skills, and doctors have diagnostic skills. It is easier to learn a skill than it is to develop a characteristic. Skills enable you to translate knowledge into action. To be successful, entrepreneurs need a variety of skills, including research, management, and relationship skills.

RESEARCH SKILLS

To run a successful venture, an entrepreneur needs to perform marketing and accounting tasks, as well as many of the other business activities covered in this textbook. Entrepreneurs must identify what they need to know, and then use research techniques to obtain this information.

Take the case of Sonja Jones, cofounder of Peninsula Farms, a small business in Lunenburg, Nova Scotia. Sonja and her husband owned a cow, which they used to keep their lawn clipped. At first, they had a problem—the cow produced milk and the Joneses didn't know how to milk it. So they learned proper milking techniques, but then another problem arose: The cow was producing more milk than they could use, and the surplus was going to waste. In this problem, Sonja saw an opportunity. She analyzed the local market to find out what kind of milk product would sell. Her research indicated that whole-milk yogurt was in demand. Sonja then learned how to make yogurt in large batches and bought more cows—enough to make Peninsula Farms a profitable business.

It is not necessary for entrepreneurs to know everything about their chosen venture before they begin. What they do need, however, is the ability to learn or acquire knowledge. The first step in knowledge acquisition is asking a good question. In fact, knowing what questions to ask is one of the most important research skills an entrepreneur can possess.

Entrepreneurs often ask questions about problems or information that most people pass over or take for granted. Entrepreneurs may wonder about something they read in a newspaper or see on a television program. Perhaps a question is sparked by a chance remark overheard in a supermarket or on the street. In any case, the entrepreneur asks questions such as "Why is that?" or "How does that work?" These initial questions often lead nowhere in particular; sometimes, however, the question is the first step in a process that leads to a venture plan.

STRETCH YOUR THINKING

The invention was fire. What was the problem? The invention was the wheel. What was the problem? The invention was the telephone. What was the problem? Reverse the answer and question, and identify a problem that concerns you. What product or service can you invent to overcome it?

Most people who struggle to find their house key in their cluster of keys day after day never wonder about the problem. An entrepreneur, however, might ask, "How could I make it easier to find the right key?" Such a question is the beginning of research.

Once you formulate your initial research question, the first step is to gather information that will help you answer it. During this process, you may discover things that lead you to ask new questions or to reformulate old ones. As your venture moves further along, your questions become more specific and focused, and may even lead to the creation of new knowledge.

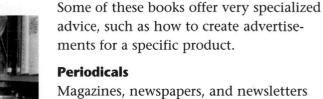

A RESEARCH MODEL: INFORMATION, CONNECTIONS, AND EXTENSIONS

Throughout this textbook, you have used information, connection, and extension questions to explore different aspects of business. You can also use this same model as a framework for your research.

Information

Once entrepreneurs form their questions, they need to know how to find answers. Often, their search begins at a library or on the Internet. Complex questions such as "How will I advertise my product?" or "What channels of distribution would be best for this item?" may require the entrepreneur to research a variety of sources.

Two young entrepreneurs look for books to help them start their jewellery business.

Books

In a library or bookstore, there are books on all aspects of business. Hundreds of books have been written about advertising, for example. Some of these books offer very specialized advice, such as how to create advertisements for a specific product.

Periodicals

Magazines, newspapers, and newsletters are good sources of business information. Some periodicals, known as trade journals, focus on a particular industry. *Convenience Store News*, for example, is written for people who are interested in the convenience store business. *Automatic Merchandiser* is a monthly magazine published for people in the vending machine industry.

Indexes and Databases

Indexes and databases are excellent research tools. A **periodical index** lists articles that have been published about a specific topic over a particular period of time. Most indexes provide the article's title, a brief description, and the name and date of the periodical in which the article appears. **Databases** are lists of information organized by category. These categories can be very specific, for example, kite manufacturers, or very broad, for example, Canadian businesses that export to the U.S. The CanCorp Financials Web site posts a database of detailed information on more than 8000 Canadian companies. Using the Thomas Register of American Manufacturers, entrepreneurs can access information on 156 000 North American manufacturers and more than 450 000 products. Some databases charge a fee, but others are free. Your public library may also provide free Internet access to some databases.

The Internet

The Internet offers many Web sites that are valuable to entrepreneurs, including government sites and association sites for people in particular businesses. One problem with the Internet is that it can provide too much information, much of it inaccurate, unedited, and dated. Nevertheless, Internet search engines such as Google, Excite, AltaVista Canada, and Copernicus can help the entrepreneur find specific information. As well, groups of people who are interested in sharing information on specific topics sometimes form special Internet chat groups called listservs. A **listserv** is an e-mail list that distributes queries and information to all the people who belong or subscribe to it. Entrepreneurs interested in starting a textile business by raising sheep, for example, could acquire information from sheep ranchers, weavers, or sweater designers. Be careful when you use the Internet: Do not give out personal or financial information to an unknown source. Unfortunately, some people use the Internet for illegal or unethical activities.

Consultants

Experts, or consultants, can help entrepreneurs gather needed information. Consultants are often entrepreneurs themselves and charge for their services. However, certain university business departments, some government departments, and most financial institutions, offer free business consulting. Local chambers of commerce and business development offices are often the best sources of free and valuable information when opening a venture in a particular city or region. They have a wealth of knowledge about topics such as business trends, available locations, and local tax rates and rental costs.

Did You Know?

Many chambers of commerce and business development offices provide a well-stocked business library and on-site consultants.

Professionals

Many different kinds of professionals can assist entrepreneurs with their research. Advertising agencies can help figure out what types of ads to create and where to place them. Accountants can give advice on maintaining financial records. Sales agents can provide information on distributing a product. Lawyers can offer advice about patents and copyrights. Professionals usually charge a fee for their services.

School

Most universities and community colleges offer extension courses in business subjects. Usually, the courses are offered at night. Many schools and community colleges also offer general interest courses, which may provide other sorts of information. If the entrepreneur has more complex information needs, he or she may need to enroll in a full-time program and obtain the necessary skills and knowledge over several years.

Connections

Not all information is usable. Once entrepreneurs gather information from a variety of sources, they need to extract data that will answer their initial question. As mentioned previously, while gathering information, entrepreneurs may ask other questions and start on new quests. They may discover alternative solutions or new opportunities. For example, Nelia was interested in textile making. Through her research, she found lots of information on this topic, but she also found information on textile dyeing and colouring. Nelia then wondered what plants are used to produce dyes. By doing research on this connection, she saw an opportunity to produce and sell potted plants that each produce a different colour of dye. She thought that she could sell these plants to crafstpeople who dye and weave their own cloth.

Extensions

The initial venture creates more questions. As the business develops, the questions and answers become more specific and focused on particular aspects of the venture. Entrepreneurs acquire new knowledge as they look for ways to solve problems: How do I adapt new equipment? find new markets? develop new products? Nelia, for example, needs a tray that can hold the plants for shipping and also display them in the customer's home. This problem is specific to the new venture. Research should be aimed at finding a practical solution. Once Nelia solves the problem, the new tray design becomes part of the venture.

E-ACTIVITY

The Web has changed and opened up the world of education. For example, it is now possible to earn an MBA by taking courses offered on the Internet. Visit www.business. nelson.com and follow the links to learn more about these programs.

MANAGEMENT SKILLS

In Chapter 7, you learned that the role of management in business is to achieve the goals of an organization by directing the allocation and use of the organization's human, financial, and material resources. Management performs five major functions for any business: planning, organizing, directing, controlling, and staffing.

The definition of management can be rephrased for entrepreneurs in this way: Entrepreneurs achieve their individual goals by applying their management skills to their personal, financial, and material resources. For entrepreneurs, management skills still involve planning, organizing, directing, controlling, and staffing.

Planning

As you will learn in Chapter 17, entrepreneurs do a great deal of planning. They develop financial, production, and marketing plans. Ultimately, they incorporate all these individual plans into an overall business plan. Entrepreneurs must be careful, however, to avoid overplanning. If they focus on every tiny detail, they may panic and give up.

Organizing

The main thing entrepreneurs need to organize is their time. Detailed schedules, "to do" lists, reminder files, and personal planners help

This entrepreneur relies on his day planner to make sure that he accomplishes everything that he needs to do during the day.

entrepreneurs keep appointments and remember all the things that need to get done such as meeting with suppliers, purchasing or repairing equipment, and interviewing potential staff. Organizing the venture is very important. Entrepreneurs need to develop job descriptions and know who is responsible for each job. Communication must be organized as well, so that each person involved in the venture knows its structure and the lines of communication.

Directing

Directing isn't simply telling people what to do. Good entrepreneurs learn to empower their staff, which means giving their employees the feeling that their work and contribution to the business are important. This task is most often accomplished by sharing the goals of the company with the employees and illustrating how their particular job fits into the overall picture. An entrepreneur who takes this approach can encourage more initiative and self-direction in his or her staff. In other words, a good boss doesn't really "boss." Instead, he or she shares the operation of the business with the people who make it work.

Would you hire a friend to work in your business? Why or why not? What are some possible advantages and disadvantages of working with friends?

Controlling

Because entrepreneurs have limited resources, they need budgets to help them control expenses, inventory, and other material resources. An accurate bookkeeping and accounting system helps an owner keep control of the finances. In fact, the inability to control spending is the primary cause of most venture failures. An entrepreneur should have accounting knowledge and skills or hire someone who does.

Staffing

Many entrepreneurs work on their own, sometimes out of home offices. As ventures grow, however, entrepreneurs need to hire staff—especially those people who have skills that they lack. Friends often ask for jobs for themselves or family members once they learn an entrepreneur has opened a business. Entrepreneurs need to be careful about hiring friends. It takes a great deal of skill to manage *any* employee, let alone friends or family.

RELATIONSHIP SKILLS

When starting and running a venture, an entrepreneur establishes many different relationships. The relationship skills that entrepreneurs need vary, depending on the kind of association the entrepreneur has with each person. Each business contact can be categorized as a staff, supplier, or customer relationship.

Staff Relationships

To maintain good relationships with their staff, entrepreneurs need the ability to motivate. Employees must feel that they are being treated fairly; they need to feel that they are being rewarded for their efforts and that their needs are being met. Each employee is unique and has different needs and different ideas about fair and equal treatment. And, as you read in Chapter 7, each employee is motivated by different rewards—money, job satisfaction, self-worth, profit sharing, holidays, employee-of-the-month awards, and so on.

Motivation skills rely on matching rewards to an employee's needs and personality. Entrepreneurs should try to get to know and empathize with their employees. **Empathy** is the ability to understand what other people think and feel. It can help entrepreneurs realize what motivates each employee to work hard and stay with their business. For example, Tawanda is single and lives alone. She likes the social aspect of her work because it allows her to meet people and develop relationships. Staff parties, casual Fridays, and organized staff events such as bowling and movie nights are all reasons why Tawanda likes coming to work. Matthew, on the other hand, is married with a young son. He likes time with his family. Friday afternoons off and additional holidays are two rewards that would motivate Matthew to make an extra effort. He would also jump at the chance to work from home more often.

Supplier Relationships

Communication is the most important relationship skill required to deal with suppliers. Regardless of who your suppliers are—the government, service providers, merchandise suppliers, or material and equipment sellers—they are all sources of information about new products, processes, and materials. They also want feedback from you if there are problems so that they can improve their service.

Paying bills when they're due is one way to maintain good relationships with suppliers. If cash flow makes prompt payment seem temporarily impossible, send a partial payment with an explanation and a request for an extension. Be sure to state the length of the extension (30 days is common) and to pay the balance before the time is up. If the problem is more serious and requires some financial restructuring, inform your suppliers and ask how you can work together to solve the problem. It's important to remember that suppliers want your business to succeed. If it doesn't, they may never receive payment. They also lose the distribution channel or source of income your business provides. Most suppliers are willing to help out their customers to some extent, as long as they feel that honest communication is taking place.

Customer Relationships

The first question an entrepreneur should ask every morning is, "How will I make my customers feel good today?"

Entrepreneurs are motivated to be independent, but they do have a boss: the customer. An entrepreneur should be able to make each customer feel important. This skill sets the standard for every member of the organization. If an entrepreneur maintains positive customer relationships, the "customer is boss" attitude is adopted by the entire staff. The restaurant owner who greets customers at the door and visits each table personally not only makes the customers feel special, but also sets an example that motivates staff to make service even better. The software manufacturer who requires employees to visit customers to see how the product is actually being used shows both staff and customers how important customers are. The first question an entrepreneur should ask every morning is, "How will I make my customers feel good today?"

INFORMATION	CONNECTION	EXTENSION
1. a) What three main skills do entrepreneurs need?	**b)** Ask two or three entrepreneurs what they consider to be the three most important skills for an entrepreneur. Make a list of all the skills they mention.	**c)** In your opinion, what is the most important skill an entrepreneur can develop? Give reasons for your choice.
2. a) List and briefly describe eight sources of information for entrepreneurs.	**b)** Think of a topic that sparks your curiosity. Ask yourself a question about that topic. Then, gather information to answer your question. Let your research lead you to raise other questions and conduct still more research. Record your experiences and discoveries in a journal.	**c)** Imagine that you are opening a sporting goods store. Working in small groups, use three of the information sources listed in this section to conduct research about the sporting goods business. As a group, prepare a report that analyzes the merits of each information source for this topic. Present your findings to the other groups.
3. a) What three business relationships are important to entrepreneurs?	**b)** Choose a local business. Find out what different suppliers the business has.	**c)** Interview three entrepreneurs. What policies do they have to ensure that "the customer is boss"?

Entrepreneurial Activities

It is the entrepreneurial spirit that drives small-business development. Entrepreneurs who take risks and work hard to start businesses and make a profit are directly responsible for Canada's economic prosperity. Entrepreneurs, however, are not always driven only by profit for themselves. Many use their skills and characteristics to fundraise; contribute to their local, provincial, national, and global communities through not-for-profit ventures; and organize school events where any gain realized goes to the charity, community group, or school. Enterprising people, too, engage in entrepreneurial activities as they organize events or take part in ventures that will benefit their community, workplace, or school.

FUNDRAISING

Entrepreneurs are needed to organize and run successful fundraising campaigns such as dances, walkathons, or car washes. **Fundraising** is the collection of money to support an identifiable cause. Most fundraising efforts are voluntary, with the money collected going directly to the chosen charity, research project, local improvement project, or other worthwhile cause. The first task of the fundraiser is to establish credibility and trust; some unethical entrepreneurs use fake fundraising as a way to cheat people out of their money. When organizing and recruiting, fundraisers must make every effort to avoid any possibility of dishonesty.

For fundraisers to succeed, they also need a great idea. Here's where entrepreneurial imagination comes into play. The challenge is difficult: How do you get people to donate their money or time to help others? A successful idea benefits both the cause and the donors. The charity receives funds to continue its work. The incentives for the donors can be fun, for example, a dance or a dinner. Prizes, donated by local businesses that receive free publicity for their contributions, are another obvious incentive, as are tax breaks. But perhaps the greatest benefit for a donor is simply the good feeling that comes from helping other people in the community.

Once fundraising entrepreneurs decide on a great idea or theme, they get approval from the community group involved with the cause. Then, they use their organizational skills to create and lead committees. Committees can be broken down into subcommittees that handle decorations, food, advertising and publicity, mailings, phone calls, accounting, and all the other organizational tasks that contribute to an event's success. When the project is over and thank-you cards, notes, flowers, or gifts have been sent to all the people who helped put the event together, most entrepreneurial fundraisers start thinking about the next year's project.

Fundraisers for the United Way, a not-for-profit organization that helps many different community agencies, sell pizza at a subway station to businesspeople and students on their way home.

NOT-FOR-PROFIT VENTURES

Entrepreneurs also start not-for-profit ventures. As you learned in Chapter 1, the major purpose of not-for-profit organizations is some gain other than making a profit. Entrepreneurs may start such ventures to provide for a community's needs. Food banks, homeless outreach programs, suicide prevention hotlines, support for the sick, and care for street youth are some examples of not-for-profit projects. These ventures require all the research, management, and relationship skills that any business requires. Entrepreneurs involved in these ventures also require all the entrepreneurial characteristics—especially persistence.

Loren Freid (left) founded the North York Harvest Food Bank in the 1980s to help feed those in need in Toronto. Here, he and a volunteer sort donations.

ORGANIZING A SCHOOL EVENT

A student who organizes a school event is an enterprising person who likely has many entrepreneurial characteristics and skills. Most school events are organized around a specific cause or theme. For example, high school student Rebekah Warner organized a Walk Against Male Violence for her school after watching a documentary on the Montreal Massacre. During the Montreal Massacre, 14 women at Montreal's Ecole Polytechnique were shot dead by Marc Lépine for being "feminists." After conducting some research, Rebekah decided to set up a committee at her school to organize the walk. She and the committee received permission from the school administration and then from the city. She contacted the police for permits. Committee members called the head of a local women's shelter and the director of the sexual assault crisis centre. They scheduled guest speakers for a school assembly to recruit walkers. Committee members photocopied pledge forms and selected a subcommittee to help distribute the forms. Rebekah arranged for staff supervisors on the walk, and another committee member ensured that buses were available to take students back to school. Rebekah and the committee took care of posters, announcements, refreshments, first aid, and many more details.

Other examples of school events include fashion shows, holiday stage shows, and student health assemblies. Every event needs an enterprising person behind it to make it work and to bring the necessary resources together. Often, student councils organize school events, but even then, they need leaders with entrepreneurial qualities to take responsibility for the event and make it work.

Not all school events have to be large. Many enterprising students in high school start clubs or interest groups. They, too, recruit members, organize meeting dates, and plan agendas and programs. Their commitment to a particular interest—for example, Spanish films or old vinyl records—sparks enthusiasm in others and makes their high school a more interesting place. Because these students contribute to the life of the school, school administrators appreciate and encourage the entrepreneurial spirit in their students.

Are You an Entrepreneur?

Before you start making decisions about your future career and education, it's important to have an idea of the traits that you possess. Many different tests can help you do this. Some of these tests are fun, and may point out characteristics or skills that you had not thought about before. If you possess entrepreneurial traits, do you want to be an entrepreneur? If you're missing some entrepreneurial traits, can you learn them? Do you want to? These are questions that you'll have to answer over the next few years.

E-ACTIVITY

Visit www.business.nelson.com and follow the links to find out whether you have what it takes to be an entrepreneur.

ACTIVITIES FOR ...

INFORMATION	**C**ONNECTION	**E**XTENSION
1. a) What challenges does an entrepreneur involved in a fundraising venture face?	**b)** With a small group, prepare a report on a local fundraiser. Be sure to interview the entrepreneur(s) involved. What problems did he or she encounter? What successes did the entrepreneur achieve? Which skills and characteristics were essential to this venture?	**c)** Describe how you could get involved in a not-for-profit business activity. Be specific.
2. a) What entrepreneurial characteristics and skills does Rebekah Warner have? Give examples to support your answer.	**b)** Describe an event that took place at your school. Who organized it? What entrepreneurial skills were involved? Explain.	**c)** In a group of five or six, brainstorm ways to raise money for a class trip or another school event. Share your ideas with the class. Together, select the best idea and sketch out a plan to organize the event.

Review

Knowledge and Understanding

1. Match each of the following terms to the correct definition:

   empathy
   enterprising
   entrepreneur
   fundraising
   intrapreneurship
   skill
   venture

   a) A person who starts a venture to solve a problem or take advantage of an opportunity.
   b) A business enterprise involving some risk, in expectation of gain.
   c) Having entrepreneurial characteristics essential to the workplace or to other organizations.
   d) The entrepreneurial spirit within a business or an organization.
   e) The ability to translate knowledge into action.
   f) The ability to understand what other people think and feel.
   g) The collection of money to support an identifiable cause.

2. What is the difference between an entrepreneur and an enterprising person?

3. How can a business encourage intrapreneurship?

4. How do the management skills that entrepreneurs need to have differ from those of an employee of a company?

5. Describe how the research process can lead to a plan for a new venture.

Thinking and Inquiry

1. List the names of 10 entrepreneurs mentioned in this chapter, as well as their businesses. For each entrepreneur, list the characteristic that best describes his or her entrepreneurial spirit. Compare your list to that of other students, and discuss any differences.

2. Select one entrepreneurial characteristic or skill. Find an entrepreneur not mentioned in the textbook who possesses this characteristic or skill. Create a profile of the person in which you explain how he or she illustrates the characteristic or skill you selected. Share your profile with a small group. Discuss how entrepreneurial characteristics and skills can be applied to all types of endeavours.

Communication

1. Write a letter to the political party of your choice asking for information on its policies and views about small business. What measures is the party taking, or would it take, if it were in power, to help entrepreneurs?

2. Using video clips, stories, poems, pictures, article titles, and any other methods you wish, create a short presentation that describes one entrepreneurial characteristic in detail. Present your work to the class, with a short explanation of your choice of characteristic.

Application

1. Speak with a local politician or community group to determine what social problem in your community most needs action. In small groups, brainstorm ways that you could help deal with this problem. Choose one or more of the suggestions and develop a plan for implementation. Be detailed and specific about the human and financial rescources that you need. Have the plan checked by your teacher or the community group involved with the issue. If the plan is feasible, carry it out. If it is not feasible, outline the problems and make the necessary changes. If possible, carry out the plan once it has been approved.

2. As a class, develop, plan, and organize an activity for the whole school. To help you decide on the activity, you might have students in your school fill out a questionnaire or you could conduct a survey. Then evaluate the opportunities to decide which venture would be most feasible.

3. With a small group, prepare a list of at least 10 local entrepreneurs. Organize the list by type of entrepreneurial activity. Then, choose one entrepreneur from each type of activity. Each group member role-plays one entrepreneur for your group, describing the goods or services that he or she produces.

REFLECT ON YOUR LEARNING

1. Go back to the list you made for the Before You Begin question on page 359. Add any entrepreneurial characteristics and skills that you learned of in this chapter.

2. Are you an entrepreneur? First, ask yourself how many of the entrepreneurial characteristics and skills you possess. Then, provide an example of when, where, and how you demonstrated each characteristic or skill. Prove to yourself whether or not you have what it takes to be an entrepreneur.

CHAPTER 16

INVENTION AND INNOVATION

STUDENT EXPECTATIONS

After completing this chapter, you will be able to
- describe several inventions that have changed the way we live
- describe a variety of Canadian inventions and innovations
- identify characteristics and skills of some Canadian inventors
- contrast the role of an inventor with the roles of an innovator and an entrepreneur
- explain the importance of invention and innovation in entrepreneurship
- explain how innovation can take place
- demonstrate how innovation has affected certain products over time
- describe how innovation and invention lead to the development and application of new technologies

Michael Duck stands in front of his invention, the SureShot Dispensing System, enjoying a cup of coffee.

HOW TOO MUCH CREAM IN YOUR COFFEE CAN JUMP-START AN INVENTION

When Michael Duck was 16 years old, his parents packed up the family home in New Jersey and said goodbye to the United States. His father also said goodbye to a secure government job because he wanted to start his own business on the east coast of Canada. Michael remembers telling his father the life of an entrepreneur was not for him. Unlike his father, he wanted a nine-to-five job. But Michael was wrong. His first (and only) nine-to-five job was working for Baxter Foods Ltd., a dairy in Dartmouth, Nova Scotia. Michael started as a general helper and worked his way up to plant engineer. Coworkers quickly discovered that he could invent the most useful gadgets. One day, after Michael complained that Tim Hortons had, yet again, put too much cream in his coffee, his boss turned to him and said, "If you don't like it, do something about it."

So he did. Working from his basement, Michael took three months to develop a machine that precisely controls the amount of cream going into a cup of hot java. Unlike the few other machines on the market, this one relies on gravity to control the flow of cream. Inventing the machine, however, was only the first step, says Michael. "I made this machine. [Then] I learned how to sell it after taking night courses in marketing."

A.C. Dispensing Equipment Inc.'s first customer was Tom Cahill, owner of the highest-volume Tim Hortons franchise in Canada, located in Halifax. "I came to him, showed him the product, then showed him how it would save him money," Michael says. After two months, Tom Cahill, who also owned the Pizza Hut franchise in Halifax, was back. He bought another cream dispenser and asked Michael if he could make a portion-control machine that could handle oil.

Indeed he could. That was 1985. Today, A.C. Dispensing, which is based in Lower Sackville, Nova Scotia, has 30 full-time employees. Its products are sold to companies throughout Canada and the U.S., including McDonald's Restaurants and Dunkin' Donuts. "We are well into millions of dollars of sales. We sell thousands of machines a year," says Michael, who is president of the company. His company is also actively involved in research and development. That is where Michael devotes most of his time and energy. He hired his old boss from the dairy to oversee the day-to-day running of A.C. Dispensing.

"My forte is as an entrepreneur. If you love what you're doing, you'll never work a day in your life."

"My forte is as an entrepreneur," Michael says. "If you love what you're doing, you'll never work a day in your life. I had to go back to doing what I do best—designing." It is precisely this love of building a business that recently earned him the title of Atlantic Entrepreneur of the Year. "Michael Duck embodies entrepreneurship," says John Carter, a partner with the Halifax office of Ernst & Young, a national consulting firm.

Since Michael gave up the nine-to-five life, he has learned two valuable lessons. The first: Put your money where your mouth is. "People say they can't get the money to start a business. Most are wasting money. You have to make sacrifices," he says. One of those sacrifices should not be time for yourself and your family. That is rule two: Get a life. "The minute you start a business, half [your time] is gone. As the business grows, it will consume all your personal time, if you let it. Balance is hard to achieve, but it is important to achieve it."

About This Profile

1. What is Michael Duck's invention? How did he come up with the idea?
2. In what way is Michael Duck both an inventor and an entrepreneur?
3. What steps did Michael take to transform his invention into a successful business venture?
4. What businesses, other than those mentioned in the profile, might be interested in Michael's invention? Why?

What Is an Invention?

BEFORE YOU BEGIN

With a partner, identify several inventions that have changed the way people live. What business opportunities developed from each invention?

Paul Nipkow, Philo Farnsworth, Vladimir Zworykin, and John Logie Baird all have something in common. They were all inventors, who experimented independently with ways to transmit pictures and moving images from one place to another. Each one is given credit for discoveries that led to the development of modern television broadcasting.

An **invention** is a product or process that does something that has never been done before. When this product or process fills a market need, it sets the stage for entrepreneurship. Entrepreneurs look for ways to use the invention in a product or service that can be sold to a consumer. Some inventors are also entrepreneurs—they build a business to produce, distribute, and market their invention. Other inventors are not entrepreneurs. They prefer to focus on experimentation and discovery. Sometimes they do not even realize, or care, that their work has commercial potential.

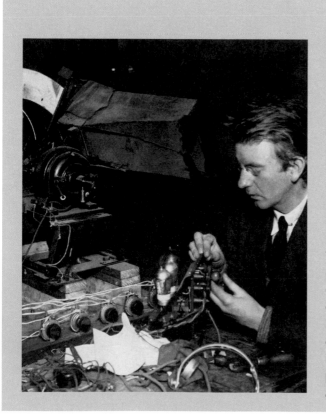

John Logie Baird

John Logie Baird was both an inventor and an entrepreneur. After his initial success with a mechanical television, he marketed his idea to private investors and used their money to start his own company, Baird Television Limited. The company developed two experimental television stations and successfully sent the first transatlantic television transmission in 1928, from London, England to an amateur radio operator in Hartsdale, New York. Next, Baird formed an association with the British Broadcasting Commission (BBC). The BBC gave Baird money to perfect his television design, called the Televisor. The BBC believed that a simple, inexpensive television would have a wide appeal to customers. However, Baird was more interested in concepts like big-screen televisions and open-air broadcasts. Gaumont British, a company that owned a chain of movie theatres, shared these interests, and provided financing for Baird to mass-produce the Televisor. Customers eventually bought about 20 000 Baird Televisors.

INVENTIONS THAT CHANGED OUR LIVES

Like the television, many inventions that have changed our lives have involved two factors—distance and communication. Devices that allow us to transport people and goods more quickly or to communicate with people over a long distance have had a tremendous impact on the way we live and on how our civilization has developed.

Each time an important invention emerges, entrepreneurs look for opportunities to market, adapt, and improve it. For example, the invention of television led to an explosion of related businesses. Companies have made money selling parts and accessories, broadcasting by cable and satellite, developing programming, and creating advertisements. Manufacturers produce colour and big-screen televisions, televisions that work in your car, and even tiny televisions that you can wear on your wrist. Related inventions, such as video games, DVD players, and Internet access over television cables, all provide opportunities for companies to serve customers and make money. Other inventions that have had a strong impact on how people live include the wheel, paper, the airplane, the automobile, the telephone, refrigeration, plastic, and computers and the Internet.

The Wheel

Most historians think that the wheel was invented about 5000 years ago. The oldest known wheel was discovered near the Persian Gulf, in an area that was once called Mesopotamia. It dates from around 3500 B.C. Over time, enterprising people have added spokes for extra strength, iron hubs that turned on greased axles, iron rims, and, most recently, rubber tires.

Early entrepreneurs recognized that wheels made it easier to move people and products from one place to another. They built and sold chariots for war, and carts to carry heavy loads. They started coach services to help people travel from one city to another. Over time, wheels led to other inventions such as gears, rollers, flywheels, and pulleys. The potential for entrepreneurship increased tremendously.

Paper

The basic process that we use for making paper was invented in China around 105 A.D., when people began using fibres from rags to make paper. The invention of the printing press in 1450 increased the need for paper, and a shortage of rags eventually developed. In 1838, a Canadian inventor named Charles Fenerty discovered a way to make paper by grinding wood fibres into a pulp. The modern pulp and paper industry was born.

Together with the printing press, paper helped spread knowledge and made it possible for more and more people to learn to read. Today, paper is big business. We print newspapers on paper, write letters on paper, and wrap presents in paper. We buy paper towels, paper napkins, and paper tissues. In fact, without the paper industry, you wouldn't be reading this book.

The Airplane

When Orville and Wilbur Wright achieved powered flight for 57 seconds over a field near Kitty Hawk, North Carolina, on December 17, 1903, no one knew that their invention would soon make it possible for people to travel great distances at incredible speeds. The development of the jet engine and of lighter metals, such as aluminum, have permitted modern planes to travel in a way that would have left the Wright brothers gasping in amazement.

Orville Wright sits at the controls while Wilbur Wright is on the ground preparing for the first heavier-than-air flight at Kitty Hawk on December 17, 1903.

Powered flight has made the world seem smaller by allowing people and products to travel across oceans in hours, rather than weeks or months. It has led to many different businesses, including travel agencies, hotels, and ground transportation services such as taxis and limousines. Whenever you buy a product that has been shipped to Canada by air, you are providing revenue not only for the manufacturer and the seller, but also for the companies that ship, package, and advertise the product.

The Automobile

You might not think that a steam-powered tricycle is an efficient means of transportation, but that's where the modern automobile got its start. The tricycle, built by Nicolas-Joseph Cugnot of France, was the first self-propelled vehicle. After the gas engine was invented in 1866, Gottfried Daimler tried installing one on a bike in 1885, and on a truck in 1896. Entrepreneurs soon realized that gas-powered vehicles could travel farther and faster than their steam- and electricity-powered predecessors.

In 1908, Henry Ford introduced the Model T, a car that was relatively inexpensive, versatile, and easy to maintain. In fact, Ford's assembly-line style of production is credited with making cars accessible to the average person. The invention of the automobile led to the development of the petroleum and trucking industries, road and highway construction companies, repair and service businesses, drive-through restaurants, and thousands of other businesses.

The Telephone

When Scottish-born Alexander Graham Bell invented the telephone in Brantford, Ontario, he made it possible for people to talk with one

another over long distances for the first time. This effectively ended the dominance of the telegraph industry. Fortunately, Bell realized the importance of obtaining legal protection for his invention: He applied for a patent for his idea in February of 1874. A **patent** entitles an inventor to legally own his or her invention and prevents others from using the invention without the inventor's permission. Only hours after Bell applied for his patent, another inventor named Elisha Gray attempted to file a patent for a similar invention. But because Bell filed first, his application was accepted. Bell's patent, issued on March 7, 1876, is one of the most valuable ever issued by the U.S. Patent Office. Bell was wise enough to apply for a patent not only for the telephone instruments, but also for his concept of a telephone system. This inclusion proved very valuable. (See pages 400–401 for more information on patents.)

Spectators look on as Alexander Graham Bell makes his first long-distance call, from New York to Chicago, in 1893.

Refrigeration

In the 18th century, scientist Michael Faraday discovered that liquefied ammonia had a cooling effect. Carl Ritter von Linde adapted Faraday's discovery, and developed the first ammonia compression refrigerator in 1873. Entrepreneurs were not far behind. In 1911, General Electric marketed the first home refrigerator.

Before the invention of the refrigerator, people used ice to keep their food cold. Food spoiled quickly, so most consumers shopped daily for products like meat and milk. Refrigeration led to the development of the supermarket—and to greater convenience for consumers. Supermarkets could stock more items because they wouldn't spoil as quickly, and consumers didn't have to shop as often. Refrigerated vehicles made it possible to transport food over long distances. Today, Canadians can buy oranges from Morocco, lamb from New Zealand, and shrimp from Thailand. The invention of the refrigerator has had a huge impact on many types of businesses, including food production and processing companies, restaurants, and shipping businesses.

Plastic

Plastic is the name given to a wide range of synthetic polymers, long molecular chains that are not found in nature but are developed from combinations of materials. Alexander Parkes invented the first plastic in 1869 in Great Britain. He sold his patent rights to John Hyatt in the

United States, who named the new product "celluloid." The discovery of polymerization led to other discoveries, including Leo Baekeland's 1907 discovery of Bakelite, a thermoset plastic. Thermoset plastics are synthetic materials that can be shaped by heat and pressure into hard, unbreakable objects that are resistant to heat, acids, and electrical currents. Other plastics quickly followed, including cellophane in 1912, vinyl in 1928, acrylic in 1936, and polyester and nylon in 1940.

Plastic is used almost everywhere. In fact, you can find it in most of the other inventions mentioned so far—in telephones, in polyester-belted tires, in refrigerator shelves and drawers, in automobile body parts, and in the interiors of airplanes. It's lightweight, so it's cheap to transport. It's resistant to breakage, so it's safer than glass. Electricians use plastic-coated wire because plastic does not conduct electricity. Plumbers use plastic pipes because they are durable and easy to work with. In one way or another, plastic has made a contribution to virtually every major industry.

Computers and the Internet

The roots of the computer date back thousands of years to the Chinese abacus, a device that allows users to make computations by sliding beads arranged on a rack. However, it wasn't until 1839 that Charles Babbage and Ada Lovelace created the first true mechanical-digital computer. Their invention set the stage for further developments. In 1945, ENIAC (the Electronic Numerical Integrator and Calculator) was born, based on ideas developed by John Mauchly and J. Presper Eckert at the University of Pennsylvania. ENIAC took up a very large room and required its own air conditioner. Later inventions, including solid-state electronics, transistors, and integrated circuits, rapidly increased computing power and reduced the size and cost of computer components. Computers became far more useful and accessible.

The Internet was originally set up in 1973 by the U.S. Department of Defense as a way to link computers in different locations. University researchers began to connect with this network and the Internet grew. Over time, home computers became more and more common, and businesses recognized that the Internet gave them a way to reach customers all around the world.

CANADIAN INVENTORS AND INVENTIONS

Many Canadians and people with Canadian connections, including Charles Fenerty and Alexander Graham Bell, have created inventions that have changed people's lives. Hundreds of Canadians have invented products that are in common use today. Examples are the

STRETCH YOUR THINKING

What new computer technologies have been invented since the Internet was introduced?

E-ACTIVITY

Visit
www.business.
nelson.com
and follow the links
to find out about
more Canadian
inventors and
Inventions.

snowmobile (invented by Armand Bombardier in 1922), the cardiac pacemaker (invented by Dr. John A. Hopps in 1950), the Jolly Jumper (invented by Olivia Poole in 1959), the goalie mask (invented by Jacques Plante in 1960), and IMAX technology (invented by Grahame Ferguson, Roman Kroiter, and Robert Kerr in 1968). Other Canadian achievements include the following:

- In 1872, Elijah McCoy received his first patent for a lubricator that allowed steam engines to be oiled while they were still in motion. His invention worked so well that people began to ask for "the real McCoy," an expression that people still use to mean "the real thing."
- In 1878, Canadian engineer Sandford Fleming developed Universal Standard Time, a system that divides the world into 24 time zones.
- In the early 1900s, Maude Abbott developed a classification system for congenital heart diseases that made it easier to diagnose and treat these diseases.
- Reginald Fessenden's pioneering work with radio broadcasting in the early 1900s paved the way for television broadcasting. During the 1920s, Fessenden worked on his own system for transmitting pictures and sounds.
- Dr. Frederick Banting and his assistant, Charles Best, discovered insulin in 1921.
- Dr. Norman Bethune devised the mobile blood-transfusion service (in Spain in 1936) and the first mobile medical unit (in China in 1938).
- In the late 1930s, University of Toronto physics professor Eli Franklin Burton and his students Cecil Hall, James Hillier, and Albert Prebus created the first practical electron microscope in North America.
- Dr. Wilbur Franks invented the antigravity suit at the University of Toronto in 1941. This pressurized flying suit made it possible for pilots to carry out high-speed manoeuvres without losing consciousness. It also led to the development of the modern space suit.
    - The cobalt "bomb" (radiotherapy) for cancer treatment was developed in 1951 by two teams of scientists working together. One team was comprised of engineers from the Eldorado Mining and Refining Company and doctors from Victoria General Hospital in London, Ontario. The other was a team of scientists from the University of Saskatchewan, led by Dr. Harold E. Johns.
    - In 1981, Spar Aerospace and the National Research Council of Canada put the Canadarm into operation. This invention has been critical to the success of more than 50 space shuttle missions and to the construction of the first international space station.

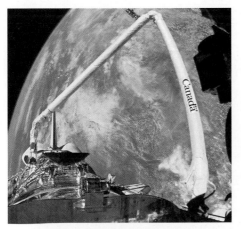

The Canadarm holds onto the Hubble Space Telescope before the telescope is sent on a 15-year mission into space.

Contemporary Issues in Canadian Business

THE ISSUE: ARE DOT.COM BUSINESSES HERE TO STAY?

The dot.com Story

In the world of business, dot.com companies seem to be on a roller coaster ride—and the ride isn't always fun. Dot.com businesses sell goods and services over the Internet rather than from traditional "bricks and mortar" locations. They are often "order-takers," acting as intermediaries between customers and the companies that actually manufacture the goods or provide the services.

In the past, businesses typically started small and grew slowly. Once established, some businesses opted to "go public" by selling shares in the ownership of the business on a stock exchange. Many dot.com companies, on the other hand, went public soon after they were formed in order to obtain capital for their online operations. Instead of buying a share of the company's assets, investors bought a share of its anticipated growth.

Why did dot.com companies take this approach? Because they had no assets, it would have been difficult for many to obtain their capital from a bank or other financial institution. Going public gave them the money they needed to set up a Web site, acquire inventory, and promote their goods and services. It also provided them with a cash flow.

The dot.com companies that moved quickly into the marketplace experienced huge initial success. However, over time, online retailing turned out to be just as difficult as traditional retailing. To increase customer loyalty, many companies made a strategic decision to sell their products at very low prices. Unfortunately, this was an expensive choice, and many businesses simply ran out of cash. Other businesses collapsed because they couldn't attract enough customers to their Web sites.

Some people argue that dot.com businesses are just a fad, while others assert that these businesses are here to stay. Who's right?

Point

Dot.com businesses, the retailing experiment of the late 1990s, have not been a complete success, but they are here to stay. Many industry experts believe that we are just reaching the end of the first wave of electronic commerce, and that online businesses will continue to grow. After all, in North America alone, e-commerce revenue is projected to reach $5.5 trillion by 2004.

Although most goods initially offered for sale by dot.com businesses were generic products, analysts say that the next stage of e-commerce will be dominated by more familiar brand names that consumers have purchased offline. Many dot.com businesses are also adding services that will help them compete more effectively with offline businesses. For example, a dot.com business may purchase a lawn mower for a customer, hire someone to tune it and sharpen the blades once a year, and even arrange for someone to cut the customer's lawn. In this way, the dot.com business hopes to attract consumers by adding value to the transaction.

With 24-hour service that can be accessed from anywhere in the world, dot.com companies have a concept that will be hard for offline retailers to beat.

Counterpoint

Would you have invested in Go.com, a Web site backed by the Walt Disney Company? If so, you would have backed a loser in the world of e-commerce. Go.com is a Web portal—an Internet "mall" where search engines help customers find what they're looking for. A competitor, Yahoo.com, outdistanced Go.com by offering a broader range of content, a friendlier style, and more incentives to customers.

Another dot.com failure was eToys. The online toy retailer experienced some initial success, but then went into a tailspin. It filed for bankruptcy in March 2001 and closed its Web site. Companies with problems like those experienced by eToys have been far from rare. In fact, in 2000 alone, over 130 dot.com companies closed down, resulting in employee layoffs and millions of dollars in losses to investors.

Even though dot.com businesses may never entirely disappear from the retailing scene, they are extremely risky investments. According to industry experts, "e-tailing" is a game of survival. The businesses that succeed are the ones that can generate a steady cash flow.

For this reason, the future of e-tailing may lie in partnerships with offline retailers. For example, Amazon.com forged a deal with Toys "R" Us to sell toys at a joint Web site. Relationships between dot.com companies and "bricks and mortar" ventures may enable some companies to survive, but e-commerce is unlikely to overtake traditional retailing as the main way in which goods are bought and sold.

A Real Life Example

Where can a Canadian entrepreneur get online help with a new business venture? Try Onvia.com—one of Canada's dot.com success stories. Onvia has established alliances with companies such as AOL Canada, Southam News Media, The Globe and Mail, and Global Television. With its Canadian head office in Vancouver, British Columbia, Onvia's electronic marketplace is designed to assist small businesses in buying products and services, finding new customers, and locating information. If a business needs help with acquiring quotations, hiring staff, financing operations, training employees, or marketing goods and services, Onvia will provide the support. Onvia has also established supplier relationships with 700 product manufacturers, making over 25 000 products readily available to small business owners.

Gary Meehan, president of Onvia in Canada, feels that one of the competitive challenges in dealing with e-commerce business is to help customers feel more comfortable with the Internet and the idea of shopping online. This effort is becoming more and more important because, according to a survey done by Dun & Bradstreet, a company that provides business information, 70% of small businesses now have access to the Internet.

Onvia was perhaps the first dot.com company to really zero in on the needs and wants of small businesses in Canada. When all is said and done, the company evaluates its own success based on the success of its customers. In fact, Onvia's Web site says, "Looking for new ways to succeed in business? Onvia is the way." Judging by customer response, Onvia has made a great start on the road to success.

Gary Meehan is energized by the challenge of the job, the constant learning, and the excitement of the dot.com industry.

Questions and Activities About This Issue

1. Paul Deninger, the chief executive officer of Broadview, a high-tech investment bank, has said, "It is true that the Internet will change everything. It is not true that everything will change." What do you think he meant?

2. If you were starting a small business, what services would you be interested in acquiring through Onvia.com?

ACTIVITIES FOR ...

INFORMATION	**C**ONNECTION	**E**XTENSION
1. a) Name three inventions that changed the world. Write briefly about changes that resulted from each one.	**b)** Choose an invention that you listed in Question 1a. Explain the impact that this invention has had on your life.	**c)** Have any inventions that changed the world contributed to our lives in a negative way? Discuss with a partner.
2. a) List five businesses that resulted from the invention of the airplane.	**b)** Choose three inventions mentioned in this section (other than the airplane). Brainstorm as many different types of businesses as you can think of that resulted from each invention.	**c)** Identify one brand name product that owes its existence to each invention you chose in Question 2b. Choose one of these products to research in more detail. Identify the company that makes the product, and prepare a one-page report on the company's history, including the name of the founder.
3. a) Name five Canadian inventors and their inventions.	**b)** What characteristics and skills do you think the inventors you listed in Question 3a had? Do some research about these inventors to find out.	**c)** Alexander Graham Bell once said, "Great discoveries and improvements invariably involve the cooperation of many minds." Select one Canadian invention. Explain what other inventions had to come first in order to make this invention possible. Find out about the earlier inventions you named. Present your findings in a labelled timeline.

What Is an Innovation?

Would Thomas Edison, who invented the phonograph in 1878, recognize the CD player as his invention? Would Alexander Graham Bell recognize the cell phone? Would Philo Farnsworth recognize today's wide-screen colour television, with digital sound and on-screen menus? No one really *invented* colour television—newer technology was simply used to improve an existing product. The colour television was an innovation. **Innovation** means using new technology, materials, or processes to improve on existing products, or on how they are produced and distributed.

Did You Know?

In the second century, Galen, a Greek doctor whose theories formed the basis of European medicine until the Renaissance, first recommended bathing with soap as a remedy for skin problems.

To see how invention and innovation work together, let's look at the history of soap. No one knows who first invented soap. Perhaps prehistoric people found foam around the ashes of their fires after a rainfall and discovered that this foam was useful for cleaning their tools. We do know that by 2800 B.C.E., the Babylonians were using soap to clean fibres that they made into cloth. The soap-making process didn't change much over the next 1500 years. By the late 17th century, early North American settlers were still making soap by creating a solution from wood ashes and then boiling this solution with animal fat. In the early 19th century, sodium hydroxide became widely available. Manufacturers began to use this compound to make firmer soaps with far less effort, changing the production process.

Over the years, people have experimented with making soap in slightly different ways, adding an endless variety of colours and scents. Soap manufacturers today create their own innovations by combining other products, such as skin lotion or lemon scent, to improve their product. Soap manufacturers have also made innovations to their distribution processes. Today, consumers can buy soap at the supermarket, at the drug store, from a catalogue, over the Internet, and even from vending machines! The person who created the soap-manufacturing process was an inventor. The people who improved the production process, as well as those who made different types of soap and first sold soap on the Internet, were innovators.

Rachel Zimmerman

In 1985, 12-year-old Rachel Zimmerman created an innovation based on Blissymbolics. Blissymbolics is a system of symbols that non-speaking people use to communicate. It was invented by Austrian engineer, Charles Bliss, in 1942. With Charles Bliss's invention, people pointed to symbols on a board or page to communicate with someone in a room. With Rachel Zimmerman's innovation, the "speaker" touches the symbols on a touch-sensitive board, then the symbols and corresponding words appear on a computer screen. The message can then be read on the screen, sent by e-mail, or printed out. Rachel's innovation allows for faster communication, and lets non-speaking people communicate with others who are not in the same room.

INNOVATORS AS ENTREPRENEURS

It is usually easier for innovators to be entrepreneurs than for inventors to be entrepreneurs. Inventors need to start from scratch as they plan ways to manufacture, distribute, and market their inventions. Innovators can build on what inventors have done.

Most innovations are spurred by a business looking for ways to gain a competitive advantage over another business. There are many ways for entrepreneurs to use innovation to gain a business advantage. For example, they can change the way a product is used, packaged, marketed, distributed, designed, or manufactured.

Changing How a Product Is Used

When was the last time you used Scotch tape? What did you use it for? When 3M introduced Scotch tape in 1948, an advertisement suggested that the tape could be used to
• cover clothespins to prevent clothing snags
• prevent plaster cracks when hanging pictures
• cover bandages
• attach coins to cards sent in the mail
• attach new window shades to old rollers
• smooth the ends of curtain rods
• fix tears in plastic aprons
• repair frayed shoelace ends
• wrap household garbage

If 3M had depended on the clothespin market for Scotch tape sales, the company would be in financial difficulty today—most people don't use clothespins any more, and the clothespins we do use don't snag clothes. Fortunately for 3M, someone decided to promote Scotch tape for other purposes, such as wrapping gifts. The company developed a whole new market by finding an innovative use for a familiar product.

Changing the Package

Changing the way a product is packaged can create a whole new industry. In 1944, two Swedish inventors, Ruben Rausing and Erik Wallenberg, created a milk package that provided maximum protection for milk using a minimum of material. Their invention was a tetrahedron-shaped paper package with a waterproof coating. Together, Rausing and Wallenberg founded a company, AB Tetra Pak, in Lund, Sweden. Since then, the company has continued to create innovations in the packaging industry, adding new package sizes and shapes, including the familiar brick-shaped drinking boxes that many people put in their lunches every day.

Package innovations occur for a variety of reasons. For example, many packages, including drink containers, are now reusable or recyclable. This kind of environmentally friendly innovation can help a product's reputation and its sales. Other packaging innovations help a

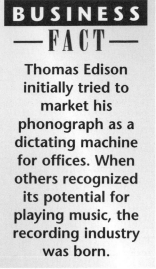

BUSINESS —FACT—

Thomas Edison initially tried to market his phonograph as a dictating machine for offices. When others recognized its potential for playing music, the recording industry was born.

company market a product to a new audience. For example, one company sells yogurt in squeeze tubes, which have become very popular among children. These squeeze tubes contain a product that is itself an innovation—yogurt that doesn't have to be refrigerated.

Changing the Marketing Strategy

As you read in Chapters 6 and 9, marketing strategies determine the target market for a product and give companies direction on how they can use advertising and promotion to encourage people in this target market to buy. For example, many breakfast cereals appeal mainly to children. Marketers try to enhance this appeal with promotions, such as contests or mascots, and with advertisements that are shown during children's television programs. In the late 1990s, Kellogg designed a series of innovative Corn Pops commercials aimed at teens as well as children. With these commercials, the company hoped to expand the market for Corn Pops and, as a result, increase the product's sales.

Advertising is certainly not limited to broadcast media. For example, Montreal's Zoom Media rents washroom wall space from universities and other places where 18- to 34-year-olds will see its ads. Companies who want to target this demographic group pay Zoom to display the ads. Over the past decade, this innovative approach has helped Zoom expand internationally.

Pepper the Clown

Companies are always looking for new ways to promote their businesses, and many innovative entrepreneurs have developed promotional ideas into personal ventures. Diane Pepper, also known as Pepper the Clown, makes kids *and* adults laugh at promotional events, such as store openings, in Toronto. She attracts large crowds of parents and children to malls and retail stores, and has lots of fun in the process.

STRETCH YOUR THINKING

Think of a local business that has changed its distribution process. Find out what impact this change has had on the business.

Changing the Distribution Process

The target market for a product is closely linked to the way the product is distributed. If the distribution process changes, then more customers, or different kinds of customers, will be able to buy the product. Suppose an entrepreneur opens an art supply store. To reach more customers, this entrepreneur might decide to start a Web site or publish a catalogue. Once the store becomes successful, the entrepreneur may decide to open a second store in another location.

Berry and Peterson, a small bookstore in Kingston, Ontario, specializes in used books. For years, the store's market was primarily local, with knowledgeable book collectors occasionally requesting certain titles by mail. A few years ago, Berry and Peterson decided to buy space on the Advanced Book Exchange Web site to display its book titles and offer them for sale. This innovative move resulted in a substantial increase in sales.

Another way for a business to reach more customers is to display products at a trade show. A **trade show** is an exhibition where a large number of manufacturers and distributors of a particular product show their goods. Some trade shows are open only to people involved in the particular industry, while others invite the general public to attend. Trade shows not only allow entrepreneurs to reach potential customers, they also help entrepreneurs make contact with retailers or distributors who may want to carry their products.

Sometimes, a business decides to expand its market by distributing its products internationally. Until the mid-1980s, most Canadians had never heard of the kiwi fruit. The popularity of this fruit in other countries encouraged overseas producers to try marketing their product in Canada. Canadians loved the taste. By the early 1990s, the taste of kiwi fruit was in products as diverse as salads, drinks, and ice cream.

Rows and rows of booths crowd a convention centre, where a trade show is taking place.

Changing the Design

There are many reasons for changing the design of a product, including improving its function and appealing to a new market segment. For example, an innovator named Alexandra Finley created The Green Box, based on the traditional composter. This air-tight plastic container was designed to make composting kitchen scraps easy—especially for apartment dwellers who have nowhere to compost. The Green Box is small enough to fit under a kitchen sink, is odour-free, and has compartments that separate solid and liquid waste.

Sometimes, simply revising the size, colour, or shape of a product can help spark or sustain customer interest. For example, some companies that sell canned pasta have changed the shapes of their pasta to look like alphabet letters, zoo animals, and cartoon characters. This innovation has increased the product's appeal to children, and has resulted in improved sales.

OXO Good Grips

OXO Good Grips swivel peeler.

The line of OXO Good Grips products was born while Sam Farber, a retired housewares executive, and his architect wife, Betsey, were on vacation, enjoying two of their favourite hobbies: cooking and entertaining. As they spent more time in the kitchen, they noticed it was difficult to find kitchen tools that felt good in their hands. Betsey's mild arthritis made it even more difficult for her to hold kitchen tools.

They reasoned that there were many other people who would appreciate kitchen tools that were comfortable to hold. Sam got in touch with Davin Stowell, founder of the industrial design firm Smart Design, and together they set out to create a line of kitchen tools that met all users' needs. The result was OXO Good Grips, a line of tools with large, soft, non-slip handles that were comfortable to hold. One feature that distinguished OXO products from earlier kitchen tools were their flexible "fins," which were added on the sides of the handles. The fins absorbed pressure when gripped, giving users more control and comfort.

Changing the Manufacturing Process

You've already learned that when sodium hydroxide became more widely available, soap manufacturers changed the process they used to make soap. As technology changes and new materials become available, manufacturers constantly review their production processes to look for innovations that make their products better or less expensive to produce.

New processes and new machinery improve efficiency and lower production costs; faster machinery makes more products in the same amount of time; and quality-control processes ensure more reliable products. A Swiss machine that processed metal to one-thousandth of a millimetre allowed Marcel Bich to make innovations to ballpoint pens. These innovations led to the development of the BIC pen.

Sometimes, a slight change to the manufacturing process can result in a wider range of products. For example, a company that makes regular potato chips can add equipment to its production facility that allows it to make chips with other flavours, such as ketchup or dill pickle. These flavours may encourage people who do not like regular potato chips to try the new products. Sales for the company could increase, resulting in increased profits.

New raw materials also have an impact on the production process. Like many other companies, Columbia Sportswear relies on the latest technology to stay in business. This company has developed and trademarked a number of fabrics, such as Omni-Tech, that make its outdoor clothing waterproof, windproof, and breathable. Columbia's innovative approach increases sales for the company, but it provides other benefits as well. By raising the standard for quality, Columbia encourages its competitors to develop better products and improve service to their customers.

ACTIVITIES FOR ...

INFORMATION	**C**ONNECTION	**E**XTENSION
1. a) What is the difference between an invention and an innovation?	**b)** Give an example of an invention. Give an example of a related innovation.	**c)** Select a retail store in your area that is privately owned. Interview the owner to discover what innovations he or she has brought to the business to make it successful.
2. a) List six ways that entrepreneurs can use innovation to gain a business advantage. Give an example of each method.	**b)** Research the history of a common household product. Prepare a list of innovations that have directly affected this product during its life cycle.	**c)** Choose a common household product. In a small group, develop a list of innovations that you think would improve this product or increase its sales.

Taking the Next Step

Inventions usually get their start when somebody asks "What if?" Once the invention is finished, it's time to ask "What now?" Inventing something new is not enough to make someone an entrepreneur. Even creating an innovation is not necessarily an entrepreneurial activity. Entrepreneurship begins when the new invention or innovation becomes the inspiration for a venture.

There are different ways for aspiring entrepreneurs to answer the question "What now?" The first step is usually to protect the invention or innovation by obtaining a patent or copyright. Then, the creator may decide to license the idea, franchise it, produce it, or sell the production rights to someone else.

PATENTS AND COPYRIGHTS

As you learned earlier in this chapter, a patent gives the holder the sole right to make, use, or sell an invention for a set period of time, preventing others from using it without permission. A **copyright** gives someone the exclusive right to publish, produce, sell, or distribute works of literature, music, art, and software.

An inventor asks his lawyer for advice about obtaining a patent.

The process of obtaining a patent is complicated and expensive. The inventor may need a lawyer's help to fill out the application form (technical drawings with exact specifications) and to perform a patent search. This search uncovers any previous patents for a similar invention that may already have been filed. If one person's invention or creative work is too similar to someone else's, the patent or copyright will not be granted. During the patenting process, the invention is considered to be legally protected as long as products are marked "patent pending" to show that an application for the patent has been filed.

Many patent services are available to new entrepreneurs. Most are reputable, but a thorough check on the company should be undertaken before any inventions or ideas are shared.

LICENSING AGREEMENTS

One of the easiest ways for an inventor to capitalize on his or her invention or innovation is to license it. As you read in Chapter 7, **licensing** an invention means that the inventor allows another business to use his or her invention for a fee. The fee, or **royalty**, can either be a fixed amount or it can be a percentage of the total sales revenue that the user pays the patent or copyright owner. The inventor is not responsible for manufacturing or distributing the product; he or she simply sells these rights to someone else.

Many computer software programs are licensed to computer manufacturers and software developers. When Sun Microsystems created JavaScript, it sought out computer companies that would benefit from its invention, such as Microsoft and IBM, and arranged licensing agreements with them.

Licensing agreements don't necessarily involve a specific invention. An entrepreneur might start a new venture by licensing an idea, an image, or a name from the owner and then use it to create an innovative product. For example, various companies hold licensing rights to Franklin, a turtle who is the main character in a popular series of children's books created by Paulette Bourgeois and Brenda Clark. These companies produce Franklin television programs, computer software, plush animals, backpacks, and many other products. Sports teams and stars, famous musicians, and fashion designers also license the use of their name, pictures, and logos on products.

Did You Know?

Canadian James Gosling was part of the team that originally developed Java, the programming language that makes it possible for many different kinds of computer systems to access the Internet.

FRANCHISING AGREEMENTS

Franchising agreements are similar to licensing agreements. In Chapter 3, you learned that a franchise agreement is an arrangement for one business to license the rights to its name and procedures to another business. The entrepreneurs in this situation are the franchiser and the franchisee. If the inventor has already launched a business, the franchiser could give the franchisee the right to sell or distribute the product in a certain area, or even to set up a similar business in another location.

PRODUCING THE INVENTION

The riskiest thing for an inventor to do is to manufacture the product that results from his or her invention. This process usually requires a large amount of capital and expertise that many inventors do not possess. Like John Logie Baird, entrepreneurial inventors who wish to minimize their personal risk can form a partnership with an established business or a financial investor. The inventor gets startup funds and business help from the venture partner, and the venture partner gets an opportunity to invest in a new invention that could become very successful. Just as trade shows bring manufacturers and distributors together in central locations, **venture capital markets** bring inventors together with financial investors who are interested in developing new ideas. This type of partnership arrangement is similar to a licensing agreement, except that the inventor has some personal control through an ownership stake in the business.

Inventors and innovators have started many famous companies. Roots, Bombardier, Clearly Canadian, and Tim Hortons are just a few examples. Although the risks are great, the rewards for the inventive or innovative entrepreneur can be great as well.

SELLING THE RIGHTS

If an inventor is prepared to completely give up control of his or her invention or a related business, then he or she may decide to sell the patent or copyright to someone else. For example, Henry Woodward and Matthew Evans, the Canadian inventors of the light bulb, sold their patent to Thomas Edison. In 1879, Edison improved the bulb's design and took out his own patent.

Inventors may sell their inventions if they prefer to receive a fairly large sum of money for the sale of their invention, rather than wait for profits from licensing or franchising to come in slowly over time. However, conflicts sometimes arise when the purchaser takes an

Did You Know?

An inventor can make money by selling the patent or copyright to his or her invention. Although this sale results in a profit, it doesn't make the inventor an entrepreneur unless the inventor makes a business out of the regular sale of patents or copyrights.

invention in a direction other than what the seller expects. There is also the risk that, over the long term, profits from licensing, franchising, or developing the business will be greater than the amount the inventor earns from a one-time sale. On the other hand, the buyer assumes the risk of financing, producing, and marketing the product.

ACTIVITIES FOR ...

INFORMATION	**C**ONNECTION	**E**XTENSION
1. a) What question do inventors ask themselves? What question do entrepreneurs ask themselves?	**b)** What characteristics and skills do inventors and entrepreneurs have in common? How would these characteristics and skills help inventors become entrepreneurs?	**c)** Profile an inventor who became an entrepreneur.
2. a) Explain the difference between a patent and a copyright. Why should you patent or copyright something that you've created?	**b)** Imagine that there were no patents or copyrights. What impact do you think this would have on inventors and innovators? on consumers?	**c)** Find out about patent protection laws in Canada. For how long can you hold a patent? What happens after that time?
3. a) Explain the difference between a licensing agreement and a franchising agreement.	**b)** Look around your home, your school, or a store. Make a list of the licensed images that you see. On what types of products do these images appear?	**c)** Choose one of the licensed images you listed in Question 3b. Find out about a business that holds a licence for that image. Why did it decide to license the image? How much did it pay for the licence? Has the venture been successful?

Review

Knowledge and Understanding

1. Match each of the following terms to the correct definition:

    copyright   patent
    innovation   royalty
    invention   trade show
    licensing

    a) The act of using new technology, materials, or processes to improve on existing products, or on how they are produced and distributed.

b) Obtaining permission from the inventor of a product to use his or her invention in return for a fee.

c) The legal right of ownership of artistic works and ideas, such as books or music.

d) An exhibition at which a large number of manufacturers and distributors of a particular product show their goods to retailers and/or customers.

e) A product or a process that does something that has never been done before.

f) A fixed amount or a percentage of the sales revenue from a product that is paid to the patent or copyright owner in return for the right to market a product.

g) The registration of the inventor's legal right of ownership of his or her invention, preventing others from using the invention without permission.

2. What roles do each of the following play: an inventor, an innovator, and an entrepreneur?

3. What potential risks are there for an inventor who wants to move into entrepreneurship? How can an inventor reduce these risks?

4. Write the names of 15 inventions mentioned in this chapter on slips of paper or index cards. On another 15 slips of paper or index cards, write the inventors' names. Use the paper or cards to play a game of Concentration in which you match each invention to its inventor.

Thinking and Inquiry

1. "Necessity is *not* the mother of invention." Explain why you agree or disagree with this statement.

2. Find out about the work of the National Research Council (NRC), an organization that promotes scientific and technological research and development in Canada. What inventions and innovations has the NRC helped create?

3. Use the news media and the Internet to identify inventions from the past 12 months. Describe one invention, and tell who invented it. How could an entrepreneur use this invention to create a venture?

4. Are all ventures innovative? Why or why not?

5. Give examples that show how innovation and invention have led to the development and application of new technologies.

E-ACTIVITY

Visit
www.business.
nelson.com
and follow the links
to find about the
National Research
Council.

Communication

1. What one invention *not* discussed in this chapter has had a significant impact on how people live? Defend your selection in a debate with a student who chose a different invention.

2. Many inventors, such as Alexander Graham Bell and Thomas Edison, have created more than one invention. Choose an inventor mentioned in this chapter and find out what else he or she created. Present your findings in a collage.

Application

1. Prepare a chart that analyzes a Canadian invention. You might choose one of the following: the Avro Arrow, Pablum, Trivial Pursuit, the goalie mask, basketball, the snowmobile, IMAX technology, or Superman. Use the following chart headings to record your information: Invention, Inventor, Brief History, How It Works, Ventures Based on the Invention, and Innovations Based on the Invention.

2. Create a visual display that shows licensed images in five categories, for example, images related to cartoons, sports teams, or food products. Include at least five images in each category. Use what you learned in Chapter 6 to describe what makes some images more recognized than others.

REFLECT ON YOUR LEARNING

1. Which one invention do you feel has had the greatest impact on people's lives? Explain your answer.

2. Which would you prefer to be—an inventor or an innovator? Explain.

CHAPTER 17

STEPS IN CREATING A VENTURE

STUDENT EXPECTATIONS

After completing this chapter, you will be able to

- describe how entrepreneurs discover opportunities in people's needs, wants, and problems
- explain the concepts of segmenting the market, data mining, and creating a product or service map
- demonstrate an understanding of the methods of collecting primary data
- describe the purpose and parts of a business plan
- identify the human and financial resources necessary to create a venture

Profile

Dean Simon, in front of Pine Tree's chalet.

KING OF THE HILL

Just outside of Stephenville, Newfoundland, entrepreneur Dean Simon toiled endlessly to build the resort of his dreams. For the past few years, Dean has lived, eaten, breathed, and slept in a cramped construction trailer on top of Table Mountain, 330 m high. His plans are to create a year-round recreation complex, complete with a downhill ski run, sports fields, a swimming pool, and a golf course for the people of western Newfoundland to enjoy.

The location high above the ocean is breathtakingly beautiful. Though the spot Dean has chosen to launch his very first business is a little remote, he has still been able to raise money for his venture.

By 1997, he had already raised close to $90 000. He's still eager to sell shares in the company to continue to finance the development of the Pine Tree Recreation Corporation. But it's slow going. Each share sale requires 20 to 30 calls. Often, construction has to stop while Dean races out to drum up more investment to cover financial obligations. He even resorts to pawning his belongings—at one point he came close to losing his class ring from St. Francis Xavier University.

For 14 months, as he attempted to build his ski-hill resort, Dean lived a hand-to-mouth existence. Food came from friends. He had no salary of his own and, consequently, no social life either. Dean waited for a large addition of cash, mainly in the form of a loan from the government. That loan never happened, but Dean still poured every penny of his own and other shareholders into construction.

Finally, by January of 1999, it looked like Dean was at the end of his towline. Life up on Pine Tree turned pretty grim, as Dean owed progressively more money at the end of each week.

After Dean's story, "King of the Hill," was aired on the CBC program *Venture*, he finally had some luck come his way. He

CONTINUED →

managed to attract a couple of large investors (and a few smaller ones too). Dean sold enough shares to make some real progress on site.

In March of 2000, Dean attempted to officially open his ski hill. Unfortunately, the weather didn't cooperate. Most of the snow had already melted away. Construction delays resulting from a lack of money also took their toll. But Dean had positive results to show for the year: He managed to build a ski chalet and he opened the Pine Tree bar and restaurant.

He also made real progress on the slopes, carving out new runs. And he's finally got the ski lift installed, ready to tow people up the hill … next year.

About This Profile

1. Describe Dean Simon's business.
2. How is his resort different from and similar to other businesses of this sort? What could Dean do to set his business apart from other ski hills or resorts?
3. How has Dean been able to finance his business?
4. What kinds of personal and financial sacrifices has Dean had to make in order to keep his business afloat?
5. If you were looking to invest in a new business, would you consider buying shares in a company like Pine Tree? Why or why not?
6. What kinds of research do you think Dean did before starting his business?

Choosing a Venture

With a small group, discuss methods that businesses use to find out what their customers think about their products and services.

If you've determined that you have the characteristics and skills necessary to be an entrepreneur, and you feel that you may enjoy starting a venture, then only two questions remain: What kind of venture will you start? How will you do it? Entrepreneurs can seek a venture opportunity in one of two ways—as an idea-driven opportunity or as a market-driven opportunity.

IDEA-DRIVEN ENTERPRISES

An **idea-driven** enterprise is one that you create as a result of an invention or innovation. Imagine that one day, while looking at a kitchen drawer organizer, you come up with a great idea for a similar device that will help people organize their ties. Your innovation—a tie organizer—is a wooden device designed to fit in a wide variety of bureau drawers. The retail price might range from $10 to $50, depending on the type of wood that's used.

Now that you have an idea for a venture, you have to find a location for your business, invest in equipment to produce the tie organizer, gather the necessary raw materials, and hire staff. Then, you can begin production. Once the tie organizers are made, you have to start selling them. At this point, idea-driven entrepreneurial ventures sometimes run into trouble. What if no one wants to buy a tie organizer? No customers have expressed a demand for the product, so you can't tell for sure if there's a market for it. Perhaps the current trend is toward *not* wearing ties. Perhaps people already have other ways to organize their ties. You hope that your idea is good enough to bring the customers you need to your business.

MARKET-DRIVEN ENTERPRISES

A **market-driven** enterprise develops in a different way. This time, imagine that you are interested in fashion. Your research indicates a real growth trend across the country in ties. Men are using ties to dress up casual clothing, wearing them with jeans or khakis and a shirt. To see whether there is a need for another tie manufacturer, you design a survey to determine how many ties most men own. The results surprise you. Most men don't know how many ties they have. They keep their ties on racks, hangers, and hooks, but the ties tend to fall off and become disorganized. The more ties men get, the more disorganized the ties become, making tie selection difficult.

You realize that what men need isn't more ties; what they need is a way to organize the ties they have. Again, you wonder. What types of tie organizers are on the market today? What types used to be available and why are they no longer sold? How do men organize their ties? How much are men willing to pay for a tie organizer?

Your new research points to a real need for a tie organizer. There is certainly a venture opportunity for anyone who can design such a system. This is the point at which market-driven entrepreneurial ventures often run into trouble. What if you can't design the product yourself? Maybe you don't know anything about woodworking, or you just aren't an inventor. You have a great market, but no idea how to tap into it.

BRINGING IDEAS AND MARKETING SKILLS TOGETHER

No successful venture can be purely idea-driven or purely market-driven. The idea person needs help with marketing, while the marketing expert needs help with ideas.

People can learn marketing skills from various sources, including courses, texts, Web sites, and magazines. If you don't want to learn these skills yourself, you can hire a marketing consultant. Advertising firms, research companies, and consulting firms all provide services to help people assess the market potential of their ideas.

In a metalworking class, you can learn skills such as welding and sheet metal bending.

People can also learn technical skills. Many high schools and community colleges hold woodworking and design classes. "How to" books are available on a wide variety of technical subjects. The Internet and magazines can help as well. If you don't want to do the technical work yourself, you can always hire someone else to do it. Drafting firms, industrial design companies, and technical consultants will, for a fee, take an idea for a product and construct a model. They will design plans and help with technical modifications. They can also advise you about which materials and manufacturing processes you will need to make the product.

When an idea person forms a partnership with a marketing person, each partner brings different strengths to a project. A partner also increases the venture's capital and shares the risks involved. You can find partners at venture capital trade fairs, which are held in major cities, or by placing an advertisement in a national newspaper or magazine. The Internet is also being widely used to bring together entrepreneurs with different types of knowledge.

Ultimately, the entrepreneur wants the answer to one question: Is my venture feasible? A **feasible** venture is one that has the potential to succeed—the entrepreneur has set reasonable goals, and there is both an idea and a market for the product.

FINDING ENTREPRENEURIAL OPPORTUNITIES

Every new venture fits into one of the following categories: manufacturing, importing or wholesaling, retail sales, or service (other than retail). When you're looking for venture opportunities, start with the area you like most. If you enjoy building things, then manufacturing may be for you. If you enjoy travel and have a good eye for merchandise that will sell, consider importing or wholesaling. If you have a great deal of knowledge or passion about a particular type of product, such as books, fashion, or sporting goods, you might enjoy selling this type of product through your own retail venture. If you like helping others or have a special talent, such as designing Web pages or gardening, you may find your place in the service sector.

A venture is feasible only when it solves a problem or satisfies a need or want. To identify problems, needs, and wants in the area you chose, you have to find out what is and what is not already available in the market. Products and services that already exist have achieved a certain level of success and acceptance. You may be able to innovate or improve on these products or services with your new venture. It's equally important to find out what's *not* available; doing so may help you identify customer needs and wants that are not currently being filled.

To investigate the market for a new business, an entrepreneur should do three things: segment the current market, perform data mining, and create a product or service map.

Segmenting

As you read in Chapter 6, a **market segment** is any part of an overall market that has common characteristics. Market segments can be large or small. For example, the carbonated soft-drink segment represents a large segment of the overall beverage market, while the caffeine-free diet cola segment is much smaller. The smaller the segmentation, the easier it is to determine what is available in a particular market. For example, it's very difficult to list all the beverages sold in North America. It's much easier to identify just the available caffeine-free diet colas.

Before you launch a new venture, it's important to analyze the segment of the market in which your business will fit. The type of

STRETCH YOUR THINKING

Name a local business that fits into each of these four categories: manufacturing, importing or wholesaling, retail sales, and service (other than retail). What problems, needs, or wants does each business address?

analysis you do depends on whether you plan to be a manufacturer, an importer or wholesaler, a retailer, or another kind of service provider.

Segmenting in Manufacturing

Manufacturers need to analyze the market to decide what category of products to make. Imagine that you plan to manufacture beverages. In such a large overall market, the segments can be defined in many different ways. You can start by categorizing beverages as juice, soft drinks, sports drinks, and bottled water. The soft drink category includes colas, fruit flavours, root beer, and so on. Within each subcategory, you can create even more categories. For example, you can classify root beer by flavour, packaging, or price.

Segmenting in Importing and Wholesaling

As you learned in Chapter 9, importers look for foreign products that might succeed in Canada, while wholesalers provide existing products at cheaper prices by eliminating stages in the distribution process. Importers might use market segmentation to look for gaps in the Canadian market that could be filled by foreign products. If they have already chosen an interesting product, they could use market segmentation to identify competing products in Canada. For example, an entrepreneur who plans to import a premium brand of root beer from another country needs to see what competing products are already being sold in Canada. With wholesalers, the segments are much broader and may cross over into several overall markets. A food distribution wholesaler, for example, might want to see how the proposed venture compares with other food distribution wholesalers. For example, one wholesaler might specialize in frozen foods, and distribute to institutions such as universities or summer camps, while another wholesaler might carry a wide range of packaged food products and distribute mainly to small grocery stores.

Segmenting in Retail

A person interested in a retailing venture must first decide what type of store to open. Then, he or she must find out what similar types of stores exist. For example, if you plan to open a convenience store, you need to determine what convenience stores already exist, and what types of products they sell.

Segmenting in Other Service Ventures

With service ventures other than retail stores, segmentation depends on the type of service you plan to offer. For example, if you plan to open a child-care facility, you need to see what types of care are already offered in the area. Segments might be categorized by where care is offered (in home/away from home), when care is offered (all day/before and after school), and the quality of service (number of staff, staff qualifications, number of other children cared for).

BUSINESS —FACT—

International trade shows, like the International Food Products Exhibition held in Paris, France, give importers a chance to see what products are available around the world.

Data Mining

Once an entrepreneur segments the market, he or she needs to gather detailed data about all the products or services that are available within the segment. Then, entrepreneurs use a research process called **data mining** to look for relationships and patterns among collected data, and to help them extract useful information. Data mining usually involves using task-specific software.

Gathering Data

The resources an entrepreneur can use to gather specific information about products and services available within a segment depend on the nature of the venture. A manufacturer could use trade magazines, books, and software to analyze the competition and make decisions about a product, including what features it should have, how it will be marketed, and how much it will cost. For example, imagine that you're planning to manufacture a new brand of root beer. You've already segmented the market and made a list of all the different brands of root beer sold in Canada. The next step is to find out everything you can about these brands and how customers respond to them. Trade journals that might help you include *Beverage Digest* (which covers the nonalcoholic beverage industry), *Beverage Retailer* (a beverage marketing and merchandising magazine), and *Beverage World* (a comprehensive magazine about the global manufacturing, marketing, and distribution of all types of beverages). You can also visit a local bookstore or library to find books about beverage manufacturing, recipes for root beer, information about the history of root beer, and so on.

An importer could gather information from foreign consulates, catalogues, government trade directories, and the Internet about products of interest in foreign markets. A wholesaler could gather information from the Yellow Pages, flyers, price lists posted on the Internet, visits to other wholesalers, and trade journals. A retailer or other service provider can use data banks developed by the provincial or federal government, especially Statistics Canada, to find out exactly what's available in the local market. Business development centres or local chambers of commerce provide excellent retail sales data and store location information, including data about walk-by traffic, rent, and parking. Private directories, such as the *Financial Post*'s "Survey of Markets," provide population estimates, retail sales statistics, and spending data for different regions of Canada.

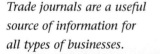

E-ACTIVITY

Visit
www.business.
nelson.com
and follow the links
to research and
report on three
different root beer
brands available
in Canada.

Trade journals are a useful source of information for all types of businesses.

Data-Mining Software

The tremendous growth in the power and speed of computer technology has made data-mining software much more accessible to entrepreneurs. Because customer profiles and purchasing records can be stored and sorted electronically, information that might once have taken days or weeks to obtain can now be assembled and retrieved at the push of a button.

Suppose you manage an office-products store. You can use data-mining software to find out when, during the month, your store sells the most notepads. If the data-mining software reveals that your highest sales of notepads are usually in the last week of the month, you could, for example, arrange to have special prices on pens and markers at the same time, or try to even out your sales patterns by reducing the price of notepads slightly during the second week of every month.

When customer profiles are correlated with data about the items customers purchase, the possibilities are endless. For example, you could ask your database to tell you how many purchases over $400 were made during weekdays by customers between 35 and 55 years of age who were purchasing managers. This information might help you develop advertising material that targets this demographic.

You can use data-mining software to ask any question that might help you understand your business better. The more knowledge you have, the better your decisions will be.

This businessperson is using data-mining software to determine the relationship between sales of a particular brand of root beer and consumers' age.

Product or Service Mapping

Product mapping allows an entrepreneur to visualize all the products or services that are available in a particular segment and to group them by a specific feature—root beer available in long-necked bottles, premium root beers, foamy root beers, and so on. This stage also involves analyzing sales statistics, taste test data, product histories, consumer motivation data, and any other information that has been found about individual brands. The aspiring root beer maker or importer looks for connections between sales figures and specific attributes, such as packaging, product history, and taste. After thorough research, the entrepreneur creates a product map. This map illustrates all the characteristics that make each type of root beer popular. When the map is complete, the new entrepreneur can decide which type of root beer to make or import in order to fill a need or want in the market. For example, an entrepreneur's product map might reveal a need for a premium, strong-flavoured root beer that is packaged in a long-necked brown bottle and yields five centimetres of frothy foam when poured into a glass. These characteristics remind consumers of old-fashioned types of root beer, with which they have positive associations. Consumers will pay more for this type of treat than they would for a beverage purchased only to quench their thirst.

Figure 17.1

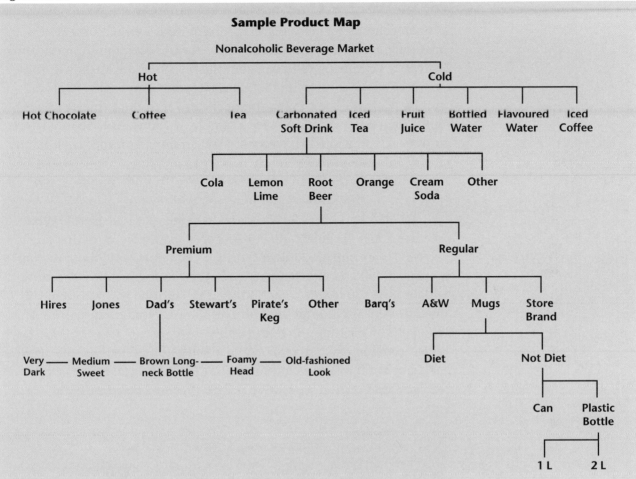

Sample Product Map

Retail entrepreneurs use a different type of product map to profile all the retail stores in a certain area that sell products in the same segment. If possible, the entrepreneur includes pictures of all the stores on the product map, and analyzes the stores in terms of location, layout, design, special features, and so on. The entrepreneur collects this data by visiting each store or by obtaining information from the local chamber of commerce. When the retailer completes the map, he or she knows exactly what's available in a particular community and why consumers shop at these stores. For example, if you wanted to open a flower shop in Halifax, you would have to map about 40 stores ranging from one-person shops to branches of major chains. Similarly, people who provide services other than retail can map their segments by listing all the businesses in a community that provide the same service. Then, they could analyze these businesses according to quality, reputation, price, and so on.

Setting Your Venture Apart

As you conduct segmenting, data mining, and product or service mapping, it's important to keep the following question in mind: How will your venture be different from the ones that are already in the market? If you're interested in manufacturing, importing, or whole-saling, you would ask "What product can I introduce that's different from what's already there?" For example, if you want to manufacture root beer, you might ask yourself, "Which Canadian root beer brands are not already available in my market area? Which brands could be imported from the U.S. or another country? Which brands would meet the need for a premium root beer with lots of foam?"

Retailers and other service providers can ask themselves, "What services could we add to set our ventures apart from ones that already exist?" For example, Kamloops, British Columbia, with a population of only 80 000 people, has about 20 video stores. A new video store would have to provide something special in order to succeed in this market. What could the store offer to draw customers away from the competition? Perhaps drive-through service, home delivery, 24-hour video vending machines, an attached laundromat, or specialty products like old movies or cult movies? In fact, there are many possible answers that could lead to a successful venture opportunity.

What could the owner of this flower shop do to set his venture apart from other flower shops?

INFORMATION	CONNECTION	EXTENSION
1. a) What is the difference between idea-driven and market-driven entrepreneurial opportunities?	**b)** Select a common household product. Outline ways in which the product may have been idea-driven and market-driven.	**c)** Which business category would you like to explore? Explain how you could develop a venture in this category that is both idea-driven and market-driven.
2. a) What is the difference between market segmentation and data mining?	**b)** What other products are in the same market segment as the household product you chose in Question 1b?	**c)** Visit a local business to find out what resources management uses for data mining. List two pieces of information that the business has discovered using each resource. Present your findings in a chart.
3. a) What is a product or service map?	**b)** Imagine that you are an entrepreneur who is considering opening an appliance repair business. What information might you look for on a service map? Be specific.	**c)** With a small group, choose a segment of the snack food market, for example, chocolate bars. Create a product map to show the different products in this segment that are available in your community. If you were going to import or manufacture a new chocolate bar, what conclusions could you draw from the product map?

Collecting Market Data

Once you identify several opportunities for successful ventures, you can analyze each opportunity to determine how well it might meet consumer needs, serve the community, and generate revenue. At this stage, market research focuses on potential customers rather than on competing products and services.

While you can conduct general research using secondary data, you need primary data to complete a plan for a specific venture.

GATHERING PRIMARY DATA

By now, you've completed months of research about root beer. You've discovered that in your community, there are no available brands of root beer that customers think of as "old-fashioned." However, you've located several brands from the United States and one from the United Kingdom that have the strong flavour and foamy appearance that true root beer experts rave about. You've decided to negotiate a distribution deal with a U.S. company to import its root beer and distribute it to specialty food stores and restaurants. Will this new venture work?

This question is important since you're now at a stage where you need money to proceed with your venture. To see whether your idea is feasible, you need to collect primary data from your potential customers. You can obtain this data through a number of techniques, such as conducting surveys, using observation, holding focus groups, and networking.

Surveys

A **survey** is a set of carefully planned questions used to gather data. People can respond orally or in writing. Surveys can be conducted in person, on the telephone, through the mail, or on the Internet.

A surveyor in a mall asks a shopper questions about her purchasing habits.

Most surveys use **closed-ended questions** that ask **respondents** to select one answer from two or more choices. These questions can be completed quickly and easily, and the responses are easy to sort and analyze. Closed-ended questions usually fit one of the following types: "yes/no"; "agree/disagree"; "select a), b), c), or d)"; or "rate on a scale of 1 to 10." Examples include

• Do you drink root beer?
• Which of the following brands of root beer do you enjoy drinking?
• On a scale of 1 to 10, how would you rate the taste of this brand of root beer?

Occasionally, surveys use **open-ended questions** to allow respondents to develop their own answers, even though these questions take longer to answer and are harder to analyze. Here are some examples of open-ended questions:

• What do you like most about root beer?
• What words do you associate with the following brands of root beer?
• When do you usually drink root beer?

No matter what type of questions they use, surveys involve a cross-section of the population that is chosen to represent the whole population. The survey is **random** if everyone in the population has

Did You Know?

In an electronic survey, the results go directly into a computer for interpretation.

an equal chance of being selected as part of the sample group. If the sample group that responds to the survey does not accurately represent the whole group that the researchers are interested in, the survey results will be misleading. A sample that does not accurately represent the target population is **biased**. For example, if a researcher wants to reflect the opinions of teenaged girls in Canada, but surveys only girls from one school, then the sample is biased and the survey results will be inaccurate.

Observation

Researchers who use **observation** collect information without directly interacting or communicating with the person who is being observed. The purpose of observation research is to see how people actually behave, rather than have them recall or predict their responses. A respondent who is asked to name a favourite brand of soft drink may be influenced by what others have said or by a desire to please the researcher. On the other hand, when a respondent chooses a favourite brand of root beer from a number of brands on a table without knowing that he or she is being watched, then the choice is a more reliable guide to the person's real preference. Observation is more accurate and less biased than surveys, but it is also more expensive and less effective in large groups because the researcher must watch too many people at once.

Observations must be carefully planned in order not to interfere with the participants' actions. If the participant knows, or even guesses at, the wishes or preferences of the observer, the results become biased and inaccurate. Survey participants often want to "get it right" or "pick the right one," even though there is no right or wrong answer. When people don't know they're being watched, their actions are a better guide to how they really feel.

In some situations, observations can be made with television cameras, audiotapes, one-way mirrors, and bar code scanners which record the items and quantities customers buy. Another observation method uses **eye-tracking** photography. Researchers use the technology to determine where a person looks first when approaching a store display or when looking at a page in a magazine. It can also show how long a person's eyes focus on certain details; how the eyes move to search a shelf, examine a package, or read an advertisement; and what the customer looks at just before making a final buying decision. Information obtained this way can be very helpful to people designing a package, advertisement, or merchandise display.

STRETCH YOUR THINKING

What characteristics would you look for in a small group of people intended to represent all the students at your school?

In Store Media Systems

In Store Media Systems developed an electronic coupon-distribution system that knows what you're going to buy before you do. The people who created the system knew that consumers develop regular purchasing patterns for most products. Purchase records and information from frequent-shopper cards help the system predict when a customer is about to run out of any product, from peanut butter to plastic wrap. When a customer inserts a frequent-shopper card into a machine, out come coupons chosen especially for him or her.

The system is a winner with manufacturers, customers, and retailers alike. Manufacturers benefit because customers are encouraged to try their brands, and because they can get detailed information about whether their coupons are being used. Customers benefit because they save money on products they need, have opportunities to win prizes, and can use their coupons right away. Retailers benefit because instead of processing coupons manually, the system allows them to process coupons electronically at the checkout. This helps them increase their profits.

Focus Groups

Sometimes people are brought together in a small group to discuss a particular product or problem. As you learned in Chapter 9, a focus group combines the features of an interview with those of the observation method of collecting data. Like survey respondents, focus group participants are carefully selected to represent a larger group. For example, a focus group for possible boat buyers might include couples who earn more than $100 000 per year. A focus group talking about a new video game might include males from 14 to 18 years old who own video-game systems.

The group's moderator asks questions that guide the discussion and help participants generate ideas. The questions must be phrased and presented so that each respondent understands what is being asked, is encouraged to respond honestly, and is not directed toward any one answer. Questions should be short, straightforward, clear, and simple. Usually, they should deal with only one concept at a time. Observers may watch the focus group during the interview to detect any behavioural traits of the participants that could be included in the final report. If the observers don't want to be seen, they will often set up the discussions in special rooms equipped with hidden microphones, video cameras, and two-way mirrors.

To set up focus groups that would help you prepare for your root beer venture, you would need three or four different brands of root beer on hand—including yours—so participants could compare taste

STRETCH YOUR THINKING

Who should you include in a focus group for possible television buyers?

The moderator of this focus group asked questions about the taste and packaging of different kinds of root beer.

and discuss details such as price and packaging. Plan discussions with groups of people in different age categories, as well as groups of restaurant operators, convenience and specialty store owners, and wholesale distributors.

Here are some key questions you could ask each focus group, and some tips about what to look for in the answers.

- **Question**: Is root beer your favourite soft drink flavour?

  What to look for: If you chose your participants carefully, they should accurately represent the total population of soft drink consumers. If 5% of the participants identify root beer as their favourite soft drink, then about 5% of all soft drink consumers favour root beer. You could use similar questions to identify the percentage of people who drink root beer every day or every week, and classify these people by age, gender, or educational background.

- **Question**: When would you drink this product?

  What to look for: If the most frequent response is "to quench my thirst on a hot day," then people don't think of your root beer as a premium brand. On the other hand, answers such as "when I watch television," "when I'm relaxing," or "with a meal" indicate a potential market for your product.

- **Question**: How much would you pay for this product?

  What to look for: The moderator should start listing prices slightly higher than the price of a regular brand and move up in 50¢ increments. Ask respondents to stop the moderator when the price gets too high. This question can help you determine the economic feasibility of importing root beer from the U.S. If people are not willing to pay enough to cover the cost of manufacturing, importing, warehousing, distributing, and promoting the product, then the business will fail.

- **Question**: If this product were a dog, what breed would it be?

  What to look for: Answers to this open-ended question may reveal some very interesting associations with the product. For example, "I think this product would be a sheepdog because I see it sitting with its head on my knee while I'm reading" and "I think of it as a terrier because it feels active and fast to me" are very different responses that indicate two different brand attitudes.

Networking

As you read in Chapter 5, networking is the process of meeting and getting to know people in a business that you are interested in.

Business organizations and events, volunteer work, meetings of service clubs such as Rotary or Kiwanis, conferences, and business luncheons all provide opportunities for the entrepreneur to network. Networking brings experts and novices together. Entrepreneurs can share their experiences, warn others about potential pitfalls, and give or get advice. Owners can discuss market trends, sales figures, suppliers, and other information that may be difficult to obtain in other ways.

Networking also allows people in one type of business to meet people in other businesses who can be of help. Sales leads, supplier contacts, and even new customers can come from meeting people in informal settings.

ANALYZING MARKET DATA

Once the data is collected, it is collated. **Collating** means forming groups based on common features observed in the data. For the root beer scenario, possible groupings include all teenaged males who chose root beer as their favourite beverage, all respondents who thought of root beer as a quiet, trustworthy breed of dog, and all participants who had a university education.

After collating the data, researchers examine it for significant **correlations**—two or more different elements that seem to affect each other. For instance, there may be a high correlation between age, gender, and soft-drink preference, with over 75% of all female respondents between the ages of 30 and 55 preferring the premium brand of root beer. Or, if 90% of the respondents who liked root beer said they would pay more for a premium brand, there may be a correlation between preference and price.

If all the signals are positive after these entrepreneurs have finished data crunching, they can begin to make a more detailed plan for the venture.

Studying data to see what interpretations can be made is called **data crunching**. This process can help the root beer entrepreneur determine if a market exists for the premium brand, whether people prefer this brand over other alternatives, how much customers are willing to pay, what characteristics customers are likely to have, and what types of promotions are likely to be successful.

INFORMATION	**C**ONNECTION	**E**XTENSION
1. a) List and describe four methods used to collect primary data.	**b)** Use the Internet, magazines, public library, or another source to find an example of a survey. What is the main purpose of the survey? List three questions from the survey and explain what information researchers could get from each one.	**c)** Work in groups of six to eight. Each person designs an open-ended question that begins "If root beer were ... " and asks the other group members the question. After the group answers all the questions, determine which one sparked the most discussion. What made the question effective? Then, summarize what the responses to the various questions revealed about root beer.
2. a) Explain how a focus group is conducted.	**b)** Identify a problem or issue at your school that could be addressed with a five-person focus group. Describe five segments of the school population that should be represented in the focus group. Explain how you would choose the representatives.	**c)** Organize the focus group that you described in Question 2b. Prepare a report on your findings from the focus group. Discuss the report with your class. What recommendations could you make to the school administration?
3. a) What is the difference between collating data and examining the data for correlations?	**b)** Ask a local entrepreneur what analysis he or she performed to determine the market potential of his or her venture before it was launched. How did the analysis help shape the venture? What questions did the entrepreneur not ask at the time, but should have?	**c)** How did the market analysis used by the entrepreneur you interviewed in Question 3b differ from the process described in this chapter? In your opinion, would this chapter have helped the entrepreneur? Why or why not? What valuable information did the entrepreneur give you that wasn't in this chapter?

The Business Plan

Once you decide what venture to pursue, it's time to write a business plan. A **business plan** outlines the objectives of the business and summarizes the strategies and resources needed to achieve these objectives. A well-prepared business plan indicates both the strengths and weaknesses of the business, and helps the business find ways to use its strengths to overcome or eliminate the weaknesses.

Your business plan is the single most important document that you will produce in the lifetime of your venture. It is the blueprint of your success. Although a business plan may seem tedious to complete, it is an important reference. Without a business plan, you waste time, energy, and money, and you may even lose sight of your objective. If you need outside financing for your business, potential lenders will ask you to provide a business plan. Financial institutions and other possible investors use the business plan to assess the risk involved in lending money to your business.

Your business plan should contain a brief summary of your venture, background information, a description of the products or services you will sell, the structure of the business, a market analysis, a resource analysis, an operating strategy, a financial strategy, references, and appendices.

BRIEF SUMMARY

This summary is often called the **executive summary**. It appears first in the business plan to provide a quick reference for a busy loans officer, manager of a financial institution, or potential investor. The summary explains what your business is going to make, sell, or do. It includes projected revenues, expenses, and profits, and explains how these projections were calculated. If the business plan is part of a loan application, the summary should end by stating how much money your business requires and how you will use this money.

BACKGROUND INFORMATION

Your business plan should outline the history of your business—when it was started, why it was started, and who started it (including the names and addresses of the owners and the percentage owned by each one). This section of the plan indicates whether your business is a sole proprietorship, a partnership, or a corporation.

PRODUCTS AND SERVICES

The business plan should provide a description of the products or services that your business will manufacture or sell. How are they unique? What patents, trade secrets, or new technologies are involved? The plan should also profile the overall industry and provide projections of how the industry is likely to grow over time.

THE STRUCTURE OF THE BUSINESS

The business plan should include a chart that shows how your business will be organized, along with brief biographies of key management personnel. It should illustrate the expertise and experience available to manage your business and ensure its success.

MARKET ANALYSIS

The market analysis begins by identifying the overall target market for your venture and by describing the related market segments in detail. It includes profiles of demographic characteristics, locations of consumers, and consumer motivations.

The plan outlines who your competitors are, where they are, and how successful they are (including the market share that each one holds). It should also explain how your business will ensure that its products or services are better than those offered by your competitors.

Your market analysis estimates the sales potential of the business and includes weekly sales projections. You can determine these projections by multiplying the size of the overall market by the estimated share percentage your venture should have, and dividing the results into weekly estimates. The estimates then need to be varied to show how sales may increase or decrease, depending on the season or special holidays and events. At this stage, it's helpful to look at sales patterns experienced by other similar businesses.

The business plan also outlines the venture's pricing policy, including the cost price (the actual cost of manufacturing the product or providing the service), the markup (the amount that you add for profit), and the selling price (the cost price + the markup) of each product or service. Policies that govern customer billing should be part of the market analysis, including payment options, discounts offered to large customers, shipping charges, and credit terms.

The market analysis needs to describe in detail how your products and services will be distributed to customers. For example, you might sell them through retail stores or over the Internet. The plan also includes any costs involved in bringing the product or service to customers.

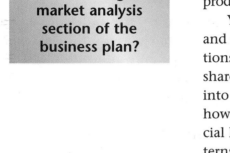

This entrepreneur studies the market analysis section of her business plan.

The market analysis must include your advertising and sales promotion plans for the product or service. This part of the plan is so important that it is often developed as a separate section. Advertising and promotion plans should include the **creative strategy** for the campaign, showing how the target consumer will be persuaded to buy your products or services. The advertising budget is included, along with the advertising and promotional schedule.

RESOURCE ANALYSIS

As you read in Chapter 1, resources are the materials, people, technology, and money that your business needs in order to function. The business plan includes a list of the capital resources, such as buildings or machines, that your business owns. If your business owns property, the plan should include the outstanding mortgage, a current market valuation of the property, and a description of the building. The plan should explain where your business is located and why this location was chosen. If your business is in manufacturing, for example, you should also include a list of all machinery, equipment, and raw materials that you will have to buy, complete with information about who will supply them and how much they will cost.

Your venture can succeed only if the right people are in place to do the work. The resource analysis outlines the jobs that have to be done and who will do them. The business plan also shows the money available to the business and indicates a need for a financial plan if not enough capital is available.

OPERATING STRATEGY

This section of the business plan describes how your business will function from day to day. If the business manufactures a product, the plan outlines production procedures, estimated manufacturing costs, and quality-control procedures. If it's a retail business, then the plan describes what the store will sell, where these products will come from, and how the selling will be done.

In this section, potential investors can read about record-keeping, purchasing practices, and human resources policies. They should also find a salary or wage schedule and some suggestions for keeping costs down.

If there are rules and regulations that apply to your business, including environmental regulations, they should be addressed in the operating strategy.

FINANCIAL STRATEGY

If your new venture needs financing, this section of the business plan will be extremely important. It lists all your capital requirements, as well as sources who have already provided money for your business, such as relatives or partners. The financial section includes projected income statements and balance sheets, cash flow projections, and a loan repayment plan.

In order to obtain a loan, your business needs collateral. Most banks accept the following as business collateral: accounts receivable, real estate, inventory, equipment, and automobiles. The owner's personal assets, such as a home or investments, may also be considered.

For a small service business that doesn't have many valuable assets, **third-party guarantees** (loan guarantees by someone outside the business who has collateral) and personal assets may be enough to secure the loan.

REFERENCES

Financial institutions, other investors, and new suppliers look for references in the business plan. The plan lists the names of financial institutions and other investors with whom you and your business have had financial dealings, along with the details of financial transactions, their terms, and payment histories. It also helps to list the names of accountants, lawyers, suppliers, or other businesses with whom you and your venture have had a financial relationship.

APPENDICES

Your business plan might include supporting documents such as résumés of key personnel, a statement of your personal net worth, an outline of the community benefits of the business, the availability of government assistance or grants, and detailed market research results. Include these documents as appendices at the end of the plan, rather than in each section.

Contemporary Issues in Canadian Business

THE ISSUE: FINANCING A NEW BUSINESS

How do new businesses get started?

Do you have an innovative idea and a sound business plan for starting a new business? If so, you have two of the three critical elements you need to get started as an entrepreneur. The third element is money or capital. Without money, your innovative idea and sound business plan won't go far.

Many new entrepreneurs assume that acquiring capital is simply a matter of deciding between debt financing (borrowing the funds you need) and equity financing (giving up ownership in exchange for investment funds). They assume that they can get the money they need simply by filling out an application or soliciting funds, and then signing on the dotted line.

Sometimes, trying to get money to start a new business is like applying for your first job. Potential lenders tell you that business experience is a necessary requirement. But how can you gain experience if no one will give you the money to get started in the first place?

Financing is difficult for new entrepreneurs because a business that hasn't yet begun to operate has no established credit. With no credit history, the lender runs a greater risk that the loan will not be repaid. On the other hand, small businesses are considered to be the backbone of the Canadian economy. They provide jobs for millions of people across the country.

Should financial institutions be more willing to lend money to first-time entrepreneurs?

Point

The idea that financial institutions are unwilling to lend money to small businesses is a myth. Financial institutions are often willing to lend money to first-time entrepreneurs, especially if the entrepreneurs can show a valid business plan and offer collateral that can be used to repay the loan if necessary. Every small business currently operating in Canada found startup funding somewhere, and a great deal of that money came from financial institutions.

During the three-month period from April to June 2000, the six largest Canadian financial institutions loaned almost $50 billion to small- and medium-sized businesses (SMEs) with fewer than 50 employees. In fact, SMEs represent approximately 95% of all businesses that borrow money from financial institutions.

Counterpoint

Financial institutions have good reason to be cautious about lending to new entrepreneurs. According to a Statistics Canada study, over 50% of new businesses will not survive their third year of operation, 70% will not survive their sixth year, and over 80% will not survive their tenth year. There are a number of reasons why a new business might fail:

- It may take more time than people expect for the business to build a reputation and attract regular customers.
- An inexperienced management team may keep inadequate records or make errors that will affect the company's cash flow.
- A competitor may be able to offer a better product or service, drawing customers away from the business.
- There may be a downturn in the economy, resulting in fewer profits than expected.

E-ACTIVITY

Visit **www.business. nelson.com** and follow the links to learn more about financing a new venture.

Even when a new business can't get the funding it needs from a financial institution, there are other ways to raise capital. According to *Business Start-Ups* magazine, the most common sources of funding are personal savings (72%), financial institutions (45%), friends (28%), individual investors (10%), government-guaranteed loans (7%), and venture capital firms (1%).

In Canada, there are a number of government programs that help finance business startups and expansions. These include
- grants and subsidies
- low- or no-interest loans
- tax refunds or credits
- government insurance against business risks
- guaranteed government purchases of a product or service

The availability of alternative sources of funding means that financial institutions can afford to be cautious about where they decide to put their money. Once a new business has achieved some degree of success, financial institutions will be more than willing to lend the business the money it needs to grow and expand.

A Real Life Example

A few years ago, Angela DeMarco decided she needed a change. For 10 years, she had been working as an administrative assistant in a busy office in downtown Vancouver. But her dream had always been to open her own bakery. So at age 34, she quit her office job and set out on her own.

She began small, setting up shop in her own kitchen and selling her bread, cookies, and other baked goods to local stores. The business grew quickly and Angela was soon thinking of expansion—while Angela enjoyed working out of her home and selling to other retailers, what she really wanted was a bakery of her own. However, renting retail space can be costly. Although Angela was earning money from the sales she was making, she had to reinvest most of this income back into the business—to pay for supplies, equipment, ingredients, and the cost of transporting her product to her customers.

Angela knew that if she wanted her business to grow, she would have to look beyond her own savings. She borrowed some money from family and friends, and also received a $10 000 loan from her bank. With this money, Angela was able to get her new bakery off the ground. She found some retail space to rent in a busy commercial area of the city, and bought new equipment and supplies. She also hired an assistant to help her with her rapidly increasing workload. Still, in the early months of the new operation, finances were tight.

Says Angela: "When you're starting a new business, it seems that every last penny you make either goes back into the business—to pay for costs and expenses—or goes toward paying off your debts. Financially, every day is a struggle. But the important thing is to stick with it. You have to be realistic about what you can accomplish in the first few years. If you put a lot of time into developing your business plan, and can prove to potential lenders that your business has a good chance of succeeding, you will eventually get the financing you need."

Questions and Activities About This Issue

1. Where did Angela DeMarco find financing for her business?
2. Do you think Angela's bakery will succeed? Why or why not?
3. Contact your local chamber of commerce or Better Business Bureau to find out how the statistics given for business failures in the Counterpoint section compare with similar statistics for your community.
4. Make a chart to show the advantages and disadvantages of each financing method mentioned in the Counterpoint section.

ACTIVITIES FOR ...

INFORMATION	CONNECTION	EXTENSION
1. a) What is the purpose of a business plan?	**b)** Use the Internet or invite a bank representative to speak to the class about what assistance is available to help a new entrepreneur complete a business plan.	**c)** You write a business plan when starting a venture. After your business is established, when might you refer to your business plan? Under what circumstances might you change your business plan?
2. a) List the different sections of a business plan.	**b)** Which section of a business plan do you think is the most important for your business? Why? Which section is the most important to financial institutions or other potential investors? Why?	**c)** In the e-activity on page 424, you used the Internet to find examples of sample business plans. Compare the structure of one plan you found with the description in this chapter. Present the plan you found for the class, pointing out any differences.

Review

Knowledge and Understanding

1. Match each of the following terms to the correct definition:

   business plan product mapping
   correlation random
   data mining survey
   market segment

   a) Having an equal chance of being selected as a representative of a population.

   b) Two or more different elements that seem to affect each other.

   c) A document that outlines the objectives of a business and summarizes the strategies and resources needed to achieve these objectives.

   d) Any part of an overall market that has common characteristics.

   e) An activity that allows an entrepreneur to visualize all the products or services that are available in a particular segment and to group them by a specific feature.

   f) A set of carefully planned questions used to gather data.

g) A research process used to look for relationships and patterns in collected data and to extract useful information, usually using task-specific software.

2. Make a labelled diagram to show the sections of a business plan and the types of information in each section.

3. List the advantages and disadvantages of each method of collecting primary data.

4. Give some examples of closed-ended questions that an entrepreneur who is thinking about opening a furniture store might ask. Give examples of open-ended questions that the same entrepreneur might ask.

Thinking and Inquiry

1. Select a retail business that you might enjoy operating. On a map of your community, mark the location of each store that already sells products similar to yours. Find out how many potential customers your store would have if the area population were divided equally among all these businesses, including yours.

2. List the brand names of five products that have existed for a long time. Then, visit a store or use the Internet to identify a recently introduced competitor for each product. Prepare a brief report on each new product, explaining who makes it and how it is different from the established product.

3. Ask several students and teachers to name their favourite movie, song, or book from the past 12 months. Which response is the most common? What patterns can you find if you group the data by gender? by age range? What other correlations can you find between people's characteristics and their choices?

4. Make a chart to show the main differences among business plans for each of the following businesses: a manufacturing business, an import business, a wholesale business, a retail business, a service business (other than retail), and a not-for-profit venture.

Communication

1. Create a networking opportunity at your school to help people discover and share information. You could hold a group study session before a test or exam, a panel discussion with local entrepreneurs, or a "careers day" where students can meet employers who hire part-time workers. Report on what you learned as you organized and supervised the event.

2. In Question 1 of Thinking and Inquiry, you chose a retail business that you might enjoy operating some day. Use photographs, videotapes, or drawings to take a close look at the appearance of some competing stores. What do you like or dislike about each one? How would you make your store different from the competition? Draw a picture of what the inside of your store might look like and label the important features.

Application

1. Eye-tracking photography can show where on a magazine page a reader first looks. How might the magazine use this information to determine where to place ads and how much to charge for these ads?

2. Design a survey that assesses the market potential for a retail store that you would consider opening. Conduct your survey, and then organize and interpret the data.

3. With a small group, choose a retail store that you'd like to open. Assign each member of the group one or more sections of the business plan to complete for the new store. Combine the sections, and have your plan evaluated for feasibility by your teacher and by one outside expert, such as a local entrepreneur or a loans officer at a financial institution.

REFLECT ON YOUR LEARNING

1. This chapter was divided into three main sections: "Choosing a Venture," "Collecting Market Data," and "The Business Plan." Summarize the most important points of each section.

2. What are some strategies that an entrepreneur can use to increase the chances that a new venture will succeed? Discuss your ideas with a partner.

INTERNATIONAL BUSINESS

"Our high level of global connectedness leads to jobs for Canadians, to enhanced competitiveness of our companies, to greater choice for consumers, and to a better quality of life for the country."

Pierre Pettigrew, Minister for International Trade, 2000

STUDENT EXPECTATIONS

After completing this chapter, you will be able to

- **define domestic and international transactions**
- **explain the reasons for doing business internationally**
- **state the advantages and disadvantages of doing business internationally**
- **analyze the impact of trade on the quality and quantity of products available**
- **identify Canada's main trade partners**
- **summarize the impact of trade on employment and job creation in Canada**
- **explain the factors that affect the flow of goods and services**
- **identify potential barriers to international business**

Beijing, Shanghai, Hong Kong

February 9-18, 2001

Beijing, Shanghai, Hong Kong

9-18 février 2001

Team Canada · Équipe Canada
2001

Profile

Grace White, president and CEO of CanJam Trading Ltd.

A PERFECT BALANCING ACT

Grace White is living proof that it is possible to have both a thriving business and a rewarding personal life. In fact, she makes it look easy. The president and CEO of CanJam Trading Ltd. built her food-products business from her basement in Dartmouth, Nova Scotia, with little more than a phone and a lot of determination. Today, White heads up a $50-million international trading business, exporting products from fish to cornmeal to the U.S., Japan, and China. Along the way, she collected a Woman Entrepreneur of the Year award and, in 2000, made *Chatelaine* magazine's list of top 100 women-owned businesses.

But in 1998, White realized she had no balance in her life. "In 1992, when my husband died, I threw myself into work to cope with the pain," she says. "For a long time, I was working seven days a week, and sometimes 15 or 16 hours a day." That took a serious toll on White.

In 1998, White met an older woman who impressed her with her serenity and sense of peace. The woman became a friend and mentor, and inspired White to reevaluate her own priorities. With 30 employees and key management in place at CanJam, White now spends less time at the office—"No more seven-day work weeks," she says—and more time with her two children.

But that doesn't mean White is not committed to growing CanJam. In fact, she has never been shy of thinking big. In 1994, CanJam started carving itself an international niche, exporting mackerel and other underutilized fish to Korea and her native Jamaica. With sales of $6.5 million, White quipped at the time: "I think $100 million is just another zero."

Today, she is on the road to making it happen. From its humble start in 1989, CanJam now exports a range of low-cost food products, from salted fish and mutton to kidney beans, worldwide. "Our

CONTINUED →

product line is expanding almost daily," she says. "When you do something well, people come back to you to fill new orders, and that's how we've gotten into a lot of different products." White also broadened her company's reach by purchasing Atlantic Pearl, a Nova Scotia fish-processing plant. While she still does business with nine other plants, White says owning Atlantic Pearl gives CanJam more control over both pricing and delivery.

To further strengthen her business, White is developing a network of agents to represent CanJam in international markets. "To expand in these markets, we need to work with people on a long-term basis, people who really know the markets," says White. "You can't expect someone here [in Canada] to have the same knowledge." Also, CanJam recently began branding some of its products under its own label. "There are plants that have production capacity, but don't have markets [for their products]," says White. "Maximizing [these plants'] unused capacity helps us grow."

"I reviewed myself to see if I have the skill level to take us to $100 million ... and I believe I do."

Now, White is gearing up for her next big challenge: reaching $100 million in sales in five years. "I reviewed myself to see if I have the skill level to take us to $100 million," says White, "and I believe I do." To get there, she says, CanJam will maximize each business relationship to build market share. "We have had customers become suppliers and suppliers become customers," she says. "Also, because these people have other customers that they sell to, we are able to connect with new sources and new markets." "And her vision won't change either, says White. "We focus on our customers' success."

About This Profile

1. What makes CanJam an international business? To what countries does CanJam export?
2. What steps has CanJam taken to strengthen its business both nationally and internationally?
3. What skills do you think White will need to help her company reach $100 million in sales in five years?
4. Why is it important to have a balance in life? What steps can people take to achieve that balance?

What Is International Business?

BEFORE YOU BEGIN

Discuss the following question with a partner: What are the advantages of selling products or services in other countries?

Every day, vast numbers of business transactions take place in Canada. If you visit a local store and buy a bicycle that has been manufactured in Canada, you engage in a domestic transaction. With **domestic transactions**, both the production and sale of an item take place in the same country. On the other hand, if you buy a pair of sneakers made in Mexico, you engage in an **international transaction**. Even if you buy the shoes at a local store, the transaction is considered to be international because the goods were produced in one country and sold in another.

International transactions involve creating, shipping, and selling goods and services across national borders. Because these transactions usually involve exchanges of one type or another, they are often referred to as **international trade** or **foreign trade**. By participating in an international transaction, you are contributing to the **global economy**.

Most countries rely on international trade for their economic survival. In fact, with a world population of over six billion people, the international market for Canadian products and services is 200 times as large as the domestic market!

The BMW X5

Parts of this BMW X5 travelled from country to country even before its wheels touched the pavement. The X5's engine was assembled in Munich, Germany, and then shipped across the ocean in finished form to the production plant in South Carolina. The rear-view mirror was manufactured by Magna in Ontario. The leather on the seats came from South Africa. And the Michelin tires? They were manufactured in France. Automotive engineers at BMW search the world for parts that will help them create the best possible products for their customers.

WHY DO BUSINESS INTERNATIONALLY?

If a country could produce all the goods and services that domestic consumers need and want, and charge prices that consumers are willing to pay, there would be no need to buy from other countries. Canada could probably produce enough fruit and vegetables for the domestic market on a year-round basis. But growing produce indoors is far more expensive than buying it from countries that have longer or different growing seasons. When each country is able to focus its efforts on what it can do best, everyone benefits. Consumers have access to a broader variety of goods and services, offered at a wider range of prices, and businesses can sell their goods and services to many more markets.

There are five major reasons for doing business internationally: product, price, proximity, preference, and promotion. These reasons are sometimes called the five Ps of international business.

Product

A country's resources determine what goods and services it can produce. Because Canada's climate isn't suited to growing citrus crops, Canadian grocery stores buy oranges and grapefruit from countries with warmer climates, such as the United States, Mexico, and Israel. On the other hand, Canada has large forests and wheat fields that can provide lumber and grain for countries that don't have an abundance of these resources, such as England and Japan.

Price

The cost of producing a particular good or service varies from one country to another. If the cost of wages, taxes, and raw materials is lower in another country than in Canada, it may be less expensive to produce something overseas and ship it to Canada than it would be to produce it domestically. If an item is less expensive to produce, then the business may be able to charge a lower price and increase sales and profits by selling a greater number of units.

Proximity

In Canada, 80% of the population lives within 170 km of the American border. In fact, many small Canadian communities are closer to large American cities than they are to large Canadian cities. For example, the city of Windsor, Ontario, and nearby Essex County have a population of about 350 000 people. They are located just across a bridge from Detroit, Michigan, a city of several million people. As a result, Detroit has a great influence on businesses located in and near Windsor.

E-ACTIVITY

Visit
www.business.
nelson.com
and follow the links
to find out about
companies that sell
their goods and
services to
international
markets.

Preference

Some countries specialize in certain types of goods or services that have a reputation for quality all over the world. Even though similar goods can be made domestically, many people still prefer to buy foreign specialties, such as Belgian chocolates, Swiss watches, Australian wine, German cars, and Canadian wheat.

Promotion

Before the invention of global communications technology, such as satellite broadcasting and the Internet, businesses found it difficult to let people far away know about the goods and services they sold. Today, technology makes it simple for businesses to promote their products anywhere in the world. Some companies spend millions of dollars to translate their television or radio advertisements into many different languages and broadcast them around the globe. Others spend comparatively small amounts of money to set up Web sites that can be accessed from anywhere. Either way, ease of promotion is an incentive for companies to reach beyond their domestic market for customers.

ADVANTAGES AND DISADVANTAGES OF INTERNATIONAL BUSINESS

Often, international business activities open a dialogue between nations that improves mutual understanding, builds lines of communication, and increases the level of respect people have for one another.

International business provides increased markets for businesses and a broader choice of products, services, and prices for consumers. As companies expand to serve new markets, they create jobs both at home and overseas. When Canadian and international businesses exchange goods and services, they also exchange knowledge. This exchange of knowledge results in new approaches to production, marketing, and selling that benefit Canadian consumers as well as producers. It may also bring political benefits. An old saying tells us, "Countries that trade with one another seldom go to war with each other." Often, international business activities open a dialogue between nations that improves mutual understanding, builds lines of communication, and increases the level of respect people have for one another.

However, some potential pitfalls accompany the advantages created by international business. If Canadian companies move their production facilities to places where labour costs are lower, Canadians may lose jobs as a result of competition from foreign enterprises. Canadians would also have less money to spend on domestic goods. At the same time, workers in the new foreign facilities may have to work under conditions that would not be tolerated in Canada.

(See Chapter 7 for information on sweatshops.) Competition, however, can also be good for consumers. As you read in Chapter 1, it can force Canadian businesses to find ways to become more productive and to improve product quality.

Sometimes, Canadian companies have trouble adapting their products to suit a foreign market. Consumers in other parts of the world have different wants and needs. A company must understand these wants and needs before it tries to sell its goods and services internationally. A standardized item that is offered in the same form in all the countries in which it is sold is called a **global product**. Some examples of global products are pencils, soccer balls, and cameras. Food items, on the other hand, are usually difficult to market as global products because people in different parts of the world have different tastes.

ACTIVITIES FOR ...

INFORMATION	CONNECTION	EXTENSION
1. a) What is a domestic transaction? an international transaction?	**b)** Call, visit, or e-mail the chamber of commerce in your community to identify some local businesses that buy or sell goods and services in international markets. Contact these businesses to find out about their international transactions. Using a map of the world, show which countries they do business with.	**c)** If Canada did not buy and sell goods internationally, how would your community be affected?
2. a) List five reasons for doing business internationally.	**b)** Look at the labels on some products in your home. Identify three that were made in Canada and three that were not.	**c)** On the international market, wheat is considered a Canadian specialty. Identify three other goods that are considered Canadian specialties. Research one of these goods in more detail.
3. a) How does proximity encourage international trade?	**b)** Windsor, Ontario, benefits from being close to Detroit, Michigan. Name three other border cities across Canada that benefit from being close to large American cities. In what ways do the Canadian and American cities benefit?	**c)** Some complex products, such as cars, are assembled partly in Canada and partly in another country. Find a Canadian business that makes its products this way. Research this business on the Internet or interview a company representative to find out how the production process works and why the company produces the product in this way. Report your findings to the class.

Canada's Trade Partners

In some ways, international trade is like collecting trading cards. You can use whatever you have in abundance to trade for whatever you need. The only difference is that countries don't usually trade goods directly. Instead, they buy and sell goods for money, as you read in Chapter 5.

Canada has trade partners all over the world, and Canadian companies continue to seek out new partners all the time. However, without a doubt, Canada's number one trade partner is the United States. Goods and services produced in one country and sold to another are called **exports**. **Imports** are goods and services produced in one country and brought into another country for sale.

Figure 18.1

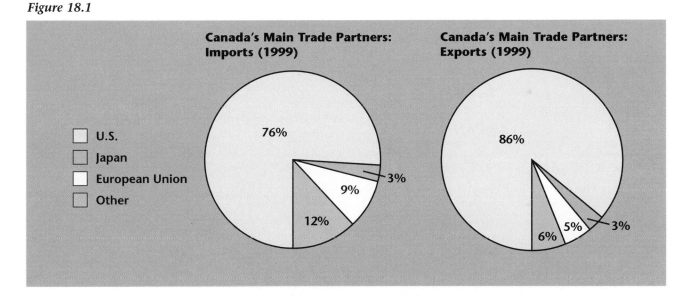

Canada's Main Trade Partners: Imports (1999)

- ☐ U.S.
- ☐ Japan
- ☐ European Union
- ☐ Other

76%
3%
9%
12%

Canada's Main Trade Partners: Exports (1999)

86%
6%
5%
3%

There are a number of reasons why it makes sense for Canadians to develop a solid trade relationship with their nearest neighbour. First, shipping costs are cheaper for nearby destinations. Second, Canadians and Americans share many of the same interests, so the same products and services will likely appeal to both groups. Canadians and Americans speak the same language, watch the same television programs, line up to see the same movies, and enjoy the same sports. Many people from both countries travel back and forth across the border regularly for business trips and vacations. Third, the U.S. population is 10 times greater than the Canadian population. As a result, Canadian businesses can sell their products and services to a much larger market. A Canadian product that is successful in both Canada and the U.S. will likely be far more profitable for its manufacturer than one sold only in Canada.

TEAM CANADA MISSIONS

One way in which Canadians have been able to establish new trade relationships is by participating in trade missions called Team Canada missions. Canadian businesspeople and government representatives on the team visit other countries to let them know what goods and services Canada has to offer. The government representatives meet with politicians in the countries they visit. Together, they try to find ways to adjust laws and regulations to make it easier for people to engage in trade. The businesspeople meet with their foreign counterparts and try to establish links that will allow them to sell goods and services to one another. Table 18.1 shows some of the highlights of various Team Canada trade missions.

Table 18.1 Team Canada Missions

Team Canada Missions (To February 2001)	Total Value of Trade Deals (Made During/ After Mission)	Related Facts
November 1994: Mission to China	$12.9 billion	China's expected economic growth is likely to lead to a significant increase in the value of trade deals made with Canada.
January 1996: Mission to India, Pakistan, Indonesia, and Malaysia	$11.2 billion	$2.5 billion came from business deals made after the mission.
January 1997: Mission to Korea, the Philippines, and Thailand	$2.1 billion	Business delegates represented 414 different companies.
January 1998: Mission to Mexico, Brazil, Argentina, and Chile	$1.8 billion	This mission signed more individual deals than any other Team Canada mission cited here.
September 1999: Mission to Japan	$3.4 billion	This Team Canada delegation included 50 women entrepreneurs, 29 young entrepreneurs, and 4 Aboriginal businesspeople.
February 2001: Mission to Beijing, Shanghai, and Hong Kong	$5.7 billion	Close to 600 business participants, 8 premiers, and 3 territorial leaders participated in this mission.

Keith Peiris

Keith Peiris, an entrepreneur from London, Ontario, participated in the Team Canada mission to Beijing, Shanghai, and Hong Kong in February 2001. Despite his young age—he was only 12 years old when the mission took place—Keith is already an accomplished businessperson. He is the founder and president of Cyberteks Design, a Web design firm that he operates out of his parents' basement.

ABSOLUTE AND COMPARATIVE ADVANTAGES

Canada trades with another country only if it enjoys an absolute or comparative advantage in producing a good or service. Enjoying an **absolute advantage** means that the good or service can be produced only in Canada, or that Canada can produce it at a better price than anyone else. Countries must either trade with Canada to get the product, pay the higher cost of buying it elsewhere, or make it themselves. For example, imagine that labour is the only resource required to manufacture a product. If Canada can produce 15 TVs using five workers, and the U.S. can manufacture the same amount of TVs with 10 workers, Canada has an absolute advantage—it can produce TVs using fewer resources (and therefore at a lower cost) than the U.S.

Now, let's imagine that, in Canada, it takes eight workers to produce 15 DVD players; in the U.S., it takes 10 workers to manufacture 15 DVD players. Canada, therefore, produces both TVs and DVD players more efficiently that the U.S. But because Canada can produce TVs more efficiently than it can produce DVD players, it has a **comparative advantage** in producing TVs. If Canada chose to specialize in the production of one product based on comparative advantage, it would use all its resources to manufacture TVs.

When Canadian businesses make plans to sell their products internationally, they need to consider both the absolute and comparative advantages they can offer to potential buyers. Since absolute advantages don't exist for every business, comparative advantages can be very important factors in planning and decision making.

ACTIVITIES FOR ...

INFORMATION	CONNECTION	EXTENSION
1. a) List some reasons why Canada's number one trade partner is the U.S. Who are Canada's other main trade partners?	**b)** Interview someone who works in a manufacturing industry in your community to find out what local goods are exported to the U.S.	**c)** Because the U.S. is so large and so close to Canada, it exerts a considerable influence on Canadian interests. Create a collage or multimedia presentation to show how American music, movies, television, magazines, and Web sites influence your life.
2. a) What is Team Canada? What was the total amount raised by Team Canada missions from 1994 to 2001?	**b)** Research Team Canada on the Internet to find out about any Team Canada missions that took place after February 2001 or about other Canada trade missions. Summarize information about the composition of the team or the results of the mission.	**c)** You have been selected to take part in a Team Canada mission to a South American country. Do some research about Canadian business and about business in the South American country. What will you say to representatives about how your two countries can help one another through trade? Make rough notes and then give the speech you will make to political and business leaders in that country.
3. a) Explain the difference between an absolute and a comparative advantage.	**b)** Would one country prefer to have an absolute advantage or a comparative advantage in a trading relationship with another country? Explain.	**c)** Choose one of these countries: Taiwan, Mexico, India, or Brazil. Conduct research to find out what absolute or comparative advantages Canada enjoys in its trade relationship with this country.

Flow of Goods and Services

Wherever international trading occurs, there are actually two streams flowing between countries. One is the flow of goods and services, and the other is the flow of funds used to pay for the goods and services. This chapter will examine the factors that have a direct impact on the flow of goods and services. The flow of funds will be dealt with in Chapter 20.

Goods and services flow into Canada as imports, and they flow out as exports. The imports coming into Canada could be raw materials, processed materials, semifinished goods, or manufactured products that are ready for sale. The less finished the imports are, the more jobs they create for Canadians. For example, an auto manufacturer might import windshields, tires, transmissions, and other parts that will be used to assemble vehicles at a Canadian plant. This situation provides jobs for workers at the assembly plant, but it doesn't provide as many jobs as there would be if the vehicles were assembled from scratch. Even if the vehicles were manufactured overseas and imported in a finished state, there might still be jobs for Canadians in design, engineering, administrative, marketing, or sales positions.

Exports also provide jobs for Canadians. In fact, more than 43% of all goods and services produced in Canada are exported, providing an estimated 11 000 jobs in Canada for every $1 billion in exports. Although the Canadian labour force benefits from importing goods that are less finished, the opposite is true for exports. The more finished a product is when it leaves Canada, the more jobs it provides for Canadian workers.

The types of goods that are imported and exported by Canadians fit into several categories. Statistics for Canadian imports and exports in 1999 are shown in Figure 18.2.

BUSINESS —FACT—

One-third of all jobs in Canada are tied to exports.

Figure 18.2

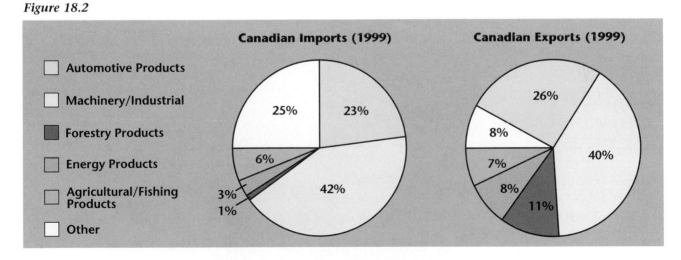

Legend:
- Automotive Products
- Machinery/Industrial
- Forestry Products
- Energy Products
- Agricultural/Fishing Products
- Other

Canadian Imports (1999)
25%, 23%, 6%, 3%, 1%, 42%

Canadian Exports (1999)
26%, 8%, 7%, 8%, 11%, 40%

BALANCE OF TRADE

Countries try to maintain a balance of trade between the value of the products they import and the value of the products they export. A **balance of trade** is the relationship between a country's total imports and total exports. If the country pays more for imports than it earns from exports, there is a **trade deficit**. If the country earns more from exports than it pays for imports, there is a **trade surplus**.

Figure 18.3

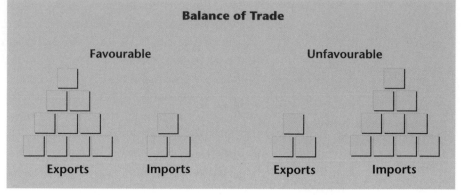

Governments usually try to reduce a high trade deficit because it means that money is flowing out of the country and fewer jobs are being provided. On the other hand, trade surpluses are beneficial to a country's economy, especially if the surplus is made up primarily of manufactured goods. Exporting manufactured goods means that many workers are required in the production process. In 1999, Canada had an overall trade surplus of about $34 billion. This surplus was the direct result of a $60 billion trade surplus with the U.S. that helped balance the $26 billion trade deficit that resulted from all other international trading.

Figure 18.4

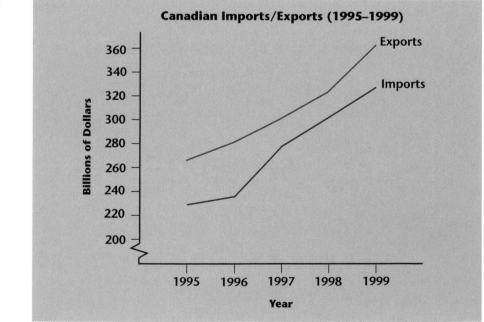

Trade Snapshot

In October 2000, Canada exported $30.5 billion of goods and services to the U.S., and imported $22.4 billion of goods and services from the U.S. When exports exceed imports, more money flows into Canada from trade than flows out. This situation places Canada in a favourable trade balance with the United States. However, during the same month, total exports to other destinations totalled approximately $4.6 billion. Total imports from those countries totalled about $8.1 billion. Luckily, the $8.1 billion trade surplus that resulted from U.S. trade was more than enough to balance the $3.5 billion loss on other international trade.

IMPORTS

A business that wants to starts importing goods for sale in Canada needs to know that there are five main ways to offset the risks involved in the import business:

- Before you fill your warehouse with imported goods, take the time to measure consumer interest in what you plan to sell. If no one is interested in buying your goods, you will find yourself with large bills to pay to your suppliers and no way to pay them.
- Choose foreign suppliers with care. You not only need to find a supplier who can provide the right goods, you need to find one who can supply them at the right price and at the right time. Government agencies such as the Department of Foreign Affairs and International Trade (DFAIT) can help you find the best possible foreign suppliers for your business.
- Make an effort to learn about the culture you will be dealing with. Cultural sensitivity can help you establish a positive relationship with your suppliers, while cultural clashes can quickly break a deal. (Chapter 20 will deal with specific cultural concerns for importers.)
- Give careful thought to the purchase agreement before you sign it. Many specifics have to be worked out when the two parties involved in a transaction are thousands of kilometres apart. Ask questions. Who pays the shipping costs? When do the goods have to be paid for? What happens if the goods are damaged during shipping? Then, make sure to word the agreement to purchase so that it covers every possible eventuality.
- When the goods arrive, check them to make sure that everything you ordered is there and in good condition. You will likely need to pay import or customs duties that are based either on the value of the goods or on other factors, such as quantity or weight. (Customs duties were discussed in Chapter 5, and will be further discussed later in this chapter.)

BUSINESS —FACT—

Vancouver and Montreal are Canada's two largest seaport cities, shipping and receiving approximately 90 million tonnes of cargo each year.

EXPORTS

The idea to export a good or service can come either from the company that produces it or from buyers in a foreign market who wish to purchase it. With **direct exporting**, the exporter deals directly with the importer and does not use an intermediary. With **indirect exporting**, goods move from the exporter to an intermediary, and then on to the importer.

Usually, established companies export directly. These businesses often have the resources to set up offices and sales staff in a foreign country, or to send a sales representative to the international market. On the other hand, many new companies use indirect exporting because they don't have the resources to establish themselves abroad. They hire an intermediary who may be more familiar with regulations and restrictions than they are. The intermediary will handle all the paperwork and may help collect money. Direct exporting can be risky; with indirect exporting, the intermediary assumes some of the risk. In certain cases, even large, established businesses use indirect exporting since some countries, including those in the Middle East, Central America, and Asia, prohibit direct exporting—probably to create jobs for local intermediaries.

Offsetting Risks

Exporters can offset risks by careful planning. If you plan to export a product to a foreign market, start by conducting market research to make sure there are consumers in the market who will buy your goods. Ask the Department of Foreign Affairs and International Trade to help you locate potential customers. You may also find it helpful to use the Internet to contact agencies such as the Asia Pacific Foundation of Canada, the Alliance of Manufacturers and Exporters of Canada, and the Canadian Association of Importers and Exporters.

Canadian embassies are also good sources of advice, and can help you get to know your potential customers. According to embassy staff, foreign clients often ask the following kinds of questions to find out about potential exporters of goods or services:

- What is unique or special about your company, product, or service? How do you market and sell your products?
- Who uses your product or service? To whom do you sell in Canada and abroad?
- Which countries or regional markets are you targeting, and why? What do you know about these markets?
- How do you plan to enter the market? Will you sell the products directly? license people to sell your products? set up a joint venture with another business? invest in a venture that already serves the market?

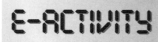

E-ACTIVITY

Visit
www.business.
nelson.com
and follow the links
to find sites
designed to guide
exporters as they
seek out markets
and potential
customers. Which of
these sites do you
think exporters
would find most
useful? Explain your
reasoning.

- How would you describe the typical buyer, distributor, agent, or partner you want to work with in this market?
- When do you plan to visit the market? How will you adapt your product-related literature to suit the needs of this market?

FACTORS AFFECTING THE FLOW OF GOODS AND SERVICES

The flow of goods and services from one country to another is driven by two forces—the need and ability of consumers to buy a product, and the ease or difficulty of moving the product to the market. Factors to consider include consumer needs and incomes, currency values, transportation costs, and government rules and regulations.

Consumer Needs and Incomes

In Chapter 1, you learned about the role business plays in getting goods and services to the consumers who need them. Figure 18.2 illustrates some types of goods that are imported or exported by Canada to meet consumer demands at home and around the world.

The amount of money that consumers have to spend has a direct impact on the flow of goods and services in a country. In some parts of the world, people have a significant amount of discretionary income to spend, while in other places, most people's disposable income barely covers—or doesn't even cover—basic needs. If a business determines how much disposable and discretionary income customers have, and how this money is usually spent, the business can make sure that it has the right goods for its market.

Currency Values

Most nations have their own banking systems and their own currency. For example, Brazil uses the real, Japan uses the yen, and Mexico uses the peso. Currency exchanges take place on the foreign exchange market. This market consists of banks and financial institutions that buy and sell different currencies. The value of one country's currency compared to another's is called the **exchange rate**.

The exchange rate is affected by supply and demand. In other words, exchange rates depend on how many banks and other financial institutions want to buy the currency of a particular country. If these institutions think that the value of a country's currency is rising because of favourable economic

What currencies can you identify in this picture?

conditions, that currency will be in high demand. If they perceive the value to be falling—because of political upheaval or an unfavourable economic situation, for example—then fewer institutions will want to buy the currency and the exchange rate will fall. Many different economic conditions influence the currency exchange rate, including a country's inflation rate, productivity level, and employment level.

The business sections of many newspapers publish the exchange rates for foreign currencies. Exchange rates are also available from banks and other institutions. An exchange rate tells you how many units of foreign currency it would take to match the value of one Canadian dollar. For example, if the value of U.S. $1 is Cdn. $1.50, then a Canadian company that wants to import American goods has to find out the price in U.S. dollars and multiply by 1.5 to determine the price in Canadian dollars. Therefore, to import a product that costs U.S. $5.00, a Canadian business would have to pay Cdn. $7.50. On the other hand, if a Canadian company plans to export goods to the U.S., it needs to divide the Canadian price by 1.5 to find out how many U.S. dollars the buyer has to pay. If the price of the product is Cdn. $5.00, the buyer would have to pay U.S. $3.33.

Transportation Costs

Just like an importer, an exporter needs to know how products will be transported and who will pay the shipping costs. Airfreight costs more than water or land transportation, but it is also much quicker. Perishable products and goods in high demand usually need to be transported by air.

E-ACTIVITY

Take a look at the business section of a newspaper or visit www.business.nelson.com and follow the links to compare the value of the Canadian dollar with the value of other currencies.

Why do you think that timber is transported by boat?

Transportation decisions are very important because unexpected transportation expenses can make the selling price of the goods too high to be competitive. In the agreement to purchase, the importer and exporter state who pays for the shipping costs.

Sometimes, the importer and exporter share the shipping costs. At other times, the importer pays for transportation costs beyond an agreed-upon point. For example, if a shipment of goods from Canada to Mexico is designated "**Free on Board (FOB)**," the importer has to pay the cost of transporting the goods from the shipping point to Mexico. The importer can then recoup the transportation costs by building them into the selling price of the goods. On the other hand, if the exporter plans to pay the cost of shipping the goods all the way to Mexico, the shipment is labelled "**Cost, Insurance, and Freight (CIF)**." Any shipment designated CIF is paid for by the exporter. The exporter factors in this added cost when deciding how much to charge for the goods.

Rules and Regulations

Did You Know?
To find out about the regulations that apply to a specific trade situation, contact the Canada Customs and Revenue Agency.

The governments of different countries have very different rules about what can be imported or exported, and in what quantities. Before any transactions are finalized, it's important for both the exporter and the importer to become familiar with any rules and regulations that may apply.

When a business decides to import or export goods, it has to complete a number of documents. A **bill of lading** records the agreement between the exporter and the transportation company, and serves as a receipt for the exported goods. A **certificate of origin** states the name of the country in which the shipped goods were produced. Customs officials may use this certificate, along with customs documents, to determine the amounts of any import taxes or customs duties that must be paid when the goods arrive at their destination. When the importer pays for the goods, the exporter needs to provide a receipt for the transaction. Since the rules and regulations regarding imports and exports can sometimes be quite complex because they involve the laws of at least two countries, businesses often seek professional advice from a trade expert, a more experienced businessperson, or Canadian embassy staff in the country where the goods will be received.

CAREER FOCUS 5: SUCCEEDING ON THE JOB

STEPS TO SUCCESS

You've been hired for the job you applied for. Now you want to do the job well and make a good impression on your employer and coworkers. First of all, remember that attitude counts—be positive and look at your job as an opportunity to learn. Here are some tips that can help you in your new position:

- Arrive on time (or early) and leave at the end of the day. If you occasionally arrive late because of factors you can't control, such as bad weather or a traffic accident, apologize for your lateness and explain what happened. If you occasionally need to leave early, for example, for a doctor's appointment, remember to ask permission in advance.

- Follow the company rules. Don't take extra-long lunch or coffee breaks even if you see others behaving irresponsibly.

- Dress neatly and appropriately. Employers often find that a sloppy appearance results in sloppy or careless work habits.

- Be friendly to the people you work with. Positive relationships will help you avoid problems on the job, and your coworkers will be more willing to help you learn new skills if you treat them in a friendly way. However, your friendships should never interfere with your work.

- Ask questions and learn from the people you work with. If you don't understand someone's directions, ask for a clearer explanation and listen carefully. Never pretend to understand if you really don't.

- Don't take on extra work or responsibilities to impress your boss unless you're sure you have enough time to do the work.

- Don't complain about your workload. If you think you have too much work to do, talk to a fellow employee before seeing your supervisor—make sure that what you think is "too much" is actually more than average for this particular company.

- Do your work well and on time since others depend on you. Take pride in your work and always try to do your best.

- Be adaptable. Because technology is changing people's jobs so quickly, being open to new opportunities is one of the most important characteristics you'll need to succeed on the job.

GETTING ALONG WITH OTHERS

As a new employee, you will find that most of your coworkers will be very helpful and cooperative, especially during your first few weeks on the job. They will want to get to know you, to see what you can do, and to see you succeed.

Maintaining self-confidence is important. If you don't feel that you can rely on yourself, then you'll have a hard time convincing others to rely on you. Remember that mistakes are natural and expected as you're learning to do a new job. When mistakes happen, don't let it shake your confidence. Try to learn from what happened and avoid repeating the same error.

Confident people are not afraid to learn new things. Listen carefully to your supervisor and follow his or her directions to the letter. Making sure that your work is done on time and consistently doing a high-quality job will help you develop strong, positive relationships with your supervisor and with your coworkers.

In addition to being friendly and self-confident, there are many other ways to gain the respect of the people you work with:

- Return telephone calls and e-mails promptly.
- Help others whenever you can.
- Remember to give and accept thanks graciously. It's very simple to say "Thank you," and it has a positive effect on both the giver and the receiver.
- Look ahead to the future, considering possibilities for advancement with your current employer or even a change in job. Remember that you may be working with some of your current coworkers for a long time—you can help each other develop and grow.

WHEN IT'S TIME TO MOVE ON

As you learned in the second Career Focus, on pages 100–101, you may have as many as seven or more jobs during your working life. Sooner or later, you are likely to leave your job for a different one. Leaving on good terms is important. Receiving a good recommendation from your employer will help, as will having positive relationships with others who may know people at your new workplace—or who may even end up working there themselves someday. Here are some suggestions that will help you make a smooth transition to a new job:

- Give at least two weeks' notice that you're planning to leave. Write a short, polite letter of resignation that includes the last day you will be working at your current job. Try to make some positive comments about the job you're leaving and explain why you've decided to move on.

- Try hard to complete all the work that you've been given to do before you leave. If it's really impossible to finish, leave a note to let your replacement know what still has to be done and where to begin.

- If possible, ask your supervisor for a letter of reference for your records. This letter may come in handy in a future job search and will provide helpful information about your work experience.

- Thank your coworkers and say goodbye. Let them know how much you appreciated their assistance and friendship.

Something to Think About

1. In the first Career Focus, on pages 14–15, you made a list of your academic, personal management, and teamwork skills. Which skills are your strongest? Which ones will help you do well as you begin a new job?

2. Meet with a small group to discuss some actions a new employee could take to build a positive working relationship with coworkers.

3. Read the following three statements:
   - "A job is more than just a way to pay the bills."
   - "In the future, people's jobs will be very different from what they are today."
   - "At work, you should do what you love to do; you should be able to follow your dreams."

   What ideas and images do these statements bring to mind? Respond to one of the statements by creating a poster, collage, or another type of visual presentation.

Coworkers help a new employee adjust to a new position and workplace.

INFORMATION	**C**ONNECTION	**E**XTENSION
1. a) Explain how imports and exports create jobs.	**b)** Using Figure 18.2, tell what you notice when you compare the imports and exports for 1999.	**c)** Figure 18.2 shows that forestry products represented about 1% of Canada's total imports in 1999. Since Canada's imports for that year totalled about $327 billion, Canadians spent over $3 billion on imported forestry products. Why might a country with such vast forest reserves import forestry products from another country?
2. a) Explain the difference between a trade deficit and a trade surplus.	**b)** Use Figure 18.4 to estimate Canada's balance of trade position for each year from 1995 through 1999. Why is it good for Canada that the line for exports is consistently higher than the line for imports?	**c)** Use information from an almanac or from the Statistics Canada Web site to answer the following questions: What were the total values of Canada's imports from and exports to the U.S. last year? For all of last year, did Canada have a trade deficit or a trade surplus with the U.S.?
3. a) What do the designations "FOB" and "CIF" mean?	**b)** Contact a business in your community that has international business dealings. Interview the manager to find the answers to as many questions on pages 448–449 as possible.	**c)** Visit the Web site of the Canadian Department of Foreign Affairs and International Trade. Make a list of ways in which the department can help a new exporter find markets in other countries.

Barriers to International Business

As you read earlier in this chapter, when foreign competitors enter the market, domestic businesses sometimes suffer. As a result, most countries
- impose controls on the types and amounts of goods and services that they are prepared to import
- prohibit the importation of certain goods
- impose customs duties
- establish tariff and non-tariff barriers
- establish embargoes
- impose excise taxes

A country may also restrict trade with another country or prohibit certain goods from entering its borders for political or cultural reasons.

PROHIBITED AND RESTRICTED GOODS

Some countries prohibit the entry of certain goods. For example, goods prohibited in Canada include narcotics, certain weapons, and certain secondhand automobiles and aircraft. Print materials that have been ruled obscene or that promote hatred or treason may also be stopped at the border.

The government allows some goods to enter the country only if they have been inspected, are accompanied by a valid permit, or having special packaging and labelling.

Table 18.2 Imported Goods That Require Permits, Inspection, or Special Packaging and Labelling

Imported Goods	Government Department
Endangered animals and plants and products made from them	Environment Canada
Agricultural and food products	Agriculture and Agri-food Canada
Fish and fish products	Fisheries and Oceans Canada
Non-food products and clothing, precious metals, and radio communications equipment	Industry Canada
Food, drugs, medicines, pharmaceuticals, medical and radiation-emitting devices	Health Canada
Hazardous waste, goods that may contain chlorofluorocarbons or leaded gas	Environment Canada
Motor vehicles	Transport Canada

In some cases, countries allow only specified quantities or dollar values of goods—known as **quotas**—to be imported or exported. Countries set quotas for various reasons. For example, countries that export oil may put quotas on crude oil so that the supply remains low and prices stay at a certain level. As you learned in Chapter 5, OPEC member countries set limits on the amount of oil they produce and export. These quotas help them control the petroleum market. At other times, a country may impose quotas on imports from another country to protect its own manufacturers of a particular product or to express disapproval of the policies of that country.

CUSTOMS DUTIES

Countries that import items charge customs duties on these goods. **Customs duties** usually represent a percent of the value or cost of the product. The list or schedule that tells what percent will be charged for different types of a similar item is called a **tariff**. The tariff rates vary according to a number of conditions. For example, a rate of 6.3% might be charged for fabric that is used to make a toy kite, but the rate for fabric used to make a woman's blouse might be 12.5%. The duty for the fabric for the blouse is higher because the Canadian clothing manufacturing industry is more protected than the Canadian toy manufacturing industry. If Canada imports cheaper clothing to compete with Canadian-made clothing, people may buy the cheaper items and the Canadian companies will suffer. To pay the duty, the producers will need to charge more for the imported clothes, giving Canadian companies an advantage.

Customs duties also vary according to where the imported materials are from. If Canada has a good trading relationship with one country and wants to encourage more trade, it lowers its duty rates on goods imported from that country. Canada's customs tariff has varying duty charges for different countries of origin, ranging from the Most-Favoured-Nation Tariff (the lowest duty rates) to the General Tariff (the highest duty rates). There is a special tariff for items imported from the United States. These items fall under the terms of trade agreements that will be discussed in more detail in Chapter 19.

E-ACTIVITY

Visit
www.business.
nelson.com
and follow the links
to find out more
about customs
duties. Why do you
think tariff rates
change so often?

TARIFF AND NON-TARIFF BARRIERS

Each country sets its own rules for dealing with imports. These rules are generally in place to protect domestic industry. **Tariff barriers** are often the subject of international negotiations, such as those conducted during the Team Canada missions. Tariff barriers are gradually being reduced as countries forge trade agreements. Here are a few examples of tariff barriers:

• Canada restricts imports of certain agricultural products, such as dairy products, poultry, eggs, and wheat.

• The **European Union**, an organization of 15 European countries that have combined into a single market, protects its biotechnology products and its aircraft industry. (See Chapter 19 for more information about the European Union.)

STRETCH YOUR THINKING

Find out how one of these tariff barriers protects industries in the given country.

- Japan protects its telecommunications and high-tech sectors.
- Korea protects its pharmaceutical industries, intellectual property, and steel production.
- Until very recently, China restricted imports of meat, poultry, wheat, and citrus products.

Tariffs are not the only barriers countries can use to protect domestic industry. **Non-tariff barriers** set standards for the quality of imported goods so high that it becomes difficult for foreign competitors to enter the market. For example, if Canada set very high standards for safety and emission controls on imported automobiles, few existing vehicles would meet the standards. Foreign competitors would either have to withdraw from the market or spend a lot of money to engineer better vehicles. A country can also impose non-tariff barriers by requiring an international business to apply for a licence to sell goods in its market. If the licence is expensive, foreign businesses will be discouraged from exporting goods. Finally, non-tariff barriers can also be imposed at the border, where goods have to pass a customs inspection in order to enter the country.

EMBARGOES

When a government wants to completely stop the import or export of a particular type of product, it imposes an **embargo.** There are many reasons why a government might impose an embargo, including

- protecting a new industry until the labour force is trained, the production process is functioning, and costs are in line so that it can remain competitive when foreign goods are imported
- protecting Canadian workers from losing their jobs to a less expensive overseas work force
- retaliating against countries that have imposed similar trade restrictions
- preventing countries from dumping goods in Canada. **Dumping** means increasing a good's market share in a country by selling the good for less than the cost of producing it.
- preventing Canadian firms from exporting products that might pose a threat to Canada's defence

EXCISE TAXES

An **excise tax** is a tax on the manufacture, sale, or consumption of a product within a country. It often represents a percentage of the dollar value of an item. For example, Canada charges an excise tax of 10% on jewellery, including diamonds and other precious stones. In other cases, the excise tax depends on the quantity or mass of an item.

Currently, for example, Canada charges an excise tax on the mass of a passenger automobile that exceeds 2007 kg.

The government mainly uses excise taxes to raise money. However, it may apply an excise tax to some products (for example, tobacco) to discourage people from engaging in a certain activity (smoking). With other products, such as imported wine and petroleum products, the government imposes excise taxes to increase the cost of these imported goods to encourage consumers to buy Canadian products.

ACTIVITIES FOR ...

INFORMATION	CONNECTION	EXTENSION
1. a) Identify six ways for a country to control its international trade.	**b)** If the tariff on fabric for making toy kites is 6.3% and the tariff on fabric for manufacturing blouses is 12.5%, how much would be owed in tariffs on a shipment of kite fabric worth $5500 and a shipment of blouse fabric worth $12 500?	**c)** Choose two items from Table 18.2. Find out about permits, inspection requirements, or special packaging and labelling of these products.
2. a) What is a quota? Why do countries set quotas?	**b)** In the past, Canada set import quotas on eggs, ice cream, and yogurt. What other types of products might Canada set quotas for? Why?	**c)** What are the current excise tax rates for tobacco and petroleum products? Use the Canada Customs and Revenue Agency Web site to assist you in your research.
3. a) Why might one country impose an embargo on another?	**b)** Suppose Country A imposed an embargo on food imports from Country B. Describe some of the possible consequences of this embargo for both countries.	**c)** Do some research to find out about a time when one country imposed an embargo on another. Why was the embargo imposed? What effects did the embargo have on both countries? Was the embargo lifted? If so, what changes in circumstances led to the lifting of the embargo?

Review

Knowledge and Understanding

1. Match each of the following terms to the correct definition:

   balance of trade   imports
   domestic transaction   international transaction
   exchange rate   non-tariff barriers
   exports   trade surplus

   a) A transaction in which both the production and sale of an item take place in the same country.
   b) The relationship between a country's total imports and total exports.
   c) Goods and services produced in one country and sold to another country.
   d) A situation in which a country's exports exceed its imports.
   e) The value of one country's currency as compared with the value of another's.
   f) A method other than customs duties that can be used to control the flow of imported goods into a country.
   g) A business transaction that is made across national borders.
   h) Goods and services produced in one country and brought into another country for sale.

2. Describe advantages and disadvantages of doing business internationally.

3. What factors affect the flow of goods and services between countries?

4. If a business plans to enter a foreign market, why would it be helpful to gather information about the discretionary incomes of potential customers?

Thinking and Inquiry

1. Make a poster that compares domestic business with international business. Show examples of each.

2. Find an international business story in the business section of a newspaper or on the Internet. Prepare a short written or oral summary of the information in this article.

3. List three reasons why Canada would want to maintain good trade relationships with foreign countries.

4. Canada has an abundance of raw materials that are greatly needed by some other countries. How could this fact be both an advantage and a disadvantage for Canada in its trading relationship with those markets?

5. If a country has a trade deficit, what actions could it take to improve its balance of trade?

Communication

1. In recent years, the Canadian textile, automobile, and electronics industries have felt the negative impact of international competition. Work in groups of three. Each group member finds out what has happened to one of these industries in Canada. Share your findings with the rest of your group.

2. Form two groups. Conduct research and hold a class debate on this issue: "Canada is working toward freer trade, not totally free trade."

Application

1. Select three products you use that are produced in Canada. Search for information on the Internet that will help you determine whether these products are sold internationally and, if so, whether they are changed or repackaged for other markets. Write and illustrate a report to present your findings.

2. Invite an expert or panel of experts to speak with your class about the impact of international business on your community. Possible guests include your MP or MPP, someone from the economic development department of your local government, or a representative from the chamber of commerce. Prepare questions in advance for your guest(s) to answer.

3. If the Canadian government put stiffer controls on imports, it could increase the number of jobs for Canadians. Describe the advantages and disadvantages of this strategy. Then, interview a businessperson in your community to get his or her opinion. Present your conclusions to the class in an oral report.

REFLECT ON YOUR LEARNING

1. What is the impact of international business on your life? Discuss your ideas with a partner.

2. What advice would you give Canadian manufacturers who are considering exporting their goods to help them minimize their financial risk?

CHAPTER 19

INTERNATIONAL TRADE AGREEMENTS AND TRADING PARTNERS

STUDENT EXPECTATIONS

After completing this chapter, you will be able to

- describe the advantages of reducing trade barriers
- analyze the effects of trade agreements and pacts on the flow of goods and services among nations
- analyze the impact of trade on the Canadian economy
- summarize the key points of several international trade agreements
- identify Canada's major trading partners
- identify the main goods and services that Canada's major trading partners import from and export to Canada
- describe the future of trading blocs

Profile

AFS technicians test the emissions produced by an engine equipped with the Eagle II fuel-management system.

AFS Clears the Air

For anyone living in a major urban centre, smog has become an unfortunate fact of life. People are asked to car pool, use public transit, or ride their bikes to work—all to cut down on emissions produced by the millions of gas- and diesel-burning vehicles that crowd city streets. Calgary-based Alternative Fuel Systems Inc. (AFS) is one Canadian high-tech company that is trying to help reduce emissions. AFS has developed technology that converts gas and diesel engines to engines that run on natural gas. Natural gas is an attractive alternative to other types of fuel because it is cleaner and, in many places, cheaper.

AFS's Eagle II fuel-management system is a computerized device that can be installed in new vehicles or fitted into old ones. The Eagle II allows a diesel engine to run on a combination of diesel and natural gas, which dramatically reduces harmful emissions. Most trucks and heavy vehicles use diesel engines because they are efficient, durable, and powerful. The Eagle II system keeps these strengths while addressing diesel's main weakness: heavy emissions. AFS's other major fuel system is called the Sparrow. This system converts gasoline engines to engines that use 100% natural gas. According to AFS, its fuel-conversion technology can be adapted to all sorts of vehicles.

As governments everywhere set tougher emissions standards to reduce air pollution, transportation authorities all over the world have begun to take notice of AFS. Free trade agreements have helped make deals between AFS and other countries a reality. For example, the 1994 North American Free Trade Agreement (NAFTA) has removed many trade barriers between Canada, the U.S., and Mexico, and has reduced import duties, allowing companies in these countries to do business with one another at a much lower cost.

AFS's ongoing project in Mexico City, the world's largest city in terms of population, is a prime example of how Canadian companies have benefited from NAFTA. Over the next 10 years, Mexico City will use AFS technology to convert more than 100 000 buses and taxis from gasoline to natural gas. Because of NAFTA, AFS was able to put in a competitive bid for the project, and had an advantage over companies from other countries that still face trade barriers.

The 1997 Canada–Chile Free Trade Agreement (CCFTA) also opened up trade opportunities for AFS. AFS is currently participating in a project in Santiago (the capital of Chile), converting some of its public transportation vehicles to natural gas. AFS's other export markets span the globe—from China to India to England. These projects have created jobs for Canadians. For example, AFS predicts that its Mexican project will create between 400 and 500 jobs in Canada.

As countries sign more and more international trade agreements and as AFS's technology continues to develop, it is likely that AFS's international business will expand. One day, in your travels, you may even find yourself riding in a bus or taxi equipped with AFS technology.

Free trade agreements have helped make deals between AFS and other countries a reality.

About This Profile
1. What trade agreements are mentioned in this profile? Explain how these agreements have benefited AFS.
2. Briefly describe the AFS Eagle II and Sparrow systems. How do these systems help decrease pollution?
3. Which country do you think benefits most from AFS's project in Mexico City—Mexico or Canada? Explain your answer.
4. Find out about other opportunities that have opened up for Canadian businesses as a result of the Canada–Chile Free Trade Agreement.

Canada and International Trade Agreements

BEFORE YOU BEGIN

Trade barriers protect domestic businesses such as AFS from foreign competition, but they can also make it more difficult for these businesses to sell their products abroad. Why?

In Chapter 18, you learned that countries often set up trade barriers, such as customs duties, quotas, and embargoes, to protect domestic businesses. Since World War II, many countries have taken part in negotiations to reduce or eliminate some of these barriers.

There are two main advantages to reducing trade barriers. The first is that domestic businesses are able to sell their products and services abroad at lower prices since customs duties are not added to the cost of domestic businesses' exports. If revenues from foreign sales are greater than the costs of shipping and marketing the product abroad, profits increase and businesses grow. The second advantage is that consumers have access to new products, and existing products must improve their quality or reduce their prices in order to compete.

Countries must come to a **trade agreement** in order to reduce trade barriers. If the countries are just beginning a trade relationship, this agreement usually deals mainly with importing and exporting products. The agreement states which tariffs each country will drop or reduce, and may include a process for resolving disputes. Over time, trade agreements grow to include much more.

In today's economy, trade in services is just as important as trade in goods. Trade agreements, therefore, need to include answers to questions such as when and why people will be permitted to work across international borders, what qualifications they will need, what standards will be applied to their work, and how people's ideas (intellectual property) will be protected.

Figure 19.1

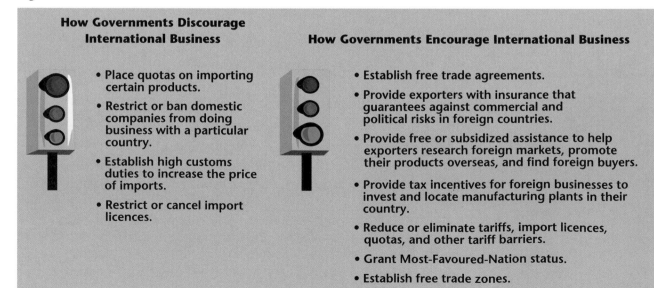

How Governments Discourage International Business

- Place quotas on importing certain products.
- Restrict or ban domestic companies from doing business with a particular country.
- Establish high customs duties to increase the price of imports.
- Restrict or cancel import licences.

How Governments Encourage International Business

- Establish free trade agreements.
- Provide exporters with insurance that guarantees against commercial and political risks in foreign countries.
- Provide free or subsidized assistance to help exporters research foreign markets, promote their products overseas, and find foreign buyers.
- Provide tax incentives for foreign businesses to invest and locate manufacturing plants in their country.
- Reduce or eliminate tariffs, import licences, quotas, and other tariff barriers.
- Grant Most-Favoured-Nation status.
- Establish free trade zones.

The Beginnings of the World Trade Organization

A very important international trade agreement called the **General Agreement on Tariffs and Trade (GATT)** came into effect in 1948. Countries that had been allies during World War II saw that it would be helpful to agree on rules that would help them strengthen their trade relationships. Canada and 22 other nations, including the U.S., signed this agreement. As a result, an international organization was set up to help the GATT member nations negotiate trade deals, resolve problems, and collect data about world trade.

Although GATT was originally intended to last only three years, it continued for nearly 50 years and grew to include 115 member states. During its lifetime, GATT was revised many times. The most important revisions occurred in Uruguay, between 1986 and 1994. At this time, the agreement was extended to include services and intellectual property as well as goods. In 1995, the **World Trade Organization (WTO)** was established to replace the earlier GATT administration. With 140 member countries, the WTO is the principal international organization that deals with the rules of trade between nations.

One important WTO agreement is the **General Agreement on Trade in Services (GATS)**. The GATS, which came into effect in 1995, sets guidelines for the trade of services, such as banking, across international borders.

E-ACTIVITY

Visit
www.business.
nelson.com
and follow the links
to learn more about
the World Trade
Organization.

The Auto Pact

The GATT rules initially required member countries to treat every other country that signed the agreement in the same way—giving everyone the same tariff privileges as they give their closest partners. In the agreement, a country's closest partners were called its **Most Favoured Nations (MFN)**.

As you read in Chapter 18, Canada's closest trading partner is its nearest neighbour, the United States. In 1965, Canada and the U.S. were permitted to become an exception to the GATT rules when they entered into the Canada–U.S. Automotive Products Agreement (usually called the **auto pact**). The auto pact dropped trade barriers between Canada and the U.S., allowing North American automobile and automobile-parts manufacturers to sell their products freely in both countries. The pact was a very important agreement because automotive vehicles and parts represent a major part of the trade between Canada and the U.S. With the auto pact, automobile production became more efficient as Canadian and U.S. production facilities were able to specialize in producing specific vehicles and parts. As a result, vehicle prices dropped. The auto pact also helped Canada turn its automotive trade deficit with the U.S. into a trade surplus. The auto pact ended in 2001 when the WTO intervened to defend the interests of automobile manufacturers, such as Toyota and Honda, not originally included in the deal.

THE NORTH AMERICAN FREE TRADE AGREEMENT

By 1986, Canada and the U.S. were ready to negotiate a free trade agreement. The agreement was intended to gradually phase out a number of tariff barriers that existed between the two countries. Canada hoped that the agreement would give Canadian businesses stable access to U.S. markets, clarify the rules about government assistance to industry, make it possible for Canadian companies to bid on U.S. government contracts, and allow Canada an equal say in the settlement of disputes. The U.S. wanted to expand previous agreements to include services and intellectual property (the revisions to GATT had not yet been made), to reduce government restrictions on American investment in Canadian industries, and to increase U.S. exports.

Then Mexican president Carlos Salinas (rear left), American president George Bush (rear middle), and Canadian prime minister Brian Mulroney (rear right) attend the signing of NAFTA along with trade representatives from each member country.

The free trade deal was an important election issue in Canada in the fall of 1988. It was supported by Brian Mulroney and the federal Conservative party. The Conservatives were elected, and the **Canada–U.S. Free Trade Agreement (FTA)** came into effect in January 1989. Soon afterward, the U.S. announced a similar agreement with Mexico, and Canada asked to be included in the negotiations. The **North American Free Trade Agreement (NAFTA)**, which came into effect in 1994, joined all three countries in a continent-wide free trade zone.

Under FTA and NAFTA, tariffs on many goods flowing between Canada and the U.S have been phased out. However, certain products are excluded from the agreement. These include dairy products and poultry in Canada, and sugar, dairy products, peanuts, and cotton in the U.S.

One important feature of NAFTA is that it applies only to goods and services produced within the borders of the three member countries. Therefore, products are duty free only if they are made in and imported from the U.S., Mexico, or Canada. If a Canadian company manufactures shoes in Brazil and exports them to the U.S., duties will apply because the shoes were not made inside the free trade zone. Conversely, if a Brazilian company manufactures shoes in Canada and then exports them to the U.S., the shoes will be duty free because they were made in Canada.

Since NAFTA, trade and investment among Canada, the U.S., and Mexico have increased by hundreds of billions of dollars, and free trade negotiations have continued to expand. Leaders from North, Central, and South America are currently negotiating a **Free Trade Area of the Americas (FTAA)** agreement, which would extend NAFTA to include all the democratic countries in the western hemisphere. Negotiators hope that the FTAA will be adopted in 2005.

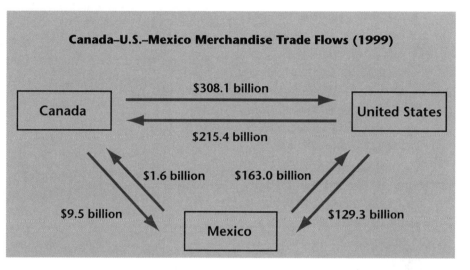

Figure 19.2

Canada–U.S.–Mexico Merchandise Trade Flows (1999)

Canada → United States: $308.1 billion
United States → Canada: $215.4 billion
Mexico → Canada: $1.6 billion
Canada → Mexico: $9.5 billion
United States → Mexico: $163.0 billion
Mexico → United States: $129.3 billion

NAFTA's Impact on Canada

In April 1999, the trade ministers of Canada, the U.S., and Mexico released "Five Years of Achievement," a joint statement on the impact of NAFTA. Much of the information focused on trade data covering the period from January 1, 1994, when NAFTA came into effect, to January 1, 1999. The following were some of the benefits of NAFTA:
- Canada's merchandise trade with the U.S. increased by 80%.
- Canada's merchandise trade with Mexico doubled.
- Canadian exports to the U.S. and Mexico increased by 80% and 65% respectively.
- More than one million jobs were created in Canada.
- Canada was particularly successful in exporting automotive equipment (trucks, cars, and parts), machinery and parts, and industrial goods.

Along with the benefits, NAFTA has had some disadvantages for Canadians. For instance, many critics of NAFTA worry that the agreement gives the U.S. and Mexico too much access to Canada's natural resources, such as minerals and timber, and that these resources will gradually be depleted. As well, Canadians are concerned about the Americanization of their cultural industries, including book and magazine publishing and television broadcasting.

NAFTA's Impact on the U.S.

Economically, the U.S. is the most powerful country in the world today, and has the largest number of internationally recognized businesses based within its borders. The U.S. is a highly industrialized nation. It exports mainly finished products such as food, consumer goods, vehicles, and machinery. It imports oil, chemicals, metals, and other types of machinery.

NAFTA has brought both advantages and disadvantages to the U.S:
- U.S. exports to NAFTA countries have risen more than 67%.
- More than 650 000 new jobs have been created as a result of the trade deal. On the other hand, more than 200 000 Americans have signed up for benefits offered to workers whose jobs disappeared as a direct result of NAFTA.
- Before NAFTA, the U.S. had a trade surplus of U.S. $1.7 billion with Mexico. Since the trade agreement was signed, U.S. imports from Mexico have increased by more than U.S. exports to Mexico. The trade surplus has been transformed into a deficit of U.S. $11.5 billion.
- When NAFTA came into effect, the U.S. already had a trade deficit with Canada. Since the agreement, this deficit has increased substantially.

The effects of NAFTA have been particularly noticeable in the U.S. agricultural and manufacturing sectors. Agricultural exports have increased, but at the same time, producers face growing competition from lower-priced products from Mexico. There are also concerns about the safety of Mexican farm products because Mexico has different environmental standards for dealing with problems such as pesticide use and pollution.

The jobs that have been lost as a result of NAFTA are mainly in the manufacturing sector. Many of these jobs were lost when companies closed their production facilities in the U.S. and opened new facilities in Mexico, where production and labour costs are lower.

NAFTA's Impact on Mexico

One of Mexico's major industries is agricultural production. In addition to exporting a wide variety of fruit and vegetables, Mexico also exports crude oil, metal products, and minerals. Machinery and equipment are Mexico's largest import items, along with iron, steel, textile products, and consumer goods such as food, beverages, and tobacco.

BUSINESS —FACT—

Between 1994, when NAFTA came into effect, and 1999, employment grew by 10.1% (1.3 million jobs) in Canada, by 22% (2.2 million jobs) in Mexico, and by more than 7% (12.8 million jobs) in the U.S.

As with Canada and the U.S., Mexico has enjoyed some benefits from free trade, and has also experienced some problems.

- Expanding markets in the U.S. and Canada have resulted in a sharp increase in Mexican exports. Overall, trade with the U.S. and Canada has nearly doubled since the agreement came into effect. One NAFTA-related success story has been the rapid growth of Mexico's automotive industry. Exports of Mexican-made cars and trucks doubled during the first three years of the trade agreement, and continue to increase each year. However, this growth hasn't been matched by overall financial gains. Soon after NAFTA came into effect, the Mexican currency, the peso, dropped sharply in value. This drop led to a recession and financial problems for Mexican businesses.

- A number of industries from Canada and the U.S. have relocated to Mexico or expanded their Mexican operations. These moves have created new jobs in Mexico, but many of the jobs are low paying. There have also been some environmental problems as a result of factory crowding along the border between the U.S. and Mexico.

A man loads his purchases into the trunk of his car after shopping at Wal-Mart in Mexico City, one of the largest Wal-Mart stores in the world.

- Large U.S. retailers, such as Wal-Mart and Sears, have expanded into Mexico, buying products from Mexican businesses and selling these products in stores across North America. These new retailers in Mexico make it possible for Mexicans to buy a broader range of products at lower prices than was possible before the trade deal came into effect.

OTHER FREE TRADE AGREEMENTS

NAFTA is only one free trade agreement that Canada has with countries around the world. Some of Canada's trade agreements are **regional** (involving groups of countries), while others are **bilateral** (involving Canada and one other country or group).

NAFTA and FTAA are examples of regional agreements. Canada is also a partner in two other regional trade organizations—the Canada–European Free Trade Association (EFTA) and the Asia–Pacific Economic Cooperation (APEC).

In addition, Canada currently has bilateral free trade agreements with Chile and Israel, and is negotiating others with Costa Rica and a trading bloc made up of four Central American countries—Guatemala, El Salvador, Honduras, and Nicaragua. (A **trading bloc** is a group of countries that share the same trade interests.)

The Canada–European Free Trade Association

The **European Free Trade Association (EFTA)** was established in 1960. It currently includes the countries of Norway, Switzerland, Iceland, and Liechtenstein. Canada's trade agreement with EFTA is less comprehensive than NAFTA. It focuses mainly on industrial goods such as aircraft and aircraft parts; natural resources such as gold, nickel, zinc, magnesium, and crude oil; and fisheries products. The countries in the Canada–European Free Trade Association also offer one another reduced barriers on imported agricultural products.

The Asia–Pacific Economic Cooperation

Canada is one of the founding members of the **Asia–Pacific Economic Cooperation (APEC)**. APEC was created in 1989 to help develop the Asia–Pacific economy and to establish a sense of community among the member countries. One of APEC's main goals is to remove all trade barriers within member economies by 2010.

APEC is a unique organization that allows many countries from different regions and trading blocs to come together to facilitate international trade. The original 12 APEC members were Australia, Brunei, Canada, Indonesia, Japan, South Korea, Malaysia, New Zealand, the Republic of the Philippines, Singapore, Thailand, and the United States. In 1991, China, Taiwan, and Hong Kong joined. Mexico and Papua New Guinea joined in 1993; Chile joined in 1994; and Peru, Russia, and Vietnam joined in 1998. Today, APEC continues to grow, with many other countries negotiating membership.

ACTIVITIES FOR ...

Information	Connection	Extension
1. a) What kind of information is included in trade agreements? Why are these agreements important?	**b)** Why do you think that adding services and intellectual property to the original GATT agreement was so significant?	**c)** Do you think that it was fair for GATT to make an exception for Canada and the U.S. so that they could sign the auto pact? Explain.
2. a) Write out the formal names of FTA and NAFTA. When were these agreements signed? What countries were involved?	**b)** Using information from the chapter, create a table to show the advantages and disadvantages of NAFTA for each of the member nations.	**c)** In your opinion, does NAFTA benefit you as a Canadian citizen? Why or why not? Use the Internet or the library to find information that supports your opinion.
3. a) What are the Canada–European Free Trade Association and the Asia–Pacific Economic Cooperation?	**b)** Besides Canada and the U.S., all the original APEC members were from Asian–Pacific countries. Why do you think that Canada and the U.S. wanted to be part of APEC?	**c)** Find out about other free trade agreements that Canada has signed or is currently negotiating. How do you think these agreements will benefit the countries involved?

Canada and the European Market

French explorer Samuel de Champlain.

Canada's relationship with Europe has a long history that is based on trade and economics. Europeans were looking for a sea route to trade with Asia when they landed in Canada. They explored rivers and mountain passes to make trading with the Aboriginal peoples easier. In 1604, Samuel de Champlain established the first permanent European settlement in Canada at Port Royal, in what is now Nova Scotia. In 1670, England's king gave a trading charter to a group of wealthy businesspeople. This charter granted them exclusive rights to trade on all lands draining into Hudson Bay. The group established the Hudson's Bay Company and began to set up trading posts.

As trade grew, so did the need for support services such as shops, farms, banks, and railways. Thousands of people left Europe and looked for opportunities in the New World. From the 1600s until the mid-1960s, the vast majority of immigrants to Canada were European, providing a strong connection with Europe. Today, Europeans still account for almost 20% of all immigrants to Canada.

Once, Great Britain and Europe were Canada's closest trading partners. Then, as roads and railways were built, it became easier to ship goods between Canada and the U.S. Over time, Canada's trade relationship with the U.S. grew closer, while trade with Europe diminished. Canada still maintains close relationships with countries in Europe, and especially with those in the European Union.

THE EUROPEAN UNION

The first step toward a European Union was taken in 1950, when French foreign minister Robert Schuman invited several countries to join together to regulate their coal and steel industries. West Germany, France, Belgium, Italy, Luxembourg, and the Netherlands formed the **European Coal and Steel Community (ECSC)** in 1952. These countries started to look for other ways to cooperate economically. In 1957, the **European Economic Community (EEC)** was established by treaty as a trade agreement between all the ECSC members. Informally, this community of nations became known as the **Common Market**.

The main goal of the EEC was to eliminate trade barriers among member nations over a 12-year period, and to develop a common tariff for imports from elsewhere in the world. The member countries also considered ways to improve their agricultural management and formed the European Atomic Energy Community (Euratom) to explore peacetime uses of nuclear energy.

Meanwhile, another trade association was forming among countries that did not belong to the EEC. In 1960, the United Kingdom (U.K.) and six other countries joined to create the **European Free Trade Association (EFTA)**.

Beginning in 1973, the EFTA and EEC negotiated a series of agreements to ensure uniformity between the two organizations in many areas of economic policy. With the ratification of the **Maastricht Treaty** in 1993, the EEC became the **European Union (EU)**. The treaty united the member states into a truly single market, not simply an area of free trade.

All the EU countries have adopted the euro, except for the U.K., Sweden, and Denmark, which each kept their own currency.

The Maastricht Treaty provided for the free movement of goods and services among member countries; once a product entered any EU country, it could enter all of them. The treaty also set uniform technical standards for items such as electrical devices, and removed financial and investment barriers for member countries. Finally, it established a single currency, the **euro**, for all member nations. In fact, the creation of the euro has been the most controversial aspect of the Maastricht Treaty.

Table 19.1 Member States of the European Union (2001)

Original Members (1993)	Joined after 1993
Belgium	Austria (1995)
Denmark	Finland (1995)
France	Sweden (1995)
Germany	
Greece	
Ireland	
Italy	
Luxembourg	
Netherlands	
Portugal	
Spain	
United Kingdom	

CANADA AND THE EUROPEAN UNION

In 1996, Canada and the EU entered into an agreement called the Joint Canada–EU Action Plan. This plan acknowledges the historical and cultural ties between Canada and Europe, and sets guidelines for cooperation in areas such as foreign trade, foreign policy, and international security.

The Action Plan states that "Canada and the EU are important economic partners who share a common outlook and philosophy with regard to international trade and commerce." Trade issues dealt with in the plan include

- reducing trade barriers, especially for government purchases
- working through the World Trade Organization to negotiate environmental policies and to promote trade and investment
- working toward an international agreement about trade in information technology
- resolving trade disputes
- reviewing market access to financial service industries
- simplifying customs procedures
- consulting on issues involving energy trade, threats to the environment related to energy, and energy technology

United Kingdom as a Trading Partner

The U.K. has closer historical ties to Canada than does any other country in the EU. Canada was a founding member of the **Commonwealth of Nations**—an international association of the U.K. and many countries that were formerly part of the British Empire. For many years, Canada's Commonwealth membership gave it Most-Favoured-Nation trade status with Britain, and Britain has traditionally been very supportive of Canadian business interests in Europe. Because Canada's legal system is based on English common law, the British understand Canada's legal system and business practices more than other European countries do.

The United Kingdom is made up of four countries: England, Scotland, Northern Ireland, and Wales. In 1999, Canada exported almost $5 billion worth of products to the U.K. Of these exports, more than 25% were in the area of machinery and electrical devices and parts. Other Canadian exports to the U.K. include aircraft parts, nickel, minerals, paper, and wood. In return, Canada imported more than $8 billion worth of products in 1999, including machinery, vehicles, medical instruments, pharmaceutical products, and chemicals.

Canadian Subsidiaries in the U.K.

A **subsidiary company** is a company that is controlled and owned by another company, called a **parent company**. Since EU countries pay lower duty rates than other countries when they export goods to other EU members, some Canadian businesses have established subsidiary companies in Britain to take advantage of lower tariffs.

Germany as a Trading Partner

Germany is Europe's largest market and Canada's fifth-largest trading partner. In 1999, Canada exported products worth about $2.4 billion to Germany, while imports from Germany were valued at about $7 billion. Exports to Germany included machinery and electrical products, wood pulp, passenger vehicles, minerals, and pharmaceuticals. Canada imported machinery and electrical products, passenger vehicles, medical instruments, and iron and steel goods from Germany.

Like Canada, Germany is a leader in the area of high technology. In fact, Germans register more patents per year than citizens in any other country. At the same time, Germany faces problems with high unemployment and high labour costs—both factors that discourage foreign companies from investing in German-based operations.

Canada and Germany have a close relationship and share similar concerns about trade policy and international security. In 1996, Germany played an important role in finalizing the Canada–EU Action Plan. Since then, Canada and Germany have cooperated on a number of initiatives, especially in the area of defence.

France is known for its fashion industry. It exports clothing by top fashion designers, such as Chanel, to countries around the world.

France as a Trading Partner

Like Canada and the U.K., Canada and France have strong economic, linguistic, historical, and cultural links. Because Canada—Quebec in particular—has close connections to France, Canadian businesses can often count on France's support for entry into European markets.

France is now Canada's sixth largest economic partner. In 1999, Canadian exports to France totalled nearly $2 billion, while imports from France totalled more than $5 billion. Products such as aircraft parts and machinery travelled both ways across the Atlantic. Other Canadian exports included telecommunications equipment, wood pulp, metal ores, and seafood. Other Canadian imports from France were beverages, metals, and pharmaceutical products.

THE GROUP OF EIGHT

The **Group of Eight (G8)**, formerly known as the Group of Seven (G7), is an association of the world's most powerful industrialized democracies. Unlike other trading blocs, G8 countries are not located close together. Instead, countries from different parts of the world work together in the global economy. The original G7 consisted of four members from the European Union (Britain, France, Germany, and Italy), two from North America (Canada and the U.S.), and one from the Asia–Pacific region (Japan). The eighth member is Russia, which joined in 1998 and caused the group's name to change from G7 to G8.

Since 1975, the leaders of these countries have met at annual summits to deal with major economic and political issues facing their own countries and the broader international community. Topics dealt with at the summits include energy, employment, the environment, human rights, and arms control. G8 summits set new priorities and directions, and define new issues for the international community. In this way, the G8 provides guidance and support to established international organizations.

STRETCH YOUR THINKING

Are global trading blocs such as the G8 likely to be the wave of the future? Why or why not?

ACTIVITIES FOR ...

INFORMATION	**C**ONNECTION	**E**XTENSION
1. a) What is the European Union? Describe how it was founded.	**b)** Explain why each of the four goals of the Maastricht Treaty, listed on page 472, is important.	**c)** In your opinion, why has the adoption of the euro been so controversial?
2. a) Identify one product or service that is imported by each EU country discussed in detail in this section, and one product or service that is exported.	**b)** Choose a product that is manufactured in Canada. Suppose you have been hired to market the product to the U.K., France, or Germany. Because of costs, you can select only one of these markets. Which country will you choose? Explain your choice.	**c)** The European Union has a great need for raw materials, and Canada has abundant natural resources to export. How could this situation place Canada at an advantage in its trading relationship with the EU?

Canada and the Asia–Pacific Market

The **Asia–Pacific market** is an area that includes all nations (other than the former Soviet Union) on the continents of Asia and Australia that have a Pacific Ocean shoreline. It includes countries as large as the People's Republic of China and as small as Brunei. The area is home to 60% of the world's population. As immigration to Canada from this region has increased, Canada has begun to develop a closer relationship with Asia–Pacific markets. After the U.S., Japan is Canada's most important trading partner.

The Asia–Pacific market is a major global economic force. Its greatest resource is labour. After World War II, the people in many Asian nations worked very hard for low wages to rebuild their war-shattered economies. As the manufacturing sector grew stronger, technological advances took place. In the 1980s and 1990s, the region became a driving force in the global economy. Today, three of the top five countries in the world in terms of gross domestic product are in the Asia–Pacific region. These countries are China, Japan, and India.

ASSOCIATION OF SOUTHEAST ASIAN NATIONS

In 1967, five Southeast Asian countries—Indonesia, Malaysia, the Republic of the Philippines, Singapore, and Thailand—formed the **Association of Southeast Asian Nations (ASEAN)**. ASEAN is an association of developing and industrialized nations. Its purpose is to promote political and economic cooperation among developing, non-communist nations in Southeast Asia. (Communist countries have centrally planned economies, with governments that make all economic and business decisions.) These nations have some of the world's largest reserves of natural resources, such as rubber, palm oil, tin, copper, timber, oil, and natural gas. ASEAN helped these nations develop their resources and export markets. Today, ASEAN has grown to a membership of 10 nations. In addition to its original members, it now includes Brunei, Cambodia, Laos, Myanmar (formerly Burma), and Vietnam. In terms of trade, Canada exports vegetable products, pulp and paper, and chemicals to ASEAN countries, and imports machinery, electrical appliances, textiles, apparel, and plastics.

A man on a plantation in Sumatra, Indonesia taps a rubber tree for its milky sap.

For many years, ASEAN members have enjoyed very successful global trade. Recently, however, ASEAN members have become concerned that trade associations such as NAFTA and the EU may shift Canadian and U.S. trade away from them and toward other countries. The ASEAN industries most at risk are businesses involved in textiles, footwear, and machinery exports. In an effort to improve economic security, ASEAN countries formed the **ASEAN Free Trade Area (AFTA)** in 1993. The AFTA agreement stipulates that tariffs on most manufacturers' imports within ASEAN countries will be reduced to 0%–5% by 2002.

The Organization for Economic Cooperation and Development

Formed in 1961, the **Organization for Economic Cooperation and Development (OECD)** brings together 30 countries that share the principles of a market economy, democracy, and respect for human rights. The founding nations of the OECD, including Canada, were all countries in Europe and North America. The OECD developed from the Organization for European Economic Cooperation (OEEC), which was formed to help rebuild Europe after World War II. Since then, the group has expanded to include Asia–Pacific members such as Japan, Australia, New Zealand, and South Korea. The OECD links countries together to help one another by conducting economic research and coordinating efforts to promote global trade and development. The main goals of the OECD are to help its member countries build strong economies, improve efficiency and market systems, expand free trade, and contribute to development in both industrialized and developing countries.

CHINA AS A TRADING PARTNER

China, or the People's Republic of China, is the largest single market in the world, with a population of more than 1.25 billion people and

a GDP of more than $4.25 trillion (second only to the U.S.). Since 1949, China has been a communist country. As a result, business dealings must be conducted with government officials. In 1978, however, China adopted an open-door policy that created new opportunities for trade and business with other countries. Canada played a key role in this development, and greatly increased its trade and investment with China.

China's economy is rapidly expanding, partly as a result of heavy foreign investment. Much of this investment comes from Chinese businesspeople who live in other parts of Asia, North America, and Europe. The economic boom has raised incomes and improved the standard of

Based on its recent growth patterns, by 2020, China could economically out-distance not only the rest of the Asia–Pacific market, but the rest of the world.

living in several regions of China. However, the overall impact is limited, and it is estimated that only 12% of people working in the major cities earn an income of more than $300 a month.

Canada's trade relationship with China began in 1960, when the two countries negotiated an agreement that allowed Canada to sell wheat to China. In 1973, China and Canada agreed to give each other Most-Favoured-Nation status in their trade exchanges and lowered tariffs to encourage trade between the two countries. In 1999, China was Canada's fourth largest export market. Exports to China were valued at more than $2.5 billion, while imports from China were worth nearly $9 billion. Canada's main exports to China include wood pulp, agricultural products, fertilizers, and machinery. Canadian imports from China include machinery, toys, sports equipment, footwear, and clothing.

JAPAN AS A TRADING PARTNER

Japan is one of the world's most highly developed nations, with a GDP that is exceeded only by those of the U.S. and China. Japan is particularly strong in manufacturing: its businesses produce and export motor vehicles, electronic devices, and household appliances around the globe. Japanese brand names such as Sony, Toyota, Panasonic, Honda, and Nintendo are well known in many countries, including Canada.

Because Japan has limited natural resources, Japanese businesses must import raw materials. For example, Japan imports iron ore from Australia and crude oil from the Middle East. Japanese manufacturing businesses then process these raw materials to make finished products for export.

In 1999, Canada exported more than $8 billion worth of goods to Japan, and imported more than $15 billion. Canada, then, had a negative trade balance with Japan. The bulk of Canada's export sales to Japan are raw or semiprocessed goods: coal, forest products, fish, uranium, and canola oil. Other exports include auto parts, aerospace equipment, computer equipment, and medical supplies.

In general, Japan exports more than it imports, giving the country a trade surplus. Japan uses much of this surplus to invest in other countries. For example, Japanese-affiliated companies in the U.S. now account for 9% of the total value of American exports and employ more than half a million Americans. In Canada, Japanese businesses such as Toyota, Honda, Suzuki, and Panasonic all have affiliated manufacturing facilities. Joint Japanese–Canadian ventures have also been initiated in areas such as oil and gas, pulp and paper, and coal mining.

TAIWAN AS A TRADING PARTNER

Taiwan is an island nation of more than 22 million people, located just off the coast of China. Its free market economy has grown steadily over the years, relying mostly on small- and medium-sized businesses as well as a few large government-owned banks and industrial firms. Today, many state-owned businesses in Taiwan are being privatized. Taiwan is moving away from traditional labour-intensive industries to more capital- and technology-intensive industries. Taiwan is a major investor in China, Thailand, Indonesia, the Philippines, Malaysia, and Vietnam.

In 1999, Taiwan's trade surplus was close to $20 billion. Its main export partners were the U.S., Hong Kong, and Europe, while its main import partners included Japan, the U.S., and Europe. Even though Canada is not one of Taiwan's main trading partners, it did import more than $4.5 billion worth of products from Taiwan during 1999— mostly machinery and electrical devices. The same year, Canada's exports to Taiwan were worth about $1.1 billion and included wood pulp, electrical machinery, chemicals, and oil.

Taiwanese businesses are interested in setting up subsidiary plants and investing in joint ventures in Canada. These kinds of undertakings will give Taiwan a link to Canada and greater access to the entire NAFTA market. Major industries in Taiwan that could expand into Canada include electronics, chemical production, and textiles.

South Korea as a Trading Partner

South Korea has achieved tremendous economic growth over the past 40 years, even with few natural resources and a tense political situation. In 1945, near the end of World War II, Korea was split into two countries, North Korea and South Korea (also called the Republic of Korea). North Korea became a communist state while South Korea became a free enterprise economy. In 1950, war erupted between North and South Korea. Many other nations, including Canada, were drawn into the conflict. Although a truce was signed in 1953, the conflict between North and South Korea has never really been resolved.

South Korea's major resource is its people. With a population of more than 47 million, South Korea has a highly skilled and hardworking labour force. South Korea's top three trading partners are the U.S., Japan, and China. In 1999, Canada exported about $2 billion worth of products to South Korea, including wood pulp, oil, organic chemicals, and machinery. That same year, Canada imported about $3.6 billion worth of products, mainly electrical machinery and vehicles, including automobiles produced by Hyundai and Kia.

In the future, there will be growing opportunities for Canadian businesses in South Korea. South Korea needs knowledge and information to further develop its high-technology sector, and Canada can offer expertise in the fields of aerospace, telecommunications, advanced agricultural technology, and defence.

Even though North Korea and South Korea have been on the verge of war a number of times since their truce was signed, they literally joined hands to carry one flag during the Olympic Summer Games in Sydney, Australia, in September 2000.

Sheep crowd a corral at a sheep farm in New Zealand.

AUSTRALIA AND NEW ZEALAND AS TRADING PARTNERS

Australia and New Zealand are very different from many of their neighbours in the Asian–Pacific region. Both Australia and New Zealand are advanced and developed nations, but their economic activities are largely land-based. Both countries have small populations. For example, Australia's geographical area is only slightly smaller than that of the U.S., yet its population is only about 19 million (compared to more than 281 million people in the U.S.).

Australia is a major exporter of agricultural products, minerals, and fossil fuels. New Zealand, with 3.8 million people, exports dairy products, meat, fish, wool, and forestry products. Both New Zealand and Australia are moving from a resource-based economy toward a more industrialized economy that can compete globally.

Canada's trade with Australia and New Zealand amounted to about $1.5 billion in exports in 1999, and about the same amount in imports. Canada's exports to these countries are mainly machinery, wood, vehicles, aircraft parts, fertilizers, meat, and wheat. Canadian imports from Australia and New Zealand include meat and dairy products (from New Zealand) and chemicals and metals (from Australia).

Australia and New Zealand have negotiated trade agreements and associations with one another. The **Closer Economic Relations Trade Agreement (CER)** came into effect in 1983. Its central provision is the creation of a free trade agreement between the two countries. Since then, all tariffs and restrictions on trade in goods have been eliminated between Australia and New Zealand. In October 2000, representatives of CER and the ASEAN Free Trade Area (AFTA) met to begin negotiations to help trade and investment flow between the two regions.

Contemporary Issues in Canadian Business

THE ISSUE: FREE TRADE

Why does Canada engage in free trade?

Earlier in this chapter, you learned that free trade agreements help Canadian businesses buy and sell products and services across international borders by reducing or eliminating trade barriers such as duties and quotas. When trade barriers decrease or disappear, the cost of doing business goes down, as do prices. Without the added expense of having to pay tariffs, a business in Canada that is exporting its products can compete on an equal basis with a similar business in another country.

However, when Canada engages in free trade, it also means that domestic businesses face more competition from abroad. So why does Canada engage in free trade? First, since Canadian businesses can't possibly provide all the goods and services that consumers will buy, free trade makes it easier to import the products and services that Canadians want and need. Free trade also gives Canadian businesses access to larger markets, in the hope that increased sales will more than offset any losses a company might experience because of foreign competition.

It isn't as easy as you might think to establish a free trade zone. It took five years of tough negotiating between Canada, the U.S., and Mexico before the North American Free Trade Agreement (NAFTA) came into effect in 1994. The implementation process has taken even longer.

Some say that freer trade in North America is an important objective for Canadians, while others say that Canada would be better off focusing on building relationships with a wide range of countries, even where trade barriers are still in place. Here are some reasons why someone might take each position.

Point

Free trade has been good for Canadian businesses. The NAFTA market—Canada, the U.S., and Mexico— has a population base of 370 million people. Although long-distance shipping costs are greater, the potential for increased sales has made it very worthwhile for Canadian businesses to sell their products across North America.

Free trade has also been good for consumers. To compete with less expensive imports, Canadian businesses have improved their products and services by, for example, offering higher-quality goods, extended warranties, and excellent after-sale service. Free trade also benefits Canada in other ways:

- New jobs are created when foreign companies choose to locate operations in Canada.
- Canadians have access to a wider range of products and pay lower prices for imports.
- The expanded market created by free trade gives Canadian businesses the opportunity to specialize in particular types of a product, for example, certain types of wheat, vehicles, or telecommunications equipment. In a smaller market, there may not have been sufficient demand to make production of the product profitable; however, the demand may exist in a larger market.

Counterpoint

Those who believe that free trade always works to Canada's advantage are wrong. NAFTA encourages Canada to depend too heavily on the U.S. and Mexico for its economic well-being. This close dependence on only two trading partners means increased risk for Canadians.

In 1994, Mexico devalued the peso by 40%. Immediately, the price of imports from Canada shot up to compensate for the difference in the exchange rate. Sales of Canadian products dropped radically.

Imagine what would happen if the U.S., which represents the market for 85% of Canada's total exports, experienced a financial crisis. Canada would immediately face a crisis of its own. To reduce this risk, Canada needs to globalize its exports, spreading its economic dependence over a broad range of countries.

Free trade has other disadvantages as well. For instance, NAFTA encourages Canadian businesses to set up manufacturing and assembly plants in countries where labour costs are lower. This could result in problems such as

- a loss of jobs in Canada
- a trade deficit, caused by exporting inexpensive raw materials and importing finished products
- air and water pollution (the result of increased operations in countries with lower environmental standards)

Because of these and other problems, free trade is not the best way for Canada to protect its economic future. Instead, Canadians should focus on building a strong domestic market and spreading Canada's reliance on foreign markets more broadly around the world.

E-ACTIVITY

Visit
www.business. nelson.com
and follow the links to learn more about free trade issues.

A Real Life Example

Prince Edward Island's Testori Americas Corporation started selling its aircraft and related components south of the border—mainly through Bombardier—just before NAFTA came into effect in 1994. Testori president Lindo Lapegna recalls the difficulties of doing business with the U.S. back then, and how NAFTA opened doors for the Summerside-based company. "Transportation and border logistics were real headaches," Lapegna says. "NAFTA has brought these issues within our control, so they no longer inhibit our ability to compete. It's basically made a level playing field of North America, where contracts are won or lost strictly on the basis of efficiency and cost effectiveness. The ones at a disadvantage now on American turf are our European competitors. As a Canadian company, we have the upper hand."

Lapegna says NAFTA has paid off—both for the

company and for Prince Edward Islanders. The agreement has created scores of new jobs. Over the past five years, Testori has become 80% export-based—primarily to the U.S.—and its staff has soared from 12 to 68 employees.

Questions and Activities About This Issue

1. Do you think that NAFTA's advantages outweigh its disadvantages for businesses? Why or why not?
2. Trade barriers exist between provinces and/or territories, as well as between countries. The Canadian Agreement on Internal Trade (AIT) took effect in July 1995. It was designed to encourage freer movement of goods, services, and people between provinces and/or territories. Find out more about this agreement. What trade barriers still exist? Why are they in place?

Building a Global Economy

In this chapter, you learned that trade blocs have become more globally oriented as nations organize themselves to enhance good trading relationships. You've read about some major trade agreements, but many others exist in the world and many more are being negotiated. These agreements and associations do not come about without controversy. They have, and always will have, critics. Some nations argue that markets have become so open that they are difficult to control. Others believe that freer trade is necessary in order for businesses to grow.

WHAT DOES THE FUTURE HOLD?

During the first decade of the 21st century, the fastest growing trade group in the world will be the Asia–Pacific market. Countries in this region already form the largest trading bloc in the world. Like all trading blocs, ASEAN is **protectionist** by nature, meaning that it protects its own members' economic interests by imposing tariffs or quotas on imports from other countries. However, experts agree that continued economic prosperity requires that individual trading blocs lower their barriers and begin a period of global cooperation.

In December 2000, European Union members met in Nice, France, and proposed a new treaty. Under the terms of the Nice Treaty, EU membership could grow to as many as 28 countries by 2010, bringing the population of the EU from the current 370 million to more than 500 million.

In North America, NAFTA seems likely to evolve in a similar way, gradually drawing more and more countries into the agreement. Cooperation with Central and South American countries in a Free Trade Area of the Americas (FTAA) agreement could make it easier for Canada and its current NAFTA partners to compete with the ever-expanding European Union and with the rapid economic growth in the Asia–Pacific region.

Like the EU, NAFTA or its FTAA successor could gradually evolve from a trade bloc into a single market. Such a change would mean that Canadians could move freely into the U.S. and Mexico. It would also mean that U.S. and Mexican workers could compete with Canadian workers for jobs in Canada. Perhaps a North American Union could even mean a single currency, similar to the euro. Whatever the future holds, it's clear that trade agreements are going to be an important force in shaping Canada's economy, and the economy of the world.

STRETCH YOUR THINKING

Find out what countries are being considered for membership in the EU. What economic strengths does each country have?

ACTIVITIES FOR ...

INFORMATION	**C**ONNECTION	**E**XTENSION
1. a) What countries are included in the Asia–Pacific market? What products does Canada export to and import from countries in this market?	**b)** Identify one product or service associated with each Japanese brand name mentioned on page 478.	**c)** Do you agree with the economists who predict that the 21st century is going to be the Asia–Pacific century? Support your opinion with facts and figures.
2. a) What does the acronym ASEAN stand for? What countries make up ASEAN?	**b)** Conduct some research about one natural resource belonging to an ASEAN member. How is this resource harvested? How much is produced each year? What is it used for domestically? Where and how is it used abroad?	**c)** Find out more about the OECD. How is this organization similar to and different from other organizations you've read about in this chapter?
3. a) How are trading blocs changing?	**b)** Do you think that the change you described in Question 3a is positive or negative? Explain.	**c)** In groups of three, role-play a television interview on the topic of free trade. One person role-plays a critic of free trade; the second person role-plays a supporter of free trade; and the third person role-plays the television interviewer. Present your role-play to the class, either "live" or on videotape.

Review

Knowledge and Understanding

1. Match each of the following terms to the correct definition:

AFTA   Maastricht Treaty
APEC   NAFTA
EU   trading bloc
euro   WTO
G8

   a) An economic union of 15 independent European states.
   b) A group of countries that share the same trade interests.
   c) An area of free trade that was formed by ASEAN countries.

d) An agreement among Canada, the U.S., and Mexico that came into effect on January 1, 1994, joining the countries into a free trade zone.

e) The name of the single common currency for the European Union.

f) The principal international group that deals with the rules of trade between nations.

g) An organization created in 1989 to help develop the Asia–Pacific economy and to establish a sense of community among the member countries.

h) An association of the world's most powerful industrialized democracies, representing different trading blocs.

i) An agreement, signed in 1993, that created the European Union, joining 12 countries into a truly single market, not just an area of free trade.

2. In a small group, make a four-column chart that summarizes the trade agreements and associations that you learned about in this chapter. Label the first column "Abbreviation of Agreement/ Association," the second column "Full Name," the third column "Effective Date," and the fourth column "Key Points."

Thinking and Inquiry

1. Why do international trade agreements usually include some type of protectionism, for example, regulations that protect intellectual property and natural resources?

2. Look at home or in stores to find products from at least five countries mentioned in this chapter. In a table, identify each product, show its country of origin, and give a reason why you think the product was imported to Canada instead of being produced domestically.

3. Use the Statistics Canada Web site to obtain the most recent data on Canada's major trading partners in terms of exports and imports. Group your findings under the headings "NAFTA," "EU," and "AFTA" partners. Present your findings graphically, and calculate the balance of trade with each group.

4. Trading blocs offer advantages to importers and exporters, but they also offer disadvantages. Identify one advantage and one disadvantage for an importer and for an exporter in dealing with a trading bloc.

Communication

1. Using the Internet, the library, or another source, prepare an oral report on how important the Asia–Pacific market will be to your province or territory in the next 10 years.

2. Select a country from either the EU or AFTA that was not described in detail in this chapter. Research this country as a market. What are its economic strengths? its weaknesses? What products and services does it import from and export to Canada? Summarize your findings in a one-page report. Create a bulletin board display or computer database titled "International Markets Around the World" and post the reports generated by your class.

3. Could Canada continue to exist as an independent nation inside a North American economic union? Research the potential impact of such a union on Canada's economy, environment, culture, and government. Then hold a debate to discuss this issue.

Application

1. A Canadian giftware manufacturer wants to sell products in the European market and has come to you for advice. Consider what you have learned in this chapter and explain, in an oral report, the pros and cons of trying to enter this market. Conclude your report by making two recommendations to the Canadian manufacturer.

2. Find out how Canadian immigration patterns have changed in the past 40 years. What effect has this had on Canada's economic relationships with various countries?

REFLECT ON YOUR LEARNING

1. Describe some problems that nations might have when trying to work together to create an economic community for international trade.

2. Which of the following statements best expresses your opinion? Give reasons for your choice.
   - "Canada should join more international trade groups and associations."
   - "Canada should maintain its current trade position."
   - "Canada should restore tariff barriers to protect domestic industries and businesses."

CHAPTER 20

INTERNATIONAL ECONOMIC RELATIONSHIPS

STUDENT EXPECTATIONS

After completing this chapter, you will be able to

- describe Canada's key economic relationships
- describe how a company's profit and growth can be affected by its international business activity and participation in the markets of other nations
- define "flow of funds"
- describe the roles played by foreign direct investment in Canada and Canadian direct investment abroad
- identify investment opportunities for Canadian businesses in foreign markets and for foreign businesses in Canada
- explain the impact of culture and customs on business activity in international markets
- understand the impact of international business on jobs in Canada

Profile

Louis Girardin shows off Discreet's technology, which was used to create special effects for Mission Kashmir.

HURRAY FOR BOLLYWOOD

On billboards for India's recent action hit, *Mission Kashmir*, a stoic hero gazes over an urban skyline. One of many ads for domestic blockbusters that loom over the congested streets of Mumbai (formerly called Bombay), it's symbolic of the world's most productive movie-producing city; with more than 700 features made here each year, it surpasses Hollywood in terms of output. And just like its southern California namesake—the film-producing quarter of Mumbai has been dubbed Bollywood—the Indian film industry is pumped on computer effects for stunts and explosions. In fact, *Mission Kashmir*'s scenes of exploding *shikara* boats on a peaceful Kashmiri lake and terrorists plunging from three-storey buildings exemplify the recent rise of computer-generated effects in Indian cinema.

Computer effects are a staple of U.S. film, but their spicing up of Indian movies is sweet for the Canadians selling the underlying technology, such as Discreet Logic Inc. Founded in Montreal in 1991, the software maker helped win an Oscar for *The Matrix* in 1999, the year it joined the umbrella of software giant Autodesk Inc. Discreet now has 18 offices around the world, but the growth in its 11-person Mumbai office is turning heads. Discreet says India is one of its fastest-growing markets.

Discreet sells video-editing software as well as hardware to big-budget houses. It sells identical software to domestic and international clients, but offers laxer terms to clients in developing nations. "People want the same stuff as Hollywood," says Louis Girardin, a product manager in Discreet's Montreal office who has peddled for Discreet in places as disparate as Brazil and Japan, "but the amount of money available to spend on special effects varies."

CONTINUED →

Discreet has long planned a foothold in India. In 1993, Hollywood's *Jurassic Park* made a big splash in the country, raising the bar of audience expectation for special effects. That's why Discreet opened an office in India in 1995. "We definitely wanted to be the first to bring the technology here," says Pankaj Kedia, business manager of the Discreet office in Mumbai. "It was felt that if we had a presence locally, the focus would probably help catalyze market growth." Film budgets are more modest than in the U.S., and effects eat a smaller slice of the cash, but Kedia says the latter gap is narrowing. Four years ago, only about five Indian productions had more than $10 000 worth of effects; today, more than 30 films in production here employ computer animation, and most effects budgets are up a least fivefold.

Discreet also got a boost from its move into Indian television. "Basically, all blockbusters—good, bad, drama, horror—somehow, somewhere, we are part of it," explains Girardin, chuckling. But with a hot market comes competition. Chief rival Alias/Wavefront, a Toronto-based subsidiary of California-based Silicon Graphics Inc., also reports explosive growth of its business in India. According to Alias/Wavefront, it sells to many existing studios in India—including the majority of new studios set up in the past 18 months. And as special effects and computer animation become more prominent in Indian films, it is likely that this market will only become more competitive.

"It was felt that if we had a presence locally, the focus would probably help catalyze market growth."

About This Profile
1. What makes India such a lucrative market for Discreet?
2. Why did Discreet decide to open offices in India, rather than simply exporting its products to India from Montreal?
3. Apart from India, what other countries might offer business opportunities for Discreet? Explain your answer.

International Investment

BEFORE YOU BEGIN

Name some businesses in your community that are owned by companies outside Canada. Find out when and where one of these companies first began operating in Canada.

In Chapter 18, you learned that when goods and services flow out of a country, funds flow back in. This exchange occurs when countries trade internationally. In other types of international business, funds flow on their own, without any exchange of goods or services.

For example, suppose you operate a successful chain of pizza restaurants in the United States. You already have outlets in every state, and you're wondering if your restaurant concept would do well in Canada. You do some market research to check out the Canadian competition and to see whether Canadians like the features offered by your restaurant. It turns out that they do, so you look for a good location for your first Canadian restaurant.

International investment means that a business from one country sets up shop in another. An investment occurs when someone lends or spends an amount of money in the hope of earning back that money, plus a profit. In this case, the pizza chain will spend money to do market research and build a new restaurant, hoping that increased revenues will exceed the amount spent.

Expanding a pizza chain into another country can benefit the business in many ways. It makes the restaurants available to more customers. If these customers like the chain, the company will have increased publicity, higher pizza sales, and greater profits. If the business is a franchise operation, Canadian operators may buy licences to set up more locations. Since the franchisees pay a portion of their monthly profits to the franchiser, more Canadian franchises would provide an ongoing source of revenue for the company.

Often, this type of foreign-based investment is good for Canadians. As well as providing a new and possibly better place to buy pizza, the restaurants contribute to the Canadian economy. Canadian workers are usually hired to build and staff the restaurants, providing Canadians with jobs and more money to put into the economy. The business may also rely on Canadian suppliers for pizza ingredients or other supplies, giving a boost to domestic industry.

There are many different ways to engage in foreign investment besides expanding into a foreign market. Options include mergers, acquisitions, partnerships, joint ventures, or new businesses. In each case, a **flow of funds** takes place between countries without an accompanying exchange of goods or services.

As you read in Chapter 6, a **merger** occurs when two or more companies join together, either because one has purchased a controlling interest in the other(s) or because the companies have combined their interests. A merger can help both companies strengthen their operations, enter new markets, and acquire new technologies, resources, and skills. If a smaller company merges with a larger one, the small company may also gain access to more capital or a larger sales force.

Foreign money that is invested in Canada, as in the pizza restaurant example, is called **foreign direct investment (FDI)**. When Canadian money is invested in another country, we call it **Canadian direct investment abroad (CDIA)**.

Pizza Hut

Pizza Hut is the largest pizza-restaurant company in the world. It has more than 12 000 restaurants in 86 countries. The Pizza Hut restaurant with the highest volume of sales is in Paris, France.

The Pizza Hut chain began when two brothers, Dan and Frank Carney, borrowed $600 from their mother in 1958 to open a small pizza restaurant in Wichita, Kansas. At the time, Dan and Frank were still in college. The name for their restaurant was chosen because after they wrote "Pizza" on the sign, there was only room for three more letters! The Carney brothers' first franchise opened one year later in the neighbouring town of Topeka.

The first Pizza Hut restaurant in Canada opened in Toronto in 1968. When Pizza Hut invests in a new franchise, it tries to find a location
• near a mall or plaza with good parking
• that is very visible and easy to access
• with neighbouring tenants who will attract customers from a wide area
• that will continue to draw customers for many years
• that has both day and night activities in the area that will draw potential customers
• with a freestanding building that can be adapted to Pizza Hut's standard shape and colours, or a site where a new restaurant can be built
• that has a 25-year lease with regular rent reviews and a stipulation that no other pizza restaurants will open in the same complex

FOREIGN DIRECT INVESTMENT IN CANADA

According to the Department of Foreign Affairs and International Trade (DFAIT), there are many reasons for foreign businesses to invest in Canada:

• Canada has a strong domestic economy.
• Canada's nearness to the U.S., along with NAFTA, gives businesses in Canada access to a market of about 400 million people.
• Canada is connected to an efficient and inexpensive North American transportation system that carries more than $1 billion per day in traded goods.
• Canada is rich in natural resources, including oil, gas, coal, and hydroelectric power. As a result, energy costs are lower than in the U.S.
• Canadian workers are highly skilled, especially in the area of technology, and Canadian businesses have a low turnover rate.
• Labour costs in Canada are lower than in any of the other G8 countries.
• Intellectual property rights are protected.
• The standard of living in Canada is high.

Where the Money Goes

What types of businesses do foreign investors support in Canada? In recent years, foreign investment has grown fastest in the high-technology, manufacturing, and service sectors—in part because of government programs designed to encourage research and development through tax breaks and government grants and loans. Table 20.1 shows how foreign investment was distributed among various industries in Canada in 1999.

STRETCH YOUR THINKING

What factors are considered when measuring a country's standard of living?

Table 20.1 Foreign Direct Investment in Canada by Industry (1999)

Industry	Percentage of FDI	FDI in Billions of Dollars
Services and retailing	8.1	19.4
Finance and insurance	20.9	50.1
Machinery and transportation equipment	11.3	27.1
Energy and metallic minerals	16.3	39.1
Wood and paper	7.7	18.5
Other industries	35.7	85.7
Total	100.0	239.9

Where the Money Comes From

Canada's largest trading partner is also our largest foreign investor—the United States. In 1999, the U.S. invested about $173.3 billion in Canada, or about 72% of the total foreign direct investment in Canada for the year.

Why does the U.S. invest so much money in Canada? Part of the answer is that the U.S. and Canada are close neighbours, linked by geography, similar cultures, a highly efficient transportation system, and favourable trade agreements. Like the pizza restaurant described earlier, many American businesses see advantages in expanding into the Canadian market by establishing branches and outlets in Canada.

Another factor in this investment relationship is the fact that the U.S. dollar is worth about one and a half times as much as the Canadian dollar. This difference means that American companies can save a significant amount of money by taking advantage of lower production and distribution costs in Canada.

Although the U.S. is Canada's closest investment partner, it is by no means our only partner. Money also flows into the country from Europe, Asia, and many other parts of the world.

Figure 20.1

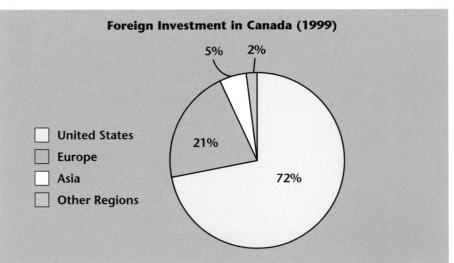

Benefits of Foreign Direct Investment

Foreign direct investment is critical to Canada's future. It provides an opportunity for Canada to compete on the global stage and, at the same time, to improve its domestic industries. Foreign direct investment not only produces jobs, it also introduces new technology and management techniques, and provides access to new markets for Canadian businesses. The rapid growth of foreign investment in high-technology industries has additional benefits, including giving Canada access to foreign capital, which has helped Canada become a global leader in the knowledge-based economy.

Why Invest in Canada?

STMicroelectronics (ST), a European-based electronics firm, is one of many companies that have made an investment in Canada. ST is one of the world's largest semiconductor suppliers, with operations in 26 countries. In 1999, the company's sales exceeded $7.7 billion worldwide. ST has Canadian offices in Calgary, Ottawa, and Toronto.

ST chose to locate in Canada because of the leadership role that Canada plays in the semiconductor industry. According to ST, Canada has
- the lowest annual location-related costs among the G8 countries for the production of electronic components
- the most highly competitive workplace in the world in terms of research and development investment
- the highest number of knowledge workers and the greatest technological potential of any G8 nation
- over 25 000 graduates per year in mathematics, engineering, and pure and applied sciences
- the highest rate of postsecondary education and the greatest per capita expenditure on training in the G8

CANADIAN DIRECT INVESTMENT ABROAD

So far, this chapter has focused mainly on foreign investments that bring capital from other countries into Canada. However, this flow of funds also travels in the other direction. Sometimes, Canadian businesses decide to invest Canadian dollars abroad.

Magna International is a worldwide supplier of automotive systems, headquartered in Aurora, Ontario. During the late 1990s, the company expanded quickly through Europe, acquiring a number of European-based automotive system suppliers. This expansion not only gave the company access to new markets for its products in Europe, but also helped Magna trade information with European companies about new technologies and processes. Since the beginning of its expansion in 1994, Magna's yearly sales have increased from just less than $6 billion to more than $20 billion (in 2000).

Like FDI, CDIA benefits Canadians both directly and indirectly. Magna's growth, for example, provides jobs for Canadians at home and around the world, increases Magna's access to international markets, and gives auto parts buyers access to a broader range of products. The

Magna International now has manufacturing facilities in a number of European countries, including Austria, Great Britain, Italy, Poland, and Turkey.

information exchange with European companies has benefited customers by improving the company's product line, distribution system, and efficiency. Magna's success also means that the company spends more money in Canada, which gives a boost to other Canadian businesses.

Magna is only one of many Canadian businesses with investments abroad. Table 20.2 shows how much various Canadian industries contributed to Canada's total foreign investment in 1999.

BUSINESS
—FACT—
Canadian direct investment abroad increased from $98.4 billion in 1990 to $257.4 billion in 1999.

Table 20.2 Canadian Direct Investment Abroad by Industry (1999)

Industry	Percentage of CDIA	CDIA in Billions of Dollars
Services and retailing	13.2	34.0
Finance and insurance	33.1	85.2
Machinery and transportation equipment	4.7	12.1
Energy and metallic minerals	21.0	54.1
Wood and paper	2.8	7.2
Other industries	25.2	64.8
Total	100.0	257.4

Not surprisingly, over half of Canada's foreign investments are made in the United States. However, significant portions of Canadian direct investment abroad also go to other regions, especially Europe and Asia.

Figure 20.2

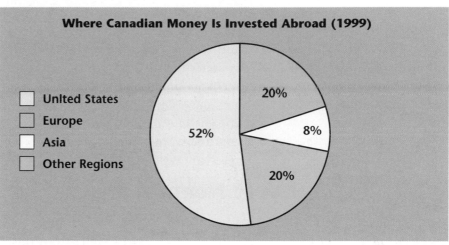

Where Canadian Money Is Invested Abroad (1999)

- United States
- Europe
- Asia
- Other Regions

52%
20%
8%
20%

ACTIVITIES FOR ...

INFORMATION

1. a) Define "merger." List several reasons why one business might want to merge with another.

2. a) What do the acronyms FDI and CDIA stand for? Explain what each term means.

3. a) List five reasons why Canada is a good place for foreign businesses to invest.

CONNECTION

b) Look for an article in a newspaper or business magazine about a merger or an acquisition. Briefly explain to the class what occurred, and why.

b) What is likely to happen to Canadian imports when FDI increases? What is likely to happen to Canadian exports when CDIA increases? Explain.

b) Refer to Tables 20.1 and 20.2. Compare the amounts of investment flowing in and out of Canada on an industry-by-industry basis. Which industries have more investment dollars flowing into Canada? flowing out of Canada?

EXTENSION

c) All foreign investors in Canada must follow the rules in the Investment Canada Act. Research this document to find out when it was passed, what its purpose was, and how it improved on the previous legislation.

c) Look for information about one of the following topics in *The Canadian Encyclopedia*: foreign investment, the Foreign Investment Review Agency, or multinational corporations. Share the information you find with classmates who researched the other topics.

c) Hold a class debate on the following topic: "Foreign investment in Canada is always good for Canadians."

Canada's International Investment Partners

In 1999, Canadian businesses invested more than $257 billion in other countries. The Department of Foreign Affairs and International Trade keeps track of trade and investments in Canada and abroad, and supplies potential investors with information that will help them make choices about where and how to invest their money. DFAIT organizes the countries of the world into six economic regions: North America, Europe, Asia–Pacific, Latin America and Caribbean, Middle East and North Africa, and sub-Saharan Africa.

IN NORTH AMERICA

Earlier in this chapter, you learned that about 72% of the foreign investment in Canada comes from the United States. In Figure 20.2, you saw that the U.S. receives about 52% of Canada's foreign investment. The United States has a labour force of over 140 million people and a wide range of natural resources. These factors, along with its large population, its nearness to Canada, and favourable trade agreements, make it a natural place for Canadian businesses to invest.

IN EUROPE

In Chapter 19, you learned about the European countries that have come together to form the European Union. Canadian businesses invested about $48 billion in EU countries in 1999, while businesses from these countries invested about $45 billion in Canada.

Many European countries, such as Switzerland and the Netherlands, have large populations spread over a relatively small area. This situation makes Europe a significant market for foreign-produced agri-foods. (The **agri-foods** industry includes farm-produced foods, as well as services associated with primary agriculture, such as supplying or transporting food, or food inspection.) In Switzerland, the agri-food import market is worth an estimated $7.5 billion annually. Currently, Canadian businesses meet about 2% of this demand.

United Kingdom

Almost half of Canada's outgoing investment to the EU goes to the United Kingdom, Canada's closest investment partner in Europe.

When two countries share a common language and close historical ties, it isn't surprising that they also share their business. Over 400 Canadian companies have investments in the United Kingdom, including Alcan, Bombardier, Magna International, and Alcatel Canada (formerly Newbridge Networks).

Netherlands

The Netherlands is one of the top five investors in Canada. Although yearly investments are much less than the investments that the U.S. or the U.K. make in Canada, Dutch direct investments in Canada had reached a total of $9.02 billion by the end of 1998. Large Dutch companies operating in Canada include Shell, Unilever, Philips, Akzo Nobel, Hoogovens, and CSM. There are also a number of smaller companies seeking to increase their market share in North America.

Canada's investment in the Netherlands is much less than Dutch investment in Canada, with a total of about $2 billion invested to the end of 1998. Canadian companies like McCain, Cognos, and TransCanada Pipelines have operations based in the Netherlands.

The Netherlands provides a growing market for telecommunications equipment and services. Several Canadian companies, including Nortel Networks, Northern Telecom, Eicon Networks, have expanded into the Netherlands to address these needs. Other Canadian telecom/data companies, such as Mitel and Ubitech, are selling their products in the Netherlands through Dutch distributors.

A sign with Nestlé's logo stands outside the company's headquarters in Vevey, Switzerland.

Switzerland

Switzerland—a country in Europe that has not joined the European Union—is the home base for many large businesses that operate

in Canada, including Nestlé, St. Lawrence Cement, Novartis, and Ciba–Geigy. In fact, Switzerland is Canada's seventh-largest foreign investor.

The costs of operating a business in Switzerland are very high, but many Canadian firms have found that the benefits of a central European location and nearby markets for their products make it worthwhile to establish Swiss operations. Canadian companies with investments in Switzerland include Alcan, Bata, and Nortel Networks.

IN THE ASIA–PACIFIC REGION

The Asia–Pacific region has tremendous potential for rapid economic growth. Team Canada's first mission to Beijing and Shanghai in 1994 demonstrated that Canadian exporters and foreign investors were very interested in this expanding market. On its 2001 mission to Beijing, Shanghai, and Hong Kong, Team Canada strengthened this commitment. As you read in Chapter 18, the 2001 mission resulted in $5.7 billion in new deals for Canadian businesses.

The Asia–Pacific region also includes Australia and New Zealand—countries with small populations but large opportunities. Canada has traditionally been a significant investor in these countries, partly because the business culture is similar to our own.

Hong Kong

Hong Kong became part of the People's Republic of China in 1997, but it still maintains its own customs organization, sets its own economic policies, and retains its membership in the World Trade Organization. In 1999, Canadian direct investment in Hong Kong was just over $3 billion—nearly as much as Hong Kong's $3.3 billion direct investment in Canada.

Banks and life insurance companies, such as Canada Life, Sun Life, Manulife, the Bank of Nova Scotia, and CIBC, together made over 70% of the Canadian investment in Hong Kong. Other Canadian businesses operating in Hong Kong include Air Canada, Maple Leaf Foods, and Bombardier.

More than half a million Canadians, mainly in Toronto and Vancouver, have family connections in Hong Kong. These ties are part of the reason why Hong Kong invests billions of dollars in Canada each year. This investment is mainly directed into real estate and hotels, the financial sector, telecommunications, and oil and gas. Examples of Hong Kong-controlled businesses in Canada include Numac Energy, Husky Energy, the Sutton Place Grande Hotel in Toronto, and the Delta Whistler Resort in Whistler, British Columbia.

Singapore

Singapore is the transportation centre of Southeast Asia, making it an exciting area for international investment. Canadian investments in Singapore amounted to about $2.2 billion in 1998, mainly in the financial services sector. There has also been considerable investment in telecommunications. Over 40% of households in Singapore own a computer, and the country is among the top 15 in the world for Internet usage. Since Canada is a world leader in the telecommunications

Banks, insurance companies, and the stock exchange are located in the city of Singapore's financial district.

field, many business opportunities exist in this area. In fact, both Mitel and Nortel Networks, two major Canadian telecommunications firms, have established operations in Singapore.

Singaporean direct investment in Canada amounted to approximately $150 million in 1997. In addition, Singapore's government holds more than $1 billion in Canadian government bonds and other securities. These investments are called **portfolio investments**—they are made only to earn interest or dividends.

One important connection between Canada and Singapore is the many Singaporean students who have studied at Canadian universities. Many of these university graduates, who number over 10 000, have jobs in government, business, and education in Singapore. This connection can be beneficial to a Canadian business that wishes to expand into the Asian market.

STRETCH YOUR THINKING

How might Canadian businesses wishing to expand into the Asian market benefit from the fact that many Singaporeans who now work in government, business, and education once went to university in Canada?

IN LATIN AMERICA AND THE CARIBBEAN

Another area where opportunities for Canadian investment are growing is in Latin America and the Caribbean. In 1998, Canada invested $14.3 billion in Barbados, $6.1 billion in Bahamas, $4.7 billion in Bermuda, and $4.2 billion in Chile. These amounts—only part of the Canadian investment picture in Latin America and the Caribbean—total more than Canadian businesses invest in the entire Asia–Pacific area, and add up to roughly two-thirds of what Canadians invest in the European Union. Several Latin American and Caribbean countries also have significant investments in Canada, including Bermuda ($1.7 billion).

As you read in Chapter 19, with the Free Trade Area of the Americas and the Canada–Chile Free Trade Agreement, it is expected that Canadian trade and investment in Central and South America will grow. In addition to these agreements, Canada has set up Foreign Investment Protection Agreements (FIPAs) with Brazil and Colombia. These agreements are designed to protect and promote Canada's foreign investments by clarifying procedures and making it easier to access foreign markets.

Brazil

Canada has invested in Brazil for more than a century. Canadians helped Brazil develop power-distribution systems in major centres, bring rapid transit systems to urban areas, and establish the first telephone company in Sao Paulo. In 1999, Canada's investments in Brazil exceeded $7 billion.

Opportunities for Canadian direct investment in Brazil exist in many economic areas, including telecommunications, environmental services, processed foods, health industries, transportation, and energy services. The Brazilian telecommunications sector is the largest in Latin America, with an estimated market of $15 billion in 1999. Canadian telecommunications companies with operations in Brazil include Bell Canada International, Teleglobe, and Nortel Networks.

Managers of a Canadian business work out the details of an expansion into Brazil.

IN THE MIDDLE EAST AND NORTH AFRICA

Although Canadian investment in this region is still quite small, there are growing opportunities in areas such as tourism, oil and gas, and mining. Iran and Israel are Canada's two closest trading partners in the region. Exports to Iran average about $725 million per year, while exports to Israel average about $250 million per year. Roughly 70% of Canada's total exports to the Middle East are in the form of consulting and engineering services to the oil and gas, power generation, and telecommunications industries.

Israel

The Canada–Israel Free Trade Agreement came into effect in January 1997, lifting tariffs on most industrial goods and making it easier for Canada to export fish and many agricultural products. Israel has a fast-growing economy fueled by development in telecommunications, the medical sector, electronics, textiles, the chemical industry, and financial services.

IN SUB-SAHARAN AFRICA

In 1997, Canada's exports to sub-Saharan Africa amounted to $876 million. At that time, there were about 75 Canadian companies with operations in South Africa, and about 30 more in Kenya and

E-ACTIVITY

Visit www.business. nelson.com and follow the links to find the most recent statistics for foreign direct investment in Canada and for Canadian direct investment abroad. What differences do you notice between these statistics and the statistics in this chapter?

Zimbabwe. Mining is an especially attractive area for Canadian investment. In fact, it's been estimated that there is some level of Canadian participation in more than 50% of the new mining ventures launched in South Africa.

Although Canadian investments in Africa are still small, they are growing rapidly. The amount invested doubled from $400 million in 1993 to $777 million in 1997, with about 25% of this amount going to South Africa.

Tips for International Success

The Canadian Trade Commissioner Service offers the following tips to Canadian businesses hoping to enter the foreign market.

1. **Zoom in on the most promising markets.** Successful companies concentrate on one foreign market at a time, moving on to the next only after succeeding in the last.

2. **Learn from experienced companies.** Talk to Canadian companies that have succeeded in your target market. Many are willing to share information about what works and what doesn't. Contact your industry association to find names of successful companies in your sector and target market.

3. **Plan for the financial resources that you'll need.** Exploring foreign markets can take longer and cost more than expected. Be prepared for additional costs for market research, product launchings, and personal visits.

4. **Gear up for demand.** Be prepared to meet increased demand from a successful foreign sale. Don't forget to plan how you will adapt your product or service to the needs and tastes of your target market.

5. **Make personal visits.** Face-to-face conversations are the best way to build a business relationship in a foreign market, while phone calls, faxes, and e-mail are great for follow-up.

6. **Study the market and the culture.** Businesspeople and customers in most foreign markets appreciate your efforts to learn about their culture.

7. **Set realistic expectations.** Developing foreign markets is a long-term commitment. It takes time, effort, and resources. Make sure that your management is committed to the venture. Be prepared for the long haul and persevere.

ACTIVITIES FOR ...

INFORMATION	**C**ONNECTION	**E**XTENSION
1. a) Name the six main economic regions of the world.	**b)** Suppose you operate a Canadian business that specializes in one of the following areas: education, mining, agri-foods, or telecommunications. In which world economic region(s) would you be most likely to invest in each case? Why?	**c)** Choose one economic region of the world to profile in more detail. What are the economic strengths and weaknesses of the region you chose?
2. a) Choose one region discussed in this chapter. What Canadian businesses operate in this region? What businesses owned by companies in this region operate in Canada?	**b)** Why might a Canadian business decide to invest in a foreign operation rather than simply export its own products to the foreign country?	**c)** Choose one Canadian business that operates internationally. Conduct some research about the business to find out when it first decided to invest in a foreign operation, why it made this decision, and how the first foreign operation began. Tell how successful the operation has been, what the business's current international status is, and how the business's international investments have affected its profits.
3. a) List some important tips for achieving business success in international markets.	**b)** Which tip that you listed in Question 3a do you think is the most important? Why?	**c)** Describe a business that you might like to start in a foreign country. Find out what similar businesses are already operating in that country and what problems they've faced. What steps would you take to give your venture the best possible chance of success?

The Impact of Cultural Differences

STRETCH YOUR THINKING

Choose a foreign country. What cultural differences must a Canadian paint company that wants to open a branch plant in that country consider?

Anyone who plans to do business in a foreign country is likely to encounter cultural differences. **Culture** is the sum of a country's way of life, beliefs, and customs. It influences how things are bought and sold. It sets the boundaries of what can and cannot be done, of what is acceptable or unacceptable. Culture is absorbed everywhere—at school, at home, and at work. Luckily, people who aren't born in a certain culture can still learn to operate within it.

Imagine, for a moment, the difficulties that might face a paint company in Mexico that wants to set up a branch plant in Canada. To begin with, the paint will need to be put into approved packages that are labelled in both French and English, with metric measurements. These requirements mean that the Mexican company will have to invest in new packaging before the sales revenues begin to flow in.

In Canada, the weather is hot in the summer, but very cold in the winter. Outdoor paints have to withstand extreme changes in temperature, along with rain, snow, and ice. The paint manufacturer whose products have only been used in warmer climates may need to develop new formulas to address this need.

Because of cultural differences, it may be difficult for the Mexican paint manufacturer to predict Canadian colour preferences or plan an advertising campaign that appeals to Canadians. To make choices, the investor needs to do considerable market research in Canada, even though similar research may already have been done in Mexico. This research should include a study of social and environmental issues that are important to Canadians, and demographic characteristics that shape the Canadian market.

Even something as simple as the name of a product may be enough to create problems in another language. For example, General Motors faced difficulties when it tried to sell its Chevrolet Nova automobile in Latin America because, in Spanish, Nova means "won't go." A culture is like an iceberg—what you see is only the tip. Most of the beliefs, values, and assumptions of a culture are hidden beneath the surface. It's easy to see reflections of a culture in clothes, music, and literature, but it's more often the things you can't see that count.

GLOBAL DEPENDENCY

The 20th century was a time of almost unimaginable growth in the communications industry. People all around the world were drawn closer together by inventions such as the television, movies, satellite communications, and the Internet. This rapid growth has put us on the path to becoming a "global community."

If you walked down the streets of Taipei, Barcelona, Cairo, or Buenos Aires, you would likely see signs of home. You might see a Pizza Hut, an advertisement for a Hollywood movie, or a copy of a Canadian newspaper. You'd see people wearing clothes with familiar logos. In a parking lot, you'd see familiar vehicles.

Why are consumers buying cars and clothing made in foreign countries? The simple answer is something called global dependency. **Global dependency** exists when customers in one country begin to demand items that are created in another country. These customers become aware of the products because of global communications. Over time, the products are incorporated into the culture of the people who buy them. But the process doesn't always go smoothly. Awareness of different cultures and preferences is the key to success in a foreign market. A North American advertisement for a brand of laundry detergent might show dirty clothes on the left, the detergent in the middle, and clean clothes on the right. If this ad were introduced in a country where people read from right to left, the result would be confusion and declining sales.

DEALING WITH PEOPLE

Doing business around the world not only means learning other languages; it also means learning the nuances of dealing with people from many countries and finding out what's important to them. Some key areas to find out about include punctuality, greetings, nonverbal communication, good manners, and decision-making processes.

Punctuality

In some cultures, such as North American cultures, people are expected to be on time for appointments. They rely on appointment books and calendars, and may even have to pay for missed appointments. In other cultures, time is considered to be flowing, flexible, and beyond people's control. What doesn't get done today can be done tomorrow. If you find out how important punctuality is in a country you plan to visit, you can set an acceptable pace, impress others with your good manners, and avoid long waits.

Greetings

In many countries, the way you greet someone is an important part of the impression you make. Handshakes are common in most countries, but not everyone shakes hands the same way. In France, for example, a single shake is all that's needed, and more may be considered rude. In most cultures, it's considered polite to make eye contact when you greet someone, but in others, averting your eyes is a sign of respect. These details are very important because the impression you create first is usually the one that stays with people over time.

Nonverbal Communication Signals

In many cultures, nonverbal signals tell far more than words. For example, in Asian cultures, refusing someone's request is considered to be rude, so Asian businesspeople may prefer not to give direct answers to questions asked during sales negotiations instead of saying "no." Businesspeople may have to rely on the body language of the person they're speaking with to tell them whether they have or have not made a sale.

Familiar gestures are not always a useful guide because they may have different meanings from one culture to another. To a Bulgarian, a nod of the head means "no," while shaking the head from side to side means "yes"—the opposite to the meaning of these gestures in North America.

Cultural rules about touching other people also vary widely from one country to another. In one place, a pat on the back may be a friendly greeting; in another place, it may be an insult. In some places, standing too close to a person is considered an invasion of personal space. In other places, it is considered rude to stand far away. In a business situation, it's important to know these rules.

Good Manners

People in Canada, the United States, and some European countries like to do business quickly and efficiently. They tend to focus on the task at hand and try to get it done so they can move on to something else. Almost anywhere else in the world—particularly in Asian and Latin American countries—it's considered polite to try to get to know the people you're doing business with before you discuss the business itself. The three F's of business—family, friends, and favours—have a very strong influence on the business decisions people make. To be successful, it's essential to spend time establishing a relationship with customers and business associates before you proceed with your work.

Although good manners everywhere are based on the ideas of showing respect for others and making them feel comfortable, specific rules and expectations differ from one culture to the next. For example, in some countries, it's considered rude to use your left hand to give something to someone. In others, it's rude to ask about someone's

> ## Did You Know?
> The "okay" sign commonly used in Canada (thumb and index finger touching to form a circle) is a symbol for money in Japan, and is considered offensive in Brazil.

E-ACTIVITY

Visit
www.business.
nelson.com
and follow the links
to travel sites to
find out about some
of the cultural
characteristics of a
country you might
like to visit or do
business in
some day.

spouse. Because it's hard to predict what people will expect from you, it's a good idea to do some research about etiquette before you travel to a foreign country.

Decision Making

In North American business, decision making is typically a top-down process. People expect the president of a company to have much more say in an important decision than someone who works in a less senior position. Latin American cultures usually take a similar approach. However, in some Asian cultures, decisions are made from the bottom up. That means that before an important decision can be made, the person who makes the decision may need to consult everyone who will be affected by the outcome. As a result, decisions may sometimes take longer to make.

International Investment and Jobs

The 1990s witnessed two major changes in the Canadian business environment. First, there was the rapid technological change that accompanied the arrival of the Internet. Second, the spread of free trade markets, through trade agreements such as NAFTA, promoted greater competition worldwide and created strong incentives for domestic businesses to look beyond Canadian borders for opportunities. This process of doing business all over the world is generally referred to as **globalization**.

Throughout this unit, you have explored the impact of foreign trade and investment on Canadian business. In Canada, one out of every three jobs is connected in some way with international trade, and one in 10 is linked directly to foreign investment in Canada. This trend is growing. In the mid-1990s, exports accounted for 30% of Canada's gross domestic product. By the end of the decade, this figure had risen to 40%—making Canada more dependent on foreign trade than any other G8 country. Foreign direct investment in Canada has experienced similar growth, almost doubling during the 1990s. As a result, the vast majority of the more than 1.9 million jobs created since 1993 have stemmed directly from the growth in exports and international investment.

How does international business benefit workers, consumers, and producers in the countries involved? As you learned in Chapter 18, at its best, international business generates lower consumer prices, creates more efficient production of goods and services, and contributes to economic growth. This economic growth, in turn, translates into new jobs. In 1999, Canada's top 10 employers (the Canadian companies that employ the most people) provided jobs for approximately 675 000 Canadians, not only in Canada, but also around the world.

Table 20.3 Canada's Top 10 Employers (1999)

Company	Approximate Number of Employees	Field of Expertise
Loblaw Companies	113 000	supermarkets
ONEX Corporation	83 000	various (electronics, insurance, sugar, etc.)
Nortel Networks	75 000	telecommunications
Laidlaw Inc.	71 400	transportation
Hudson's Bay Company	70 000	department stores
Quebecor Inc.	60 000	media
Bombardier Inc.	53 000	transportation
Royal Bank of Canada	52 000	banking
Brascade Resources	51 000	mining, forestry
Magna International	51 000	automotive systems

On the other hand, if Canadian businesses can no longer survive because of increased global competition, Canadian workers may lose their jobs and domestic businesses may fold. Fortunately, these job losses are usually offset by job and income growth in other businesses.

BUSINESS
—FACT—

According to a U.S. report, the top five fastest-growing occupations are computer engineers, computer support specialists, systems analysts, database administrators, and desktop publishing specialists.

HOW CANADA'S JOBS ARE CHANGING

Statistical data provided by the World Trade Organization shows that the types of jobs done by Canadians changed significantly from the 1980s to the 1990s. In the 1990s, most new jobs were for self-employed people. Company hirings accounted for only 18% of new job creation in the 1990s, compared with 47% in the 1980s.

One reason for this difference is that, during the 1990s, many industries **downsized**, or reduced their labour forces. At the same time, the business services and manufacturing sectors flourished because of international competition. People who left full-time jobs with companies found ways to take advantage of opportunities in these sectors and became self-employed.

Producers of computer software, such as this person who's developing Web-based videoconferencing software, will continue to be in great demand in the new economy.

Another reason for the increase in self-employment is the advances in computer technology that took place during this period. The rapid expansion of e-mail and the Internet made it possible for more people to work from home, and created new entrepreneurial opportunities in the field of e-commerce.

Today, jobs continue to change. There is currently a great deal of growth in the manufacturing sector, particularly in businesses that manufacture industrial machinery, electronics, telecommunications systems, and transportation equipment. Thanks in part to these industries, Canada's exports are increasing dynamically. Experts predict that, in the future, more jobs will open up in companies that produce chemicals, communications systems, and computer software.

CANADA'S FUTURE

The Conference Board of Canada reports annually on Canada's performance and potential. This board is an independent membership-based agency that brings together representatives from business, government, and public-sector organizations. Its purpose is to provide insights that will allow its members to anticipate and respond to an increasingly challenging global economy.

In its annual report of 2000, the Conference Board identified five areas that are critical to Canada's overall economic and social performance: lifelong learning, foreign investment, innovation, social policy, and health care.

It's clear from these conclusions that the future of Canada depends on business, and that the future of business depends on Canadians. The inclusion of foreign investment on the Conference Board's list shows its critical importance to the continued development of the Canadian economy and job market. Lifelong learning and innovation are related goals that will help Canadian businesses grow and flourish in new markets, and that will attract foreign investors to Canada. Earlier in this chapter, you learned that one of the features investors find most attractive about Canada is that it is a great place to live. Canadian social policy and health care provide Canadians with one of the highest standards of living in the world. By continuing to learn, innovate, and grow, we can ensure that Canadians will enjoy an exceptional lifestyle for a very long time.

ACTIVITIES FOR ...

INFORMATION	CONNECTION	EXTENSION
1. a) What is "global dependency"? How does it influence international business?	**b)** Culture has an influence on many aspects of people's everyday life, including music, clothing, and entertainment. Choose one of these areas. What can you learn about Canadian culture by examining this area? Then, choose another country and tell what you know about its culture by examining the same area.	**c)** Suppose a business promotes its products in Canada by advertising in the newspaper and on radio, and by distributing flyers door to door. How might differences in culture and customs in a foreign country make it necessary to change this approach?
2. a) Describe several ways in which you could find out about the culture of another country.	**b)** Why is it important to watch body language when communicating with someone from another culture? Give some examples of the types of body language you might look for in a business meeting with someone from another country.	**c)** Besides punctuality, greetings, nonverbal communication, good manners, and decision making, what cultural factors should you consider when doing business with another country?
3. a) How did the types of jobs done by Canadians change during the 1990s? Give some reasons for these changes.	**b)** What types of jobs do you think Canadians will be doing in the future? Why?	**c)** Which of the top 10 Canadian employers have operations in your area? Write a short profile of one local operation, explaining what the company does, how many people it employs, and what contributions it has made to your community.

Review

Knowledge and Understanding

1. Match each of the following terms to the correct definition:

    CDIA   flow of funds
    culture   globalization
    FDI   merger

    a) Money invested in Canada by foreign businesses.
    b) A trend toward doing business worldwide.
    c) A set of beliefs and conventions that can influence buying decisions and set boundaries for what is and is not acceptable.

d) The joining of two or more companies to form one larger company.

e) A movement of funds, as in international business transactions.

f) Canadian money that's invested in foreign countries.

2. In 1999, which types of foreign businesses invested the most money in Canada? Which types of Canadian businesses invested the most money abroad?

3. Explain several ways in which Canadians benefit from foreign investment in Canada and from Canadian investment abroad. Describe at least two problems for Canadians that could result from each type of investment.

Thinking and Inquiry

1. If you're planning to do business with people from another part of the world, why is it important to find out as much as you can about their culture?

2. Invite someone who does business in Canada and at least one other country to visit your class and talk about similarities and differences in culture. Prepare questions for this person in advance.

3. Choose one country in any economic region. Gather as much information as you can about this country's investment relationship with Canada. Then, create a visual display or multimedia presentation designed to help investors who might be interested in doing business there.

4. What courses available at your school would help you prepare for one of the "Top Five" careers listed in the Business Fact on page 509?

Communication

1. Review this chapter and explore business periodicals to identify one current trend in Canadian foreign investment abroad. Research this trend and set up a class debate to discuss the pros and cons of such a shift in foreign investment by Canada.

2. Conduct a survey of the banks and other financial institutions in your community to find out which ones lend money to businesses that sell or invest in foreign countries. Is the demand for these loans increasing, decreasing, or remaining steady? With which countries is Canada doing the most business?

3. Use what you've learned from this course to set up a heritage fair at your school, with special events presented by people from various cultures. Start by creating a business plan to show what resources you will need, how the event will operate, and how you will finance it. You may find it helpful to contact heritage language representatives in your community.

Application

1. Select one of Canada's top 10 employers from Table 20.3. Research the company and prepare a report outlining its domestic business interests and, if applicable, its international business interests. Your report should describe the products or services that this company produces, its investments, its profit picture, and any other companies that it owns or controls.

2. Investigate how the Government of Quebec has tried to preserve the French language and Quebec culture. What effect have these efforts had on business and foreign direct investment in Quebec? in the rest of Canada? What effect might these efforts have in the future? Report your findings to the class.

3. With the whole class, compile a guide to "Doing Business in Canada" that will help people from other countries understand some of the conventions of Canadian culture.

4. Based on newspaper and magazine articles, advertisements, and Internet links, prepare a list of international job opportunities. What types of skills would help someone succeed in an international business career? Create a bulletin-board display to showcase available job opportunities and to point out the skills needed for each one.

REFLECT ON YOUR LEARNING

1. Would you like to work at a branch of a Canadian company set up in another country? Why or why not?

2. Using information from this chapter and from the rest of this book, create a scenario to show what you think business will be like in Canada in 20 years. What jobs do you think people will be doing? How will the nature of their work have changed? What will the Canadian foreign investment picture look like? What political issues will have an impact on the business world? You may wish to write your scenario, or you could present it in the form of visual images, a dramatic monologue, or a futuristic news report.

Glossary

absolute advantage An advantage that a country enjoys when dealing in goods and services if it is the only country that can provide the good or service, or if it can produce the good or service at a lower cost than other countries. An absolute advantage can also apply to a person.

abuse of dominant position Anticompetitive activities by a dominant firm.

account statement A monthly record of all transactions in a bank account.

accountability The principle that employees with access to cash are responsible for the money they handle and must explain any losses or discrepancies.

accounting The process of recording, analyzing, and interpreting the financial or economic activities of a business.

accounts payable Money that a business owes.

accounts receivable Money owed to a business.

acquisition A process or transaction in which one company takes over control of another company; also known as a takeover.

advertising The paid use of various types of media (such as television, radio, newspapers, and magazines) to try to convince consumers to buy a particular product or service.

advertising research Research that provides information on how to get a product message to potential consumers effectively.

agri-foods Farm-produced foods and services associated with primary agriculture.

annual report A publication that presents a company's financial statements for the year to shareholders and potential investors.

ASEAN Free Trade Area (AFTA) A trade agreement established in 1993 by the ASEAN member countries. It provides for the phased-in reduction of tariffs on most manufacturers' imports within ASEAN countries.

Asia-Pacific Economic Cooperation (APEC) An economic development organization based on consensus and voluntary participation that was formed in 1989.

Asia-Pacific market The region that includes all nations (other than the former Soviet Union) on the continents of Asia and Australia that have a Pacific Ocean shoreline.

ask price The lowest price that any shareholder is currently willing to accept for a particular stock.

assets Things of value that a business or person owns.

Association of Southeast Asian Nations (ASEAN) An association formed in 1967 whose initial members were Indonesia, Malaysia, the Philippines, Singapore, and Thailand.

auto pact The usual term for the Canada–U.S. Automotive Products Agreement, a trade agreement between Canada and the United States that established freer trade in automobile components and completed vehicles. The pact was signed in 1965 and remained in force until 2001.

autocratic leader A leader who makes all the decisions and expects employees to do as they are told.

automated banking machine (ABM) A computer terminal that allows customers to withdraw, deposit, and transfer money with a coded access card.

baby-boom group The large group of people born after World War Two, between 1945 and 1965.

balance of payments The total flow of money coming into a country minus the total flow of money going out.

balance of trade The relationship between a country's imports and exports.

balance sheet A financial statement that shows the financial position of a business on a specific date.

bank notes Paper money issued by the Bank of Canada and accepted as legal tender.

Bank of Canada A bank operated by the federal government that is Canada's central bank; it controls the money supply.

bank rate The minimum rate of interest charged by the Bank of Canada for loans made to the chartered banks; also called the prime lending rate.

barriers to entry Factors that prevent competition from being profitable in a given market.

barter To trade one thing for another without using money.

bear market A period of falling prices in the stock market.

biased Not random; not accurately representing a target population.

bid price The highest price anyone is currently prepared to pay for a particular stock.

bid rigging An unfair pricing practice, in which companies bidding for business arrange bids between themselves instead of truly competing.

big-box store A large retail store that sells a wide range of products at low prices.

bilateral Involving two parties or countries.

bill of lading A document that records the agreement between the person shipping goods and the transportation company.

blank cheque A cheque with no details filled in.

blank endorsement A cheque endorsement consisting only of the signature of the payee.

blue chip company A company with a long record of good earnings, regular dividend payments, stable growth patterns, and an active market for its shares.

blue-collar worker A worker whose work primarily involves the operation of machinery and equipment.

board of directors A group of individuals who run a corporation or cooperative and make decisions on behalf of the shareholders.

bond A long-term loan made to a government or a large business on which interest is paid to the lender (the purchaser of the bond); a definite promise to repay borrowed money on a certain date, along with interest.

bonus A reward for good performance.

bookkeeping The method of recording all transactions for a business in a specific format.

branch banking A banking system in which there is a head office and interconnected branches or outlets providing financial services in different parts of the country.

brand extension Transferring the image created for one product to other products made by the same company.

brand management Grouping all the activities related to a particular brand into one department.

brand name A word or group of words chosen by a manufacturer or retailer to distinguish its products from its competitors.

brand trial Encouragement to consumers, through advertising, to try a product in its early stages.

budget A plan for how income will be spent.

bull market A period of rising prices in the stock market.

business The production and/or sale of goods and/or services to satisfy the needs, wants, and demands of consumers with the purpose of making a profit; an organization set up to do this.

business cycle The four phases or periods of economic activity, namely, peak, recession, trough, and recovery.

business form A method of describing a business by its ownership, such as a sole proprietorship, partnership, corporation, or cooperative form of business.

business plan A document that describes the objectives of a business and summarizes the strategies and resources needed to achieve these objectives. Also referred to as a venture plan.

Business Practices Act An Ontario law that protects consumers from fraud and from salespeople who make misleading statements about the quality of the merchandise they are selling or the terms of the sale.

business type A method of describing a business by its function, such as a merchandising, manufacturing, or service type of business.

buying factors These include time spent, contact time, and waiting time. They are used to help gauge consumer behaviour.

buying quota A limit on the amount of money a business should spend on inventory.

caisse populaire A type of credit union, located mainly in Quebec.

Canada Savings Bond (CSB) A loan from the purchaser to the Government of Canada, in return for a promise that the purchaser will receive the face value of the bond, plus interest, on or before the maturity date.

Canada–U.S. Free Trade Agreement (FTA) A trade agreement that came into effect in January of 1989, and was replaced by NAFTA in 1994.

Canadian direct investment abroad (CDIA) Canadian money invested in other countries.

cancelled cheque A cheque that has been cashed and paid by the financial institution.

capacity A borrower's ability to carry a debt and pay the debt when it is due (one of the three Cs of credit).

capital The value of a borrower's assets that could be used to repay a debt (one of the three Cs of credit).

capital assets Assets that businesses keep for a long time and that last longer than a year. Sometimes referred to as fixed assets.

capital gain Money made when an asset is sold for more than it cost to purchase it.

capital resource A resource such as equipment, a building, or money, that is used to produce goods and services.

capitalist form of government
This form of government tends to let the marketplace dictate the control and the decision making in terms of answering the basic economic questions.

career A goal in life that is fulfilled through an occupation or a series of occupations.

career planning The process of studying career options, assessing one's career skills, and making decisions about a future career.

carpal tunnel syndrome A serious and painful injury to nerves in the hand, often caused or made worse by repeated use of a keyboard.

cartel A group formed to control the supply, and therefore the price, of a product or service within a particular industry.

cash cow A mature product that generates high profits for a business.

cash flow The movement of cash in and out of a business, or cash that is available to the owner for the purpose of running the business on a daily basis and is used to pay for costs and expenses.

cash-flow statement A summary of the cash-in and cash-out transactions of a business in order to predict whether the business will have enough cash to meet its obligations.

caveat emptor A term meaning "Let the buyer beware."

central bank A country's main bank, such as the Bank of Canada, that deals only with the federal government and the chartered banks.

certificate of origin A document that states the country in which shipped goods were produced. It may be used to determine the amount of any import taxes or custom duties.

chamber of commerce An agency that is supported by its chamber members from the business community. It takes responsibility for promotional activities, providing leadership opportunities, and helping its members to network with one another.

channels of distribution See distribution channels.

character A borrower's reliability and willingness to repay a debt when it is due (one of the three Cs of credit).

charge account A contract between a consumer and a retailer for sales in its own stores.

charter school A school run by a private business while receiving funds from the provincial government. It is accountable for money spent, as well as for meeting standards and guidelines set by the government.

chartered bank A financial institution that has received a charter or licence from the federal government to operate in Canada; operates under the federal Bank Act; entitled to use the word "bank."

choice The opportunity to select from several alternatives.

CIF See cost, insurance, and freight.

clearance sale A sale in which seasonal goods are sold below their regular prices to clear the shelves for stock that will sell best during the new season; also called end-of-season sale.

clearing The processing of cheques and settling of accounts among financial institutions through the Canadian Payments Association.

closed-ended questions Questions for which respondents must select an answer from two or more choices they are given.

Closer Economic Relations Trade Agreement (CER) A trade agreement between Australia and New Zealand that came into force in 1983. Its central provision was the creation of a free trade zone eliminating all tariffs and restrictions on trade in goods.

co-branding The sharing of business premises by two or more businesses.

code of ethics A document that describes specifically how a company's employees should respond to different situations.

collate To form groups based on common features.

collateral Something of value offered as security for a loan, which the lender can take and sell if the loan is not repaid on time.

collectible Any item of personal interest to a collector that can increase in value over time; for example, sports cards, stamps, and coins.

combination account An account that offers both savings and chequing features and that may pay interest on deposits.

combination service package A package plan from a financial institution that offers a variety of services for a flat monthly fee.

commission A form of pay based on the amount of sales generated by the employee.

common stock Stock that represents general ownership in a corporation, carries voting privileges, and includes a right to share in its profits, but with no stated or fixed dividend rate.

Commonwealth of Nations An international association of nations (including Canada) that were formerly part of the British Empire. The Queen is the Head of the Commonwealth.

comparative advantage An advantage in producing one good or service rather than another.

comparison shopping Comparing the price, quality, and services of one product or store with those of another.

compensation The money and other benefits received by employees in exchange for their work.

competition A situation in which two or more businesses try to sell the same type of product or service to the same customer.

Competition Act A federal law governing business conduct in Canada.

competitive edge An obvious advantage over the competition.

competitive image The way the consumer sees the business or thinks about the products made and/or sold by the business.

competitive market Specific types of products as well as the companies that produce them.

competitive research Research into all the similar products on the market.

compound interest Interest calculated on the amount saved or borrowed plus any interest already accumulated.

comptroller The manager of the financial department of a business.

consolidation loan A consumer loan that combines all of a borrower's debts into one more manageable loan.

conspicuous consumption The purchase of products or services with the primary purpose of impressing others.

consumer A person who buys goods and services. Also referred to as a customer.

consumer market All the potential users of a product or service.

consumer product Any product intended for a non-industrial consumer.

Consumer Protection Act An Ontario law that, among other things, regulates door-to-door selling by providing a two-day cooling-off period for cancelling contracts.

consumer research Research whose purpose is to discover possible products consumers would purchase and to predict overall sales potential.

convenience store A neighbourhood store that sells a limited number of items but has long operating hours.

cooperative A business owned by members who utilize the goods and services offered.

copyright The exclusive right to publish, produce, sell, or distribute an original work of literature, art, music, software, design, etc.

corporate citizen A business in the context of its relationship with its community.

corporation A business owned by, but existing separately from, its shareholders.

corrective interview An interview with an employee who is having difficulties, in which problems are discussed openly and a plan for improvement is made.

correlation Two or more different elements in a set of data that seem to affect each other.

cost The amount of money that is required for each stage of production.

cost cutting A method of controlling expenses and making more profit.

cost, insurance, and freight (CIF) A shipping term that means the selling price includes the cost of transportation all the way to the purchaser's premises.

cost of goods sold The cost of inventory that was sold to generate business revenue for a specific period of time.

counterfeiting The production of fake money.

creative strategy A plan for an advertising or promotional campaign that outlines how the target consumer will be persuaded to buy the product or service.

credit The borrowing capacity of an individual or company; also, a situation in which someone receives something of value now and agrees to pay for it later.

credit application An information form that a borrower must complete to help a lender make a decision about granting credit or approving a loan.

credit bureau A business that gathers credit information on borrowers.

credit counselling service A not-for-profit consumer debt counselling service that provides unbiased assistance for individuals and families experiencing money and credit problems.

credit rating An indication of the level of risk that a consumer, business, or government will pose if credit is granted.

credit union A financial institution organized, owned, and controlled by people with a common bond, such as employees of a private business or government organization.

creditor A person or business that is owed money; one who lends money or sells on credit.

credit worthiness A person's ability to take on and repay a debt.

crown corporation A business owned and operated by the provincial or federal government.

culture The sum of a country's way of life, beliefs, and customs.

current account An account in a financial institution for business, not personal, use.

current assets Assets that are held for a short period of time and that can quickly be converted into cash. A company funds its day-to-day operations from current assets.

current liability A debt that should be paid quickly, usually within a year.

current ratio The number of dollars of liquid assets (cash or near cash) a business has for every dollar of its short-term debt (total current assets divided by the total current liabilities).

custom A habit, routine, or accepted way of doing things.

customs duty An amount added by a country to the cost of an imported product. The duty is usually a percent of the price of the product, depending on the tariff of the country.

customer loyalty cards Cards that are stamped with each purchase and, when full, entitle the customer to a discount or a free product.

data crunching The process of studying data to see what interpretations can be taken from it.

data mining A research process used to look for unknown relationships and patterns among collected data.

database A list of information organized by category.

debit card Another name for a bank card that allows customers to access their accounts electronically at ABMs or at retailers using the Interac direct payment service.

debt financing Borrowing money to finance operations of the business.

debtor Any person or business that buys on credit or receives a loan.

decision-making model A five-step procedure that assists in making the most appropriate choice among competing alternatives.

decision ownership A type of employee participation in which employees make decisions that directly affect them.

deep selection A lot of different sizes, colours, etc. of one specific product.

delegating Telling others what they should do.

demand The quantity of a good or service that consumers are willing and able to buy.

demand loan A loan, usually for a short term, for which repayment of the entire sum owing can be demanded by the lender at any time.

democratic leader A leader who encourages employees to participate in the decision-making process.

demographics The study of obvious characteristics that categorize human beings.

department store A store that offers a wide variety of goods and services; also called a full-service store.

departmentalization Grouping similar activities in an organization together in order to achieve related goals.

deposit A sum of money placed in an account at a financial institution.

depression A severe form of recession, in which unemployment is high and the sales of goods and services are weak, even though prices are declining.

direct channel of distribution A direct connection between the consumer and the producer of a good or service; also known as a maker-user relationship.

direct competition Competition between products that are very similar.

direct deposit A banking service that allows funds such as wages or government payments to be transferred directly into a specific account.

direct exporting Exporting a product directly to an importer, without using an intermediary.

direct labour Labour that is directly involved in the manufacturing process.

direct-to-home advertisement An advertising message that comes directly to a person's residence.

discount store A store that sells name brand products at prices usually lower than its competitors.

discretionary income The portion of one's disposable income that is not already committed to paying for necessities, and can be used to buy things for pleasure, satisfaction, and comfort.

disposable income The amount of income that is left after taxes have been paid. This income can be used to pay for the basic necessities such as, food, clothing, and shelter.

distribution chain See distribution channels.

distribution channels The paths of ownership or control that goods follow as they pass from the producer or manufacturer to the consumer.

dividend The part of a corporation's profit after taxes that each shareholder receives.

domain name The name given to a Web site; a Web address.

domestic business The producing, distributing, or selling of goods and/or services within a country.

domestic transaction A transaction in which the production and sale of an item occur within the same country.

downsize To reduce the size of a labour force or other aspect of a business.

draft A secure method of sending a large amount of money.

drawee The financial institution on which a cheque is drawn.

drawer The person or business from whose chequing account money will be taken.

early adopter A marketing term for a consumer who likes to be one of the first to try a new product.

e-cash A form of money equivalent to cash, that can be used in an electronic transaction.

e-commerce A method of direct distribution that uses the Internet to sell products directly to consumers.

Economic Development Corporation A type of business, often a Crown Corporation, that is established in a community for the purpose of attracting new businesses and industries to that community.

economic resource The means through which goods and services are made available to consumers; natural resources, human resources, and capital resources are considered to be the three kinds of economic resources. Also known as factors of production.

economic system The way business and government work together to provide goods and services to consumers.

economies of scale The tendency of the cost per item to go down when the items are bought or produced in large quantities.

electronic bill presentment The sending and paying of bills over the Internet.

electronic funds transfer system (EFTS) A computerized system of electronic deposit and withdrawal of funds that reduces need for written cheques.

embargo A complete stoppage of the importing or exporting of a good or service.

empathy The ability to understand what other people think and feel.

employee layoff Dismissing staff to reduce expenses.

employee referral program An incentive program that pays employees a bonus if they find qualified applicants for new positions with the company.

employee turnover The rate at which employees leave a company voluntarily.

endorsement The signature of the payee on the back of a cheque, providing written evidence that payment has been received or has been transferred to a third party.

enterprising person Someone who brings entrepreneurial characteristics to the workplace or another organization.

entrepreneur A person who takes risks and starts a venture to solve a problem or to take advantage of an opportunity; a person who provides an innovative product or service to meet a consumer want or need.

equity financing Raising money using the owner's resources or money from investors.

equity The net value of property or assets after subtracting any mortgage or liabilities.

essential good An item that can be seen and touched and is necessary for survival.

essential service A service that is essential for survival, such as lighting, heating, and water.

ethics The principles of morality and proper conduct that people or businesses use to guide their behaviour.

euro The name of the single common currency for the European Union.

European Coal and Steel Community A trade agreement signed in 1952 that was one of the first steps toward the European Union.

European Economic Community (EEC) This organization was established in 1958 by treaty between Belgium, France, Italy, Luxembourg, the Netherlands, and West Germany; it was known informally as the Common Market.

European Free Trade Association (EFTA) Britain engineered the formation of this association in 1960 and was joined by other European nations that did not belong to the Common Market. The current members are Norway, Switzerland, Iceland, and Liechtenstein.

European Union (EU) In 1993, the European Union united its 12 member states (Belgium, Denmark, France, Germany, Greece, Ireland, Italy, Luxembourg, the Netherlands, Portugal, Spain, and the United Kingdom) into a true single market, not simply an area of free trade. Today the EU is composed of 15 independent states (Austria, Finland, Sweden joined after 1993) with a total population of more than 370 million people.

exchange rate The value of one currency compared to the value of another currency.

exclusive dealing An illegal requirement by a manufacturer that a dealer carry its products exclusively, thereby reducing competition and consumer choice.

excise tax A tax on the manufacture, sale, or consumption of a product within a country.

executive summary A brief summary of a document that allows busy readers to grasp the main points quickly.

exit interview An interview with a departing employee.

expenses Expenditures that help a business generate revenue; assets that are consumed in the process of generating revenue.

export A product or service produced in one country and sold in another.

eye-tracking photography A research technique that records where a person's eyes look first when approaching a store display or looking at a page in a magazine.

face value The value of a bond that appears on the face or front of the bond. It is the amount the issuer promises to pay the purchaser on the maturity date.

factor of production Another name for economic resource.

factory outlet A store that sells goods directly from the manufacturer's factory.

factory overhead The expenses involved in operating all production facilities.

fad A product that is extremely popular for a very short period of time.

feasible Having the potential to succeed.

financial institution A bank, trust company, credit union, or other organization that accepts money from depositors and lends it to borrowers.

fiscal year Business year; the 12-month period used for financial calculations and comparisons by a business.

fixed cost An expense that does not change depending on the quantity produced.

fixed expenses Expenses that occur regularly and for the same amount each time; for example, rent or mortgage payments.

flow of funds The process of paying for imported and exported goods and services; the movement of funds in international investment transactions.

focus group A company-arranged meeting of potential consumers that the marketer observes during an organized discussion.

forecasting Predicting future conditions.

foreign direct investment (FDI) Foreign money invested in Canada.

foreign trade See international business.

form What a product looks like.

franchisee A person who runs a franchise operation and is under contract, or licensing agreement, with the franchiser.

franchiser The parent company who grants the franchise and provides goods and/or services to the franchisees.

free enterprise An economic system in which economic resources are privately owned and decisions about what to produce are made freely by individual owners.

free on board (FOB) A shipping term that means the selling price of the product includes the cost of transportation only as far as the specified point.

free trade zone A designated area, usually around a seaport or airport, where products can be imported duty-free and then stored, assembled, and/or used in manufacturing.

Free Trade Area of the Americas (FTAA) A proposed trade agreement that would extend NAFTA to all the democratic countries in the Western Hemisphere.

freedom of choice The freedom to enter into a business or career of one's own choice, to own property, to make a profit, and to compete in the marketplace.

FTA See Canada–U.S. Free Trade Agreement.

FTAA See Free Trade Area of the Americas.

function What a product is designed to do.

fundraising Collecting money to support an identifiable cause.

gatekeeper A person who makes buying decisions for others.

General Agreement on Tariffs and Trade (GATT) A trade agreement that was originally signed by 23 nations after World War Two. It was designed to encourage economic growth through international trade and grew to 115 member states before it was replaced by the World Trade Organization in 1995.

General Agreement on Trade in Services (GATS) A WTO agreement that came into effect in 1995 and that set guidelines for the trade of services across international borders.

general partnership The most common form of partnership, in which the partners share in responsibility, decision-making, and profits. However, the partners have unlimited liability for the debts of the business.

generic brand A product packaged in a very plain container; also called a no-name brand.

gentrification The revitalization of a poor urban neighbourhood by renovating or replacing the existing dwellings.

glass ceiling The invisible barriers said to be faced by women, the disabled, or people from visible minorities as they approach senior leadership positions in companies.

global dependency The phenomenon that occurs when many items consumers need and want are created in countries other than their own.

global economy The exchange of goods and services among people in different countries throughout the world.

global product A standardized item offered in the same form in all the countries in which it is sold.

globalization A term used to describe the process of doing business all over the world.

goal An objective; something that one works to achieve or attain.

good An item that can be seen and touched.

goods and services tax (GST) A tax imposed by the federal government on the purchase of most goods and services in Canada.

goods in process All partially finished goods in the plant at inventory time.

gross domestic product (GDP) The total value of all goods and services produced in a country during a specific period of time (including items produced by foreign-owned companies).

gross pay The total amount of money received from one's employer, before any deductions.

gross profit All the money left over after deducting the cost of goods sold from revenue, but before deducting the business expenses that helped generate the revenue.

Group of Eight (G8) An association of the world's most powerful industrialized nations: Britain, France, Germany, Italy, Canada, the United States, Japan, and Russia.

growth company A company that directs its profits back into the company's operations instead of paying dividends, and has prospects for above-average future growth.

GST See goods and services tax.

guarantee A promise by a manufacturer or retailer, usually in writing, about the performance or quality of a product; also called a warranty.

guaranteed investment certificate (GIC) A savings plan similar to a term deposit, but usually involving a larger sum of money invested for a longer period of time.

harassment Making a particular person or group feel uncomfortable in a work situation because of their race, religion, gender, etc.

headhunter A recruitment agency or executive search company.

hidden job market Jobs that are never advertised; about 85% of all available jobs.

hold A delay in clearing a cheque, imposed by a financial institution.

homogeneous market A market in which everyone requires the same types of goods and services, regardless of age, gender, or income.

human resource People who work to produce goods and services in a business; also known as work force or labour.

Human Resources Development Canada (HRDC) The department of the federal government responsible for workforce issues and programs.

idea-driven enterprise A venture that begins as the result of an invention or innovation.

image The consumer's perception of a business or its products.

import A good or service brought into a country for sale.

importer Someone who seeks out foreign products to bring into his or her own country.

impulse buying Purchasing an item on the spur of the moment without considering whether it is a wise purchase.

incentive Something added to the pay of an employee to encourage harder work or particular types of work.

income The money that an individual or business receives from various sources, such as wages or sales, interest, and dividends.

income statement A financial statement that shows a business's profit (or loss) over a stated period of time.

indirect channel of distribution The presence of one or more intermediaries between the producer and the consumer.

indirect competition Competition between products or services that are not directly related to each other.

indirect exporting Exporting a product to an intermediary, who then conveys the product to the importer.

indirect labour Labour in departments of a business not directly involved in the manufacturing process.

inflation The reduction in purchasing power of a given amount of money when wages and prices increase.

informal structure Organization based on personal contacts rather than formal role divisions.

innovation Using new technology, materials, or processes to improve on existing products, or on how they are produced and distributed.

installment sales credit A credit plan that requires a down payment and fixed regular payments, with finance charges added to the purchase price.

intangible Not capable of being seen or touched.

Interac Direct Payment (IDP) A method of paying for goods and services electronically that uses customers' banking cards to immediately and directly transfer funds from their bank accounts to those of merchants or other service providers.

interception rate The average amount of time a customer will spend with a salesperson in a store.

interdependent Mutually dependent; relying on others who also rely on you.

interest The money paid for the use of borrowed or loaned money over a period of time.

intermediary A business that takes possession of the goods before the consumer does.

international business All the business transactions necessary for creating, shipping, and selling goods and services across national borders. Also referred as international trade or foreign trade.

international investment Investing that occurs across national borders.

international trade See international business.

international transaction A transaction in which the production and sale of an item take place in different countries.

intrapreneurship The entrepreneurial spirit within a business or an organization.

invention A product or process that does something that has never been done before.

inventory Goods and materials kept on hand.

inventory management Balancing product quantity with sales; having merchandise when it is needed and not having merchandise when it is no longer needed.

investing Using savings to earn extra income.

invoice A bill for goods and services either bought by or sold to the business.

jingle A short, catchy tune, often incorporating a slogan, that is used in advertising and easily remembered by the consumer.

joint account A financial institution account shared by two or more people.

just in time A process by which required items are delivered immediately before they are needed, rather than kept on hand.

knockoff A cheaper version of a product that is experiencing a fad.

labour force The total number of people working or looking for work.

labour market The way connections are established between buyers of skills (employers) and sellers of skills (employees).

launch The introduction of a product.

law of demand The economic principle that demand goes up when prices come down, and comes down when prices go up.

law of supply The economic principle that supply goes up when prices go up, and comes down when prices come down.

layaway plan A buying plan in which a product is "laid away" or set aside until its full price has been paid over weeks or months.

lease An agreement to rent something for a period of time at an agreed price.

legal tender Coins and paper money, as defined by the Government of Canada, that must be accepted as payment for goods and services.

liability A debt of the business.

licensee Someone who has obtained a licence.

licensing Permission from the inventor of a product that allows another business to use his or her invention for a fee.

licensing fee Money paid to obtain a licence.

lifestyle advertising Advertising that implies that using the product or service being promoted will improve one's lifestyle.

lifestyle The way people live, including their values, beliefs, and motivations.

limited liability A restriction on the extent to which the shareholders (owners) of a corporation are personally responsible for its debts, limiting their liability to the amount they originally invested.

limited partnership A partnership in which the liability of each partner is limited to the amount of his or her investment.

line of credit A form of borrowing that allows access to credit up to a maximum amount agreed on between the borrower and the financial institution.

liquid Easily turned into cash.

liquidity The ability to convert an asset or investment into cash quickly and easily.

listserv A kind of e-mailing list that distributes queries and information to all the people who belong or subscribe to it.

loans payable Debt acquired by borrowing money from investors, banks, or other financial institutions; also called notes payable.

logo A special symbol that is associated with a product or company.

long-term assets See capital assets.

long-term liability A debt that takes longer than a year to pay in full.

long-term goal A plan intended to be achieved within a long period, such as a year or more.

luxury good An item which can be seen and touched but is not necessary for survival.

luxury service A service that is not necessary for survival.

Maastricht Treaty A treaty signed in 1993 that converted the 12 member states of the European Union into a truly single market, not just an area of free trade.

magnetic ink character recognition (MICR) Special coded characters printed across the bottom of cheques and read by cheque-sorting machines.

maker-user relationship See direct channel of distribution.

management Those who decide how best to use an organization's human, financial, and material resources.

managers People who get things done by directing others.

manufacturing business A business that produces goods for sale.

margin The difference between the cost of the product and the selling price of the product.

marginal business A business that is barely profitable.

market-driven enterprise A venture that begins with an idea about the market rather than about a product.

market research Research used to identify specific groups of consumers who would use a particular product or service.

market segment Any part of an overall market that has common characteristics.

market share The amount spent on one company's product, expressed as a percent of the total amount spent by consumers on all products of that type.

market value The price at which a share of stock or a bond can be bought or sold; the amount people pay for a good or a service.

marketing All the activities involved in getting goods and services from the businesses that produce them to the consumers who wish to purchase them.

marketing board A government organization that controls the manufacturing, processing, distribution, and supply of a product or service.

marketing research The collection and analysis of information relevant to the marketing strategy or process.

matching principle The principle that accurate profit reporting can be done only if all the costs of doing business in a particular period are matched with the revenue generated during that period.

maturity date The date on which a bond or loan becomes due and must be repaid.

medium of exchange A function of money when it is exchanged for goods and services.

merger A process whereby one company combines with or takes over the ownership of one or more other companies.

minimum wage The lowest hourly wage an employer can pay an employee.

minted Manufactured, as in the minting of coins by the Royal Canadian Mint.

modern mixed economy An economy that contains elements of several different economic systems, such as socialism and free enterprise.

money management Daily financial activities aimed at satisfying one's needs and wants within a limited income.

money order A form of payment, like a cheque, in which the issuing institution guarantees to pay the amount shown on the form to a payee.

money supply The total amount of money in circulation in Canada, including cash and deposits and savings in financial institutions.

monopoly A business that is the only supplier of a good or service.

mortgage The legal document in which the borrower of a mortgage loan gives the lender a claim against the property purchased if the loan is not repaid as agreed.

mortgage loan A long-term credit plan for purchasing real estate.

most favoured nation A term applied to a country's closest trading partners.

motivation research Psychological research into the behaviour of consumers.

multiple intelligences A theory that each person has varying amounts of eight different kinds of intelligence.

municipal corporation The formal name for a city or town.

mutual fund A pool of money from many investors set up and managed by an investment company to buy and sell securities from other corporations.

name brand A well-known brand that is advertised nationally and available in most communities; also called a national brand.

national brand See name brand.

natural resource Those raw materials that we get from the earth, the water, and the air.

need An item necessary for survival such as food, clothing, or shelter.

net income See net profit.

net pay The amount of money received from one's employer after deductions such as those for income tax, Canada Pension Plan contributions, and employment insurance.

net profit The money left over once operating expenses have been deducted from the gross profit.

networking The process of meeting new people and establishing business relationships with them.

niche A section of the market in which a product dominates and into which few competitors enter; a place or position particularly suitable to the person or thing.

night depository A secure, locked deposit facility at a financial institution that lets business clients make deposits at any time, especially after hours.

no-name brand See generic brand.

not-for-profit organization An organization, often a charitable organization, that does not seek to make a profit from the operations of the business.

non-tariff barriers Controls, other than tariff barriers, to restrict or deter the importing of goods and services.

North American Free Trade Agreement (NAFTA) An agreement among Canada, the United States, and Mexico to allow freer trade among the three countries, which came into effect on January 1, 1994.

notes payable See loans payable.

NSF cheque A cheque for an amount that is greater than the amount of funds in the account it is drawn on.

observation The collection of information by recording a person's actions without interacting or communicating with that person.

obsolete A product or service that consumers no longer want because it has become outdated or outmoded or has been replaced by a new or improved product.

occupation Something one does to provide a good or a service; a job.

occupational forecasts Predictions about jobs.

online Linked electronically, especially over the Internet. To "go online" is to establish oneself on the Internet.

online banking A service that allows customers to conduct banking activities from their personal computers through their financial institution's Web site.

OPEC The Organization of Petroleum Exporting Countries; a cartel composed of nations that produce and export oil.

open-ended question A question that allows respondents to develop their own answers.

open job market The jobs that are advertised and for which people apply; about 15% of all available jobs.

operating expenses The cost of doing business for a particular period.

organization A method of combining people, finances, and physical resources.

organization chart A graphic representation of the structure of an organization or business.

Organization for Economic Cooperation and Development (OECD) An organization formed in 1961 to promote the principles of a market economy, democracy, and respect for human rights.

orientation A familiarization period for new employees.

out-of-home advertising An advertising message that the consumer is supposed to receive while not at home.

outplacement counselling Assistance given to laid off or terminated employees in finding a new job.

outsourcing The practice of subcontracting work to other companies.

outstanding cheque A cheque that has not been cashed and deducted from your bank statement balance.

overdraft A temporary loan from a financial institution that results when the institution pays a cheque written for more money than is in the drawer's account.

overtime A higher hourly rate for working longer than the regular scheduled time or on holidays.

owner's equity The owner's investment in the business or the financial portion of the business that actually belongs to the owner.

parent company A company that owns or controls other companies.

partnership A business with two or more owners who share the responsibilities and profits/losses.

partnership agreement The legal document that establishes a partnership and each partner's responsibilities.

passbook A customer's record of transactions for accounts in financial institutions.

patent pending A warning that an application for a patent has been filed, giving the patent owner legal protection for his or her invention.

patent The registration of an inventor's legal right of ownership of his or her invention, preventing others from using the invention without permission.

patronage refund If a cooperative makes a profit, members may receive a return in the form of a patronage refund. The amount of refund is tied to how much each member uses the cooperative.

payables See accounts payable.

payee The person or business to whom a cheque is made payable.

peak The phase of the business cycle when economic activity is at its highest level.

peer pressure The strong influence of people from one's own social group.

pension Income paid to an employee who has retired from a company.

periodical index A list of all articles published about specific topics over a particular period of time.

perk A special benefit beyond ordinary compensation.

personal identification number (PIN) A special customer code number or electronic signature used with a coded card to operate an ABM.

piecework A form of pay based on the amount of a particular product a person can make.

portfolio investment An investment made solely to earn interest or dividends.

postdating Putting a future date on a cheque.

preauthorized debit A regular, automatic withdrawal from a bank account.

preauthorized payment plan The process of paying regular monthly bills like loans, car and home insurance, and utilities automatically from one's account on specified dates.

preferred stock Stock that has priority over common stock in the payment of fixed rate dividends and gives its holders certain additional privileges.

premium Something a consumer gets free with the purchase of a product.

price The value of a product or service expressed in dollars and cents.

price fixing An illegal action by companies who agree on the quantity of a product they will supply and the prices they will charge their customers, in order to reduce competition.

pricing research Research into the possible price to charge for a business's product.

primary data Current information collected and analyzed for a specific purpose.

prime lending rate See bank rate.

principal The original amount of money deposited or borrowed.

private brand A product that is manufactured by another company but is sold with a store's brand name; also called a store brand or private-label brand.

private corporation A corporation owned by a small number of shareholders.

private enterprise The right of an individual to choose whether to own a business, what business to enter, and what to produce with only limited government direction.

private label See private brand.

private property A principle of the free market system that permits people to own, use, or dispose of things of value, including the tools and machinery used in production, as long as they do not violate any laws in the process.

private sector The economic sector represented by individually owned and operated businesses rather than government.

privatization The sale to the private sector of a business formerly owned by the government.

producer An individual or business that makes a product.

product life cycle The changes in the popularity of a product over time.

product mapping An activity that allows the entrepreneur to visualize all the products or services that are available in a particular segment and to group them by specific features.

product research The examination of each detail of a product or service and the analysis of its potential impact on the market.

productivity A comparison of the resources used with the products or services that result. If fewer resources are used per unit produced, productivity increases.

professional labour Highly trained people in specific occupations such as accountants and electricians.

profit The reward that an owner receives for taking risks. It is the money left over from sales after the costs and expenses of operating a business have been paid.

profit equation Selling Price – Cost of Goods Sold – Expenses.

promotional sale A sale in which goods are sold below their regular price, for example to build acceptance for a new product or to publicize the opening of a new store.

protected grounds Characteristics of an employee that, by law, cannot lead to harassment or discrimination.

protectionist Tending to protect one's own economic interests by imposing trade barriers.

provincial sales tax (PST) A tax imposed by a provincial government, usually payable on retail purchases.

provincial sales tax number
An identification number for a business that must charge provincial sales tax on its products.

psychographics The study of lifestyles.

public corporation A corporation with many shareholders, whose shares can be bought and sold on a stock exchange.

public relations firm A business that is hired to manage the publicity of another company.

public sector The sector of the economy consisting of agencies or departments controlled by the different levels of government.

publicity Information about a business, either positive or negative, that appears in the media and is not paid for by the business.

public–private partnerships These partnerships, sometimes called P3s, are businesses from the public and private sector that have pooled resources and gone into business together.

pull strategy A marketing strategy whose main objective is to increase consumer demand.

purchases The total goods bought by the business in a year, calculated by examining invoices for the year, as recorded in the books of the business.

purchasing power The amount and quality of goods and services that money will buy.

pure command economy An economy in which the central government owns all the resources and makes all the economic decisions.

pure market economy An economy in which resources are privately owned and buyers and sellers make all the economic decisions.

push strategy A marketing strategy whose objective is to sell products to the retailer.

quota A specified quantity that cannot be exceeded, such as a limit on the number of items to be imported or their dollar value.

random Without bias; offering an equal chance for anyone in a population to be selected as a representative of that population.

rate of return Interest expressed as a percent of the original investment; also called yield.

rate of return on average owner's equity A figure calculated in order to determine the success of a business. Rate of Return on Average Owner's Equity = (Net Profit ÷ Average Owner's Equity) X 100. See owner's equity.

rate of return on net sales Net profit divided by total revenue in order to show the portion of business sales that are kept as profit.

raw materials Ingredients that are transformed into another product.

real estate Land and anything attached to it.

receivables See accounts receivable.

recession The phase of the business cycle when demand begins to decrease, businesses lower production of goods and services, and jobs tend to disappear.

reconciliation In relation to financial institutions, checking bank statements against personal records to ensure that they agree.

recovery The phase of the business cycle when jobs begin to reappear, demand for goods and services is on the increase, and confidence is restored in the economy.

redemption rate The percentage of coupons issued in a sales promotion that are used by consumers.

refusal to deal An illegal practice of refusing to sell products to small retailers, thereby reducing competition.

regional relating to a geographic area or to a group of countries.

registered education savings plan (RESP) A long-term, tax-sheltered savings plan to finance a child's postsecondary education.

registered retirement savings plan (RRSP) A long-term savings plan that builds up a savings fund for a person's retirement. Tax is deferred on money earned in the plan until it is withdrawn.

respondent A person who responds to a survey.

restrictive endorsement A cheque endorsement that limits the use of the cheque to the purpose given in the endorsement; for example, "For deposit only."

retail business A business that buys goods and resells them to consumers.

return on sales Profit expressed as a percent of sales.

revenue The money a business receives for the products and/ or services it sells or from its investments.

revolving credit account A credit plan that allows consumers to charge purchases at any time but requires that a minimum part of the debt be repaid every month.

royalty The fee paid to the owner of a patent or copyright by a someone who used it.

Rule of 72 A formula to determine how many years it will take to double your money if you let your investment compound. If you divide 72 by the interest rate being earned, the result is the number of years until your principal doubles.

safety deposit box A box located in a financial institution's vault that is rented by an individual or business to store important documents and valuables.

salary A fixed amount of money paid to an employee on a regular schedule.

sales pitch A scripted sales presentation that anticipates all possible consumer responses.

sales promotion Any attempt to sell a product.

sales quota A performance goal an employee is expected to achieve.

saving Putting money aside for future use; the opposite of consuming; the difference between the money you earn and the money you spend.

savings plan Putting money aside in a regular way to reach a financial goal.

secondary data Information collected by others.

secondhand shopping Purchasing goods that have already been owned by someone else.

securities A general term for stocks and bonds that are sold by corporations and governments to raise large sums of money.

semiskilled labour Labour required for a job that needs some instruction. Employees will be productive after a few days of training.

seniority Length of service with a company.

service Assistance provided, usually in return for payment, that satisfies needs and wants of people or businesses but that does not result in a product that can be touched.

service business A business that provides a service to satisfy the needs or wants of consumers.

service charge A fee charged for a service provided; a processing fee.

service sector The part of the economy composed of businesses that provide mainly services.

set of books Accurate accounting records of each transaction the business makes.

severance package Final compensation paid to a laid-off or terminated employee.

share A unit of ownership in a corporation.

shareholder A person who owns shares in a corporation; also called a stockholder.

shareholders' equity The shareholders' investment in a corporation or the financial portion of the corporation that actually belongs to the shareholders

shelf allowance A special fee paid by a manufacturer to help a retail store offset the costs of advertising and rearranging the shelves to stock the product.

short-term goal A plan intended to be achieved within a short time, usually less than one year.

sick pay Wages paid to an employee who is absent from work due to illness.

signature card A financial institution's official record of a customer's handwritten name, used to verify a customer's identity.

simple interest Interest calculated only on the principal amount loaned or deposited.

skill The ability to do something specific or to translate knowledge into action.

skilled labour Labour required for positions that need training from an educational institution and/or previous employment.

slogan A short, catchy advertising phrase associated with a company or product.

smart card A plastic card with a computer chip that stores information.

social responsibility The obligation of a business to contribute to a community's well-being.

sole proprietorship A business directly owned by one person who receives all profits and is responsible for all liabilities.

solvent Having the ability to pay all debts and other obligations.

specialty channel of distribution Any indirect channel of distribution that does not involve a retail store.

specialty store A store that carries a specific type or line of products.

stakeholder Someone affected by or with an interest in a decision or activity.

standard of future payment A function of money that allows a consumer to calculate the future value of a current transaction.

standard of living The way one lives, as measured by the kinds and quality of goods and services one can afford.

standard of value A function of money that determines the worth or value of goods and services.

statement In relation to financial institutions, a computer printout that lists all transactions in an account each month.

statement of cash flow See cash-flow statement.

stock See shares.

stock exchange A trading market in which investors buy and sell shares and other investments through stockbrokers.

stockholder See shareholder.

stop payment An order requesting a financial institution not to pay a particular cheque.

store brand See private brand.

store of value A function of money in which its value can be saved until a later time.

strategy A plan for achieving goals.

style curve A graphic representation of a product's success in the market, illustrating the volume of sales over time.

subsidiary company A company that is controlled and owned by another company.

subsidy A financial benefit given to a business by a government.

supermarket A large full-service food store that carries a wide variety of name brand, private brand, and generic products.

supply The quantity of a good or service that producers can provide, determined by the costs of producing it and by the price people are willing to pay for it.

supply quota The amount of a product that producers agree to make available to consumers.

survey A planned set of questions used to gather data that can be analyzed to help solve problems.

sweatshop A piecework factory with low wages and unsafe or unhealthy working conditions.

takeover See acquisition.

tangible Capable of being seen and touched.

tariff A list or schedule of the percent of the product price to be charged as customs duty.

tariff barrier An effort by a country to protect its domestic industry by increasing the cost of imported goods.

Team Canada The name given to trade missions to foreign countries, led by senior members of the government, that have taken place since 1994.

tender An invitation to bid on a contract and to do the necessary work as outlined in the "request to tender" document.

term The period of time over which a loan is to be repaid.

term deposit A savings plan in which a fixed sum of money is deposited for a specific length of time, paying a fixed rate of interest higher than that paid on regular savings accounts.

term loan A form of borrowing in which the borrower agrees to make fixed payments over a set period of time.

third-party guarantee A loan guaranteed by someone other than the borrower who has collateral.

three Cs of credit The three qualities of a potential borrower that a lender considers when making a decision about credit worthiness: character, capacity, and capital.

trade agreement An agreement between countries to allow goods and services to flow more freely across their borders.

trade deficit A situation in which a country pays more for its imports than it earns from its exports.

trade show An exhibition where a large number of manufacturers and distributors show their goods.

trade surplus A situation in which a country pays less for its imports than it earns from its exports.

trademark A word, symbol, or design, or a combination of these, used to distinguish one company's goods or services from other goods or services.

tradeoff Something one gives up in order to have something more important.

trading bloc A group of countries that share the same trade interests.

transaction The process of exchanging something of value for something else that has value.

transaction account A type of account in a financial institution used to deposit money needed for everyday use, such as paying bills, rather than for savings.

transaction register A record similar to a passbook, used with a transaction account.

traveller's cheques A cheque-like form that can be purchased at financial institutions and used in place of cash to pay for items in most countries of the world; similar to a cheque but accepted like cash around the world.

trough The phase of the business cycle when economic activity is at its lowest level.

trust company A financial institution that manages estates, acts as a trustee in business transactions, and provides a number of financial services similar to those provided by banks.

unemployment rates The number of able-to-work people who do not have jobs, expressed as a percent of the labour force.

unlimited liability Responsibility for claims against the business that goes beyond the amount invested in the business and extends to one's personal assets.

unskilled labour Labour required for a job that almost anyone could do because it requires very little training.

value A personal or corporate belief about what is important.

value-added service An extra service added to attract or retain customers.

variable cost An expense that changes depending on the quantity produced.

variable expense An expense that differs each time and is usually difficult to estimate in advance; for example, food, clothing, and entertainment.

venture A business enterprise involving some risk, established with the expectation of gain or profit.

venture capital market A market that brings together inventors and financial investors who are interested in developing new ideas.

want An item not necessary for survival but that adds pleasure and comfort to life.

warehouse club A no-frills retail outlet that offers bulk quantities of products at prices lower than those of most supermarkets. Shoppers often pay a membership fee to join the club.

Web page A portion of the information posted on a Web site.

Web site A place, or site, on the Internet where a business can be established and accessed by consumers. A Web site consists of one or more Web pages designed to provide information about the business and display goods or services offered for sale.

Web site hit A visit to a Web site by someone using the Internet. The number of hits indicates the popularity or usefulness of the site.

wellness program A program that promotes and encourages the physical and emotional health of employees.

white-collar worker A worker whose work involves considerable contact with other people and the processing and handling of information.

wholesaler Someone who buys goods from producers or importers and resells them to retailers.

wide selection A large number of different brands or types of merchandise.

withdrawal The act of taking money out of an account at a financial institution.

work team A group of qualified people brought together for a specific task.

working capital The funds a business uses to pay its short-term debts (working capital = current assets − current liabilities).

World Trade Organization (WTO) The principal international organization that deals with the rules of trade between nations. It was created in 1995 and replaced the General Agreement on Tariffs and Trade (GATT).

yield See rate of return.

zoning regulations Controls that municipal governments place on where a business can locate and what sorts of activities can be done there.

Index

A

AB Tetra Pak, 396
Absolute advantage, 443
Abuse of dominant position, 118
A.C. Dispensing Equipment Inc., 384–385
Accountability, 176
Accounting
  business failure and, 107–108
  defined, 176
  in manufacturing businesses, 182–183
  in product-sales businesses, 180–182
  in retail businesses, 180–182
  in service businesses, 179–180
Accounting equation, 186
Accounts payable, 185
Accounts receivable, 184
Addiction treatment, 151
Advertising
  creative strategy for, 426
  defined, 220
  direct-to-home, 221, 223
  lifestyle, 34
  in magazines, 222, 223
  in newspapers, 222, 223
  out-of-home, 221, 223
  purposes of, 220–221
  on radio, 222, 223
  research, 213
  on television, 222, 223
  types of, 221–223
Africa, Sub-Saharan
  Canadian investment in, 502–503
Age, markets and, 131–132
Agri-foods industry, 498
Air Canada, 69
Airplanes, invention of, 388
Akol, Günseli, 331–332
Allowances, 238
Alternative Fuel Systems Inc. (AFS), 462–463
Annual reports, 178
Antismoking programs, 151
Antitrust legislation, 104
Arbib, Walter, 143–144

ASEAN Free Trade Area (AFTA), 477
Asia–Pacific Economic Cooperation (APEC), 469, 470
Asia–Pacific market, 476, 484
Asia–Pacific region
  investment relations with Canada, 500–501
Assets, 67, 184–185
Association of Southeast Asian Nations (ASEAN), 476–477, 484
Attitude, positive, 147–150
Australia, trade with Canada, 481
Auto Pact, 465–466
Autocratic leaders, 166
Automated banking machines (ABMs), 300, 301, 322
Automobiles, invention of, 388
Ayotte, Sharlyn, 287–288

B

Babra, Surjit, 143–144
Baby-boom group, 132
Baird, John Logie, 386
Balance of trade, 445–446
Balance sheet, 184–189
Bank Act, 290
Bank notes, 233
Bank of Canada, 104, 292–293
Bank rate, 293
Banking
  branch, 291–292
  history of, 289–291
  online, 324
  by telephone, 323–324
Banks
  acquisitions of, 294–295
  chartered, 290
  mergers of, 294–295
  in the United States, 292
Barriers to entry, 208
Barter, 235
Bear market, 276
Berry and Peterson, 397–398
Bias, in samples, 419
BIC pen, 399

Bich, Marcel, 399
Bid rigging, 117–118
Big-box stores, 110, 195, 231–232, 245
Bill of lading, 451
Blank cheques, 313
Blast Radius, 115–116
Bliss Spa, 83–84
Blissymbolics, 395
Blue-collar workers, 14
Board of directors, 53
Boland, Mike, 174–175
Bonds
  Canada Savings, 274
  corporate, 275
Bonus, incentive, 149
Bookkeeping, 176
Books, on business, 371
Brand extension, 138
Brand identification, 138
Brand management, 164, 203–206, 209–210
Brand names, 136, 250
Brand trials, 220
Branding, 215. *See also* Co-branding
Brazil, investment by Canada in, 502
Budgeting, 87, 177, 253–257
Budman, Michael, 93, 363
Bull market, 275
Business cycles, 72
Business plans, 423–427
Business Practices Act, 106
Business(es)
  defined, 5
  failures of, 107–111, 428–429
  financing, 47, 428–429
  government influence on, 102–106
  home-based, 49
  impact on community, 70–77
  manufacturing, 50
  marginal, 95–96
  new, 428–429
  ownership of, 52–55
  quality of life and, 74
  resources needed, 49

Credits

Every reasonable effort to trace the copyright holders of materials appearing in this book has been made. Information that will enable the publisher to rectify any error or omission will be welcomed.

Cover Images: Russell Illiq/PhotoDisc (maple leaf), Ken Davies/Masterfile (globe)

Table of Contents: p. vii Courtesy Mountain Equipment Co-op; p. viii NASA; p. ix Courtesy A.C. Dispensing Equipment Inc.; p. x Jack Wilson

Photo credits

Unit One: p. 1 Dick Hemingway; **Chapter One**: p. 2 Dick Hemingway; p. 3 Courtesy Manoucher Food & Co.; p. 4 Manoucher is a trademark of Manoucher Food & Co. and is used with permission; p. 6 Courtesy Home Depot; p. 7 Dick Hemingway; p. 10 "Speedbump" by permission of Dave Coverly and Creators Syndicate Inc.; p. 12 Mark Tuschman/First Light; **Chapter Two**: p. 24 Mug Shots/First Light; p. 25 Steve Uhraney © 2001 Brunico Communications Inc. Reprinted with permission. STRATEGY and "The Canadian Marketing Report" are trademarks of Brunico Communications Inc.; p. 27 John A. Rizzo/PhotoDisc; p. 29 Images/First Light; p. 33 Superstock; p. 37 Courtesy Grocery Gateway Inc.; **Chapter Three**: p. 42 Dick Hemingway; p. 43 Communications Nova Scotia; p. 48 Dick Hemingway; p. 51 Courtesy General Motors of Canada; p. 52 Dick Hemingway; p. 53 Francisco Cruz/Superstock; p. 54 Courtesy Mountain Equipment Co-op; **Chapter Four**: p. 60 CP Picture Archives/Mike Ridewood; p. 61 Courtesy Emmie Leung, International Paper Industries; p. 65 CBC Still Photo Collection, Toronto, Ben Flock; p. 66 Boily Photo; p. 69 Images/First Light; p. 70 Chuck Savage/First Light; p. 74 Dick Hemingway; p. 76 Courtesy University of Western Ontario; **Unit Two:** p. 81 Courtesy Sobeys Inc.; **Chapter Five**: p. 82 Dick Hemingway; p. 83 CP Picture Archives/Phill Snel; p. 86 Geographical Visual Aids; p. 88 Courtesy Glaxo Wellcome Inc.; p. 91 Courtesy G.A.P Adventures; p. 93 F. Scott Grant: Canadian Sport Images; p. 94 Jon Feingersh/First Light; p. 97 Russell Illiq/PhotoDisc; p. 98 Dick Hemingway; p. 101 Dick Hemingway; p. 103 Courtesy of Dairy Farmer's of Ontario; p. 109 CP Picture Archives/Kim Stallknecht; **Chapter Six**: p. 114 Dick Hemingway; p. 115 © 2000 Verve Photograph Inc. Photographer: Paul Joseph; p. 119 Dick Hemingway; p. 120 Courtesy Escabèche Restaurant at the Prince of Wales Hotel, Niagara-On-The-Lake, Ontario, Canada; p. 122 Used under licence from Billy Bee Honey Products Ltd., the registered owner of such trademarks; p. 125 Seaman's Beverages, Charlottetown, Prince Edward Island; p. 132 Nancy Santullo/First Light; p. 133 Dick Hemingway; p. 136 Dick Hemingway; p. 137 CP Picture Archives/Dan Loh; **Chapter Seven:** p. 142 Ryan McVay/PhotoDisc; p. 143 Photo by Al M. Gilbert; p. 146 Randy Duchaine/First Light; p. 152 Courtesy Husky Injection Molding Systems; p. 155 Courtesy General Motors of Canada; p. 161 UN/DPI Photo; p. 165 Francisco Cruz/Superstock; **Chapter Eight**: p. 173 Superstock; p. 174 © Daniel Cremin; p. 180 Bob Rowan/Corbis/Magma; p. 181 David Buffington/PhotoDisc; p. 185 CP Photo Archive/Phill Snel; p. 195 Dick Hemingway; **Chapter Nine:** p. 200 CP Picture Archives/Marty Lederhandler; p. 201 © Derek Shapton; p. 206 CP Picture Archives/Atsushi Tsukada; p. 211 Dick Hemingway/Courtesy Consumer Vision; p. 214 Courtesy Arizona Beverage Company; p. 215 Courtesy Jones Soda Co.; p. 216 Dick Hemingway; p. 220 Dick Hemingway; p. 221 Dick Hemingway; **Unit Three**: p. 229 Dick Hemingway; **Chapter Ten**: p. 230 CP Picture Archives; p. 231 Rick Chard, photographer; p. 234 Bank of Canada; p. 240 © Koko Press Inc.; p. 242 Rick Chard, photographer; p. 243 CP Picture Archives/Ray Smith; p. 244 Chuck Savage/First Light; p. 251 Dick Hemingway; **Chapter Eleven**: p. 260 Dick Hemingway; p. 261 *National Post*; p. 263 Karl Weatherly/Photo Disc; p. 264 Dick Hemingway; p. 269 Ron Watts/First Light; p. 271 Dick Hemingway; p. 274 Reproduced with the permission of the Minister of Finance; p. 277 Dick Hemingway; p. 279 CP Picture Archive/Marty Lederhandler; p. 281 Toronto Blue Jays Baseball Club/The Topps Company, Inc.; **Chapter Twelve**: p. 286 Dick Hemingway/Courtesy Scotiabank; p. 287 Chris Mikula, *Ottawa Citizen*; p. 289 Canadian Press; p. 295 CP Picture Archives/Rene Johnston; p. 299 Reprinted with permission of the Bank of Montreal; p. 300 Dick Hemingway; **Chapter Thirteen:** p. 304 Charles Gupton/First Light; p. 305 Steve Chenn/First Light; p. 307 Reprinted with permission from the Bank of Montreal; p. 308 Courtesy Scotiabank; p. 310 Courtesy Scotiabank; p. 311t CP Picture Archives/Annette Young; p. 311b Reprinted with permission from the Bank of Montreal; p. 318 Dick Hemingway/Courtesy Scotiabank; p. 320 CP Picture Archives/Michael Euler; p. 325 CP Picture Archives/Phill Snel; **Chapter Fourteen**: p. 330 Dick Hemingway; p. 331 Dick Hemingway; p. 338 CP Picture Archive; p. 347 Reprinted with permission from the Bank of Montreal; **Unit Four:** p. 355 Dick Hemingway; **Chapter Fifteen:** p. 356 CP Picture Archives/Beth A. Keiser; p. 357, 358 Courtesy Gros Morne Adventure Guides; p. 360 Peanuts © UFS; p. 362 CP Picture Archives/Phill Snel; p. 363 Jeff Zaruba/First Light; p. 369 R.W. Jones/First Light; p. 371 Dick Hemingway; p. 374 Ryan McVay/PhotoDisc; p. 378 Dick Hemingway; p. 379 Colin McConnell/*The Toronto Star*; **Chapter Sixteen:** p. 383 William Taufic/First Light; p. 384 Courtesy A.C. Dispensing Equipment Inc.; p. 386 Hulton-Deutsch/Corbis/Magma; p. 388 The Granger Collection, New York; p. 389 The Granger Collection, New York; p. 391 NASA; p. 393 Onvia.com; p. 398 Geostock/PhotoDisc; p. 399 Courtesy OXO International; p. 401 Keith Brofsky/PhotoDisc; **Chapter Seventeen**: p. 406 Dick Hemingway; p. 407 Courtesy Dean Simon; p. 410 Courtesy Sheridan College, School of Crafts & Design; p. 413 David Raymer/First Light; p. 414 David Raymer/First Light; p. 416 Peter Beck/First Light; p. 418 Dick Hemingway; p. 421 Dick Hemingway;

p. 422 Rob Lewine/First Light; p. 425 LWA/Dann Tardiff/First Light; **Unit Five:** p. 433 Phillip Spears/PhotoDisc; **Chapter Eighteen:** p. 434 CP Picture Archives/Fred Chartrand; p. 435 Courtesy Grace White, CanJam Trading Co.; p. 437 Jack Wilson; p. 443 CP Picture Archives/Suzanne Bird; p. 449 C. Goldie/First Light; p. 450 Dan Lamont/Corbis/Magma; p. 453 Paul Barton/First Light; **Chapter Nineteen:** p. 461 Agence France Presse/Corbis/Magma; p. 462 Courtesy Alternative Fuel Systems Inc.; p. 466 Bettmann/Corbis/Magma; p. 469 Sergio Dorantes/Corbis/Magma; p. 471 Bettmann Archive/Corbis/Magma; p. 472 Mark Langenstein/First Light; p. 474 Reuters/Corbis/Magma; p. 477 Wolfgang Kaehler/Corbis/Magma; p. 478 A. deLeiva/First Light; p. 480 CP Picture Archives/David Guttenfelder; p. 481 Vince Streano/Corbis/Magma; **Chapter 20:** p. 488 Charles O'Rear/Corbis/Magma; p. 489 Yves Medam; p. 492 Dick Hemingway; p. 495 Courtesy STMicroelectronics; p. 496 source: Magna International Inc. p. 499 France Presse/Corbis/Magma; p. 501 Geographical Visual Aids; p. 502 Jeff Zaruba/First Light; p. 510 Jon Feingersh/First Light

Text Credits

Chapter 1: pp. 3–4 Madhavi Acharya, August 3, 1998. Reprinted with permission-The Toronto Star Syndicate; p. 15 The Multiple Intelligences Chart has been reproduced (adapted from *Canada Prospects* 1999–2000. *Canada Prospects* is published by Canada Career Consortium; **Chapter 2:** pp. 25–26 CBC Television's *Venture*; **Chapter 3:** pp. 43–44 Reprinted with permission of Nova Scotia Economic Development & Tourism; p. 56 "Top 10 Checklist for Startups" from the *Getting Started in Small Business* publication, second edition, November 2000, Canadian Bankers Association; **Chapter 4:** pp. 61–62 Christine Hanlon, *Alumni Journal: Alumni Association of the University of Manitoba*, April 2000; **Chapter 5:** pp. 83–84 Jane O'Hara, *Maclean's*, February 14, 2000; **Chapter 6:** pp. 115–116 Andrew Wahl, *Canadian Business*, May 1, 2000; p. 126 Table 6.1 The Service Sector. Adapted from Statistics Canada Internet site, www.statcan.ca, www.statcan.ca/english/Subjects/Standard/81.htm; **Chapter 7:** pp. 143–144 John Gray, *Canadian Business*, November 26, 1999; **Chapter 8:** pp. 174–175 © David Menzies, from *Canadian Business*, September 4, 2000; **Chapter 9:** pp. 201–202 © John Lorinc, from *ROB Magazine*, August 2000; **Chapter 10:** pp. 231–232 D'arcy Jenish, *Maclean's*; p. 242 Danylo Hawaleshka, *Maclean's*; **Chapter 11:** pp. 261–262 Tracy LeMay, *National Post/Financial Post*, December 2, 2000; p. 272 Table 11.1 Student Living at Home and Table 11.2 Student Living Away from Home. TD Financial Group and Association of Universities and Colleges of Canada; **Chapter 12:** pp. 287–288 Keith Woolhouse, *The Ottawa Citizen*; p. 297 Table 12.1 Credit Unions and *Caisses Populaires* in Canada. Credit Union Central of Canada; **Chapter 13:** p. 301 Adapted from Canadian Bankers Association's "Security Tips for Using ABM/Debit Cards," *Safeguarding Your Money*, Canadian Bankers Association Web site: www.cba.ca; **Chapter 14:** p. 334 Table 14.1 Total Business and Consumer Credit in Canada. Adapted from

Statistics Canada Internet site, www.statcan.ca, www.statcan.ca/english/Pgdb/Economy/Finance/fin21.htm and www.statcan.ca/english/Pgdb/Economy/Finance/fin21.htm; p. 339 "Ten Steps to Stay Fraud Free." Adapted from Canadian Bankers Association's "Safeguarding Your Money," Canadian Bankers Association Web site: www.cba.ca; p. 343 Table 14.2 Cost of Borrowing $10 000 for a Car. *There's Something About Money,* Canadian Bankers Association, www.yourmoney.cba.ca; **Chapter 15:** pp. 357–358 Greg Roberts, NEW SHOES, Vol.2 #1, 1999, p. 40; p. 364 "The Flexibility to Change," Royal Bank Financial Group; p. 367 Code of Ethics, Canadian Information Processing Society; **Chapter 16:** pp. 384–385 © Donalee Moulton, *National Post*, March 15, 2000; **Chapter 17:** pp. 407–408 CBC Television's *Venture*; **Chapter 18:** pp. 435–436 Hilary Davidson, PROFIT Magazine, April 2000; p. 441 Figure 18.1 Canada's Main Trade Partners: Imports (1999). Adapted from "Imports of goods on a balance-of-payment basis." Statistics Canada, CANSIM database, Matrix 3651. Canada's Main Trade Partners: Exports (1999). Adapted from "Exports of goods on a balance-of-payment basis." Statistics Canada, CANSIM database, Matrix 3685; p. 445 Figure 18.2 Canadian Imports (1999). "Imports of goods on a balance-of-payment basis." Statistics Canada, CANSIM database, Matrix 3651. Canadian Exports (1999). "Exports of goods on a balance-of-payment basis." Statistics Canada, CANSIM database, Matrix 3685; p. 455 Table 18.2 Goods that Require Permits, Inspection, or Special Packaging and Labelling. Canada Customs and Revenue Agency; **Chapter 19:** p. 483 Real Life Example. Department of Foreign Affairs and International Trade; **Chapter 20:** pp. 489–490 © Sarah Elton; p. 493 Table 20.1 Foreign Direct Investment in Canada by Industry (1999). Adapted from Statistics Canada, CANSIM database, Matrix 4189: D58849, D65271, D65272, D65272, D65375, D65280, D65281, D65282; p. 494 Figure 20.1 Foreign Investment in Canada (1999). Adapted from Statistics Canada, CANSIM database, Matrix 4189: D58849, D67443; p. 496 Table 20.2 Canadian Direct Investment Abroad by Industry (1999). Adapted from Statistics Canada, CANSIM database, Matrix 4188: D58093, D65238, D65239, D65242, D65248, D65250, D65251; p. 497 Figure 20.2 Where Canadian Money is Invested Abroad (1999). Adapted from Statistics Canada, CANSIM database, Matrix 4180: D65201; p. 503 "Tips for International Success." Adapted from Tips for Client Success from the Canadian Trade Commissioner Service, Department of Foreign Affairs and International Trade

Statistics Canada information is used with the permission of the Minister of Industry, as Minister responsible for Statistics Canada. Information on the availability of the wide range of data from Statistics Canada can be obtained from Statistics Canada's Regional Offices, its World Wide Web site at http://www.statcan.ca, and its toll-free access number 1-800-263-1136.